Windows® Internals, Sixth Edition, Part 1

Mark Russinovich
David A. Solomon
Alex Ionescu

PUBLISHED BY
Microsoft Press
A Division of Microsoft Corporation
One Microsoft Way
Redmond, Washington 98052-6399

Library of Congress Control Number: 2012933511
ISBN: 978-0-7356-4873-9

Microsoft Press books are available through booksellers and distributors worldwide. If you need support related to this book, email Microsoft Press Book Support at mspinput@microsoft.com. Please tell us what you think of this book at http://www.microsoft.com/learning/booksurvey.

Microsoft and the trademarks listed at http://www.microsoft.com/about/legal/en/us/IntellectualProperty /Trademarks/EN-US.aspx are trademarks of the Microsoft group of companies. All other marks are property of their respective owners.

The example companies, organizations, products, domain names, email addresses, logos, people, places, and events depicted herein are fictitious. No association with any real company, organization, product, domain name, email address, logo, person, place, or event is intended or should be inferred.

This book expresses the author's views and opinions. The information contained in this book is provided without any express, statutory, or implied warranties. Neither the authors, Microsoft Corporation, nor its resellers, or distributors will be held liable for any damages caused or alleged to be caused either directly or indirectly by this book.

Acquisitions Editor: Devon Musgrave
Developmental Editor: Devon Musgrave
Project Editor: Carol Dillingham
Technical Reviewer: Christophe Nasarre; Technical Review services provided by Content Master, a member of CM Group, Ltd.
Copy Editor: Roger LeBlanc
Indexer: Christina Yeager
Editorial Production: Waypoint Press
Cover: Twist Creative • Seattle

To our parents, who guided and inspired us to follow our dreams

Contents at a Glance

Windows Internals, Sixth Edition, Part 1

Windows Internals, Sixth Edition, Part 2 *(available separately)*

Contents

Windows Internals, Sixth Edition, Part 1

What do you think of this book? We want to hear from you!

Microsoft is interested in hearing your feedback so we can continually improve our books and learning resources for you. To participate in a brief online survey, please visit:

> microsoft.com/learning/booksurvey

Chapter 5 Processes, Threads, and Jobs 359

Chapter 6   Security   487

Windows Internals, Sixth Edition, Part 2 *(available separately)*

Introduction

Chapter 8   I/O System

I/O System Components

Device Drivers

I/O Processing

Kernel-Mode Driver Framework (KMDF)

User-Mode Driver Framework (UMDF)

The Plug and Play (PnP) Manager

The Power Manager

Conclusion

Chapter 9   Storage Management

Storage Terminology

Disk Drivers

Volume Management

BitLocker Drive Encryption

Volume Shadow Copy Service

Conclusion

What do you think of this book? We want to hear from you!

Microsoft is interested in hearing your feedback so we can continually improve our books and learning resources for you. To participate in a brief online survey, please visit:

microsoft.com/learning/booksurvey

Introduction

Windows Internals, Sixth Edition is intended for advanced computer professionals (both developers and system administrators) who want to understand how the core components of the Microsoft Windows 7 and Windows Server 2008 R2 operating systems work internally. With this knowledge, developers can better comprehend the rationale behind design choices when building applications specific to the Windows platform. Such knowledge can also help developers debug complex problems. System administrators can benefit from this information as well, because understanding how the operating system works "under the covers" facilitates understanding the performance behavior of the system and makes troubleshooting system problems much easier when things go wrong. After reading this book, you should have a better understanding of how Windows works and why it behaves as it does.

Structure of the Book

For the first time, Windows Internals has been divided into two parts. Updating the book for each release of Windows takes considerable time so producing it in two parts allows us to publish the first part earlier.

This book, Part 1, begins with two chapters that define key concepts, introduce the tools used in the book, and describe the overall system architecture and components. The next two chapters present key underlying system and management mechanisms. Part 1 wraps up by covering three core components of the operating system: processes, threads, and jobs; security; and networking.

Part 2, which is available separately, covers the remaining core subsystems: I/O, storage, memory management, the cache manager, and file systems. Part 2 concludes with a description of the startup and shutdown processes and a description of crash-dump analysis.

History of the Book

This is the sixth edition of a book that was originally called *Inside Windows NT* (Microsoft Press, 1992), written by Helen Custer (prior to the initial release of Microsoft Windows NT 3.1). *Inside Windows NT* was the first book ever published about Windows NT and provided key insights into the architecture and design of the system. *Inside Windows NT, Second Edition* (Microsoft Press, 1998) was written by David Solomon. It updated the original book to cover Windows NT 4.0 and had a greatly increased level of technical depth.

Inside Windows 2000, Third Edition (Microsoft Press, 2000) was authored by David Solomon and Mark Russinovich. It added many new topics, such as startup and shutdown, service internals, registry internals, file-system drivers, and networking. It also covered kernel changes in Windows 2000, such as the Windows Driver Model (WDM), Plug and Play, power management, Windows Management Instrumentation (WMI), encryption, the job object, and Terminal Services. *Windows Internals, Fourth Edition* was the Windows XP and Windows Server 2003 update and added more content focused on helping IT professionals make use of their knowledge of Windows internals, such as using key tools from Windows Sysinternals (*www.microsoft.com/technet /sysinternals*) and analyzing crash dumps. *Windows Internals, Fifth Edition* was the update for Windows Vista and Windows Server 2008. New content included the image loader, user-mode debugging facility, and Hyper-V.

Sixth Edition Changes

This latest edition has been updated to cover the kernel changes made in Windows 7 and Windows Server 2008 R2. Hands-on experiments have been updated to reflect changes in tools.

Hands-on Experiments

Even without access to the Windows source code, you can glean much about Windows internals from tools such as the kernel debugger and tools from Sysinternals and Winsider Seminars & Solutions. When a tool can be used to expose or demonstrate some aspect of the internal behavior of Windows, the steps for trying the tool yourself are listed in "EXPERIMENT" boxes. These appear throughout the book, and we encourage you to try these as you're reading—seeing visible proof of how Windows works internally will make much more of an impression on you than just reading about it will.

Topics Not Covered

Windows is a large and complex operating system. This book doesn't cover everything relevant to Windows internals but instead focuses on the base system components. For example, this book doesn't describe COM+, the Windows distributed object-oriented programming infrastructure, or the Microsoft .NET Framework, the foundation of managed code applications.

Because this is an internals book and not a user, programming, or system administration book, it doesn't describe how to use, program, or configure Windows.

A Warning and a Caveat

Because this book describes undocumented behavior of the internal architecture and the operation of the Windows operating system (such as internal kernel structures and functions), this content is subject to change between releases. (External interfaces, such as the Windows API, are not subject to incompatible changes.)

By "subject to change," we don't necessarily mean that details described in this book will change between releases, but you can't count on them not changing. Any software that uses these undocumented interfaces might not work on future releases of Windows. Even worse, software that runs in kernel mode (such as device drivers) and uses these undocumented interfaces might experience a system crash when running on a newer release of Windows.

Acknowledgments

First, thanks to Jamie Hanrahan and Brian Catlin of Azius, LLC for joining us on this project—the book would not have been finished without their help. They did the bulk of the updates on the "Security" and "Networking" chapters and contributed to the update of the "Management Mechanisms" and "Processes and Threads" chapters. Azius provides Windows-internals and device-driver training. See *www.azius.com* for more information.

We want to recognize Alex Ionescu, who for this edition is a full coauthor. This is a reflection of Alex's extensive work on the fifth edition, as well as his continuing work on this edition.

Thanks to Eric Traut and Jon DeVaan for continuing to allow David Solomon access to the Windows source code for his work on this book as well as continued development of his Windows Internals courses.

Three key reviewers were not acknowledged for their review and contributions to the fifth edition: Arun Kishan, Landy Wang, and Aaron Margosis—thanks again to them! And thanks again to Arun and Landy for their detailed review and helpful input for this edition.

This book wouldn't contain the depth of technical detail or the level of accuracy it has without the review, input, and support of key members of the Microsoft Windows development team. Therefore, we want to thank the following people, who provided technical review and input to the book:

- Greg Cottingham

- Joe Hamburg

- Jeff Lambert

- Pavel Lebedynskiy

- Joseph East

- Adi Oltean

- Alexey Pakhunov

- Valerie See

For the "Networking" chapter, a special thanks to Gianluigi Nusca and Tom Jolly, who really went beyond the call of duty: Gianluigi for his extraordinary help with the BranchCache material and the amount of suggestions (and many paragraphs of material he wrote), and Tom Jolly not only for his own review and suggestions (which were excellent), but for getting many other developers to assist with the review. Here are all those who reviewed and contributed to the "Networking" chapter:

- Roopesh Battepati

- Molly Brown

- Greg Cottingham

- Dotan Elharrar

- Eric Hanson

- Tom Jolly

- Manoj Kadam

- Greg Kramer

- David Kruse

- Jeff Lambert

- Darene Lewis

- Dan Lovinger

- Gianluigi Nusca

- Amos Ortal

- Ivan Pashov

- Ganesh Prasad

- Paul Swan

- Shiva Kumar Thangapandi

Amos Ortal and Dotan Elharrar were extremely helpful on NAP, and Shiva Kumar Thangapandi helped extensively with EAP.

The detailed checking Christophe Nasarre, overall technical reviewer, performed contributed greatly to the technical accuracy and consistency in the book.

We would like to again thank Ilfak Guilfanov of Hex-Rays (*www.hex-rays.com*) for the IDA Pro Advanced and Hex-Rays licenses they granted to Alex Ionescu so that he could speed up his reverse engineering of the Windows kernel.

Finally, the authors would like to thank the great staff at Microsoft Press who have been behind turning this book into a reality. Devon Musgrave served double duty as acquisitions editor and developmental editor, while Carol Dillingham oversaw the title as its project editor. Editorial and production manager Steve Sagman, copy editor Roger LeBlanc, proofreader Audrey Marr, and indexer Christina Yeager also contributed to the quality of this book.

Last but not least, thanks to Ben Ryan, publisher of Microsoft Press, who continues to believe in the importance of providing this level of detail about Windows to their readers!

Errata & Book Support

We've made every effort to ensure the accuracy of this book. Any errors that have been reported since this book was published are listed on our Microsoft Press site at oreilly.com:

http://go.microsoft.com/FWLink/?Linkid=245675

If you find an error that is not already listed, you can report it to us through the same page.

If you need additional support, email Microsoft Press Book Support at *mspinput@microsoft.com*.

Please note that product support for Microsoft software is not offered through the addresses above.

We Want to Hear from You

At Microsoft Press, your satisfaction is our top priority, and your feedback our most valuable asset. Please tell us what you think of this book at:

http://www.microsoft.com/learning/booksurvey

The survey is short, and we read every one of your comments and ideas. Thanks in advance for your input!

Stay in Touch

Let's keep the conversation going! We're on Twitter: *http://twitter.com/MicrosoftPress*.

CHAPTER 1

Concepts and Tools

In this chapter, we'll introduce the key Microsoft Windows operating system concepts and terms we'll be using throughout this book, such as the Windows API, processes, threads, virtual memory, kernel mode and user mode, objects, handles, security, and the registry. We'll also introduce the tools that you can use to explore Windows internals, such as the kernel debugger, the Performance Monitor, and key tools from Windows Sysinternals (*www.microsoft.com/technet/sysinternals*). In addition, we'll explain how you can use the Windows Driver Kit (WDK) and the Windows Software Development Kit (SDK) as resources for finding further information on Windows internals.

Be sure that you understand everything in this chapter—the remainder of the book is written assuming that you do.

Windows Operating System Versions

This book covers the most recent version of the Microsoft Windows client and server operating systems: Windows 7 (32-bit and 64-bit versions) and Windows Server 2008 R2 (64-bit version only). Unless specifically stated, the text applies to all versions. As background information, Table 1-1 lists the Windows product names, their internal version number, and their release date.

TABLE 1-1 Windows Operating System Releases

Product Name	Internal Version Number	Release Date
Windows NT 3.1	3.1	July 1993
Windows NT 3.5	3.5	September 1994
Windows NT 3.51	3.51	May 1995
Windows NT 4.0	4.0	July 1996
Windows 2000	5.0	December 1999
Windows XP	5.1	August 2001
Windows Server 2003	5.2	March 2003
Windows Vista	6.0 (Build 6000)	January 2007
Windows Server 2008	6.0 (Build 6001)	March 2008
Windows 7	6.1 (Build 7600)	October 2009
Windows Server 2008 R2	6.1 (Build 7600)	October 2009

Note The "7" in the "Windows 7" product name does not refer to the internal version number, but is rather a generational index. In fact, to minimize application compatibility issues, the version number for Windows 7 is actually 6.1, as shown in Table 1-1. This allows applications checking for the major version number to continue behaving on Windows 7 as they did on Windows Vista. In fact, Windows 7 and Server 2008 R2 have identical version/build numbers because they were built from the same Windows code base.

Foundation Concepts and Terms

In the course of this book, we'll be referring to some structures and concepts that might be unfamiliar to some readers. In this section, we'll define the terms we'll be using throughout. You should become familiar with them before proceeding to subsequent chapters.

Windows API

The Windows application programming interface (API) is the user-mode system programming interface to the Windows operating system family. Prior to the introduction of 64-bit versions of Windows, the programming interface to the 32-bit versions of the Windows operating systems was called the *Win32 API* to distinguish it from the original 16-bit Windows API, which was the programming interface to the original 16-bit versions of Windows. In this book, the term *Windows API* refers to both the 32-bit and 64-bit programming interfaces to Windows.

Note The Windows API is described in the Windows Software Development Kit (SDK) documentation. (See the section "Windows Software Development Kit" later in this chapter.) This documentation is available for free viewing online at *www.msdn.microsoft.com*. It is also included with all subscription levels to the Microsoft Developer Network (MSDN), Microsoft's support program for developers. For more information, see *www.msdn.microsoft.com*. An excellent description of how to program the Windows base API is in the book *Windows via C/C++*, Fifth Edition by Jeffrey Richter and Christophe Nasarre (Microsoft Press, 2007).

The Windows API consists of thousands of callable functions, which are divided into the following major categories:

- Base Services
- Component Services
- User Interface Services

- Graphics and Multimedia Services

- Messaging and Collaboration

- Networking

- Web Services

This book focuses on the internals of the key base services, such as processes and threads, memory management, I/O, and security.

What About .NET?

The Microsoft .NET Framework consists of a library of classes called the Framework Class Library (FCL) and a Common Language Runtime (CLR) that provides a managed code execution environment with features such as just-in-time compilation, type verification, garbage collection, and code access security. By offering these features, the CLR provides a development environment that improves programmer productivity and reduces common programming errors. For an excellent description of the .NET Framework and its core architecture, see *CLR via C#, Third Edition* by Jeffrey Richter (Microsoft Press, 2010).

The CLR is implemented as a classic COM server whose code resides in a standard user-mode Windows DLL. In fact, all components of the .NET Framework are implemented as standard user-mode Windows DLLs layered over unmanaged Windows API functions. (None of the .NET Framework runs in kernel mode.) Figure 1-1 illustrates the relationship between these components:

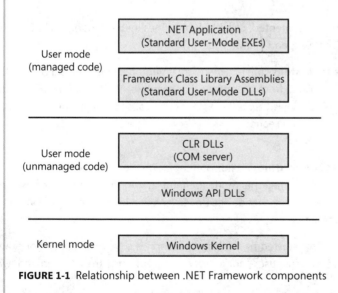

FIGURE 1-1 Relationship between .NET Framework components

History of the Win32 API

Interestingly, Win32 wasn't slated to be the original programming interface to what was then called Windows NT. Because the Windows NT project started as a replacement for OS/2 version 2, the primary programming interface was the 32-bit OS/2 Presentation Manager API. A year into the project, however, Microsoft Windows 3.0 hit the market and took off. As a result, Microsoft changed direction and made Windows NT the future replacement for the Windows family of products as opposed to the replacement for OS/2. It was at this juncture that the need to specify the Windows API arose—before this, in Windows 3.0, the API existed only as a 16-bit interface.

Although the Windows API would introduce many new functions that hadn't been available on Windows 3.1, Microsoft decided to make the new API compatible with the 16-bit Windows API function names, semantics, and use of data types whenever possible to ease the burden of porting existing 16-bit Windows applications to Windows NT. This explains why many function names and interfaces might seem inconsistent: this was required to ensure that the then new Windows API was compatible with the old 16-bit Windows API.

Services, Functions, and Routines

Several terms in the Windows user and programming documentation have different meanings in different contexts. For example, the word *service* can refer to a callable routine in the operating system, a device driver, or a server process. The following list describes what certain terms mean in this book:

- **Windows API functions**   Documented, callable subroutines in the Windows API. Examples include *CreateProcess*, *CreateFile*, and *GetMessage*.

- **Native system services (or system calls)**   The undocumented, underlying services in the operating system that are callable from user mode. For example, *NtCreateUserProcess* is the internal system service the Windows *CreateProcess* function calls to create a new process. For a definition of *system calls*, see the section "System Service Dispatching" in Chapter 3, "System Mechanisms."

- **Kernel support functions (or routines)**   Subroutines inside the Windows operating system that can be called only from kernel mode (defined later in this chapter). For example, *ExAllocatePoolWithTag* is the routine that device drivers call to allocate memory from the Windows system heaps (called *pools*).

- **Windows services**   Processes started by the Windows service control manager. For example, the Task Scheduler service runs in a user-mode process that supports the *at* command (which is similar to the UNIX commands *at* or *cron*). (Note: although the registry defines Windows device drivers as "services," they are not referred to as such in this book.)

- **DLLs (dynamic-link libraries)**   A set of callable subroutines linked together as a binary file that can be dynamically loaded by applications that use the subroutines. Examples include Msvcrt.dll (the C run-time library) and Kernel32.dll (one of the Windows API subsystem libraries). Windows user-mode components and applications use DLLs extensively. The advantage DLLs provide over static libraries is that applications can share DLLs, and Windows ensures that there is only one in-memory copy of a DLL's code among the applications that are referencing it. Note that nonexecutable .NET assemblies are compiled as DLLs but without any exported subroutines. Instead, the CLR parses compiled metadata to access the corresponding types and members.

Processes, Threads, and Jobs

Although programs and processes appear similar on the surface, they are fundamentally different. A *program* is a static sequence of instructions, whereas a *process* is a container for a set of resources used when executing the instance of the program. At the highest level of abstraction, a Windows process comprises the following:

- A *private virtual address space*, which is a set of virtual memory addresses that the process can use

- An executable program, which defines initial code and data and is mapped into the process' virtual address space

- A list of open handles to various system resources—such as semaphores, communication ports, and files—that are accessible to all threads in the process

- A security context called an *access token* that identifies the user, security groups, privileges, User Account Control (UAC) virtualization state, session, and limited user account state associated with the process

- A unique identifier called a *process ID* (internally part of an identifier called a *client ID*)

- At least one thread of execution (although an "empty" process is possible, it is not useful)

Each process also points to its parent or creator process. If the parent no longer exists, this information is not updated. Therefore, it is possible for a process to refer to a nonexistent parent. This is not a problem, because nothing relies on this information being kept current. In the case of ProcessExplorer, the start time of the parent process is taken into account to avoid attaching a child process based on a reused process ID. The following experiment illustrates this behavior.

EXPERIMENT: Viewing the Process Tree

One unique attribute about a process that most tools don't display is the parent or creator process ID. You can retrieve this value with the Performance Monitor (or programmatically) by querying the Creating Process ID. The Tlist.exe tool (in the Debugging Tools for Windows) can show the process tree by using the /t switch. Here's an example of output from *tlist /t*:

```
C:\>tlist /t
System Process (0)
System (4)
  smss.exe (224)
csrss.exe (384)
csrss.exe (444)
  conhost.exe (3076) OleMainThreadWndName
winlogon.exe (496)
wininit.exe (504)
  services.exe (580)
    svchost.exe (696)
    svchost.exe (796)
    svchost.exe (912)
    svchost.exe (948)
    svchost.exe (988)
    svchost.exe (244)
      WUDFHost.exe (1008)
      dwm.exe (2912) DWM Notification Window
    btwdins.exe (268)
    svchost.exe (1104)
    svchost.exe (1192)
    svchost.exe (1368)
    svchost.exe (1400)
    spoolsv.exe (1560)
    svchost.exe (1860)
    svchost.exe (1936)
    svchost.exe (1124)
    svchost.exe (1440)
    svchost.exe (2276)
    taskhost.exe (2816) Task Host Window
    svchost.exe (892)
  lsass.exe (588)
  lsm.exe (596)
explorer.exe (2968) Program Manager
  cmd.exe (1832) Administrator: C:\Windows\system32\cmd.exe - "c:\tlist.exe"  /t
    tlist.exe (2448)
```

The list indents each process to show its parent/child relationship. Processes whose parents aren't alive are left-justified (as is Explorer.exe in the preceding example) because even if a grandparent process exists, there's no way to find that relationship. Windows maintains only the creator process ID, not a link back to the creator of the creator, and so forth.

To demonstrate the fact that Windows doesn't keep track of more than just the parent process ID, follow these steps:

1. Open a Command Prompt window.

2. Type **title Parent** (to change the window title to Parent).

3. Type **start cmd** (which starts a second command prompt).

4. Type **title Child** in the second command prompt.

5. Bring up Task Manager.

6. Type **mspaint** (which runs Microsoft Paint) in the second command prompt.

7. Go back to the second command prompt and type **exit**. (Notice that Paint remains.)

8. Switch to Task Manager.

9. Click on the Applications tab.

10. Right-click on the Parent task, and select Go To Process.

11. Right-click on this cmd.exe process, and select End Process Tree.

12. Click End Process Tree in the Task Manager confirmation message box.

The first command prompt window will disappear, but you should still see the Paint window because it was the grandchild of the command prompt process you terminated; and because the intermediate process (the parent of Paint) was terminated, there was no link between the parent and the grandchild.

A number of tools for viewing (and modifying) processes and process information are available. The following experiments illustrate the various views of process information you can obtain with some of these tools. While many of these tools are included within Windows itself and within the Debugging Tools for Windows and the Windows SDK, others are stand-alone tools from Sysinternals. Many of these tools show overlapping subsets of the core process and thread information, sometimes identified by different names.

Probably the most widely used tool to examine process activity is Task Manager. (Because there is no such thing as a "task" in the Windows kernel, the name of this tool, Task Manager, is a bit odd.) The following experiment shows the difference between what Task Manager lists as applications and processes.

EXPERIMENT: Viewing Process Information with Task Manager

The built-in Windows Task Manager provides a quick list of the processes on the system. You can start Task Manager in one of four ways: (1) press Ctrl+Shift+Esc, (2) right-click on the taskbar and click Start Task Manager, (3) press Ctrl+Alt+Delete and click the Start Task Manager button, or (4) start the executable Taskmgr.exe. Once Task Manager has started, click on the Processes tab to see the list of processes. Notice that processes are identified by the name of the image of which they are an instance. Unlike some objects in Windows, processes can't be given global names. To display additional details, choose Select Columns from the View menu and select additional columns to be added, as shown here:

Although the Task Manager Processes tab shows a list of processes, what the Applications tab displays isn't as obvious. The Applications tab lists the top-level visible windows on all the desktops in the interactive window station you are connected to. (By default, there is only one interactive desktop—an application can create more by using the Windows *CreateDesktop* function, as is done by the Sysinternals Desktops tool.) The Status column indicates whether or not the thread that owns the window is in a window message wait state. "Running" means the thread is waiting for windowing input; "Not Responding" means the thread isn't waiting for windowing input (for example, the thread might be running or waiting for I/O or some Windows synchronization object).

On the Applications tab, you can match a task to the process that owns the thread that owns the task window by right-clicking on the task name and choosing Go To Process as shown in the previous tlist experiment.

Process Explorer, from Sysinternals, shows more details about processes and threads than any other available tool, which is why you will see it used in a number of experiments throughout the book. The following are some of the unique things that Process Explorer shows or enables:

- Process security token (such as lists of groups and privileges and the virtualization state)
- Highlighting to show changes in the process and thread list
- List of services inside service-hosting processes, including the display name and description
- Processes that are part of a job and job details
- Processes hosting .NET applications and .NET-specific details (such as the list of AppDomains, loaded assemblies, and CLR performance counters)
- Start time for processes and threads
- Complete list of memory-mapped files (not just DLLs)
- Ability to suspend a process or a thread
- Ability to kill an individual thread

- Easy identification of which processes were consuming the most CPU time over a period of time (The Performance Monitor can display process CPU utilization for a given set of processes, but it won't automatically show processes created after the performance monitoring session has started—only a manual trace in binary output format can do that.)

Process Explorer also provides easy access to information in one place, such as:

- Process tree (with the ability to collapse parts of the tree)

- Open handles in a process (including unnamed handles)

- List of DLLs (and memory-mapped files) in a process

- Thread activity within a process

- User-mode and kernel-mode thread stacks (including the mapping of addresses to names using the Dbghelp.dll that comes with the Debugging Tools for Windows)

- More accurate CPU percentage using the thread cycle count (an even better representation of precise CPU activity, as explained in Chapter 5, "Processes and Threads")

- Integrity level

- Memory manager details such as peak commit charge and kernel memory paged and nonpaged pool limits (other tools show only current size)

An introductory experiment using Process Explorer follows.

EXPERIMENT: Viewing Process Details with Process Explorer

Download the latest version of Process Explorer from Sysinternals and run it. The first time you run it and go to the the Threads tab of a process' property page, you will receive a message that symbols are not currently configured. If properly configured, Process Explorer can access symbol information to display the symbolic name of the thread start function and functions on a thread's call stack (available by double-clicking on a process and clicking on the Threads tab). This is useful for identifying what threads are doing within a process. To access symbols, you must have the Debugging Tools for Windows installed (described later in this chapter). Then click on Options, choose Configure Symbols, and fill in the path to the Dbghelp.dll in the Debugging Tools folder and a valid symbol path. For example, on a 64-bit system this configuration is correct:

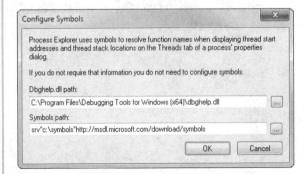

In the preceding example, the on-demand symbol server is being used to access symbols and a copy of the symbol files is being stored on the local machine in the c:\symbols folder. For more information on configuring the use of the symbol server, see *http://msdn.microsoft.com /en-us/windows/hardware/hh852360.aspx*.

When Process Explorer starts, it shows by default the process tree view. It has an optional lower pane that can show open handles or mapped DLLs and memory-mapped files. (These are explored in Chapter 3, "System Mechanisms" in Part 1 and Chapter 10, "Memory Management" in Part 2.) It also shows tooltips for several kinds of hosting processes:

- The services inside a service-hosting process (Svchost.exe) if you hover your mouse over the name

- The COM object tasks inside a Taskeng.exe process (started by the Task Scheduler)

- The target of a Rundll32.exe process (used for things such as Control Panel items)

- The COM object being hosted inside a Dllhost.exe process

- Internet Explorer tab processes

- Console host processes

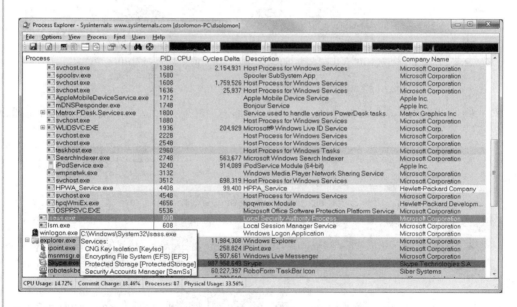

Here are a few steps to walk you through some basic capabilities of Process Explorer:

1. Notice that processes hosting services are highlighted by default in pink. Your own processes are highlighted in blue. (These colors can be configured.)

2. Hover your mouse pointer over the image name for processes, and notice the full path displayed by the tooltip. As noted earlier, certain types of processes have additional details in the tooltip.

3. Click on View, Select Columns from the Process Image tab, and add the image path.

4. Sort by clicking on the process column, and notice the tree view disappears. (You can either display tree view or sort by any of the columns shown.) Click again to sort from Z to A. Then click again, and the display returns to tree view.

5. Deselect View, Show Processes From All Users to show only your processes.

6. Go to Options, Difference Highlight Duration, and change the value to 5 seconds. Then launch a new process (anything), and notice the new process highlighted in green for 5 seconds. Exit this new process, and notice the process is highlighted in red for 5 seconds before disappearing from the display. This can be useful to see processes being created and exiting on your system.

7. Finally, double-click on a process and explore the various tabs available from the process properties display. (These will be referenced in various experiments throughout the book where the information being shown is being explained.)

A *thread* is the entity within a process that Windows schedules for execution. Without it, the process' program can't run. A thread includes the following essential components:

- The contents of a set of CPU registers representing the state of the processor.

- Two stacks—one for the thread to use while executing in kernel mode and one for executing in user mode.

- A private storage area called *thread-local storage* (TLS) for use by subsystems, run-time libraries, and DLLs.

- A unique identifier called a *thread ID* (part of an internal structure called a *client ID*—process IDs and thread IDs are generated out of the same namespace, so they never overlap).

- Threads sometimes have their own security context, or token, that is often used by multi-threaded server applications that impersonate the security context of the clients that they serve.

The volatile registers, stacks, and private storage area are called the thread's *context*. Because this information is different for each machine architecture that Windows runs on, this structure, by necessity, is architecture-specific. The Windows *GetThreadContext* function provides access to this architecture-specific information (called the CONTEXT block).

Note The threads of a 32-bit application running on a 64-bit version of Windows will contain both 32-bit and 64-bit contexts, which Wow64 will use to switch the application from running in 32-bit to 64-bit mode when required. These threads will have two user stacks and two CONTEXT blocks, and the usual Windows API functions will return the 64-bit context instead. The *Wow64GetThreadContext* function, however, will return the 32-bit context. See Chapter 3 for more information on Wow64.

Fibers and User-Mode Scheduler Threads

Because switching execution from one thread to another involves the kernel scheduler, it can be an expensive operation, especially if two threads are often switching between each other. Windows implements two mechanisms for reducing this cost: *fibers* and *user-mode scheduling* (UMS).

Fibers allow an application to schedule its own "threads" of execution rather than rely on the priority-based scheduling mechanism built into Windows. Fibers are often called "light-weight" threads, and in terms of scheduling, they're invisible to the kernel because they're implemented in user mode in Kernel32.dll. To use fibers, a call is first made to the Windows *ConvertThreadToFiber* function. This function converts the thread to a running fiber. Afterward, the newly converted fiber can create additional fibers with the *CreateFiber* function. (Each fiber can have its own set of fibers.) Unlike a thread, however, a fiber doesn't begin execution until it's manually selected through a call to the *SwitchToFiber* function. The new fiber runs until it exits or until it calls *SwitchToFiber*, again selecting another fiber to run. For more information, see the Windows SDK documentation on fiber functions.

UMS threads, which are available only for 64-bit applications on 64-bit versions of Windows, provide the same basic advantages as fibers, without many of the disadvantages. UMS threads have their own kernel thread state and are therefore visible to the kernel, which allows multiple UMS threads to issue blocking system calls, share and contend on resources, and have per-thread state. However, as long as two or more UMS threads only need to perform work in user mode, they can periodically switch execution contexts (by yielding from one thread to another) without involving the scheduler: the context switch is done in user mode. From the kernel's perspective, the same kernel thread is still running and nothing has changed. When a UMS thread performs an operation that requires entering the kernel (such as a system call), it switches to its dedicated kernel-mode thread (called a *directed context switch*).

Although threads have their own execution context, every thread within a process shares the process' virtual address space (in addition to the rest of the resources belonging to the process), meaning that all the threads in a process have full read-write access to the process virtual address space. Threads cannot accidentally reference the address space of another process, however, unless the other process makes available part of its private address space as a *shared memory section* (called a *file mapping object* in the Windows API) or unless one process has the right to open another process to use cross-process memory functions such as *ReadProcessMemory* and *WriteProcessMemory*.

In addition to a private address space and one or more threads, each process has a security context and a list of open handles to kernel objects such as files, shared memory sections, or one of the synchronization objects such as mutexes, events, or semaphores, as illustrated in Figure 1-2.

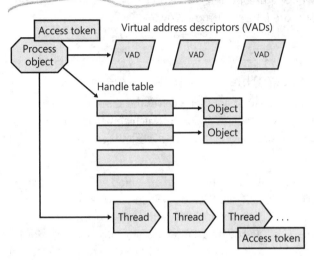

FIGURE 1-2 A process and its resources

Each process' security context is stored in an object called an *access token*. The process access token contains the security identification and credentials for the process. By default, threads don't have their own access token, but they can obtain one, thus allowing individual threads to impersonate the security context of another process—including processes on a remote Windows system—without affecting other threads in the process. (See Chapter 6, "Security," for more details on process and thread security.)

The *virtual address descriptors* (VADs) are data structures that the memory manager uses to keep track of the virtual addresses the process is using. These data structures are described in more depth in Chapter 10 in Part 2.

Windows provides an extension to the process model called a *job*. A job object's main function is to allow groups of processes to be managed and manipulated as a unit. A job object allows control of certain attributes and provides limits for the process or processes associated with the job. It also records basic accounting information for all processes associated with the job and for all processes that were associated with the job but have since terminated. In some ways, the job object compensates for the lack of a structured process tree in Windows—yet in many ways it is more powerful than a UNIX-style process tree.

You'll find out much more about the internal structure of jobs, processes, and threads; the mechanics of process and thread creation; and the thread-scheduling algorithms in Chapter 5.

Virtual Memory

Windows implements a virtual memory system based on a flat (linear) address space that provides each process with the illusion of having its own large, private address space. Virtual memory provides a logical view of memory that might not correspond to its physical layout. At run time, the memory manager, with assistance from hardware, translates, or *maps*, the virtual addresses into physical addresses, where the data is actually stored. By controlling the protection and mapping, the operating system can ensure that individual processes don't bump into one another or overwrite operating system data. Figure 1-3 illustrates three virtually contiguous pages mapped to three discontiguous pages in physical memory.

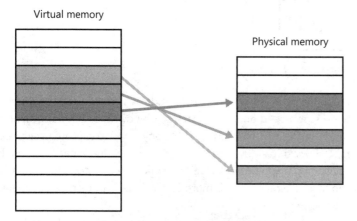

FIGURE 1-3 Mapping virtual memory to physical memory

Because most systems have much less physical memory than the total virtual memory in use by the running processes, the memory manager transfers, or *pages*, some of the memory contents to disk. Paging data to disk frees physical memory so that it can be used for other processes or for the operating system itself. When a thread accesses a virtual address that has been paged to disk, the virtual memory manager loads the information back into memory from disk. Applications don't have to be altered in any way to take advantage of paging because hardware support enables the memory manager to page without the knowledge or assistance of processes or threads.

The size of the virtual address space varies for each hardware platform. On 32-bit x86 systems, the total virtual address space has a theoretical maximum of 4 GB. By default, Windows allocates half this address space (the lower half of the 4-GB virtual address space, from 0x00000000 through 0x7FFFFFFF) to processes for their unique private storage and uses the other half (the upper half, addresses 0x80000000 through 0xFFFFFFFF) for its own protected operating system memory utilization. The mappings of the lower half change to reflect the virtual address space of the currently executing process, but the mappings of the upper half always consist of the operating system's virtual memory. Windows supports boot-time options (the *increaseuserva* qualifier in the Boot Configuration Database, described in Chapter 13, "Startup and Shutdown," in Part 2) that give processes running specially marked programs (the large address space aware flag must be set in the header of the executable image) the ability to use up to 3 GB of private address space (leaving 1 GB for the operating system). This option allows applications such as database servers to keep larger portions of a database in the process address space, thus reducing the need to map subset views of the database. Figure 1-4 shows the two typical virtual address space layouts supported by 32-bit Windows. (The *increaseuserva* option allows anywhere from 2 to 3 GB to be used by marked applications.)

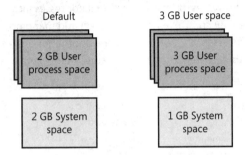

FIGURE 1-4 Typical address space layouts for 32-bit Windows

Although 3 GB is better than 2 GB, it's still not enough virtual address space to map very large (multigigabyte) databases. To address this need on 32-bit systems, Windows provides a mechanism called *Address Windowing Extension* (AWE), which allows a 32-bit application to allocate up to 64 GB of physical memory and then map views, or windows, into its 2-GB virtual address space. Although using AWE puts the burden of managing mappings of virtual to physical memory on the programmer, it does address the need of being able to directly access more physical memory than can be mapped at any one time in a 32-bit process address space.

64-bit Windows provides a much larger address space for processes: 7152 GB on IA-64 systems and 8192 GB on x64 systems. Figure 1-5 shows a simplified view of the 64-bit system address space layouts. (For a detailed description, see Chapter 10 in Part 2.) Note that these sizes do not represent the architectural limits for these platforms. Sixty-four bits of address space is over 17 billion GB, but current 64-bit hardware limits this to smaller values. And Windows implementation limits in the current versions of 64-bit Windows further reduce this to 8192 GB (8 TB).

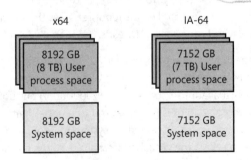

FIGURE 1-5 Address space layouts for 64-bit Windows

Details of the implementation of the memory manager, including how address translation works and how Windows manages physical memory, are described in Chapter 10 in Part 2.

Kernel Mode vs. User Mode

To protect user applications from accessing and/or modifying critical operating system data, Windows uses two processor access modes (even if the processor on which Windows is running supports more than two): *user mode* and *kernel mode*. User application code runs in user mode, whereas operating system code (such as system services and device drivers) runs in kernel mode. *Kernel mode* refers to a mode of execution in a processor that grants access to all system memory and all CPU instructions. By providing the operating system software with a higher privilege level than the application software has, the processor provides a necessary foundation for operating system designers to ensure that a misbehaving application can't disrupt the stability of the system as a whole.

> **Note** The architectures of the x86 and x64 processors define four privilege levels (or rings) to protect system code and data from being overwritten either inadvertently or maliciously by code of lesser privilege. Windows uses privilege level 0 (or ring 0) for kernel mode and privilege level 3 (or ring 3) for user mode. The reason Windows uses only two levels is that some hardware architectures that were supported in the past (such as Compaq Alpha and Silicon Graphics MIPS) implemented only two privilege levels.

Although each Windows process has its own private memory space, the kernel-mode operating system and device driver code share a single virtual address space. Each page in virtual memory is tagged to indicate what access mode the processor must be in to read and/or write the page. Pages in system space can be accessed only from kernel mode, whereas all pages in the user address space are accessible from user mode. Read-only pages (such as those that contain static data) are not writable from any mode. Additionally, on processors that support no-execute memory protection, Windows marks pages containing data as nonexecutable, thus preventing inadvertent or malicious code execution in data areas.

32-bit Windows doesn't provide any protection to private read/write system memory being used by components running in kernel mode. In other words, once in kernel mode, operating system and device driver code has complete access to system space memory and can bypass Windows security to access objects. Because the bulk of the Windows operating system code runs in kernel mode, it is vital that components that run in kernel mode be carefully designed and tested to ensure that they don't violate system security or cause system instability.

This lack of protection also emphasizes the need to take care when loading a third-party device driver, because once in kernel mode the software has complete access to all operating system data. This weakness was one of the reasons behind the driver-signing mechanism introduced in Windows, which warns (and, if configured as such, blocks) the user if an attempt is made to add an unsigned Plug and Play driver. (See Chapter 8, "I/O System," in Part 2 for more information on driver signing.) Also, a mechanism called Driver Verifier helps device driver writers to find bugs (such as buffer overruns or memory leaks) that can cause security or reliability issues. Driver Verifier is explained in Chapter 10 in Part 2.

On 64-bit versions of Windows, the Kernel Mode Code Signing (KMCS) policy dictates that any 64-bit device drivers (not just Plug and Play) must be signed with a cryptographic key assigned by one of the major code certification authorities. The user cannot explicitly force the installation of an unsigned driver, even as an administrator, but, as a one-time exception, this restriction can be disabled manually at boot time by pressing F8 and choosing the advanced boot option Disable Driver Signature Enforcement. This causes a watermark on the desktop wallpaper and certain digital rights management (DRM) features to be disabled.

As you'll see in Chapter 2, "System Architecture," user applications switch from user mode to kernel mode when they make a system service call. For example, a Windows *ReadFile* function eventually needs to call the internal Windows routine that actually handles reading data from a file. That routine, because it accesses internal system data structures, must run in kernel mode. The transition from user mode to kernel mode is accomplished by the use of a special processor instruction that causes the processor to switch to kernel mode and enter the system service dispatching code in the kernel which calls the appropriate internal function in Ntoskrnl.exe or Win32k.sys. Before returning control to the user thread, the processor mode is switched back to user mode. In this way, the operating system protects itself and its data from perusal and modification by user processes.

Note A transition from user mode to kernel mode (and back) does *not* affect thread scheduling per se—a mode transition is *not* a context switch. Further details on system service dispatching are included in Chapter 3.

Thus, it's normal for a user thread to spend part of its time executing in user mode and part in kernel mode. In fact, because the bulk of the graphics and windowing system also runs in kernel mode, graphics-intensive applications spend more of their time in kernel mode than in user mode. An easy way to test this is to run a graphics-intensive application such as Microsoft Paint or Microsoft Chess Titans and watch the time split between user mode and kernel mode using one of the performance counters listed in Table 1-2. More advanced applications can use newer technologies such as Direct2D and compositing, which perform bulk computations in user mode and send only the raw surface data to the kernel, reducing the time spent transitioning between user and kernel modes.

TABLE 1-2 Mode-Related Performance Counters

Object: Counter	Function
Processor: % Privileged Time	Percentage of time that an individual CPU (or all CPUs) has run in kernel mode during a specified interval
Processor: % User Time	Percentage of time that an individual CPU (or all CPUs) has run in user mode during a specified interval
Process: % Privileged Time	Percentage of time that the threads in a process have run in kernel mode during a specified interval
Process: % User Time	Percentage of time that the threads in a process have run in user mode during a specified interval
Thread: % Privileged Time	Percentage of time that a thread has run in kernel mode during a specified interval
Thread: % User Time	Percentage of time that a thread has run in user mode during a specified interval

EXPERIMENT: Kernel Mode vs. User Mode

You can use the Performance Monitor to see how much time your system spends executing in kernel mode vs. in user mode. Follow these steps:

1. Run the Performance Monitor by opening the Start menu and selecting All Programs /Administrative Tools/Performance Monitor. Select the Performance Monitor node under Performance/Monitoring Tools on the left-side tree.

2. Click the Add button (+) on the toolbar.

3. Expand the Processor counter section, click the % Privileged Time counter and, while holding down the Ctrl key, click the % User Time counter.

4. Click Add, and then click OK.

5. Open a command prompt, and do a directory scan of your C drive over the network by typing **dir \\%computername%\c$ /s**.

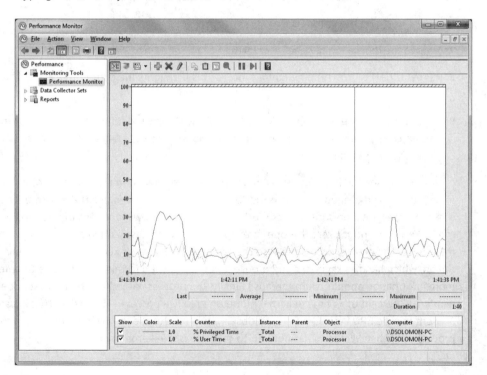

6. When you're finished, just close the tool.

You can also quickly see this by using Task Manager. Just click the Performance tab, and then select Show Kernel Times from the View menu. The CPU usage bar will show total CPU usage in green and kernel-mode time in red.

To see how the Performance Monitor itself uses kernel time and user time, run it again, but add the individual Process counters % User Time and % Privileged Time for every process in the system:

1. If it's not already running, run the Performance Monitor again. (If it is already running, start with a blank display by right-clicking in the graph area and selecting Remove All Counters.)

2. Click the Add button (+) on the toolbar.

3. In the available counters area, expand the Process section.

4. Select the % Privileged Time and % User Time counters.

5. Select a few processes in the Instance box (such as mmc, csrss, and Idle).

6. Click Add, and then click OK.

7. Move the mouse rapidly back and forth.

8. Press Ctrl+H to turn on highlighting mode. This highlights the currently selected counter in black.

9. Scroll through the counters at the bottom of the display to identify the processes whose threads were running when you moved the mouse, and note whether they were running in user mode or kernel mode.

You should see the Performance Monitor process (by looking in the Instance column for the mmc process) kernel-mode *and* user-mode time go up when you move the mouse because it is executing application code in user mode and calling Windows functions that run in kernel mode. You'll also notice kernel-mode thread activity in a process named csrss when you move the mouse. This activity occurs because the Windows subsystem's kernel-mode raw input thread, which handles keyboard and mouse input, is attached to this process. (See Chapter 2 for more information about system threads.) Finally, the process named Idle that you see spending nearly 100 percent of its time in kernel mode isn't really a process—it's a fake process used to account for idle CPU cycles. As you can observe from the mode in which the threads in the Idle process run, when Windows has nothing to do, it does it in kernel mode.

Terminal Services and Multiple Sessions

Terminal Services refers to the support in Windows for multiple interactive user sessions on a single system. With Windows Terminal Services, a remote user can establish a session on another machine, log in, and run applications on the server. The server transmits the graphical user interface to the client (as well as other configurable resources such as audio and clipboard), and the client transmits the user's input back to the server. (Similar to the X Window System, Windows permits running individual applications on a server system with the display remoted to the client instead of remoting the entire desktop.)

The first session is considered the services session, or session zero, and contains system service hosting processes (explained in further detail in Chapter 4, "Management Mechanisms"). The first login session at the physical console of the machine is session one, and additional sessions can be created through the use of the remote desktop connection program (Mstsc.exe) or through the use of fast user switching (described later).

Windows client editions permits a single remote user to connect to the machine, but if someone is logged in at the console, the workstation is locked (that is, someone can be using the system either locally or remotely, but not at the same time). Windows editions that include Windows Media Center allow one interactive session and up to four Windows Media Center Extender sessions.

Windows server systems support two simultaneous remote connections (to facilitate remote management—for example, use of management tools that require being logged in to the machine being managed) and more than two remote sessions if it's appropriately licensed and configured as a terminal server.

All Windows client editions support multiple sessions created locally through a feature called *fast user switching* that can be used one at a time. When a user chooses to disconnect her session instead of log off (for example, by clicking Start and choosing Switch User from the Shutdown submenu or by holding down the Windows key and pressing L and then clicking the Switch User button), the current session (that is, the processes running in that session and all the sessionwide data structures that describe the session) remains active in the system and the system returns to the main logon screen. If a new user logs in, a new session is created.

For applications that want to be aware of running in a terminal server session, there are a set of Windows APIs for programmatically detecting that as well as for controlling various aspects of Terminal Services. (See the Windows SDK and the Remote Desktop Services API for details.)

Chapter 2 describes briefly how sessions are created and has some experiments showing how to view session information with various tools, including the kernel debugger. The "Object Manager" section in Chapter 3 describes how the system namespace for objects is instantiated on a per-session basis and how applications that need to be aware of other instances of themselves on the same system can accomplish that. Finally, Chapter 10 in Part 2 covers how the memory manager sets up and manages sessionwide data.

Objects and Handles

In the Windows operating system, a kernel *object* is a single, run-time instance of a statically defined object type. An *object type* comprises a system-defined data type, functions that operate on instances of the data type, and a set of object attributes. If you write Windows applications, you might encounter process, thread, file, and event objects, to name just a few examples. These objects are based on lower-level objects that Windows creates and manages. In Windows, a process is an instance of the process object type, a file is an instance of the file object type, and so on.

An *object attribute* is a field of data in an object that partially defines the object's state. An object of type *process*, for example, would have attributes that include the process ID, a base scheduling priority, and a pointer to an access token object. *Object methods*, the means for manipulating objects, usually read or change the object attributes. For example, the *open* method for a process would accept a process identifier as input and return a pointer to the object as output.

> **Note** Although there is a parameter named *ObjectAttributes* that a caller supplies when creating an object using the kernel object manager APIs, that parameter shouldn't be confused with the more general meaning of the term as used in this book.

The most fundamental difference between an object and an ordinary data structure is that the internal structure of an object is opaque. You must call an object service to get data out of an object or to put data into it. You can't directly read or change data inside an object. This difference separates the underlying implementation of the object from code that merely uses it, a technique that allows object implementations to be changed easily over time.

Objects, through the help of a kernel component called the *object manager*, provide a convenient means for accomplishing the following four important operating system tasks:

- Providing human-readable names for system resources

- Sharing resources and data among processes

- Protecting resources from unauthorized access

- Reference tracking, which allows the system to know when an object is no longer in use so that it can be automatically deallocated

Not all data structures in the Windows operating system are objects. Only data that needs to be shared, protected, named, or made visible to user-mode programs (via system services) is placed in objects. Structures used by only one component of the operating system to implement internal functions are not objects. Objects and handles (references to an instance of an object) are discussed in more detail in Chapter 3.

Security

Windows was designed from the start to be secure and to meet the requirements of various formal government and industry security ratings, such as the Common Criteria for Information Technology Security Evaluation (CCITSE) specification. Achieving a government-approved security rating allows an operating system to compete in that arena. Of course, many of these capabilities are advantageous features for any multiuser system.

The core security capabilities of Windows include discretionary (need-to-know) and mandatory integrity protection for all shareable system objects (such as files, directories, processes, threads, and so forth), security auditing (for accountability of subjects, or users and the actions they initiate), user authentication at logon, and the prevention of one user from accessing uninitialized resources (such as free memory or disk space) that another user has deallocated.

Windows has three forms of access control over objects. The first form—discretionary access control—is the protection mechanism that most people think of when they think of operating system security. It's the method by which owners of objects (such as files or printers) grant or deny access to others. When users log in, they are given a set of security credentials, or a security context. When they attempt to access objects, their security context is compared to the access control list on the object they are trying to access to determine whether they have permission to perform the requested operation.

Privileged access control is necessary for those times when discretionary access control isn't enough. It's a method of ensuring that someone can get to protected objects if the owner isn't available. For example, if an employee leaves a company, the administrator needs a way to gain access to files that might have been accessible only to that employee. In that case, under Windows, the administrator can take ownership of the file so that he can manage its rights as necessary.

Finally, mandatory integrity control is required when an additional level of security control is required to protect objects that are being accessed from within the same user account. It's used both to isolate Protected Mode Internet Explorer from a user's configuration and to protect objects created by an elevated administrator account from access by a nonelevated administrator account. (See Chapter 6 for more information on User Account Control—UAC.)

Security pervades the interface of the Windows API. The Windows subsystem implements object-based security in the same way the operating system does; the Windows subsystem protects shared Windows objects from unauthorized access by placing Windows security descriptors on them. The first time an application tries to access a shared object, the Windows subsystem verifies the application's right to do so. If the security check succeeds, the Windows subsystem allows the application to proceed.

For a comprehensive description of Windows security, see Chapter 6.

Registry

If you've worked at all with Windows operating systems, you've probably heard about or looked at the registry. You can't talk much about Windows internals without referring to the registry because it's the system database that contains the information required to boot and configure the system, systemwide software settings that control the operation of Windows, the security database, and per-user configuration settings (such as which screen saver to use).

In addition, the registry is a window into in-memory volatile data, such as the current hardware state of the system (what device drivers are loaded, the resources they are using, and so on) as well as the Windows performance counters. The performance counters, which aren't actually "in" the registry, are accessed through the registry functions. See Chapter 4 for more on how performance counter information is accessed from the registry.

Although many Windows users and administrators will never need to look directly into the registry (because you can view or change most configuration settings with standard administrative utilities), it is still a useful source of Windows internals information because it contains many settings that affect system performance and behavior. (If you decide to directly change registry settings, you must exercise extreme caution; any changes might adversely affect system performance or, worse, cause the system to fail to boot successfully.) You'll find references to individual registry keys throughout this book as they pertain to the component being described. Most registry keys referred to in this book are under the systemwide configuration, HKEY_LOCAL_MACHINE, which we'll abbreviate throughout as HKLM.

For further information on the registry and its internal structure, see Chapter 4.

Unicode

Windows differs from most other operating systems in that most internal text strings are stored and processed as 16-bit-wide Unicode characters. Unicode is an international character set standard that defines unique 16-bit values for most of the world's known character sets.

Because many applications deal with 8-bit (single-byte) ANSI character strings, many Windows functions that accept string parameters have two entry points: a Unicode (wide, 16-bit) version and an ANSI (narrow, 8-bit) version. If you call the narrow version of a Windows function, there is a slight performance impact as input string parameters are converted to Unicode before being processed by the system and output parameters are converted from Unicode to ANSI before being returned to the application. Thus, if you have an older service or piece of code that you need to run on Windows but this code is written using ANSI character text strings, Windows will convert the ANSI characters into Unicode for its own use. However, Windows never converts the *data* inside files—it's up to the application to decide whether to store data as Unicode or as ANSI.

Regardless of language, all versions of Windows contain the same functions. Instead of having separate language versions, Windows has a single worldwide binary so that a single installation can support multiple languages (by adding various language packs). Applications can also take advantage of Windows functions that allow single worldwide application binaries that can support multiple languages.

For more information about Unicode, see *www.unicode.org* as well as the programming documentation in the MSDN Library.

Digging into Windows Internals

Although much of the information in this book is based on reading the Windows source code and talking to the developers, you don't have to take *everything* on faith. Many details about the internals of Windows can be exposed and demonstrated by using a variety of available tools, such as those that come with Windows and the Windows debugging tools. These tool packages are briefly described later in this section.

To encourage your exploration of Windows internals, we've included "Experiment" sidebars throughout the book that describe steps you can take to examine a particular aspect of Windows internal behavior. (You already saw a few of these sections earlier in this chapter.) We encourage you to try these experiments so that you can see in action many of the internals topics described in this book.

Table 1-3 shows a list of the principal tools used in this book and where they come from.

TABLE 1-3 Tools for Viewing Windows Internals

Tool	Image Name	Origin
Startup Programs Viewer	AUTORUNS	Sysinternals
Access Check	ACCESSCHK	Sysinternals
Dependency Walker	DEPENDS	*www.dependencywalker.com*
Global Flags	GFLAGS	Debugging tools
Handle Viewer	HANDLE	Sysinternals
Kernel debuggers	WINDBG, KD	Debugging tools, Windows SDK
Object Viewer	WINOBJ	Sysinternals
Performance Monitor	PERFMON.MSC	Windows built-in tool
Pool Monitor	POOLMON	Windows Driver Kit
Process Explorer	PROCEXP	Sysinternals
Process Monitor	PROCMON	Sysinternals
Task (Process) List	TLIST	Debugging tools
Task Manager	TASKMGR	Windows built-in tool

Performance Monitor

We'll refer to the Performance Monitor found in the Administrative Tools folder on the Start menu (or via Control Panel) throughout this book; specifically, we'll focus on the Performance Monitor and Resource Monitor. The Performance Monitor has three functions: system monitoring, viewing performance counter logs, and setting alerts (by using data collector sets, which also contain performance counter logs and trace and configuration data). For simplicity, when we refer to the Performance Monitor, we are referring to the System Monitor function within the tool.

The Performance Monitor provides more information about how your system is operating than any other single utility. It includes hundreds of base and extensible counters for various objects. For each major topic described in this book, a table of the relevant Windows performance counters is included.

The Performance Monitor contains a brief description for each counter. To see the descriptions, select a counter in the Add Counters window and select the Show Description check box.

Although all the low-level system monitoring we'll do in this book can be done with the Performance Monitor, Windows also includes a Resource Monitor utility (accessible from the start menu or from the Task Manager Performance tab) that shows four primary system resources: CPU, Disk, Network, and Memory. In their basic states, these resources are displayed with the same level of information that you would find in Task Manager. However, they also provide sections that can be expanded for more information.

When expanded, the CPU tab displays information about per-process CPU usage, just like Task Manager. However, it adds a column for average CPU usage, which can give you a better idea of which processes are most active. The CPU tab also includes a separate display of services and their associated CPU usage and average. Each service hosting process is identified by the service group it is hosting. As with Process Explorer, selecting a process (by clicking its associated check box) will display a list of named handles opened by the process, as well as a list of modules (such as DLLs) that are loaded in the process address space. The Search Handles box can also be used to search for which processes have opened a handle to a given named resource.

The Memory section displays much of the same information that one can obtain with Task Manager, but it is organized for the entire system. A physical memory bar graph displays the current organization of physical memory into either hardware reserved, in use, modified, standby, and free memory. See Chapter 10 in Part 2 for the exact meaning of these terms.

The Disk section, on the other hand, displays per-file information for I/Os in a way that makes it easy to identify the most accessed, written to, or read from files on the system. These results can be further filtered down by process.

The Networking section displays the active network connections and which processes own them, as well as how much data is going through them. This information makes it possible to see background network activity that might be hard to detect otherwise. In addition, the TCP connections that are active on the system are shown, organized by process, with data such as the remote and local port and address, and packet latency. Finally, a list of listening ports is displayed by process, allowing an administrator to see which services (or applications) are currently waiting for connections on a given port. The protocol and firewall policy for each port and process is also shown.

Note that all of the Windows performance counters are accessible programmatically. The section "HKEY_PERFORMANCE_DATA" in Chapter 4 has a brief description of the components involved in retrieving performance counters through the Windows API.

Kernel Debugging

Kernel debugging means examining internal kernel data structures and/or stepping through functions in the kernel. It is a useful way to investigate Windows internals because you can display internal system information not available through any other tools and get a clearer idea of code flows within the kernel.

Before describing the various ways you can debug the kernel, let's examine a set of files that you'll need in order to perform any type of kernel debugging.

Symbols for Kernel Debugging

Symbol files contain the names of functions and variables and the layout and format of data structures. They are generated by the linker and used by debuggers to reference and display these names during a debug session. This information is not usually stored in the binary image because it is not needed to execute the code. This means that binaries are smaller and faster. However, this means that when debugging, you must make sure that the debugger can access the symbol files that are associated with the images you are referencing during a debugging session.

To use any of the kernel debugging tools to examine internal Windows kernel data structures (such as the process list, thread blocks, loaded driver list, memory usage information, and so on), you must have the correct symbol files for at least the kernel image, Ntoskrnl.exe. (The section "Architecture Overview" in Chapter 2 explains more about this file.) Symbol table files must match the version of the image they were taken from. For example, if you install a Windows Service Pack or hot fix that updates the kernel, you must obtain the matching, updated symbol files.

While it is possible to download and install symbols for various versions of Windows, updated symbols for hot fixes are not always available. The easiest solution to obtain the correct version of symbols for debugging is to use the Microsoft on-demand symbol server by using a special syntax for the symbol path that you specify in the debugger. For example, the following symbol path causes the debugging tools to load required symbols from the Internet symbol server and keep a local copy in the c:\symbols folder:

```
srv*c:\symbols*http://msdl.microsoft.com/download/symbols
```

For detailed instructions on how to use the symbol server, see the debugging tools help file or the Web page *http://msdn.microsoft.com/en-us/windows/hardware/gg462988.aspx*.

Debugging Tools for Windows

The Debugging Tools for Windows package contains advanced debugging tools used in this book to explore Windows internals. The latest version is included as part of the Windows Software Development Kit (SDK). These tools can be used to debug user-mode processes as well as the kernel. (See the following sidebar.)

 Note The Debugging Tools for Windows are updated frequently and released independently of Windows operating system versions, so check often for new versions.

User-Mode Debugging

The debugging tools can also be used to attach to a user-mode process and examine and/or change process memory. There are two options when attaching to a process:

- **Invasive** Unless specified otherwise, when you attach to a running process, the DebugActiveProcess Windows function is used to establish a connection between the debugger and the debugee. This permits examining and/or changing process memory, setting breakpoints, and performing other debugging functions. Windows allows you to stop debugging without killing the target process, as long as the debugger is detached, not killed.

- **Noninvasive** With this option, the debugger simply opens the process with the *OpenProcess* function. It does not attach to the process as a debugger. This allows you to examine and/or change memory in the target process, but you cannot set breakpoints.

You can also open user-mode process dump files with the debugging tools. User-mode dump files are explained in Chapter 3 in the section on exception dispatching.

There are two debuggers that can be used for kernel debugging: a command-line version (Kd.exe) and a graphical user interface (GUI) version (Windbg.exe). Both provide the same set of commands, so which one you choose is a matter of personal preference. You can perform three types of kernel debugging with these tools:

- Open a crash dump file created as a result of a Windows system crash. (See Chapter 14, "Crash Dump Analysis," in Part 2 for more information on kernel crash dumps.)

- Connect to a live, running system and examine the system state (or set breakpoints if you're debugging device driver code). This operation requires two computers—a target and a host. The target is the system being debugged, and the host is the system running the debugger. The target system can be connected to the host via a null modem cable, an IEEE 1394 cable, or a USB 2.0 debugging cable. The target system must be booted in debugging mode (either by pressing F8 during the boot process and selecting Debugging Mode or by configuring the system to boot in debugging mode using Bcdedit or Msconfig.exe). You can also connect through a named pipe, which is useful when debugging through a virtual machine product such as Hyper-V, Virtual PC, or VMWare, by exposing the guest operating system's serial port as a named pipe device.

- Windows systems also allow you to connect to the local system and examine the system state. This is called *local kernel debugging*. To initiate local kernel debugging with WinDbg, open the File menu, choose Kernel Debug, click on the Local tab, and then click OK. The target system must be booted in debugging mode. An example output screen is shown in Figure 1-6. Some kernel debugger commands do not work when used in local kernel debugging mode (such as creating a memory dump with the .dump command—however, this can be done with LiveKd, described later in this section).

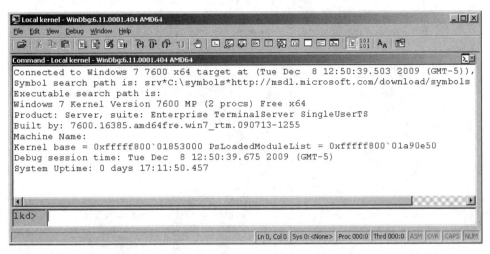

FIGURE 1-6 Local kernel debugging

Once connected in kernel debugging mode, you can use one of the many *debugger extension commands* (commands that begin with "!") to display the contents of internal data structures such as threads, processes, I/O request packets, and memory management information. Throughout this book, the relevant kernel debugger commands and output are included as they apply to each topic being discussed. An excellent companion reference is the Debugger.chm help file, contained in the WinDbg installation folder, which documents all the kernel debugger functionality and extensions. In addition, the *dt* (display type) command can format over 1000 kernel structures because the kernel symbol files for Windows contain type information that the debugger can use to format structures.

EXPERIMENT: Displaying Type Information for Kernel Structures

To display the list of kernel structures whose type information is included in the kernel symbols, type **dt nt!_*** in the kernel debugger. A sample partial output is shown here:

```
lkd> dt nt!_*
        nt!_LIST_ENTRY
        nt!_LIST_ENTRY
        nt!_IMAGE_NT_HEADERS
        nt!_IMAGE_FILE_HEADER
        nt!_IMAGE_OPTIONAL_HEADER
        nt!_IMAGE_NT_HEADERS
        nt!_LARGE_INTEGER
```

You can also use the *dt* command to search for specific structures by using its wildcard lookup capability. For example, if you were looking for the structure name for an interrupt object, type **dt nt!_*interrupt***:

```
lkd> dt nt!_*interrupt*
        nt!_KINTERRUPT
        nt!_KINTERRUPT_MODE
        nt!_KINTERRUPT_POLARITY
        nt!_UNEXPECTED_INTERRUPT
```

Then you can use *dt* to format a specific structure as shown next:

```
lkd> dt nt!_kinterrupt
nt!_KINTERRUPT
   +0x000 Type                 : Int2B
   +0x002 Size                 : Int2B
   +0x008 InterruptListEntry   : _LIST_ENTRY
   +0x018 ServiceRoutine       : Ptr64      unsigned char
   +0x020 MessageServiceRoutine : Ptr64        unsigned char
   +0x028 MessageIndex         : Uint4B
   +0x030 ServiceContext       : Ptr64 Void
   +0x038 SpinLock             : Uint8B
   +0x040 TickCount            : Uint4B
   +0x048 ActualLock           : Ptr64 Uint8B
   +0x050 DispatchAddress      : Ptr64        void
   +0x058 Vector               : Uint4B
   +0x05c Irql                 : UChar
   +0x05d SynchronizeIrql      : UChar
   +0x05e FloatingSave         : UChar
   +0x05f Connected            : UChar
   +0x060 Number               : Uint4B
   +0x064 ShareVector          : UChar
   +0x065 Pad                  : [3] Char
   +0x068 Mode                 : _KINTERRUPT_MODE
   +0x06c Polarity             : _KINTERRUPT_POLARITY
   +0x070 ServiceCount         : Uint4B
   +0x074 DispatchCount        : Uint4B
   +0x078 Rsvd1                : Uint8B
   +0x080 TrapFrame            : Ptr64 _KTRAP_FRAME
   +0x088 Reserved             : Ptr64 Void
   +0x090 DispatchCode         : [4] Uint4B
```

Note that *dt* does not show substructures (structures within structures) by default. To recurse through substructures, use the *–r* switch. For example, using this switch to display the kernel interrupt object shows the format of the _LIST_ENTRY structure stored at the *InterruptListEntry* field:

```
lkd> dt nt!_kinterrupt -r
nt!_KINTERRUPT
   +0x000 Type                 : Int2B
   +0x002 Size                 : Int2B
   +0x008 InterruptListEntry   : _LIST_ENTRY
      +0x000 Flink              : Ptr64 _LIST_ENTRY
         +0x000 Flink             : Ptr64 _LIST_ENTRY
         +0x008 Blink             : Ptr64 _LIST_ENTRY
      +0x008 Blink              : Ptr64 _LIST_ENTRY
         +0x000 Flink             : Ptr64 _LIST_ENTRY
         +0x008 Blink             : Ptr64 _LIST_ENTRY
```

The Debugging Tools for Windows help file also explains how to set up and use the kernel debuggers. Additional details on using the kernel debuggers that are aimed primarily at device driver writers can be found in the Windows Driver Kit documentation.

LiveKd Tool

LiveKd is a free tool from Sysinternals that allows you to use the standard Microsoft kernel debuggers just described to examine the running system without booting the system in debugging mode. This approach might be useful when kernel-level troubleshooting is required on a machine that wasn't booted in debugging mode—certain issues might be hard to reproduce reliably, so a reboot with the *debug* option enabled might not readily exhibit the error.

You run LiveKd just as you would WinDbg or Kd. LiveKd passes any command-line options you specify to the debugger you select. By default, LiveKd runs the command-line kernel debugger (Kd). To have it run WinDbg, specify the *–w* switch. To see the help files for LiveKd switches, specify the *–?* switch.

LiveKd presents a simulated crash dump file to the debugger, so you can perform any operations in LiveKd that are supported on a crash dump. Because LiveKd is relying on physical memory to back the simulated dump, the kernel debugger might run into situations in which data structures are in the middle of being changed by the system and are inconsistent. Each time the debugger is launched, it starts with a fresh view of the system state. If you want to refresh the snapshot, quit the debugger (with the *q* command), and LiveKd will ask you whether you want to start it again. If the debugger enters a loop in printing output, press Ctrl+C to interrupt the output and quit. If it hangs, press Ctrl+Break, which will terminate the debugger process. LiveKd will then ask you whether you want to run the debugger again.

Windows Software Development Kit

The Windows Software Development Kit (SDK) is available as part of the MSDN subscription program or can be downloaded for free from *msdn.microsoft.com*. Besides the Debugging Tools, it contains the documentation, C header files, and libraries necessary to compile and link Windows applications. (Although Microsoft Visual C++ comes with a copy of these header files, the versions contained in the Windows SDK always match the latest version of the Windows operating systems, whereas the version that comes with Visual C++ might be an older version that was current when Visual C++ was released.) From an internals perspective, items of interest in the Windows SDK include the Windows API header files (\Program Files\Microsoft SDKs\Windows\v7.0A\Include). A few of these tools are also shipped as sample source code in both the Windows SDK and the MSDN Library.

Windows Driver Kit

The Windows Driver Kit (WDK) is also available through the MSDN subscription program, and just like the Windows SDK, it is available for free download. The Windows Driver Kit documentation is included in the MSDN Library.

Although the WDK is aimed at device driver developers, it is an abundant source of Windows internals information. For example, while Chapter 8 in Part 2 describes the I/O system architecture, driver model, and basic device driver data structures, it does not describe the individual kernel support functions in detail. The WDK documentation contains a comprehensive description of all the Windows kernel support functions and mechanisms used by device drivers in both a tutorial and reference form.

Besides including the documentation, the WDK contains header files (in particular, ntddk.h, ntifs.h, and wdm.h) that define key internal data structures and constants as well as interfaces to many internal system routines. These files are useful when exploring Windows internal data structures with the kernel debugger because although the general layout and content of these structures are shown in this book, detailed field-level descriptions (such as size and data types) are not. A number of these data structures (such as object dispatcher headers, wait blocks, events, mutants, semaphores, and so on) are, however, fully described in the WDK.

So if you want to dig into the I/O system and driver model beyond what is presented in this book, read the WDK documentation (especially the Kernel-Mode Driver Architecture Design Guide and Reference manuals). You might also find useful *Programming the Microsoft Windows Driver Model, Second Edition* by Walter Oney (Microsoft Press, 2002) and *Developing Drivers with the Windows Driver Foundation* by Penny Orwick and Guy Smith (Microsoft Press, 2007).

Sysinternals Tools

Many experiments in this book use freeware tools that you can download from Sysinternals. Mark Russinovich, coauthor of this book, wrote most of these tools. The most popular tools include Process Explorer and Process Monitor. Note that many of these utilities involve the installation and execution of kernel-mode device drivers and thus require (elevated) administrator privileges, though they can run with limited functionality and output in a standard (or nonelevated) user account.

Since the Sysinternals tools are updated frequently, it is best to make sure you have the latest version. To be notified of tool updates, you can follow the Sysinternals Site Blog (which has an RSS feed).

For a description of all the tools, a description of how to use them, and case studies of problems solved, see *Windows Sysinternals Administrator's Reference* (Microsoft Press, 2011) by Mark Russinovich and Aaron Margosis.

For questions and discussions on the tools, use the Sysinternals Forums.

Conclusion

In this chapter, you've been introduced to the key Windows technical concepts and terms that will be used throughout the book. You've also had a glimpse of the many useful tools available for digging into Windows internals. Now we're ready to begin our exploration of the internal design of the system, beginning with an overall view of the system architecture and its key components.

CHAPTER 2

System Architecture

Now that we've covered the terms, concepts, and tools you need to be familiar with, we're ready to start our exploration of the internal design goals and structure of the Microsoft Windows operating system. This chapter explains the overall architecture of the system—the key components, how they interact with each other, and the context in which they run. To provide a framework for understanding the internals of Windows, let's first review the requirements and goals that shaped the original design and specification of the system.

Requirements and Design Goals

The following requirements drove the specification of Windows NT back in 1989:

- Provide a true 32-bit, preemptive, reentrant, virtual memory operating system

- Run on multiple hardware architectures and platforms

- Run and scale well on symmetric multiprocessing systems

- Be a great distributed computing platform, both as a network client and as a server

- Run most existing 16-bit MS-DOS and Microsoft Windows 3.1 applications

- Meet government requirements for POSIX 1003.1 compliance

- Meet government and industry requirements for operating system security

- Be easily adaptable to the global market by supporting Unicode

To guide the thousands of decisions that had to be made to create a system that met these requirements, the Windows NT design team adopted the following design goals at the beginning of the project:

- **Extensibility**   The code must be written to comfortably grow and change as market requirements change.

- **Portability**   The system must be able to run on multiple hardware architectures and must be able to move with relative ease to new ones as market demands dictate.

- **Reliability and robustness**   The system should protect itself from both internal malfunction and external tampering. Applications should not be able to harm the operating system or other applications.

- **Compatibility**   Although Windows NT should extend existing technology, its user interface and APIs should be compatible with older versions of Windows and with MS-DOS. It should also interoperate well with other systems, such as UNIX, OS/2, and NetWare.

- **Performance**   Within the constraints of the other design goals, the system should be as fast and responsive as possible on each hardware platform.

As we explore the details of the internal structure and operation of Windows, you'll see how these original design goals and market requirements were woven successfully into the construction of the system. But before we start that exploration, let's examine the overall design model for Windows and compare it with other modern operating systems.

Operating System Model

In most multiuser operating systems, applications are separated from the operating system itself—the operating system kernel code runs in a privileged processor mode (referred to as *kernel mode* in this book), with access to system data and to the hardware; application code runs in a nonprivileged processor mode (called *user mode*), with a limited set of interfaces available, limited access to system data, and no direct access to hardware. When a user-mode program calls a system service, the processor executes a special instruction that switches the calling thread to kernel mode. When the system service completes, the operating system switches the thread context back to user mode and allows the caller to continue.

Windows is similar to most UNIX systems in that it's a monolithic operating system in the sense that the bulk of the operating system and device driver code shares the same kernel-mode protected memory space. This means that any operating system component or device driver can potentially corrupt data being used by other operating system components. However, Windows does implement some kernel protection mechanisms, such as PatchGuard and Kernel Mode Code Signing (both described in Chapter 3, "System Mechanisms"), which help in the mitigation and prevention of issues related to the shared kernel-mode address space.

All these operating system components are, of course, fully protected from errant applications because applications don't have direct access to the code and data of the privileged part of the operating system (although they can quickly call other kernel services). This protection is one of the reasons that Windows has the reputation for being both robust and stable as an application server and as a workstation platform, yet fast and nimble from the perspective of core operating system services, such as virtual memory management, file I/O, networking, and file and print sharing.

The kernel-mode components of Windows also embody basic object-oriented design principles. For example, in general they don't reach into one another's data structures to access information maintained by individual components. Instead, they use formal interfaces to pass parameters and access and/or modify data structures.

Despite its pervasive use of objects to represent shared system resources, Windows is not an object-oriented system in the strict sense. Most of the operating system code is written in C for portability. The C programming language doesn't directly support object-oriented constructs such as dynamic binding of data types, polymorphic functions, or class inheritance. Therefore, the C-based implementation of objects in Windows borrows from, but doesn't depend on, features of particular object-oriented languages.

Architecture Overview

With this brief overview of the design goals and packaging of Windows, let's take a look at the key system components that make up its architecture. A simplified version of this architecture is shown in Figure 2-1. Keep in mind that this diagram is basic—it doesn't show everything. (For example, the networking components and the various types of device driver layering are not shown.)

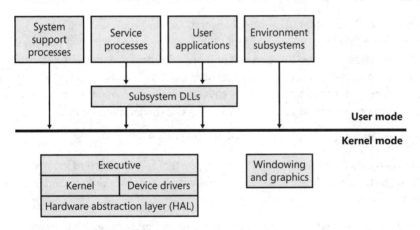

FIGURE 2-1 Simplified Windows architecture

In Figure 2-1, first notice the line dividing the user-mode and kernel-mode parts of the Windows operating system. The boxes above the line represent user-mode processes, and the components below the line are kernel-mode operating system services. As mentioned in Chapter 1, "Concepts and Tools," user-mode threads execute in a protected process address space (although while they are executing in kernel mode, they have access to system space). Thus, system support processes, service processes, user applications, and environment subsystems each have their own private process address space.

The four basic types of user-mode processes are described as follows:

- Fixed (or hardwired) *system support processes*, such as the logon process and the Session Manager, that are not Windows services. (That is, they are not started by the service control manager. Chapter 4, "Management and Mechanisms," describes services in detail.)

- *Service processes* that host Windows services, such as the Task Scheduler and Print Spooler services. Services generally have the requirement that they run independently of user logons. Many Windows server applications, such as Microsoft SQL Server and Microsoft Exchange Server, also include components that run as services.

- *User applications*, which can be one of the following types: Windows 32-bit or 64-bit, Windows 3.1 16-bit, MS-DOS 16-bit, or POSIX 32-bit or 64-bit. Note that 16-bit applications can be run only on 32-bit Windows.

- *Environment subsystem server processes*, which implement part of the support for the operating system *environment*, or personality, presented to the user and programmer. Windows NT originally shipped with three environment subsystems: Windows, POSIX, and OS/2. However, the POSIX and OS/2 subsystems last shipped with Windows 2000. The Ultimate and Enterprise editions of Windows client as well as all of the server versions include support for an enhanced POSIX subsystem called Subsystem for Unix-based Applications (SUA).

In Figure 2-1, notice the "Subsystem DLLs" box below the "Service processes" and "User applications" boxes. Under Windows, user applications don't call the native Windows operating system services directly; rather, they go through one or more *subsystem dynamic-link libraries* (DLLs). The role of the subsystem DLLs is to translate a documented function into the appropriate internal (and generally undocumented) native system service calls. This translation might or might not involve sending a message to the environment subsystem process that is serving the user application.

The kernel-mode components of Windows include the following:

- The Windows *executive* contains the base operating system services, such as memory management, process and thread management, security, I/O, networking, and interprocess communication.

- The Windows *kernel* consists of low-level operating system functions, such as thread scheduling, interrupt and exception dispatching, and multiprocessor synchronization. It also provides a set of routines and basic objects that the rest of the executive uses to implement higher-level constructs.

- *Device drivers* include both hardware device drivers, which translate user I/O function calls into specific hardware device I/O requests, as well as nonhardware device drivers such as file system and network drivers.

- The *hardware abstraction layer* (HAL) is a layer of code that isolates the kernel, the device drivers, and the rest of the Windows executive from platform-specific hardware differences (such as differences between motherboards).

- The *windowing and graphics system* implements the graphical user interface (GUI) functions (better known as the Windows USER and GDI functions), such as dealing with windows, user interface controls, and drawing.

Table 2-1 lists the file names of the core Windows operating system components. (You'll need to know these file names because we'll be referring to some system files by name.) Each of these components is covered in greater detail both later in this chapter and in the chapters that follow.

TABLE 2-1 Core Windows System Files

File Name	Components
Ntoskrnl.exe	Executive and kernel
Ntkrnlpa.exe (32-bit systems only)	Executive and kernel, with support for Physical Address Extension (PAE), which allows 32-bit systems to address up to 64 GB of physical memory and to mark memory as nonexecutable (see the section "No Execute Page Prevention" in Chapter 10, "Memory Management," in Part 2)
Hal.dll	Hardware abstraction layer
Win32k.sys	Kernel-mode part of the Windows subsystem
Ntdll.dll	Internal support functions and system service dispatch stubs to executive functions
Kernel32.dll, Advapi32.dll, User32.dll, Gdi32.dll	Core Windows subsystem DLLs

Before we dig into the details of these system components, though, let's examine some basics about the Windows kernel design, starting with how Windows achieves portability across multiple hardware architectures.

Portability

Windows was designed to run on a variety of hardware architectures. The initial release of Windows NT supported the x86 and MIPS architectures. Support for the Digital Equipment Corporation (which was bought by Compaq, which later merged with Hewlett-Packard) Alpha AXP was added shortly thereafter. (Although Alpha AXP was a 64-bit processor, Windows NT ran in 32-bit mode. During the development of Windows 2000, a native 64-bit version was running on Alpha AXP, but this was never released.) Support for a fourth processor architecture, the Motorola PowerPC, was added in Windows NT 3.51. Because of changing market demands, however, support for the MIPS and PowerPC architectures was dropped before development began on Windows 2000. Later, Compaq withdrew support for the Alpha AXP architecture, resulting in Windows 2000 being supported only on the x86 architecture. Windows XP and Windows Server 2003 added support for three 64-bit processor families: the Intel Itanium IA-64 family, the AMD64 family, and the Intel 64-bit Extension Technology (EM64T) for x86 (which is compatible with the AMD64 architecture, although there are slight differences in instructions supported). The latter two processor families are called *64-bit extended systems* and in this book are referred to as *x64*. (How Windows runs 32-bit applications on 64-bit Windows is explained in Chapter 3.)

Windows achieves portability across hardware architectures and platforms in two primary ways:

- Windows has a layered design, with low-level portions of the system that are processor-architecture-specific or platform-specific isolated into separate modules so that upper layers of the system can be shielded from the differences between architectures and among hardware platforms. The two key components that provide operating system portability are the kernel (contained in Ntoskrnl.exe) and the hardware abstraction layer (or HAL, contained in Hal.dll). Both these components are described in more detail later in this chapter. Functions that are architecture-specific (such as thread context switching and trap dispatching) are implemented in the kernel. Functions that can differ among systems within the same architecture (for example, different motherboards) are implemented in the HAL. The only other component with a significant amount of architecture-specific code is the memory manager, but even that is a small amount compared to the system as a whole.

- The vast majority of Windows is written in C, with some portions in C++. Assembly language is used only for those parts of the operating system that need to communicate directly with system hardware (such as the interrupt trap handler) or that are extremely performance-sensitive (such as context switching). Assembly language code exists not only in the kernel and the HAL but also in a few other places within the core operating system (such as the routines that implement interlocked instructions as well as one module in the local procedure call facility), in the kernel-mode part of the Windows subsystem, and even in some user-mode libraries, such as the process startup code in Ntdll.dll (a system library explained later in this chapter).

Symmetric Multiprocessing

Multitasking is the operating system technique for sharing a single processor among multiple threads of execution. When a computer has more than one processor, however, it can execute multiple threads simultaneously. Thus, whereas a multitasking operating system only appears to execute multiple threads at the same time, a multiprocessing operating system actually does it, executing one thread on each of its processors.

As mentioned at the beginning of this chapter, one of the key design goals for Windows was that it had to run well on multiprocessor computer systems. Windows is a *symmetric multiprocessing* (SMP) operating system. There is no master processor—the operating system as well as user threads can be scheduled to run on any processor. Also, all the processors share just one memory space. This model contrasts with *asymmetric multiprocessing* (ASMP), in which the operating system typically selects one processor to execute operating system kernel code while other processors run only user code. The differences in the two multiprocessing models are illustrated in Figure 2-2.

Windows also supports three modern types of multiprocessor systems: multicore, Hyper-Threading enabled, and NUMA (non-uniform memory architecture). These are briefly mentioned in the following paragraphs. (For a complete, detailed description of the scheduling support for these systems, see the thread scheduling section in Chapter 5, "Processes and Threads".)

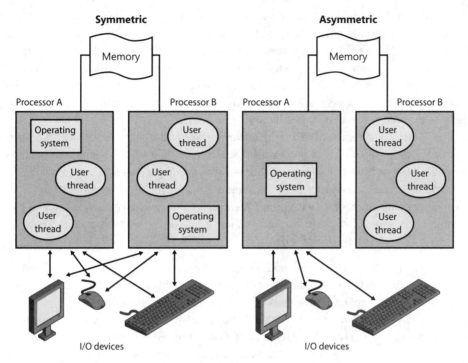

FIGURE 2-2 Symmetric vs. asymmetric multiprocessing

Hyper-Threading is a technology introduced by Intel that provides two logical processors for each physical core. Each logical processor has its own CPU state, but the execution engine and onboard cache are shared. This permits one logical CPU to make progress while the other logical CPU is stalled (such as after a cache miss or branch misprediction). The scheduling algorithms are enhanced to make optimal use of Hyper-Threading-enabled machines, such as by scheduling threads on an idle physical processor versus choosing an idle logical processor on a physical processor whose other logical processors are busy. For more details on thread scheduling, see Chapter 5.

In NUMA systems, processors are grouped in smaller units called *nodes*. Each node has its own processors and memory and is connected to the larger system through a cache-coherent interconnect bus. Windows on a NUMA system still runs as an SMP system, in that all processors have access to all memory—it's just that node-local memory is faster to reference than memory attached to other nodes. The system attempts to improve performance by scheduling threads on processors that are in the same node as the memory being used. It attempts to satisfy memory-allocation requests from within the node, but it will allocate memory from other nodes if necessary.

Naturally, Windows also natively supports multicore systems—because these systems have real physical cores (simply on the same package), the original SMP code in Windows treats them as discrete processors, except for certain accounting and identification tasks (such as licensing, described shortly) that distinguish between cores on the same processor and cores on different sockets.

Windows was not originally designed with a specific processor number limit in mind, other than the licensing policies that differentiate the various Windows editions. However, for convenience and efficiency, Windows does keep track of processors (total number, idle, busy, and other such details) in a bitmask (sometimes called an *affinity mask*) that is the same number of bits as the native data type of the machine (32-bit or 64-bit), which allows the processor to manipulate bits directly within a register. Due to this fact, Windows systems were originally limited to the number of CPUs in a native word, because the affinity mask couldn't arbitrarily be increased. To maintain compatibility, as well as support larger processor systems, Windows implements a higher-order construct called a *processor group*. The processor group is a set of processors that can all be defined by a single affinity bitmask, and the kernel as well as the applications can choose which group they refer to during affinity updates. Compatible applications can query the number of supported groups (currently limited to 4) and then enumerate the bitmask for each group. Meanwhile, legacy applications continue to function by seeing only their current group. More information on how exactly Windows assigns processors to groups (which is also related to NUMA) is detailed in Chapter 5.

As mentioned, the actual number of supported *licensed* processors depends on the edition of Windows being used. (See Table 2-2 later in this chapter.) This number is stored in the system license policy file (\Windows\ServiceProfiles\NetworkService\AppData\Roaming\Microsoft \SoftwareProtectionPlatform\tokens.dat) as a policy value called "Kernel-RegisteredProcessors." (Keep in mind that tampering with that data is a violation of the software license, and modifying licensing policies to allow the use of more processors involves more than just changing this value.)

Scalability

One of the key issues with multiprocessor systems is *scalability*. To run correctly on an SMP system, operating system code must adhere to strict guidelines and rules. Resource contention and other performance issues are more complicated in multiprocessing systems than in uniprocessor systems and must be accounted for in the system's design. Windows incorporates several features that are crucial to its success as a multiprocessor operating system:

- The ability to run operating system code on any available processor and on multiple processors at the same time

- Multiple threads of execution within a single process, each of which can execute simultaneously on different processors

- Fine-grained synchronization within the kernel (such as spinlocks, queued spinlocks, and pushlocks, described in Chapter 3) as well as within device drivers and server processes, which allows more components to run concurrently on multiple processors

- Programming mechanisms such as I/O completion ports (described in Chapter 8, "I/O System," in Part 2) that facilitate the efficient implementation of multithreaded server processes that can scale well on multiprocessor systems

The scalability of the Windows kernel has evolved over time. For example, Windows Server 2003 introduced per-CPU scheduling queues, which permit thread scheduling decisions to occur in parallel on multiple processors. Windows 7 and Windows Server 2008 R2 eliminated global locking on the scheduling database. This step-wise improvement of the granularity of locking has also occurred in other areas, such as the memory manager. Further details on multiprocessor synchronization can be found in Chapter 3.

Differences Between Client and Server Versions

Windows ships in both client and server retail packages. As of this writing, there are six client versions of Windows 7: Windows 7 Home Basic, Windows 7 Home Premium, Windows 7 Professional, Windows 7 Ultimate, Windows 7 Enterprise, and Windows 7 Starter.

There are seven different versions of Windows Server 2008 R2: Windows Server 2008 R2 Foundation, Windows Server 2008 R2 Standard, Windows Server 2008 R2 Enterprise, Windows Server 2008 R2 Datacenter, Windows Web Server 2008 R2, Windows HPC Server 2008 R2, and Windows Server 2008 R2 for Itanium-Based Systems (which is the last release of Windows to support the Intel Itanium processor).

Additionally, there are "N" versions of the client that do not include Windows Media Player. Finally, the Standard, Enterprise, and Datacenter editions of Windows Server 2008 R2 also include "with Hyper-V" editions, which include Hyper-V. (Hyper-V virtualization is discussed in Chapter 3.)

These versions differ by

- The number of processors supported (in terms of sockets, not cores or threads)

- The amount of physical memory supported (actually highest physical address usable for RAM—see Chapter 10 in Part 2 for more information on physical memory limits)

- The number of concurrent network connections supported (For example, a maximum of 10 concurrent connections are allowed to the file and print services in the client version.)

- Support for Media Center

- Support for Multi-Touch, Aero, and Desktop Compositing

- Support for features such as BitLocker, VHD Booting, AppLocker, Windows XP Compatibility Mode, and more than 100 other configurable licensing policy values

- Layered services that come with Windows Server editions that don't come with the client editions (for example, directory services and clustering)

Table 2-2 lists the differences in memory and processor support for Windows 7 and Windows Server 2008 R2. For a detailed comparison chart of the different editions of Windows Server 2008 R2, see *www.microsoft.com/windowsserver2008/en/us/r2-compare-specs.aspx*.

TABLE 2-2 Differences Between Windows 7 and Windows Server 2008 R2

	Number of Sockets Supported (32-Bit Edition)	Physical Memory Supported (32-Bit Edition)	Number of Sockets Supported (64-Bit Edition)	Physical Memory Supported (Itanium Editions)	Physical Memory Supported (x64 Editions)
Windows 7 Starter	1	2 GB	Not available	Not available	2 GB
Windows 7 Home Basic	1	4 GB	1	Not available	8 GB
Windows 7 Home Premium	1	4 GB	1	Not available	16 GB
Windows 7 Professional	2	4 GB	2	Not available	192 GB
Windows 7 Enterprise	2	4 GB	2	Not available	192 GB
Windows 7 Ultimate	2	4 GB	2	Not available	192 GB
Windows Server 2008 R2 Foundation	Not available	Not available	1	Not available	8 GB
Windows Web Server 2008 R2	Not available	Not available	4	Not available	32 GB
Windows Server 2008 R2 Standard	Not available	Not available	4	Not available	32 GB
Windows HPC Server 2008 R2	Not available	Not available	4	Not available	128 GB
Windows Server 2008 R2 Enterprise	Not available	Not available	8	Not available	2048 GB
Windows Server 2008 R2 Datacenter	Not available	Not available	64	Not available	2048 GB
Windows Server 2008 R2 for Itanium-Based Systems	Not available	Not available	64	2048 GB	Not available

Although there are several client and server retail packages of the Windows operating system, they share a common set of core system files, including the kernel image, Ntoskrnl.exe (and the PAE version, Ntkrnlpa.exe); the HAL libraries; the device drivers; and the base system utilities and DLLs. These files are identical for all editions of Windows 7 and Windows Server 2008 R2.

With so many different editions of Windows and each having the same kernel image, how does the system know which edition is booted? By querying the registry values ProductType and ProductSuite under the HKLM\SYSTEM\CurrentControlSet\Control\ProductOptions key. ProductType is used to distinguish whether the system is a client system or a server system (of any flavor). These values are loaded into the registry based on the licensing policy file described earlier. The valid values are listed in Table 2-3. This can be queried from the user-mode *GetVersionEx* function or from a device driver using the kernel-mode support function *RtlGetVersion*.

TABLE 2-3 ProductType Registry Values

Edition of Windows	Value of ProductType
Windows client	WinNT
Windows server (domain controller)	LanmanNT
Windows server (server only)	ServerNT

A different registry value, ProductPolicy, contains a cached copy of the data inside the tokens.dat file, which differentiates between the editions of Windows and the features that they enable.

If user programs need to determine which edition of Windows is running, they can call the Windows *VerifyVersionInfo* function, documented in the Windows Software Development Kit (SDK). Device drivers can call the kernel-mode function *RtlVerifyVersionInfo*, documented in the WDK.

So if the core files are essentially the same for the client and server versions, how do the systems differ in operation? In short, server systems are optimized by default for system throughput as high-performance application servers, whereas the client version (although it has server capabilities) is optimized for response time for interactive desktop use. For example, based on the product type, several resource allocation decisions are made differently at system boot time, such as the size and number of operating system heaps (or pools), the number of internal system worker threads, and the size of the system data cache. Also, run-time policy decisions, such as the way the memory manager trades off system and process memory demands, differ between the server and client editions. Even some thread scheduling details have different default behavior in the two families (the default length of the time slice, or thread *quantum*—see Chapter 5 for details). Where there are significant operational differences in the two products, these are highlighted in the pertinent chapters throughout the rest of this book. Unless otherwise noted, everything in this book applies to both the client and server versions.

EXPERIMENT: Determining Features Enabled by Licensing Policy

As mentioned earlier, Windows supports more than 100 different features that can be enabled through the software licensing mechanism. These policy settings determine the various differences not only between a client and server installation, but also between each edition (or SKU) of the operating system, such as BitLocker support (available on Windows server as well as the Ultimate and Enterprise editions of Windows client). You can use the SlPolicy tool available from Winsider Seminars & Solutions (*www.winsiderss.com/tools/slpolicy.htm*) to display these policy values on your machine.

Policy settings are organized by a *facility*, which represents the owner module for which the policy applies. You can display a list of all facilities on your system by running Slpolicy.exe with the *–f* switch:

```
C:\>SlPolicy.exe -f
SlPolicy v1.05 - Show Software Licensing Policies
Copyright (C) 2008-2011 Winsider Seminars & Solutions Inc.
www.winsiderss.com

Software Licensing Facilities:

Kernel
Licensing and Activation
Core
DWM
SMB
IIS
.
.
.
```

You can then add the name of any facility after the switch to display the policy value for that facility. For example, to look at the limitations on CPUs and available memory, use the Kernel facility. Here's the expected output on a machine running Windows 7 Ultimate:

```
C:\>SlPolicy.exe -f Kernel


SlPolicy v1.05 - Show Software Licensing Policies
Copyright (C) 2008-2011 Winsider Seminars & Solutions Inc.
www.winsiderss.com

Kernel
------
Processor Limit: 2
Maximum Memory Allowed (x86): 4096
Maximum Memory Allowed (x64): 196608
Maximum Memory Allowed (IA64): 196608
Maximum Physical Page: 4096
Addition of Physical Memory Allowed: No
Addition of Physical Memory Allowed, if virtualized: Yes
Product Information: 1
Dynamic Partitioning Supported: No
Virtual Dynamic Partitioning Supported: No
Memory Mirroring Supported: No
Native VHD Boot Supported: Yes
Bad Memory List Persistance Supported: No
Number of MUI Languages Allowed: 1000
List of Allowed Languages: EMPTY
List of Disallowed Languages: EMPTY
MUI Language SKU:
Expiration Date: 0
```

Checked Build

There is a special debug version of Windows called the *checked build* (available only with an MSDN Operating Systems subscription). It is a recompilation of the Windows source code with a compile-time flag defined called "DBG" (to cause compile-time, conditional debugging and tracing code to be included). Also, to make it easier to understand the machine code, the post-processing of the Windows binaries to optimize code layout for faster execution is not performed. (See the section "Debugging Performance-Optimized Code" in the Debugging Tools for Windows help file.)

The checked build is provided primarily to aid device driver developers because it performs more stringent error checking on kernel-mode functions called by device drivers or other system code. For example, if a driver (or some other piece of kernel-mode code) makes an invalid call to a system function that is checking parameters (such as acquiring a spinlock at the wrong interrupt level), the system will stop execution when the problem is detected rather than allow some data structure to be corrupted and the system to possibly crash at a later time.

EXPERIMENT: Determining If You Are Running the Checked Build

There is no built-in tool to display whether you are running the checked build or the retail build (called the *free build*). However, this information is available through the "Debug" property of the Windows Management Instrumentation (WMI) Win32_OperatingSystem class. The following sample Microsoft Visual Basic script displays this property:

```
strComputer = "."
Set objWMIService = GetObject("winmgmts:" _
 & "{impersonationLevel=impersonate}!\\" & strComputer & "\root\cimv2")
Set colOperatingSystems = objWMIService.ExecQuery _
 ("SELECT * FROM Win32_OperatingSystem")
For Each objOperatingSystem in colOperatingSystems
 Wscript.Echo "Caption: " & objOperatingSystem.Caption
 Wscript.Echo "Debug: " & objOperatingSystem.Debug
 Wscript.Echo "Version: " & objOperatingSystem.Version
Next
```

To try this, type in the preceding script and save it as file. The following is the output from running the script:

```
C:\>cscript osversion.vbs
Microsoft (R) Windows Script Host Version 5.8
Copyright (C) Microsoft Corporation. All rights reserved.

Caption: Microsoft Windows Server 2008 R2 Enterprise
Debug: False
Version: 6.1.7600
```

This system is not running the checked build, because the Debug flag shown here says False.

Much of the additional code in the checked-build binaries is a result of using the ASSERT and/or NT_ASSERT macros, which are defined in the WDK header file Wdm.h and documented in the WDK documentation. These macros test a condition (such as the validity of a data structure or parameter), and if the expression evaluates to FALSE, the macros call the kernel-mode function *RtlAssert*, which calls *DbgPrintEx* to send the text of the debug message to a debug message buffer. If a kernel debugger is attached, this message is displayed automatically followed by a prompt asking the user what to do about the assertion failure (breakpoint, ignore, terminate process, or terminate thread). If the system wasn't booted with the kernel debugger (using the *debug* option in the Boot Configuration Database—BCD) and no kernel debugger is currently attached, failure of an ASSERT test will bug-check the system. For a list of ASSERT checks made by some of the kernel support routines, see the section "Checked Build ASSERTs" in the WDK documentation.

The checked build is also useful for system administrators because of the additional detailed informational tracing that can be enabled for certain components. (For detailed instructions, see the Microsoft Knowledge Base Article number 314743, titled *HOWTO: Enable Verbose Debug Tracing in Various Drivers and Subsystems*.) This information output is sent to an internal debug message buffer using the *DbgPrintEx* function referred to earlier. To view the debug messages, you can either attach a kernel debugger to the target system (which requires booting the target system in debugging mode), use the *!dbgprint* command while performing local kernel debugging, or use the Dbgview.exe tool from Sysinternals (*www.microsoft.com/technet/sysinternals*).

You don't have to install the entire checked build to take advantage of the debug version of the operating system. You can just copy the checked version of the kernel image (Ntoskrnl.exe) and the appropriate HAL (Hal.dll) to a normal retail installation. The advantage of this approach is that device drivers and other kernel code get the rigorous checking of the checked build without having to run the slower debug versions of all components in the system. For detailed instructions on how to do this, see the section "Installing Just the Checked Operating System and HAL" in the WDK documentation.

Finally, the checked build can also be useful for testing user-mode code only because the timing of the system is different. (This is because of the additional checking taking place within the kernel and the fact that the components are compiled without optimizations.) Often, multithreaded synchronization bugs are related to specific timing conditions. By running your tests on a system running the checked build (or at least the checked kernel and HAL), the fact that the timing of the whole system is different might cause latent timing bugs to surface that do not occur on a normal retail system.

Key System Components

Now that we've looked at the high-level architecture of Windows, let's delve deeper into the internal structure and the role each key operating system component plays. Figure 2-3 is a more detailed and complete diagram of the core Windows system architecture and components than was shown earlier in the chapter (in Figure 2-1). Note that it still does not show all components (networking in particular, which is explained in Chapter 7, "Networking."

The following sections elaborate on each major element of this diagram. Chapter 3 explains the primary control mechanisms the system uses (such as the object manager, interrupts, and so forth). Chapter 13, "Startup and Shutdown," in Part 2 describes the process of starting and shutting down

Windows, and Chapter 4 details management mechanisms such as the registry, service processes, and Windows Management Instrumentation. Other chapters explore in even more detail the internal structure and operation of key areas such as processes and threads, memory management, security, the I/O manager, storage management, the cache manager, the Windows file system (NTFS), and networking.

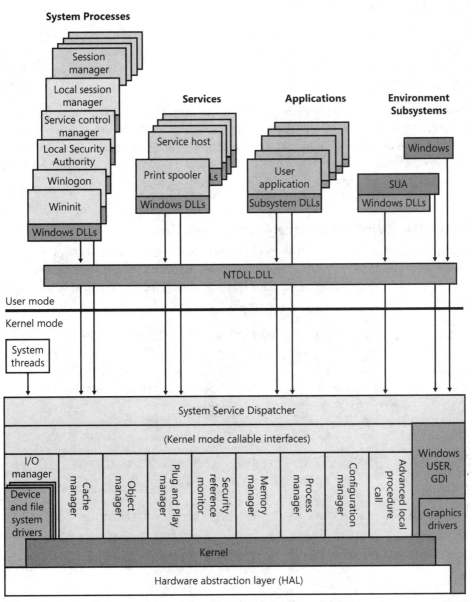

FIGURE 2-3 Windows architecture

Environment Subsystems and Subsystem DLLs

The role of an environment subsystem is to expose some subset of the base Windows executive system services to application programs. Each subsystem can provide access to different subsets of the native services in Windows. That means that some things can be done from an application built on one subsystem that can't be done by an application built on another subsystem. For example, a Windows application can't use the SUA *fork* function.

Each executable image (.exe) is bound to one and only one subsystem. When an image is run, the process creation code examines the subsystem type code in the image header so that it can notify the proper subsystem of the new process. This type code is specified with the /SUBSYSTEM qualifier of the *link* command in Microsoft Visual C++.

As mentioned earlier, user applications don't call Windows system services directly. Instead, they go through one or more subsystem DLLs. These libraries export the documented interface that the programs linked to that subsystem can call. For example, the Windows subsystem DLLs (such as Kernel32.dll, Advapi32.dll, User32.dll, and Gdi32.dll) implement the Windows API functions. The SUA subsystem DLL (Psxdll.dll) implements the SUA API functions.

EXPERIMENT: Viewing the Image Subsystem Type

You can see the image subsystem type by using the Dependency Walker tool (Depends.exe) (available at *www.dependencywalker.com*). For example, notice the image types for two different Windows images, Notepad.exe (the simple text editor) and Cmd.exe (the Windows command prompt):

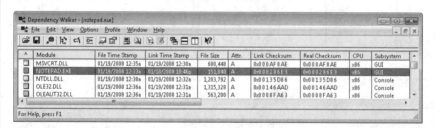

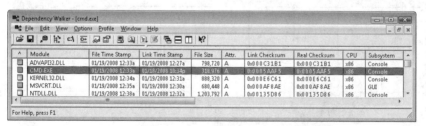

This shows that Notepad is a GUI program, while Cmd is a console, or character-based, program. And although this implies there are two different subsystems for GUI and character-based programs, there is just one Windows subsystem, and GUI programs can have consoles, just like console programs can display GUIs.

When an application calls a function in a subsystem DLL, one of three things can occur:

- The function is entirely implemented in user mode inside the subsystem DLL. In other words, no message is sent to the environment subsystem process, and no Windows executive system services are called. The function is performed in user mode, and the results are returned to the caller. Examples of such functions include *GetCurrentProcess* (which always returns −1, a value that is defined to refer to the current process in all process-related functions) and *GetCurrentProcessId*. (The process ID doesn't change for a running process, so this ID is retrieved from a cached location, thus avoiding the need to call into the kernel.)

- The function requires one or more calls to the Windows executive. For example, the Windows *ReadFile* and *WriteFile* functions involve calling the underlying internal (and undocumented) Windows I/O system services *NtReadFile* and *NtWriteFile*, respectively.

- The function requires some work to be done in the environment subsystem process. (The environment subsystem processes, running in user mode, are responsible for maintaining the state of the client applications running under their control.) In this case, a client/server request is made to the environment subsystem via a message sent to the subsystem to perform some operation. The subsystem DLL then waits for a reply before returning to the caller.

Some functions can be a combination of the second and third items just listed, such as the Windows *CreateProcess* and *CreateThread* functions.

Subsystem Startup

Subsystems are started by the Session Manager (Smss.exe) process. The subsystem startup information is stored under the registry key HKLM\SYSTEM\CurrentControlSet\Control \Session Manager\SubSystems. Figure 2-4 shows the values under this key.

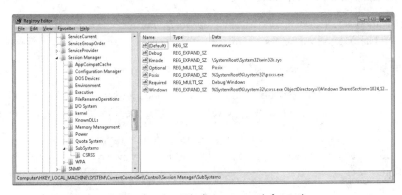

FIGURE 2-4 Registry Editor showing Windows startup information

The *Required* value lists the subsystems that load when the system boots. The value has two strings: Windows and Debug. The Windows value contains the file specification of the Windows subsystem, Csrss.exe, which stands for Client/Server Run-Time Subsystem. *Debug* is blank (because it's used for internal testing) and therefore does nothing. The *Optional* value indicates that the

SUA subsystem will be started on demand. The registry value *Kmode* contains the file name of the kernel-mode portion of the Windows subsystem, Win32k.sys (explained later in this chapter).

Let's take a closer look at each of the environment subsystems.

Windows Subsystem

Although Windows was designed to support multiple, independent environment subsystems, from a practical perspective, having each subsystem implement all the code to handle windowing and display I/O would result in a large amount of duplication of system functions that, ultimately, would negatively affect both system size and performance. Because Windows was the primary subsystem, the Windows designers decided to locate these basic functions there and have the other subsystems call on the Windows subsystem to perform display I/O. Thus, the SUA subsystem calls services in the Windows subsystem to perform display I/O.

As a result of this design decision, the Windows subsystem is a required component for any Windows system, even on server systems with no interactive users logged in. Because of this, the process is marked as a critical process (which means if for any reason it exits, the system crashes).

The Windows subsystem consists of the following major components:

- For each session, an instance of the environment subsystem process (Csrss.exe) loads three DLLs (Basesrv.dll, Winsrv.dll, and Csrsrv.dll) that contain support for the following:

  - Creating and deleting processes and threads

  - Portions of the support for 16-bit virtual DOS machine (VDM) processes (32-bit Windows only)

  - Side-by-Side (SxS)/Fusion and manifest support

  - Other miscellaneous functions—such as *GetTempFile*, *DefineDosDevice*, *ExitWindowsEx*, and several natural language support functions

- A kernel-mode device driver (Win32k.sys) that contains the following:

  - The window manager, which controls window displays; manages screen output; collects input from keyboard, mouse, and other devices; and passes user messages to applications.

  - The Graphics Device Interface (GDI), which is a library of functions for graphics output devices. It includes functions for line, text, and figure drawing and for graphics manipulation.

  - Wrappers for DirectX support that is implemented in another kernel driver (Dxgkrnl.sys).

- The console host process (Conhost.exe), which provides support for console (character cell) applications.

- Subsystem DLLs (such as Kernel32.dll, Advapi32.dll, User32.dll, and Gdi32.dll) that translate documented Windows API functions into the appropriate and mostly undocumented kernel-mode system service calls in Ntoskrnl.exe and Win32k.sys.

- Graphics device drivers for hardware-dependent graphics display drivers, printer drivers, and video miniport drivers.

> **Note** As part of a refactoring effort in the Windows architecture called MinWin, the subsystem DLLs are now generally composed of specific libraries that implement *API Sets*, which are then linked together into the subsystem DLL and resolved using a special redirection scheme. More information on this refactoring is available in Chapter 5 in the "Image Loader" section.

Applications call the standard USER functions to create user interface controls, such as windows and buttons, on the display. The window manager communicates these requests to the GDI, which passes them to the graphics device drivers, where they are formatted for the display device. A display driver is paired with a video miniport driver to complete video display support.

The GDI provides a set of standard two-dimensional functions that let applications communicate with graphics devices without knowing anything about the devices. GDI functions mediate between applications and graphics devices such as display drivers and printer drivers. The GDI interprets application requests for graphic output and sends the requests to graphics display drivers. It also provides a standard interface for applications to use varying graphics output devices. This interface enables application code to be independent of the hardware devices and their drivers. The GDI tailors its messages to the capabilities of the device, often dividing the request into manageable parts. For example, some devices can understand directions to draw an ellipse; others require the GDI to interpret the command as a series of pixels placed at certain coordinates. For more information about the graphics and video driver architecture, see the "Design Guide" section of the "Display (Adapters and Monitors)" chapter in the Windows Driver Kit.

Because much of the subsystem—in particular, display I/O functionality—runs in kernel mode, only a few Windows functions result in sending a message to the Windows subsystem process: process and thread creation and termination, network drive letter mapping, and creation of temporary files. In general, a running Windows application won't be causing many, if any, context switches to the Windows subsystem process.

Console Window Host

In the original Windows subsystem design, the subsystem process (Csrss.exe) was responsible for the managing of console windows and each console application (such as Cmd.exe, the command prompt) communicated with Csrss. Windows now uses a separate process, the console window host (Conhost.exe), for each console window on the system. (A single console window can be shared by multiple console applications, such as when you launch a command prompt from the command prompt. By default, the second command prompt shares the console window of the first.)

Whenever a console application registers itself with the Csrss instance running in the current session, Csrss creates a new instance of Conhost using the client process' security token instead of Csrss' System token. It then maps a shared memory section that is used to allow all Conhosts to share part of their memory with Csrss for efficient buffer handling (because these threads do not live within Csrss anymore) and creates a named Asynchronous Local Procedure Call (ALPC) port in the \RPC Control object directory. (For more information on ALPC, see Chapter 3.) The name of the port is of the format *console-PID-lpc-handle*, where *PID* is the process ID of the Conhost process. It then registers its PID with the kernel process structure associated with the user application, which can then query this information to open the newly created ALPC port. This process also creates a mapping of a shared section memory object between the command-line application and its Conhost so that the two can share data. Finally, a wait event is created in the session 0 BaseNamedObjects directory (named *ConsoleEvent-PID*) so that the command-line application and the Conhost can notify each other of new buffer data. The following figure shows a Conhost process with handles open to its ALPC port and event.

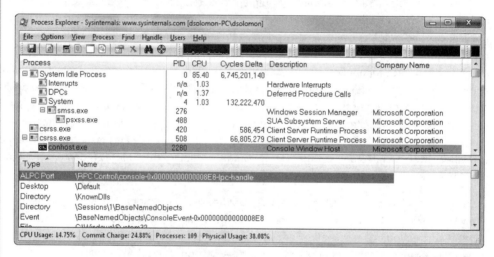

Because the Conhost is running with the user's credentials (which also implies the user's privilege level), as well as in a process associated with the console application itself, the User Interface Privilege Isolation (UIPI, described in Chapter 6, "Security") security mechanism covers console processes. In addition, CPU-bound console applications can be identified with their supporting console host process (which a user can kill if needed). As a side effect, because Conhost processes now run outside the special enclave of the Csrss subsystem, console applications (whose windows are actually owned by Conhost) can be fully themed, load third-party DLLs, and run with full windowing capabilities.

Subsystem for Unix-based Applications

The Subsystem for UNIX-based Applications (SUA) enables compiling and running custom UNIX-based applications on a computer running Windows Server or the Enterprise or Ultimate editions of Windows client. SUA provides nearly 2000 UNIX functions and 300 UNIX-like tools and utilities. (See *http://technet.microsoft.com/en-us/library/cc771470.aspx* for more information on SUA.) For more information on how Windows handles running SUA applications, see the section "Flow of *CreateProcess*" in Chapter 5.

Original POSIX Subsystem

POSIX, an acronym loosely defined as "a portable operating system interface based on UNIX," refers to a collection of international standards for UNIX-style operating system interfaces. The POSIX standards encourage vendors implementing UNIX-style interfaces to make them compatible so that programmers can move their applications easily from one system to another.

Windows initially implemented only one of the many POSIX standards, POSIX.1, formally known as ISO/IEC 9945-1:1990 or IEEE POSIX standard 1003.1-1990. This standard was included primarily to meet U.S. government procurement requirements set in the mid-to-late 1980s that mandated POSIX.1 compliance as specified in Federal Information Processing Standard (FIPS) 151-2, developed by the National Institute of Standards and Technology. Windows NT 3.5, 3.51, and 4 were formally tested and certified according to FIPS 151-2.

Because POSIX.1 compliance was a mandatory goal for Windows, the operating system was designed to ensure that the required base system support was present to allow for the implementation of a POSIX.1 subsystem (such as the *fork* function, which is implemented in the Windows executive, and the support for hard file links in the Windows file system).

Ntdll.dll

Ntdll.dll is a special system support library primarily for the use of subsystem DLLs. It contains two types of functions:

- System service dispatch stubs to Windows executive system services

- Internal support functions used by subsystems, subsystem DLLs, and other native images

The first group of functions provides the interface to the Windows executive system services that can be called from user mode. There are more than 400 such functions, such as *NtCreateFile*, *NtSetEvent*, and so on. As noted earlier, most of the capabilities of these functions are accessible through the Windows API. (A number are not, however, and are for use only within the operating system.)

For each of these functions, Ntdll contains an entry point with the same name. The code inside the function contains the architecture-specific instruction that causes a transition into kernel mode to invoke the system service dispatcher (explained in more detail in Chapter 3), which, after verifying some parameters, calls the actual kernel-mode system service that contains the real code inside Ntoskrnl.exe.

Ntdll also contains many support functions, such as the image loader (functions that start with *Ldr*), the heap manager, and Windows subsystem process communication functions (functions that start with *Csr*). Ntdll also includes general run-time library routines (functions that start with *Rtl*), support for user-mode debugging (functions that start with *DbgUi*), and Event Tracing for Windows (functions starting in *Etw*), and the user-mode asynchronous procedure call (APC) dispatcher and exception dispatcher. (APCs and exceptions are explained in Chapter 3.) Finally, you'll find a small subset of the C Run-Time (CRT) routines in Ntdll, limited to those routines that are part of the string and standard libraries (such as *memcpy, strcpy, itoa*, and so on).

Executive

The Windows executive is the upper layer of Ntoskrnl.exe. (The kernel is the lower layer.) The executive includes the following types of functions:

- Functions that are exported and callable from user mode. These functions are called *system services* and are exported via Ntdll. Most of the services are accessible through the Windows API or the APIs of another environment subsystem. A few services, however, aren't available through any documented subsystem function. (Examples include ALPC and various query functions such as *NtQueryInformationProcess*, specialized functions such as *NtCreatePagingFile*, and so on.)

- Device driver functions that are called through the use of the *DeviceIoControl* function. This provides a general interface from user mode to kernel mode to call functions in device drivers that are not associated with a read or write.

- Functions that can be called only from kernel mode that are exported and are documented in the WDK.

- Functions that are exported and callable from kernel mode but are not documented in the WDK (such as the functions called by the boot video driver, which start with *Inbv*).

- Functions that are defined as global symbols but are not exported. These include internal support functions called within Ntoskrnl, such as those that start with *Iop* (internal I/O manager support functions) or *Mi* (internal memory management support functions).

- Functions that are internal to a module that are not defined as global symbols.

The executive contains the following major components, each of which is covered in detail in a subsequent chapter of this book:

- The *configuration manager* (explained in Chapter 4) is responsible for implementing and managing the system registry.

- The *process manager* (explained in Chapter 5) creates and terminates processes and threads. The underlying support for processes and threads is implemented in the Windows kernel; the executive adds additional semantics and functions to these lower-level objects.

- The *security reference monitor* (or SRM, described in Chapter 6) enforces security policies on the local computer. It guards operating system resources, performing run-time object protection and auditing.

- The *I/O manager* (explained in Chapter 8 in Part 2) implements device-independent I/O and is responsible for dispatching to the appropriate device drivers for further processing.

- The *Plug and Play (PnP) manager* (explained in Chapter 8 in Part 2) determines which drivers are required to support a particular device and loads those drivers. It retrieves the hardware resource requirements for each device during enumeration. Based on the resource require- ments of each device, the PnP manager assigns the appropriate hardware resources such as I/O ports, IRQs, DMA channels, and memory locations. It is also responsible for sending proper event notification for device changes (addition or removal of a device) on the system.

- The *power manager* (explained in Chapter 8 in Part 2) coordinates power events and generates power management I/O notifications to device drivers. When the system is idle, the power manager can be configured to reduce power consumption by putting the CPU to sleep. Changes in power consumption by individual devices are handled by device drivers but are coordinated by the power manager.

- The *Windows Driver Model Windows Management Instrumentation routines* (explained in Chapter 4) enable device drivers to publish performance and configuration information and receive commands from the user-mode WMI service. Consumers of WMI information can be on the local machine or remote across the network.

- The *cache manager* (explained in Chapter 11, "Cache Manager," in Part 2) improves the performance of file-based I/O by causing recently referenced disk data to reside in main memory for quick access (and by deferring disk writes by holding the updates in memory for a short time before sending them to the disk). As you'll see, it does this by using the memory manager's support for mapped files.

- The *memory manager* (explained in Chapter 10 in Part 2) implements *virtual memory*, a memory management scheme that provides a large, private address space for each pro- cess that can exceed available physical memory. The memory manager also provides the underlying support for the cache manager.

- The *logical prefetcher* and *Superfetch* (explained in Chapter 10 in Part 2) accelerate system and process startup by optimizing the loading of data referenced during the startup of the system or a process.

In addition, the executive contains four main groups of support functions that are used by the executive components just listed. About a third of these support functions are documented in the WDK because device drivers also use them. These are the four categories of support functions:

- The *object manager*, which creates, manages, and deletes Windows executive objects and abstract data types that are used to represent operating system resources such as processes, threads, and the various synchronization objects. The object manager is explained in Chapter 3.

- The *Advanced LPC facility* (ALPC, explained in Chapter 3) passes messages between a client process and a server process on the same computer. Among other things, ALPC is used as a local transport for *remote procedure call* (RPC), an industry-standard communication facility for client and server processes across a network.

- A broad set of common *run-time library* functions, such as string processing, arithmetic operations, data type conversion, and security structure processing.

- Executive support routines, such as system memory allocation (paged and nonpaged pool), interlocked memory access, as well as three special types of synchronization objects: resources, fast mutexes, and pushlocks.

The executive also contains a variety of other infrastructure routines, some of which we will mention only briefly throughout the book:

- The *kernel debugger* library, which allows debugging of the kernel from a debugger supporting KD, a portable protocol supported over a variety of transports (such as USB and IEEE 1394) and implemented by WinDbg and the Kd.exe utilities.

- The *user-mode debugging framework*, which is responsible for sending events to the user-mode debugging API and allowing breakpoints and stepping through code to work, as well as for changing contexts of running threads.

- The *kernel transaction manager*, which provides a common, two-phase commit mechanism to resource managers, such as the transactional registry (TxR) and transactional NTFS (TxF).

- The *hypervisor library*, part of the Hyper-V stack in Windows Server 2008, provides kernel support for the virtual machine environment and optimizes certain parts of the code when the system knows it's running in a client partition (virtual environment).

- The *errata manager* provides workarounds for nonstandard or noncompliant hardware devices.

- The *Driver Verifier* implements optional integrity checks of kernel-mode drivers and code.

- *Event Tracing for Windows* provides helper routines for systemwide event tracing for kernel-mode and user-mode components.

- The *Windows diagnostic infrastructure* enables intelligent tracing of system activity based on diagnostic scenarios.

- The *Windows hardware error architecture* support routines provide a common framework for reporting hardware errors.

- The *file-system runtime library* provides common support routines for file system drivers.

Kernel

The kernel consists of a set of functions in Ntoskrnl.exe that provides fundamental mechanisms (such as thread scheduling and synchronization services) used by the executive components, as well as low-level hardware architecture–dependent support (such as interrupt and exception dispatching) that is different on each processor architecture. The kernel code is written primarily in C, with assembly code reserved for those tasks that require access to specialized processor instructions and registers not easily accessible from C.

Like the various executive support functions mentioned in the preceding section, a number of functions in the kernel are documented in the WDK (and can be found by searching for functions beginning with *Ke*) because they are needed to implement device drivers.

Kernel Objects

The kernel provides a low-level base of well-defined, predictable operating system primitives and mechanisms that allow higher-level components of the executive to do what they need to do. The kernel separates itself from the rest of the executive by implementing operating system mechanisms and avoiding policy making. It leaves nearly all policy decisions to the executive, with the exception of thread scheduling and dispatching, which the kernel implements.

Outside the kernel, the executive represents threads and other shareable resources as objects. These objects require some policy overhead, such as object handles to manipulate them, security checks to protect them, and resource quotas to be deducted when they are created. This overhead is eliminated in the kernel, which implements a set of simpler objects, called *kernel objects*, that help the kernel control central processing and support the creation of executive objects. Most executive-level objects encapsulate one or more kernel objects, incorporating their kernel-defined attributes.

One set of kernel objects, called *control objects*, establishes semantics for controlling various operating system functions. This set includes the APC object, the *deferred procedure call* (DPC) object, and several objects the I/O manager uses, such as the interrupt object.

Another set of kernel objects, known as *dispatcher objects*, incorporates synchronization capabilities that alter or affect thread scheduling. The dispatcher objects include the kernel thread, mutex (called *mutant* internally), event, kernel event pair, semaphore, timer, and waitable timer. The executive uses kernel functions to create instances of kernel objects, to manipulate them, and to construct the more complex objects it provides to user mode. Objects are explained in more detail in Chapter 3, and processes and threads are described in Chapter 5.

Kernel Processor Control Region and Control Block (KPCR and KPRCB)

The kernel uses a data structure called the *processor control region*, or KPCR, to store processor-specific data. The KPCR contains basic information such as the processor's interrupt dispatch table (IDT), task-state segment (TSS), and global descriptor table (GDT). It also includes the interrupt controller state, which it shares with other modules, such as the ACPI driver and the HAL. To provide easy access to the KPCR, the kernel stores a pointer to it in the *fs* register on 32-bit Windows and in the *gs* register on an x64 Windows system. On IA64 systems, the KPCR is always located at 0xe0000000ffff0000.

The KPCR also contains an embedded data structure called the *kernel processor control block* (KPRCB). Unlike the KPCR, which is documented for third-party drivers and other internal Windows kernel components, the KPRCB is a private structure used only by the kernel code in Ntoskrnl.exe. It contains scheduling information such as the current, next, and idle threads scheduled for execution on the processor; the dispatcher database for the processor (which includes the ready queues for each priority level); the DPC queue; CPU vendor and identifier information (model, stepping, speed, feature bits); CPU and NUMA topology (node information, cores per package, logical processors per core, and so on); cache sizes; time accounting information (such as the DPC and interrupt time); and more. The KPRCB also contains all the statistics for the processor, such as I/O statistics, cache manager statistics (see Chapter 11, "Cache Manager," in Part 2 for a description of these), DPC statistics, and memory manager statistics. (See Chapter 10 in Part 2 for more information.) Finally, the KPRCB is sometimes used to store cache-aligned, per-processor structures to optimize memory access, especially on NUMA systems. For example, the nonpaged and paged-pool system look-aside lists are stored in the KPRCB.

EXPERIMENT: Viewing the KPCR and KPRCB

You can view the contents of the KPCR and KPRCB by using the *!pcr* and *!prcb* kernel debugger commands. If you don't include flags, the debugger will display information for CPU 0 by default; otherwise, you can specify a CPU by adding its number after the command (for example, *!pcr 2*). The following example shows what the output of the *!pcr* and *!prcb* commands looks like. If the system had pending DPCs, those would also be shown.

```
lkd> !pcr
KPCR for Processor 0 at 81d09800:
    Major 1 Minor 1
    NtTib.ExceptionList: 9b31ca3c
        NtTib.StackBase: 00000000
       NtTib.StackLimit: 00000000
     NtTib.SubSystemTib: 80150000
          NtTib.Version: 1c47209e
      NtTib.UserPointer: 00000001
         NtTib.SelfTib: 7ffde000

               SelfPcr: 81d09800
                  Prcb: 81d09920
                  Irql: 00000002
                   IRR: 00000000
                   IDR: ffffffff
```

```
          InterruptMode: 00000000
                    IDT: 82fb8400
                    GDT: 82fb8000
                    TSS: 80150000

          CurrentThread: 86d317e8
             NextThread: 00000000
             IdleThread: 81d0d640

              DpcQueue:

lkd> !prcb
PRCB for Processor 0 at 81d09920:
Current IRQL -- 0
Threads-- Current 86d317e8 Next 00000000 Idle 81d0d640
Number 0 SetMember 1
Interrupt Count -- 294ccce0
Times -- Dpc    0002a87f Interrupt 00010b87
        Kernel 026270a1 User        00140e5e
```

You can use the *dt* command to directly dump the _KPCR and _KPRCB data structures because both debugger commands give you the address of the structure (shown in bold for clarity in the previous output). For example, if you wanted to determine the speed of the processor, you could look at the MHz field with the following command:

```
lkd> dt nt!_KPRCB 81d09920 MHz

   +0x3c4 MHz : 0xbb4
lkd> ? bb4
Evaluate expression: 2996 = 00000bb4
```

On this machine, the processor was running at about 3 GHz.

Hardware Support

The other major job of the kernel is to abstract or isolate the executive and device drivers from variations between the hardware architectures supported by Windows. This job includes handling variations in functions such as interrupt handling, exception dispatching, and multiprocessor synchronization.

Even for these hardware-related functions, the design of the kernel attempts to maximize the amount of common code. The kernel supports a set of interfaces that are portable and semantically identical across architectures. Most of the code that implements these portable interfaces is also identical across architectures.

Some of these interfaces are implemented differently on different architectures or are partially implemented with architecture-specific code. These architecturally independent interfaces can be called on any machine, and the semantics of the interface will be the same whether or not the code varies by architecture. Some kernel interfaces (such as spinlock routines, which are described in Chapter 3) are actually implemented in the HAL (described in the next section) because their implementation can vary for systems within the same architecture family.

The kernel also contains a small amount of code with x86-specific interfaces needed to support old MS-DOS programs. These x86 interfaces aren't portable in the sense that they can't be called on a machine based on any other architecture; they won't be present. This x86-specific code, for example, supports calls to manipulate global descriptor tables (GDTs) and local descriptor tables (LDTs), which are hardware features of the x86.

Other examples of architecture-specific code in the kernel include the interfaces to provide translation buffer and CPU cache support. This support requires different code for the different architectures because of the way caches are implemented.

Another example is context switching. Although at a high level the same algorithm is used for thread selection and context switching (the context of the previous thread is saved, the context of the new thread is loaded, and the new thread is started), there are architectural differences among the implementations on different processors. Because the context is described by the processor state (registers and so on), what is saved and loaded varies depending on the architecture.

Hardware Abstraction Layer

As mentioned at the beginning of this chapter, one of the crucial elements of the Windows design is its portability across a variety of hardware platforms. The hardware abstraction layer (HAL) is a key part of making this portability possible. The HAL is a loadable kernel-mode module (Hal.dll) that provides the low-level interface to the hardware platform on which Windows is running. It hides hardware-dependent details such as I/O interfaces, interrupt controllers, and multiprocessor communication mechanisms—any functions that are both architecture-specific and machine-dependent.

So rather than access hardware directly, Windows internal components as well as user-written device drivers maintain portability by calling the HAL routines when they need platform-dependent information. For this reason, the HAL routines are documented in the WDK. To find out more about the HAL and its use by device drivers, refer to the WDK.

Although several HALs are included (as shown in Table 2-4), Windows has the ability to detect at boot-up time which HAL should be used, eliminating the problem that existed on earlier versions of Windows when attempting to boot a Windows installation on a different kind of system.

TABLE 2-4 List of x86 HALs

HAL File Name	Systems Supported
Halacpi.dll	Advanced Configuration and Power Interface (ACPI) PCs. Implies uniprocessor-only machine, without APIC support (the presence of either one would make the system use the HAL below instead).
Halmacpi.dll	Advanced Programmable Interrupt Controller (APIC) PCs with an ACPI. The existence of an APIC implies SMP support.

Note On x64 machines, there is only one HAL image, called Hal.dll. This results from all x64 machines having the same motherboard configuration, because the processors require ACPI and APIC support. Therefore, there is no need to support machines without ACPI or with a standard PIC.

EXPERIMENT: Determining Which HAL You're Running

You can determine which version of the HAL you're running by using WinDbg and opening a local kernel debugging session. Be sure you have the symbols loaded by entering **.reload**, and then typing **lm vm hal**. For example, the following output is from a system running the ACPI HAL:

```
lkd> lm vm hal
start     end          module name
fffff800'0181b000 fffff800'01864000   hal           (deferred)
    Loaded symbol image file: halmacpi.dll
    Image path: halmacpi.dll
    Image name: halmacpi.dll
    Timestamp:        Mon Jul 13 21:27:36 2009 (4A5BDF08)
    CheckSum:         0004BD36
    ImageSize:        00049000
    File version:     6.1.7600.16385
    Product version:  6.1.7600.16385
    File flags:       0 (Mask 3F)
    File OS:          40004 NT Win32
    File type:        2.0 Dll
    File date:        00000000.00000000
    Translations:     0409.04b0
    CompanyName:      Microsoft Corporation
    ProductName:      Microsoft® Windows® Operating System
    InternalName:     halmacpi.dll
    OriginalFilename: halmacpi.dll
    ProductVersion:   6.1.7600.16385
    FileVersion:      6.1.7600.16385 (win7_rtm.090713-1255)
    FileDescription:  Hardware Abstraction Layer DLL
    LegalCopyright:   © Microsoft Corporation. All rights reserved.
```

EXPERIMENT: Viewing NTOSKRNL and HAL Image Dependencies

You can view the relationship of the kernel and HAL images by examining their export and import tables using the Dependency Walker tool (Depends.exe). To examine an image in the Dependency Walker, select Open from the File menu to open the desired image file.

Here is a sample of output you can see by viewing the dependencies of Ntoskrnl using this tool:

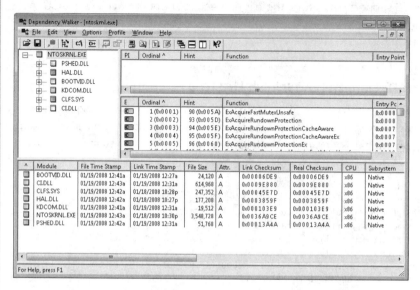

Notice that Ntoskrnl is linked against the HAL, which is in turn linked against Ntoskrnl. (They both use functions in each other.) Ntoskrnl is also linked to the following binaries:

- Pshed.dll, the Platform-Specific Hardware Error Driver. PSHED provides an abstraction of the hardware error reporting facilities of the underlying platform by hiding the details of a platform's error-handling mechanisms from the operating system and exposing a consistent interface to the Windows operating system.

- On 32-bit systems only, Bootvid.dll, the Boot Video Driver. Bootvid provides support for the VGA commands required to display boot text and the boot logo during startup. On x64 systems, this library is built into the kernel to avoid conflicts with Kernel Patch Protection (KPP). (See Chapter 3 for more information on KPP and PatchGuard.)

- Kdcom.dll, the Kernel Debugger Protocol (KD) Communications Library.

- Ci.dll, the code integrity library. (See Chapter 3 for more information on code integrity.)

- Clfs.sys, the common logging file system driver, used by, among other things, the Kernel Transaction Manager (KTM). (See Chapter 3 for more information on the KTM.)

For a detailed description of the information displayed by this tool, see the Dependency Walker help file (Depends.hlp).

Device Drivers

Although device drivers are explained in detail in Chapter 8 in Part 2, this section provides a brief overview of the types of drivers and explains how to list the drivers installed and loaded on your system.

Device drivers are loadable kernel-mode modules (typically ending in .sys) that interface between the I/O manager and the relevant hardware. They run in kernel mode in one of three contexts:

- In the context of the user thread that initiated an I/O function

- In the context of a kernel-mode system thread

- As a result of an interrupt (and therefore not in the context of any particular process or thread—whichever process or thread was current when the interrupt occurred)

As stated in the preceding section, device drivers in Windows don't manipulate hardware directly, but rather they call functions in the HAL to interface with the hardware. Drivers are typically written in C (sometimes C++) and therefore, with proper use of HAL routines, can be source-code portable across the CPU architectures supported by Windows and binary portable within an architecture family.

There are several types of device drivers:

- *Hardware device drivers* manipulate hardware (using the HAL) to write output to or retrieve input from a physical device or network. There are many types of hardware device drivers, such as bus drivers, human interface drivers, mass storage drivers, and so on.

- *File system drivers* are Windows drivers that accept file-oriented I/O requests and translate them into I/O requests bound for a particular device.

- *File system filter drivers*, such as those that perform disk mirroring and encryption, intercept I/Os, and perform some added-value processing before passing the I/O to the next layer.

- *Network redirectors and servers* are file system drivers that transmit file system I/O requests to a machine on the network and receive such requests, respectively.

- *Protocol drivers* implement a networking protocol such as TCP/IP, NetBEUI, and IPX/SPX.

- *Kernel streaming filter drivers* are chained together to perform signal processing on data streams, such as recording or displaying audio and video.

Because installing a device driver is the only way to add user-written kernel-mode code to the system, some programmers have written device drivers simply as a way to access internal operating system functions or data structures that are not accessible from user mode (but that are documented and supported in the WDK). For example, many of the utilities from Sysinternals combine a Windows GUI application and a device driver that is used to gather internal system state and call kernel-mode-only accessible functions not available from the user-mode Windows API.

Windows Driver Model (WDM)

Windows 2000 added support for Plug and Play, Power Options, and an extension to the Windows NT driver model called the Windows Driver Model (WDM). Windows 2000 and later can run legacy Windows NT 4 drivers, but because these don't support Plug and Play and Power Options, systems running these drivers will have reduced capabilities in these two areas.

From the WDM perspective, there are three kinds of drivers:

- A *bus driver* services a bus controller, adapter, bridge, or any device that has child devices. Bus drivers are required drivers, and Microsoft generally provides them; each type of bus (such as PCI, PCMCIA, and USB) on a system has one bus driver. Third parties can write bus drivers to provide support for new buses, such as VMEbus, Multibus, and Futurebus.

- A *function driver* is the main device driver and provides the operational interface for its device. It is a required driver unless the device is used raw (an implementation in which I/O is done by the bus driver and any bus filter drivers, such as SCSI PassThru). A function driver is by definition the driver that knows the most about a particular device, and it is usually the only driver that accesses device-specific registers.

- A *filter driver* is used to add functionality to a device (or existing driver) or to modify I/O requests or responses from other drivers (and is often used to fix hardware that provides incorrect information about its hardware resource requirements). Filter drivers are optional and can exist in any number, placed above or below a function driver and above a bus driver. Usually, system original equipment manufacturers (OEMs) or independent hardware vendors (IHVs) supply filter drivers.

In the WDM driver environment, no single driver controls all aspects of a device: a bus driver is concerned with reporting the devices on its bus to the PnP manager, while a function driver manipulates the device.

In most cases, lower-level filter drivers modify the behavior of device hardware. For example, if a device reports to its bus driver that it requires 4 I/O ports when it actually requires 16 I/O ports, a lower-level, device-specific function filter driver could intercept the list of hardware resources reported by the bus driver to the PnP manager and update the count of I/O ports.

Upper-level filter drivers usually provide added-value features for a device. For example, an upper-level device filter driver for a keyboard can enforce additional security checks.

Interrupt processing is explained in Chapter 3. Further details about the I/O manager, WDM, Plug and Play, and Power Options are included in Chapter 8 in Part 2.

Windows Driver Foundation

The Windows Driver Foundation (WDF) simplifies Windows driver development by providing two frameworks: the Kernel-Mode Driver Framework (KMDF) and the User-Mode Driver Framework (UMDF). Developers can use KMDF to write drivers for Windows 2000 SP4 and later, while UMDF supports Windows XP and later.

KMDF provides a simple interface to WDM and hides its complexity from the driver writer without modifying the underlying bus/function/filter model. KMDF drivers respond to events that they can register and call into the KMDF library to perform work that isn't specific to the hardware they are managing, such as generic power management or synchronization. (Previously, each driver had to implement this on its own.) In some cases, more than 200 lines of WDM code can be replaced by a single KMDF function call.

UMDF enables certain classes of drivers (mostly USB-based or other high-latency protocol buses)—such as those for video cameras, MP3 players, cell phones, PDAs, and printers—to be implemented as user-mode drivers. UMDF runs each user-mode driver in what is essentially a user-mode service, and it uses ALPC to communicate to a kernel-mode wrapper driver that provides actual access to hardware. If a UMDF driver crashes, the process dies and usually restarts, so the system doesn't become unstable—the device simply becomes unavailable while the service hosting the driver restarts. Finally, UMDF drivers are written in C++ using COM-like classes and semantics, further lowering the bar for programmers to write device drivers.

EXPERIMENT: Viewing the Installed Device Drivers

You can list the installed drivers by running Msinfo32. (To launch this, click Start and then type **Msinfo32** and then press Enter.) Under System Summary, expand Software Environment and open System Drivers. Here's an example output of the list of installed drivers:

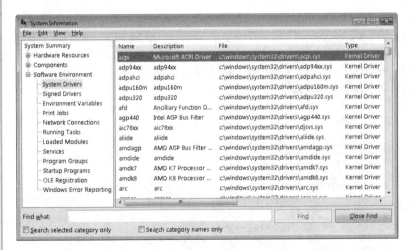

This window displays the list of device drivers defined in the registry, their type, and their state (Running or Stopped). Device drivers and Windows service processes are both defined in the same place: HKLM\SYSTEM\CurrentControlSet\Services. However, they are distinguished by a type code—for example, *type 1* is a kernel-mode device driver. (For a complete list of the information stored in the registry for device drivers, see Table 4-7 in Chapter 4.)

Alternatively, you can list the currently loaded device drivers by selecting the System process in Process Explorer and opening the DLL view.

Peering into Undocumented Interfaces

Examining the names of the exported or global symbols in key system images (such as Ntoskrnl.exe, Hal.dll, or Ntdll.dll) can be enlightening—you can get an idea of the kinds of things Windows can do versus what happens to be documented and supported today. Of course, just because you know the names of these functions doesn't mean that you can or should call them—the interfaces are undocumented and are subject to change. We suggest that you look at these functions purely to gain more insight into the kinds of internal functions Windows performs, not to bypass supported interfaces.

For example, looking at the list of functions in Ntdll.dll gives you the list of all the system services that Windows provides to user-mode subsystem DLLs versus the subset that each subsystem exposes. Although many of these functions map clearly to documented and supported Windows functions, several are not exposed via the Windows API.

Conversely, it's also interesting to examine the imports of Windows subsystem DLLs (such as Kernel32.dll or Advapi32.dll) and which functions they call in Ntdll.

Another interesting image to dump is Ntoskrnl.exe—although many of the exported routines that kernel-mode device drivers use are documented in the Windows Driver Kit, quite a few are not. You might also find it interesting to take a look at the import table for Ntoskrnl and the HAL; this table shows the list of functions in the HAL that Ntoskrnl uses and vice versa.

Table 2-5 lists most of the commonly used function name prefixes for the executive components. Each of these major executive components also uses a variation of the prefix to denote internal functions—either the first letter of the prefix followed by an *i* (for *internal*) or the full prefix followed by a *p* (for *private*). For example, *Ki* represents internal kernel functions, and *Psp* refers to internal process support functions.

TABLE 2-5 Commonly Used Prefixes

Prefix	Component
Alpc	Advanced Local Inter-Process Communication
Cc	Common Cache
Cm	Configuration manager
Dbgk	Debugging Framework for User-Mode
Em	Errata Manager
Etw	Event Tracing for Windows
Ex	Executive support routines
FsRtl	File system driver run-time library

Prefix	Component
Hvl	Hypervisor Library
Io	I/O manager
Kd	Kernel Debugger
Ke	Kernel
Lsa	Local Security Authority
Mm	Memory manager
Nt	NT system services (most of which are exported as Windows functions)
Ob	Object manager
Pf	Prefetcher
Po	Power manager
Pp	PnP manager
Ps	Process support
Rtl	Run-time library
Se	Security
Sm	Store Manager
Tm	Transaction Manager
Vf	Verifier
Wdi	Windows Diagnostic Infrastructure
Whea	Windows Hardware Error Architecture
Wmi	Windows Management Instrumentation
Zw	Mirror entry point for system services (beginning with Nt) that sets previous access mode to kernel, which eliminates parameter validation, because Nt system services validate parameters only if previous access mode is user

You can decipher the names of these exported functions more easily if you understand the naming convention for Windows system routines. The general format is

    <Prefix><Operation><Object>

In this format, *Prefix* is the internal component that exports the routine, *Operation* tells what is being done to the object or resource, and *Object* identifies what is being operated on.

For example, *ExAllocatePoolWithTag* is the executive support routine to allocate from a paged or nonpaged pool. *KeInitializeThread* is the routine that allocates and sets up a kernel thread object.

System Processes

The following system processes appear on every Windows system. (Two of these—Idle and System—are not full processes because they are not running a user-mode executable.)

- Idle process (contains one thread per CPU to account for idle CPU time)

- System process (contains the majority of the kernel-mode system threads)

- Session manager (Smss.exe)

- Local session manager (Lsm.exe)

- Windows subsystem (Csrss.exe)

- Session 0 initialization (Wininit.exe)

- Logon process (Winlogon.exe)

- Service control manager (Services.exe) and the child service processes it creates (such as the system-supplied generic service-host process, Svchost.exe)

- Local security authentication server (Lsass.exe)

To understand the relationship of these processes, it is helpful to view the process "tree"—that is, the parent/child relationship between processes. Seeing which process created each process helps to understand where each process comes from. Figure 2-5 is a screen snapshot of the process tree viewed after taking a Process Monitor boot trace. Using Process Monitor allows you to see processes that have since exited (indicated by the muted icon).

FIGURE 2-5 Initial system process tree

The next sections explain the key system processes shown in Figure 2-5. Although these sections briefly indicate the order of process startup, Chapter 13 in Part 2 contains a detailed description of the steps involved in booting and starting Windows.

System Idle Process

The first process listed in Figure 2-5 is the system idle process. As we'll explain in Chapter 5, processes are identified by their image name. However, this process (as well as the process named System) isn't running a real user-mode image (in that there is no "System Idle Process.exe" in the \Windows directory). In addition, the name shown for this process differs from utility to utility (because of implementation details). Table 2-6 lists several of the names given to the Idle process (process ID 0). The Idle process is explained in detail in Chapter 5.

TABLE 2-6 Names for Process ID 0 in Various Utilities

Utility	Name for Process ID 0
Task Manager	System Idle Process
Process Status (Pstat.exe)	Idle Process
Process Explorer (Procexp.exe)	System Idle Process
Task List (Tasklist.exe)	System Idle Process
Tlist (Tlist.exe)	System Process

Now let's look at system threads and the purpose of each of the system processes that are running real images.

System Process and System Threads

The System process (process ID 4) is the home for a special kind of thread that runs only in kernel mode: a *kernel-mode system thread*. System threads have all the attributes and contexts of regular user-mode threads (such as a hardware context, priority, and so on) but are different in that they run only in kernel-mode executing code loaded in system space, whether that is in Ntoskrnl.exe or in any other loaded device driver. In addition, system threads don't have a user process address space and hence must allocate any dynamic storage from operating system memory heaps, such as a paged or nonpaged pool.

System threads are created by the *PsCreateSystemThread* function (documented in the WDK), which can be called only from kernel mode. Windows, as well as various device drivers, create system threads during system initialization to perform operations that require thread context, such as issuing and waiting for I/Os or other objects or polling a device. For example, the memory manager uses system threads to implement such functions as writing dirty pages to the page file or mapped files, swapping processes in and out of memory, and so forth. The kernel creates a system thread called the *balance set manager* that wakes up once per second to possibly initiate various scheduling and memory management related events. The cache manager also uses system threads to implement both read-ahead and write-behind I/Os. The file server device driver (Srv2.sys) uses system threads to respond to network I/O requests for file data on disk partitions shared to the network. Even the floppy driver has a system thread to poll the floppy device. (Polling is more efficient in this case because an interrupt-driven floppy driver consumes a large amount of system resources.) Further information on specific system threads is included in the chapters in which the component is described.

By default, system threads are owned by the System process, but a device driver can create a system thread in any process. For example, the Windows subsystem device driver (Win32k.sys) creates a system thread inside the Canonical Display Driver (Cdd.dll) part of the Windows subsystem process (Csrss.exe) so that it can easily access data in the user-mode address space of that process.

When you're troubleshooting or going through a system analysis, it's useful to be able to map the execution of individual system threads back to the driver or even to the subroutine that contains the code. For example, on a heavily loaded file server, the System process will likely be consuming considerable CPU time. But the knowledge that when the System process is running that "some system thread" is running isn't enough to determine which device driver or operating system component is running.

So if threads in the System process are running, first determine which ones are running (for example, with the Performance Monitor tool). Once you find the thread (or threads) that is running, look up in which driver the system thread began execution (which at least tells you which driver likely created the thread) or examine the call stack (or at least the current address) of the thread in question, which would indicate where the thread is currently executing.

Both of these techniques are illustrated in the following experiment.

EXPERIMENT: Mapping a System Thread to a Device Driver

In this experiment, we'll see how to map CPU activity in the System process to the responsible system thread (and the driver it falls in) generating the activity. This is important because when the System process is running, you must go to the thread granularity to really understand what's going on. For this experiment, we will generate system thread activity by generating file server activity on your machine. (The file server driver, Srv2.sys, creates system threads to handle inbound requests for file I/O. See Chapter 7 for more information on this component.)

1. Open a command prompt.

2. Do a directory listing of your entire C drive using a network path to access your C drive. For example, if your computer name is COMPUTER1, type **dir \\computer1\c$ /s** (The /s switch lists all subdirectories.)

3. Run Process Explorer, and double-click on the System process.

4. Click on the Threads tab.

5. Sort by the CSwitch Delta (context switch delta) column. You should see one or more threads in Srv2.sys running, such as the following:

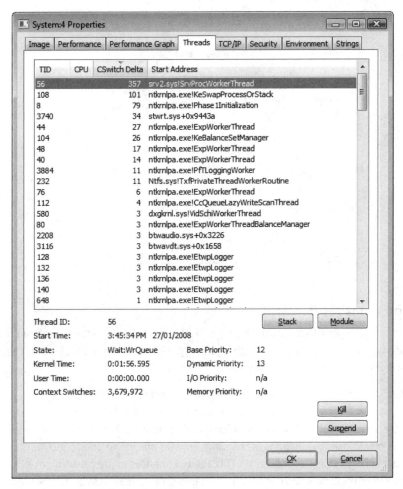

If you see a system thread running and you are not sure what the driver is, click the Module button, which will bring up the file properties. Clicking the Module button while highlighting the thread in the Srv2.sys previously shown results in the following display.

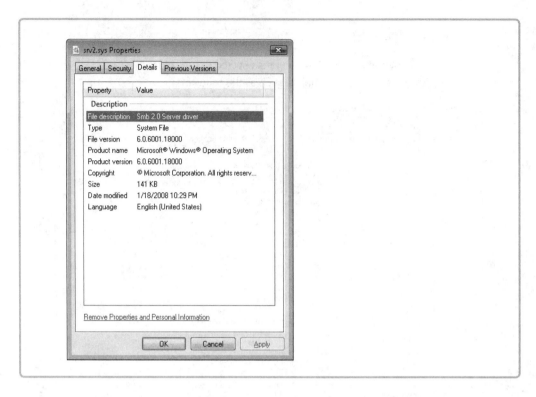

Session Manager (Smss)

The session manager (%SystemRoot%\System32\Smss.exe) is the first user-mode process created in the system. The kernel-mode system thread that performs the final phase of the initialization of the executive and kernel creates this process.

When Smss starts, it checks whether it is the first instance (the master Smss) or an instance of itself that the master Smss launched to create a session. (If command-line arguments are present, it is the latter.) By creating multiple instances of itself during boot-up and Terminal Services session creation, Smss can create multiple sessions at the same time (at maximum, four concurrent sessions, plus one more for each extra CPU beyond one). This ability enhances logon performance on Terminal Server systems where multiple users connect at the same time. Once a session finishes initializing, the copy of Smss terminates. As a result, only the initial Smss.exe process remains active. (For a description of Terminal Services, see the section "Terminal Services and Multiple Sessions" in Chapter 1.)

The master Smss performs the following one-time initialization steps:

1. Marks the process and the initial thread as critical. (If a process or thread marked critical exits for any reason, Windows crashes. See Chapter 5 for more information.)

2. Increases the process base priority to 11.

3. If the system supports hot processor add, enables automatic processor affinity updates so that if new processors are added new sessions will take advantage of the new processors. (For more information about dynamic processor additions, see Chapter 5.)

4. Creates named pipes and mailslots used for communication between Smss, Csrss, and Lsm (described in upcoming paragraphs).

5. Creates ALPC port to receive commands.

6. Creates systemwide environment variables as defined in HKLM\SYSTEM\CurrentControlSet \Control\Session Manager\Environment.

7. Creates symbolic links for devices defined in HKLM\SYSTEM\CurrentControlSet\Control \Session Manager\DOS Devices under the \Global?? directory in the Object Manager namespace.

8. Creates root \Sessions directory in the Object Manager namespace.

9. Runs the programs in HKLM\SYSTEM\CurrentControlSet\Control\Session Manager \BootExecute. (The default is Autochk.exe, which performs a check disk.)

10. Processes pending file renames as specified in HKLM\SYSTEM\CurrentControlSet\Control \Session Manager\PendingFileRenameOperations.

11. Initializes paging file(s).

12. Initializes the rest of the registry (HKLM Software, SAM, and Security hives).

13. Runs the programs in HKLM\SYSTEM\CurrentControlSet\Control\Session Manager \SetupExecute.

14. Opens known DLLs (HKLM\SYSTEM\CurrentControlSet\Control\Session Manager\KnownDLLs) and maps them as permanent sections (mapped files).

15. Creates a thread to respond to session create requests.

16. Creates the Smss to initialize session 0 (noninteractive session).

17. Creates the Smss to initialize session 1 (interactive session).

Once these steps have been completed, Smss waits forever on the handle to the session 0 instance of Csrss.exe. Because Csrss is marked as a critical process (see Chapter 5), if Csrss exits, this wait will never complete because the system will crash.

A session startup instance of Smss does the following:

1. Calls *NtSetSystemInformation* with a request to set up kernel-mode session data structures. This in turn calls the internal memory manager function *MmSessionCreate*, which sets up the session virtual address space that will contain the session paged pool and the per-session data structures allocated by the kernel-mode part of the Windows subsystem (Win32k.sys) and other session-space device drivers. (See Chapter 10 in Part 2 for more details.)

2. Creates the subsystem process(es) for the session (by default, the Windows subsystem Csrss.exe).

3. Creates an instance of Winlogon (interactive sessions) or Wininit (for session 0). See the upcoming paragraphs for more information on these two processes.

Then this intermediate Smss process exits (leaving the subsystem processes and Winlogon or Wininit as parent-less processes).

Windows Initialization Process (Wininit.exe)

The Wininit.exe process performs the following system initialization functions:

- Marks itself critical so that if it exits prematurely and the system is booted in debugging mode, it will break into the debugger (if not, the system will crash).

- Initializes the user-mode scheduling infrastructure.

- Creates the %windir%\temp folder.

- Creates a window station (Winsta0) and two desktops (Winlogon and Default) for processes to run on in session 0.

- Creates Services.exe (Service Control Manager or SCM). See upcoming paragraphs for a brief description or Chapter 4 for more details.

- Starts Lsass.exe (Local Security Authentication Subsystem Server). See Chapter 6 for more information on Lsass.

- Starts Lsm.exe (Local Session Manager). See the upcoming "Local Session Manager (Lsm.exe)," section for a brief description.

- Waits forever for system shutdown.

Service Control Manager (SCM)

Recall from earlier in the chapter that "services" on Windows can refer either to a server process or to a device driver. This section deals with services that are user-mode processes. Services are like UNIX "daemon processes" or VMS "detached processes" in that they can be configured to start automatically at system boot time without requiring an interactive logon. They can also be started manually (such as by running the Services administrative tool or by calling the Windows *StartService* function). Typically, services do not interact with the logged-on user, although there are special conditions when this is possible. (See Chapter 4.)

The service control manager is a special system process running the image %SystemRoot% \System32\Services.exe that is responsible for starting, stopping, and interacting with service processes. Service programs are really just Windows images that call special Windows functions to interact with the service control manager to perform such actions as registering the service's successful startup, responding to status requests, or pausing or shutting down the service. Services are defined in the registry under HKLM\SYSTEM\CurrentControlSet\Services.

Keep in mind that services have three names: the process name you see running on the system, the internal name in the registry, and the display name shown in the Services administrative tool. (Not all services have a display name—if a service doesn't have a display name, the internal name is shown.) With Windows, services can also have a description field that further details what the service does.

To map a service process to the services contained in that process, use the *tlist /s* or *tasklist /svc* command. Note that there isn't always one-to-one mapping between service processes and running services, however, because some services share a process with other services. In the registry, the type code indicates whether the service runs in its own process or shares a process with other services in the image.

A number of Windows components are implemented as services, such as the Print Spooler, Event Log, Task Scheduler, and various networking components. For more details on services, see Chapter 4.

EXPERIMENT: Listing Installed Services

To list the installed services, select Administrative Tools from Control Panel, and then select Services. You should see output like this:

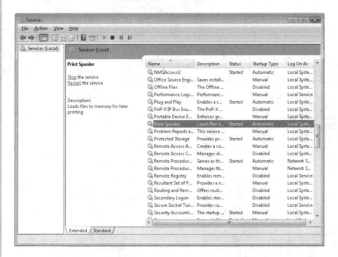

To see the detailed properties about a service, right-click on a service and select Properties. For example, here are the properties for the Print Spooler service (highlighted in the previous screen shot):

Notice that the Path To Executable field identifies the program that contains this service. Remember that some services share a process with other services—mapping isn't always one to one.

EXPERIMENT: Viewing Service Details Inside Service Processes

Process Explorer highlights processes hosting one service or more. (You can configure this by selecting the Configure Colors entry in the Options menu.) If you double-click on a service-hosting process, you will see a Services tab that lists the services inside the process, the name of the registry key that defines the service, the display name seen by the administrator, the description text for that service (if present), and for Svchost services, the path to the DLL that implements the service. For example, listing the services in a Svchost.exe process running under the System account looks like the following:

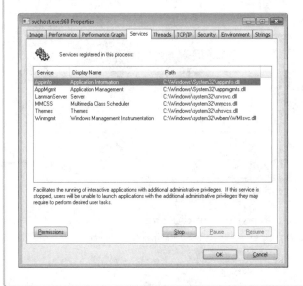

Local Session Manager (Lsm.exe)

The Local Session Manager (Lsm.exe) manages the state of terminal server sessions on the local machine. It sends requests to Smss through the ALPC port SmSsWinStationApiPort to start new sessions (for example, creating the Csrss and Winlogon processes) such as when a user selects Switch User from Explorer. Lsm also communicates with Winlogon and Csrss (using a local system RPC). It notifies Csrss of events such as connect, disconnect, terminate, and broadcast system message. It receives notification from Winlogon for the following events:

- Logon and logoff

- Shell start and termination

- Connect to a session

- Disconnect from a session

- Lock or unlock desktop

Winlogon, LogonUI, and Userinit

The Windows logon process (%SystemRoot%\System32\Winlogon.exe) handles interactive user logons and logoffs. Winlogon is notified of a user logon request when the *secure attention sequence* (SAS) keystroke combination is entered. The default SAS on Windows is the combination Ctrl+Alt+Delete. The reason for the SAS is to protect users from password-capture programs that simulate the logon process, because this keyboard sequence cannot be intercepted by a user-mode application.

The identification and authentication aspects of the logon process are implemented through DLLs called *credential providers*. The standard Windows credential providers implement the default Windows authentication interfaces: password and smartcard. However, developers can provide their own credential providers to implement other identification and authentication mechanisms in place of the standard Windows user name/password method (such as one based on a voice print or a biometric device such as a fingerprint reader). Because Winlogon is a critical system process on which the system depends, credential providers and the UI to display the logon dialog box run inside a child process of Winlogon called LogonUI. When Winlogon detects the SAS, it launches this process, which initializes the credential providers. Once the user enters her credentials or dismisses the logon interface, the LogonUI process terminates.

In addition, Winlogon can load additional network provider DLLs that need to perform secondary authentication. This capability allows multiple network providers to gather identification and authentication information all at one time during normal logon.

Once the user name and password have been captured, they are sent to the local security authentication server process (%SystemRoot%\System32\Lsass.exe, described in Chapter 6) to be authenticated. LSASS calls the appropriate authentication package (implemented as a DLL) to perform the actual verification, such as checking whether a password matches what is stored in the Active Directory or the SAM (the part of the registry that contains the definition of the local users and groups).

Upon a successful authentication, LSASS calls a function in the security reference monitor (for example, *NtCreateToken*) to generate an access token object that contains the user's security profile. If User Account Control (UAC) is used and the user logging on is a member of the administrators group or has administrator privileges, LSASS will create a second, *restricted* version of the token. This access token is then used by Winlogon to create the initial process(es) in the user's session. The initial process(es) are stored in the registry value *Userinit* under the registry key HKLM\SOFTWARE \Microsoft\Windows NT\CurrentVersion\Winlogon. (The default is Userinit.exe, but there can be more than one image in the list.)

Userinit performs some initialization of the user environment (such as running the login script and reestablishing network connections) and then looks in the registry at the *Shell* value (under the same Winlogon key referred to previously) and creates a process to run the system-defined shell (by default, Explorer.exe). Then Userinit exits. This is the reason Explorer.exe is shown with no parent—its parent has exited, and as explained in Chapter 1, tlist left-justifies processes whose parent isn't running. (Another way of looking at it is that Explorer is the grandchild of Winlogon.)

Winlogon is active not only during user logon and logoff but also whenever it intercepts the SAS from the keyboard. For example, when you press Ctrl+Alt+Delete while logged on, the Windows Security screen comes up, providing the options to log off, start the Task Manager, lock the workstation, shut down the system, and so forth. Winlogon and LogonUI are the processes that handle this interaction.

For a complete description of the steps involved in the logon process, see the section "Smss, Csrss, and Wininit" in Chapter 13 in Part 2. For more details on security authentication, see Chapter 6. For details on the callable functions that interface with LSASS (the functions that start with *Lsa*), see the documentation in the Windows SDK.

Conclusion

In this chapter, we've taken a broad look at the overall system architecture of Windows. We've examined the key components of Windows and seen how they interrelate. In the next chapter, we'll look in more detail at the core system mechanisms that these components are built on, such as the object manager and synchronization.

CHAPTER 3

System Mechanisms

The Windows operating system provides several base mechanisms that kernel-mode components such as the executive, the kernel, and device drivers use. This chapter explains the following system mechanisms and describes how they are used:

- Trap dispatching, including interrupts, deferred procedure calls (DPCs), asynchronous procedure calls (APCs), exception dispatching, and system service dispatching

- The executive object manager

- Synchronization, including spinlocks, kernel dispatcher objects, how waits are implemented, as well as user-mode-specific synchronization primitives that avoid trips to kernel mode (unlike typical dispatcher objects)

- System worker threads

- Miscellaneous mechanisms such as Windows global flags

- Advanced Local Procedure Calls (ALPCs)

- Kernel event tracing

- Wow64

- User-mode debugging

- The image loader

- Hypervisor (Hyper-V)

- Kernel Transaction Manager (KTM)

- Kernel Patch Protection (KPP)

- Code integrity

Trap Dispatching

Interrupts and exceptions are operating system conditions that divert the processor to code outside the normal flow of control. Either hardware or software can detect them. The term *trap* refers to a processor's mechanism for capturing an executing thread when an exception or an interrupt occurs and transferring control to a fixed location in the operating system. In Windows, the processor transfers control to a *trap handler*, which is a function specific to a particular interrupt or exception. Figure 3-1 illustrates some of the conditions that activate trap handlers.

The kernel distinguishes between interrupts and exceptions in the following way. An *interrupt* is an asynchronous event (one that can occur at any time) that is unrelated to what the processor is executing. Interrupts are generated primarily by I/O devices, processor clocks, or timers, and they can be enabled (turned on) or disabled (turned off). An *exception*, in contrast, is a synchronous condition that usually results from the execution of a particular instruction. (Aborts, such as machine checks, is a type of processor exception that's typically not associated with instruction execution.) Running a program a second time with the same data under the same conditions can reproduce exceptions. Examples of exceptions include memory-access violations, certain debugger instructions, and divide-by-zero errors. The kernel also regards system service calls as exceptions (although technically they're system traps).

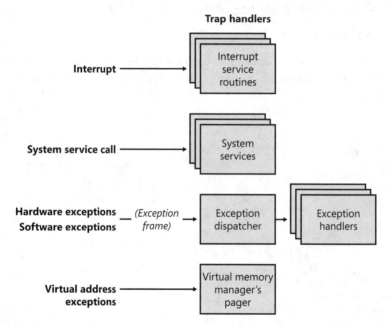

FIGURE 3-1 Trap dispatching

Either hardware or software can generate exceptions and interrupts. For example, a bus error exception is caused by a hardware problem, whereas a divide-by-zero exception is the result of a software bug. Likewise, an I/O device can generate an interrupt, or the kernel itself can issue a software interrupt (such as an APC or DPC, both of which are described later in this chapter).

When a hardware exception or interrupt is generated, the processor records enough machine state on the kernel stack of the thread that's interrupted to return to that point in the control flow and continue execution as if nothing had happened. If the thread was executing in user mode, Windows switches to the thread's kernel-mode stack. Windows then creates a *trap frame* on the kernel stack of the interrupted thread into which it stores the execution state of the thread. The trap frame is a subset of a thread's complete context, and you can view its definition by typing **dt nt!_ktrap_frame** in the kernel debugger. (Thread context is described in Chapter 5, "Processes and Threads.") The kernel handles software interrupts either as part of hardware interrupt handling or synchronously when a thread invokes kernel functions related to the software interrupt.

In most cases, the kernel installs front-end, trap-handling functions that perform general trap-handling tasks before and after transferring control to other functions that field the trap. For example, if the condition was a device interrupt, a kernel hardware interrupt trap handler transfers control to the *interrupt service routine* (ISR) that the device driver provided for the interrupting device. If the condition was caused by a call to a system service, the general system service trap handler transfers control to the specified system service function in the executive. The kernel also installs trap handlers for traps that it doesn't expect to see or doesn't handle. These trap handlers typically execute the system function *KeBugCheckEx*, which halts the computer when the kernel detects problematic or incorrect behavior that, if left unchecked, could result in data corruption. (For more information on bug checks, see Chapter 14, "Crash Dump Analysis," in Part 2.) The following sections describe interrupt, exception, and system service dispatching in greater detail.

Interrupt Dispatching

Hardware-generated interrupts typically originate from I/O devices that must notify the processor when they need service. Interrupt-driven devices allow the operating system to get the maximum use out of the processor by overlapping central processing with I/O operations. A thread starts an I/O transfer to or from a device and then can execute other useful work while the device completes the transfer. When the device is finished, it interrupts the processor for service. Pointing devices, printers, keyboards, disk drives, and network cards are generally interrupt driven.

System software can also generate interrupts. For example, the kernel can issue a software interrupt to initiate thread dispatching and to asynchronously break into the execution of a thread. The kernel can also disable interrupts so that the processor isn't interrupted, but it does so only infrequently—at critical moments while it's programming an interrupt controller or dispatching an exception, for example.

The kernel installs interrupt trap handlers to respond to device interrupts. Interrupt trap handlers transfer control either to an external routine (the ISR) that handles the interrupt or to an internal kernel routine that responds to the interrupt. Device drivers supply ISRs to service device interrupts, and the kernel provides interrupt-handling routines for other types of interrupts.

In the following subsections, you'll find out how the hardware notifies the processor of device interrupts, the types of interrupts the kernel supports, the way device drivers interact with the kernel (as a part of interrupt processing), and the software interrupts the kernel recognizes (plus the kernel objects that are used to implement them).

Hardware Interrupt Processing

On the hardware platforms supported by Windows, external I/O interrupts come into one of the lines on an interrupt controller. The controller, in turn, interrupts the processor on a single line. Once the processor is interrupted, it queries the controller to get the *interrupt request* (IRQ). The interrupt controller translates the IRQ to an interrupt number, uses this number as an index into a structure called the *interrupt dispatch table* (IDT), and transfers control to the appropriate interrupt dispatch routine. At system boot time, Windows fills in the IDT with pointers to the kernel routines that handle each interrupt and exception.

Windows maps hardware IRQs to interrupt numbers in the IDT, and the system also uses the IDT to configure trap handlers for exceptions. For example, the x86 and x64 exception number for a page fault (an exception that occurs when a thread attempts to access a page of virtual memory that isn't defined or present) is 0xe (14). Thus, entry 0xe in the IDT points to the system's page-fault handler. Although the architectures supported by Windows allow up to 256 IDT entries, the number of IRQs a particular machine can support is determined by the design of the interrupt controller the machine uses.

EXPERIMENT: Viewing the IDT

You can view the contents of the IDT, including information on what trap handlers Windows has assigned to interrupts (including exceptions and IRQs), using the *!idt* kernel debugger command. The *!idt* command with no flags shows simplified output that includes only registered hardware interrupts (and, on 64-bit machines, the processor trap handlers).

The following example shows what the output of the *!idt* command looks like:

```
lkd> !idt

Dumping IDT:


00:    fffff80001a7ec40 nt!KiDivideErrorFault
01:    fffff80001a7ed40 nt!KiDebugTrapOrFault
02:    fffff80001a7ef00 nt!KiNmiInterrupt     Stack = 0xFFFFF80001865000
03:    fffff80001a7f280 nt!KiBreakpointTrap
04:    fffff80001a7f380 nt!KiOverflowTrap
05:    fffff80001a7f480 nt!KiBoundFault
06:    fffff80001a7f580 nt!KiInvalidOpcodeFault
07:    fffff80001a7f7c0 nt!KiNpxNotAvailableFault
08:    fffff80001a7f880 nt!KiDoubleFaultAbort     Stack = 0xFFFFF80001863000
09:    fffff80001a7f940 nt!KiNpxSegmentOverrunAbort
0a:    fffff80001a7fa00 nt!KiInvalidTssFault
0b:    fffff80001a7fac0 nt!KiSegmentNotPresentFault
0c:    fffff80001a7fc00 nt!KiStackFault
0d:    fffff80001a7fd40 nt!KiGeneralProtectionFault
0e:    fffff80001a7fe80 nt!KiPageFault
10:    fffff80001a80240 nt!KiFloatingErrorFault
11:    fffff80001a803c0 nt!KiAlignmentFault
12:    fffff80001a804c0 nt!KiMcheckAbort     Stack = 0xFFFFF80001867000
```

```
13:     fffff80001a80840 nt!KiXmmException
1f:     fffff80001a5ec10 nt!KiApcInterrupt
2c:     fffff80001a80a00 nt!KiRaiseAssertion
2d:     fffff80001a80b00 nt!KiDebugServiceTrap
2f:     fffff80001acd590 nt!KiDpcInterrupt
37:     fffff8000201c090 hal!PicSpuriousService37 (KINTERRUPT fffff8000201c000)
3f:     fffff8000201c130 hal!PicSpuriousService37 (KINTERRUPT fffff8000201c0a0)
51:     fffffa80045babd0 dxgkrnl!DpiFdoLineInterruptRoutine (KINTERRUPT fffffa80045bab40)
52:     fffffa80029f1390 USBPORT!USBPORT_InterruptService (KINTERRUPT fffffa80029f1300)
62:     fffffa80029f15d0 USBPORT!USBPORT_InterruptService (KINTERRUPT fffffa80029f1540)
                        USBPORT!USBPORT_InterruptService (KINTERRUPT fffffa80029f1240)
72:     fffffa80029f1e10 ataport!IdePortInterrupt (KINTERRUPT fffffa80029f1d80)
81:     fffffa80045bae10 i8042prt!I8042KeyboardInterruptService (KINTERRUPT
fffffa80045bad80)
82:     fffffa80029f1ed0 ataport!IdePortInterrupt (KINTERRUPT fffffa80029f1e40)
90:     fffffa80045bad50 Vid+0x7918 (KINTERRUPT fffffa80045bacc0)
91:     fffffa80045baed0 i8042prt!I8042MouseInterruptService (KINTERRUPT fffffa80045bae40)
a0:     fffffa80045bac90 vmbus!XPartPncIsr (KINTERRUPT fffffa80045bac00)
a2:     fffffa80029f1210 sdbus!SdbusInterrupt (KINTERRUPT fffffa80029f1180)
                        rimmpx64+0x9FFC (KINTERRUPT fffffa80029f10c0)
                        rimspx64+0x7A14 (KINTERRUPT fffffa80029f1000)
                        rixdpx64+0x9C50 (KINTERRUPT fffffa80045baf00)
a3:     fffffa80029f1510 USBPORT!USBPORT_InterruptService (KINTERRUPT fffffa80029f1480)
                        HDAudBus!HdaController::Isr (KINTERRUPT fffffa80029f1c00)
a8:     fffffa80029f1bd0 NDIS!ndisMiniportMessageIsr (KINTERRUPT fffffa80029f1b40)
a9:     fffffa80029f1b10 NDIS!ndisMiniportMessageIsr (KINTERRUPT fffffa80029f1a80)
aa:     fffffa80029f1a50 NDIS!ndisMiniportMessageIsr (KINTERRUPT fffffa80029f19c0)
ab:     fffffa80029f1990 NDIS!ndisMiniportMessageIsr (KINTERRUPT fffffa80029f1900)
ac:     fffffa80029f18d0 NDIS!ndisMiniportMessageIsr (KINTERRUPT fffffa80029f1840)
ad:     fffffa80029f1810 NDIS!ndisMiniportMessageIsr (KINTERRUPT fffffa80029f1780)
ae:     fffffa80029f1750 NDIS!ndisMiniportMessageIsr (KINTERRUPT fffffa80029f16c0)
af:     fffffa80029f1690 NDIS!ndisMiniportMessageIsr (KINTERRUPT fffffa80029f1600)
b0:     fffffa80029f1d50 NDIS!ndisMiniportMessageIsr (KINTERRUPT fffffa80029f1cc0)
b1:     fffffa80029f1f90 ACPI!ACPIInterruptServiceRoutine (KINTERRUPT fffffa80029f1f00)
b3:     fffffa80029f1450 USBPORT!USBPORT_InterruptService (KINTERRUPT fffffa80029f13c0)
c1:     fffff8000201c3b0 hal!HalpBroadcastCallService (KINTERRUPT fffff8000201c320)
d1:     fffff8000201c450 hal!HalpHpetClockInterrupt (KINTERRUPT fffff8000201c3c0)
d2:     fffff8000201c4f0 hal!HalpHpetRolloverInterrupt (KINTERRUPT fffff8000201c460)
df:     fffff8000201c310 hal!HalpApicRebootService (KINTERRUPT fffff8000201c280)
e1:     fffff80001a8e1f0 nt!KiIpiInterrupt
e2:     fffff8000201c270 hal!HalpDeferredRecoveryService (KINTERRUPT fffff8000201c1e0)
e3:     fffff8000201c1d0 hal!HalpLocalApicErrorService (KINTERRUPT fffff8000201c140)
fd:     fffff8000201c590 hal!HalpProfileInterrupt (KINTERRUPT fffff8000201c500)
fe:     fffff8000201c630 hal!HalpPerfInterrupt (KINTERRUPT fffff8000201c5a0)
```

On the system used to provide the output for this experiment, the keyboard device driver's (I8042prt.sys) keyboard ISR is at interrupt number 0x81. You can also see that interrupt 0xe corresponds to *KiPageFault*, as explained earlier.

Each processor has a separate IDT so that different processors can run different ISRs, if appropriate. For example, in a multiprocessor system, each processor receives the clock interrupt, but only one processor updates the system clock in response to this interrupt. All the processors, however, use the interrupt to measure thread quantum and to initiate rescheduling when a thread's quantum ends.

Similarly, some system configurations might require that a particular processor handle certain device interrupts.

x86 Interrupt Controllers

Most x86 systems rely on either the i8259A Programmable Interrupt Controller (PIC) or a variant of the i82489 Advanced Programmable Interrupt Controller (APIC); today's computers include an APIC. The PIC standard originates with the original IBM PC. The i8259A PIC works only with uniprocessor systems and has only eight interrupt lines. However, the IBM PC architecture defined the addition of a second PIC, called the *slave*, whose interrupts are multiplexed into one of the master PIC's interrupt lines. This provides 15 total interrupts (seven on the master and eight on the slave, multiplexed through the master's eighth interrupt line). APICs and Streamlined Advanced Programmable Interrupt Controllers (SAPICs, discussed shortly) work with multiprocessor systems and have 256 interrupt lines. Intel and other companies have defined the Multiprocessor Specification (MP Specification), a design standard for x86 multiprocessor systems that centers on the use of APIC. To provide compatibility with uniprocessor operating systems and boot code that starts a multiprocessor system in uniprocessor mode, APICs support a PIC compatibility mode with 15 interrupts and delivery of interrupts to only the primary processor. Figure 3-2 depicts the APIC architecture.

The APIC actually consists of several components: an I/O APIC that receives interrupts from devices, local APICs that receive interrupts from the I/O APIC on the bus and that interrupt the CPU they are associated with, and an i8259A-compatible interrupt controller that translates APIC input into PIC-equivalent signals. Because there can be multiple I/O APICs on the system, motherboards typically have a piece of core logic that sits between them and the processors. This logic is responsible for implementing interrupt routing algorithms that both balance the device interrupt load across processors and attempt to take advantage of locality, delivering device interrupts to the same processor that has just fielded a previous interrupt of the same type. Software programs can reprogram the I/O APICs with a fixed routing algorithm that bypasses this piece of chipset logic. Windows does this by programming the APICs in an "interrupt one processor in the following set" routing mode.

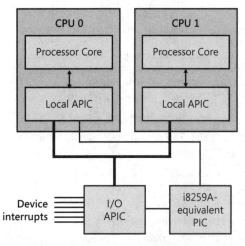

FIGURE 3-2 x86 APIC architecture

x64 Interrupt Controllers

Because the x64 architecture is compatible with x86 operating systems, x64 systems must provide the same interrupt controllers as the x86. A significant difference, however, is that the x64 versions of Windows will not run on systems that do not have an APIC because they use the APIC for interrupt control.

IA64 Interrupt Controllers

The IA64 architecture relies on the Streamlined Advanced Programmable Interrupt Controller (SAPIC), which is an evolution of the APIC. Even if load balancing and routing are present in the firmware, Windows does not take advantage of it; instead, it statically assigns interrupts to processors in a round-robin manner.

EXPERIMENT: Viewing the PIC and APIC

You can view the configuration of the PIC on a uniprocessor and the current local APIC on a multiprocessor by using the *!pic* and *!apic* kernel debugger commands, respectively. Here's the output of the *!pic* command on a uniprocessor. (Note that the *!pic* command doesn't work if your system is using an APIC HAL.)

```
lkd> !pic
----- IRQ Number ----- 00 01 02 03 04 05 06 07 08 09 0A 0B 0C 0D 0E 0F
Physically in service:  .  .  .  .  .  .  .  .  .  .  .  .  .  .  .  .
Physically masked:      .  .  .  Y  .  .  Y  Y  .  .  Y  .  .  Y  .  .
Physically requested:   .  .  .  .  .  .  .  .  .  .  .  .  .  .  .  .
Level Triggered:        .  .  .  .  .  Y  .  .  .  Y  .  Y  .  .  .  .
```

Here's the output of the *!apic* command on a system running with an APIC HAL. Note that during local kernel debugging, this command shows the APIC associated with the current processor—in other words, whichever processor the debugger's thread happens to be running on as you enter the command. When looking at a crash dump or remote system, you can use the ~(tilde) command followed by the processor number to switch the processor of whose local APIC you want to see.

```
lkd> !apic
Apic @ fffe0000  ID:0 (50014)  LogDesc:01000000  DestFmt:ffffffff  TPR 20
TimeCnt: 00000000clk  SpurVec:3f  FaultVec:e3  error:0
Ipi Cmd: 01000000'0000002f  Vec:2F  FixedDel  Ph:01000000    edg high
Timer..: 00000000'000300fd  Vec:FD  FixedDel    Dest=Self    edg high    m
Linti0.: 00000000'0001003f  Vec:3F  FixedDel    Dest=Self    edg high    m
Linti1.: 00000000'000004ff  Vec:FF  NMI         Dest=Self    edg high
TMR: 51-52, 62, A3, B1, B3
IRR:
ISR::
```

The various numbers following the *Vec* labels indicate the associated vector in the IDT with the given command. For example, in this output, interrupt number 0xFD is associated with the APIC Timer, and interrupt number 0xE3 handles APIC errors. Because this experiment was run on the same machine as the earlier *!idt* experiment, you can notice that 0xFD is the HAL's Profiling Interrupt (which uses a timer for profile intervals), and 0xe3 is the HAL's Local APIC Error Handler, as expected.

The following output is for the *!ioapic* command, which displays the configuration of the I/O APICs, the interrupt controller components connected to devices:

```
lkd> !ioapic
IoApic @ FEC00000  ID:0 (51)  Arb:A951
Inti00.: 0000a951'0000a951  Vec:51  LowestD1  Lg:0000a951       lvl low
```

Software Interrupt Request Levels (IRQLs)

Although interrupt controllers perform interrupt prioritization, Windows imposes its own interrupt priority scheme known as *interrupt request levels* (IRQLs). The kernel represents IRQLs internally as a number from 0 through 31 on x86 and from 0 to 15 on x64 and IA64, with higher numbers representing higher-priority interrupts. Although the kernel defines the standard set of IRQLs for software interrupts, the HAL maps hardware-interrupt numbers to the IRQLs. Figure 3-3 shows IRQLs defined for the x86 architecture, and Figure 3-4 shows IRQLs for the x64 and IA64 architectures.

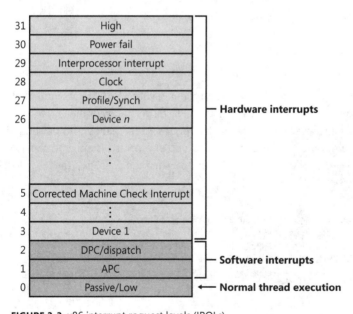

FIGURE 3-3 x86 interrupt request levels (IRQLs)

Interrupts are serviced in priority order, and a higher-priority interrupt preempts the servicing of a lower-priority interrupt. When a high-priority interrupt occurs, the processor saves the interrupted thread's state and invokes the trap dispatchers associated with the interrupt. The trap dispatcher raises the IRQL and calls the interrupt's service routine. After the service routine executes, the interrupt dispatcher lowers the processor's IRQL to where it was before the interrupt occurred and then loads the saved machine state. The interrupted thread resumes executing where it left off. When the kernel lowers the IRQL, lower-priority interrupts that were masked might materialize. If this happens, the kernel repeats the process to handle the new interrupts.

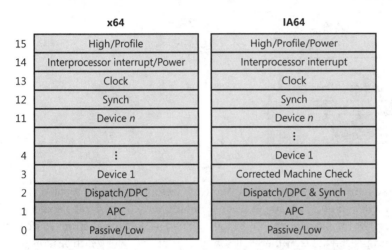

FIGURE 3-4 x64 and IA64 interrupt request levels (IRQLs)

IRQL priority levels have a completely different meaning than thread-scheduling priorities (which are described in Chapter 5). A scheduling priority is an attribute of a thread, whereas an IRQL is an attribute of an interrupt source, such as a keyboard or a mouse. In addition, each processor has an IRQL setting that changes as operating system code executes.

Each processor's IRQL setting determines which interrupts that processor can receive. IRQLs are also used to synchronize access to kernel-mode data structures. (You'll find out more about synchronization later in this chapter.) As a kernel-mode thread runs, it raises or lowers the processor's IRQL either directly by calling *KeRaiseIrql* and *KeLowerIrql* or, more commonly, indirectly via calls to functions that acquire kernel synchronization objects. As Figure 3-5 illustrates, interrupts from a source with an IRQL above the current level interrupt the processor, whereas interrupts from sources with IRQLs equal to or below the current level are *masked* until an executing thread lowers the IRQL.

Because accessing a PIC is a relatively slow operation, HALs that require accessing the I/O bus to change IRQLs, such as for PIC and 32-bit Advanced Configuration and Power Interface (ACPI) systems, implement a performance optimization, called *lazy IRQL*, that avoids PIC accesses. When the IRQL is raised, the HAL notes the new IRQL internally instead of changing the interrupt mask. If a lower-priority interrupt subsequently occurs, the HAL sets the interrupt mask to the settings appropriate for the first interrupt and does not quiesce the lower-priority interrupt until the IRQL is lowered (thus keeping the interrupt pending). Thus, if no lower-priority interrupts occur while the IRQL is raised, the HAL doesn't need to modify the PIC.

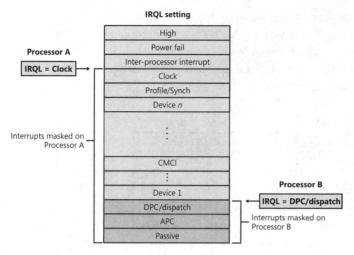

FIGURE 3-5 Masking interrupts

A kernel-mode thread raises and lowers the IRQL of the processor on which it's running, depending on what it's trying to do. For example, when an interrupt occurs, the trap handler (or perhaps the processor) raises the processor's IRQL to the assigned IRQL of the interrupt source. This elevation masks all interrupts at and below that IRQL (on that processor only), which ensures that the processor servicing the interrupt isn't waylaid by an interrupt at the same level or a lower level. The masked interrupts are either handled by another processor or held back until the IRQL drops. Therefore, all components of the system, including the kernel and device drivers, attempt to keep the IRQL at *passive* level (sometimes called *low* level). They do this because device drivers can respond to hardware interrupts in a timelier manner if the IRQL isn't kept unnecessarily elevated for long periods.

Note An exception to the rule that raising the IRQL blocks interrupts of that level and lower relates to APC-level interrupts. If a thread raises the IRQL to APC level and then is rescheduled because of a dispatch/DPC-level interrupt, the system might deliver an APC-level interrupt to the newly scheduled thread. Thus, APC level can be considered a thread-local rather than processor-wide IRQL.

EXPERIMENT: Viewing the IRQL

You can view a processor's saved IRQL with the *!irql* debugger command. The saved IRQL represents the IRQL at the time just before the break-in to the debugger, which raises the IRQL to a static, meaningless value:

```
kd> !irql
Debugger saved IRQL for processor 0x0 -- 0 (LOW_LEVEL)
```

Note that the IRQL value is saved in two locations. The first, which represents the current IRQL, is the processor control region (PCR), while its extension, the processor region control block (PRCB), contains the saved IRQL in the *DebuggerSaveIrql* field. The PCR and PRCB contain information about the state of each processor in the system, such as the current IRQL, a pointer to the hardware IDT, the currently running thread, and the next thread selected to run. The kernel and the HAL use this information to perform architecture-specific and machine-specific actions. Portions of the PCR and PRCB structures are defined publicly in the Windows Driver Kit (WDK) header file Ntddk.h.

You can view the contents of the current processor's PCR with the kernel debugger by using the *!pcr* command. To view the PCR of a specific processor, add the processor's number after the command, separated with a space:

```
lkd> !pcr 0
KPCR for Processor 0 at fffff80001bfad00:
    Major 1 Minor 1
    NtTib.ExceptionList: fffff80001853000
         NtTib.StackBase: fffff80001854080
        NtTib.StackLimit: 000000000026ea28
    NtTib.SubSystemTib: fffff80001bfad00
          NtTib.Version: 0000000001bfae80
      NtTib.UserPointer: fffff80001bfb4f0
        NtTib.SelfTib: 000007fffffdb000

                SelfPcr: 0000000000000000
                   Prcb: fffff80001bfae80
                   Irql: 0000000000000000
                    IRR: 0000000000000000
                    IDR: 0000000000000000
          InterruptMode: 0000000000000000
                    IDT: 0000000000000000
                    GDT: 0000000000000000
                    TSS: 0000000000000000

          CurrentThread: fffff80001c08c40
             NextThread: 0000000000000000
             IdleThread: fffff80001c08c40

       DpcQueue:
```

Because changing a processor's IRQL has such a significant effect on system operation, the change can be made only in kernel mode—user-mode threads can't change the processor's IRQL. This means that a processor's IRQL is always at passive level when it's executing user-mode code. Only when the processor is executing kernel-mode code can the IRQL be higher.

Each interrupt level has a specific purpose. For example, the kernel issues an *interprocessor interrupt* (IPI) to request that another processor perform an action, such as dispatching a particular thread for execution or updating its translation look-aside buffer (TLB) cache. The system clock generates an interrupt at regular intervals, and the kernel responds by updating the clock and measuring thread execution time. If a hardware platform supports two clocks, the kernel adds another clock interrupt level to measure performance. The HAL provides a number of interrupt levels for use by interrupt-driven devices; the exact number varies with the processor and system configuration. The kernel uses software interrupts (described later in this chapter) to initiate thread scheduling and to asynchronously break into a thread's execution.

Mapping Interrupts to IRQLs

IRQL levels aren't the same as the interrupt requests (IRQs) defined by interrupt controllers—the architectures on which Windows runs don't implement the concept of IRQLs in hardware. So how does Windows determine what IRQL to assign to an interrupt? The answer lies in the HAL. In Windows, a type of device driver called a *bus driver* determines the presence of devices on its bus (PCI, USB, and so on) and what interrupts can be assigned to a device. The bus driver reports this information to the Plug and Play manager, which decides, after taking into account the acceptable interrupt assignments for all other devices, which interrupt will be assigned to each device. Then it calls a Plug and Play interrupt arbiter, which maps interrupts to IRQLs. (The root arbiter is used on non-ACPI systems, while the ACPI HAL has its own arbiter on ACPI-compatible systems.)

The algorithm for assignment differs for the various HALs that Windows includes. On ACPI systems (including x86, x64, and IA64), the HAL computes the IRQL for a given interrupt by dividing the interrupt vector assigned to the IRQ by 16. As for selecting an interrupt vector for the IRQ, this depends on the type of interrupt controller present on the system. On today's APIC systems, this number is generated in a round-robin fashion, so there is no computable way to figure out the IRQ based on the interrupt vector or the IRQL. However, an experiment later in this section shows how the debugger can query this information from the interrupt arbiter.

Predefined IRQLs

Let's take a closer look at the use of the predefined IRQLs, starting from the highest level shown in Figure 3-4:

- The kernel uses *high* level only when it's halting the system in *KeBugCheckEx* and masking out all interrupts.

- *Power fail* level originated in the original Windows NT design documents, which specified the behavior of system power failure code, but this IRQL has never been used.

- *Interprocessor interrupt* level is used to request another processor to perform an action, such as updating the processor's TLB cache, system shutdown, or system crash.

- *Clock* level is used for the system's clock, which the kernel uses to track the time of day as well as to measure and allot CPU time to threads.

- The system's real-time clock (or another source, such as the local APIC timer) uses *profile* level when kernel profiling (a performance-measurement mechanism) is enabled. When kernel profiling is active, the kernel's profiling trap handler records the address of the code that was executing when the interrupt occurred. A table of address samples is constructed over time that tools can extract and analyze. You can obtain Kernrate, a kernel profiling tool that you can use to configure and view profiling-generated statistics, from the Windows Driver Kit (WDK). See the Kernrate experiment for more information on using this tool.

- The *synchronization* IRQL is internally used by the dispatcher and scheduler code to protect access to global thread scheduling and wait/synchronization code. It is typically defined as the highest level right after the device IRQLs.

- The *device* IRQLs are used to prioritize device interrupts. (See the previous section for how hardware interrupt levels are mapped to IRQLs.)

- The *corrected machine check interrupt* level is used to signal the operating system after a serious but corrected hardware condition or error that was reported by the CPU or firmware through the *Machine Check Error (MCE)* interface.

- *DPC/dispatch*-level and *APC*-level interrupts are software interrupts that the kernel and device drivers generate. (DPCs and APCs are explained in more detail later in this chapter.)

- The lowest IRQL, *passive* level, isn't really an interrupt level at all; it's the setting at which normal thread execution takes place and all interrupts are allowed to occur.

EXPERIMENT: Using Kernel Profiler (Kernrate) to Profile Execution

You can use the Kernel Profiler tool (Kernrate) to enable the system-profiling timer, collect samples of the code that is executing when the timer fires, and display a summary showing the frequency distribution across image files and functions. It can be used to track CPU usage consumed by individual processes and/or time spent in kernel mode independent of processes (for example, interrupt service routines). Kernel profiling is useful when you want to obtain a breakdown of where the system is spending time.

In its simplest form, Kernrate samples where time has been spent in each kernel module (for example, Ntoskrnl, drivers, and so on). For example, after installing the Windows Driver Kit, try performing the following steps:

1. Open a command prompt.

2. Type **cd C:\WinDDK\7600.16385.1\tools\other** (the path to your installation of the Windows 7/Server 2008R2 WDK).

3. Type **dir**. (You will see directories for each platform.)

4. Run the image that matches your platform (with no arguments or switches). For example, *i386\kernrate.exe* is the image for an x86 system.

5. While Kernrate is running, perform some other activity on the system. For example, run Windows Media Player and play some music, run a graphics-intensive game, or perform network activity such as doing a directory listing of a remote network share.

6. Press Ctrl+C to stop Kernrate. This causes Kernrate to display the statistics from the sampling period.

In the following sample output from Kernrate, Windows Media Player was running, playing a recorded movie from disk:

```
C:\WinDDK\7600.16385.1\tools\Other\i386>kernrate.exe

 /===============================\
<          KERNRATE LOG          >
 \===============================/
Date: 2011/03/09   Time: 16:44:24
Machine Name: TEST-LAPTOP
Number of Processors: 2
PROCESSOR_ARCHITECTURE: x86
PROCESSOR_LEVEL: 6
PROCESSOR_REVISION: 0f06
Physical Memory: 3310 MB
Pagefile Total: 7285 MB
Virtual Total: 2047 MB
PageFile1: \??\C:\pagefile.sys, 4100MB
OS Version: 6.1 Build 7601 Service-Pack: 1.0
WinDir: C:\Windows


Kernrate Executable Location: C:\WINDDK\7600.16385.1\TOOLS\OTHER\I386


Kernrate User-Specified Command Line:
kernrate.exe


Kernel Profile (PID = 0): Source= Time,
Using Kernrate Default Rate of 25000 events/hit
Starting to collect profile data

***> Press ctrl-c to finish collecting profile data
===> Finished Collecting Data, Starting to Process Results

-----------Overall Summary:--------------

P0     K 0:00:00.000 ( 0.0%)  U 0:00:00.234 ( 4.7%)  I 0:00:04.789 (95.3%)
DPC 0:00:00.000 ( 0.0%)  Interrupt 0:00:00.000 ( 0.0%)
        Interrupts= 9254, Interrupt Rate= 1842/sec.

P1     K 0:00:00.031 ( 0.6%)  U 0:00:00.140 ( 2.8%)  I 0:00:04.851 (96.6%)
DPC 0:00:00.000 ( 0.0%)  Interrupt 0:00:00.000 ( 0.0%)
        Interrupts= 7051, Interrupt Rate= 1404/sec.

TOTAL  K 0:00:00.031 ( 0.3%)  U 0:00:00.374 ( 3.7%)  I 0:00:09.640 (96.0%)
DPC 0:00:00.000 ( 0.0%)  Interrupt 0:00:00.000 ( 0.0%)
        Total Interrupts= 16305, Total Interrupt Rate= 3246/sec.
```

```
Total Profile Time = 5023 msec

                                    BytesStart        BytesStop       BytesDiff.
      Available Physical Memory  ,   1716359168,      1716195328,      -163840
      Available Pagefile(s)      ,   5973733376,      5972783104,      -950272
      Available Virtual          ,   2122145792,      2122145792,            0
      Available Extended Virtual ,            0,               0,            0
      Committed Memory Bytes     ,   1665404928,      1666355200,       950272
      Non Paged Pool Usage Bytes ,     66211840,        66211840,            0
      Paged Pool Usage Bytes     ,    189083648,       189087744,         4096
      Paged Pool Available Bytes ,    150593536,       150593536,            0
      Free System PTEs           ,        37322,           37322,            0

                                Total           Avg. Rate
      Context Switches     ,     30152,          6003/sec.
      System Calls         ,    110807,         22059/sec.
      Page Faults          ,       226,            45/sec.
      I/O Read Operations  ,       730,           145/sec.
      I/O Write Operations ,      1038,           207/sec.
      I/O Other Operations ,       858,           171/sec.
      I/O Read Bytes       ,   2013850,         2759/ I/O
      I/O Write Bytes      ,     28212,           27/ I/O
      I/O Other Bytes      ,     19902,           23/ I/O


----------------------------


Results for Kernel Mode:
----------------------------


OutputResults: KernelModuleCount = 167
Percentage in the following table is based on the Total Hits for the Kernel

Time    3814 hits, 25000 events per hit --------
Module                         Hits      msec   %Total   Events/Sec
NTKRNLPA                       3768      5036    98 %     18705321
NVLDDMKM                         12      5036     0 %        59571
HAL                              12      5036     0 %        59571
WIN32K                           10      5037     0 %        49632
DXGKRNL                           9      5036     0 %        44678
NETW4V32                          2      5036     0 %         9928
FLTMGR                            1      5036     0 %         4964

=============================== END OF RUN ===================================
=========================== NORMAL END OF RUN ===============================
```

The overall summary shows that the system spent 0.3 percent of the time in kernel mode, 3.7 percent in user mode, 96.0 percent idle, 0.0 percent at DPC level, and 0.0 percent at interrupt level. The module with the highest hit rate was Ntkrnlpa.exe, the kernel for machines with Physical Address Extension (PAE) or NX support. The module with the second highest hit rate was nvlddmkm.sys, the driver for the video card on the machine used for the test. This makes sense because the major activity going on in the system was Windows Media Player sending video I/O to the video driver.

If you have symbols available, you can zoom in on individual modules and see the time spent by function name. For example, profiling the system while rapidly dragging a window around the screen resulted in the following (partial) output:

```
C:\WinDDK\7600.16385.1\tools\Other\i386>kernrate.exe -z ntkrnlpa -z win32k
/==============================\
<        KERNRATE LOG          >
\==============================/
Date: 2011/03/09   Time: 16:49:56

Time    4191 hits, 25000 events per hit --------
Module                          Hits      msec   %Total  Events/Sec
NTKRNLPA                        3623      5695    86 %    15904302
WIN32K                          303       5696     7 %     1329880
INTELPPM                        141       5696     3 %      618855
HAL                             61        5695     1 %      267778
CDD                             30        5696     0 %      131671
NVLDDMKM                        13        5696     0 %       57057


----- Zoomed module WIN32K.SYS (Bucket size = 16 bytes, Rounding Down) --------
Module                          Hits      msec   %Total  Events/Sec
BltLnkReadPat                   34        5696    10 %      149227
memmove                         21        5696     6 %       92169
vSrcTranCopyS8D32               17        5696     5 %       74613
memcpy                          12        5696     3 %       52668
RGNOBJ::bMerge                  10        5696     3 %       43890
HANDLELOCK::vLockHandle         8         5696     2 %       35112

----- Zoomed module NTKRNLPA.EXE (Bucket size = 16 bytes, Rounding Down) --------
Module                          Hits      msec   %Total  Events/Sec
KiIdleLoop                      3288      5695    87 %    14433713
READ_REGISTER_USHORT            95        5695     2 %      417032
READ_REGISTER_ULONG             93        5695     2 %      408252
RtlFillMemoryUlong              31        5695     0 %      136084
KiFastCallEntry                 18        5695     0 %       79016
```

The module with the second hit rate was Win32k.sys, the windowing system driver. Also high on the list were the video driver and Cdd.dll, a global video driver used for the 3D-accelerated Aero desktop theme. These results make sense because the main activity in the system was drawing on the screen. Note that in the zoomed display for Win32k.sys, the functions with the highest hits are related to merging, copying, and moving bits, the main GDI operations for painting a window dragged on the screen.

One important restriction on code running at DPC/dispatch level or above is that it can't wait for an object if doing so necessitates the scheduler to select another thread to execute, which is an illegal operation because the scheduler relies on DPC-level software interrupts to schedule threads. Another restriction is that only nonpaged memory can be accessed at IRQL DPC/dispatch level or higher.

This rule is actually a side effect of the first restriction because attempting to access memory that isn't resident results in a page fault. When a page fault occurs, the memory manager initiates a disk I/O and then needs to wait for the file system driver to read the page in from disk.

This wait would, in turn, require the scheduler to perform a context switch (perhaps to the idle thread if no user thread is waiting to run), thus violating the rule that the scheduler can't be invoked (because the IRQL is still DPC/dispatch level or higher at the time of the disk read). A further problem results in the fact that I/O completion typically occurs at APC_LEVEL, so even in cases where a wait wouldn't be required, the I/O would never complete because the completion APC would not get a chance to run.

If either of these two restrictions is violated, the system crashes with an IRQL_NOT_LESS_OR_EQUAL or a DRIVER_IRQL_NOT_LESS_OR_EQUAL crash code. (See Chapter 14 in Part 2 for a thorough discussion of system crashes.) Violating these restrictions is a common bug in device drivers. The Windows Driver Verifier (explained in the section "Driver Verifier" in Chapter 10, "Memory Management," in Part 2) has an option you can set to assist in finding this particular type of bug.

Interrupt Objects

The kernel provides a portable mechanism—a kernel control object called an *interrupt object*—that allows device drivers to register ISRs for their devices. An interrupt object contains all the information the kernel needs to associate a device ISR with a particular level of interrupt, including the address of the ISR, the IRQL at which the device interrupts, and the entry in the kernel's interrupt dispatch table (IDT) with which the ISR should be associated. When an interrupt object is initialized, a few instructions of assembly language code, called the *dispatch code*, are copied from an interrupt-handling template, *KiInterruptTemplate*, and stored in the object. When an interrupt occurs, this code is executed.

This interrupt-object resident code calls the real interrupt dispatcher, which is typically either the kernel's *KiInterruptDispatch* or *KiChainedDispatch* routine, passing it a pointer to the interrupt object. *KiInterruptDispatch* is the routine used for interrupt vectors for which only one interrupt object is registered, and *KiChainedDispatch* is for vectors shared among multiple interrupt objects. The interrupt object contains information that this second dispatcher routine needs to locate and properly call the ISR the device driver provides.

The interrupt object also stores the IRQL associated with the interrupt so that *KiInterruptDispatch* or *KiChainedDispatch* can raise the IRQL to the correct level before calling the ISR and then lower the IRQL after the ISR has returned. This two-step process is required because there's no way to pass a pointer to the interrupt object (or any other argument for that matter) on the initial dispatch because the initial dispatch is done by hardware. On a multiprocessor system, the kernel allocates and initializes an interrupt object for each CPU, enabling the local APIC on that CPU to accept the particular interrupt.

On x64 Windows systems, the kernel optimizes interrupt dispatch by using specific routines that save processor cycles by omitting functionality that isn't needed, such as *KiInterruptDispatchNoLock*, which is used for interrupts that do not have an associated kernel-managed spinlock (typically used by drivers that want to synchronize with their ISRs), and *KiInterruptDispatchNoEOI*, which is used for interrupts that have programmed the APIC in *"Auto-End-of-Interrupt"* (*Auto-EOI*) mode—because the interrupt controller will send the EOI signal automatically, the kernel does not need to the extra code to do perform the EOI itself. Finally, for the performance/profiling interrupt specifically, the *KiInterruptDispatchLBControl* handler is used, which supports the *Last Branch Control* MSR available on modern CPUs. This register enables the kernel to track/save the branch instruction when tracing; during an interrupt, this information would be lost because it's not stored in the normal thread register context, so special code must be added to preserve it. The HAL's performance and profiling interrupts use this functionality, for example, while the other HAL interrupt routines take advantage of the "no-lock" dispatch code, because the HAL does not require the kernel to synchronize with its ISR.

Another kernel interrupt handler is *KiFloatingDispatch,* which is used for interrupts that require saving the floating-point state. Unlike kernel-mode code, which typically is not allowed to use floating-point (MMX, SSE, 3DNow!) operations because these registers won't be saved across context switches, ISRs might need to use these registers (such as the video card ISR performing a quick drawing operation). When connecting an interrupt, drivers can set the *FloatingSave* argument to *TRUE*, requesting that the kernel use the floating-point dispatch routine, which will save the floating registers. (However, this greatly increases interrupt latency.) Note that this is supported only on 32-bit systems.

Figure 3-6 shows typical interrupt control flow for interrupts associated with interrupt objects.

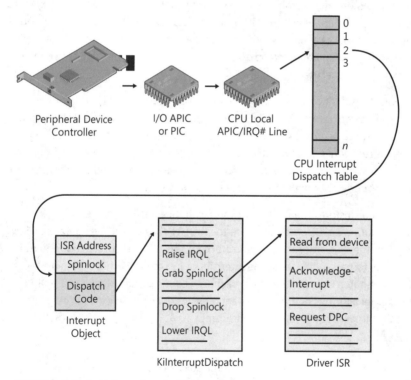

FIGURE 3-6 Typical interrupt control flow

EXPERIMENT: Examining Interrupt Internals

Using the kernel debugger, you can view details of an interrupt object, including its IRQL, ISR address, and custom interrupt-dispatching code. First, execute the *!idt* command and locate the entry that includes a reference to *I8042KeyboardInterruptService*, the ISR routine for the PS/2 keyboard device:

```
81:    fffffa80045bae10 i8042prt!I8042KeyboardInterruptService (KINTERRUPT
fffffa80045bad80)
```

To view the contents of the interrupt object associated with the interrupt, execute *dt nt!_kinterrupt* with the address following KINTERRUPT:

```
lkd> dt nt!_KINTERRUPT fffffa80045bad80
   +0x000 Type             : 22
   +0x002 Size             : 160
   +0x008 InterruptListEntry : _LIST_ENTRY [ 0x00000000'00000000 - 0x0 ]
   +0x018 ServiceRoutine   : 0xfffff880'0356ca04      unsigned char
 i8042prt!I8042KeyboardInterruptService+0
   +0x020 MessageServiceRoutine : (null)
   +0x028 MessageIndex     : 0
   +0x030 ServiceContext   : 0xfffffa80'02c839f0
   +0x038 SpinLock         : 0
   +0x040 TickCount        : 0
   +0x048 ActualLock       : 0xfffffa80'02c83b50  -> 0
   +0x050 DispatchAddress  : 0xfffff800'01a7db90      void  nt!KiInterruptDispatch+0
   +0x058 Vector           : 0x81
   +0x05c Irql             : 0x8 ''
   +0x05d SynchronizeIrql  : 0x9 ''
   +0x05e FloatingSave     : 0 ''
   +0x05f Connected        : 0x1 ''
   +0x060 Number           : 0
   +0x064 ShareVector      : 0 ''
   +0x065 Pad              : [3]  ""
   +0x068 Mode             : 1 ( Latched )
   +0x06c Polarity         : 0 ( InterruptPolarityUnknown )
   +0x070 ServiceCount     : 0
   +0x074 DispatchCount    : 0
   +0x078 Rsvd1            : 0
   +0x080 TrapFrame        : 0xfffff800'0185ab00 _KTRAP_FRAME
   +0x088 Reserved         : (null)
   +0x090 DispatchCode     : [4] 0x8d485550
```

In this example, the IRQL that Windows assigned to the interrupt is 8. Although there is no direct mapping between an interrupt vector and an IRQ, Windows does keep track of this translation when managing device resources through what are called *arbiters*. For each resource type, an arbiter maintains the relationship between virtual resource usage (such as an interrupt vector) and physical resources (such as an interrupt line). As such, you can query either the root

IRQ arbiter (on systems without ACPI) or the ACPI IRQ arbiter and obtain this mapping. Use the *!apciirqarb* command to obtain information on the ACPI IRQ arbiter:

```
lkd> !acpiirqarb

Processor 0 (0, 0):
Device Object: 0000000000000000
Current IDT Allocation:
...
    0000000000000081 - 0000000000000081   D   fffffa80029b4c20  (i8042prt)
A:0000000000000000 IRQ:0
...
```

If you don't have an ACPI system, you can use *!arbiter 4* (*4* tells the debugger to display only IRQ arbiters):

```
lkd> !arbiter 4

DEVNODE fffffa80027c6d90 (HTREE\ROOT\0)
  Interrupt Arbiter "RootIRQ" at fffff80001c82500
    Allocated ranges:
      0000000000000081 - 0000000000000081   Owner   fffffa80029b4c20  (i8042prt)
```

In both cases, you will be given the owner of the vector, in the type of a *device object*. You can then use the *!devobj* command to get information on the i8042prt device in this example (which corresponds to the PS/2 driver):

```
lkd> !devobj fffffa80029b4c20
Device object (fffffa80029b4c20) is for:
 00000061 \Driver\ACPI DriverObject fffffa8002888e70
Current Irp 00000000 RefCount 1 Type 00000032 Flags 00003040
Dacl fffff9a100096a41 DevExt fffffa800299f740 DevObjExt fffffa80029b4d70 DevNode
fffffa80029b54b0
```

The device object is associated to a *device node*, which stores all the device's physical resources. You can now dump these resources with the *!devnode* command, and using the 6 flag to ask for resource information:

```
lkd> !devnode fffffa80029b54b0 6
DevNode 0xfffffa80029b54b0 for PDO 0xfffffa80029b4c20
  Parent 0xfffffa800299b390   Sibling 0xfffffa80029b5230   Child 0000000000
  InstancePath is "ACPI\PNP0303\4&17aa870d&0"
  ServiceName is "i8042prt"
...
  CmResourceList at 0xfffff8a00185bf40  Version 1.1  Interface 0xf  Bus #0
    Entry 0 - Port (0x1) Device Exclusive (0x1)
      Flags (0x11) - PORT_MEMORY PORT_IO 16_BIT_DECODE
      Range starts at 0x60 for 0x1 bytes
    Entry 1 - Port (0x1) Device Exclusive (0x1)
      Flags (0x11) - PORT_MEMORY PORT_IO 16_BIT_DECODE
      Range starts at 0x64 for 0x1 bytes
    Entry 2 - Port (0x1) Device Exclusive (0x1)
      Flags (0x11) - PORT_MEMORY PORT_IO 16_BIT_DECODE
      Range starts at 0x62 for 0x1 bytes
```

```
    Entry 3 - Port (0x1) Device Exclusive (0x1)
      Flags (0x11) - PORT_MEMORY PORT_IO 16_BIT_DECODE
      Range starts at 0x66 for 0x1 bytes
    Entry 4 - Interrupt (0x2) Device Exclusive (0x1)
      Flags (0x01) - LATCHED
      Level 0x1, Vector 0x1, Group 0, Affinity 0xffffffff
```

The device node tells you that this device has a resource list with 4 entries, one of which is an interrupt entry corresponding to IRQ 1. (The level and vector numbers represent the IRQ vector, not the interrupt vector.) IRQ 1 is the traditional PC/AT IRQ number associated with the PS/2 keyboard device, so this is the expected value. (A USB keyboard would have a different interrupt.)

On ACPI systems, you can obtain this information in a slightly easier way by reading the extended output of the *!acpiirqarb* command introduced earlier. As part of its output, it displays the IRQ to IDT mapping table:

```
Interrupt Controller (Inputs: 0x0-0x17 Dev: 0000000000000000):
    (00)Cur:IDT-a1 Ref-1 edg hi   Pos:IDT-00 Ref-0 edg hi
    (01)Cur:IDT-81 Ref-1 edg hi   Pos:IDT-00 Ref-0 edg hi
    (02)Cur:IDT-00 Ref-0 edg hi   Pos:IDT-00 Ref-0 edg hi
    (03)Cur:IDT-00 Ref-0 edg hi   Pos:IDT-00 Ref-0 edg hi
    (04)Cur:IDT-00 Ref-0 edg hi   Pos:IDT-00 Ref-0 edg hi
    (05)Cur:IDT-00 Ref-0 edg hi   Pos:IDT-00 Ref-0 edg hi
    (06)Cur:IDT-00 Ref-0 edg hi   Pos:IDT-00 Ref-0 edg hi
    (07)Cur:IDT-00 Ref-0 edg hi   Pos:IDT-00 Ref-0 edg hi
    (08)Cur:IDT-71 Ref-1 edg hi   Pos:IDT-00 Ref-0 edg hi
    (09)Cur:IDT-b1 Ref-1 lev hi   Pos:IDT-00 Ref-0 edg hi
    (0a)Cur:IDT-00 Ref-0 edg hi   Pos:IDT-00 Ref-0 edg hi
    (0b)Cur:IDT-00 Ref-0 edg hi   Pos:IDT-00 Ref-0 edg hi
    (0c)Cur:IDT-91 Ref-1 edg hi   Pos:IDT-00 Ref-0 edg hi
    (0d)Cur:IDT-61 Ref-1 edg hi   Pos:IDT-00 Ref-0 edg hi
    (0e)Cur:IDT-82 Ref-1 edg hi   Pos:IDT-00 Ref-0 edg hi
    (0f)Cur:IDT-72 Ref-1 edg hi   Pos:IDT-00 Ref-0 edg hi
    (10)Cur:IDT-51 Ref-3 lev low  Pos:IDT-00 Ref-0 edg hi
    (11)Cur:IDT-b2 Ref-1 lev low  Pos:IDT-00 Ref-0 edg hi
    (12)Cur:IDT-a2 Ref-5 lev low  Pos:IDT-00 Ref-0 edg hi
    (13)Cur:IDT-92 Ref-1 lev low  Pos:IDT-00 Ref-0 edg hi
    (14)Cur:IDT-62 Ref-2 lev low  Pos:IDT-00 Ref-0 edg hi
    (15)Cur:IDT-a3 Ref-2 lev low  Pos:IDT-00 Ref-0 edg hi
    (16)Cur:IDT-b3 Ref-1 lev low  Pos:IDT-00 Ref-0 edg hi
    (17)Cur:IDT-52 Ref-1 lev low  Pos:IDT-00 Ref-0 edg hi
```

As expected, IRQ 1 is associated with IDT entry 0x81. For more information on device objects, resources, and other related concepts, see Chapter 8, "I/O System," in Part 2.

The ISR's address for the interrupt object is stored in the *ServiceRoutine* field (which is what *!idt* displays in its output), and the interrupt code that actually executes when an interrupt occurs is stored in the *DispatchCode* array at the end of the interrupt object. The interrupt code stored there is programmed to build the trap frame on the stack and then call the function stored in the *DispatchAddress* field (*KiInterruptDispatch* in the example), passing it a pointer to the interrupt object.

Windows and Real-Time Processing

Deadline requirements, either hard or soft, characterize real-time environments. Hard real-time systems (for example, a nuclear power plant control system) have deadlines the system must meet to avoid catastrophic failures, such as loss of equipment or life. Soft real-time systems (for example, a car's fuel-economy optimization system) have deadlines the system can miss, but timeliness is still a desirable trait. In real-time systems, computers have sensor input devices and control output devices. The designer of a real-time computer system must know worst-case delays between the time an input device generates an interrupt and the time the device's driver can control the output device to respond. This worst-case analysis must take into account the delays the operating system introduces as well as the delays the application and device drivers impose.

Because Windows doesn't enable controlled prioritization of device IRQs and user-level applications execute only when a processor's IRQL is at passive level, Windows isn't typically suitable as a real-time operating system. The system's devices and device drivers—not Windows—ultimately determine the worst-case delay. This factor becomes a problem when the real-time system's designer uses off-the-shelf hardware. The designer can have difficulty determining how long every off-the-shelf device's ISR or DPC might take in the worst case. Even after testing, the designer can't guarantee that a special case in a live system won't cause the system to miss an important deadline. Furthermore, the sum of all the delays a system's DPCs and ISRs can introduce usually far exceeds the tolerance of a time-sensitive system.

Although many types of embedded systems (for example, printers and automotive computers) have real-time requirements, Windows Embedded Standard 7 doesn't have real-time characteristics. It is simply a version of Windows 7 that makes it possible to produce small-footprint versions of Windows 7 suitable for running on devices with limited resources. For example, a device that has no networking capability would omit all the Windows 7 components related to networking, including network management tools and adapter and protocol stack device drivers.

Still, there are third-party vendors that supply real-time kernels for Windows. The approach these vendors take is to embed their real-time kernel in a custom HAL and to have Windows run as a task in the real-time operating system. The task running Windows serves as the user interface to the system and has a lower priority than the tasks responsible for managing the device.

Associating an ISR with a particular level of interrupt is called *connecting an interrupt object*, and dissociating an ISR from an IDT entry is called *disconnecting an interrupt object*. These operations, accomplished by calling the kernel functions *IoConnectInterruptEx* and *IoDisconnectInterruptEx*, allow a device driver to "turn on" an ISR when the driver is loaded into the system and to "turn off" the ISR if the driver is unloaded.

Using the interrupt object to register an ISR prevents device drivers from fiddling directly with interrupt hardware (which differs among processor architectures) and from needing to know any details about the IDT. This kernel feature aids in creating portable device drivers because it eliminates the need to code in assembly language or to reflect processor differences in device drivers.

Interrupt objects provide other benefits as well. By using the interrupt object, the kernel can synchronize the execution of the ISR with other parts of a device driver that might share data with the ISR. (See Chapter 8 in Part 2 for more information about how device drivers respond to interrupts.)

Furthermore, interrupt objects allow the kernel to easily call more than one ISR for any interrupt level. If multiple device drivers create interrupt objects and connect them to the same IDT entry, the interrupt dispatcher calls each routine when an interrupt occurs at the specified interrupt line. This capability allows the kernel to easily support *daisy-chain* configurations, in which several devices share the same interrupt line. The chain breaks when one of the ISRs claims ownership for the interrupt by returning a status to the interrupt dispatcher.

If multiple devices sharing the same interrupt require service at the same time, devices not acknowledged by their ISRs will interrupt the system again once the interrupt dispatcher has lowered the IRQL. Chaining is permitted only if all the device drivers wanting to use the same interrupt indicate to the kernel that they can share the interrupt; if they can't, the Plug and Play manager reorganizes their interrupt assignments to ensure that it honors the sharing requirements of each. If the interrupt vector is shared, the interrupt object invokes *KiChainedDispatch*, which will invoke the ISRs of each registered interrupt object in turn until one of them claims the interrupt or all have been executed. In the earlier sample *!idt* output (in the "EXPERIMENT: Viewing the IDT" section), vector 0xa2 is connected to several chained interrupt objects. On the system it was run on, it happens to correspond to an integrated 7-in-1 media card reader, which is a combination of Secure Digital (SD), Compact Flash (CF), MultiMedia Card (MMC) and other types of readers, each having their individual interrupt. Because it's packaged as one device by the same vendor, it makes sense that its interrupts share the same vector.

Line-Based vs. Message Signaled-Based Interrupts

Shared interrupts are often the cause of high interrupt latency and can also cause stability issues. They are typically undesirable and a side effect of the limited number of physical interrupt lines on a computer. For example, in the previous example of the 7-in-1 media card reader, a much better solution is for each device to have its own interrupt and for one driver to manage the different interrupts knowing which device they came from. However, consuming four IRQ lines for a single device quickly leads to IRQ line exhaustion. Additionally, PCI devices are each connected to only one IRQ line anyway, so the media card reader cannot use more than one IRQ in the first place.

Other problems with generating interrupts through an IRQ line is that incorrect management of the IRQ signal can lead to interrupt storms or other kinds of deadlocks on the machine, because the signal is driven "high" or "low" until the ISR acknowledges it. (Furthermore, the interrupt controller must typically receive an EOI signal as well.) If either of these does not happen due to a bug, the system can end up in an interrupt state forever, further interrupts could be masked away, or both. Finally, line-based interrupts provide poor scalability in multiprocessor environments. In many cases, the hardware has the final decision as to which processor will be interrupted out of the possible set that the Plug and Play manager selected for this interrupt, and there is little device drivers can do.

A solution to all these problems is a new interrupt mechanism first introduced in the PCI 2.2 standard called *message-signaled interrupts (MSI)*. Although it remains an optional component of the standard that is seldom found in client machines, an increasing number of servers and workstations implement MSI support, which is fully supported by the all recent versions of Windows. In the MSI model, a device delivers a message to its driver by writing to a specific memory address. This action causes an interrupt, and Windows then calls the ISR with the message content (value) and the address where the message was delivered. A device can also deliver multiple messages (up to 32) to the memory address, delivering different payloads based on the event.

Because communication is based across a memory value, and because the content is delivered with the interrupt, the need for IRQ lines is removed (making the total system limit of MSIs equal to the number of interrupt vectors, not IRQ lines), as is the need for a driver ISR to query the device for data related to the interrupt, decreasing latency. Due to the large number of device interrupts available through this model, this effectively nullifies any benefit of sharing interrupts, decreasing latency further by directly delivering the interrupt data to the concerned ISR.

Finally, MSI-X, an extension to the MSI model, which is introduced in PCI 3.0, adds support for 32-bit messages (instead of 16-bit), a maximum of 2048 different messages (instead of just 32), and more importantly, the ability to use a different address (which can be dynamically determined) for each of the MSI payloads. Using a different address allows the MSI payload to be written to a different physical address range that belongs to a different processor, or a different set of target processors, effectively enabling nonuniform memory access (NUMA)-aware interrupt delivery by sending the interrupt to the processor that initiated the related device request. This improves latency and scalability by monitoring both load and closest NUMA node during interrupt completion.

Interrupt Affinity and Priority

On systems that both support ACPI and contain an APIC, Windows enables driver developers and administrators to somewhat control the processor affinity (selecting the processor or group of processors that receives the interrupt) and affinity policy (selecting how processors will be chosen and which processors in a group will be chosen). Furthermore, it enables a primitive mechanism of interrupt prioritization based on IRQL selection. Affinity policy is defined according to Table 3-1, and it's configurable through a registry value called InterruptPolicyValue in the Interrupt Management\Affinity Policy key under the device's instance key in the registry. Because of this, it does not require any code to configure—an administrator can add this value to a given driver's key to influence its behavior. Microsoft provides such a tool, called the Interrupt Affinity policy Tool, which can be downloaded from *http://www.microsoft.com/whdc /system/sysperf/intpolicy.mspx*.

TABLE 3-1 IRQ Affinity Policies

Policy	Meaning
IrqPolicyMachineDefault	The device does not require a particular affinity policy. Windows uses the default machine policy, which (for machines with less than eight logical processors) is to select any available processor on the machine.
IrqPolicyAllCloseProcessors	On a NUMA machine, the Plug and Play manager assigns the interrupt to all the processors that are close to the device (on the same node). On non-NUMA machines, this is the same as IrqPolicyAllProcessorsInMachine.
IrqPolicyOneCloseProcessor	On a NUMA machine, the Plug and Play manager assigns the interrupt to one processor that is close to the device (on the same node). On non-NUMA machines, the chosen processor will be any available on the system.
IrqPolicyAllProcessorsInMachine	The interrupt is processed by any available processor on the machine.
IrqPolicySpecifiedProcessors	The interrupt is processed only by one of the processors specified in the affinity mask under the AssignmentSetOverride registry value.
IrqPolicySpreadMessagesAcrossAllProcessors	Different message-signaled interrupts are distributed across an optimal set of eligible processors, keeping track of NUMA topology issues, if possible. This requires MSI-X support on the device and platform.

Other than setting this affinity policy, another registry value can also be used to set the interrupt's priority, based on the values in Table 3-2.

TABLE 3-2 IRQ Priorities

Priority	Meaning
IrqPriorityUndefined	No particular priority is required by the device. It receives the default priority (IrqPriorityNormal).
IrqPriorityLow	The device can tolerate high latency and should receive a lower IRQL than usual.
IrqPriorityNormal	The device expects average latency. It receives the default IRQL associated with its interrupt vector.
IrqPriorityHigh	The device requires as little latency as possible. It receives an elevated IRQL beyond its normal assignment.

As discussed earlier, it is important to note that Windows is not a real-time operating system, and as such, these IRQ priorities are hints given to the system that control only the IRQL associated with the interrupt and provide no extra priority other than the Windows IRQL priority-scheme mechanism. Because the IRQ priority is also stored in the registry, administrators are free to set these values for drivers should there be a requirement of lower latency for a driver not taking advantage of this feature.

Software Interrupts

Although hardware generates most interrupts, the Windows kernel also generates software interrupts for a variety of tasks, including these:

- Initiating thread dispatching

- Non-time-critical interrupt processing

- Handling timer expiration

- Asynchronously executing a procedure in the context of a particular thread

- Supporting asynchronous I/O operations

These tasks are described in the following subsections.

Dispatch or Deferred Procedure Call (DPC) Interrupts   When a thread can no longer continue executing, perhaps because it has terminated or because it voluntarily enters a wait state, the kernel calls the dispatcher directly to effect an immediate context switch. Sometimes, however, the kernel detects that rescheduling should occur when it is deep within many layers of code. In this situation, the kernel requests dispatching but defers its occurrence until it completes its current activity. Using a DPC software interrupt is a convenient way to achieve this delay.

The kernel always raises the processor's IRQL to DPC/dispatch level or above when it needs to synchronize access to shared kernel structures. This disables additional software interrupts and thread dispatching. When the kernel detects that dispatching should occur, it requests a DPC/dispatch-level interrupt; but because the IRQL is at or above that level, the processor holds the interrupt in check. When the kernel completes its current activity, it sees that it's going to lower the IRQL below DPC/dispatch level and checks to see whether any dispatch interrupts are pending. If there are, the IRQL drops to DPC/dispatch level and the dispatch interrupts are processed. Activating the thread dispatcher by using a software interrupt is a way to defer dispatching until conditions are right. However, Windows uses software interrupts to defer other types of processing as well.

In addition to thread dispatching, the kernel also processes deferred procedure calls (DPCs) at this IRQL. A DPC is a function that performs a system task—a task that is less time-critical than the current one. The functions are called *deferred* because they might not execute immediately.

DPCs provide the operating system with the capability to generate an interrupt and execute a system function in kernel mode. The kernel uses DPCs to process timer expiration (and release threads waiting for the timers) and to reschedule the processor after a thread's quantum expires. Device drivers use DPCs to process interrupts. To provide timely service for hardware interrupts, Windows—with the cooperation of device drivers—attempts to keep the IRQL below device IRQL levels. One way that this goal is achieved is for device driver ISRs to perform the minimal work necessary to acknowledge their device, save volatile interrupt state, and defer data transfer or other less time-critical interrupt processing activity for execution in a DPC at DPC/dispatch IRQL. (See Chapter 8 in Part 2 for more information on DPCs and the I/O system.)

A DPC is represented by a *DPC object*, a kernel control object that is not visible to user-mode programs but is visible to device drivers and other system code. The most important piece of information the DPC object contains is the address of the system function that the kernel will call when it processes the DPC interrupt. DPC routines that are waiting to execute are stored in kernel-managed queues, one per processor, called *DPC queues*. To request a DPC, system code calls the kernel to initialize a DPC object and then places it in a DPC queue.

By default, the kernel places DPC objects at the end of the DPC queue of the processor on which the DPC was requested (typically the processor on which the ISR executed). A device driver can override this behavior, however, by specifying a DPC priority (low, medium, medium-high, or high, where medium is the default) and by targeting the DPC at a particular processor. A DPC aimed at a specific CPU is known as a *targeted DPC*. If the DPC has a high priority, the kernel inserts the DPC object at the front of the queue; otherwise, it is placed at the end of the queue for all other priorities.

When the processor's IRQL is about to drop from an IRQL of DPC/dispatch level or higher to a lower IRQL (APC or passive level), the kernel processes DPCs. Windows ensures that the IRQL remains at DPC/dispatch level and pulls DPC objects off the current processor's queue until the queue is empty (that is, the kernel "drains" the queue), calling each DPC function in turn. Only when the queue is empty will the kernel let the IRQL drop below DPC/dispatch level and let regular thread execution continue. DPC processing is depicted in Figure 3-7.

DPC priorities can affect system behavior another way. The kernel usually initiates DPC queue draining with a DPC/dispatch-level interrupt. The kernel generates such an interrupt only if the DPC is directed at the current processor (the one on which the ISR executes) and the DPC has a priority higher than low. If the DPC has a low priority, the kernel requests the interrupt only if the number of outstanding DPC requests for the processor rises above a threshold or if the number of DPCs requested on the processor within a time window is low.

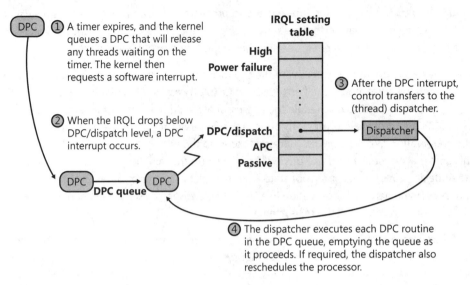

FIGURE 3-7 Delivering a DPC

If a DPC is targeted at a CPU different from the one on which the ISR is running and the DPC's priority is either high or medium-high, the kernel immediately signals the target CPU (by sending it a dispatch IPI) to drain its DPC queue, but only as long as the target processor is idle. If the priority is medium or low, the number of DPCs queued on the target processor must exceed a threshold for the kernel to trigger a DPC/dispatch interrupt. The system idle thread also drains the DPC queue for the processor it runs on. Although DPC targeting and priority levels are flexible, device drivers rarely need to change the default behavior of their DPC objects. Table 3-3 summarizes the situations that initiate DPC queue draining. Medium-high and high appear and are, in fact, equal priorities when looking at the generation rules. The difference comes from their insertion in the list, with high interrupts being at the head and medium-high interrupts at the tail.

TABLE 3-3 DPC Interrupt Generation Rules

DPC Priority	DPC Targeted at ISR's Processor	DPC Targeted at Another Processor
Low	DPC queue length exceeds maximum DPC queue length, or DPC request rate is less than minimum DPC request rate	DPC queue length exceeds maximum DPC queue length, or system is idle
Medium	Always	DPC queue length exceeds maximum DPC queue length, or system is idle
Medium-High	Always	Target processor is idle
High	Always	Target processor is idle

Because user-mode threads execute at low IRQL, the chances are good that a DPC will interrupt the execution of an ordinary user's thread. DPC routines execute without regard to what thread is running, meaning that when a DPC routine runs, it can't assume what process address space is currently mapped. DPC routines can call kernel functions, but they can't call system services, generate page faults, or create or wait for dispatcher objects (explained later in this chapter). They can, however, access nonpaged system memory addresses, because system address space is always mapped regardless of what the current process is.

DPCs are provided primarily for device drivers, but the kernel uses them too. The kernel most frequently uses a DPC to handle quantum expiration. At every tick of the system clock, an interrupt occurs at clock IRQL. The *clock interrupt handler* (running at clock IRQL) updates the system time and then decrements a counter that tracks how long the current thread has run. When the counter reaches 0, the thread's time quantum has expired and the kernel might need to reschedule the processor, a lower-priority task that should be done at DPC/dispatch IRQL. The clock interrupt handler queues a DPC to initiate thread dispatching and then finishes its work and lowers the processor's IRQL. Because the DPC interrupt has a lower priority than do device interrupts, any pending device interrupts that surface before the clock interrupt completes are handled before the DPC interrupt occurs.

Because DPCs execute regardless of whichever thread is currently running on the system (much like interrupts), they are a primary cause for perceived system unresponsiveness of client systems or workstation workloads because even the highest-priority thread will be interrupted by a pending DPC. Some DPCs run long enough that users might perceive video or sound lagging, and even abnormal mouse or keyboard latencies, so for the benefit of drivers with long-running DPCs, Windows supports *threaded DPCs*.

Threaded DPCs, as their name implies, function by executing the DPC routine at passive level on a real-time priority (priority 31) thread. This allows the DPC to preempt most user-mode threads (because most application threads don't run at real-time priority ranges), but it allows other interrupts, nonthreaded DPCs, APCs, and higher-priority threads to preempt the routine.

The threaded DPC mechanism is enabled by default, but you can disable it by adding a DWORD value HKEY_LOCAL_MACHINE\System\CurrentControlSet\Control\Session Manager\kernel \ThreadDpcEnable and setting it to 0. Because threaded DPCs can be disabled, driver developers who make use of threaded DPCs must write their routines following the same rules as for nonthreaded DPC routines and cannot access paged memory, perform dispatcher waits, or make assumptions about the IRQL level at which they are executing. In addition, they must not use the *KeAcquire/ReleaseSpinLockAtDpcLevel* APIs because the functions assume the CPU is at dispatch level. Instead, threaded DPCs must use *KeAcquire/ReleaseSpinLockForDpc*, which performs the appropriate action after checking the current IRQL.

EXPERIMENT: Monitoring Interrupt and DPC Activity

You can use Process Explorer to monitor interrupt and DPC activity by opening the System Information dialog and switching to the CPU tab, where it lists the number of interrupts and DPCs executed each time Process Explorer refreshes the display (1 second by default):

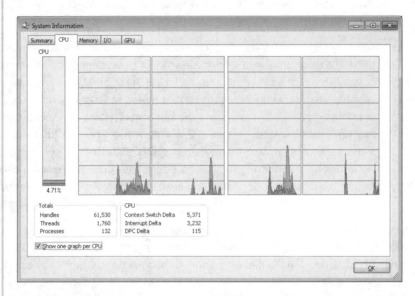

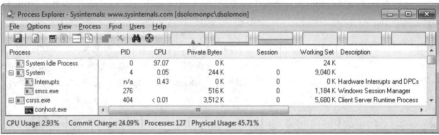

You can also trace the execution of specific interrupt service routines and deferred procedure calls with the built-in event tracing support (described later in this chapter):

1. Start capturing events by opening an elevated command prompt, navigating to the Microsoft Windows Performance Toolkit directory (typically in c:\Program Files) and typing the following command (make sure no other program is capturing events, such as Process Explorer or Process Monitor, or this will fail with an error):

   ```
   xperf -on PROC_THREAD+LOADER+DPC+INTERRUPT
   ```

2. Stop capturing events by typing the following:

   ```
   xperf -d dpcisr.etl
   ```

3. Generate reports for the event capture by typing this:

```
xperf dpcisr.etl
tracerpt \kernel.etl -report dpcisr.html -f html
```

This will generate a web page called dpcisr.html.

4. Open report.html, and expand the DPC/ISR subsection. Expand the DPC/ISR Breakdown area, and you will see summaries of the time spent in ISRs and DPCs by each driver. For example:

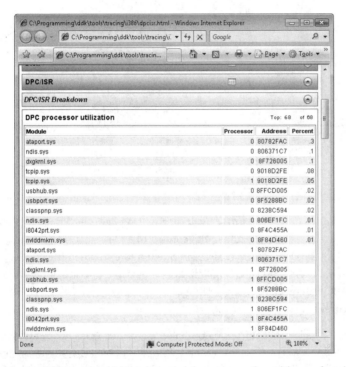

Running an *ln* command in the kernel debugger on the address of each event record shows the name of the function that executed the DPC or ISR:

```
lkd> ln 0x806321C7
(806321c7)   ndis!ndisInterruptDpc

lkd> ln 0x820AED3F
(820aed3f)   nt!IopTimerDispatch

lkd> ln 0x82051312
(82051312)   nt!PpmPerfIdleDpc
```

The first is a DPC queued by a network card NDIS miniport driver. The second is a DPC for a generic I/O timer expiration. The third address is the address of a DPC for an idle performance operation.

Other than using it to get an HTML report, you can use the Xperf Viewer to show a detailed overview of all DPC and ISR events by right-clicking on the DPC and/or ISR CPU Usage graphs in the main Xperf window and choosing Summary Table. You will be able to see a per-driver view of each DPC and ISR in detail, along with its duration and count, just as shown in the following graphic:

Asynchronous Procedure Call Interrupts   Asynchronous procedure calls (APCs) provide a way for user programs and system code to execute in the context of a particular user thread (and hence a particular process address space). Because APCs are queued to execute in the context of a particular thread and run at an IRQL less than DPC/dispatch level, they don't operate under the same restrictions as a DPC. An APC routine can acquire resources (objects), wait for object handles, incur page faults, and call system services.

APCs are described by a kernel control object, called an *APC object*. APCs waiting to execute reside in a kernel-managed *APC queue*. Unlike the DPC queue, which is systemwide, the APC queue is thread-specific—each thread has its own APC queue. When asked to queue an APC, the kernel inserts it into the queue belonging to the thread that will execute the APC routine. The kernel, in turn, requests a software interrupt at APC level, and when the thread eventually begins running, it executes the APC.

There are two kinds of APCs: kernel mode and user mode. Kernel-mode APCs don't require permission from a target thread to run in that thread's context, while user-mode APCs do. Kernel-mode APCs interrupt a thread and execute a procedure without the thread's intervention or consent. There are also two types of kernel-mode APCs: normal and special. Special APCs execute at APC level and allow the APC routine to modify some of the APC parameters. Normal APCs execute at passive level and receive the modified parameters from the special APC routine (or the original parameters if they weren't modified).

Both normal and special APCs can be disabled by raising the IRQL to APC level or by calling *KeEnterGuardedRegion*. *KeEnterGuardedRegion* disables APC delivery by setting the *SpecialApcDisable* field in the calling thread's KTHREAD structure (described further in Chapter 5). A thread can disable normal APCs only by calling *KeEnterCriticalRegion*, which sets the *KernelApcDisable* field in the thread's KTHREAD structure. Table 3-4 summarizes the APC insertion and delivery behavior for each type of APC.

The executive uses kernel-mode APCs to perform operating system work that must be completed within the address space (in the context) of a particular thread. It can use special kernel-mode APCs to direct a thread to stop executing an interruptible system service, for example, or to record the results of an asynchronous I/O operation in a thread's address space. Environment subsystems use special kernel-mode APCs to make a thread suspend or terminate itself or to get or set its user-mode execution context. The Subsystem for UNIX Applications uses kernel-mode APCs to emulate the delivery of UNIX signals to Subsystem for UNIX Application processes.

Another important use of kernel-mode APCs is related to thread suspension and termination. Because these operations can be initiated from arbitrary threads and directed to other arbitrary threads, the kernel uses an APC to query the thread context as well as to terminate the thread. Device drivers often block APCs or enter a critical or guarded region to prevent these operations from occurring while they are holding a lock; otherwise, the lock might never be released, and the system would hang.

TABLE 3-4 APC Insertion and Delivery

APC Type	Insertion Behavior	Delivery Behavior
Special (kernel)	Inserted at the tail of the kernel-mode APC list	Delivered at APC level as soon as IRQL drops and the thread is not in a guarded region. It is given pointers to arguments specified when inserting the APC.
Normal (kernel)	Inserted right after the last special APC (at the head of all other normal APCs)	Delivered at PASSIVE_LEVEL after the associated special APC was executed. It is given arguments returned by the associated special APC (which can be the original arguments used during insertion or new ones).
Normal (user)	Inserted at the tail of the user-mode APC list	Delivered at PASSIVE_LEVEL as soon as IRQL drops, the thread is not in a critical (or guarded) region, and the thread is in an alerted state. It is given arguments returned by the associated special APC (which can be the original arguments used during insertion or new ones).
Normal (user) Thread Exit (PsExitSpecialApc)	Inserted at the head of the user-mode APC list	Delivered at PASSIVE_LEVEL on return to user mode, if the thread is doing an alerted user-mode wait. It is given arguments returned by the thread-termination special APC.

Device drivers also use kernel-mode APCs. For example, if an I/O operation is initiated and a thread goes into a wait state, another thread in another process can be scheduled to run. When the device finishes transferring data, the I/O system must somehow get back into the context of the thread that initiated the I/O so that it can copy the results of the I/O operation to the buffer in the address space of the process containing that thread. The I/O system uses a special kernel-mode APC to perform this action, unless the application used the *SetFileIoOverlappedRange* API or I/O completion ports—in which case, the buffer will either be global in memory or copied only after the thread pulls a completion item from the port. (The use of APCs in the I/O system is discussed in more detail in Chapter 8 in Part 2.)

Several Windows APIs—such as *ReadFileEx*, *WriteFileEx*, and *QueueUserAPC*—use user-mode APCs. For example, the *ReadFileEx* and *WriteFileEx* functions allow the caller to specify a completion routine to be called when the I/O operation finishes. The I/O completion is implemented by queuing an APC to the thread that issued the I/O. However, the callback to the completion routine doesn't necessarily take place when the APC is queued because user-mode APCs are delivered to a thread only when it's in an *alertable wait state*. A thread can enter a wait state either by waiting for an object handle and specifying that its wait is alertable (with the Windows *WaitForMultipleObjectsEx* function) or by testing directly whether it has a pending APC (using *SleepEx*). In both cases, if a user-mode APC is pending, the kernel interrupts (alerts) the thread, transfers control to the APC routine, and resumes the thread's execution when the APC routine completes. Unlike kernel-mode APCs, which can execute at APC level, user-mode APCs execute at passive level.

APC delivery can reorder the wait queues—the lists of which threads are waiting for what, and in what order they are waiting. (Wait resolution is described in the section "Low-IRQL Synchronization," later in this chapter.) If the thread is in a wait state when an APC is delivered, after the APC routine completes, the wait is reissued or re-executed. If the wait still isn't resolved, the thread returns to the wait state, but now it will be at the end of the list of objects it's waiting for. For example, because APCs are used to suspend a thread from execution, if the thread is waiting for any objects, its wait is removed until the thread is resumed, after which that thread will be at the end of the list of threads waiting to access the objects it was waiting for. A thread performing an alertable kernel-mode wait will also be woken up during thread termination, allowing such a thread to check whether it woke up as a result of termination or for a different reason.

Timer Processing

The system's clock interval timer is probably the most important device on a Windows machine, as evidenced by its high IRQL value (CLOCK_LEVEL) and due to the critical nature of the work it is responsible for. Without this interrupt, Windows would lose track of time, causing erroneous results in calculations of uptime and clock time—and worse, causing timers not to expire anymore and threads never to lose their quantum anymore. Windows would also not be a preemptive operating system, and unless the current running thread yielded the CPU, critical background tasks and scheduling could never occur on a given processor.

Windows programs the system clock to fire at the most appropriate interval for the machine, and subsequently allows drivers, applications, and administrators to modify the clock interval for their needs. Typically, the system clock is maintained either by the PIT (Programmable Interrupt Timer) chip that is present on all computers since the PC/AT, or the RTC (Real Time Clock). The PIT works on a crystal that is tuned at one-third the NTSC color carrier frequency (because it was originally used for TV-Out on the first CGA video cards), and the HAL uses various achievable multiples to reach millisecond-unit intervals, starting at 1 ms all the way up to 15 ms. The RTC, on the other hand, runs at 32.768 KHz, which, by being a power of two, is easily configured to run at various intervals that are also powers of two. On today's machines, the APIC Multiprocessor HAL configures the RTC to fire every 15.6 milliseconds, which corresponds to about 64 times a second.

Some types of Windows applications require very fast response times, such as multimedia applications. In fact, some multimedia tasks require rates as low as 1 ms. For this reason, Windows implements APIs and mechanisms that enable lowering the interval of the system's clock interrupt, which results in more clock interrupts (at least on processor 0). Note that this increases the resolution of all timers in the system, potentially causing other timers to expire more frequently.

Windows tries its best to restore the clock timer back to its original value whenever it can. Each time a process requests a clock interval change, Windows increases an internal reference count and associates it with the process. Similarly, drivers (which can also change the clock rate) get added to the global reference count. When all drivers have restored the clock and all processes that modified the clock either have exited or restored it, Windows restores the clock to its default value (or, barring that, to the next highest value that's been required by a process or driver).

EXPERIMENT: Identifying High-Frequency Timers

Due to the problems that high-frequency timers can cause, Windows uses Event Tracing for Windows (ETW) to trace all processes and drivers that request a change in the system's clock interval, displaying the time of the occurrence and the requested interval. The current interval is also shown. This data is of great use to both developers and system administrators in identifying the causes of poor battery performance on otherwise healthy systems, and to decrease overall power consumption on large systems as well. To obtain it, simply run **powercfg /energy** and you should obtain an HTML file called *energy-report.html* similar to the one shown here:

Scroll down to the section on Platform Timer Resolution, and you will be shown all the applications that have modified the timer resolution and are still active, along with the call stacks that caused this call. Timer resolutions are shown in hundreds of nanoseconds, so a period of 20,000 corresponds to 2 ms. In the sample shown, two applications—namely, Microsoft PowerPoint and the UltraVNC remote desktop server—each requested a higher resolution.

You can also use the debugger to obtain this information. For each process, the EPROCESS structure contains a number of fields, shown next, that help identify changes in timer resolution:

```
+0x4a8 TimerResolutionLink : _LIST_ENTRY [ 0xfffffa80'05218fd8 - 0xfffffa80'059cd508 ]
+0x4b8 RequestedTimerResolution : 0
+0x4bc ActiveThreadsHighWatermark : 0x1d
+0x4c0 SmallestTimerResolution : 0x2710
+0x4c8 TimerResolutionStackRecord : 0xfffff8a0'0476ecd0 _PO_DIAG_STACK_RECORD
```

Note that the debugger shows you an additional piece of information: the smallest timer resolution that was ever requested by a given process. In this example, the process shown corresponds to PowerPoint 2010, which typically requests a lower timer resolution during slideshows, but not during slide editing mode. The EPROCESS fields of PowerPoint, shown in the preceding code, prove this, and the stack could be parsed by dumping the PO_DIAG_STACK_RECORD structure.

Finally, the *TimerResolutionLink* field connects all processes that have made changes to timer resolution, through the *ExpTimerResolutionListHead* doubly linked list. Parsing this list with the *!list* debugger command can reveal all processes on the system that have, or had, made changes to the timer resolution, when the *powercfg* command is unavailable or information on past processes is required:

```
lkd> !list "-e -x \"dt nt!_EPROCESS @$extret-@@(#FIELD_OFFSET(nt!_EPROCESS,
TimerResolutionLink))
ImageFileName SmallestTimerResolution RequestedTimerResolution\"
nt!ExpTimerResolutionListHead"

dt nt!_EPROCESS @$extret-@@(#FIELD_OFFSET(nt!_EPROCESS, TimerResolutionLink))
ImageFileName
SmallestTimerResolution RequestedTimerResolution
   +0x2e0 ImageFileName          : [15]  "audiodg.exe"
   +0x4b8 RequestedTimerResolution : 0
   +0x4c0 SmallestTimerResolution  : 0x2710

dt nt!_EPROCESS @$extret-@@(#FIELD_OFFSET(nt!_EPROCESS, TimerResolutionLink))
ImageFileName
SmallestTimerResolution RequestedTimerResolution
   +0x2e0 ImageFileName          : [15]  "chrome.exe"
   +0x4b8 RequestedTimerResolution : 0
   +0x4c0 SmallestTimerResolution  : 0x2710

dt nt!_EPROCESS @$extret-@@(#FIELD_OFFSET(nt!_EPROCESS, TimerResolutionLink))
ImageFileName
SmallestTimerResolution RequestedTimerResolution
```

```
    +0x2e0 ImageFileName          : [15]  "calc.exe"
    +0x4b8 RequestedTimerResolution : 0
    +0x4c0 SmallestTimerResolution  : 0x2710

dt nt!_EPROCESS @$extret-@@(#FIELD_OFFSET(nt!_EPROCESS, TimerResolutionLink))
ImageFileName
SmallestTimerResolution RequestedTimerResolution
    +0x2e0 ImageFileName          : [15]  "devenv.exe"
    +0x4b8 RequestedTimerResolution : 0
    +0x4c0 SmallestTimerResolution  : 0x2710

dt nt!_EPROCESS @$extret-@@(#FIELD_OFFSET(nt!_EPROCESS, TimerResolutionLink))
ImageFileName
SmallestTimerResolution RequestedTimerResolution
    +0x2e0 ImageFileName          : [15]  "POWERPNT.EXE"
    +0x4b8 RequestedTimerResolution : 0
    +0x4c0 SmallestTimerResolution  : 0x2710

dt nt!_EPROCESS @$extret-@@(#FIELD_OFFSET(nt!_EPROCESS, TimerResolutionLink))
ImageFileName
SmallestTimerResolution RequestedTimerResolution
    +0x2e0 ImageFileName          : [15]  "winvnc.exe"
    +0x4b8 RequestedTimerResolution : 0x2710
    +0x4c0 SmallestTimerResolution  : 0x2710
```

Timer Expiration

As we said, one of the main tasks of the ISR associated with the interrupt that the RTC or PIT will generate is to keep track of system time, which is mainly done by the *KeUpdateSystemTime* routine. Its second job is to keep track of logical run time, such as process/thread execution times and the system *tick time*, which is the underlying number used by APIs such as *GetTickCount* that developers use to time operations in their applications. This part of the work is performed by *KeUpdateRunTime*. Before doing any of that work, however, *KeUpdateRunTime* checks whether any timers have expired.

Windows timers can be either *absolute* timers, which implies a distinct expiration time in the future, or *relative* timers, which contain a negative expiration value used as a positive offset from the current time during timer insertion. Internally, all timers are converted to an absolute expiration time, although the system keeps track of whether or not this is the "true" absolute time or a converted relative time. This difference is important in certain scenarios, such as Daylight Saving Time (or even manual clock changes). An absolute timer would still fire at "8PM" if the user moved the clock from 1PM to 7PM, but a relative timer—say, one set to expire "in two hours"—would not feel the effect of the clock change because two hours haven't really elapsed. During system time-change events such as these, the kernel reprograms the absolute time associated with relative timers to match the new settings.

Because the clock fires at known interval multiples, the bottom bits of the current system time will be at one of 64 known positions (on an APIC HAL). Windows uses that fact to organize all driver and application timers into linked lists based on an array where each entry corresponds to a possible multiple of the system time. This table, called the *timer table*, is located in the PRCB, which enables each processor to perform its own independent timer expiration without needing to acquire a global lock, as shown in Figure 3-8. Later, you will see what determines which logical processor's timer table a timer is inserted on. Because each processor has its own timer table, each processor also does its own timer expiration work. As each processor gets initialized, the table is filled with absolute timers with an infinite expiration time, to avoid any incoherent state. Each multiple of the system time that a timer can be associated with is called the *hand*, and it's stored in the timer object's dispatcher header. Therefore, to determine if a clock has expired, it is only necessary to check if there are any timers on the linked list associated with the current hand.

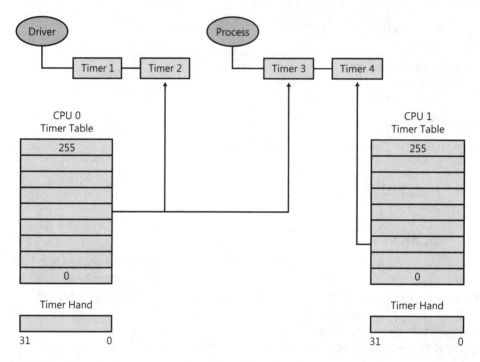

FIGURE 3-8 Example of per-processor timer lists

Although updating counters and checking a linked list are fast operations, going through every timer and expiring it is a potentially costly operation—keep in mind that all this work is currently being performed at CLOCK_LEVEL, an exceptionally elevated IRQL. Similarly to how a driver ISR queues a DPC to defer work, the clock ISR requests a DPC software interrupt, setting a flag in the PRCB so that the DPC draining mechanism knows timers need expiration. Likewise, when updating process/thread runtime, if the clock ISR determines that a thread has expired its quantum, it also queues a DPC software interrupt and sets a different PRCB flag. These flags are per-PRCB because each processor normally does its own processing of run-time updates, because each processor is running a different thread and has different tasks associated with it. Table 3-5 displays the various fields used in timer expiration and processing.

Once the IRQL eventually drops down back to DISPATCH_LEVEL, as part of DPC processing, these two flags will be picked up.

TABLE 3-5 Timer Processing KPRCB Fields

KPRCB Field	Type	Description
ReadySummary	Bitmask (32 bits)	Bitmask of priority levels that have one or more ready threads
DeferredReadyListHead	Singly linked list	Single list head for the deferred ready queue
DispatcherReadyListHead	Array of 32 list entries	List heads for the 32 ready queues

Chapter 5 covers the actions related to thread scheduling and quantum expiration. Here we will take a look at the timer expiration work. Because the timers are linked together by hand, the expiration code (executed by the DPC associated with the PRCB in the *TimerExpiryDpc* field) parses this list from head to tail. (At insertion time, the timers nearest to the clock interval multiple will be first, followed by timers closer and closer to the next interval, but still within this hand.) There are two primary tasks to expiring a timer:

- The timer is treated as a dispatcher synchronization object (threads are waiting on the timer as part of a timeout or directly as part of a wait). The wait-testing and wait-satisfaction algorithms will be run on the timer. This work is described in a later section on synchronization in this chapter. This is how user-mode applications, and some drivers, make use of timers.

- The timer is treated as a control object associated with a DPC callback routine that executes when the timer expires. This method is reserved only for drivers and enables very low latency response to timer expiration. (The wait/dispatcher method requires all the extra logic of wait signaling.) Additionally, because timer expiration itself executes at DISPATCH_LEVEL, where DPCs also run, it is perfectly suited as a timer callback.

As each processor wakes up to handle the clock interval timer to perform system-time and run-time processing, it therefore also processes timer expirations after a slight latency/delay in which the IRQL drops from CLOCK_LEVEL to DISPATCH_LEVEL. Figure 3-9 shows this behavior on two processors—the solid arrows indicate the clock interrupt firing, while the dotted arrows indicate any timer expiration processing that might occur if the processor had associated timers.

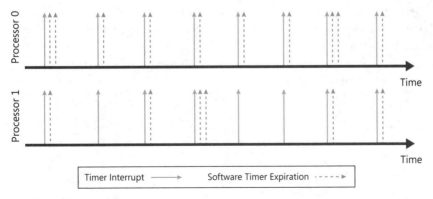

FIGURE 3-9 Timer expiration

Processor Selection

A critical determination that must be made when a timer is inserted is to pick the appropriate table to use—in other words, the most optimal processor choice. If the timer has no DPC associated with it, the kernel scans all processors in the current processor's group that have not been parked. (For more information on Core Parking, see Chapter 5.) If the current processor is parked, it picks the next processor in the group; otherwise, the current processor is used. On the other hand, if the timer does have an associated DPC, the insertion code simply looks at the target processor associated with the DPC and selects that processor's timer table.

In the case where the driver developer did not specify a target processor for the DPC, the kernel must make the choice. Because driver developers typically expect the DPC to execute on the same processor as the one the driver code was running on at insertion time, the kernel typically chooses CPU 0, since CPU 0 is the timekeeping processor that will always be active to pick up clock interrupts (more on this later). However, on server systems, the kernel picks a processor, just as it normally does when there is no DPC, by using the same checks just described.

This behavior is intended to improve performance and scalablity on server systems that make use of Hyper-V, although it can improve performance on any heavily loaded system. As system timers pile up—because most drivers do not affinitize their DPCs—CPU 0 becomes more and more congested with the execution of timer expiration code, which increases latency and can even cause heavy delays or missed DPCs. Additionally, the timer expiration can start competing with the DPC timer typically associated with driver interrupt processing, such as network packet code, causing systemwide slowdowns. This process is exacerbated in a Hyper-V scenario, where CPU 0 must process the timers and DPCs associated with potentially numerous virtual machines, each with their own timers and associated devices.

By spreading the timers across processors, as shown in Figure 3-10, each processor's timer-expiration load is fully distributed among unparked logical processors. The timer object stores its associated processor number in the dispatcher header on 32-bit systems and in the object itself on 64-bit systems.

Note This behavior is controlled by the kernel variable *KiDistributeTimers*, which is initialized based on a registry key whose value is different between a server and client installation. By modifying, or creating, the value *DistributeTimers* under HKLM\SYSTEM\ CurrentControlSet\Control\Session Manager\kernel, this behavior can be configured differently from its SKU-based default.

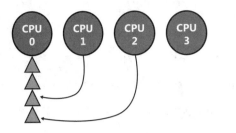

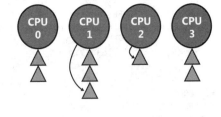

Timers Queue on CPU 0 · Timers Queued on Current CPU

FIGURE 3-10 Timer queuing behaviors

EXPERIMENT: Listing System Timers

You can use the kernel debugger to dump all the current registered timers on the system, as well as information on the DPC associated with each timer (if any). See the following output for a sample:

```
[lkd> !timer
Dump system timers

Interrupt time: 61876995 000003df [ 4/ 5/2010 18:58:09.189]

List Timer    Interrupt Low/High    Fire Time              DPC/thread
PROCESSOR 0 (nt!_KTIMER_TABLE fffff80001bfd080)
  5 fffffa8003099810    627684ac 000003df [ 4/ 5/2010 18:58:10.756]
NDIS!ndisMTimerObjectDpc (DPC @ fffffa8003099850)
 13 fffffa8003027278    272dde78 000004cf [ 4/ 6/2010 23:34:30.510]  NDIS!ndisMWakeUpDpcX
(DPC @ fffffa80030272b8)
    fffffa8003029278    272e0588 000004cf [ 4/ 6/2010 23:34:30.511]  NDIS!ndisMWakeUpDpcX
(DPC @ fffffa80030292b8)
    fffffa8003025278    272e0588 000004cf [ 4/ 6/2010 23:34:30.511]  NDIS!ndisMWakeUpDpcX
(DPC @ fffffa80030252b8)
    fffffa8003023278    272e2c99 000004cf [ 4/ 6/2010 23:34:30.512]  NDIS!ndisMWakeUpDpcX
(DPC @ fffffa80030232b8)
 16 fffffa8006096c20    6c1613a6 000003df [ 4/ 5/2010 18:58:26.901]  thread
fffffa8006096b60
 19 fffff80001c85c40    64f9aeb5 000003df [ 4/ 5/2010 18:58:14.971]
nt!CmpLazyFlushDpcRoutine (DPC @ fffff80001c85c00)
 31 fffffa8002c43660 P dc527b9b 000003e8 [ 4/ 5/2010 20:06:00.673]
intelppm!LongCapTraceDpc (DPC @ fffffa8002c436a0)
 40 fffff80001c86f60    62ca1080 000003df [ 4/ 5/2010 18:58:11.304]  nt!CcScanDpc (DPC @
fffff80001c86f20)
    fffff88004039710    62ca1080 000003df [ 4/ 5/2010 18:58:11.304]
luafv!ScavengerTimerRoutine (DPC @ fffff88004039750)
...
252 fffffa800458ed50    62619a91 000003df [ 4/ 5/2010 18:58:10.619]  netbt!TimerExpiry (DPC
@ fffffa800458ed10)
    fffffa8004599b60    fe2fc6ce 000003e0 [ 4/ 5/2010 19:09:41.514]  netbt!TimerExpiry (DPC
@ fffffa8004599b20)
```

```
PROCESSOR 1 (nt!_KTIMER_TABLE fffff880009ba380)
   0 fffffa8004ec9700   626be121 000003df [ 4/ 5/2010 18:58:10.686]  thread
fffffa80027f3060
     fffff80001c84dd0 P 70b3f446 000003df [ 4/ 5/2010 18:58:34.647]
nt!IopIrpStackProfilerTimer (DPC @ fffff80001c84e10)
  11 fffffa8005c26cd0   62859842 000003df [ 4/ 5/2010 18:58:10.855]  afd!AfdTimeoutPoll (DPC
@ fffffa8005c26c90)
     fffffa8002ce8160   6e6c45f4 000003df [ 4/ 5/2010 18:58:30.822]  thread
fffffa80053c2b60
     fffffa8004fdb3d0   77f0c2cb 000003df [ 4/ 5/2010 18:58:46.789]  thread
fffffa8004f4bb60
  13 fffffa8005051c20   60713a93 800003df [          NEVER         ]  thread
fffffa8005051b60
  15 fffffa8005ede120   77f9fb8c 000003df [ 4/ 5/2010 18:58:46.850]  thread
fffffa8005ede060
  20 fffffa8004f40ef0   629a3748 000003df [ 4/ 5/2010 18:58:10.990]  thread
fffffa8004f4bb60
  22 fffffa8005195120   6500ec7a 000003df [ 4/ 5/2010 18:58:15.019]  thread
fffffa8005195060
  28 fffffa8004760e20   62ad4e07 000003df [ 4/ 5/2010 18:58:11.115]  btaudio (DPC @
fffffa8004760e60)+12d10
  31 fffffa8002c40660 P dc527b9b 000003e8 [ 4/ 5/2010 20:06:00.673]
intelppm!LongCapTraceDpc (DPC @ fffffa8002c406a0)
  ...
 232 fffff80001c85040 P 62317a00 000003df [ 4/ 5/2010 18:58:10.304]  nt!IopTimerDispatch
(DPC @ fffff80001c85080)
     fffff80001c26fc0 P 6493d400 000003df [ 4/ 5/2010 18:58:14.304]
nt!EtwpAdjustBuffersDpcRoutine (DPC @ fffff80001c26f80)
 235 fffffa80047471a8   6238ba5c 000003df [ 4/ 5/2010 18:58:10.351]  stwrt64 (DPC @
fffffa80047471e8)+67d4
 242 fffff880023ae480   11228580 000003e1 [ 4/ 5/2010 19:10:13.304]  dfsc!DfscTimerDispatch
(DPC @ fffff880023ae4c0)
 245 fffff800020156b8 P 72fb2569 000003df [ 4/ 5/2010 18:58:38.469]
hal!HalpCmcDeferredRoutine (DPC @ fffff800020156f8)
 248 fffffa80029ee460 P 62578455 000003df [ 4/ 5/2010 18:58:10.553]
ataport!IdePortTickHandler (DPC @ fffffa80029ee4a0)
     fffffa8002776460 P 62578455 000003df [ 4/ 5/2010 18:58:10.553]
ataport!IdePortTickHandler (DPC @ fffffa80027764a0)
     fffff88001678500   fe2f836f 000003e0 [ 4/ 5/2010 19:09:41.512]  cng!seedFileDpcRoutine
(DPC @ fffff880016784c0)
     fffff80001c25b80   885e52b3 0064a048 [12/31/2099 23:00:00.008]
nt!ExpCenturyDpcRoutine (DPC @ fffff80001c25bc0)


Total Timers: 254, Maximum List: 8
```

In this example, there are multiple driver-associated timers, due to expire shortly, associated
with the Ndis.sys and Afd.sys drivers (both related to networking), as well as audio, Bluetooth,
and ATA/IDE drivers. There are also background housekeeping timers due to expire, such as
those related to power management, ETW, registry flushing, and Users Account Control (UAC)
virtualization. Additionally, there are a dozen or so timers that don't have any DPC associated with them—this likely indicates user-mode or kernel-mode timers that are used for wait

dispatching. You can use *!thread* on the thread pointers to verify this. Finally, three interesting timers that are always present on a Windows system are the timer that checks for Daylight Savings Time time-zone changes, the timer that checks for the arrival of the upcoming year, and the timer that checks for entry into the next century. One can easily locate them based on their typically distant expiration time, unless this experiment is performed on the eve of one of these events.

Intelligent Timer Tick Distribution

Figure 3-11, which shows processors handling the clock ISR and expiring timers, reveals that processor 1 wakes up a number of times (the solid arrows) even when there are no associated expiring timers (the dotted arrows). Although that behavior is required as long as processor 1 is running (to update the thread/process run times and scheduling state), what if processor 1 is idle (and has no expiring timers). Does it still need to handle the clock interrupt? Because the only other work required that was referenced earlier is to update the overall system time/clock ticks, it's sufficient to designate merely one processor as the time-keeping processor (in this case, processor 0) and allow other processors to remain in their sleep state; if they wake, any time-related adjustments can be performed by resynchronizing with processor 0.

Windows does, in fact, make this realization (internally called *intelligent timer tick distribution*), and Figure 3-11 shows the processor states under the scenario where processor 1 is sleeping (unlike earlier, when we assumed it was running code). As you can see, processor 1 wakes up only 5 times to handle its expiring timers, creating a much larger gap (sleeping period). The kernel uses a variable *KiPendingTimer*, which contains an array of affinity mask structures that indicate which logical processors need to receive a clock interval for the given timer hand (clock-tick interval). It can then appropriately program the interrupt controller, as well as determine to which processors it will send an IPI to initiate timer processing.

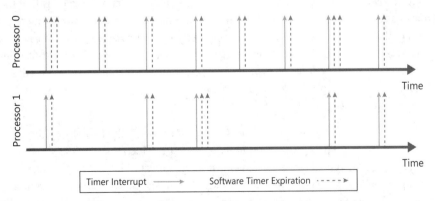

FIGURE 3-11 Intelligent timer tick distribution applied to processor 1

Leaving as large a gap as possible is important due to the way power management works in processors: as the processor detects that the work load is going lower and lower, it decreases its power consumption (P states), until it finally reaches an idle state. The processor then has the ability to selectively turn off parts of itself and enter deeper and deeper idle/sleep states, such as turning off caches. However, if the processor has to wake again, it will consume energy and take time to power up; for this reason, processor designers will risk entering these lower idle/sleep states (C states) only if the time spent in a given state outweighs the time and energy it takes to enter and exit the state. Obviously, it makes no sense to spend 10 ms to enter a sleep state that will last only 1 ms. By preventing clock interrupts from waking sleeping processors unless needed (due to timers), they can enter deeper C-states and stay there longer.

Timer Coalescing

Although minimizing clock interrupts to sleeping processors during periods of no timer expiration gives a big boost to longer C-state intervals, with a timer granularity of 15 ms, many timers likely will be queued at any given hand and expiring often, even if just on processor 0. Reducing the amount of software timer-expiration work would both help to decrease latency (by requiring less work at DISPATCH_LEVEL) as well as allow other processors to stay in their sleep states even longer (because we've established that the processors wake up only to handle expiring timers, fewer timer expirations result in longer sleep times). In truth, it is not just the amount of expiring timers that really affects sleep state (it does affect latency), but the periodicity of these timer expirations—six timers all expiring at the same hand is a better option than six timers expiring at six different hands. Therefore, to fully optimize idle-time duration, the kernel needs to employ a *coalescing* mechanism to combine separate timer hands into an individual hand with multiple expirations.

Timer coalescing works on the assumption that most drivers and user-mode applications do not particularly care about the exact firing period of their timers (except in the case of multimedia applications, for example). This "don't care" region actually grows as the original timer period grows—an application waking up every 30 seconds probably doesn't mind waking up every 31 or 29 seconds instead, while a driver polling every second could probably poll every second plus or minus 50 ms without too many problems. The important guarantee most periodic timers depend on is that their firing period remains constant within a certain range—for example, when a timer has been changed to fire every second plus 50 ms, it continues to fire within that range forever, not sometimes at every two seconds and other times at half a second. Even so, not all timers are ready to be coalesced into coarser granularities, so Windows enables this mechanism only for timers that have marked themselves as coalescable, either through the *KeSetCoalescableTimer* kernel API or through its user-mode counterpart, *SetWaitableTimerEx*.

With these APIs, driver and application developers are free to provide the kernel with the maximum *tolerance* (or tolerably delay) that their timer will endure, which is defined as the maximum amount of time past the requested period at which the timer will still function correctly. (In the previous example, the 1-second timer had a tolerance of 50 milliseconds.) The recommended minimum tolerance is 32 ms, which corresponds to about twice the 15.6-ms clock tick—any smaller value wouldn't really result in any coalescing, because the expiring timer could not be moved even from one clock tick to the next. Regardless of the tolerance that is specified, Windows aligns the timer to one of four *preferred coalescing intervals*: 1 second, 250 ms, 100 ms, or 50 ms.

When a tolerable delay is set for a periodic timer, Windows uses a process called *shifting*, which causes the timer to drift between periods until it gets aligned to the most optimal multiple of the period interval within the preferred coalescing interval associated with the specified tolerance (which is then encoded in the dispatcher header). For absolute timers, the list of preferred coalescing intervals is scanned, and a preferred expiration time is generated based on the closest acceptable coalescing interval to the maximum tolerance the caller specified. This behavior means that absolute timers are always pushed out as far as possible past their real expiration point, which spreads out timers as far as possible and creates longer sleep times on the processors.

Now with timer coalescing, refer back to Figure 3-11 and assume all the timers specified tolerances and are thus coalescable. In one scenario, Windows could decide to coalesce the timers as shown in Figure 3-12. Notice that now, processor 1 receives a total of only three clock interrupts, significantly increasing the periods of idle sleep, thus achieving a lower C-state. Furthermore, there is less work to do for some of the clock interrupts on processor 0, possibly removing the latency of requiring a drop to DISPATCH_LEVEL at each clock interrupt.

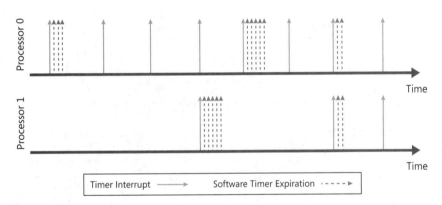

FIGURE 3-12 Timer coalescing

Exception Dispatching

In contrast to interrupts, which can occur at any time, exceptions are conditions that result directly from the execution of the program that is running. Windows uses a facility known as *structured exception handling*, which allows applications to gain control when exceptions occur. The application can then fix the condition and return to the place the exception occurred, unwind the stack (thus terminating execution of the subroutine that raised the exception), or declare back to the system that the exception isn't recognized and the system should continue searching for an exception handler that might process the exception. This section assumes you're familiar with the basic concepts behind Windows structured exception handling—if you're not, you should read the overview in the Windows API reference documentation in the Windows SDK or Chapters 23 through 25 in Jeffrey Richter and Christophe Nasarre's book *Windows via C/C++* (Microsoft Press, 2007) before proceeding. Keep in mind that although exception handling is made accessible through language extensions (for example, the __try construct in Microsoft Visual C++), it is a system mechanism and hence isn't language specific.

On the x86 and x64 processors, all exceptions have predefined interrupt numbers that directly correspond to the entry in the IDT that points to the trap handler for a particular exception. Table 3-6 shows x86-defined exceptions and their assigned interrupt numbers. Because the first entries of the IDT are used for exceptions, hardware interrupts are assigned entries later in the table, as mentioned earlier.

All exceptions, except those simple enough to be resolved by the trap handler, are serviced by a kernel module called the *exception dispatcher*. The exception dispatcher's job is to find an exception handler that can dispose of the exception. Examples of architecture-independent exceptions that the kernel defines include memory-access violations, integer divide-by-zero, integer overflow, floating-point exceptions, and debugger breakpoints. For a complete list of architecture-independent exceptions, consult the Windows SDK reference documentation.

TABLE 3-6 x86 Exceptions and Their Interrupt Numbers

Interrupt Number	Exception
0	Divide Error
1	Debug (Single Step)
2	Non-Maskable Interrupt (NMI)
3	Breakpoint
4	Overflow
5	Bounds Check
6	Invalid Opcode
7	NPX Not Available
8	Double Fault
9	NPX Segment Overrun
10	Invalid Task State Segment (TSS)
11	Segment Not Present
12	Stack Fault
13	General Protection
14	Page Fault
15	Intel Reserved
16	Floating Point
17	Alignment Check
18	Machine Check
19	SIMD Floating Point

The kernel traps and handles some of these exceptions transparently to user programs. For example, encountering a breakpoint while executing a program being debugged generates an exception, which the kernel handles by calling the debugger. The kernel handles certain other exceptions by returning an unsuccessful status code to the caller.

A few exceptions are allowed to filter back, untouched, to user mode. For example, certain types of memory-access violations or an arithmetic overflow generate an exception that the operating system doesn't handle. 32-bit applications can establish *frame-based exception handlers* to deal with these exceptions. The term *frame-based* refers to an exception handler's association with a particular procedure activation. When a procedure is invoked, a *stack frame* representing that activation of the procedure is pushed onto the stack. A stack frame can have one or more exception handlers associated with it, each of which protects a particular block of code in the source program. When an exception occurs, the kernel searches for an exception handler associated with the current stack frame. If none exists, the kernel searches for an exception handler associated with the previous stack frame, and so on, until it finds a frame-based exception handler. If no exception handler is found, the kernel calls its own default exception handlers.

For 64-bit applications, structured exception handling does not use frame-based handlers. Instead, a table of handlers for each function is built into the image during compilation. The kernel looks for handlers associated with each function and generally follows the same algorithm we described for 32-bit code.

Structured exception handling is heavily used within the kernel itself so that it can safely verify whether pointers from user mode can be safely accessed for read or write access. Drivers can make use of this same technique when dealing with pointers sent during I/O control codes (IOCTLs).

Another mechanism of exception handling is called *vectored exception handling*. This method can be used only by user-mode applications. You can find more information about it in the Windows SDK or the MSDN Library.

When an exception occurs, whether it is explicitly raised by software or implicitly raised by hardware, a chain of events begins in the kernel. The CPU hardware transfers control to the kernel trap handler, which creates a trap frame (as it does when an interrupt occurs). The trap frame allows the system to resume where it left off if the exception is resolved. The trap handler also creates an exception record that contains the reason for the exception and other pertinent information.

If the exception occurred in kernel mode, the exception dispatcher simply calls a routine to locate a frame-based exception handler that will handle the exception. Because unhandled kernel-mode exceptions are considered fatal operating system errors, you can assume that the dispatcher always finds an exception handler. Some traps, however, do not lead into an exception handler because the kernel always assumes such errors to be fatal—these are errors that could have been caused only by severe bugs in the internal kernel code or by major inconsistencies in driver code (that could have occurred only through deliberate, low-level system modifications that drivers should not be responsible for). Such fatal errors will result in a bug check with the UNEXPECTED_KERNEL_MODE_TRAP code.

If the exception occurred in user mode, the exception dispatcher does something more elaborate. As you'll see in Chapter 5, the Windows subsystem has a debugger port (this is actually a debugger object, which will be discussed later) and an exception port to receive notification of user-mode exceptions in Windows processes. (In this case, by "port" we mean an LPC port object, which will be discussed later in this chapter.) The kernel uses these ports in its default exception handling, as illustrated in Figure 3-13.

Debugger breakpoints are common sources of exceptions. Therefore, the first action the exception dispatcher takes is to see whether the process that incurred the exception has an associated debugger process. If it does, the exception dispatcher sends a debugger object message to the *debug object* associated with the process (which internally the system refers to as a "port" for compatibility with programs that might rely on behavior in Windows 2000, which used an LPC port instead of a debug object).

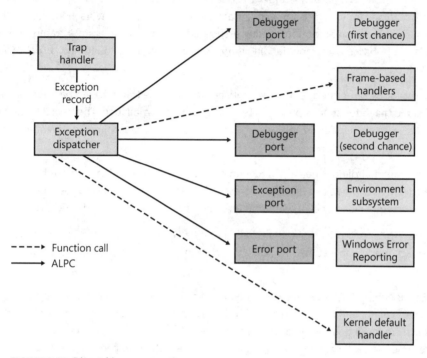

FIGURE 3-13 Dispatching an exception

If the process has no debugger process attached or if the debugger doesn't handle the exception, the exception dispatcher switches into user mode, copies the trap frame to the user stack formatted as a CONTEXT data structure (documented in the Windows SDK), and calls a routine to find a structured or vectored exception handler. If none is found or if none handles the exception, the exception dispatcher switches back into kernel mode and calls the debugger again to allow the user to do more debugging. (This is called the *second-chance notification*.)

If the debugger isn't running and no user-mode exception handlers are found, the kernel sends a message to the exception port associated with the thread's process. This exception port, if one exists, was registered by the environment subsystem that controls this thread. The exception port gives the environment subsystem, which presumably is listening at the port, the opportunity to translate the exception into an environment-specific signal or exception. For example, when Subsystem for UNIX Applications gets a message from the kernel that one of its threads generated an exception, Subsystem for UNIX Applications sends a UNIX-style signal to the thread that caused the exception. However, if the kernel progresses this far in processing the exception and the subsystem doesn't handle the exception, the kernel sends a message to a systemwide *error port* that Csrss (Client/Server Run-Time Subsystem) uses for Windows Error Reporting (WER)—which will be discussed shortly—and executes a default exception handler that simply terminates the process whose thread caused the exception.

Unhandled Exceptions

All Windows threads have an exception handler that processes unhandled exceptions. This exception handler is declared in the internal Windows *start-of-thread* function. The start-of-thread function runs when a user creates a process or any additional threads. It calls the environment-supplied thread start routine specified in the initial thread context structure, which in turn calls the user-supplied thread start routine specified in the *CreateThread* call.

EXPERIMENT: Viewing the Real User Start Address for Windows Threads

The fact that each Windows thread begins execution in a system-supplied function (and not the user-supplied function) explains why the start address for thread 0 is the same for every Windows process in the system (and why the start addresses for secondary threads are also the same). To see the user-supplied function address, use Process Explorer or the kernel debugger.

Because most threads in Windows processes start at one of the system-supplied wrapper functions, Process Explorer, when displaying the start address of threads in a process, skips the initial call frame that represents the wrapper function and instead shows the second frame on the stack. For example, notice the thread start address of a process running Notepad.exe:

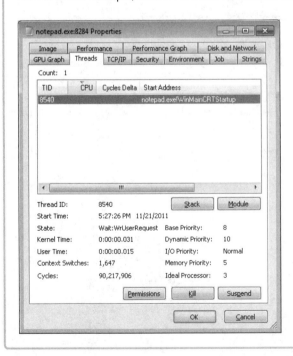

Process Explorer does display the complete call hierarchy when it displays the call stack. Notice the following results when the Stack button is clicked:

Line 18 in the preceding screen shot is the first frame on the stack—the start of the internal thread wrapper. The second frame (line 17) is the environment subsystem's thread wrapper—in this case, kernel32, because you are dealing with a Windows subsystem application. The third frame (line 16) is the main entry point into Notepad.exe.

The generic code for the internal thread start functions is shown here:

```
VOID RtlUserThreadStart(VOID)
{
    LPVOID lpStartAddr = (R/E)AX; // Located in the initial thread context structure
    LPVOID lpvThreadParam = (R/E)BX; // Located in the initial thread context structure
    LPVOID lpWin32StartAddr;

    lpWin32StartAddr = Kernel32ThreadInitThunkFunction ? Kernel32ThreadInitThunkFunction :
lpStartAddr;
    __try
    {
        DWORD dwThreadExitCode = lpWin32StartAddr(lpvThreadParam);
        RtlExitUserThread(dwThreadExitCode);
    }
    __except(RtlpGetExceptionFilter(GetExceptionInformation()))
    {
        NtTerminateProcess(NtCurrentProcess(), GetExceptionCode());
    }
}
```

```
VOID Win32StartOfProcess(
    LPTHREAD_START_ROUTINE lpStartAddr,
    LPVOID lpvThreadParam)
{
    lpStartAddr(lpvThreadParam);
}
```

Notice that the Windows unhandled exception filter is called if the thread has an exception that it doesn't handle. The purpose of this function is to provide the system-defined behavior for what to do when an exception is not handled, which is to launch the WerFault.exe process. However, in a default configuration the Windows Error Reporting service, described next, will handle the exception and this unhandled exception filter never executes.

WerFault.exe checks the contents of the HKLM\SOFTWARE\Microsoft\Windows NT \CurrentVersion\AeDebug registry key and makes sure that the process isn't on the exclusion list. There are two important values in the key: *Auto* and *Debugger*. *Auto* tells the unhandled exception filter whether to automatically run the debugger or ask the user what to do. Installing development tools, such as Microsoft Visual Studio, changes this value to *0* if it is already set. (If the value was not set, *0* is the default option.) The *Debugger* value is a string that points to the path of the debugger executable to run in the case of an unhandled exception, and *WerFault* passes the process ID of the crashing process and an event name to signal when the debugger has started as command-line arguments when it starts the debugger.

Windows Error Reporting

Windows Error Reporting (WER) is a sophisticated mechanism that automates the submission of both user-mode process crashes as well as kernel-mode system crashes. (For a description of how this applies to system crashes, see Chapter 14 in Part 2.)

Windows Error Reporting can be configured by going to Control Panel, choosing Action Center, Change Action Center settings, and then Problem Reporting Settings.

When an unhandled exception is caught by the unhandled exception filter (described in the previous section), it builds context information (such as the current value of the registers and stack) and opens an ALPC port connection to the WER service. This service begins to analyze the crashed program's state and performs the appropriate actions to notify the user. As described previously, in most cases this means launching the WerFault.exe program, which executes with the current user's credentials and, unless the system is configured not to, displays a message box informing the user of the crash. On systems where a debugger is installed, an additional option to debug the process is shown, as you can see in Figure 3-14. When you click the Debug button, the debugger (registered in the Debugger string value described earlier in the *AeDebug* key) will be launched so that it can attach to the crashing process.

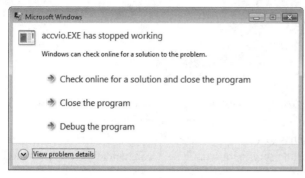

FIGURE 3-14 Windows Error Reporting dialog box

On default configured systems, an error report (a minidump and an XML file with various details, such as the DLL version numbers loaded in the process) is sent to Microsoft's online crash analysis server. Eventually, as the service is notified of a solution for a problem, it will display a tooltip to the user informing her of steps that should be taken to solve the problem. An entry will also be displayed in the Action Center. Furthermore, the Reliability Monitor will also show all instances of application and system crashes.

Note WER will actively (visually) inform the user of a crashed application only if the application has at least one visible/interactive window; otherwise, the crash will be logged, but the user will have to manually visit the Action Center to view it. This behavior attempts to avoid user confusion by not displaying a WER dialog box about an invisible crashed process the user might not be aware of, such as a background service.

In environments where systems are not connected to the Internet or where the administrator wants to control which error reports are submitted to Microsoft, the destination for the error report can be configured to be an internal file server. Microsoft System Center Desktop Error Monitoring understands the directory structure created by Windows Error Reporting and provides the administrator with the option to take selective error reports and submit them to Microsoft.

If all the operations we've described had to occur within the crashing thread's context—that is, as part of the unhandled exception filter that was initially set up—these complex steps would sometimes become impossible for a badly damaged thread to perform, and the unhandled exception filter itself would crash. This "silent process death" would be impossible to log, making it hard to debug and also resulting in invisible crashes in cases where no user was present on the machine. To avoid such issues, Windows' WER mechanism performs this work externally from the crashed thread if the unhandled exception filter itself crashes, which allows any kind of process or thread crash to be logged and for the user to be notified.

WER contains many customizable settings that can be configured by the user through the Group Policy editor or by manually making changes to the registry. Table 3-7 lists the WER registry configuration options, their use, and possible values. These values are located under the HKLM\SOFTWARE\Microsoft\Windows\Windows Error Reporting subkey for computer configuration and in the equivalent path under HKEY_CURRENT_USER for per-user configuration.

TABLE 3-7 WER Registry Settings

Setting	Meaning	Values
ConfigureArchive	Contents of archived data	1 for parameters, 2 for all data
Consent\DefaultConsent	What kind of data should require consent	1 for any data, 2 for parameters only, 3 for parameters and safe data, 4 for all data.
Consent\DefaultOverrideBehavior	Whether the *DefaultConsent* over-rides WER plug-in consent values	1 to enable override
Consent\PluginName	Consent value for a specific WER plug-in	Same as *DefaultConsent*
CorporateWERDirectory	Directory for a corporate WER store	String containing the path
CorporateWERPortNumber	Port to use for a corporate WER store	Port number
CorporateWERServer	Name to use for a corporate WER store	String containing the name
CorporateWERUseAuthentication	Use Windows Integrated Authentication for corporate WER store	1 to enable built-in authentication
CorporateWERUseSSL	Use Secure Sockets Layer (SSL) for corporate WER store	1 to enable SSL
DebugApplications	List of applications that require the user to choose between Debug and Continue	1 to require the user to choose
DisableArchive	Whether the archive is enabled	1 to disable archive
Disabled	Whether WER is disabled	1 to disable WER
DisableQueue	Determines whether reports are to be queued	1 to disable queue
DontShowUI	Disables or enables the WER UI	1 to disable UI
DontSendAdditionalData	Prevents additional crash data from being sent	1 not to send
ExcludedApplications\AppName	List of applications excluded from WER	String containing the application list
ForceQueue	Whether reports should be sent to the user queue	1 to send reports to the queue
LocalDumps\DumpFolder	Path at which to store the dump files	String containing the path
LocalDumps\DumpCount	Maximum number of dump files in the path	Count
LocalDumps\DumpType	Type of dump to generate during a crash	0 for a custom dump, 1 for a minidump, 2 for a full dump
LocalDumps\CustomDumpFlags	For custom dumps, specifies custom options	Values defined in MINIDUMP_TYPE (see Chapter 13, "Startup and Shutdown," in Part 2 for more information)

Setting	Meaning	Values
LoggingDisabled	Enables or disables logging	1 to disable logging
MaxArchiveCount	Maximum size of the archive (in files)	Value between 1–5000
MaxQueueCount	Maximum size of the queue	Value between 1–500
QueuePesterInterval	Days between requests to have the user check for solutions	Number of days

Note The values listed under *LocalDumps* can also be configured per application by adding the application name in the subkey path between *LocalDumps* and the relevant value. However, they cannot be configured per user; they exist only in the HKLM path.

As discussed, the WER service uses an ALPC port for communicating with crashed processes. This mechanism uses a systemwide error port that the WER service registers through *NtSetInformationProcess (*which uses *DbgkRegisterErrorPort)*. As a result, all Windows processes now have an error port that is actually an ALPC port object registered by the WER service. The kernel, which is first notified of an exception, uses this port to send a message to the WER service, which then analyzes the crashing process. This means that even in severe cases of thread state damage, WER will still be able to receive notifications and launch WerFault.exe to display a user interface instead of having to do this work within the crashing thread itself. Additionally, WER will be able to generate a crash dump for the process, and a message will be written to the Event Log. This solves all the problems of silent process death: users are notified, debugging can occur, and service administrators can see the crash event.

System Service Dispatching

As Figure 3-1 illustrated, the kernel's trap handlers dispatch interrupts, exceptions, and system service calls. In the preceding sections, you saw how interrupt and exception handling work; in this section, you'll learn about system services. A system service dispatch is triggered as a result of executing an instruction assigned to system service dispatching. The instruction that Windows uses for system service dispatching depends on the processor on which it's executing.

System Service Dispatching

On x86 processors prior to the Pentium II, Windows uses the *int 0x2e* instruction (46 decimal), which results in a trap. Windows fills in entry 46 in the IDT to point to the system service dispatcher. (Refer to Table 3-3.) The trap causes the executing thread to transition into kernel mode and enter the system service dispatcher. A numeric argument passed in the EAX processor register indicates the system service number being requested. The EDX register points to the list of parameters the caller passes to the system service. To return to user mode, the system service dispatcher uses the *iret* (interrupt return instruction).

On x86 Pentium II processors and higher, Windows uses the *sysenter* instruction, which Intel defined specifically for fast system service dispatches. To support the instruction, Windows stores at boot time the address of the kernel's system service dispatcher routine in a *machine-specific register* (MSR) associated with the instruction. The execution of the instruction causes the change to kernel mode and execution of the system service dispatcher. The system service number is passed in the EAX processor register, and the EDX register points to the list of caller arguments. To return to user mode, the system service dispatcher usually executes the *sysexit* instruction. (In some cases, like when the single-step flag is enabled on the processor, the system service dispatcher uses the *iret* instead because *sysexit* does not allow returning to user-mode with a different EFLAGS register, which is needed if *sysenter* was executed while the *trap flag* was set as a result of a user-mode debugger tracing or stepping over a system call.)

> **Note** Because certain older applications might have been hardcoded to use the *int 0x2e* instruction to manually perform a system call (an unsupported operation), 32-bit Windows keeps this mechanism usable even on systems that support the *sysenter* instruction by still having the handler registered.

On the x64 architecture, Windows uses the *syscall* instruction, passing the system call number in the EAX register, the first four parameters in registers, and any parameters beyond those four on the stack.

On the IA64 architecture, Windows uses the *epc* (Enter Privileged Mode) instruction. The first eight system call arguments are passed in registers, and the rest are passed on the stack.

EXPERIMENT: Locating the System Service Dispatcher

As mentioned, 32-bit system calls occur through an interrupt, which means that the handler needs to be registered in the IDT or through a special *sysenter* instruction that uses an MSR to store the handler address at boot time. On certain 32-bit AMD systems, Windows uses the *syscall* instruction instead, which is similar to the 64-bit *syscall* instruction. Here's how you can locate the appropriate routine for either method:

1. To see the handler on 32-bit systems for the interrupt 2E version of the system call dispatcher, type **!idt 2e** in the kernel debugger.

    ```
    lkd> !idt 2e

    Dumping IDT:

    2e:    8208c8ee nt!KiSystemService
    ```

2. To see the handler for the *sysenter* version, use the *rdmsr* debugger command to read from the MSR register 0x176, which stores the handler:

    ```
    lkd> rdmsr 176
    msr[176] = 00000000'8208c9c0
    ```

```
lkd> ln 00000000'8208c9c0
(8208c9c0)   nt!KiFastCallEntry
```

If you have a 64-bit machine, you can look at the 64-bit service call dispatcher by repeating this step, but using the 0xC0000082 MSR instead, which is used by the *syscall* version for 64-bit code. You will see it corresponds to *nt!KiSystemCall64*:

```
lkd> rdmsr c0000082
msr[c0000082] = fffff800'01a71ec0
lkd> ln fffff800'01a71ec0
(fffff800'01a71ec0)   nt!KiSystemCall64
```

3. You can disassemble the *KiSystemService* or *KiSystemCall64* routine with the *u* command. On a 32-bit system, you'll eventually notice the following instructions:

```
nt!KiSystemService+0x7b:
8208c969 897d04          mov       dword ptr [ebp+4],edi
8208c96c fb              sti
8208c96d e9dd000000      jmp       nt!KiFastCallEntry+0x8f (8208ca4f)
```

Because the actual system call dispatching operations are common regardless of the mechanism used to reach the handler, the older interrupt-based handler simply calls into the middle of the newer *sysenter*-based handler to perform the same generic tasks. The only parts of the handlers that are different are related to the generation of the trap frame and the setup of certain registers.

At boot time, 32-bit Windows detects the type of processor on which it's executing and sets up the appropriate system call code to use by storing a pointer to the correct code in the *SharedUserData* structure. The system service code for *NtReadFile* in user mode looks like this:

```
0:000> u ntdll!NtReadFile
ntdll!ZwReadFile:
77020074 b802010000      mov      eax,102h
77020079 ba0003fe7f      mov      edx,offset SharedUserData!SystemCallStub (7ffe0300)
7702007e ff12            call     dword ptr [edx]
77020080 c22400          ret      24h
77020083 90              nop
```

The system service number is 0x102 (258 in decimal), and the *call* instruction executes the system service dispatch code set up by the kernel, whose pointer is at address 0x7ffe0300. (This corresponds to the *SystemCallStub* member of the KUSER_SHARED_DATA structure, which starts at 0x7FFE0000.) Because the following output was taken from an Intel Core 2 Duo, it contains a pointer to *sysenter*:

```
0:000> dd SharedUserData!SystemCallStub l 1
7ffe0300  77020f30
0:000> u 77020f30
ntdll!KiFastSystemCall:
77020f30 8bd4            mov      edx,esp
77020f32 0f34            sysenter
```

Because 64-bit systems have only one mechanism for performing system calls, the system service entry points in Ntdll.dll use the *syscall* instruction directly, as shown here:

```
ntdll!NtReadFile:
00000000'77f9fc60 4c8bd1          mov     r10,rcx
00000000'77f9fc63 b810200000      mov     eax,0x102
00000000'77f9fc68 0f05            syscall
00000000'77f9fc6a c3              ret
```

Kernel-Mode System Service Dispatching

As Figure 3-15 illustrates, the kernel uses the system call number to locate the system service information in the *system service dispatch table*. On 32-bit systems, this table is similar to the interrupt dispatch table described earlier in the chapter except that each entry contains a pointer to a system service rather than to an interrupt-handling routine. On 64-bit systems, the table is implemented slightly differently—instead of containing pointers to the system service, it contains offsets relative to the table itself. This addressing mechanism is more suited to the x64 application binary interface (ABI) and instruction-encoding format.

 Note System service numbers can change between service packs—Microsoft occasionally adds or removes system services, and the system service numbers are generated automatically as part of a kernel compile.

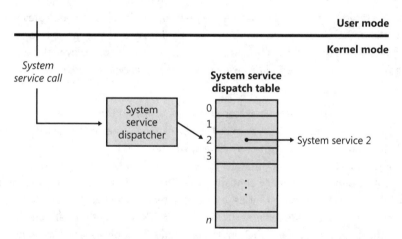

FIGURE 3-15 System service exceptions

The system service dispatcher, *KiSystemService*, copies the caller's arguments from the thread's user-mode stack to its kernel-mode stack (so that the user can't change the arguments as the kernel is accessing them) and then executes the system service. The kernel knows how many stack bytes require copying by using a second table, called the *argument table,* which is a byte array (instead of a pointer array like the dispatch table), each entry describing the number of bytes to copy. On 64-bit systems, Windows actually encodes this information within the service table itself through a process called *system call table compaction*. If the arguments passed to a system service point to buffers in user space, these buffers must be probed for accessibility before kernel-mode code can copy data to or from them. This probing is performed only if the *previous mode* of the thread is set to user mode. The *previous mode* is a value (kernel or user) that the kernel saves in the thread whenever it executes a trap handler and identifies the privilege level of the incoming exception, trap, or system call. As an optimization, if a system call comes from a driver or the kernel itself, the probing and capturing of parameters is skipped, and all parameters are assumed to be pointing to valid kernel-mode buffers (also, access to kernel-mode data is allowed).

Because kernel-mode code can also make system calls, let's look at the way these are done. Because the code for each system call is in kernel mode and the caller is already in kernel mode, you can see that there shouldn't be a need for an interrupt or *sysenter* operation: the CPU is already at the right privilege level, and drivers, as well as the kernel, should only be able to directly call the function required. In the executive's case, this is actually what happens: the kernel has access to all its own routines and can simply call them just like standard routines. Externally, however, drivers can access these system calls only if they have been exported just like other standard kernel-mode APIs. In fact, quite a few of the system calls are exported. Drivers, however, are not supposed to access system calls this way. Instead, drivers must use the *Zw* versions of these calls—that is, instead of *NtCreateFile*, they must use *ZwCreateFile*. These *Zw* versions must also be manually exported by the kernel, and only a handful are, but they are fully documented and supported.

The *Zw* versions are officially available only for drivers because of the *previous mode* concept discussed earlier. Because this value is updated only each time the kernel builds a trap frame, its value won't actually change across a simple API call—no trap frame is being generated. By calling a function such as *NtCreateFile* directly, the kernel preserves the *previous mode* value that indicates that it is user mode, detects that the address passed is a kernel-mode address, and fails the call, correctly asserting that user-mode applications should not pass kernel-mode pointers. However, this is not actually what happens, so how can the kernel be aware of the correct *previous mode*? The answer lies in the *Zw* calls.

These exported APIs are not actually simple aliases or wrappers around the *Nt* versions. Instead, they are "trampolines" to the appropriate *Nt* system call, which use the same system call-dispatching mechanism. Instead of generating an interrupt or a *sysenter*, which would be slow and/or unsupported, they build a fake interrupt stack (the stack that the CPU would generate after an interrupt) and call the *KiSystemService* routine directly, essentially emulating the CPU interrupt. The handler executes the same operations as if this call came from user mode, except it detects the actual privilege level this call came from and set the *previous mode* to kernel. Now *NtCreateFile* sees that the call came from the kernel and does not fail anymore. Here's what the kernel-mode trampolines look like on both 32-bit and 64-bit systems. The system call number is highlighted in bold.

```
lkd> u nt!ZwReadFile
nt!ZwReadFile:
8207f118 b802010000       mov       eax,102h
8207f11d 8d542404         lea       edx,[esp+4]
8207f121 9c               pushfd
8207f122 6a08             push      8
8207f124 e8c5d70000       call      nt!KiSystemService (8208c8ee)
8207f129 c22400           ret       24h
```

```
lkd> uf nt!ZwReadFile
nt!ZwReadFile:
fffff800'01a7a520 488bc4        mov     rax,rsp
fffff800'01a7a523 fa            cli
fffff800'01a7a524 4883ec10      sub     rsp,10h
fffff800'01a7a528 50            push    rax
fffff800'01a7a529 9c            pushfq
fffff800'01a7a52a 6a10          push    10h
fffff800'01a7a52c 488d05bd310000  lea   rax,[nt!KiServiceLinkage (fffff800'01a7d6f0)]
fffff800'01a7a533 50            push    rax
fffff800'01a7a534 b803000000    mov     eax,3
fffff800'01a7a539 e902690000    jmp     nt!KiServiceInternal (fffff800'01a80e40)
```

As you'll see in Chapter 5, Windows has two system service tables, and third-party drivers cannot extend the tables or insert new ones to add their own service calls. On 32-bit and IA64 versions of Windows, the system service dispatcher locates the tables via a pointer in the thread kernel structure, and on x64 versions it finds them via their global addresses. The system service dispatcher determines which table contains the requested service by interpreting a 2-bit field in the 32-bit system service number as a table index. The low 12 bits of the system service number serve as the index into the table specified by the table index. The fields are shown in Figure 3-16.

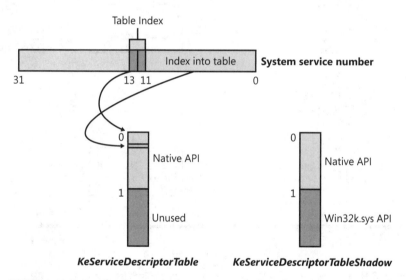

FIGURE 3-16 System service number to system service translation

Service Descriptor Tables

A primary default array table, *KeServiceDescriptorTable*, defines the core executive system services implemented in Ntosrknl.exe. The other table array, *KeServiceDescriptorTableShadow*, includes the Windows USER and GDI services implemented in the kernel-mode part of the Windows subsystem, Win32k.sys. On 32-bit and IA64 versions of Windows, the first time a Windows thread calls a Windows USER or GDI service, the address of the thread's system service table is changed to point to a table that includes the Windows USER and GDI services. The *KeAddSystemServiceTable* function allows Win32k.sys to add a system service table.

The system service dispatch instructions for Windows executive services exist in the system library Ntdll.dll. Subsystem DLLs call functions in Ntdll to implement their documented functions. The exception is Windows USER and GDI functions, for which the system service dispatch instructions are implemented in User32.dll and Gdi32.dll—Ntdll.dll is not involved. These two cases are shown in Figure 3-17.

As shown in Figure 3-17, the Windows *WriteFile* function in Kernel32.dll imports and calls the *WriteFile* function in API-MS-Win-Core-File-L1-1-0.dll, one of the MinWin redirection DLLs (see the next section for more information on API redirection), which in turn calls the *WriteFile* function in KernelBase.dll, where the actual implementation lies. After some subsystem-specific parameter checks, it then calls the *NtWriteFile* function in Ntdll.dll, which in turn executes the appropriate instruction to cause a system service trap, passing the system service number representing *NtWriteFile*. The system service dispatcher (function *KiSystemService* in Ntoskrnl.exe) then calls the real *NtWriteFile* to process the I/O request. For Windows USER and GDI functions, the system service dispatch calls functions in the loadable kernel-mode part of the Windows subsystem, Win32k.sys.

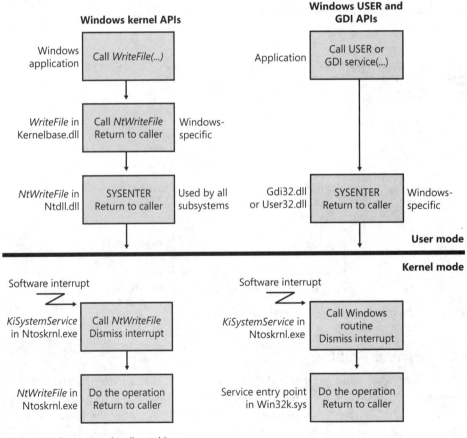

FIGURE 3-17 System service dispatching

EXPERIMENT: Mapping System Call Numbers to Functions and Arguments

You can duplicate the same lookup performed by the kernel when dealing with a system call ID to figure out which function is responsible for handling it and how many arguments it takes

1. The *KeServiceDescriptorTable* and *KeServiceDescriptorTableShadow* tables both point to the same array of pointers (or offsets, on 64-bit) for kernel system calls, called *KiServiceTable*, and the same array of stack bytes, called *KiArgumentTable*. On a 32-bit system, you can use the kernel debugger command *dds* to dump the data along with symbolic information. The debugger attempts to match each pointer with a symbol. Here's a partial output:

```
lkd> dds KiServiceTable
820807d0  821be2e5 nt!NtAcceptConnectPort
820807d4  820659a6 nt!NtAccessCheck
820807d8  8224a953 nt!NtAccessCheckAndAuditAlarm
820807dc  820659dd nt!NtAccessCheckByType
820807e0  8224a992 nt!NtAccessCheckByTypeAndAuditAlarm
820807e4  82065a18 nt!NtAccessCheckByTypeResultList
820807e8  8224a9db nt!NtAccessCheckByTypeResultListAndAuditAlarm
820807ec  8224aa24 nt!NtAccessCheckByTypeResultListAndAuditAlarmByHandle
820807f0  822892af nt!NtAddAtom
```

2. As described earlier, 64-bit Windows organizes the system call table differently and uses relative pointers (an offset) to system calls instead of the absolute addresses used by 32-bit Windows. The base of the pointer is the *KiServiceTable* itself, so you'll have to dump the data in its raw format with the *dq* command. Here's an example of output from a 64-bit system:

```
lkd> dq nt!KiServiceTable
fffff800'01a73b00  02f6f000'04106900 031a0105'fff72d00
```

3. Instead of dumping the entire table, you can also look up a specific number. On 32-bit Windows, because each system call number is an index into the table and because each element is 4 bytes, you can use the following calculation: *Handler = KiServiceTable + Number * 4*. Let's use the number 0x102, obtained during our description of the *NtReadFile* stub code in Ntdll.dll.

```
lkd> ln poi(KiServiceTable + 102 * 4)
(82193023)   nt!NtReadFile
```

On 64-bit Windows, each offset can be mapped to each function with the *ln* command, by shifting right by 4 bits (used as described earlier) and adding the remaining value to the base of *KiServiceTable* itself, as shown here:

```
lkd> ln @@c++(((int*)@@(nt!KiServiceTable))[3] >> 4) + nt!KiServiceTable
(fffff800'01d9cb10)   nt!NtReadFile  |  (fffff800'01d9d24c)   nt!NtOpenFile
Exact matches:
    nt!NtReadFile = <no type information>
```

4. Because drivers, including kernel-mode rootkits, are able to patch this table on 32-bit versions of Windows, which is something the operating system does not support, you can use *dds* to dump the entire table and look for any values outside the range of valid kernel addresses (*dds* will also make this clear by not being able to look up a symbol for the function). On 64-bit Windows, Kernel Patch Protection monitors the system service tables and crashes the system when it detects modifications.

EXPERIMENT: Viewing System Service Activity

You can monitor system service activity by watching the System Calls/Sec performance counter in the System object. Run the Performance Monitor, click on Performance Monitor under Monitoring Tools, and click the Add button to add a counter to the chart. Select the System object, select the System Calls/Sec counter, and then click the Add button to add the counter to the chart.

Object Manager

As mentioned in Chapter 2, "System Architecture," Windows implements an object model to provide consistent and secure access to the various internal services implemented in the executive. This section describes the Windows *object manager*, the executive component responsible for creating, deleting, protecting, and tracking objects. The object manager centralizes resource control operations that otherwise would be scattered throughout the operating system. It was designed to meet the goals listed on the next page.

EXPERIMENT: Exploring the Object Manager

Throughout this section, you'll find experiments that show you how to peer into the object manager database. These experiments use the following tools, which you should become familiar with if you aren't already:

■ WinObj (available from Sysinternals) displays the internal object manager's namespace and information about objects (such as the reference count, the number of open handles, security descriptors, and so forth).

■ Process Explorer and Handle from Sysinternals, as well as Resource Monitor (introduced in Chapter 1) display the open handles for a process.

■ The *Openfiles /query* command displays the open file handles for a process, but it requires a global flag to be set in order to operate.

■ The kernel debugger *!handle* command displays the open handles for a process.

WinObj provides a way to traverse the namespace that the object manager maintains. (As we'll explain later, not all objects have names.) Run WinObj, and examine the layout, shown next.

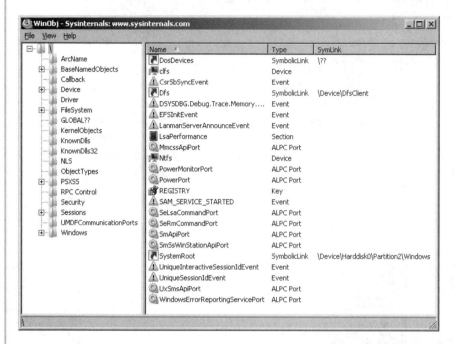

As noted previously, the Windows *Openfiles /query* command requires that a Windows global flag called *maintain objects list* be enabled. (See the "Windows Global Flags" section later in this chapter for more details about global flags.) If you type **Openfiles /Local**, it will tell you whether the flag is enabled. You can enable it with the *Openfiles /Local ON* command. In either case, you must reboot the system for the setting to take effect. Process Explorer, Handle, and Resource Monitor do not require object tracking to be turned on because they query all system handles and create a per-process object list.

The object manager was designed to meet the following goals:

- Provide a common, uniform mechanism for using system resources

- Isolate object protection to one location in the operating system to ensure uniform and consistent object access policy

- Provide a mechanism to charge processes for their use of objects so that limits can be placed on the usage of system resources

- Establish an object-naming scheme that can readily incorporate existing objects, such as the devices, files, and directories of a file system, or other independent collections of objects

- Support the requirements of various operating system environments, such as the ability of a process to inherit resources from a parent process (needed by Windows and Subsystem for

UNIX Applications) and the ability to create case-sensitive file names (needed by Subsystem for UNIX Applications)

- Establish uniform rules for object retention (that is, for keeping an object available until all processes have finished using it)

- Provide the ability to isolate objects for a specific session to allow for both local and global objects in the namespace

Internally, Windows has three kinds of objects: *executive objects*, *kernel objects,* and *GDI/User objects*. Executive objects are objects implemented by various components of the executive (such as the process manager, memory manager, I/O subsystem, and so on). Kernel objects are a more primitive set of objects implemented by the Windows kernel. These objects are not visible to user-mode code but are created and used only within the executive. Kernel objects provide fundamental capabilities, such as synchronization, on which executive objects are built. Thus, many executive objects contain (encapsulate) one or more kernel objects, as shown in Figure 3-18.

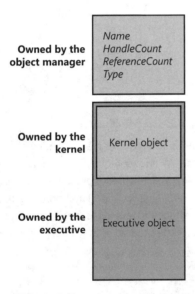

FIGURE 3-18 Executive objects that contain kernel objects

  Note GDI/User objects, on the other hand, belong to the Windows subsystem (Win32k.sys) and do not interact with the kernel. For this reason, they are outside the scope of this book, but you can get more information on them from the Windows SDK.

Details about the structure of kernel objects and how they are used to implement synchronization are given later in this chapter. The remainder of this section focuses on how the object manager works and on the structure of executive objects, handles, and handle tables and just briefly describes how objects are involved in implementing Windows security access checking; Chapter 6 thoroughly covers that topic.

Executive Objects

Each Windows environment subsystem projects to its applications a different image of the operating system. The executive objects and object services are primitives that the environment subsystems use to construct their own versions of objects and other resources.

Executive objects are typically created either by an environment subsystem on behalf of a user application or by various components of the operating system as part of their normal operation. For example, to create a file, a Windows application calls the Windows *CreateFileW* function, implemented in the Windows subsystem DLL Kernelbase.dll. After some validation and initialization, *CreateFileW* in turn calls the native Windows service *NtCreateFile* to create an executive file object.

The set of objects an environment subsystem supplies to its applications might be larger or smaller than the set the executive provides. The Windows subsystem uses executive objects to export its own set of objects, many of which correspond directly to executive objects. For example, the Windows mutexes and semaphores are directly based on executive objects (which, in turn, are based on corresponding kernel objects). In addition, the Windows subsystem supplies named pipes and mailslots, resources that are based on executive file objects. Some subsystems, such as Subsystem for UNIX Applications, don't support objects as objects at all. Subsystem for UNIX Applications uses executive objects and services as the basis for presenting UNIX-style processes, pipes, and other resources to its applications.

Table 3-8 lists the primary objects the executive provides and briefly describes what they represent. You can find further details on executive objects in the chapters that describe the related executive components (or in the case of executive objects directly exported to Windows, in the Windows API reference documentation). You can see the full list of object types by running Winobj with elevated rights and navigating to the ObjectTypes directory.

> **Note** The executive implements a total of 4242 object types. Many of these objects are for use only by the executive component that defines them and are not directly accessible by Windows APIs. Examples of these objects include *Driver*, *Device*, and *EventPair*.

TABLE 3-8 Executive Objects Exposed to the Windows API

Object Type	Represents
Process	The virtual address space and control information necessary for the execution of a set of thread objects.
Thread	An executable entity within a process.
Job	A collection of processes manageable as a single entity through the job.
Section	A region of shared memory (known as a file-mapping object in Windows).
File	An instance of an opened file or an I/O device.
Token	The security profile (security ID, user rights, and so on) of a process or a thread.
Event	An object with a persistent state (signaled or not signaled) that can be used for synchronization or notification.

Object Type	Represents
Semaphore	A counter that provides a resource gate by allowing some maximum number of threads to access the resources protected by the semaphore.
Mutex	A synchronization mechanism used to serialize access to a resource.
Timer	A mechanism to notify a thread when a fixed period of time elapses.
IoCompletion	A method for threads to enqueue and dequeue notifications of the completion of I/O operations (known as an I/O completion port in the Windows API).
Key	A mechanism to refer to data in the registry. Although keys appear in the object manager namespace, they are managed by the configuration manager, in a way similar to that in which file objects are managed by file system drivers. Zero or more key values are associated with a key object; key values contain data about the key.
Directory	A virtual directory in the object manager's namespace responsible for containing other objects or object directories.
TpWorkerFactory	A collection of threads assigned to perform a specific set of tasks. The kernel can manage the number of work items that will be performed on the queue, how many threads should be responsible for the work, and dynamic creation and termination of worker threads, respecting certain limits the caller can set. Windows exposes the worker factory object through *thread pools*.
TmRm (Resource Manager), TmTx (Transaction), TmTm (Transaction Manager), TmEn (Enlistment)	Objects used by the Kernel Transaction Manager (KTM) for various *transactions* and/or *enlistments* as part of a *resource manager* or *transaction manager*. Objects can be created through the *CreateTransactionManager, CreateResourceManager, CreateTransaction,* and *CreateEnlistment* APIs.
WindowStation	An object that contains a clipboard, a set of global atoms, and a group of Desktop objects.
Desktop	An object contained within a window station. A desktop has a logical display surface and contains windows, menus, and hooks.
PowerRequest	An object associated with a thread that executes, among other things, a call to *SetThreadExecutionState* to request a given power change, such as blocking sleeps (due to a movie being played, for example).
EtwConsumer	Represents a connected ETW real-time consumer that has registered with the *StartTrace* API (and can call *ProcessTrace* to receive the events on the object queue).
EtwRegistration	Represents the registration object associated with a user-mode (or kernel-mode) ETW provider that registered with the *EventRegister* API.

Note Because Windows NT was originally supposed to support the OS/2 operating system, the mutex had to be compatible with the existing design of OS/2 mutual-exclusion objects, a design that required that a thread be able to abandon the object, leaving it inaccessible. Because this behavior was considered unusual for such an object, another kernel object—the *mutant*—was created. Eventually, OS/2 support was dropped, and the object became used by the Windows 32 subsystem under the name *mutex* (but it is still called *mutant* internally).

Object Structure

As shown in Figure 3-19, each object has an object header and an object body. The object manager controls the object headers, and the owning executive components control the object bodies of the object types they create. Each object header also contains an index to a special object, called the *type object*, that contains information common to each instance of the object. Additionally, up to five optional subheaders exist: the name information header, the quota information header, the process information header, the handle information header, and the creator information header.

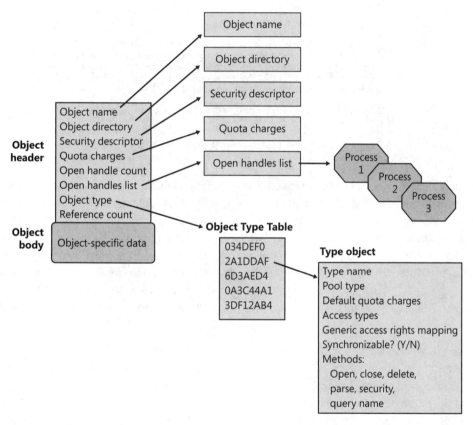

FIGURE 3-19 Structure of an object

Object Headers and Bodies

The object manager uses the data stored in an object's header to manage objects without regard to their type. Table 3-9 briefly describes the object header fields, and Table 3-10 describes the fields found in the optional object subheaders.

TABLE 3-9 Object Header Fields

Field	Purpose
Handle count	Maintains a count of the number of currently opened handles to the object.
Pointer count	Maintains a count of the number of references to the object (including one reference for each handle). Kernel-mode components can reference an object by pointer without using a handle.
Security descriptor	Determines who can use the object and what they can do with it. Note that unnamed objects, by definition, cannot have security.
Object type index	Contains the index to a type object that contains attributes common to objects of this type. The table that stores all the type objects is ObTypeIndexTable.
Subheader mask	Bitmask describing which of the optional subheader structures described in Table 3-10 are present, except for the creator information subheader, which, if present, always precedes the object. The bitmask is converted to a negative offset by using the ObpInfoMaskToOffset table, with each subheader being associated with a 1-byte index that places it relative to the other subheaders present.
Flags	Characteristics and object attributes for the object. See Table 3-12 for a list of all the object flags.
Lock	Per-object lock used when modifying fields belonging to this object header or any of its subheaders.

In addition to the object header, which contains information that applies to any kind of object, the subheaders contain optional information regarding specific aspects of the object. Note that these structures are located at a variable offset from the start of the object header, the value of which depends on the number of subheaders associated with the main object header (except, as mentioned earlier, for creator information). For each subheader that is present, the *InfoMask* field is updated to reflect its existence. When the object manager checks for a given subheader, it checks if the corresponding bit is set in the *InfoMask* and then uses the remaining bits to select the correct offset into the *ObpInfoMaskToOffset* table, where it finds the offset of the subheader from the start of the object header.

These offsets exist for all possible combinations of subheader presence, but because the subheaders, if present, are always allocated in a fixed, constant order, a given header will have only as many possible locations as the maximum number of subheaders that precede it. For example, because the name information subheader is always allocated first, it has only one possible offset. On the other hand, the handle information subheader (which is allocated third) has three possible locations, because it might or might not have been allocated after the quota subheader, itself having possibly been allocated after the name information. Table 3-10 describes all the optional object subheaders and their location. In the case of creator information, a value in the object header flags determines whether the subheader is present. (See Table 3-12 for information about these flags.)

TABLE 3-10 Optional Object Subheaders

Name	Purpose	Bit	Location
Creator information	Links the object into a list for all the objects of the same type, and records the process that created the object, along with a back trace.	0 (0x1)	Object header - *ObpInfoMaskToOffset*[0])

Name	Purpose	Bit	Location
Name information	Contains the object name, responsible for making an object visible to other processes for sharing, and a pointer to the object directory, which provides the hierarchical structure in which the object names are stored.	1 (0x2)	Object header - *ObpInfoMaskToOffset* - *ObpInfoMaskToOffset*[InfoMask & 0x3]
Handle information	Contains a database of entries (or just a single entry) for a process that has an open handle to the object (along with a per-process handle count).	2 (0x4)	Object header - *ObpInfoMaskToOffset*[InfoMask & 0x7]
Quota information	Lists the resource charges levied against a process when it opens a handle to the object.	3 (0x8)	Object header - *ObpInfoMaskToOffset*[InfoMask & 0xF]
Process information	Contains a pointer to the owning process if this is an exclusive object. More information on exclusive objects follows later in the chapter.	4 (0x10)	Object header - *ObpInfoMaskToOffset*[InfoMask & 0x1F]

Each of these subheaders is optional and is present only under certain conditions, either during system boot up or at object creation time. Table 3-11 describes each of these conditions.

TABLE 3-11 Conditions Required for Presence of Object Subheaders

Name	Condition
Name information	The object must have been created with a name.
Quota information	The object must not have been created by the initial (or idle) system process.
Process information	The object must have been created with the *exclusive object* flag. (See Table 3-12 for information about object flags.)
Handle information	The object type must have enabled the *maintain handle count* flag. File objects, ALPC objects, WindowStation objects, and Desktop objects have this flag set in their object type structure.
Creator information	The object type must have enabled the *maintain type list* flag. Driver objects have this flag set if the Driver Verifier is enabled. However, enabling the *maintain object type list* global flag (discussed earlier) will enable this for all objects, and *Type* objects always have the flag set.

Finally, a number of attributes and/or flags determine the behavior of the object during creation time or during certain operations. These flags are received by the object manager whenever any new object is being created, in a structure called the *object attributes*. This structure defines the object name, the root object directory where it should be inserted, the security descriptor for the object, and the *object attribute flags*. Table 3-12 lists the various flags that can be associated with an object.

> **Note** When an object is being created through an API in the Windows subsystem (such as *CreateEvent* or *CreateFile)*, the caller does not specify any object attributes—the subsystem DLL performs the work behind the scenes. For this reason, all named objects created through Win32 go in the *BaseNamedObjects* directory, either the global or per-session instance, because this is the root object directory that Kernelbase.dll specifies as part of the object attributes structure. More information on *BaseNamedObjects* and how it relates to the per-session namespace will follow later in this chapter.

TABLE 3-12 Object Flags

Attributes Flag	Header Flag	Purpose
OBJ_INHERIT	Saved in the handle table entry	Determines whether the handle to the object will be inherited by child processes, and whether a process can use *DuplicateHandle* to make a copy.
OBJ_PERMANENT	OB_FLAG_PERMANENT_OBJECT	Defines object retention behavior related to reference counts, described later.
OBJ_EXCLUSIVE	OB_FLAG_EXCLUSIVE_OBJECT	Specifies that the object can be used only by the process that created it.
OBJ_CASE_INSENSITIVE	Stored in the handle table entry	Specifies that lookups for this object in the namespace should be case insensitive. It can be overridden by the *case insensitive* flag in the object type.
OBJ_OPENIF	Not stored, used at run time	Specifies that a create operation for this object name should result in an open, if the object exists, instead of a failure.
OBJ_OPENLINK	Not stored, used at run time	Specifies that the object manager should open a handle to the symbolic link, not the target.
OBJ_KERNEL_HANDLE	OB_FLAG_KERNEL_OBJECT	Specifies that the handle to this object should be a *kernel handle* (more on this later).
OBJ_FORCE_ACCESS_CHECK	Not stored, used at run time	Specifies that even if the object is being opened from kernel mode, full access checks should be performed.
OBJ_KERNEL_EXCLUSIVE	OB_FLAG_KERNEL_ONLY_ACCESS	Disables any user-mode process from opening a handle to the object; used to protect the */Device/PhysicalMemory* section object.
N/A	OF_FLAG_DEFAULT_SECURITY_QUOTA	Specifies that the object's security descriptor is using the default 2-KB quota.
N/A	OB_FLAG_SINGLE_HANDLE_ENTRY	Specifies that the handle information subheader contains only a single entry and not a database.
N/A	OB_FLAG_NEW_OBJECT	Specifies that the object has been created but not yet inserted into the object namespace.
N/A	OB_FLAG_DELETED_INLINE	Specifies that the object is being deleted through the *deferred deletion worker thread*.

In addition to an object header, each object has an object body whose format and contents are unique to its object type; all objects of the same type share the same object body format. By creating an object type and supplying services for it, an executive component can control the manipulation of data in all object bodies of that type. Because the object header has a static and well-known size, the object manager can easily look up the object header for an object simply by subtracting the size of the header from the pointer of the object. As explained earlier, to access the subheaders, the object manager subtracts yet another well-known value from the pointer of the object header.

Because of the standardized object header and subheader structures, the object manager is able to provide a small set of generic services that can operate on the attributes stored in any object header and can be used on objects of any type (although some generic services don't make sense for certain objects). These generic services, some of which the Windows subsystem makes available to Windows applications, are listed in Table 3-13.

Although these generic object services are supported for all object types, each object has its own create, open, and query services. For example, the I/O system implements a create file service for its file objects, and the process manager implements a create process service for its process objects.

Although a single create object service could have been implemented, such a routine would have been quite complicated, because the set of parameters required to initialize a file object, for example, differs markedly from that required to initialize a process object. Also, the object manager would have incurred additional processing overhead each time a thread called an object service to determine the type of object the handle referred to and to call the appropriate version of the service.

TABLE 3-13 Generic Object Services

Service	Purpose
Close	Closes a handle to an object
Duplicate	Shares an object by duplicating a handle and giving it to another process
Make permanent/temporary	Changes the retention of an object (described later)
Query object	Gets information about an object's standard attributes
Query security	Gets an object's security descriptor
Set security	Changes the protection on an object
Wait for a single object	Synchronizes a thread's execution with one object
Signal an object and wait for another	Signals an object (such as an event), and synchronizes a thread's execution with another
Wait for multiple objects	Synchronizes a thread's execution with multiple objects

Type Objects

Object headers contain data that is common to all objects but that can take on different values for each instance of an object. For example, each object has a unique name and can have a unique security descriptor. However, objects also contain some data that remains constant for all objects of a particular type. For example, you can select from a set of access rights specific to a type of object when you open a handle to objects of that type. The executive supplies terminate and suspend access (among others) for thread objects and read, write, append, and delete access (among others) for file objects. Another example of an object-type-specific attribute is synchronization, which is described shortly.

To conserve memory, the object manager stores these static, object-type-specific attributes once when creating a new object type. It uses an object of its own, a type object, to record this data. As Figure 3-20 illustrates, if the object-tracking debug flag (described in the "Windows Global Flags" section later in this chapter) is set, a type object also links together all objects of the same type (in this case, the process type), allowing the object manager to find and enumerate them, if necessary. This functionality takes advantage of the creator information subheader discussed previously.

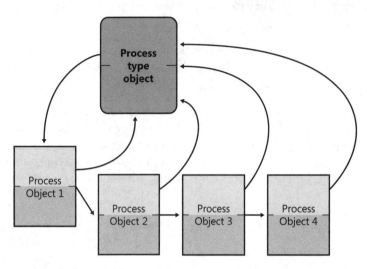

FIGURE 3-20 Process objects and the process type object

EXPERIMENT: Viewing Object Headers and Type Objects

You can look at the process object type data structure in the kernel debugger by first identifying a process object with the *!process* command:

```
lkd> !process 0 0
**** NT ACTIVE PROCESS DUMP ****
PROCESS fffffa800279cae0
    SessionId: none  Cid: 0004    Peb: 00000000  ParentCid: 0000
    DirBase: 00187000  ObjectTable: fffff8a000001920  HandleCount: 541.
    Image: System
```

Then execute the *!object* command with the process object address as the argument:

```
lkd> !object fffffa800279cae0
Object: fffffa800279cae0  Type: (fffffa8002755b60) Process
    ObjectHeader: fffffa800279cab0 (new version)
    HandleCount: 3  PointerCount: 172 3172
```

Notice that on 32-bit Windows, the object header starts 0x18 (24 decimal) bytes prior to the start of the object body, and on 64-bit Windows, it starts 0x30 (48 decimal) bytes prior—the size of the object header itself. You can view the object header with this command:

```
lkd> dt nt!_OBJECT_HEADER fffffa800279cab0
   +0x000 PointerCount    : 172
   +0x008 HandleCount     : 33
   +0x008 NextToFree      : 0x000000000x00000000'00000003
   +0x010 Lock            : _EX_PUSH_LOCK
```

```
+0x018 TypeIndex          : 0x7 ''
+0x019 TraceFlags         : 0 ''
+0x01a InfoMask           : 0 ''
+0x01b Flags              : 0x2 ''
+0x020 ObjectCreateInfo   : 0xffff800'01c53a80 _OBJECT_CREATE_INFORMATION
+0x020 QuotaBlockCharged  : 0xffff800'01c53a80
+0x028 SecurityDescriptor : 0xffff8a0'00004b29
+0x030 Body               : _QUAD
```

Now look at the object type data structure by obtaining its address from the *ObTypeIndexTable* table for the entry associated with the *TypeIndex* field of the object header data structure:

```
lkd> ?? ((nt!_OBJECT_TYPE**)@@(nt!ObTypeIndexTable))[((nt!_OBJECT_
HEADER*)0xffffa800279cab0)->TypeIndex]
struct _OBJECT_TYPE * 0xffffa80'02755b60
   +0x000 TypeList         : _LIST_ENTRY [ 0xffffa80'02755b60 - 0xffffa80'02755b60 ]
   +0x010 Name             : _UNICODE_STRING "Process"
   +0x020 DefaultObject    : (null)
   +0x028 Index            : 0x70x7 ''
   +0x02c TotalNumberOfObjects : 0x380x38
   +0x030 TotalNumberOfHandles : 0x1320x132
   +0x034 HighWaterNumberOfObjects : 0x3d
   +0x038 HighWaterNumberOfHandles : 0x13c
   +0x040 TypeInfo         : _OBJECT_TYPE_INITIALIZER
   +0x0b0 TypeLock         : _EX_PUSH_LOCK
   +0x0b8 Key              : 0x636f7250
   +0x0c0 CallbackList     : _LIST_ENTRY [ 0xffffa80'02755c20 - 0xffffa80'02755c20 ]
```

The output shows that the object type structure includes the name of the object type, tracks the total number of active objects of that type, and tracks the peak number of handles and objects of that type. The *CallbackList* also keeps track of any object manager filtering callbacks that are associated with this object type. The *TypeInfo* field stores the pointer to the data structure that stores attributes common to all objects of the object type as well as pointers to the object type's methods:

```
lkd> ?? ((nt!_OBJECT_TYPE*)0xffffa8002755b60)->TypeInfo*)
   +0x000 Length           : 0x70
   +0x002 ObjectTypeFlags  : 0x4a 'J'
   +0x002 CaseInsensitive  : 0y0
   +0x002 UnnamedObjectsOnly : 0y1
   +0x002 UseDefaultObject : 0y0
   +0x002 SecurityRequired : 0y1
   +0x002 MaintainHandleCount : 0y0
   +0x002 MaintainTypeList : 0y0
   +0x002 SupportsObjectCallbacks : 0y1
   +0x004 ObjectTypeCode   : 0
   +0x008 InvalidAttributes : 0xb0
   +0x00c GenericMapping   : _GENERIC_MAPPING
   +0x01c ValidAccessMask  : 0x1fffff
   +0x020 RetainAccess     : 0x101000
   +0x024 PoolType         : 0 ( NonPagedPool )
   +0x028 DefaultPagedPoolCharge : 0x1000
```

```
+0x02c DefaultNonPagedPoolCharge : 0x528
+0x030 DumpProcedure     : (null)
+0x038 OpenProcedure     : 0xfffff800'01d98d58   long  nt!PspProcessOpen+0
+0x040 CloseProcedure    : 0xfffff800'01d833c4   void  nt!PspProcessClose+0
+0x048 DeleteProcedure   : 0xfffff800'01d83090   void  nt!PspProcessDelete+0
+0x050 ParseProcedure    : (null)
+0x058 SecurityProcedure : 0xfffff800'01d8bb50   long  nt!SeDefaultObjectMethod+0
+0x060 QueryNameProcedure : (null)
+0x068 OkayToCloseProcedure : (null)
```

Type objects can't be manipulated from user mode because the object manager supplies no services for them. However, some of the attributes they define are visible through certain native services and through Windows API routines. The information stored in the type initializers is described in Table 3-14.

TABLE 3-14 Type Initializer Fields

Attribute	Purpose
Type name	The name for objects of this type ("process," "event," "port," and so on).
Pool type	Indicates whether objects of this type should be allocated from paged or nonpaged memory.
Default quota charges	Default paged and nonpaged pool values to charge to process quotas.
Valid access mask	The types of access a thread can request when opening a handle to an object of this type ("read," "write," "terminate," "suspend," and so on).
Generic access rights mapping	A mapping between the four generic access rights (read, write, execute, and all) to the type-specific access rights.
Flags	Indicate whether objects must never have names (such as process objects), whether their names are case-sensitive, whether they require a security descriptor, whether they support object-filtering callbacks, and whether a handle database (handle information subheader) and/or a type-list linkage (creator information subheader) should be maintained. The *use default object* flag also defines the behavior for the *default object* field shown later in this table.
Object type code	Used to describe the type of object this is (versus comparing with a well-known name value). File objects set this to *1*, synchronization objects set this to *2*, and thread objects set this to *4*. This field is also used by ALPC to store handle attribute information associated with a message.
Invalid attributes	Specifies object attribute flags (shown earlier in Table 3-12) that are invalid for this object type.
Default object	Specifies the internal object manager event that should be used during waits for this object, if the object type creator requested one. Note that certain objects, such as File objects and ALPC port objects already contain their own embedded dispatcher object; in this case, this field is an offset into the object body. For example, the event inside the FILE_OBJECT structure is embedded in a field called *Event*.
Methods	One or more routines that the object manager calls automatically at certain points in an object's lifetime.

Synchronization, one of the attributes visible to Windows applications, refers to a thread's ability to synchronize its execution by waiting for an object to change from one state to another. A thread can synchronize with executive job, process, thread, file, event, semaphore, mutex, and timer objects. Other executive objects don't support synchronization. An object's ability to support synchronization is based on three possibilities:

- The executive object is a wrapper for a dispatcher object and contains a dispatcher header, a kernel structure that is covered in the section "Low-IRQL Synchronization" later in this chapter.

- The creator of the object type requested a *default object*, and the object manager provided one.

- The executive object has an embedded dispatcher object, such as an event somewhere inside the object body, and the object's owner supplied its offset to the object manager when registering the object type (described in Table 3-14).

Object Methods

The last attribute in Table 3-14, methods, comprises a set of internal routines that are similar to C++ constructors and destructors—that is, routines that are automatically called when an object is created or destroyed. The object manager extends this idea by calling an object method in other situations as well, such as when someone opens or closes a handle to an object or when someone attempts to change the protection on an object. Some object types specify methods whereas others don't, depending on how the object type is to be used.

When an executive component creates a new object type, it can register one or more methods with the object manager. Thereafter, the object manager calls the methods at well-defined points in the lifetime of objects of that type, usually when an object is created, deleted, or modified in some way. The methods that the object manager supports are listed in Table 3-15.

The reason for these object methods is to address the fact that, as you've seen, certain object operations are generic (close, duplicate, security, and so on). Fully generalizing these generic routines would have required the designers of the object manager to anticipate all object types. However, the routines to create an object type are exported by the kernel, enabling external kernel components to create their own object types. Although this functionality is not documented for driver developers, it is internally used by Win32k.sys to define WindowStation and Desktop objects. Through object-method extensibility, Win32k.sys defines its routines for handling operations such as create and query.

One exception to this rule is the *security* routine, which does, unless otherwise instructed, default to *SeDefaultObjectMethod*. This routine does not need to know the internal structure of the object because it deals only with the security descriptor for the object, and you've seen that the pointer to the security descriptor is stored in the generic object header, not inside the object body. However, if an object does require its own additional security checks, it can define a custom security routine. The other reason for having a generic security method is to avoid complexity, because most objects rely on the security reference monitor to manage their security.

TABLE 3-15 Object Methods

Method	When Method Is Called
Open	When an object handle is opened
Close	When an object handle is closed
Delete	Before the object manager deletes an object
Query name	When a thread requests the name of an object, such as a file, that exists in a secondary object namespace
Parse	When the object manager is searching for an object name that exists in a secondary object namespace
Dump	Not used
Okay to close	When the object manager is instructed to close a handle
Security	When a process reads or changes the protection of an object, such as a file, that exists in a secondary object namespace

The object manager calls the open method whenever it creates a handle to an object, which it does when an object is created or opened. The WindowStation and Desktop objects provide an open method; for example, the WindowStation object type requires an open method so that Win32k.sys can share a piece of memory with the process that serves as a desktop-related memory pool.

An example of the use of a close method occurs in the I/O system. The I/O manager registers a close method for the file object type, and the object manager calls the close method each time it closes a file object handle. This close method checks whether the process that is closing the file handle owns any outstanding locks on the file and, if so, removes them. Checking for file locks isn't something the object manager itself can or should do.

The object manager calls a delete method, if one is registered, before it deletes a temporary object from memory. The memory manager, for example, registers a delete method for the section object type that frees the physical pages being used by the section. It also verifies that any internal data structures the memory manager has allocated for a section are deleted before the section object is deleted. Once again, the object manager can't do this work because it knows nothing about the internal workings of the memory manager. Delete methods for other types of objects perform similar functions.

The parse method (and similarly, the query name method) allows the object manager to relinquish control of finding an object to a secondary object manager if it finds an object that exists outside the object manager namespace. When the object manager looks up an object name, it suspends its search when it encounters an object in the path that has an associated parse method. The object manager calls the parse method, passing to it the remainder of the object name it is looking for. There are two namespaces in Windows in addition to the object manager's: the registry namespace, which the configuration manager implements, and the file system namespace, which the I/O manager implements with the aid of file system drivers. (See Chapter 4, "Management Mechanisms," for more information on the configuration manager and Chapter 8 in Part 2 for more details about the I/O manager and file system drivers.)

For example, when a process opens a handle to the object named \Device\HarddiskVolume1\docs\resume.doc, the object manager traverses its name tree until it reaches the device object named *HarddiskVolume1*. It sees that a parse method is associated with this object, and it calls the method, passing to it the rest of the object name it was searching for—in this case, the string *docs\resume.doc*. The parse method for device objects is an I/O routine because the I/O manager defines the device object type and registers a parse method for it. The I/O manager's parse routine takes the name string and passes it to the appropriate file system, which finds the file on the disk and opens it.

The security method, which the I/O system also uses, is similar to the parse method. It is called whenever a thread tries to query or change the security information protecting a file. This information is different for files than for other objects because security information is stored in the file itself rather than in memory. The I/O system, therefore, must be called to find the security information and read or change it.

Finally, the okay-to-close method is used as an additional layer of protection around the malicious—or incorrect—closing of handles being used for system purposes. For example, each process has a handle to the Desktop object or objects on which its thread or threads have windows visible. Under the standard security model, it is possible for those threads to close their handles to their desktops because the process has full control of its own objects. In this scenario, the threads end up without a desktop associated with them—a violation of the windowing model. Win32k.sys registers an okay-to-close routine for the Desktop and WindowStation objects to prevent this behavior.

Object Handles and the Process Handle Table

When a process creates or opens an object by name, it receives a *handle* that represents its access to the object. Referring to an object by its handle is faster than using its name because the object manager can skip the name lookup and find the object directly. Processes can also acquire handles to objects by inheriting handles at process creation time (if the creator specifies the inherit handle flag on the *CreateProcess* call and the handle was marked as inheritable, either at the time it was created or afterward by using the Windows *SetHandleInformation* function) or by receiving a duplicated handle from another process. (See the Windows *DuplicateHandle* function.)

All user-mode processes must own a handle to an object before their threads can use the object. Using handles to manipulate system resources isn't a new idea. C and Pascal (an older programming language similar to Delphi) run-time libraries, for example, return handles to opened files. Handles serve as indirect pointers to system resources; this indirection keeps application programs from fiddling directly with system data structures.

Object handles provide additional benefits. First, except for what they refer to, there is no difference between a file handle, an event handle, and a process handle. This similarity provides a consistent interface to reference objects, regardless of their type. Second, the object manager has the exclusive right to create handles and to locate an object that a handle refers to. This means that the object manager can scrutinize every user-mode action that affects an object to see whether the security profile of the caller allows the operation requested on the object in question.

Note Executive components and device drivers can access objects directly because they are running in kernel mode and therefore have access to the object structures in system memory. However, they must declare their usage of the object by incrementing the reference count so that the object won't be de-allocated while it's still being used. (See the section "Object Retention" later in this chapter for more details.) To successfully make use of this object, however, device drivers need to know the internal structure definition of the object, and this is not provided for most objects. Instead, device drivers are encouraged to use the appropriate kernel APIs to modify or read information from the object. For example, although device drivers can get a pointer to the Process object (EPROCESS), the structure is opaque, and *Ps** APIs must be used. For other objects, the type itself is opaque (such as most executive objects that wrap a dispatcher object—for example, events or mutexes). For these objects, drivers must use the same system calls that user-mode applications end up calling (such as *ZwCreateEvent)* and use handles instead of object pointers.

EXPERIMENT: Viewing Open Handles

Run Process Explorer, and make sure the lower pane is enabled and configured to show open handles. (Click on View, Lower Pane View, and then Handles). Then open a command prompt and view the handle table for the new Cmd.exe process. You should see an open file handle to the current directory. For example, assuming the current directory is C:\Users\Administrator, Process Explorer shows the following:

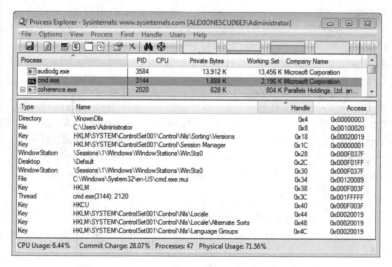

Now pause Process Explorer by pressing the space bar or clicking on View, Update Speed and choosing Pause. Then change the current directory with the *cd* command and press F5 to refresh the display. You will see in Process Explorer that the handle to the previous current directory is closed and a new handle is opened to the new current directory. The previous handle is highlighted in red and the new handle is highlighted in green.

Process Explorer's differences-highlighting feature makes it easy to see changes in the handle table. For example, if a process is leaking handles, viewing the handle table with Process Explorer can quickly show what handle or handles are being opened but not closed. (Typically, you see a long list of handles to the same object.) This information can help the programmer find the handle leak.

Resource Monitor also shows open handles to named handles for the processes you select by checking the boxes next to their names. Here are the command prompt's open handles:

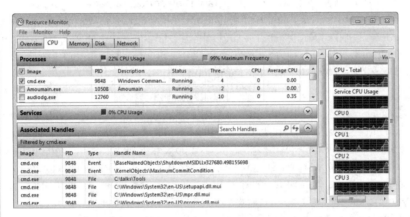

You can also display the open handle table by using the command-line Handle tool from Sysinternals. For example, note the following partial output of Handle when examining the file object handles located in the handle table for a Cmd.exe process before and after changing the directory. By default, Handle filters out nonfile handles unless the –a switch is used, which displays all the handles in the process, similar to Process Explorer.

```
C:\>handle -p cmd.exe

Handle v3.46
Copyright (C) 1997-2011 Mark Russinovich
Sysinternals - www.sysinternals.com

------------------------------------------------------------------------
cmd.exe pid: 5124 Alex-Laptop\Alex Ionescu
   3C: File  (R-D)   C:\Windows\System32\en-US\KernelBase.dll.mui
   44: File  (RW-)   C:\

C:\>cd windows

C:\Windows>handle -p cmd.exe

Handle v3.46
Copyright (C) 1997-2011 Mark Russinovich
Sysinternals - www.sysinternals.com

------------------------------------------------------------------------
cmd.exe pid: 5124 Alex-Laptop\Alex Ionescu
   3C: File  (R-D)   C:\Windows\System32\en-US\KernelBase.dll.mui
   40: File  (RW-)   C:\Windows
```

An *object handle* is an index into a process-specific *handle table*, pointed to by the executive process (EPROCESS) block (described in Chapter 5). The first handle index is 4, the second 8, and so on. A process' handle table contains pointers to all the objects that the process has opened a handle to. Handle tables are implemented as a three-level scheme, similar to the way that the x86 memory management unit implements virtual-to-physical address translation, giving a maximum of more than 16,000,000 handles per process. (See Chapter 10 in Part 2 for details about memory management in x86 systems.)

> **Note** With a three-table scheme, the top-level table can contain a page full of pointers to mid-level tables, allowing for well over half a billion handles. However, to maintain compatibility with Windows 2000's handle scheme and inherent limitation of 16,777,216 handles, the top-level table only contains up to a maximum of 32 pointers to the mid-level tables, capping newer versions of Windows at the same limit.

Only the lowest-level handle table is allocated on process creation—the other levels are created as needed. The subhandle table consists of as many entries as will fit in a page minus one entry that is used for handle auditing. For example, for x86 systems a page is 4096 bytes, divided by the size of a handle table entry (8 bytes), which is 512, minus 1, which is a total of 511 entries in the lowest-level handle table. The mid-level handle table contains a full page of pointers to subhandle tables, so the number of subhandle tables depends on the size of the page and the size of a pointer for the platform. Figure 3-21 describes the handle table layout on Windows.

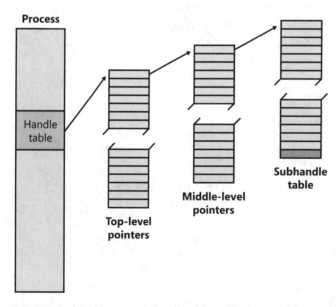

FIGURE 3-21 Windows process handle table architecture

EXPERIMENT: Creating the Maximum Number of Handles

The test program Testlimit from Sysinternals has an option to open handles to an object until it cannot open any more handles. You can use this to see how many handles can be created in a single process on your system. Because handle tables are allocated from paged pool, you might run out of paged pool before you hit the maximum number of handles that can be created in a single process. To see how many handles you can create on your system, follow these steps:

1. Download the Testlimit executable file corresponding to the 32/64 bit Windows you need from *http://live.sysinternals.com/WindowsInternals*.

2. Run Process Explorer, click View and then System Information, and then click on the Memory tab. Notice the current and maximum size of paged pool. (To display the maximum pool size values, Process Explorer must be configured properly to access the symbols for the kernel image, Ntoskrnl.exe.) Leave this system information display running so that you can see pool utilization when you run the Testlimit program.

3. Open a command prompt.

4. Run the Testlimit program with the *–h* switch (do this by typing **testlimit –h**). When Testlimit fails to open a new handle, it displays the total number of handles it was able to create. If the number is less than approximately 16 million, you are probably running out of paged pool before hitting the theoretical per-process handle limit.

5. Close the Command Prompt window; doing this kills the Testlimit process, thus closing all the open handles.

As shown in Figure 3-22, on x86 systems, each handle entry consists of a structure with two 32-bit members: a pointer to the object (with flags), and the granted access mask. On 64-bit systems, a handle table entry is 12 bytes long: a 64-bit pointer to the object header and a 32-bit access mask. (Access masks are described in Chapter 6, "Security.")

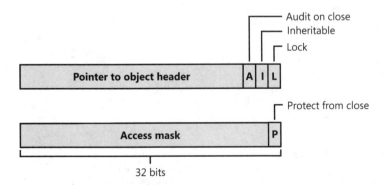

FIGURE 3-22 Structure of a handle table entry

The first flag is a lock bit, indicating whether the entry is currently in use. The second flag is the inheritance designation—that is, it indicates whether processes created by this process will get a copy of this handle in their handle tables. As already noted, handle inheritance can be specified on handle creation or later with the *SetHandleInformation* function. The third flag indicates whether closing the object should generate an audit message. (This flag isn't exposed to Windows—the object manager uses it internally.) Finally, the protect-from-close bit, stored in an unused portion of the access mask, indicates whether the caller is allowed to close this handle. (This flag can be set with the *NtSetInformationObject* system call.)

System components and device drivers often need to open handles to objects that user-mode applications shouldn't have access to. This is done by creating handles in the *kernel handle table* (referenced internally with the name *ObpKernelHandleTable*). The handles in this table are accessible only from kernel mode and in any process context. This means that a kernel-mode function can reference the handle in any process context with no performance impact. The object manager recognizes references to handles from the kernel handle table when the high bit of the handle is set—that is, when references to kernel-handle-table handles have values greater than 0x80000000. The kernel handle table also serves as the handle table for the System process, and all handles created by the System process (such as code running in system threads) are automatically marked as kernel handles because they live in the kernel handle table by definition.

EXPERIMENT: Viewing the Handle Table with the Kernel Debugger

The *!handle* command in the kernel debugger takes three arguments:

```
!handle <handle index> <flags> <processid>
```

The handle index identifies the handle entry in the handle table. (Zero means "display all handles.") The first handle is index 4, the second 8, and so on. For example, typing **!handle 4** will show the first handle for the current process.

The flags you can specify are a bitmask, where bit 0 means "display only the information in the handle entry," bit 1 means "display free handles (not just used handles)," and bit 2 means "display information about the object that the handle refers to." The following command displays full details about the handle table for process ID 0x62C:

```
lkd> !handle 0 7 62c
processor number 0, process 000000000000062c
Searching for Process with Cid == 62c
PROCESS fffffa80052a7060
    SessionId: 1  Cid: 062c    Peb: 7fffffdb000  ParentCid: 0558
    DirBase: 7e401000  ObjectTable: fffff8a00381fc80  HandleCount: 111.
    Image: windbg.exe

Handle table at fffff8a0038fa000 with 113 Entries in use
0000: free handle, Entry address fffff8a0038fa000, Next Entry 00000000ffffffffe
0004: Object: fffff8a005022b70  GrantedAccess: 00000003 Entry: fffff8a0038fa010
Object: fffff8a005022b70  Type: (fffffa8002778f30) Directory
    ObjectHeader: fffff8a005022b40fffff8a005022b40 (new version)
        HandleCount: 25  PointerCount: 63
```

```
         Directory Object: fffff8a000004980  Name: KnownDlls

0008: Object: ffffa8005226070  GrantedAccess: 00100020 Entry: fffff8a0038fa020
Object: ffffa8005226070  Type: (ffffa80027b3080) File
    ObjectHeader: ffffa8005226040ffffa8005226040 (new version)
        HandleCount: 1 PointerCount: 1
        Directory Object: 00000000  Name: \Program Files\Debugging Tools for Windows (x64)
{HarddiskVolume2}
```

EXPERIMENT: Searching for Open Files with the Kernel Debugger

Although you can use Process Explorer, Handle, and the OpenFiles.exe utility to search for open file handles, these tools are not available when looking at a crash dump or analyzing a system remotely. You can instead use the *!devhandles* command to search for handles opened to files on a specific volume. (See Chapter 8 in Part 2 for more information on devices, files, and volumes.)

1. First you need to pick the drive letter you are interested in and obtain the pointer to its *Device object*. You can use the *!object* command as shown here:

   ```
   1: kd> !object \Global??\C:
   Object: fffff8a00016ea40  Type: (ffffa8000c38bb0) SymbolicLink
       ObjectHeader: fffff8a00016ea10 (new version)
       HandleCount: 0  PointerCount: 1
       Directory Object: fffff8a000008060  Name: C
       Target String is '\Device\HarddiskVolume1'
       Drive Letter Index is 3 (C:)
   ```

2. Next use the *!object* command to get the *Device* object of the target volume name:

   ```
   1: kd> !object \Device\HarddiskVolume1
   Object: ffffa8001bd3cd0  Type: (ffffa8000ca0750) Device
   ```

3. Now you can use the pointer of the *Device* object with the *!devhandles* command. Each object shown points to a file:

   ```
   !devhandles ffffa8001bd3cd0
   Checking handle table for process 0xffffa8000c819e0
   Kernel handle table at fffff8a000001830 with 434 entries in use

   PROCESS ffffa8000c819e0
       SessionId: none  Cid: 0004     Peb: 00000000   ParentCid: 0000
       DirBase: 00187000  ObjectTable: fffff8a000001830  HandleCount: 434.
       Image: System

   0048: Object: ffffa8001d4f2a0  GrantedAccess: 0013008b Entry: fffff8a000003120
   Object: ffffa8001d4f2a0  Type: (ffffa8000ca0360) File
       ObjectHeader: ffffa8001d4f270 (new version)
           HandleCount: 1 PointerCount: 19
           Directory Object: 00000000  Name: \Windows\System32\LogFiles\WMI\
   RtBackup\EtwRTEventLog-Application.etl {HarddiskVolume1}
   ```

Reserve Objects

Because objects represent anything from events to files to interprocess messages, the ability for applications and kernel code to create objects is essential to the normal and desired runtime behavior of any piece of Windows code. If an object allocation fails, this usually causes anywhere from loss of functionality (the process cannot open a file) to data loss or crashes (the process cannot allocate a synchronization object). Worse, in certain situations, the reporting of errors that led to object creation failure might themselves require new objects to be allocated. Windows implements two special *reserve objects* to deal with such situations: the User APC reserve object and the I/O Completion packet reserve object. Note that the reserve-object mechanism itself is fully extensible, and future versions of Windows might add other reserve object types—from a broad view, the reserve object is a mechanism enabling any kernel-mode data structure to be wrapped as an object (with an associated handle, name, and security) for later use.

As was discussed in the APC section earlier in this chapter, APCs are used for operations such as suspension, termination, and I/O completion, as well as communication between user-mode applications that want to provide asynchronous callbacks. When a user-mode application requests a User APC to be targeted to another thread, it uses the *QueueUserApc* API in Kernelbase.dll, which calls the *NtQueueUserApcThread* system call. In the kernel, this system call attempts to allocate a piece of paged pool in which to store the *KAPC* control object structure associated with an APC. In low-memory situations, this operation fails, preventing the delivery of the APC, which, depending on what the APC was used for, could cause loss of data or functionality.

To prevent this, the user-mode application, can, on startup, use the *NtAllocateReserveObject* system call to request the kernel to pre-allocate the KAPC structure. Then the application uses a different system call, *NtQueueUserApcThreadEx*, that contains an extra parameter that is used to store the handle to the reserve object. Instead of allocating a new structure, the kernel attempts to acquire the reserve object (by setting its *InUse* bit to *true*) and use it until the KAPC object is not needed anymore, at which point the reserve object is released back to the system. Currently, to prevent mismanagement of system resources by third-party developers, the reserve object API is available only internally through system calls for operating system components. For example, the RPC library uses reserved APC objects to guarantee asynchronous callbacks will still be able to return in low-memory situations.

A similar scenario can occur when applications need failure-free delivery of an I/O completion port message, or packet. Typically, packets are sent with the *PostQueuedCompletionStatus* API in Kernelbase.dll, which calls the *NtSetIoCompletion* API. Similarly to the user APC, the kernel must allocate an I/O manager structure to contain the completion-packet information, and if this allocation fails, the packet cannot be created. With reserve objects, the application can use the *NtAllocateReserveObject* API on startup to have the kernel pre-allocate the I/O completion packet, and the *NtSetIoCompletionEx* system call can be used to supply a handle to this reserve object, guaranteeing a success path. Just like User APC reserve objects, this functionality is reserved for system components and is used both by the RPC library and the Windows Peer-To-Peer BranchCache service (see Chapter 7, "Networking," for more information on networking) to guarantee completion of asynchronous I/O operations.

Object Security

When you open a file, you must specify whether you intend to read or to write. If you try to write to a file that is opened for read access, you get an error. Likewise, in the executive, when a process creates an object or opens a handle to an existing object, the process must specify a set of *desired access rights*—that is, what it wants to do with the object. It can request either a set of standard access rights (such as read, write, and execute) that apply to all object types or specific access rights that vary depending on the object type. For example, the process can request delete access or append access to a file object. Similarly, it might require the ability to suspend or terminate a thread object.

When a process opens a handle to an object, the object manager calls the *security reference monitor*, the kernel-mode portion of the security system, sending it the process' set of desired access rights. The security reference monitor checks whether the object's security descriptor permits the type of access the process is requesting. If it does, the reference monitor returns a set of *granted access rights* that the process is allowed, and the object manager stores them in the object handle it creates. How the security system determines who gets access to which objects is explored in Chapter 6.

Thereafter, whenever the process' threads use the handle through a service call, the object manager can quickly check whether the set of granted access rights stored in the handle corresponds to the usage implied by the object service the threads have called. For example, if the caller asked for read access to a section object but then calls a service to write to it, the service fails.

EXPERIMENT: Looking at Object Security

You can look at the various permissions on an object by using either Process Explorer, WinObj, or AccessCheck, which are all tools from Sysinternals. Let's look at different ways you can display the access control list (ACL) for an object:

■ You can use WinObj to navigate to any object on the system, including object directories, right-click on the object, and select Properties. For example, select the BaseNamedObjects directory, select Properties, and click on the Security tab. You should see a dialog box similar to the one shown next.

By examining the settings in the dialog box, you can see that the Everyone group doesn't have *delete* access to the directory, for example, but the SYSTEM account does (because this is where session 0 services with SYSTEM privileges will store their objects).

- Instead of using WinObj, you can view the handle table of a process using Process Explorer, as shown in the experiment "Viewing Open Handles" earlier in the chapter. Look at the handle table for the Explorer.exe process. You should notice a Directory object handle to the \Sessions\n\BaseNamedObjects directory. (We'll describe the per-session namespace shortly.) You can double-click on the object handle and then click on the Security tab and see a similar dialog box (with more users and rights granted). Process Explorer cannot decode the specific object directory access rights, so all you'll see are generic rights.

- Finally, you can use AccessCheck to query the security information of any object by using the –o switch as shown in the following output. Note that using AccessCheck will also show you the *integrity level* of the object. (See Chapter 6 for more information on integrity levels and the security reference monitor.)

```
C:\Windows>accesschk -o \Sessions\1\BaseNamedObjects

Accesschk v5.02 - Reports effective permissions for securable objects
Copyright (C) 2006-2011 Mark Russinovich
Sysinternals - www.sysinternals.com

\sessions\2\BaseNamedObjects
  Type: Directory
  RW NT AUTHORITY\SYSTEM
  RW NTDEV\markruss
  RW NTDEV\S-1-5-5-0-5491067-markruss
  RW BUILTIN\Administrators
  R  Everyone
     NT AUTHORITY\RESTRICTED
```

Windows also supports *Ex* (Extended) versions of the APIs—*CreateEventEx, CreateMutexEx, CreateSemaphoreEx*—that add another argument for specifying the access mask. This makes it possible for applications to properly use discretionary access control lists (DACLs) to secure their objects without breaking their ability to use the create object APIs to open a handle to them. You might be wondering why a client application would not simply use *OpenEvent*, which does support a desired access argument. Using the open object APIs leads to an inherent race condition when dealing with a failure in the open call—that is, when the client application has attempted to open the event before it has been created. In most applications of this kind, the open API is followed by a create API in the failure case. Unfortunately, there is no guaranteed way to make this create operation *atomic*—in other words, to occur only once. Indeed, it would be possible for multiple threads and/or processes to have executed the create API concurrently and all attempt to create the event at the same time. This race condition and the extra complexity required to try and handle it makes using the open object APIs an inappropriate solution to the problem, which is why the *Ex* APIs should be used instead.

Object Retention

There are two types of objects: temporary and permanent. Most objects are temporary—that is, they remain while they are in use and are freed when they are no longer needed. Permanent objects remain until they are explicitly freed. Because most objects are temporary, the rest of this section describes how the object manager implements *object retention*—that is, retaining temporary objects only as long as they are in use and then deleting them. Because all user-mode processes that access an object must first open a handle to it, the object manager can easily track how many of these processes, and even which ones, are using an object. Tracking these handles represents one part of implementing retention. The object manager implements object retention in two phases. The first phase is called *name retention*, and it is controlled by the number of open handles to an object that exist. Every time a process opens a handle to an object, the object manager increments the open handle counter in the object's header. As processes finish using the object and close their handles to it, the object manager decrements the open handle counter. When the counter drops to 0, the object manager deletes the object's name from its global namespace. This deletion prevents processes from opening a handle to the object.

The second phase of object retention is to stop retaining the objects themselves (that is, to delete them) when they are no longer in use. Because operating system code usually accesses objects by using pointers instead of handles, the object manager must also record how many object pointers it has dispensed to operating system processes. It increments a *reference count* for an object each time it gives out a pointer to the object; when kernel-mode components finish using the pointer, they call the object manager to decrement the object's reference count. The system also increments the reference count when it increments the handle count, and likewise decrements the reference count when the handle count decrements, because a handle is also a reference to the object that must be tracked.

Figure 3-23 illustrates two event objects that are in use. Process A has the first event open. Process B has both events open. In addition, the first event is being referenced by some kernel-mode structure; thus, the reference count is 3. So even if Processes A and B closed their handles to the first event object, it would continue to exist because its reference count is 1. However, when Process B closes its handle to the second event object, the object would be deallocated.

So even after an object's open handle counter reaches 0, the object's reference count might remain positive, indicating that the operating system is still using the object. Ultimately, when the reference count drops to 0, the object manager deletes the object from memory. This deletion has to respect certain rules and also requires cooperation from the caller in certain cases. For example, because objects can be present both in paged or nonpaged pool memory (depending on the settings located in their object type), if a dereference occurs at an IRQL level of dispatch or higher and this dereference causes the pointer count to drop to 0, the system would crash if it attempted to immediately free the memory of a paged-pool object. (Recall that such access is illegal because the page fault will never be serviced.) In this scenario, the object manager performs a *deferred delete* operation, queuing the operation on a worker thread running at passive level (IRQL 0). We'll describe more about system worker threads later in this chapter.

Another scenario that requires deferred deletion is when dealing with Kernel Transaction Manager (KTM) objects. In some scenarios, certain drivers might hold a lock related to this object, and attempting to delete the object will result in the system attempting to acquire this lock. However, the driver might never get the chance to release its lock, causing a deadlock. When dealing with KTM objects, driver developers must use *ObDereferenceObjectDeferDelete* to force deferred deletion regardless of IRQL level. Finally, the I/O manager also uses this mechanism as an optimization so that certain I/Os can complete more quickly, instead of waiting for the object manager to delete the object.

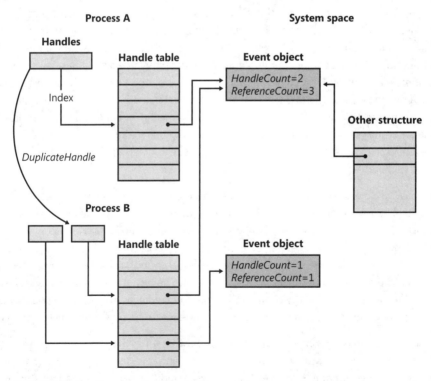

FIGURE 3-23 Handles and reference counts

Because of the way object retention works, an application can ensure that an object and its name remain in memory simply by keeping a handle open to the object. Programmers who write applications that contain two or more cooperating processes need not be concerned that one process might delete an object before the other process has finished using it. In addition, closing an application's object handles won't cause an object to be deleted if the operating system is still using it. For example, one process might create a second process to execute a program in the background; it then immediately closes its handle to the process. Because the operating system needs the second process to run the program, it maintains a reference to its process object. Only when the background program finishes executing does the object manager decrement the second process' reference count and then delete it.

Because object leaks can be dangerous to the system by leaking kernel pool memory and eventually causing systemwide memory starvation—and can also break applications in subtle ways—Windows includes a number of debugging mechanisms that can be enabled to monitor, analyze, and debug issues with handles and objects. Additionally, Debugging Tools for Windows come with two extensions that tap into these mechanisms and provide easy graphical analysis. Table 3-16 describes them.

TABLE 3-16 Debugging Mechanisms for Object Handles

Mechanism	Enabled By	Kernel Debugger Extension
Handle Tracing Database	Kernel Stack Trace systemwide and/or per-process with the User Stack Trace option checked with Gflags.exe.	*!htrace <handle value> <process ID>*
Object Reference Tracing	Per-process-name(s), or per-object-type-pool-tag(s), with Gflags.exe, under Object Reference Tracing.	*!obtrace <object pointer>*
Object Reference Tagging	Drivers must call appropriate API.	N/A

Enabling the handle-tracing database is useful when attempting to understand the use of each handle within an application or the system context. The *!htrace* debugger extension can display the stack trace captured at the time a specified handle was opened. After you discover a handle leak, the stack trace can pinpoint the code that is creating the handle, and it can be analyzed for a missing call to a function such as *CloseHandle*.

The object-reference-tracing *!obtrace* extension monitors even more by showing the stack trace for each new handle created as well as each time a handle is referenced by the kernel (and also each time it is opened, duplicated, or inherited) and dereferenced. By analyzing these patterns, misuse of an object at the system level can be more easily debugged. Additionally, these reference traces provide a way to understand the behavior of the system when dealing with certain objects. Tracing processes, for example, display references from all the drivers on the system that have registered callback notifications (such as Process Monitor) and help detect rogue or buggy third-party drivers that might be referencing handles in kernel mode but never dereferencing them.

> **Note** When enabling object-reference tracing for a specific object type, you can obtain the name of its pool tag by looking at the *key* member of the OBJECT_TYPE structure when using the *dt* command. Each object type on the system has a global variable that references this structure—for example, *PsProcessType*. Alternatively, you can use the *!object* command, which displays the pointer to this structure.

Unlike the previous two mechanisms, object-reference tagging is not a debugging feature that must be enabled with global flags or the debugger, but rather a set of APIs that should be used by device-driver developers to reference and dereference objects, including *ObReferenceObjectWithTag* and *ObDereferenceObjectWithTag*. Similar to pool tagging (see Chapter 10 in Part 2 for more information on pool tagging), these APIs allow developers to supply a four-character tag identifying each reference/dereference pair. When using the *!obtrace* extension just described, the tag for each reference or dereference operation is also shown, which avoids solely using the call stack as a mechanism to identify where leaks or under-references might occur, especially if a given call is performed thousands of times by the driver.

Resource Accounting

Resource accounting, like object retention, is closely related to the use of object handles. A positive open handle count indicates that some process is using that resource. It also indicates that some process is being charged for the memory the object occupies. When an object's handle count and reference count drop to 0, the process that was using the object should no longer be charged for it.

Many operating systems use a quota system to limit processes' access to system resources. However, the types of quotas imposed on processes are sometimes diverse and complicated, and the code to track the quotas is spread throughout the operating system. For example, in some operating systems, an I/O component might record and limit the number of files a process can open, whereas a memory component might impose a limit on the amount of memory a process' threads can allocate. A process component might limit users to some maximum number of new processes they can create or a maximum number of threads within a process. Each of these limits is tracked and enforced in different parts of the operating system.

In contrast, the Windows object manager provides a central facility for resource accounting. Each object header contains an attribute called *quota charges* that records how much the object manager subtracts from a process' allotted paged and/or nonpaged pool quota when a thread in the process opens a handle to the object.

Each process on Windows points to a quota structure that records the limits and current values for nonpaged-pool, paged-pool, and page-file usage. These quotas default to 0 (no limit) but can be specified by modifying registry values. (You need to add/edit *NonPagedPoolQuota*, *PagedPoolQuota*, and *PagingFileQuota* under HKLM\SYSTEM\CurrentControlSet\Control\Session Manager\Memory Management.) Note that all the processes in an interactive session share the same quota block (and there's no documented way to create processes with their own quota blocks).

Object Names

An important consideration in creating a multitude of objects is the need to devise a successful system for keeping track of them. The object manager requires the following information to help you do so:

- A way to distinguish one object from another

- A method for finding and retrieving a particular object

The first requirement is served by allowing names to be assigned to objects. This is an extension of what most operating systems provide—the ability to name selected resources, files, pipes, or a block of shared memory, for example. The executive, in contrast, allows any resource represented by an object to have a name. The second requirement, finding and retrieving an object, is also satisfied by object names. If the object manager stores objects by name, it can find an object by looking up its name.

Object names also satisfy a third requirement, which is to allow processes to share objects. The executive's object namespace is a global one, visible to all processes in the system. One process can create an object and place its name in the global namespace, and a second process can open a handle to the object by specifying the object's name. If an object isn't meant to be shared in this way, its creator doesn't need to give it a name.

To increase efficiency, the object manager doesn't look up an object's name each time someone uses the object. Instead, it looks up a name under only two circumstances. The first is when a process creates a named object: the object manager looks up the name to verify that it doesn't already exist before storing the new name in the global namespace. The second is when a process opens a handle to a named object: the object manager looks up the name, finds the object, and then returns an object handle to the caller; thereafter, the caller uses the handle to refer to the object. When looking up a name, the object manager allows the caller to select either a case-sensitive or case-insensitive search, a feature that supports Subsystem for UNIX Applications and other environments that use case-sensitive file names.

Object Directories

The object directory object is the object manager's means for supporting this hierarchical naming structure. This object is analogous to a file system directory and contains the names of other objects, possibly even other object directories. The object directory object maintains enough information to translate these object names into pointers to the objects themselves. The object manager uses the pointers to construct the object handles that it returns to user-mode callers. Both kernel-mode code (including executive components and device drivers) and user-mode code (such as subsystems) can create object directories in which to store objects. For example, the I/O manager creates an object directory named \Device, which contains the names of objects representing I/O devices.

Where the names of objects are stored depends on the object type. Table 3-17 lists the standard object directories found on all Windows systems and what types of objects have their names stored there. Of the directories listed, only \BaseNamedObjects and \Global?? are visible to standard Windows applications. (See the "Session Namespace" section later in this chapter for more information.)

TABLE 3-17 Standard Object Directories

Directory	Types of Object Names Stored
\ArcName	Symbolic links mapping ARC-style paths to NT-style paths.
\BaseNamedObjects	Global mutexes, events, semaphores, waitable timers, jobs, ALPC ports, symbolic links, and section objects.
\Callback	Callback objects.
\Device	Device objects.
\Driver	Driver objects.
\FileSystem	File-system driver objects and file-system-recognizer device objects. The Filter Manager also creates its own device objects under the Filters subkey.
\GLOBAL??	MS-DOS device names. (The \Sessions\0\DosDevices\<LUID>\Global directories are symbolic links to this directory.)
\KernelObjects	Contains event objects that signal low resource conditions, memory errors, the completion of certain operating system tasks, as well as objects representing Sessions.
\KnownDlls	Section names and path for known DLLs (DLLs mapped by the system at startup time).
\KnownDlls32	On a 64-bit Windows installation, \KnownDlls contains the native 64-bit binaries, so this directory is used instead to store Wow64 32-bit versions of those DLLs.
\Nls	Section names for mapped national language support tables.
\ObjectTypes	Names of types of objects.
\PSXSS	If Subsystem for UNIX Applications is enabled (through installation of the SUA component), this contains ALPC ports used by Subsystem for UNIX Applications.
\RPC Control	ALPC ports used by remote procedure calls (RPCs), and events used by Conhost.exe as part of the console isolation mechanism.
\Security	ALPC ports and events used by names of objects specific to the security subsystem.
\Sessions	Per-session namespace directory. (See the next subsection.)
\UMDFCommunicationPorts	ALPC ports used by the User-Mode Driver Framework (UMDF).
\Windows	Windows subsystem ALPC ports, shared section, and window stations.

Because the base kernel objects such as mutexes, events, semaphores, waitable timers, and sections have their names stored in a single object directory, no two of these objects can have the same name, even if they are of a different type. This restriction emphasizes the need to choose names carefully so that they don't collide with other names. For example, you could prefix names with a GUID and/or combine the name with the user's security identifier (SID).

Object names are global to a single computer (or to all processors on a multiprocessor computer), but they're not visible across a network. However, the object manager's parse method makes it possible to access named objects that exist on other computers. For example, the I/O manager, which supplies file-object services, extends the functions of the object manager to remote files. When asked to open a remote file object, the object manager calls a parse method, which allows the I/O manager to intercept the request and deliver it to a network redirector, a driver that accesses files across the network. Server code on the remote Windows system calls the object manager and the I/O manager on that system to find the file object and return the information back across the network.

One security consideration to keep in mind when dealing with named objects is the possibility of *object name squatting*. Although object names in different sessions are protected from each other, there's no standard protection inside the current session namespace that can be set with the standard Windows API. This makes it possible for an unprivileged application running in the same session as a privileged application to access its objects, as described earlier in the object security subsection. Unfortunately, even if the object creator used a proper DACL to secure the object, this doesn't help against the *squatting* attack, in which the unprivileged application creates the object *before* the privileged application, thus denying access to the legitimate application.

Windows exposes the concept of a *private namespace* to alleviate this issue. It allows user-mode applications to create object directories through the *CreatePrivateNamespace* API and associate these directories with *boundary descriptors*, which are special data structures protecting the directories. These descriptors contain SIDs describing which security principals are allowed access to the object directory. In this manner, a privileged application can be sure that unprivileged applications will not be able to conduct a denial-of-service attack against its objects. (This doesn't stop a privileged application from doing the same, however, but this point is moot.) Additionally, a boundary descriptor can also contain an integrity level, protecting objects possibly belonging to the same user account as the application, based on the integrity level of the process. (See Chapter 6 for more information on integrity levels.)

EXPERIMENT: Looking at the Base Named Objects

You can see the list of base objects that have names with the WinObj tool from Sysinternals. Run Winobj.exe., and click on \BaseNamedObjects, as shown here:

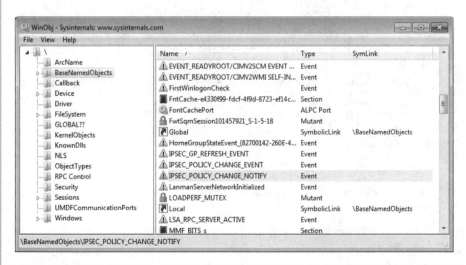

The named objects are shown on the right. The icons indicate the object type:

- Mutexes are indicated with a lock sign.

- Sections (Windows file-mapping objects) are shown as memory chips.

- Events are shown as exclamation points.

- Semaphores are indicated with an icon that resembles a traffic signal.

- Symbolic links have icons that are curved arrows.

- Folders indicate object directories.

- Gears indicate other objects, such as ALPC ports.

EXPERIMENT: Tampering with Single Instancing

Applications such as Windows Media Player and those in Microsoft Office are common examples of single-instancing enforcement through named objects. Notice that when launching the Wmplayer.exe executable, Windows Media Player appears only once—every other launch simply results in the window coming back into focus. You can tamper with the handle list by using Process Explorer to turn the computer into a media mixer! Here's how:

1. Launch Windows Media Player and Process Explorer to view the handle table (by clicking View, Lower Pane View, and then Handles). You should see a handle whose name column contains CheckForOtherInstanceMutex.

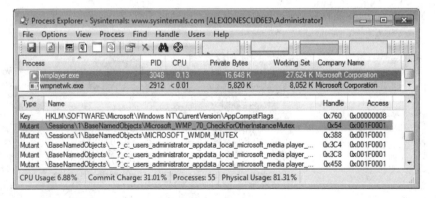

2. Right-click on the handle, and select Close Handle. Confirm the action when asked.

3. Now run Windows Media Player again. Notice that this time a second process is created.

4. Go ahead and play a different song in each instance. You can also use the Sound Mixer in the system tray (click on the Volume icon) to select which of the two processes will have greater volume, effectively creating a mixing environment.

Instead of closing a handle to a named object, an application could have run on its own before Windows Media Player and created an object with the same name. In this scenario, Windows Media Player would never run, fooled into believing it was already running on the system.

Symbolic Links   In certain file systems (on NTFS and some UNIX systems, for example), a symbolic link lets a user create a file name or a directory name that, when used, is translated by the operating system into a different file or directory name. Using a symbolic link is a simple method for allowing users to indirectly share a file or the contents of a directory, creating a cross-link between different directories in the ordinarily hierarchical directory structure.

The object manager implements an object called a *symbolic link object*, which performs a similar function for object names in its object namespace. A symbolic link can occur anywhere within an object name string. When a caller refers to a symbolic link object's name, the object manager traverses its object namespace until it reaches the symbolic link object. It looks inside the symbolic link and finds a string that it substitutes for the symbolic link name. It then restarts its name lookup.

One place in which the executive uses symbolic link objects is in translating MS-DOS-style device names into Windows internal device names. In Windows, a user refers to hard disk drives using the names C:, D:, and so on and serial ports as COM1, COM2, and so on. The Windows subsystem makes these symbolic link objects protected, global data by placing them in the object manager namespace under the \Global?? directory.

Session Namespace

Services have access to the *global* namespace, a namespace that serves as the first instance of the namespace. Additional sessions are given a session-private view of the namespace known as a *local* namespace. The parts of the namespace that are localized for each session include \DosDevices, \Windows, and \BaseNamedObjects. Making separate copies of the same parts of the namespace is known as *instancing* the namespace. Instancing \DosDevices makes it possible for each user to have different network drive letters and Windows objects such as serial ports. On Windows, the global \DosDevices directory is named \Global?? and is the directory to which \DosDevices points, and local \DosDevices directories are identified by the logon session ID.

The \Windows directory is where Win32k.sys inserts the interactive window station created by Winlogon, \WinSta0. A Terminal Services environment can support multiple interactive users, but each user needs an individual version of WinSta0 to preserve the illusion that he is accessing the predefined interactive window station in Windows. Finally, applications and the system create shared objects in \BaseNamedObjects, including events, mutexes, and memory sections. If two users are running an application that creates a named object, each user session must have a private version of the object so that the two instances of the application don't interfere with one another by accessing the same object.

The object manager implements a local namespace by creating the private versions of the three directories mentioned under a directory associated with the user's session under \Sessions*n* (where *n* is the session identifier). When a Windows application in remote session two creates a named event, for example, the object manager transparently redirects the object's name from \BaseNamedObjects to \Sessions\2\BaseNamedObjects.

All object-manager functions related to namespace management are aware of the instanced directories and participate in providing the illusion that all sessions use the same namespace. Windows subsystem DLLs prefix names passed by Windows applications that reference objects in \DosDevices with *??* (for example, C:\Windows becomes \??\C:\Windows). When the object manager sees the special \?? prefix, the steps it takes depends on the version of Windows, but it always relies on a field named *DeviceMap* in the executive process object (EPROCESS, which is described further in Chapter 5) that points to a data structure shared by other processes in the same session.

The *DosDevicesDirectory* field of the *DeviceMap* structure points at the object manager directory that represents the process' local \DosDevices. When the object manager sees a reference to \??, it locates the process' local \DosDevices by using the *DosDevicesDirectory* field of the *DeviceMap*. If the object manager doesn't find the object in that directory, it checks the *DeviceMap* field of the directory object. If it's valid, it looks for the object in the directory pointed to by the *GlobalDosDevicesDirectory* field of the *DeviceMap* structure, which is always \Global??.

Under certain circumstances, applications that are session–aware need to access objects in the global session even if the application is running in another session. The application might want to do this to synchronize with instances of itself running in other remote sessions or with the console session (that is, session 0). For these cases, the object manager provides the special override "\Global" that an application can prefix to any object name to access the global namespace. For example, an application in session two opening an object named \Global\ApplicationInitialized is directed to \BaseNamedObjects\ApplicationInitialized instead of \Sessions\2\BaseNamedObjects \ApplicationInitialized.

An application that wants to access an object in the global \DosDevices directory does not need to use the \Global prefix as long as the object doesn't exist in its local \DosDevices directory. This is because the object manager automatically looks in the global directory for the object if it doesn't find it in the local directory. However, an application can force checking the global directory by using \GLOBALROOT.

Session directories are isolated from each other, and administrative privileges are required to create a global object (except for section objects). A special privilege named *create global object* is verified before allowing such operations.

EXPERIMENT: Viewing Namespace Instancing

You can see the separation between the session 0 namespace and other session namespaces as soon as you log in. The reason you can is that the first console user is logged in to session 1 (while services run in session 0). Run Winobj.exe, and click on the \Sessions directory. You'll see a subdirectory with a numeric name for each active session. If you open one of these directories, you'll see subdirectories named \DosDevices, \Windows, and \BaseNamedObjects, which are the local namespace subdirectories of the session. The following screen shot shows a local namespace:

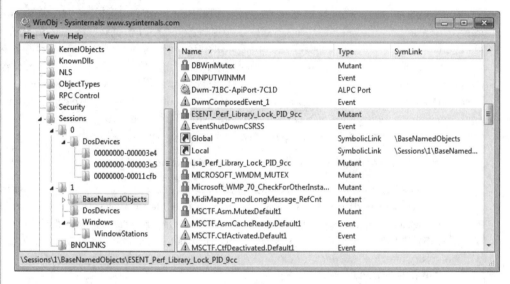

Next run Process Explorer and select a process in your session (such as Explorer.exe), and then view the handle table (by clicking View, Lower Pane View, and then Handles). You should see a handle to \Windows\WindowStations\WinSta0 underneath \Sessions\n, where n is the session ID.

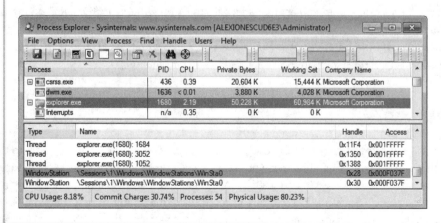

Object Filtering

Windows includes a filtering model in the object manager, similar to the file system minifilter model described in Chapter 8 in Part 2. One of the primary benefits of this filtering model is the ability to use the *altitude* concept that these existing filtering technologies use, which means that multiple drivers can filter object-manager events at appropriate locations in the filtering stack. Additionally, drivers are permitted to intercept calls such as *NtOpenThread* and *NtOpenProcess* and even to modify the access masks being requested from the process manager. This allows protection against certain operations on an open handle—however, an open operation cannot be entirely blocked because doing so would too closely resemble a malicious operation (processes that could never be managed).

Furthermore, drivers are able to take advantage of both *pre* and *post* callbacks, allowing them to prepare for a certain operation before it occurs, as well as to react or finalize information after the operation has occurred. These callbacks can be specified for each operation (currently, only open, create, and duplicate are supported) and be specific for each object type (currently, only process and thread objects are supported). For each callback, drivers can specify their own internal context value, which can be returned across all calls to the driver or across a pre/post pair. These callbacks can be registered with the *ObRegisterCallbacks* API and unregistered with the *ObUnregisterCallbacks* API—it is the responsibility of the driver to ensure deregistration happens.

Use of the APIs is restricted to images that have certain characteristics:

- The image must be signed, even on 32-bit computers, according to the same rules set forth in the Kernel Mode Code Signing (KMCS) policy. (Code integrity will be discussed later in this chapter.) The image must be compiled with the */integritycheck* linker flag, which sets the IMAGE_DLLCHARACTERISTICS_FORCE_INTEGRITY value in the PE header. This instructs the memory manager to check the signature of the image regardless of any other defaults that might not normally result in a check.

- The image must be signed with a catalog containing cryptographic per-page hashes of the executable code. This allows the system to detect changes to the image after it has been loaded in memory.

Before executing a callback, the object manager calls the *MmVerifyCallbackFunction* on the target function pointer, which in turn locates the loader data table entry associated with the module owning this address, and verifies whether or not the LDRP_IMAGE_INTEGRITY_FORCED flag is set. (See the "Loaded Module Database" section in this chapter for more information.)

Synchronization

The concept of *mutual exclusion* is a crucial one in operating systems development. It refers to the guarantee that one, and only one, thread can access a particular resource at a time. Mutual exclusion is necessary when a resource doesn't lend itself to shared access or when sharing would result in an unpredictable outcome. For example, if two threads copy a file to a printer port at the same time, their output could be interspersed. Similarly, if one thread reads a memory location while another one writes to it, the first thread will receive unpredictable data. In general, writable resources can't be shared without restrictions, whereas resources that aren't subject to modification can be shared. Figure 3-24 illustrates what happens when two threads running on different processors both write data to a circular queue.

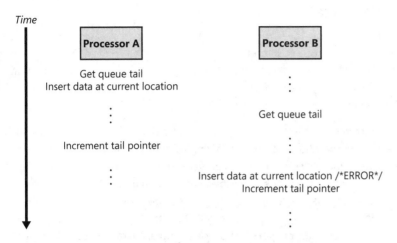

FIGURE 3-24 Incorrect sharing of memory

Because the second thread obtained the value of the queue tail pointer before the first thread finished updating it, the second thread inserted its data into the same location that the first thread used, overwriting data and leaving one queue location empty. Even though Figure 3-24 illustrates what could happen on a multiprocessor system, the same error could occur on a single-processor system if the operating system performed a context switch to the second thread before the first thread updated the queue tail pointer.

Sections of code that access a nonshareable resource are called *critical* sections. To ensure correct code, only one thread at a time can execute in a critical section. While one thread is writing to a file, updating a database, or modifying a shared variable, no other thread can be allowed to access the same resource. The pseudocode shown in Figure 3-24 is a critical section that incorrectly accesses a shared data structure without mutual exclusion.

The issue of mutual exclusion, although important for all operating systems, is especially important (and intricate) for a *tightly coupled, symmetric multiprocessing* (SMP) operating system such as Windows, in which the same system code runs simultaneously on more than one processor, sharing certain data structures stored in global memory. In Windows, it is the kernel's job to provide mechanisms that system code can use to prevent two threads from modifying the same structure at the same time. The kernel provides mutual-exclusion primitives that it and the rest of the executive use to synchronize their access to global data structures.

Because the scheduler synchronizes access to its data structures at DPC/dispatch level IRQL, the kernel and executive cannot rely on synchronization mechanisms that would result in a page fault or reschedule operation to synchronize access to data structures when the IRQL is DPC/dispatch level or higher (levels known as an *elevated* or *high* IRQL). In the following sections, you'll find out how the kernel and executive use mutual exclusion to protect their global data structures when the IRQL is high and what mutual-exclusion and synchronization mechanisms the kernel and executive use when the IRQL is *low* (below DPC/dispatch level).

High-IRQL Synchronization

At various stages during its execution, the kernel must guarantee that one, and only one, processor at a time is executing within a critical section. Kernel critical sections are the code segments that modify a global data structure such as the kernel's dispatcher database or its DPC queue. The operating system can't function correctly unless the kernel can guarantee that threads access these data structures in a mutually exclusive manner.

The biggest area of concern is interrupts. For example, the kernel might be updating a global data structure when an interrupt occurs whose interrupt-handling routine also modifies the structure. Simple single-processor operating systems sometimes prevent such a scenario by disabling all interrupts each time they access global data, but the Windows kernel has a more sophisticated solution. Before using a global resource, the kernel temporarily masks the interrupts whose interrupt handlers also use the resource. It does so by raising the processor's IRQL to the highest level used by any potential interrupt source that accesses the global data. For example, an interrupt at DPC/dispatch level causes the dispatcher, which uses the dispatcher database, to run. Therefore, any other part of the kernel that uses the dispatcher database raises the IRQL to DPC/dispatch level, masking DPC/dispatch-level interrupts before using the dispatcher database.

This strategy is fine for a single-processor system, but it's inadequate for a multiprocessor configuration. Raising the IRQL on one processor doesn't prevent an interrupt from occurring on another processor. The kernel also needs to guarantee mutually exclusive access across several processors.

Interlocked Operations

The simplest form of synchronization mechanisms rely on hardware support for multiprocessor-safe manipulation of integer values and for performing comparisons. They include functions such as *InterlockedIncrement*, *InterlockedDecrement*, *InterlockedExchange*, and *InterlockedCompareExchange*. The *InterlockedDecrement* function, for example, uses the x86 *lock* instruction prefix (for example, *lock xadd*) to lock the multiprocessor bus during the subtraction operation so that another processor that's also modifying the memory location being decremented won't be able to modify it between the decrementing processor's read of the original value and its write of the decremented value. This form of basic synchronization is used by the kernel and drivers. In today's Microsoft compiler suite, these functions are called *intrinsic* because the code for them is generated in an inline assembler, directly during the compilation phase, instead of going through a function call. (It's likely that pushing the parameters onto the stack, calling the function, copying the parameters into registers, and then popping the parameters off the stack and returning to the caller would be a more expensive operation than the actual work the function is supposed to do in the first place.)

Spinlocks

The mechanism the kernel uses to achieve multiprocessor mutual exclusion is called a *spinlock*. A spinlock is a locking primitive associated with a global data structure such as the DPC queue shown in Figure 3-25.

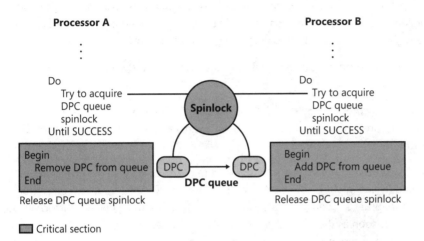

FIGURE 3-25 Using a spinlock

Before entering either critical section shown in Figure 3-25, the kernel must acquire the spinlock associated with the protected DPC queue. If the spinlock isn't free, the kernel keeps trying to acquire the lock until it succeeds. The spinlock gets its name from the fact that the kernel (and thus, the processor) waits, "spinning," until it gets the lock.

Spinlocks, like the data structures they protect, reside in nonpaged memory mapped into the system address space. The code to acquire and release a spinlock is written in assembly language for speed and to exploit whatever locking mechanism the underlying processor architecture provides. On many architectures, spinlocks are implemented with a hardware-supported test-and-set operation, which tests the value of a lock variable and acquires the lock in one atomic instruction. Testing and acquiring the lock in one instruction prevents a second thread from grabbing the lock between the time the first thread tests the variable and the time it acquires the lock. Additionally, the *lock* instruction mentioned earlier can also be used on the test-and-set operation, resulting in the combined *lock bts* assembly operation, which also locks the multiprocessor bus; otherwise, it would be possible for more than one processor to atomically perform the operation. (Without the *lock*, the operation is guaranteed to be atomic only on the current processor.)

All kernel-mode spinlocks in Windows have an associated IRQL that is always DPC/dispatch level or higher. Thus, when a thread is trying to acquire a spinlock, all other activity at the spinlock's IRQL or lower ceases on that processor. Because thread dispatching happens at DPC/dispatch level, a thread that holds a spinlock is never preempted because the IRQL masks the dispatching mechanisms. This masking allows code executing in a critical section protected by a spinlock to continue executing so that it will release the lock quickly. The kernel uses spinlocks with great care, minimizing the number of instructions it executes while it holds a spinlock. Any processor that attempts to acquire the spinlock will essentially be busy, waiting indefinitely, consuming power (a busy wait results in 100% CPU usage) and performing no actual work.

On x86 and x64 processors, a special *pause* assembly instruction can be inserted in busy wait loops. This instruction offers a *hint* to the processor that the loop instructions it is processing are part of a spinlock (or a similar construct) acquisition loop. The instruction provides three benefits:

- It significantly reduces power usage by delaying the core ever so slightly instead of continuously looping.

- On HyperThreaded cores, it allows the CPU to realize that the "work" being done by the spinning logical core is not terribly important and awards more CPU time to the second logical core instead.

- Because a busy wait loop results in a storm of read requests coming to the bus from the waiting thread (which might be generated out of order), the CPU attempts to correct for violations of memory order as soon as it detects a write (that is, when the owning thread releases the lock). Thus, as soon as the spinlock is released, the CPU reorders any pending memory read operations to ensure proper ordering. This reordering results in a large penalty in system performance and can be avoided with the pause instruction.

The kernel makes spinlocks available to other parts of the executive through a set of kernel functions, including *KeAcquireSpinLock* and *KeReleaseSpinLock*. Device drivers, for example, require spinlocks to guarantee that device registers and other global data structures are accessed by only one part of a device driver (and from only one processor) at a time. Spinlocks are not for use by user programs—user programs should use the objects described in the next section. Device drivers also need to protect access to their own data structures from interrupts associated with themselves. Because the spinlock APIs typically raise the IRQL only to DPC/dispatch level, this isn't enough to protect against interrupts. For this reason, the kernel also exports the *KeAcquireInterruptSpinLock* and *KeReleaseInterruptSpinLock* APIs that take as a parameter the KINTERRUPT object discussed at the beginning of this chapter. The system looks inside the interrupt object for the associated DIRQL with the interrupt and raises the IRQL to the appropriate level to ensure correct access to structures shared with the ISR. Devices can use the *KeSynchronizeExecution* API to synchronize an entire function with an ISR, instead of just a critical section. In all cases, the code protected by an interrupt spinlock must execute extremely quickly—any delay causes higher-than-normal interrupt latency and will have significant negative performance effects.

Kernel spinlocks carry with them restrictions for code that uses them. Because spinlocks always have an IRQL of DPC/dispatch level or higher, as explained earlier, code holding a spinlock will crash the system if it attempts to make the scheduler perform a dispatch operation or if it causes a page fault.

Queued Spinlocks

To increase the scalability of spinlocks, a special type of spinlock, called a *queued spinlock,* is used in most circumstances instead of a standard spinlock. A queued spinlock works like this: When a processor wants to acquire a queued spinlock that is currently held, it places its identifier in a queue associated with the spinlock. When the processor that's holding the spinlock releases it, it hands the lock over to the first processor identified in the queue. In the meantime, a processor waiting for a busy spinlock checks the status not of the spinlock itself but of a per-processor flag that the processor ahead of it in the queue sets to indicate that the waiting processor's turn has arrived.

The fact that queued spinlocks result in spinning on per-processor flags rather than global spinlocks has two effects. The first is that the multiprocessor's bus isn't as heavily trafficked by interprocessor synchronization. The second is that instead of a random processor in a waiting group acquiring a spinlock, the queued spinlock enforces first-in, first-out (FIFO) ordering to the lock. FIFO ordering means more consistent performance across processors accessing the same locks.

Windows defines a number of global queued spinlocks by storing pointers to them in an array contained in each processor's *processor region control block* (PRCB). A global spinlock can be acquired by calling *KeAcquireQueuedSpinLock* with the index into the PRCB array at which the pointer to the spinlock is stored. The number of global spinlocks has grown in each release of the operating system, and the table of index definitions for them is published in the WDK header file Wdm.h. Note, however, that acquiring one of these queued spinlocks from a device driver is an unsupported and heavily frowned-upon operation. These locks are reserved for the kernel's own internal use.

EXPERIMENT: Viewing Global Queued Spinlocks

You can view the state of the global queued spinlocks (the ones pointed to by the queued spinlock array in each processor's PCR) by using the *!qlocks* kernel debugger command. In the following example, the page frame number (PFN) database queued spinlock is held by processor 1, and the other queued spinlocks are not acquired. (The PFN database is described in Chapter 10 in Part 2.)

```
1kd> !qlocks
Key: 0 = Owner, 1-n = Wait order, blank = not owned/waiting, C = Corrupt

                        Processor Number
     Lock Name          0  1

KE   - Unused Spare
MM   - Expansion
MM   - Unused Spare
MM   - System Space
CC   - Vacb
CC   - Master
```

Instack Queued Spinlocks

Device drivers can use dynamically allocated queued spinlocks with the *KeAcquireInStackQueuedSpinLock* and *KeReleaseInStackQueuedSpinLock* functions. Several components—including the cache manager, executive pool manager, and NTFS—take advantage of these types of locks instead of using global queued spinlocks.

KeAcquireInStackQueuedSpinLock takes a pointer to a spinlock data structure and a spinlock queue handle. The spinlock handle is actually a data structure in which the kernel stores information about the lock's status, including the lock's ownership and the queue of processors that might be waiting for the lock to become available. For this reason, the handle shouldn't be a global variable. It is usually a stack variable, guaranteeing *locality* to the caller thread and is responsible for the *InStack* part of the spinlock and API name.

Executive Interlocked Operations

The kernel supplies a number of simple synchronization functions constructed on spinlocks for more advanced operations, such as adding and removing entries from singly and doubly linked lists. Examples include *ExInterlockedPopEntryList* and *ExInterlockedPushEntryList* for singly linked lists, and *ExInterlockedInsertHeadList* and *ExInterlockedRemoveHeadList* for doubly linked lists. All these functions require a standard spinlock as a parameter and are used throughout the kernel and device drivers.

Instead of relying on the standard APIs to acquire and release the spinlock parameter, these functions place the code required inline and also use a different ordering scheme. Whereas the *Ke* spinlock APIs first test and set the bit to see whether the lock is released and then atomically do a locked test-and-set operation to actually make the acquisition, these routines disable interrupts on the processor and immediately attempt an atomic test-and-set. If the initial attempt fails, interrupts are enabled again, and the standard busy waiting algorithm continues until the test-and-set operation returns 0—in which case, the whole function is restarted again. Because of these subtle differences, a spinlock used for the executive interlocked functions must not be used with the standard kernel APIs discussed previously. Naturally, noninterlocked list operations must not be mixed with interlocked operations.

> **Note** Certain executive interlocked operations silently ignore the spinlock when possible. For example, the *ExInterlockedIncrementLong* or *ExInterlockedCompareExchange* APIs actually use the same *lock* prefix used by the standard interlocked functions and the intrinsic functions. These functions were useful on older systems (or non-x86 systems) where the *lock* operation was not suitable or available. For this reason, these calls are now deprecated in favor of the intrinsic functions.

Low-IRQL Synchronization

Executive software outside the kernel also needs to synchronize access to global data structures in a multiprocessor environment. For example, the memory manager has only one page frame database, which it accesses as a global data structure, and device drivers need to ensure that they can gain exclusive access to their devices. By calling kernel functions, the executive can create a spinlock, acquire it, and release it.

Spinlocks only partially fill the executive's needs for synchronization mechanisms, however. Because waiting for a spinlock literally stalls a processor, spinlocks can be used only under the following strictly limited circumstances:

- The protected resource must be accessed quickly and without complicated interactions with other code.

- The critical section code can't be paged out of memory, can't make references to pageable data, can't call external procedures (including system services), and can't generate interrupts or exceptions.

These restrictions are confining and can't be met under all circumstances. Furthermore, the executive needs to perform other types of synchronization in addition to mutual exclusion, and it must also provide synchronization mechanisms to user mode.

There are several additional synchronization mechanisms for use when spinlocks are not suitable:

- Kernel dispatcher objects

- Fast mutexes and guarded mutexes

- Pushlocks

- Executive resources

Additionally, user-mode code, which also executes at low IRQL, must be able to have its own locking primitives. Windows supports various user-mode-specific primitives:

- Condition variables (CondVars)

- Slim Reader-Writer Locks (SRW Locks)

- Run-once initialization (InitOnce)

- Critical sections

We'll take a look at the user-mode primitives and their underlying kernel-mode support later; for now, we'll focus on kernel-mode objects. Table 3-18 serves as a reference that compares and contrasts the capabilities of these mechanisms and their interaction with kernel-mode APC delivery.

TABLE 3-18 Kernel Synchronization Mechanisms

	Exposed for Use by Device Drivers	Disables Normal Kernel-Mode APCs	Disables Special Kernel-Mode APCs	Supports Recursive Acquisition	Supports Shared and Exclusive Acquisition
Kernel dispatcher mutexes	Yes	Yes	No	Yes	No
Kernel dispatcher semaphores or events	Yes	No	No	No	No
Fast mutexes	Yes	Yes	Yes	No	No
Guarded mutexes	Yes	Yes	Yes	No	No
Pushlocks	No	No	No	No	Yes
Executive resources	Yes	No	No	Yes	Yes

Kernel Dispatcher Objects

The kernel furnishes additional synchronization mechanisms to the executive in the form of kernel objects, known collectively as *dispatcher objects*. The Windows API-visible synchronization objects acquire their synchronization capabilities from these kernel dispatcher objects. Each Windows API-visible object that supports synchronization encapsulates at least one kernel dispatcher object. The executive's synchronization semantics are visible to Windows programmers through the *WaitForSingleObject* and *WaitForMultipleObjects* functions, which the Windows subsystem implements by calling analogous system services that the object manager supplies. A thread in a Windows application can synchronize with a variety of objects, including a Windows process, thread, event, semaphore, mutex, waitable timer, I/O completion port, ALPC port, registry key, or file object. In fact, almost all objects exposed by the kernel can be waited on. Some of these are proper dispatcher objects, while others are larger objects that have a dispatcher object within them (such as ports, keys, or files). Table 3-19 shows the proper dispatcher objects, so any other object that the Windows API allows waiting on probably internally contains one of those primitives.

One other type of executive synchronization object worth noting is called an *executive resource*. Executive resources provide exclusive access (like a mutex) as well as shared read access (multiple readers sharing read-only access to a structure). However, they're available only to kernel-mode code and thus are not accessible from the Windows API. The remaining subsections describe the implementation details of waiting for dispatcher objects.

Waiting for Dispatcher Objects

A thread can synchronize with a dispatcher object by waiting for the object's handle. Doing so causes the kernel to put the thread in a wait state.

At any given moment, a synchronization object is in one of two states: *signaled state* or *nonsignaled state*. A thread can't resume its execution until its wait is satisfied, a condition that occurs when the dispatcher object whose handle the thread is waiting for also undergoes a state change, from the nonsignaled state to the signaled state (when another thread sets an event object, for example). To synchronize with an object, a thread calls one of the wait system services that the object manager supplies, passing a handle to the object it wants to synchronize with. The thread can wait for one or several objects and can also specify that its wait should be canceled if it hasn't ended within a certain amount of time. Whenever the kernel sets an object to the signaled state, one of the kernel's signal routines checks to see whether any threads are waiting for the object and not also waiting for other objects to become signaled. If there are, the kernel releases one or more of the threads from their waiting state so that they can continue executing.

The following example of setting an event illustrates how synchronization interacts with thread dispatching:

- A user-mode thread waits for an event object's handle.

- The kernel changes the thread's scheduling state to waiting and then adds the thread to a list of threads waiting for the event.

- Another thread sets the event.

- The kernel marches down the list of threads waiting for the event. If a thread's conditions for waiting are satisfied (see the following note), the kernel takes the thread out of the waiting state. If it is a variable-priority thread, the kernel might also boost its execution priority. (For details on thread scheduling, see Chapter 5.)

> **Note** Some threads might be waiting for more than one object, so they continue waiting, unless they specified a *WaitAny* wait, which will wake them up as soon as one object (instead of all) is signaled.

What Signals an Object?

The signaled state is defined differently for different objects. A thread object is in the nonsignaled state during its lifetime and is set to the signaled state by the kernel when the thread terminates. Similarly, the kernel sets a process object to the signaled state when the process' last thread terminates. In contrast, the timer object, like an alarm, is set to "go off" at a certain time. When its time expires, the kernel sets the timer object to the signaled state.

When choosing a synchronization mechanism, a program must take into account the rules governing the behavior of different synchronization objects. Whether a thread's wait ends when an object is set to the signaled state varies with the type of object the thread is waiting for, as Table 3-19 illustrates.

TABLE 3-19 Definitions of the Signaled State

Object Type	Set to Signaled State When	Effect on Waiting Threads
Process	Last thread terminates	All are released.
Thread	Thread terminates	All are released.
Event (notification type)	Thread sets the event	All are released.
Event (synchronization type)	Thread sets the event	One thread is released and might receive a boost; the event object is reset.
Gate (locking type)	Thread signals the gate	First waiting thread is released and receives a boost.
Gate (signaling type)	Thread signals the type	First waiting thread is released.
Keyed event	Thread sets event with a key	Thread that's waiting for the key and which is of the same process as the signaler is released.
Semaphore	Semaphore count increases by 1	One or more threads are released.
Timer (notification type)	Set time arrives, or time interval expires	All are released.
Timer (synchronization type)	Set time arrives, or time interval expires	One thread is released.
Mutex	Thread releases the mutex	One thread is released and takes ownership of the mutex.
Queue	Item is placed on queue	One thread is released.

When an object is set to the signaled state, waiting threads are generally released from their wait states immediately. Some of the kernel dispatcher objects and the system events that induce their state changes are shown in Figure 3-26.

For example, a notification event object (called a *manual reset event* in the Windows API) is used to announce the occurrence of some event. When the event object is set to the signaled state, all threads waiting for the event are released. The exception is any thread that is waiting for more than one object at a time; such a thread might be required to continue waiting until additional objects reach the signaled state.

In contrast to an event object, a mutex object has ownership associated with it (unless it was acquired during a DPC). It is used to gain mutually exclusive access to a resource, and only one thread at a time can hold the mutex. When the mutex object becomes free, the kernel sets it to the signaled state and then selects one waiting thread to execute, while also inheriting any priority boost that had been applied. (See Chapter 5 for more information on priority boosting.) The thread selected by the kernel acquires the mutex object, and all other threads continue waiting.

A mutex object can also be abandoned: this occurs when the thread currently owning it becomes terminated. When a thread terminate, the kernel enumerates all mutexes owned by the thread and sets them to the abandoned state, which, in terms of signaling logic, is treated as a signaled state in that ownership of the mutex is transferred to a waiting thread.

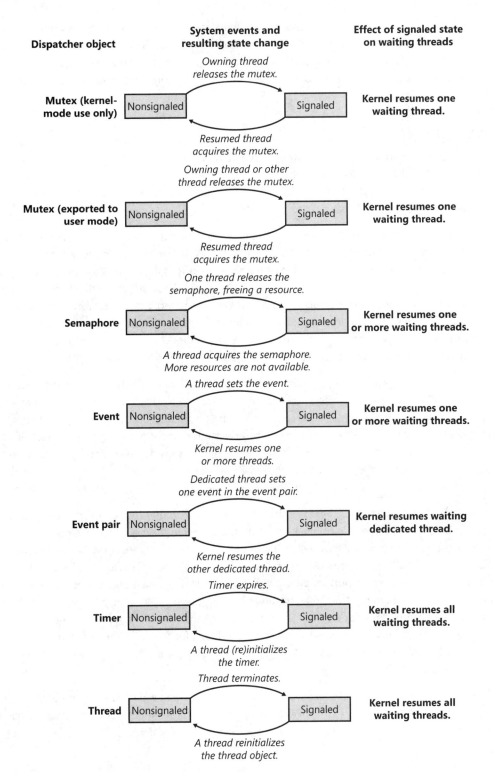

Dispatcher object	System events and resulting state change	Effect of signaled state on waiting threads

Mutex (kernel-mode use only) — *Owning thread releases the mutex.* — Nonsignaled → Signaled — *Resumed thread acquires the mutex.* — **Kernel resumes one waiting thread.**

Mutex (exported to user mode) — *Owning thread or other thread releases the mutex.* — Nonsignaled → Signaled — *Resumed thread acquires the mutex.* — **Kernel resumes one waiting thread.**

Semaphore — *One thread releases the semaphore, freeing a resource.* — Nonsignaled → Signaled — *A thread acquires the semaphore. More resources are not available.* — **Kernel resumes one or more waiting threads.**

Event — *A thread sets the event.* — Nonsignaled → Signaled — *Kernel resumes one or more threads.* — **Kernel resumes one or more waiting threads.**

Event pair — *Dedicated thread sets one event in the event pair.* — Nonsignaled → Signaled — *Kernel resumes the other dedicated thread.* — **Kernel resumes waiting dedicated thread.**

Timer — *Timer expires.* — Nonsignaled → Signaled — *A thread (re)initializes the timer.* — **Kernel resumes all waiting threads.**

Thread — *Thread terminates.* — Nonsignaled → Signaled — *A thread reinitializes the thread object.* — **Kernel resumes all waiting threads.**

FIGURE 3-26 Selected kernel dispatcher objects

This brief discussion wasn't meant to enumerate all the reasons and applications for using the various executive objects but rather to list their basic functionality and synchronization behavior. For information on how to put these objects to use in Windows programs, see the Windows reference documentation on synchronization objects or Jeffrey Richter and Christophe Nasarre's book *Windows via C/C++*.

Data Structures

Three data structures are key to tracking *who* is waiting, *how* they are waiting, *what* they are waiting for, and *which state* the entire wait operation is at. These three structures are the *dispatcher header,* the *wait block*, and the *wait status register.* The former two structures are publicly defined in the WDK include file Wdm.h, while the latter is not documented.

The dispatcher header is a packed structure because it needs to hold lots of information in a fixed-size structure. (See the upcoming "EXPERIMENT: Looking at Wait Queues" section to see the definition of the dispatcher header data structure.) One of the main tricks is to define mutually exclusive flags at the same memory location (offset) in the structure. By using the *Type* field, the kernel knows which of these fields actually applies. For example, a mutex can be abandoned, but a timer can be absolute or relative. Similarly, a timer can be inserted into the timer list, but the *Debug Active* field makes sense only for processes. On the other hand, the dispatcher header does contain information generic for any dispatcher object: the object type, signaled state, and a list of the threads waiting for that object.

The wait block represents a thread waiting for an object. Each thread that is in a wait state has a list of the wait blocks that represent the objects the thread is waiting for. Each dispatcher object has a list of the wait blocks that represent which threads are waiting for the object. This list is kept so that when a dispatcher object is signaled, the kernel can quickly determine who is waiting for that object. Finally, because the balance-set-manager thread running on each CPU (see Chapter 5 for more information about the balance set manager) needs to analyze the time that each thread has been waiting for (in order to decide whether or not to page out the kernel stack), each PRCB has a list of waiting threads.

The wait block has a pointer to the object being waited for, a pointer to the thread waiting for the object, and a pointer to the next wait block (if the thread is waiting for more than one object). It also records the type of wait (any or all) as well as the position of that entry in the array of handles passed by the thread on the *WaitForMultipleObjects* call (position 0 if the thread was waiting for only one object). The wait type is very important during wait satisfaction, because it determines whether or not all the wait blocks belonging to the thread waiting on the signaled object should be processed: for a *wait any*, the dispatcher does not care what the state of the other objects is because at least one (the current one) of the objects is now signaled. On the other hand, for a *wait all*, the dispatcher can wake the thread only if *all* the other objects are also in a signaled state, which requires traversing the wait blocks and associated objects.

The wait block also contains a volatile *wait block state*, which defines the current state of this wait block in the transactional wait operation it is currently being engaged in. The different states, their meaning, and their effects in the wait logic code, are explained in Table 3-20.

TABLE 3-20 Wait Block States

State	Meaning	Effect
WaitBlockActive (2)	This wait block is actively linked to an object as part of a thread that is in a wait state.	During wait satisfaction, this wait block will be unlinked from the wait block list.
WaitBlockInactive (3)	The thread wait associated with this wait block has been satisfied (or the timeout has already expired while setting it up).	During wait satisfaction, this wait block will not be unlinked from the wait block list because the wait satisfaction must have already unlinked during its active state.
WaitBlockBypassStart (0)	A signal is being delivered to the thread while the wait has not yet been committed.	During wait satisfaction (which would be immediate, before the thread enters the true wait state), the waiting thread must synchronize with the signaler because there is a risk that the wait object might be on the stack—marking the wait block as inactive would cause the waiter to unwind the stack while the signaler might still be accessing it.
WaitBlockBypassComplete (1)	The thread wait associated with this wait block has now been properly synchronized (the wait satisfaction has completed), and the bypass scenario is now completed.	The wait block is now essentially treated the same as an inactive wait block (ignored).

Because the overall state of the thread (or any of the objects it is being required to start waiting on) can change while wait operations are still being set up (because there is nothing blocking another thread executing on a different logical processor from attempting to signal one of the objects, or possibly alerting the thread, or even sending it an APC), the kernel dispatcher needs to keep track of two additional pieces of data for each waiting thread: the current fine-grained wait state of the thread, as well as any pending state changes that could modify the result of the attempted wait operation.

When a thread is instructed to wait for a given object (such as due to a *WaitForSingleObject* call), it first attempts to enter the in-progress wait state (*WaitInProgress*) by beginning the wait. This operation succeeds if there are no pending alerts to the thread at the moment (based on the alertability of the wait and the current processor mode of the wait, which determine whether or not the alert can preempt the wait). If there is an alert, the wait is not even entered at all, and the caller receives the appropriate status code; otherwise, the thread now enters the *WaitInProgress* state, at which point the main thread state is set to *Waiting*, and the wait reason and wait time are recorded, with any timeout specified also being registered.

Once the wait is in progress, the thread can initialize the wait blocks as needed (and mark them as *WaitBlockActive* in the process) and then proceed to lock all the objects that are part of this wait. Because each object has its own lock, it is important that the kernel be able to maintain a consistent locking ordering scheme when multiple processors might be analyzing a wait chain consisting of many objects (caused by a *WaitForMultipleObjects* call). The kernel uses a technique known as *address ordering* to achieve this: because each object has a distinct and static kernel-mode address, the objects can be ordered in monotonically increasing address order, guaranteeing that locks are always acquired and released in the same order by all callers. This means that the caller-supplied array of objects will be duplicated and sorted accordingly.

The next step is to check for immediate satisfaction of the wait, such as when a thread is being told to wait on a mutex that has already been released or an event that is already signaled. In such cases, the wait is immediately satisfied, which involves unlinking the associated wait blocks (however, in this case, no wait blocks have yet been inserted) and performing a wait exit (processing any pending scheduler operations marked in the wait status register). If this shortcut fails, the kernel next attempts to check whether the timeout specified for the wait (if any) has actually already expired. In this case, the wait is not "satisfied" but merely "timed out," which results in slightly faster processing of the exit code, albeit with the same result.

If none of these shortcuts were effective, the wait block is inserted into the thread's wait list, and the thread now attempts to commit its wait. (Meanwhile, the object lock or locks have been released, allowing other processors to modify the state of any of the objects that the thread is now supposed to attempt waiting on.) Assuming a noncontended scenario, where other processors are not interested in this thread or its wait objects, the wait switches into the committed state as long as there are no pending changes marked by the wait status register. The commit operation links the waiting thread in the PRCB list, activates an extra wait queue thread if needed, and inserts the timer associated with the wait timeout, if any. Because potentially quite a lot of cycles have elapsed by this point, it is again possible that the timeout has already elapsed. In this scenario, inserting the timer will cause immediate signaling of the thread, and thus a wait satisfaction on the timer, and the overall timeout of the wait. Otherwise, in the much more common scenario, the CPU now context switches away to the next thread that is ready for execution. (See Chapter 5 for more information on scheduling.)

In highly contended code paths on multiprocessor machines, it is possible and likely that the thread attempting to commit its wait has experienced a change while its wait was still in progress. One possible scenario is that one of the objects it was waiting on has just been signaled. As touched upon earlier, this causes the associated wait block to enter the *WaitBlockBypassStart* state, and the thread's wait status register now shows the *WaitAborted* wait state. Another possible scenario is for an alert or APC to have been issued to the waiting thread, which does not set the *WaitAborted* state but enables one of the corresponding bits in the wait status register. Because APCs can break waits (depending on the type of APC, wait mode, and alertability), the APC is delivered and the wait is aborted. Other operations that will modify the wait status register without generating a full abort cycle include modifications to the thread's priority or affinity, which will be processed when exiting the wait due to failure to commit, as with the previous cases mentioned.

Figure 3-27 shows the relationship of dispatcher objects to wait blocks to threads to PRCB. In this example, CPU 0 has two waiting (committed) threads: thread 1 is waiting for object B, and thread 2 is waiting for objects A *and* B. If object A is signaled, the kernel sees that because thread 2 is also waiting for another object, thread 2 can't be readied for execution. On the other hand, if object B is signaled, the kernel can ready thread 1 for execution right away because it isn't waiting for any other objects. (Alternatively, if thread 1 was also waiting for other objects but its wait type was a *WaitAny*, the kernel could still wake it up.)

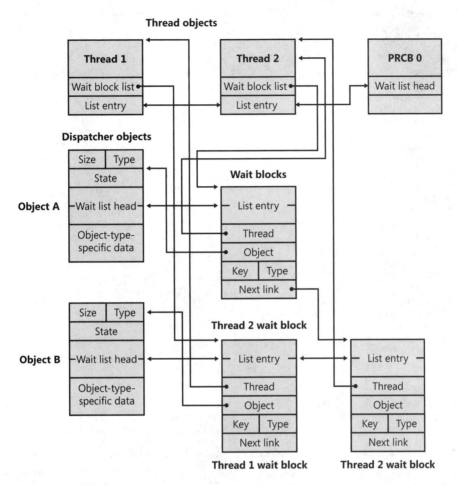

FIGURE 3-27 Wait data structures

EXPERIMENT: Looking at Wait Queues

You can see the list of objects a thread is waiting for with the kernel debugger's *!thread* command. For example, the following excerpt from the output of a *!process* command shows that the thread is waiting for an event object:

```
kd> !process
§
        THREAD fffffa8005292060  Cid 062c062c.0660  Teb: 000007fffffde000 Win32Thread:
fffff900c01c68f0 WAIT: (WrUserRequest) UserMode Non-Alertable
            fffffa80047b8240  SynchronizationEvent
```

You can use the *dt* command to interpret the dispatcher header of the object like this:

```
lkd> dt nt!_DISPATCHER_HEADER fffffa80047b8240
   +0x000 Type                    : 0x1 ''
   +0x001 TimerControlFlags       : 0 ''
   +0x001 Absolute                : 0y0
   +0x001Coalescable             : 0y0
   +0x001 KeepShifting            : 0y0
   +0x001 EncodedTolerableDelay   : 0y00000 (0)
   +0x001 Abandoned               : 0 ''
   +0x001 Signalling              : 0 ''
   +0x002 ThreadControlFlags      : 0x6 ''
   +0x002 CpuThrottled            : 0y0
   +0x002 CycleProfiling          : 0y1
   +0x002 CounterProfiling        : 0y1
   +0x002 Reserved                : 0y00000 (0)
   +0x002 Hand                    : 0x6 ''
   +0x002 Size                    : 0x6
   +0x003 TimerMiscFlags          : 0 ''
   +0x003 Index                   : 0y000000 (0)
   +0x003 Inserted                : 0y0
   +0x003 Expired                 : 0y0
   +0x003 DebugActive             : 0 ''
   +0x003 ActiveDR7               : 0y0
   +0x003 Instrumented            : 0y0
   +0x003 Reserved2               : 0y0000
   +0x003 UmsScheduled            : 0y0
   +0x003 UmsPrimary              : 0y0
   +0x003 DpcActive               : 0 ''
   +0x000 Lock                    : 393217
   +0x004 SignalState             : 0
   +0x008 WaitListHead            : _LIST_ENTRY [ 0xfffffa80'047b8248 - 0xfffffa80'047b8248 ]
```

You should ignore any values that do not correspond to the given object type, because they might be either incorrectly decoded by the debugger (because the wrong type or field is being used) or simply contain stale or invalid data from a previous allocation value. There is no defined correlation you can see between which fields apply to which object, other than by looking at the Windows kernel source code or the WDK header files' comments. For convenience, Table 3-21 lists the dispatcher header flags and the objects to which they apply.

TABLE 3-21 Usage and Meaning of the Dispatcher Header Flags

Flag	Applies To	Meaning
Absolute	Timers	The expiration time is absolute, not relative.
Coalescable	Periodic Timers	Indicates whether coalescing should be used for this timer.
KeepShifting	Coalescable Timers	Indicates whether or not the kernel dispatcher should continue attempting to shift the timer's expiration time. When alignment is reached with the machine's periodic interval, this eventually becomes FALSE.
EncodedTolerableDelay	Coalescable Timers	The maximum amount of tolerance (shifted as a power of two) that the timer can support when running outside of its expected periodicity.

Flag	Applies To	Meaning
Abandoned	Mutexes	The thread holding the mutex was terminated.
Signaling	Gates	A priority boost should be applied to the woken thread when the gate is signaled.
CpuThrottled	Threads	CPU throttling has been enabled for this thread, such as when running under DFSS mode (Dynamic Fair-Share Scheduler).
CycleProfiling	Threads	CPU cycle profiling has been enabled for this thread.
CounterProfiling	Threads	Hardware CPU performance counter monitoring/profiling has been enabled for this thread.
Size	All objects	Size of the object divided by 4, to fit in a single byte.
Hand	Timers	Index into the timer handle table.
Index	Timers	Index into the timer expiration table.
Inserted	Timers	Set if the timer was inserted into the timer handle table.
Expired	Timers	Set if the timer has already expired.
DebugActive	Processes	Specifies whether the process is being debugged.
ActiveDR7	Thread	Hardware breakpoints are being used, so DR7 is active and should be sanitized during context operations.
Instrumented	Thread	Specifies whether the thread has a user-mode instrumentation callback (supported only on Windows for x64 processors).
UmsScheduled	Thread	This thread is a UMS Worker (scheduled) thread.
UmsPrimary	Thread	This thread is a UMS Scheduler (primary) thread.
DpcActive	Mutexes	The mutex was acquired during a DPC.
Lock	All objects	Used for locking an object during wait operations which need to modify its state or linkage; actually corresponds to bit 7 (0x80) of the Type field.

Apart from these flags, the Type field contains the identifier for the object. This identifier corresponds to a number in the KOBJECTS enumeration, which you can dump with the debugger:

```
lkd> dt nt!_KOBJECTS
    EventNotificationObject = 0
    EventSynchronizationObject = 1
    MutantObject = 2
    ProcessObject = 3
    QueueObject = 4
    SemaphoreObject = 5
    ThreadObject = 6
    GateObject = 7
    TimerNotificationObject = 8
    TimerSynchronizationObject = 9
    Spare2Object = 10
```

```
         Spare3Object = 11
         Spare4Object = 12
         Spare5Object = 13
         Spare6Object = 14
         Spare7Object = 15
         Spare8Object = 16
         Spare9Object = 17
         ApcObject = 18
         DpcObject = 19
         DeviceQueueObject = 20
         EventPairObject = 21
         InterruptObject = 22
         ProfileObject = 23
         ThreadedDpcObject = 24
         MaximumKernelObject = 25
```

When the wait list head pointers are identical, there are either zero threads or one thread waiting on this object. Dumping a wait block for an object that is part of a multiple wait from a thread, or that multiple threads are waiting on, can yield the following:

```
dt nt!_KWAIT_BLOCK 0xfffffa80'053cf628
   +0x000 WaitListEntry   : _LIST_ENTRY [ 0xfffffa80'02efe568 - 0xfffffa80'02803468 ]
   +0x010 Thread          : 0xfffffa80'053cf520 _KTHREAD
   +0x018 Object          : 0xfffffa80'02803460
   +0x020 NextWaitBlock   : 0xfffffa80'053cf628 _KWAIT_BLOCK
   +0x028 WaitKey         : 0
   +0x02a WaitType        : 0x1 ''
   +0x02b BlockState      : 0x2 ''
   +0x02c SpareLong       : 8
```

If the wait list has more than one entry, you can execute the same command on the second pointer value in the *WaitListEntry* field of each wait block (by executing *!thread* on the thread pointer in the wait block) to traverse the list and see what other threads are waiting for the object. This would indicate more than one thread waiting on this object. On the other hand, when dealing with an object that's part of a collection of objects being waited on by a single thread, you have to parse the *NextWaitBlock* field instead.

Keyed Events

A synchronization object called a *keyed event* bears special mention because of the role it plays in user-mode-exclusive synchronization primitives. Keyed events were originally implemented to help processes deal with low-memory situations when using critical sections, which are user-mode synchronization objects that we'll see more about shortly. A keyed event, which is not documented, allows a thread to specify a "key" for which it waits, where the thread wakes when another thread of the same process signals the event with the same key.

If there is contention, *EnterCriticalSection* dynamically allocates an event object, and the thread wanting to acquire the critical section waits for the thread that owns the critical section to signal it in *LeaveCriticalSection*. Unfortunately, this introduces a new problem. Without keyed events, the system could be critically out of memory and critical-section acquisition could fail because the system was unable to allocate the event object required. The low-memory condition itself might have been caused by the application trying to acquire the critical section, so the system would deadlock in this situation. Low memory isn't the only scenario that could cause this to fail: a less likely scenario is handle exhaustion. If the process reaches its 16-million-handle limit, the new handle for the event object could fail.

The failure caused by low-memory conditions typically are an exception from the code responsible for acquiring the critical section. Unfortunately, the result is also a damaged critical section, which makes the situation hard to debug and makes the object useless for a reacquisition attempt. Attempting a *LeaveCriticalSection* results in another event-object allocation attempt, further generating exceptions and corrupting the structure.

Allocating a global standard event object would not fix the issue because standard event primitives can be used only for a single object. Each critical section in the process still requires its own event object, so the same problem would resurface. The implementation of keyed events allows multiple critical sections (waiters) to use the same global (per-process) keyed event handle. This allows the critical section functions to operate properly even when memory is temporarily low.

When a thread signals a keyed event or performs a wait on it, it uses a unique identifier called a *key*, which identifies the instance of the keyed event (an association of the keyed event to a single critical section). When the owner thread releases the keyed event by signaling it, only a single thread waiting on the key is woken up (the same behavior as *synchronization events*, in contrast to *notification events*). Additionally, only the waiters in the current process are awakened, so the key is even isolated across processes, meaning that there is actually only a single keyed event object for the entire system. When a critical section uses the keyed event, *EnterCriticalSection* sets the key as the address of the critical section and performs a wait.

When *EnterCriticalSection* calls *NtWaitForKeyedEvent* to perform a wait on the keyed event, it can now give a NULL handle as parameter for the keyed event, telling the kernel that it was unable to create a keyed event. The kernel recognizes this behavior and uses a global keyed event named *ExpCritSecOutOfMemoryEvent*. The primary benefit is that processes don't need to waste a handle for a named keyed event anymore because the kernel keeps track of the object and its references.

However, keyed events are more than just fallback objects for low-memory conditions. When multiple waiters are waiting on the same key and need to be woken up, the key is actually signaled multiple times, which requires the object to keep a list of all the waiters so that it can perform a "wake" operation on each of them. (Recall that the result of signaling a keyed event is the same as that of signaling a synchronization event.) However, a thread can signal a keyed event without any threads on the waiter list. In this scenario, the signaling thread instead waits on the event itself. Without this fallback, a signaling thread could signal the keyed event during the time that the user-mode code saw the keyed event as unsignaled and attempt a wait. The wait might have come *after* the signaling thread signaled the keyed event, resulting in a missed pulse, so the waiting thread would deadlock. By forcing the signaling thread to wait in this scenario, it actually signals the keyed event only when someone is looking (waiting).

Note When the keyed-event wait code itself needs to perform a wait, it uses a built-in semaphore located in the kernel-mode thread object (ETHREAD) called *KeyedWaitSemaphore*. (This semaphore actually shares its location with the ALPC wait semaphore.) See Chapter 5 for more information on thread objects.

Keyed events, however, do not replace standard event objects in the critical section implementation. The initial reason, during the Windows XP timeframe, was that keyed events do not offer scalable performance in heavy-usage scenarios. Recall that all the algorithms described were meant to be used only in critical, low-memory scenarios, when performance and scalability aren't all that important. To replace the standard event object would place strain on keyed events that they weren't implemented to handle. The primary performance bottleneck was that keyed events maintained the list of waiters described in a doubly linked list. This kind of list has poor *traversal speed*, meaning the time required to loop through the list. In this case, this time depended on the number of waiter threads. Because the object is global, dozens of threads could be on the list, requiring long traversal times every single time a key was set or waited on.

Note The head of the list is kept in the keyed event object, while the threads are actually linked through the *KeyedWaitChain* field (which is actually shared with the thread's exit time, stored as a LARGE_INTEGER, the same size as a doubly linked list) in the kernel-mode thread object (ETHREAD). See Chapter 5 for more information on this object.

Windows improves keyed-event performance by using a hash table instead of a linked list to hold the waiter threads. This optimization allows Windows to include three new lightweight user-mode synchronization primitives (to be discussed shortly) that all depend on the keyed event. Critical sections, however, still continue to use event objects, primarily for application compatibility and debugging, because the event object and internals are well known and documented, while keyed events are opaque and not exposed to the Win32 API.

Fast Mutexes and Guarded Mutexes

Fast mutexes, which are also known as *executive mutexes*, usually offer better performance than mutex objects because, although they are built on dispatcher event objects, they perform a wait through the dispatcher only if the fast mutex is contended—unlike a standard mutex, which always attempts the acquisition through the dispatcher. This gives the fast mutex especially good performance in a multiprocessor environment. Fast mutexes are used widely in device drivers.

However, fast mutexes are suitable only when normal kernel-mode APC (described earlier in this chapter) delivery can be disabled. The executive defines two functions for acquiring them: *ExAcquireFastMutex* and *ExAcquireFastMutexUnsafe*. The former function blocks all APC delivery by raising the IRQL of the processor to APC level. The latter expects to be called with normal kernel-mode APC delivery disabled, which can be done by raising the IRQL to APC level. *ExTryToAcquireFastMutex* performs similarly to the first, but it does not actually wait if the fast mutex is already held, returning FALSE instead. Another limitation of fast mutexes is that they can't be acquired recursively, like mutex objects can.

Guarded mutexes are essentially the same as fast mutexes (although they use a different synchronization object, the KGATE, internally). They are acquired with the *KeAcquireGuardedMutex* and *KeAcquireGuardedMutexUnsafe* functions, but instead of disabling APCs by raising the IRQL to APC level, they disable all kernel-mode APC delivery by calling *KeEnterGuardedRegion*. Similarly to fast mutexes, a *KeTryToAcquireGuardedMutex* method also exists. Recall that a guarded region, unlike a critical region, disables both special and normal kernel-mode APCs, which allows the guarded mutex to avoid raising the IRQL.

Three differences make guarded mutexes faster than fast mutexes:

- By avoiding raising the IRQL, the kernel can avoid talking to the local APIC of every processor on the bus, which is a significant operation on large SMP systems. On uniprocessor systems, this isn't a problem because of lazy IRQL evaluation, but lowering the IRQL might still require accessing the PIC.

- The gate primitive is an optimized version of the event. By not having both synchronization and notification versions and by being the exclusive object that a thread can wait on, the code for acquiring and releasing a gate is heavily optimized. Gates even have their own dispatcher lock instead of acquiring the entire dispatcher database.

- In the noncontended case, the acquisition and release of a guarded mutex works on a single bit, with an atomic bit test-and-reset operation instead of the more complex integer operations fast mutexes perform.

> **Note** The code for a fast mutex is also optimized to account for almost all these optimizations—it uses the same *atomic lock* operation, and the event object is actually a gate object (although by dumping the type in the kernel debugger, you would still see an event object structure; this is actually a compatibility lie). However, fast mutexes still raise the IRQL instead of using guarded regions.

Because the flag responsible for special kernel APC delivery disabling (and the guarded-region functionality) was not added until Windows Server 2003, many drivers do not take advantage of guarded mutexes. Doing so would raise compatibility issues with earlier versions of Windows, which require a recompiled driver making use only of fast mutexes. Internally, however, the Windows kernel has replaced almost all uses of fast mutexes with guarded mutexes because the two have identical semantics and can be easily interchanged.

Another problem related to the guarded mutex was the kernel function *KeAreApcsDisabled*. Prior to Windows Server 2003, this function indicated whether normal APCs were disabled by checking whether the code was running inside a critical section. In Windows Server 2003, this function was changed to indicate whether the code was in a critical, or guarded, region, changing the functionality to also return TRUE if special kernel APCs are also disabled.

Because there are certain operations that drivers should not perform when special kernel APCs are disabled, it makes sense to call *KeGetCurrentIrql* to check whether the IRQL is APC level or not, which is the only way special kernel APCs could have been disabled. However, because the memory manager makes use of guarded mutexes instead, this check fails because guarded mutexes do not raise IRQL. Drivers should instead call *KeAreAllApcsDisabled* for this purpose. This function checks whether special kernel APCs are disabled and/or whether the IRQL is APC level—the sure-fire way to detect both guarded mutexes and fast mutexes.

Executive Resources

Executive resources are a synchronization mechanism that supports shared and exclusive access; like fast mutexes, they require that normal kernel-mode APC delivery be disabled before they are acquired. They are also built on dispatcher objects that are used only when there is contention. Executive resources are used throughout the system, especially in file-system drivers, because such drivers tend to have long-lasting wait periods in which I/O should still be allowed to some extent (such as reads).

Threads waiting to acquire an executive resource for shared access wait for a semaphore associated with the resource, and threads waiting to acquire an executive resource for exclusive access wait for an event. A semaphore with unlimited count is used for shared waiters because they can all be woken and granted access to the resource when an exclusive holder releases the resource simply by signaling the semaphore. When a thread waits for exclusive access of a resource that is currently owned, it waits on a synchronization event object because only one of the waiters will wake when the event is signaled. In the earlier section on synchronization events, it was mentioned that some event unwait operations can actually cause a priority boost: this scenario occurs when executive resources are used, which is one reason why they also track ownership like mutexes do. (See Chapter 5 for more information on the executive resource priority boost.)

Because of the flexibility that shared and exclusive access offer, there are a number of functions for acquiring resources: *ExAcquireResourceSharedLite*, *ExAcquireResourceExclusiveLite*, *ExAcquireSharedStarveExclusive*, *ExAcquireShareWaitForExclusive*. These functions are documented in the WDK.

EXPERIMENT: Listing Acquired Executive Resources

The kernel debugger *!locks* command searches paged pool for executive resource objects and dumps their state. By default, the command lists only executive resources that are currently owned, but the *–d* option lists all executive resources. Here is partial output of the command:

```
lkd> !locks
**** DUMP OF ALL RESOURCE OBJECTS ****
KD: Scanning for held locks.

Resource @ 0x89929320    Exclusively owned
    Contention Count = 3911396
     Threads: 8952d030-01<*>
```

```
KD: Scanning for held locks.......................................

Resource @ 0x89da1a68    Shared 1 owning threads
    Threads: 8a4cb533-01<*> *** Actual Thread 8a4cb530
```

Note that the contention count, which is extracted from the resource structure, records the number of times threads have tried to acquire the resource and had to wait because it was already owned.

You can examine the details of a specific resource object, including the thread that owns the resource and any threads that are waiting for the resource, by specifying the –v switch and the address of the resource:

```
lkd> !locks -v 0x89929320

Resource @ 0x89929320    Exclusively owned
    Contention Count = 3913573
    Threads: 8952d030-01<*>

    THREAD 8952d030  Cid 0acc.050c  Teb: 7ffdf000 Win32Thread: fe82c4c0 RUNNING on
processor 0
    Not impersonating
    DeviceMap              9aa0bdb8
    Owning Process         89e1ead8      Image:          windbg.exe
    Wait Start TickCount   24620588      Ticks: 12 (0:00:00.187)
    Context Switch Count   772193
    UserTime               00:00:02.293
    KernelTime             00:00:09.828
    Win32 Start Address windbg (0x006e63b8)
    Stack Init a7eba000 Current a7eb9c10 Base a7eba000 Limit a7eb7000 Call 0
    Priority 10 BasePriority 8 PriorityDecrement 0 IoPriority 2 PagePriority 5
Unable to get context for thread running on processor 1, HRESULT 0x80004001
1 total locks, 1 locks currently held
```

Pushlocks

Pushlocks are another optimized synchronization mechanism built on gate objects; like guarded mutexes, they wait for a gate object only when there's contention on the lock. They offer advantages over the guarded mutex in that they can be acquired in shared or exclusive mode. However, their main advantage is their size: a resource object is 56 bytes, but a pushlock is pointer-size. Unfortunately, they are not documented in the WDK and are therefore reserved for use by the operating system (although the APIs are exported, so internal drivers do use them).

There are two types of pushlocks: normal and cache-aware. Normal pushlocks require only the size of a pointer in storage (4 bytes on 32-bit systems, and 8 bytes on 64-bit systems). When a thread acquires a normal pushlock, the pushlock code marks the pushlock as owned if it is not currently owned. If the pushlock is owned exclusively or the thread wants to acquire the thread exclusively and the pushlock is owned on a shared basis, the thread allocates a wait block on the thread's stack, initializes a gate object in the wait block, and adds the wait block to the wait list associated with the pushlock. When a thread releases a pushlock, the thread wakes a waiter, if any are present, by signaling the event in the waiter's wait block.

Because a pushlock is only pointer-sized, it actually contains a variety of bits to describe its state. The meaning of those bits changes as the pushlock changes from being contended to noncontended. In its initial state, the pushlock contains the following structure:

- One lock bit, set to 1 if the lock is acquired

- One waiting bit, set to 1 if the lock is contended and someone is waiting on it

- One waking bit, set to 1 if the lock is being granted to a thread and the waiter's list needs to be optimized

- One multiple shared bit, set to 1 if the pushlock is shared and currently acquired by more than one thread

- 28 (on 32-bit Windows) or 60 (on 64-bit Windows) share count bits, containing the number of threads that have acquired the pushlock

As discussed previously, when a thread acquires a pushlock exclusively while the pushlock is already acquired by either multiple readers or a writer, the kernel allocates a pushlock wait block. The structure of the pushlock value itself changes. The share count bits now become the pointer to the wait block. Because this wait block is allocated on the stack and the header files contain a special alignment directive to force it to be 16-byte aligned, the bottom 4 bits of any pushlock wait-block structure will be all zeros. Therefore, those bits are ignored for the purposes of pointer dereferencing; instead, the 4 bits shown earlier are combined with the pointer value. Because this alignment removes the share count bits, the share count is now stored in the wait block instead.

A cache-aware pushlock adds layers to the normal (basic) pushlock by allocating a pushlock for each processor in the system and associating it with the cache-aware pushlock. When a thread wants to acquire a cache-aware pushlock for shared access, it simply acquires the pushlock allocated for its current processor in shared mode; to acquire a cache-aware pushlock exclusively, the thread acquires the pushlock for each processor in exclusive mode.

Other than a much smaller memory footprint, one of the large advantages that pushlocks have over executive resources is that in the noncontended case they do not require lengthy accounting and integer operations to perform acquisition or release. By being as small as a pointer, the kernel can use atomic CPU instructions to perform these tasks. (*lock cmpxchg* is used, which atomically compares and exchanges the old lock with a new lock.) If the atomic compare and exchange fails, the lock contains values the caller did not expect (callers usually expect the lock to be unused or acquired as shared), and a call is then made to the more complex contended version. To improve performance even further, the kernel exposes the pushlock functionality as inline functions, meaning that no function calls are ever generated during noncontended acquisition—the assembly code is directly inserted in each function. This increases code size slightly, but it avoids the slowness of a function call. Finally, pushlocks use several algorithmic tricks to avoid lock convoys (a situation that can occur when multiple threads of the same priority are all waiting on a lock and little actual work gets done), and they are also self-optimizing: the list of threads waiting on a pushlock will be periodically rearranged to provide fairer behavior when the pushlock is released.

Areas in which pushlocks are used include the object manager, where they protect global object-manager data structures and object security descriptors, and the memory manager, where their cache-aware counterpart is used to protect Address Windowing Extension (AWE) data structures.

Deadlock Detection with Driver Verifier

A deadlock is a synchronization issue resulting from two threads or processors holding resources that the other wants and neither yielding what it has. This situation might result in system or process hangs. Driver Verifier, described in Chapter 8 in Part 2 and Chapter 9 in Part 2, has an option to check for deadlocks involving spinlocks, fast mutexes, and mutexes. For information on when to enable Driver Verifier to help resolve system hangs, see Chapter 14 in Part 2.

Critical Sections

Critical sections are one of the main synchronization primitives that Windows provides to user-mode applications on top of the kernel-based synchronization primitives. Critical sections and the other user-mode primitives you'll see later have one major advantage over their kernel counterparts, which is saving a round-trip to kernel mode in cases in which the lock is noncontended (which is typically 99 percent of the time or more). Contended cases still require calling the kernel, however, because it is the only piece of the system that is able to perform the complex waking and dispatching logic required to make these objects work.

Critical sections are able to remain in user mode by using a local bit to provide the main exclusive locking logic, much like a spinlock. If the bit is 0, the critical section can be acquired, and the owner sets the bit to 1. This operation doesn't require calling the kernel but uses the interlocked CPU operations discussed earlier. Releasing the critical section behaves similarly, with bit state changing from 1 to 0 with an interlocked operation. On the other hand, as you can probably guess, when the bit is already 1 and another caller attempts to acquire the critical section, the kernel must be called to put the thread in a wait state.Finally, because critical sections are not kernel objects, they have certain limitations. The primary one is that you cannot obtain a kernel handle to a critical section; as such, no security, naming, or other object manager functionality can be applied to a critical section. Two processes cannot use the same critical section to coordinate their operations, nor can duplication or inheritance be used.

User-Mode Resources

User-mode resources also provide more fine-grained locking mechanisms than kernel primitives. A resource can be acquired for shared mode or for exclusive mode, allowing it to function as a multiple-reader (shared), single-writer (exclusive) lock for data structures such as databases. When a resource is acquired in shared mode and other threads attempt to acquire the same resource, no trip to the kernel is required because none of the threads will be waiting. Only when a thread attempts to acquire the resource for exclusive access, or the resource is already locked by an exclusive owner, will this be required.

To make use of the same dispatching and synchronization mechanism you saw in the kernel, resources actually make use of existing kernel primitives. A resource data structure (RTL_RESOURCE) contains handles to a kernel mutex as well as a kernel semaphore object. When the resource is acquired exclusively by more than one thread, the resource uses the mutex because it permits only one owner. When the resource is acquired in shared mode by more than one thread, the resource uses a semaphore because it allows multiple owner counts. This level of detail is typically hidden from the programmer, and these internal objects should never be used directly.

Resources were originally implemented to support the SAM (or Security Account Manager, which is discussed in Chapter 6) and not exposed through the Windows API for standard applications. Slim Reader-Writer Locks (SRW Locks), described next, were implemented in Windows Vista to expose a similar locking primitive through a documented API, although some system components still use the resource mechanism.

Condition Variables

Condition variables provide a Windows native implementation for synchronizing a set of threads that are waiting on a specific result to a conditional test. Although this operation was possible with other user-mode synchronization methods, there was no *atomic* mechanism to check the result of the conditional test and to begin waiting on a change in the result. This required that additional synchronization be used around such pieces of code.

A user-mode thread initializes a condition variable by calling *InitializeConditionVariable* to set up the initial state. When it wants to initiate a wait on the variable, it can call *SleepConditionVariableCS*, which uses a critical section (that the thread must have initialized) to wait for changes to the variable. The setting thread must use *WakeConditionVariable* (or *WakeAllConditionVariable*) after it has modified the variable. (There is no automatic detection mechanism.) This call releases the critical section of either one or all waiting threads, depending on which function was used.

Before condition variables, it was common to use either a *notification event* or a *synchronization event* (recall that these are referred to as *auto-reset* or *manual-reset* in the Windows API) to signal the change to a variable, such as the state of a worker queue. Waiting for a change required a critical section to be acquired and then released, followed by a wait on an event. After the wait, the critical section had to be re-acquired. During this series of acquisitions and releases, the thread might have switched contexts, causing problems if one of the threads called *PulseEvent* (a similar problem to the one that keyed events solve by forcing a wait for the signaling thread if there is no waiter). With condition variables, acquisition of the critical section can be maintained by the application while *SleepConditionVariableCS* is called and can be released only after the actual work is done. This makes writing work-queue code (and similar implementations) much simpler and predictable.

Internally, condition variables can be thought of as a port of the existing pushlock algorithms present in kernel mode, with the additional complexity of acquiring and releasing critical sections in the *SleepConditionVariableCS* API. Condition variables are pointer-size (just like pushlocks), avoid using the dispatcher (which requires a ring transition to kernel mode in this scenario, making the advantage even more noticeable), automatically optimize the wait list during wait operations, and protect against lock convoys. Additionally, condition variables make full use of keyed events instead of the regular event object that developers would have used on their own, which makes even contended cases more optimized.

Slim Reader-Writer Locks

Although condition variables are a synchronization mechanism, they are not fully primitive locking objects. As you've seen, they still depend on the critical section lock, whose acquisition and release uses standard dispatcher event objects, so trips through kernel mode can still happen and callers still require the initialization of the large critical section object. If condition variables share a lot of similarities with pushlocks, Slim Reader-Writer Locks (SRW Locks) are nearly identical. They are also pointer-size, use atomic operations for acquisition and release, rearrange their waiter lists, protect against lock convoys, and can be acquired both in shared and exclusive mode. Some differences from pushlocks, however, include the fact that SRW Locks cannot be "upgraded" or converted from shared to exclusive or vice versa. Additionally, they cannot be recursively acquired. Finally, SRW Locks are exclusive to user-mode code, while pushlocks are exclusive to kernel-mode code, and the two cannot be shared or exposed from one layer to the other.

Not only can SRW Locks entirely replace critical sections in application code, but they also offer multiple-reader, single-writer functionality. SRW Locks must first be initialized with *InitializeSRWLock*, after which they can be acquired or released in either exclusive or shared mode with the appropriate APIs: *AcquireSRWLockExclusive*, *ReleaseSRWLockExclusive*, *AcquireSRWLockShared*, and *ReleaseSRWLockShared*.

> **Note** Unlike most other Windows APIs, the SRW locking functions do not return with a value—instead they generate exceptions if the lock could not be acquired. This makes it obvious that an acquisition has failed so that code that assumes success will terminate instead of potentially proceeding to corrupt user data.

The Windows SRW Locks do not prefer readers or writers, meaning that the performance for either case should be the same. This makes them great replacements for critical sections, which are writer-only or *exclusive* synchronization mechanisms, and they provide an optimized alternative to resources. If SRW Locks were optimized for readers, they would be poor exclusive-only locks, but this isn't the case. As a result, the design of the condition variable mechanism introduced earlier also allows for the use of SRW Locks instead of critical sections, through the *SleepConditionVariableSRW* API. Finally, SRW Locks also use keyed events instead of standard event objects, so the combination of condition variables and SRW Locks results in scalable, pointer-size synchronization mechanisms with very few trips to kernel mode—except in contended cases, which are optimized to take less time and memory to wake and set because of the use of keyed events.

Run Once Initialization

The ability to guarantee the *atomic* execution of a piece of code responsible for performing some sort of initialization task—such as allocating memory, initializing certain variables, or even creating objects on demand—is a typical problem in multithreaded programming. In a piece of code that can be called simultaneously by multiple threads (a good example is the *DllMain* routine, which initializes a DLL), there are several ways of attempting to ensure the correct, atomic, and unique execution of initialization tasks.

In this scenario, Windows implements *init once,* or *one-time initialization* (also called *run once initialization* internally). This mechanism allows for both synchronous (meaning that the other threads must wait for initialization to complete) execution of a certain piece of code, as well as asynchronous (meaning that the other threads can attempt to do their own initialization and race) execution. We'll look at the logic behind asynchronous execution after explaining the synchronous mechanism.

In the synchronous case, the developer writes the piece of code that would normally execute after double-checking the global variable in a dedicated function. Any information that this routine needs can be passed through the *parameter* variable that the init-once routine accepts. Any output information is returned through the *context* variable. (The status of the initialization itself is returned as a Boolean.) All the developer has to do to ensure proper execution is call *InitOnceExecuteOnce* with the *parameter, context,* and run-once function pointer after initializing an INIT_ONCE object with *InitOnceInitialize* API. The system will take care of the rest.

For applications that want to use the asynchronous model instead, the threads call *InitOnceBeginInitialize* and receive a BOOLEAN *pending status* and the *context* described earlier. If the *pending status* is FALSE, initialization has already taken place, and the thread uses the context value for the result. (It's also possible for the function itself to return FALSE, meaning that initialization failed.) However, if the pending status comes back as TRUE, the thread should *race* to be the first to create the object. The code that follows performs whatever initialization tasks are required, such as creating objects or allocating memory. When this work is done, the thread calls *InitOnceComplete* with the result of the work as the context and receives a BOOLEAN *status.* If the status is TRUE, the thread won the race, and the object that it created or allocated is the one that will be the global object. The thread can now save this object or return it to a caller, depending on the usage.

In the more complex scenario when the status is FALSE, this means that the thread lost the race. The thread must undo all the work it did, such as deleting objects or freeing memory, and then call *InitOnceBeginInitialize* again. However, instead of requesting to start a race as it did initially, it uses the *INIT_ONCE_CHECK_ONLY* flag, knowing that it has lost, and requests the winner's context instead (for example, the objects or memory that were created or allocated by the winner). This returns another *status,* which can be TRUE, meaning that the context is valid and should be used or returned to the caller, or FALSE, meaning that initialization failed and nobody has actually been able to perform the work (such as in the case of a low-memory condition, perhaps).

In both cases, the mechanism for run-once initialization is similar to the mechanism for condition variables and SRW Locks. The *init once* structure is pointer-size, and inline assembly versions of the

SRW acquisition/release code are used for the noncontended case, while keyed events are used when contention has occurred (which happens when the mechanism is used in synchronous mode) and the other threads must wait for initialization. In the asynchronous case, the locks are used in shared mode, so multiple threads can perform initialization at the same time.

System Worker Threads

During system initialization, Windows creates several threads in the System process, called *system worker threads*, which exist solely to perform work on behalf of other threads. In many cases, threads executing at DPC/dispatch level need to execute functions that can be performed only at a lower IRQL. For example, a DPC routine, which executes in an arbitrary thread context (because DPC execution can usurp any thread in the system) at DPC/dispatch level IRQL, might need to access paged pool or wait for a dispatcher object used to synchronize execution with an application thread. Because a DPC routine can't lower the IRQL, it must pass such processing to a thread that executes at an IRQL below DPC/dispatch level.

Some device drivers and executive components create their own threads dedicated to processing work at passive level; however, most use system worker threads instead, which avoids the unnecessary scheduling and memory overhead associated with having additional threads in the system. An executive component requests a system worker thread's services by calling the executive functions *ExQueueWorkItem* or *IoQueueWorkItem*. Device drivers should use only the latter (because this associates the work item with a Device object, allowing for greater accountability and the handling of scenarios in which a driver unloads while its work item is active). These functions place a *work item* on a queue dispatcher object where the threads look for work. (Queue dispatcher objects are described in more detail in the section "I/O Completion Ports" in Chapter 8 in Part 2.)

The *IoQueueWorkItemEx, IoSizeofWorkItem, IoInitializeWorkItem,* and *IoUninitializeWorkItem* APIs act similarly, but they create an association with a driver's Driver object or one of its Device objects.

Work items include a pointer to a routine and a parameter that the thread passes to the routine when it processes the work item. The device driver or executive component that requires passive-level execution implements the routine. For example, a DPC routine that must wait for a dispatcher object can initialize a work item that points to the routine in the driver that waits for the dispatcher object, and perhaps points to a pointer to the object. At some stage, a system worker thread will remove the work item from its queue and execute the driver's routine. When the driver's routine finishes, the system worker thread checks to see whether there are more work items to process. If there aren't any more, the system worker thread blocks until a work item is placed on the queue. The DPC routine might or might not have finished executing when the system worker thread processes its work item.

There are three types of system worker threads:

- *Delayed worker threads* execute at priority 12, process work items that aren't considered time-critical, and can have their stack paged out to a paging file while they wait for work items. The object manager uses a delayed work item to perform deferred object deletion, which deletes kernel objects after they have been scheduled for freeing.

- *Critical worker threads* execute at priority 13, process time-critical work items, and on Windows Server systems have their stacks present in physical memory at all times.

- A single hypercritical worker thread executes at priority 15 and also keeps its stack in memory. The process manager uses the hypercritical work item to execute the thread "reaper" function that frees terminated threads.

The number of delayed and critical worker threads created by the executive's *ExpWorkerInitialization* function, which is called early in the boot process, depends on the amount of memory present on the system and whether the system is a server. Table 3-22 shows the initial number of threads created on default configurations. You can specify that *ExpInitializeWorker* create up to 16 additional delayed and 16 additional critical worker threads with the *AdditionalDelayedWorkerThreads* and *AdditionalCriticalWorkerThreads* values under the registry key HKLM\SYSTEM\CurrentControlSet\Control\Session Manager\Executive.

TABLE 3-22 Initial Number of System Worker Threads

Work Queue Type	Default Number of Threads
Delayed	7
Critical	5
Hypercritical	1

The executive tries to match the number of critical worker threads with changing workloads as the system executes. Once every second, the executive function *ExpWorkerThreadBalanceManager* determines whether it should create a new critical worker thread. The critical worker threads that are created by *ExpWorkerThreadBalanceManager* are called *dynamic worker threads*, and all the following conditions must be satisfied before such a thread is created:

- Work items exist in the critical work queue.

- The number of inactive critical worker threads (ones that are either blocked waiting for work items or that have blocked on dispatcher objects while executing a work routine) must be less than the number of processors on the system.

- There are fewer than 16 dynamic worker threads.

Dynamic worker threads exit after 10 minutes of inactivity. Thus, when the workload dictates, the executive can create up to 16 dynamic worker threads.

EXPERIMENT: Listing System Worker Threads

You can use the *!exqueue* kernel debugger command to see a listing of system worker threads classified by their type:

```
1kd> !exqueue
Dumping ExWorkerQueue: 820FDE40

**** Critical WorkQueue( current = 0 maximum = 2 )
THREAD 861160b8  Cid 0004.001c  Teb: 00000000 Win32Thread: 00000000 WAIT
THREAD 8613b020  Cid 0004.0020  Teb: 00000000 Win32Thread: 00000000 WAIT
THREAD 8613bd78  Cid 0004.0024  Teb: 00000000 Win32Thread: 00000000 WAIT
THREAD 8613bad0  Cid 0004.0028  Teb: 00000000 Win32Thread: 00000000 WAIT
THREAD 8613b828  Cid 0004.002c  Teb: 00000000 Win32Thread: 00000000 WAIT

**** Delayed WorkQueue( current = 0 maximum = 2 )
THREAD 8613b580  Cid 0004.0030  Teb: 00000000 Win32Thread: 00000000 WAIT
THREAD 8613b2d8  Cid 0004.0034  Teb: 00000000 Win32Thread: 00000000 WAIT
THREAD 8613c020  Cid 0004.0038  Teb: 00000000 Win32Thread: 00000000 WAIT
THREAD 8613cd78  Cid 0004.003c  Teb: 00000000 Win32Thread: 00000000 WAIT
THREAD 8613cad0  Cid 0004.0040  Teb: 00000000 Win32Thread: 00000000 WAIT
THREAD 8613c828  Cid 0004.0044  Teb: 00000000 Win32Thread: 00000000 WAIT
THREAD 8613c580  Cid 0004.0048  Teb: 00000000 Win32Thread: 00000000 WAIT

**** HyperCritical WorkQueue( current = 0 maximum = 2 )
THREAD 8613c2d8  Cid 0004.004c  Teb: 00000000 Win32Thread: 00000000 WAIT
```

Windows Global Flags

Windows has a set of flags stored in a systemwide global variable named *NtGlobalFlag* that enable various internal debugging, tracing, and validation support in the operating system. The system variable *NtGlobalFlag* is initialized from the registry key HKLM\SYSTEM\CurrentControlSet\Control \Session Manager in the value *GlobalFlag* at system boot time. By default, this registry value is 0, so it's likely that on your systems, you're not using any global flags. In addition, each image has a set of global flags that also turn on internal tracing and validation code (although the bit layout of these flags is entirely different from the systemwide global flags).

Fortunately, the debugging tools contains a utility named Gflags.exe you can use to view and change the system global flags (either in the registry or in the running system) as well as image global flags. Gflags has both a command-line and a GUI interface. To see the command-line flags, type **gflags /?**. If you run the utility without any switches, the dialog box shown in Figure 3-28 is displayed.

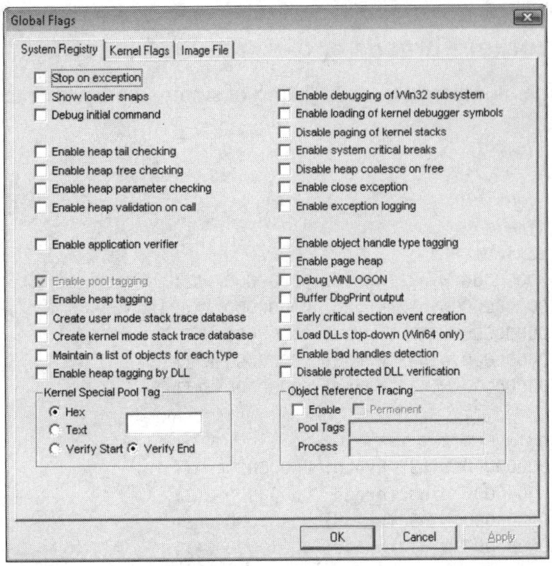

FIGURE 3-28 Setting system debugging options with Gflags

You can configure a variable's settings in the registry on the System Registry page or the current value of a variable in system memory on the Kernel Flags page.

The Image File page requires you to fill in the file name of an executable image. Use this option to change a set of global flags that apply to an individual image (rather than to the whole system). In Figure 3-29, notice that the flags are different from the operating system ones shown in Figure 3-28.

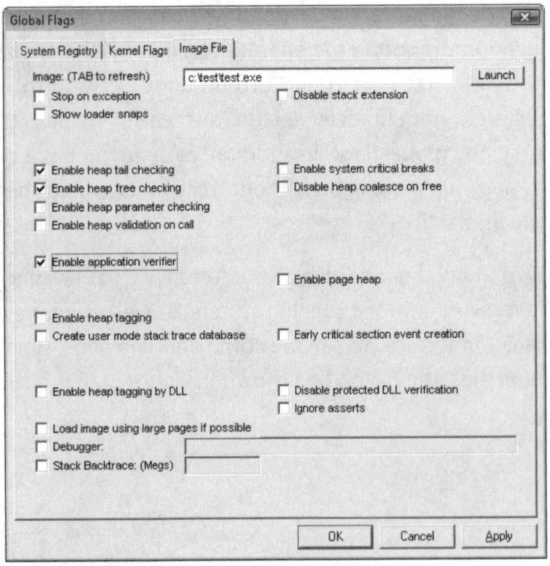

FIGURE 3-29 Setting image global flags with Gflags

EXPERIMENT: Viewing and Setting *NtGlobalFlag*

You can use the *!gflag* kernel debugger command to view and set the state of the *NtGlobalFlag* kernel variable. The *!gflag* command lists all the flags that are enabled. You can use *!gflag -?* to get the entire list of supported global flags.

Advanced Local Procedure Call

All modern operating systems require a mechanism for securely transferring data between one or more processes in user mode, as well as between a service in the kernel and clients in user mode. Typically, UNIX mechanisms such as mailslots, files, named pipes, and sockets are used for portability, while other developers use window messages for graphical applications. Windows implements an internal IPC mechanism called Advanced Local Procedure Call, or ALPC, which is a high-speed, scalable, and secured facility for message passing arbitrary-size messages. Although it is internal, and thus not available for third-party developers, ALPC is widely used in various parts of Windows:

- Windows applications that use remote procedure call (RPC), a documented API, indirectly use ALPC when they specify *local-RPC* over the *ncalrpc* transport, a form of RPC used to communicate between processes on the same system. Kernel-mode RPC, used by the network stack, also uses ALPC.

- Whenever a Windows process and/or thread starts, as well as during any Windows subsystem operation (such as all console I/O), ALPC is used to communicate with the subsystem process (CSRSS). All subsystems communicate with the session manager (SMSS) over ALPC.

- Winlogon uses ALPC to communicate with the local security authentication process, LSASS.

- The security reference monitor (an executive component explained in Chapter 6) uses ALPC to communicate with the LSASS process.

- The user-mode power manager and power monitor communicate with the kernel-mode power manager over ALPC, such as whenever the LCD brightness is changed.

- Windows Error Reporting uses ALPC to receive context information from crashing processes.

- The User-Mode Driver Framework (UMDF) enables user-mode drivers to communicate using ALPC.

Note ALPC is the replacement for an older IPC mechanism initially shipped with the very first kernel design of Windows NT, called LPC, which is why certain variables, fields, and functions might still refer to "LPC" today. Keep in mind that LPC is now emulated on top of ALPC for compatibility and has been removed from the kernel (legacy system calls still exist, which get wrapped into ALPC calls).

Connection Model

Typically, ALPCs are used between a server process and one or more client processes of that server. An ALPC connection can be established between two or more user-mode processes or between a kernel-mode component and one or more user-mode processes. ALPC exports a single executive object called the *port object* to maintain the state needed for communication. Although this is just one object, there are actually several kinds of ALPC ports that it can represent:

- **Server connection port** A named port that is a server connection request point. Clients can connect to the server by connecting to this port.

- **Server communication port** An unnamed port a server uses to communicate with a particular client. The server has one such port per active client.

- **Client communication port** An unnamed port a particular client thread uses to communicate with a particular server.

- **Unconnected communication port** An unnamed port a client can use to communicate locally with itself.

ALPC follows a connection and communication model that's somewhat reminiscent of BSD socket programming. A server first creates a server connection port (*NtAlpcCreatePort*), while a client attempts to connect to it (*NtAlpcConnectPort*). If the server was in a listening state, it receives a connection request message and can choose to accept it (*NtAlpcAcceptPort*). In doing so, both the client and server communication ports are created, and each respective endpoint process receives a handle to its communication port. Messages are then sent across this handle (*NtAlpcSendWaitReceiveMessage*), typically in a dedicated thread, so that the server can continue listening for connection requests on the original connection port (unless this server expects only one client).

The server also has the ability to deny the connection, either for security reasons or simply due to protocol or versioning issues. Because clients can send a custom payload with a connection request, this is usually used by various services to ensure that the correct client, or only one client, is talking to the server. If any anomalies are found, the server can reject the connection, and, optionally, return a payload containing information on why the client was rejected (allowing the client to take corrective action, if possible, or for debugging purposes).

Once a connection is made, a connection information structure (actually, a blob, as will be described shortly) stores the linkage between all the different ports, as shown in Figure 3-30.

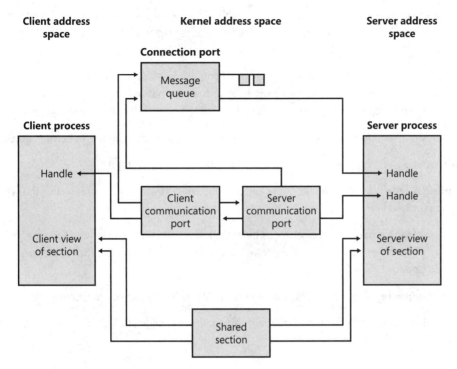

Client address space   **Kernel address space**   **Server address space**

Connection port

Message queue

Client process   **Server process**

Handle

Client communication port

Server communication port

Handle

Handle

Client view of section

Server view of section

Shared section

FIGURE 3-30 Use of ALPC ports

Message Model

Using ALPC, a client and thread using blocking messages each take turns performing a loop around the *NtAlpcSendWaitReplyPort* system call, in which one side sends a request and waits for a reply while the other side does the opposite. However, because ALPC supports asynchronous messages, it's possible for either side not to block and choose instead to perform some other runtime task and check for messages later (some of these methods will be described shortly). ALPC supports the following three methods of exchanging payloads sent with a message:

- A message can be sent to another process through the standard double-buffering mechanism, in which the kernel maintains a copy of the message (copying it from the source process), switches to the target process, and copies the data from the kernel's buffer. For compatibility, if legacy LPC is being used, only messages up to 256 bytes can be sent this way, while ALPC has the ability to allocate an *extension buffer* for messages up to ~64KB.

- A message can be stored in an ALPC section object from which the client and server processes map views. (See Chapter 10 in Part 2 for more information on section mappings.)

- A message can be stored in a *message zone*, which is an Memory Descriptor List (MDL) that backs the physical pages containing the data and that is mapped into the kernel's address space.

An important side effect of the ability to send asynchronuos messages is that a message can be canceled—for example, when a request takes too long or the user has indicated that she wants to cancel the operation it implements. ALPC supports this with the *NtAlpcCancelMessage* system call.

An ALPC message can be on one of four different queues implemented by the ALPC port object:

- **Main queue** A message has been sent, and the client is processing it.

- **Pending queue** A message has been sent and the caller is waiting for a reply, but the reply has not yet been sent.

- **Large message queue** A message has been sent, but the caller's buffer was too small to receive it. The caller gets another chance to allocate a larger buffer and request the message payload again.

- **Canceled queue** A message that was sent to the port, but has since been canceled.

Note that a fifth queue, called the *wait queue*, does not link messages together; instead, it links all the threads waiting on a message.

EXPERIMENT: Viewing Subsystem ALPC Port Objects

You can see named ALPC port objects with the WinObj tool from Sysinternals. Run Winobj.exe, and select the root directory. A gear icon identifies the port objects, as shown here:

You should see the ALPC ports used by the power manager, the security manager, and other internal Windows services. If you want to see the ALPC port objects used by RPC, you can select the \RPC Control directory. One of the primary users of ALPC, outside of Local RPC, is the Windows subsystem, which uses ALPC to communicate with the Windows subsystem DLLs that are present in all Windows processes. (Subsystem for UNIX Applications uses a similar mechanism.) Because CSRSS loads once for each session, you will find its ALPC port objects under the appropriate \Sessions\X\Windows directory, such as shown here:

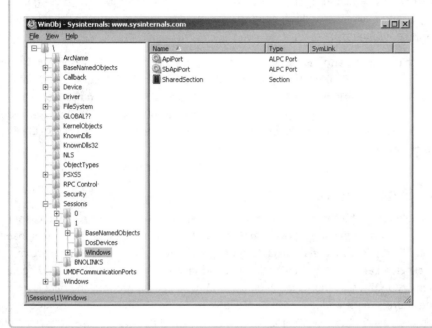

Asynchronous Operation

The synchronous model of ALPC is tied to the original LPC architecture in the early NT design, and is similar to other blocking IPC mechanisms, such as Mach ports. Although it is simple to design, a blocking IPC algorithm includes many possibilities for deadlock, and working around those scenarios creates complex code that requires support for a more flexible asynchronous (nonblocking) model. As such, ALPC was primarily designed to support asynchronous operation as well, which is a requirement for scalable RPC and other uses, such as support for pending I/O in user-mode drivers. A basic feature of ALPC, which wasn't originally present in LPC, is that blocking calls can have a timeout parameter. This allows legacy applications to avoid certain deadlock scenarios.

However, ALPC is optimized for asynchronous messages and provides three different models for asynchronous notifications. The first doesn't actually notify the client or server, but simply copies the data payload. Under this model, it's up to the implementor to choose a reliable synchronization method. For example, the client and the server can share a notification event object, or the client can poll for data arrival. The data structure used by this model is the ALPC *completion list* (not to be confused with the Windows I/O completion port). The ALPC completion list is an efficient, nonblocking data structure that enables atomic passing of data between clients, and its internals are described further in the "Performance" section.

The next notification model is a waiting model that uses the Windows completion-port mechanism (on top of the ALPC completion list). This enables a thread to retrieve multiple payloads at once, control the maximum number of concurrent requests, and take advantage of native completion-port functionality. The user-mode thread pool (described later in this chapter) implementation provides internal APIs that processes use to manage ALPC messages within the same infrastructure as worker threads, which are implemented using this model. The RPC system in Windows, when using Local RPC (over *ncalrpc*), also makes use of this functionality to provide efficient message delivery by taking advantage of this kernel support.

Finally, because drivers can also use asynchronous ALPC, but do not typically support completion ports at such a high-level, ALPC also provides a mechanism for a more basic, kernel-based notification using executive callback objects. A driver can register its own callback and context with *NtAlpcSetInformation*, after which it will get called whenever a message is received. The user-mode, power-manager interfaces in the kernel employ this mechanism for asynchronous LCD backlight operation on laptops, for example.

Views, Regions, and Sections

Instead of sending message buffers between their two respective processes, a server and client can choose a more efficient data-passing mechanism that is at the core of Windows' memory manager: the *section* object. (More information is available in Chapter 10 in Part 2.) This allows a piece of memory to be allocated as shared, and for both client and server to have a consistent, and equal, view of this memory. In this scenario, as much data as can fit can be transferred, and data is merely copied into one address range and immediately available in the other. Unfortunately, shared-memory communication, such as LPC traditionally provided, has its share of drawbacks, especially when considering security ramifications. For one, because both client and server must have access to the shared memory, an unprivileged client can use this to corrupt the server's shared memory, and even build executable payloads for potential exploits. Additionally, because the client knows the location of the server's data, it can use this information to bypass ASLR protections. (See Chapter 8 in Part 2 for more information.)

ALPC provides its own security on top of what's provided by section objects. With ALPC, a specific ALPC section object must be created with the appropriate *NtAlpcCreatePortSection* API, which will create the correct references to the port, as well as allow for automatic section garbage collection. (A manual API also exists for deletion.) As the owner of the ALPC section object begins using the section, the allocated chunks are created as ALPC regions, which represent a range of used addresses within the section and add an extra reference to the message. Finally, within a range of shared memory, the clients obtain views to this memory, which represents the local mapping within their address space.

Regions also support a couple of security options. First of all, regions can be mapped either using a secure mode or an unsecure mode. In the secure mode, only two views (mappings) are allowed to the region. This is typically used when a server wants to share data privately with a single client process. Additionally, only one region for a given range of shared memory can be opened from within the context of a given port. Finally, regions can also be marked with write-access protection, which enables only one process context (the server) to have write access to the view (by using *MmSecureVirtualMemoryAgainstWrites*). Other clients, meanwhile, will have read-only access only. These settings mitigate many privilege-escalation attacks that could happen due to attacks on shared memory, and they make ALPC more resilient than typical IPC mechanisms.

Attributes

ALPC provides more than simple message passing: it also enables specific contextual information to be added to each message and have the kernel track the validity, lifetime, and implementation of that information. Users of ALPC have the ability to assign their own custom context information as well. Whether it's system-managed or user-managed, ALPC calls this data *attributes*. There are three of these that the kernel manages:

- The security attribute, which holds key information to allow impersonation of clients, as well as advanced ALPC security functionality (which is described later)

- The data view attribute, responsible for managing the different views associated with the regions of an ALPC section

- The handle attribute, which contains information about which handles to associate with the message (which is described in more detail later in the "Security" section).

Normally, these attributes are initially passed in by the server or client when the message is sent and converted into the kernel's own internal ALPC representation. If the ALPC user requests this data back, it is *exposed* back securely. By implementing this kind of model and combining it with its own internal handle table, described next, ALPC can keep critical data opaque between clients and servers, while still maintaining the true pointers in kernel mode.

Finally, a fourth attribute is supported, called the *context attribute*. This attribute supports the traditional, LPC-style, user-specific context pointer that could be associated with a given message, and it is still supported for scenarios where custom data needs to be associated with a client/server pair.

To define attributes correctly, a variety of APIs are available for internal ALPC consumers, such as *AlpcInitializeMessageAttribute* and *AlpcGetMessageAttribute*.

Blobs, Handles, and Resources

Although the ALPC library exposes only one Object Manager object type (the port), it internally must manage a number of data structures that allow it to perform the tasks required by its mechanisms. For example, ALPC needs to allocate and track the messages associated with each port, as well as the message attributes, which it must track for the duration of their lifetime. Instead of using the Object Manager's routines for data management, ALPC implements its own lightweight objects called *blobs*. Just like objects, blobs can automatically be allocated and garbage collected, reference tracked, and locked through synchronization. Additionally, blobs can have custom allocation and deallocation callbacks, which let their owners control extra information that might need to be tracked for each blob. Finally, ALPC also uses the executive's handle table implementation (used for objects and PIDs/TIDs) to have an ALPC-specific handle table, which allows ALPC to generate private handles for blobs, instead of using pointers.

In the ALPC model, messages are blobs, for example, and their constructor generates a message ID, which is itself a handle into ALPC's handle table. Other ALPC blobs include the following:

- The connection blob, which stores the client and server communication ports, as well as the server connection port and ALPC handle table.

- The security blob, which stores the security data necessary to allow impersonation of a client. It stores the security attribute.

- The section, region, and view blobs, which describe ALPC's shared-memory model. The view blob is ultimately responsible for storing the data view attribute.

- The reserve blob, which implements support for ALPC Reserve Objects. (See the "Reserve Objects" section in this chapter.)

- The handle data blob, which contains the information that enables ALPC's handle attribute support.

Because blobs are allocated from pageable memory, they must carefully be tracked to ensure their deletion at the appropriate time. For certain kinds of blobs, this is easy: for example, when an ALPC message is freed, the blob used to contain it is also deleted. However, certain blobs can represent numerous attributes attached to a single ALPC message, and the kernel must manage their lifetime appropriately. For example, because a message can have multiple views associated with it (when many clients have access to the same shared memory), the views must be tracked with the messages that reference them. ALPC implements this functionality by using a concept of *resources*. Each message is associated with a resource list, and whenever a blob associated with a message (that isn't a simple pointer) is allocated, it is also added as a resource of the message. In turn, the ALPC library provides functionality for looking up, flushing, and deleting associated resources. Security blobs, reserve blobs, and view blobs are all stored as resources.

Security

ALPC implements several security mechanisms, full security boundaries, and mitigations to prevent attacks in case of generic IPC parsing bugs. At a base level, ALPC port objects are managed by the same object manager interfaces that manage object security, preventing nonprivileged applications from obtaining handles to server ports with ACL. On top of that, ALPC provides a SID-based trust model, inherited from the original LPC design. This model enables clients to validate the server they are connecting to by relying on more than just the port name. With a secured port, the client process submits to the kernel the SID of the server process it expects on the side of the endpoint. At connection time, the kernel validates that the client is indeed connecting to the expected server, mitigating namespace squatting attacks where an untrusted server creates a port to spoof a server.

ALPC also allows both clients and servers to atomically and uniquely identify the thread and process responsible for each message. It also supports the full Windows impersonation model through the *NtAlpcImpersonateClientThread* API. Other APIs give an ALPC server the ability to query the SIDs associated with all connected clients and to query the LUID (locally unique identifier) of the client's security token (which is further described in Chapter 6).

Performance

ALPC uses several strategies to enhance performance, primarily through its support of completion lists, which were briefly described earlier. At the kernel level, a completion list is essentially a user MDL that's been probed and locked and then mapped to an address. (For more information on Memory Descriptor Lists, see Chapter 10 in Part 2.) Because it's associated with an MDL (which tracks physical pages), when a client sends a message to a server, the payload copy can happen directly at the physical level, instead of requiring the kernel to double-buffer the message, as is common in other IPC mechanisms.

The completion list itself is implemented as a 64-bit queue of completed entries, and both user-mode and kernel-mode consumers can use an interlocked compare-exchange operation to insert and remove entries from the queue. Furthermore, to simplify allocations, once an MDL has been initialized, a bitmap is used to identify available areas of memory that can be used to hold new messages that are still being queued. The bitmap algorithm also uses native lock instructions on the processor to provide atomic allocation and de-allocation of areas of physical memory that can be used by completion lists.

Another ALPC performance optimization is the use of *message zones*. A message zone is simply a pre-allocated kernel buffer (also backed by an MDL) in which a message can be stored until a server or client retrieves it. A message zone associates a system address with the message, allowing it to be made visible in any process address space. More importantly, in the case of asynchronous operation, it does not require the complex setup of delayed payloads because no matter when the consumer finally retrieves the message data, the message zone will still be valid. Both completion lists and message zones can be set up with *NtAlpcSetInformation*.

A final optimization worth mentioning is that instead of copying data as soon as it is sent, the kernel sets up the payload for a delayed copy, capturing only the needed information, but without any copying. The message data is copied only when the receiver requests the message. Obviously, if a message zone or shared memory is being used, there's no advantage to this method, but in asynchronous, kernel-buffer message passing, this can be used to optimize cancellations and high-traffic scenarios.

Debugging and Tracing

On checked builds of the kernel, ALPC messages can be logged. All ALPC attributes, blobs, message zones, and dispatch transactions can be individually logged, and undocumented *!alpc* commands in WinDbg can dump the logs. On retail systems, IT administrators and troubleshooters can enable the ALPC Event Tracing for Windows (ETW) logger to monitor ALPC messages. ETW events do not include payload data, but they do contain connection, disconnection, and send/receive and wait/unblock information. Finally, even on retail systems, certain *!alpc* commands obtain information on ALPC ports and messages.

EXPERIMENT: Dumping a Connection Port

In this experiment, you'll use the CSRSS API port for Windows processes running in Session 1, which is the typical interactive session for the console user. Whenever a Windows application launches, it connects to CSRSS's API port in the appropriate session.

1. Start by obtaining a pointer to the connection port with the *!object* command:

```
0: kd> !object \Sessions\1\Windows\ApiPort
Object: fffffa8004dc2090  Type: (fffffa80027a2ed0) ALPC Port
    ObjectHeader: fffffa8004dc2060 (new version)
    HandleCount: 1  PointerCount: 50
    Directory Object: fffff8a001a5fb30  Name: ApiPort
```

2. Now dump information on the port object itself with *!alpc /p*. This will confirm, for example, that CSRSS is the owner:

```
0: kd> !alpc /p fffffa8004dc2090
Port @ fffffa8004dc2090
  Type                      : ALPC_CONNECTION_PORT
  CommunicationInfo         : fffff8a001a22560
   ConnectionPort           : fffffa8004dc2090
   ClientCommunicationPort  : 0000000000000000
   ServerCommunicationPort  : 0000000000000000
  OwnerProcess              : fffffa800502db30 (csrss.exe)
  SequenceNo                : 0x000003C9 (969)
  CompletionPort            : 0000000000000000
  CompletionList            : 0000000000000000
  MessageZone               : 0000000000000000
  ConnectionPending         : No
  ConnectionRefused         : No
  Disconnected              : No
  Closed                    : No
  FlushOnClose              : Yes

  ReturnExtendedInfo        : No
  Waitable                  : No
  Security                  : Static
  Wow64CompletionList       : No
```

```
Main queue is empty.
Large message queue is empty.
Pending queue is empty.
Canceled queue is empty.
```

3. You can see what clients are connected to the port, which will include all Windows processes running in the session, with the undocumented *!alpc /lpc* command. You will also see the server and client communication ports associated with each connection and any pending messages on any of the queues:

```
0: kd> !alpc /lpc fffffa8004dc2090

Port @fffffa8004dc2090 has 14 connections

SRV:fffffa8004809c50 (m:0, p:0, l:0) <-> CLI:fffffa8004809e60 (m:0, p:0, l:0),
  Process=fffffa8004ffcb30 ('winlogon.exe')
SRV:fffffa80054dfb30 (m:0, p:0, l:0) <-> CLI:fffffa80054dfe60 (m:0, p:0, l:0),
  Process=fffffa80054de060 ('dwm.exe')
SRV:fffffa8005394dd0 (m:0, p:0, l:0) <-> CLI:fffffa80054e1440 (m:0, p:0, l:0),
  Process=fffffa80054e2290 ('winvnc.exe')
SRV:fffffa80053965d0 (m:0, p:0, l:0) <-> CLI:fffffa8005396900 (m:0, p:0, l:0),
  Process=fffffa80054ed060 ('explorer.exe')
SRV:fffffa80045a8070 (m:0, p:0, l:0) <-> CLI:fffffa80045af070 (m:0, p:0, l:0),
  Process=fffffa80045b1340 ('logonhlp.exe')
SRV:fffffa8005197940 (m:0, p:0, l:0) <-> CLI:fffffa800519a900 (m:0, p:0, l:0),
  Process=fffffa80045da060 ('TSVNCache.exe')
SRV:fffffa800470b070 (m:0, p:0, l:0) <-> CLI:fffffa800470f330 (m:0, p:0, l:0),
  Process=fffffa8004713060 ('vmware-tray.ex')
SRV:fffffa80045d7670 (m:0, p:0, l:0) <-> CLI:fffffa80054b16f0 (m:0, p:0, l:0),
  Process=fffffa80056b8b30 ('WINWORD.EXE')
SRV:fffffa80050e0e60 (m:0, p:0, l:0) <-> CLI:fffffa80056fee60 (m:0, p:0, l:0),
  Process=fffffa800478f060 ('Winobj.exe')
SRV:fffffa800482e670 (m:0, p:0, l:0) <-> CLI:fffffa80047b7680 (m:0, p:0, l:0),
  Process=fffffa80056aab30 ('cmd.exe')
SRV:fffffa8005166e60 (m:0, p:0, l:0) <-> CLI:fffffa80051481e0 (m:0, p:0, l:0),
  Process=fffffa8002823b30 ('conhost.exe')
SRV:fffffa80054a2070 (m:0, p:0, l:0) <-> CLI:fffffa80056e6210 (m:0, p:0, l:0),
  Process=fffffa80055669e0 ('livekd.exe')
SRV:fffffa80056aa390 (m:0, p:0, l:0) <-> CLI:fffffa80055a6c00 (m:0, p:0, l:0),
  Process=fffffa80051b28b0 ('livekd64.exe')
SRV:fffffa8005551d90 (m:0, p:0, l:0) <-> CLI:fffffa80055bfc60 (m:0, p:0, l:0),
  Process=fffffa8002a69b30 ('kd.exe')
```

4. Note that if you have other sessions, you can repeat this experiment on those sessions also (as well as with session 0, the system session). You will eventually get a list of all the Windows processes on your machine. If you are using Subsystem for UNIX Applications, you can also use this technique on the \PSXSS\ApiPort object.

Kernel Event Tracing

Various components of the Windows kernel and several core device drivers are instrumented to record trace data of their operations for use in system troubleshooting. They rely on a common infrastructure in the kernel that provides trace data to the user-mode Event Tracing for Windows (ETW) facility. An application that uses ETW falls into one or more of three categories:

- **Controller** A controller starts and stops logging sessions and manages buffer pools. Example controllers include Reliability and Performance Monitor (see the "EXPERIMENT: Tracing TCP/IP Activity with the Kernel Logger" section, later in this section) and XPerf from the Windows Performance Toolkit (see the "EXPERIMENT: Monitoring Interrupt and DPC Activity" section, earlier in this chapter).

- **Provider** A provider defines GUIDs (globally unique identifiers) for the event classes it can produce traces for and registers them with ETW. The provider accepts commands from a controller for starting and stopping traces of the event classes for which it's responsible.

- **Consumer** A consumer selects one or more trace sessions for which it wants to read trace data. Consumers can receive the events in buffers in real time or in log files.

Windows includes dozens of user-mode providers, for everything from Active Directory to the Service Control Manager to Explorer. ETW also defines a logging session with the name NT Kernel Logger (also known as the kernel logger) for use by the kernel and core drivers. The providers for the NT Kernel Logger are implemented by ETW code in Ntoskrnl.exe and the core drivers.

When a controller in user mode enables the kernel logger, the ETW library (which is implemented in \Windows\System32\Ntdll.dll) calls the *NtTraceControl* system function, telling the ETW code in the kernel which event classes the controller wants to start tracing. If file logging is configured (as opposed to in-memory logging to a buffer), the kernel creates a system thread in the system process that creates a log file. When the kernel receives trace events from the enabled trace sources, it records them to a buffer. If it was started, the file logging thread wakes up once per second to dump the contents of the buffers to the log file.

Trace records generated by the kernel logger have a standard ETW trace event header, which records time stamp, process, and thread IDs, as well as information on what class of event the record corresponds to. Event classes can provide additional data specific to their events. For example, disk event class trace records indicate the operation type (read or write), disk number at which the operation is directed, and sector offset and length of the operation.

Some of the trace classes that can be enabled for the kernel logger and the component that generates each class include the following:

- **Disk I/O** Disk class driver
- **File I/O** File system drivers

- **File I/O Completion**   File system drivers

- **Hardware Configuration**   Plug and Play manager (See Chapter 9 in Part 2 for information on the Plug and Play manager.)

- **Image Load/Unload**   The system image loader in the kernel

- **Page Faults**   Memory manager (See Chapter 10 in Part 2 for more information on page faults.)

- **Hard Page Faults**   Memory manager

- **Process Create/Delete**   Process manager (See Chapter 5 for more information on the process manager.)

- **Thread Create/Delete**   Process manager

- **Registry Activity**   Configuration manager (See "The Registry" section in Chapter 4 for more information on the configuration manager.)

- **Network TCP/IP**   TCP/IP driver

- **Process Counters**   Process manager

- **Context Switches**   Kernel dispatcher

- **Deferred Procedure Calls**   Kernel dispatcher

- **Interrupts**   Kernel dispatcher

- **System Calls**   Kernel dispatcher

- **Sample Based Profiling**   Kernel dispatcher and HAL

- **Driver Delays**   I/O manager

- **Split I/O**   I/O manager

- **Power Events**   Power manager

- **ALPC**   Advanced local procedure call

- **Scheduler and Synchronization**   Kernel dispatcher (See Chapter 5 for more information about thread scheduling)

You can find more information on ETW and the kernel logger, including sample code for controllers and consumers, in the Windows SDK.

EXPERIMENT: Tracing TCP/IP Activity with the Kernel Logger

To enable the kernel logger and have it generate a log file of TCP/IP activity, follow these steps:

1. Run the Performance Monitor, and click on Data Collector Sets, User Defined.

2. Right-click on User Defined, choose New, and select Data Collector Set.

3. When prompted, enter a name for the data collector set (for example, **experiment**), and choose Create Manually (Advanced) before clicking Next.

4. In the dialog box that opens, select Create Data Logs, check Event Trace Data, and then click Next. In the Providers area, click Add, and locate Windows Kernel Trace. In the Properties list, select Keywords(Any), and then click Edit.

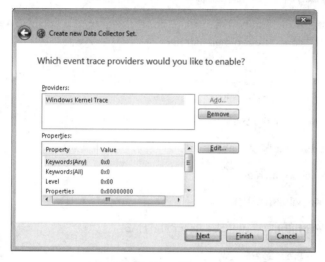

5. From this list, select only Net for Network TCP/IP, and then click OK.

6. Click Next to select a location where the files are saved. By default, this location is C:\Perflogs\<User>\experiment\, if this is how you named the data collector set. Click Next, and in the Run As edit box, enter the Administrator account name and set the password to match it. Click Finish. You should now see a window similar to the one shown here:

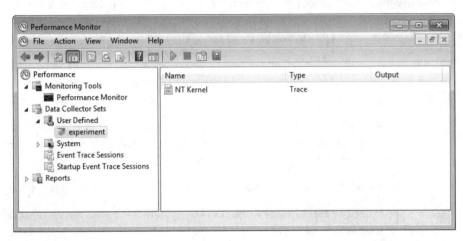

7. Right-click on "experiment" (or whatever name you gave your data collector set), and then click Start. Now generate some network activity by opening a browser and visiting a web site.

8. Right-click on the data collector set node again, and then click Stop.

9. Open a command prompt, and change to the C:\Perflogs\experiment\00001 directory (or the directory into which you specified that the trace log file be stored).

10. Run *tracerpt*, and pass it the name of the trace log file:

```
tracerpt DataCollector01.etl –o dumpfile.csv –of CSV
```

11. Open dumpfile.csv in Microsoft Excel or in a text editor. You should see TCP and/or UDP trace records like the following:

Tcplp	SendIPV4	0xFFFFFFFF	1.28663E+17	0	0	1992	1388	157.54.86.28	172.31.234.35	80	49414	646659	646661
Udplp	RecvIPV4	0xFFFFFFFF	1.28663E+17	0	0	4	50	172.31.239.255	172.31.233.110	137	137	0	0x0
Udplp	RecvIPV4	0xFFFFFFFF	1.28663E+17	0	0	4	50	172.31.239.255	172.31.234.162	137	137	0	0x0
Tcplp	RecvIPV4	0xFFFFFFFF	1.28663E+17	0	0	1992	1425	157.54.86.28	172.31.234.35	80	49414	0	0x0
Tcplp	RecvIPV4	0xFFFFFFFF	1.28663E+17	0	0	1992	1380	157.54.86.28	172.31.234.35	80	49414	0	0x0
Tcplp	RecvIPV4	0xFFFFFFFF	1.28663E+17	0	0	1992	45	157.54.86.28	172.31.234.35	80	49414	0	0x0
Tcplp	RecvIPV4	0xFFFFFFFF	1.28663E+17	0	0	1992	1415	157.54.86.28	172.31.234.35	80	49414	0	0x0
Tcplp	RecvIPV4	0xFFFFFFFF	1.28663E+17	0	0	1992	740	157.54.86.28	172.31.234.35	80	49414	0	0x0

Wow64

Wow64 (Win32 emulation on 64-bit Windows) refers to the software that permits the execution of 32-bit x86 applications on 64-bit Windows. It is implemented as a set of user-mode DLLs, with some support from the kernel for creating 32-bit versions of what would normally only be 64-bit data structures, such as the process environment block (PEB) and thread environment block (TEB). Changing Wow64 contexts through *Get/SetThreadContext* is also implemented by the kernel. Here are the user-mode DLLs responsible for Wow64:

- **Wow64.dll**   Manages process and thread creation, and hooks exception-dispatching and base system calls exported by Ntoskrnl.exe. It also implements file-system redirection and registry redirection.

- **Wow64Cpu.dll**   Manages the 32-bit CPU context of each running thread inside Wow64, and provides processor architecture-specific support for switching CPU mode from 32-bit to 64-bit and vice versa.

- **Wow64Win.dll**   Intercepts the GUI system calls exported by Win32k.sys.

- **IA32Exec.bin and Wowia32x.dll on IA64 systems**   Contain the IA-32 software emulator and its interface library. Because Itanium processors cannot natively execute x86 32-bit in-structions in an efficient manner (performance is worse than 30 percent), software emulation (through binary translation) is required through the use of these two additional components.

The relationship of these DLLs is shown in Figure 3-31.

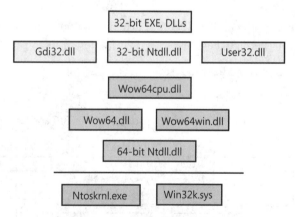

FIGURE 3-31 Wow64 architecture

Wow64 Process Address Space Layout

Wow64 processes can run with 2 GB or 4 GB of virtual space. If the image header has the large-address-aware flag set, the memory manager reserves the user-mode address space above the 4-GB boundary through the end of the user-mode boundary. If the image is not marked as large address space aware, the memory manager reserves the user-mode address space above 2 GB. (For more information on large-address-space support, see the section "x86 User Address Space Layouts" in Chapter 10 in Part 2.)

System Calls

Wow64 hooks all the code paths where 32-bit code would transition to the native 64-bit system or when the native system needs to call into 32-bit user-mode code. During process creation, the process manager maps into the process address space the native 64-bit Ntdll.dll, as well as the 32-bit Ntdll.dll for Wow64 processes. When the loader initialization is called, it calls the Wow64 initialization code inside Wow64.dll. Wow64 then sets up the startup context required by the 32-bit Ntdll, switches the CPU mode to 32-bits, and starts executing the 32-bit loader. From this point onward, execution continues as if the process is running on a native 32-bit system.

Special 32-bit versions of Ntdll.dll, User32.dll, and Gdi32.dll are located in the \Windows\Syswow64 folder (as well as certain other DLLs that perform interprocess communication, such as Rpcrt4.dll). These call into Wow64 rather than issuing the native 32-bit system call instruction. Wow64 transitions to native 64-bit mode, captures the parameters associated with the system call (converting 32-bit pointers to 64-bit pointers), and issues the corresponding native 64-bit system call. When the native system call returns, Wow64 converts any output parameters if necessary from 64-bit to 32-bit formats before returning to 32-bit mode.

Exception Dispatching

Wow64 hooks exception dispatching through Ntdll's *KiUserExceptionDispatcher*. Whenever the 64-bit kernel is about to dispatch an exception to a Wow64 process, Wow64 captures the native exception and context record in user mode and then prepares a 32-bit exception and context record and dispatches it the same way the native 32-bit kernel would.

User APC Dispatching

Wow64 also hooks user-mode APC delivery through Ntdll's *KiUserApcDispatcher*. Whenever the 64-bit kernel is about to dispatch a user-mode APC to a Wow64 process, it maps the 32-bit APC address to a higher range of 64-bit address space. The 64-bit Ntdll then captures the native APC and context record in user mode and maps it back to a 32-bit address. It then prepares a 32-bit user-mode APC and context record and dispatches it the same way the native 32-bit kernel would.

Console Support

Because console support is implemented in user mode by Csrss.exe, of which only a single native binary exists, 32-bit applications would be unable to perform console I/O while on 64-bit Windows. Similarly to how a special rpcrt4.dll exits to thunk 32-bit to 64-bit RPCs, the 32-bit Kernel.dll for Wow64 contains special code to call into Wow, for thunking parameters during interaction with Csrss and Conhost.exe.

User Callbacks

Wow64 intercepts all callbacks from the kernel into user mode. Wow64 treats such calls as system calls; however, the data conversion is done in the reverse order: input parameters are converted from 64 bits to 32 bits, and output parameters are converted when the callback returns from 32 bits to 64 bits.

File System Redirection

To maintain application compatibility and to reduce the effort of porting applications from Win32 to 64-bit Windows, system directory names were kept the same. Therefore, the \Windows\System32 folder contains native 64-bit images. Wow64, as it hooks all the system calls, translates all the path-related APIs and replaces the path name of the \Windows\System32 folder with \Windows\Syswow64. Wow64 also redirects \Windows\LastGood to \Windows\LastGood\syswow64 and \Windows \Regedit.exe to \Windows\syswow64\Regedit.exe. Through the use of system environment variables, the %PROGRAMFILES% variable is also set to \Program Files (x86) for 32-bit applications, while it is set to \Program Files folder for 64-bit applications. CommonProgramFiles and CommonProgramFiles (x86) also exist, which always point to the 32-bit location, while ProgramW6432 and CommonProgramW6432 point to the 64-bit locations unconditionally.

> **Note** Because certain 32-bit applications might indeed be aware and able to deal with 64-bit images, a virtual directory, \Windows\Sysnative, allows any I/Os originating from a 32-bit application to this directory to be exempted from file redirection. This directory doesn't actually exist—it is a virtual path that allows access to the real System32 directory, even from an application running under Wow64.

There are a few subdirectories of \Windows\System32 that, for compatibility reasons, are exempted from being redirected such that access attempts to them made by 32-bit applications actually access the real one. These directories include the following:

- %windir%\system32\drivers\etc
- %windir%\system32\spool
- %windir%\system32\catroot and %windir%\system32\catroot2
- %windir%\system32\logfiles
- %windir%\system32\driverstore

Finally, Wow64 provides a mechanism to control the file system redirection built into Wow64 on a per-thread basis through the *Wow64DisableWow64FsRedirection* and *Wow64RevertWow64FsRedirection* functions. This mechanism can have issues with delay-loaded DLLs, opening files through the common file dialog and even internationalization—because once redirection is disabled, the system no longer users it during internal loading either, and certain 64-bit-only files would then fail to be found. Using the c:\windows\sysnative path or some of the other consistent paths introduced earlier is usually a safer methodology for developers to use.

Registry Redirection

Applications and components store their configuration data in the registry. Components usually write their configuration data in the registry when they are registered during installation. If the same component is installed and registered both as a 32-bit binary and a 64-bit binary, the last component registered will override the registration of the previous component because they both write to the same location in the registry.

To help solve this problem transparently without introducing any code changes to 32-bit components, the registry is split into two portions: Native and Wow64. By default, 32-bit components access the 32-bit view and 64-bit components access the 64-bit view. This provides a safe execution environment for 32-bit and 64-bit components and separates the 32-bit application state from the 64-bit one if it exists.

To implement this, Wow64 intercepts all the system calls that open registry keys and retranslates the key path to point it to the Wow64 view of the registry. Wow64 splits the registry at these points:

- HKLM\SOFTWARE

- HKEY_CLASSES_ROOT

However, note that many of the subkeys are actually shared between 32-bit and 64-bit apps—that is, not the entire hive is split.

Under each of these keys, Wow64 creates a key called Wow6432Node. Under this key is stored 32-bit configuration information. All other portions of the registry are shared between 32-bit and 64-bit applications (for example, HKLM\SYSTEM).

As an extra help, if a 32-bit application writes a REG_SZ or REG_EXPAND_SZ value that starts with the data "%ProgramFiles%" or "%commonprogramfiles%" to the registry, Wow64 modifies the actual values to "%ProgramFiles(x86)%" and "%commonprogramfiles(x86)%" to match the file system redirection and layout explained earlier. The 32-bit application must write exactly these strings using this case—any other data will be ignored and written normally. Finally, any key containing "system32" is replaced with "syswow64" in all cases, regardless of flags and case sensitivity, unless KEY_WOW64_64KEY is used and the key is on the list of "reflected keys", which is available on MSDN.

For applications that need to explicitly specify a registry key for a certain view, the following flags on the *RegOpenKeyEx*, *RegCreateKeyEx*, *RegOpenKeyTransacted*, *RegCreateKeyTransacted*, and *RegDeleteKeyEx* functions permit this:

- KEY_WOW64_64KEY—Explicitly opens a 64-bit key from either a 32-bit or 64-bit application, and disables the REG_SZ or REG_EXPAND_SZ interception explained earlier

- KEY_WOW64_32KEY—Explicitly opens a 32-bit key from either a 32-bit or 64-bit application

I/O Control Requests

Besides normal read and write operations, applications can communicate with some device drivers through device I/O control functions using the Windows *DeviceIoControl* API. The application might specify an input and/or output buffer along with the call. If the buffer contains pointer-dependent data and the process sending the control request is a Wow64 process, the view of the input and/or output structure is different between the 32-bit application and the 64-bit driver, because pointers are 4 bytes for 32-bit applications and 8 bytes for 64-bit applications. In this case, the kernel driver is expected to convert the associated pointer-dependent structures. Drivers can call the *IoIs32bitProcess* function to detect whether or not an I/O request originated from a Wow64 process. Look for "Supporting 32-Bit I/O in Your 64-Bit Driver" on MSDN for more details.

16-Bit Installer Applications

Wow64 doesn't support running 16-bit applications. However, because many application installers are 16-bit programs, Wow64 has special case code to make references to certain well-known 16-bit installers work. These installers include the following:

- Microsoft ACME Setup version: 1.2, 2.6, 3.0, and 3.1

- InstallShield version 5.x (where *x* is any minor version number)

Whenever a 16-bit process is about to be created using the *CreateProcess()* API, Ntvdm64.dll is loaded and control is transferred to it to inspect whether the 16-bit executable is one of the supported installers. If it is, another *CreateProcess* is issued to launch a 32-bit version of the installer with the same command-line arguments.

Printing

32-bit printer drivers cannot be used on 64-bit Windows. Print drivers must be ported to native 64-bit versions. However, because printer drivers run in the user-mode address space of the requesting process and only native 64-bit printer drivers are supported on 64-bit Windows, a special mechanism is needed to support printing from 32-bit processes. This is done by redirecting all printing functions to Splwow64.exe, the Wow64 RPC print server. Because Splwow64 is a 64-bit process, it can load 64-bit printer drivers.

Restrictions

Wow64 does not support the execution of 16-bit applications (this is supported on 32-bit versions of Windows) or the loading of 32-bit kernel-mode device drivers (they must be ported to native 64-bits). Wow64 processes can load only 32-bit DLLs and can't load native 64-bit DLLs. Likewise, native 64-bit processes can't load 32-bit DLLs. The one exception is the ability to load *resource or data-only DLLs* cross-architecture, which is allowed because those DLLs contain only data, not code.

In addition to the above, due to page size differences, Wow64 on IA64 systems does not support the *ReadFileScatter*, *WriteFileGather*, *GetWriteWatch*, AVX registers, XSAVE, and AWE functions. Also, hardware acceleration through DirectX is not available. (Software emulation is provided for Wow64 processes.)

User-Mode Debugging

Support for user-mode debugging is split into three different modules. The first one is located in the executive itself and has the prefix *Dbgk*, which stands for *Debugging Framework*. It provides the necessary internal functions for registering and listening for debug events, managing the debug object, and packaging the information for consumption by its user-mode counterpart. The user-mode component that talks directly to *Dbgk* is located in the native system library, Ntdll.dll, under a set of APIs that begin with the prefix *DbgUi*. These APIs are responsible for wrapping the underlying debug object implementation (which is opaque), and they allow all subsystem applications to use debugging by wrapping their own APIs around the *DbgUi* implementation. Finally, the third component in user-mode debugging belongs to the subsystem DLLs. It is the exposed, documented API (located in KernelBase.dll for the Windows subsystem) that each subsystem supports for performing debugging of other applications.

Kernel Support

The kernel supports user-mode debugging through an object mentioned earlier, the *debug object*. It provides a series of system calls, most of which map directly to the Windows debugging API, typically accessed through the *DbgUi* layer first. The debug object itself is a simple construct, composed of a series of flags that determine state, an event to notify any waiters that debugger events are present, a doubly linked list of debug events waiting to be processed, and a fast mutex used for locking the object. This is all the information that the kernel requires for successfully receiving and sending debugger events, and each debugged process has a *debug port* member in its structure pointing to this debug object.

Once a process has an associated debug port, the events described in Table 3-23 can cause a debug event to be inserted into the list of events.

TABLE 3-23 Kernel-Mode Debugging Events

Event Identifier	Meaning	Triggered By
DbgKmExceptionApi	An exception has occurred.	*KiDispatchException* during an exception that occurred in user mode
DbgKmCreateThreadApi	A new thread has been created.	Startup of a user-mode thread
DbgKmCreateProcessApi	A new process has been created.	Startup of a user-mode thread that is the first thread in the process
DbgKmExitThreadApi	A thread has exited.	Death of a user-mode thread
DbgKmExitProcessApi	A process has exited.	Death of a user-mode thread that was the last thread in the process
DbgKmLoadDllApi	A DLL was loaded.	*NtMapViewOfSection* when the section is an image file (could be an EXE as well)
DbgKmUnloadDllApi	A DLL was unloaded.	*NtUnmapViewOfSection* when the section is an image file (could be an EXE as well)
DbgKmErrorReportApi	An exception needs to be forwarded to Windows Error Reporting (WER).	*KiDispatchException* during an exception that occurred in user mode, after the debugger was unable to handle it

Apart from the causes mentioned in the table, there are a couple of special triggering cases outside the regular scenarios that occur at the time a debugger object first becomes associated with a process. The first *create process* and *create thread* messages will be manually sent when the debugger is attached, first for the process itself and its main thread and followed by create thread messages for all the other threads in the process. Finally, *load dll* events for the executable being debugged (Ntdll.dll) and then all the current DLLs loaded in the debugged process will be sent.

Once a debugger object has been associated with a process, all the threads in the process are suspended. At this point, it is the debugger's responsibility to start requesting that debug events be sent through. Debuggers request that debug events be sent back to user mode by performing a *wait* on the debug object. This call loops the list of debug events. As each request is removed from the list, its contents are converted from the internal *dbgk* structure to the *native* structure that the next layer up understands. As you'll see, this structure is different from the Win32 structure as well, and another layer of conversion has to occur. Even after all pending debug messages have been processed by the debugger, the kernel does not automatically resume the process. It is the debugger's responsibility to call the *ContinueDebugEvent* function to resume execution.

Apart from some more complex handling of certain multithreading issues, the basic model for the framework is a simple matter of *producers*—code in the kernel that generates the debug events in the previous table—and *consumers*—the debugger waiting on these events and acknowledging their receipt.

Native Support

Although the basic protocol for user-mode debugging is quite simple, it's not directly usable by Windows applications—instead, it's wrapped by the *DbgUi* functions in Ntdll.dll. This abstraction is required to allow native applications, as well as different subsystems, to use these routines (because code inside Ntdll.dll has no dependencies). The functions that this component provides are mostly analogous to the Windows API functions and related system calls. Internally, the code also provides the functionality required to create a debug object associated with the thread. The handle to a debug object that is created is never exposed. It is saved instead in the thread environment block (TEB) of the debugger thread that performs the attachment. (For more information on the TEB, see Chapter 5.) This value is saved in *DbgSsReserved[1]*.

When a debugger attaches to a process, it expects the process to be *broken into*—that is, an *int 3* (breakpoint) operation should have happened, generated by a thread injected into the process. If this didn't happen, the debugger would never actually be able to take control of the process and would merely see debug events flying by. Ntdll.dll is responsible for creating and injecting that thread into the target process.

Finally, Ntdll.dll also provides APIs to convert the native structure for debug events into the structure that the Windows API understands.

EXPERIMENT: Viewing Debugger Objects

Although you've been using WinDbg to do kernel-mode debugging, you can also use it to debug user-mode programs. Go ahead and try starting Notepad.exe with the debugger attached using these steps:

1. Run WinDbg, and then click File, Open Executable.

2. Navigate to the \Windows\System32\ directory, and choose Notepad.exe.

3. You're not going to do any debugging, so simply ignore whatever might come up. You can type **g** in the command window to instruct WinDbg to continue executing Notepad.

Now run Process Explorer, and be sure the lower pane is enabled and configured to show open handles. (Click on View, Lower Pane View, and then Handles.) You also want to look at unnamed handles, so click on View, Show Unnamed Handles And Mappings.

Next, click on the Windbg.exe process and look at its handle table. You should see an open, unnamed handle to a debug object. (You can organize the table by Type to find this entry more readily.) You should see something like the following:

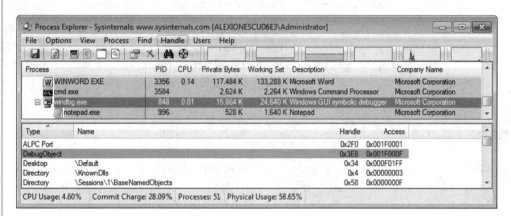

You can try right-clicking on the handle and closing it. Notepad should disappear, and the following message should appear in WinDbg:

```
ERROR: WaitForEvent failed, NTSTATUS 0xC0000354
This usually indicates that the debuggee has been
killed out from underneath the debugger.
You can use .tlist to see if the debuggee still exists.
WaitForEvent failed
```

In fact, if you look at the description for the NTSTATUS code given, you will find the text: "An attempt to do an operation on a debug port failed because the port is in the process of being deleted," which is exactly what you've done by closing the handle.

As you can see, the native *DbgUi* interface doesn't do much work to support the framework except for this abstraction. The most complicated task it does is the conversion between native and Win32 debugger structures. This involves several additional changes to the structures.

Windows Subsystem Support

The final component responsible for allowing debuggers such as Microsoft Visual Studio or WinDbg to debug user-mode applications is in Kernel32.dll. It provides the documented Windows APIs. Apart from this trivial conversion of one function name to another, there is one important management job that this side of the debugging infrastructure is responsible for: managing the duplicated file and thread handles.

Recall that each time a *load DLL* event is sent, a handle to the image file is duplicated by the kernel and handed off in the event structure, as is the case with the handle to the process executable during the *create process* event. During each *wait* call, Kernel32.dll checks whether this is an event that results in new duplicated process and/or thread handles from the kernel (the two *create* events). If so, it allocates a structure in which it stores the process ID, thread ID, and the thread and/or process handle associated with the event. This structure is linked into the first *DbgSsReserved* array index in the TEB, where we mentioned the debug object handle is stored. Likewise, Kernel32.dll also checks for *exit* events. When it detects such an event, it "marks" the handles in the data structure.

Once the debugger is finished using the handles and performs the *continue* call, Kernel32.dll parses these structures, looks for any handles whose threads have exited, and closes the handles for the debugger. Otherwise, those threads and processes would actually never exit, because there would always be open handles to them as long as the debugger was running.

Image Loader

When a process is started on the system, the kernel creates a *process object* to represent it (see Chapter 5 for more information on processes) and performs various kernel-related initialization tasks. However, these tasks do not result in the execution of the application, merely in the preparation of its context and environment. In fact, unlike drivers, which are kernel-mode code, applications execute in user mode. So most of the actual initialization work is done outside the kernel. This work is performed by the *image loader*, also internally referred to as *Ldr*.

The image loader lives in the user-mode system DLL *Ntdll.dll* and not in the kernel library. Therefore, it behaves just like standard code that is part of a DLL, and it is subject to the same restrictions in terms of memory access and security rights. What makes this code special is the guaranty that it will always be present in the running process (Ntdll.dll is always loaded) and that it is the first piece of code to run in user mode as part of a new application. (When the system builds the initial context, the program counter, or instruction pointer, is set to an initialization function inside Ntdll.dll. See Chapter 5 for more information.)

Because the loader runs before the actual application code, it is usually invisible to users and developers. Additionally, although the loader's initialization tasks are hidden, a program typically does interact with its interfaces during the run time of a program—for example, whenever loading or unloading a DLL or querying the base address of one. Some of the main tasks the loader is responsible for include these:

- Initializing the user-mode state for the application, such as creating the initial heap and setting up the thread-local storage (TLS) and fiber-local storage (FLS) slots

- Parsing the import table (IAT) of the application to look for all DLLs that it requires (and then recursively parsing the IAT of each DLL), followed by parsing the export table of the DLLs to make sure the function is actually present (Special *forwarder entries* can also redirect an export to yet another DLL.)

- Loading and unloading DLLs at run time, as well as on demand, and maintaining a list of all loaded modules (the module database)

- Allowing for run-time patching (called *hotpatching)* support, explained later in the chapter

- Handling manifest files

- Reading the application compatibility database for any shims, and loading the shim engine DLL if required

- Enabling support for API sets and API redirection, a core part of the MinWin refactoring effort

- Enabling dynamic runtime compatibility mitigations through the SwitchBranch mechanism

As you can see, most of these tasks are critical to enabling an application to actually run its code; without them, everything from calling external functions to using the heap would immediately fail. After the process has been created, the loader calls a special native API to continue execution based on a context frame located on the stack. This context frame, built by the kernel, contains the actual entry point of the application. Therefore, because the loader doesn't use a standard call or jump into the running application, you'll never see the loader initialization functions as part of the call tree in a stack trace for a thread.

EXPERIMENT: Watching the Image Loader

In this experiment, you'll use global flags to enable a debugging feature called *loader snaps.* This allows you to see debug output from the image loader while debugging application startup.

1. From the directory where you've installed WinDbg, launch the Gflags.exe application, and then click on the Image File tab.

2. In the Image field, type **Notepad.exe**, and then press the Tab key. This should enable the check boxes. Select the Show Loader Snaps option, and then click OK to dismiss the dialog box.

3. Now follow the steps in the "EXPERIMENT: Viewing Debugger Objects" section to start debugging the Notepad.exe application.

4. You should now see a couple of screens of debug information similar to that shown here:

```
0924:0248 @ 116983652 - LdrpInitializeProcess - INFO: Initializing process 0x924
0924:0248 @ 116983652 - LdrpInitializeProcess - INFO: Beginning execution of
        notepad.exe (C:\Windows\notepad.exe)
0924:0248 @ 116983652 - LdrpLoadDll - INFO: Loading DLL "kernel32.dll" from path
        "C:\Windows;C:\Windows\system32;C:\Windows\system;C:\Windows;
0924:0248 @ 116983652 - LdrpMapDll - INFO: Mapped DLL "kernel32.dll" at address
        76BD000
0924:0248 @ 116983652 - LdrGetProcedureAddressEx - INFO: Locating procedure
        "BaseThreadInitThunk" by name
0924:0248 @ 116983652 - LdrpRunInitializeRoutines - INFO: Calling init routine
        76C14592 for DLL "C:\Windows\system32\kernel32.dll"
0924:0248 @ 116983652 - LdrGetProcedureAddressEx - INFO: Locating procedure
        "BaseQueryModuleData" by name
```

5. Eventually, the debugger breaks somewhere inside the loader code, at a special place where the image loader checks whether a debugger is attached and fires a breakpoint. If you press the G key to continue execution, you will see more messages from the loader, and Notepad will appear.

6. Try interacting with Notepad and see how certain operations invoke the loader. A good experiment is to open the Save/Open dialog. That demonstrates that the loader not only runs at startup, but continuously responds to thread requests that can cause *delayed loads* of other modules (which can then be unloaded after use).

Early Process Initialization

Because the loader is present in Ntdll.dll, which is a native DLL that's not associated with any particular subsystem, all processes are subject to the same loader behavior (with some minor differences). In Chapter 5, we'll look in detail at the steps that lead to the creation of a process in kernel mode, as well as some of the work performed by the Windows function *CreateProcess*. Here, however, we'll cover the work that takes place in user mode, independent of any subsystem, as soon as the first user-mode instruction starts execution. When a process starts, the loader performs the following steps:

1. Build the image path name for the application, and query the Image File Execution Options key for the application, as well as the DEP and SEH validation linker settings.

2. Look inside the executable's header to see whether it is a .NET application (specified by the presence of a .NET-specific image directory).

3. Initialize the National Language Support (NLS for internationalization) tables for the process.

4. Initialize the Wow64 engine if the image is 32-bit and is running on 64-bit Windows.

5. Load any configuration options specified in the executable's header. These options, which a developer can define when compiling the application, control the behavior of the executable.

6. Set the affinity mask if one was specified in the executable header.

7. Initialize FLS and TLS.

8. Initialize the heap manager for the process, and create the first process heap.

9. Allocate an SxS (Side-by-Side Assembly)/Fusion activation context for the process. This allows the system to use the appropriate DLL version file, instead of defaulting to the DLL that shipped with the operating system. (See Chapter 5 for more information.)

10. Open the \KnownDlls object directory, and build the known DLL path. For a Wow64 process, \KnownDlls32 is used instead.

11. Determine the process' current directory and default load path (used when loading images and opening files).

12. Build the first loader data table entries for the application executable and Ntdll.dll, and insert them into the module database.

At this point, the image loader is ready to start parsing the import table of the executable belonging to the application and start loading any DLLs that were dynamically linked during the compilation of the application. Because each imported DLL can also have its own import table, this operation will continue recursively until all DLLs have been satisfied and all functions to be imported have been found. As each DLL is loaded, the loader will keep state information for it and build the module database.

DLL Name Resolution and Redirection

Name resolution is the process by which the system converts the name of a PE-format binary to a physical file in situations where the caller has not specified or cannot specify a unique file identity. Because the locations of various directories (the application directory, the system directory, and so on) cannot be hardcoded at link time, this includes the resolution of all binary dependencies as well as *LoadLibrary* operations in which the caller does not specify a full path.

When resolving binary dependencies, the basic Windows application model locates files in a search path—a list of locations that is searched sequentially for a file with a matching base name—although various system components override the search path mechanism in order to extend the default application model. The notion of a search path is a holdover from the era of the command line, when an application's current directory was a meaningful notion; this is somewhat anachronistic for modern GUI applications.

However, the placement of the current directory in this ordering allowed load operations on system binaries to be overridden by placing malicious binaries with the same base name in the application's current directory. To prevent security risks associated with this behavior, a feature known as *safe DLL search mode* was added to the path search computation and, starting with Windows XP SP2, is enabled by default for all processes. Under safe search mode, the current directory is moved behind the three system directories, resulting in the following path ordering:

1. The directory from which the application was launched

2. The native Windows system directory (for example, C:\Windows\System32)

3. The 16-bit Windows system directory (for example, C:\Windows\System)

4. The Windows directory (for example, C:\Windows)

5. The current directory at application launch time

6. Any directories specified by the %PATH% environment variable

The DLL search path is recomputed for each subsequent DLL load operation. The algorithm used to compute the search path is the same as the one used to compute the default search path, but the application can change specific path elements by editing the %PATH% variable using the *SetEnvironmentVariable* API, changing the current directory using the *SetCurrentDirectory* API, or using the *SetDllDirectory* API to specify a DLL directory for the process. When a DLL directory is specified, the directory replaces the current directory in the search path and the loader ignores the safe DLL search mode setting for the process.

Callers can also modify the DLL search path for specific load operations by supplying the LOAD_WITH_ALTERED_SEARCH_PATH flag to the *LoadLibraryEx* API. When this flag is supplied and the DLL name supplied to the API specifies a full path string, the path containing the DLL file is used in place of the application directory when computing the search path for the operation.

DLL Name Redirection

Before attempting to resolve a DLL name string to a file, the loader attempts to apply DLL name redirection rules. These redirection rules are used to extend or override portions of the DLL namespace—which normally corresponds to the Win32 file system namespace—to extend the Windows application model. In order of application, they are

- **MinWin API Set Redirection** The API set mechanism is designed to allow the Windows team to change the binary that exports a given system API in a manner that is transparent to applications.

- **.LOCAL Redirection** The .LOCAL redirection mechanism allows applications to redirect all loads of a specific DLL base name, regardless of whether a full path is specified, to a local copy of the DLL in the application directory—either by creating a copy of the DLL with the same base name followed by *.local* (for example, MyLibrary.dll.local) or by creating a file folder with the name .local under the application directory and placing a copy of the local DLL in the folder (for example, C:\Program Files\My App\.LOCAL\MyLibrary.dll). DLLs redirected by the .LOCAL mechanism are handled identically to those redirected by SxS. (See the next bullet point.) The loader honors .LOCAL redirection of DLLs only when the executable does not have an associated manifest, either embedded or external.

- **Fusion (SxS) Redirection**   Fusion (also referred to as *side-by-side, or SxS*) is an extension to the Windows application model that allows components to express more detailed binary dependency information (usually versioning information) by embedding binary resources known as *manifests*. The Fusion mechanism was first used so that applications could load the correct version of the Windows common controls package (comctl32.dll) after that binary was split into different versions that could be installed alongside one another; other binaries have since been versioned in the same fashion. As of Visual Studio 2005, applications built with the Microsoft linker will use Fusion to locate the appropriate version of the C runtime libraries.

  The Fusion runtime tool reads embedded dependency information from a binary's resource section using the Windows resource loader, and it packages the dependency information into lookup structures known as *activation contexts*. The system creates default activation contexts at the system and process level at boot and process startup time, respectively; in addition, each thread has an associated activation context stack, with the activation context structure at the top of the stack considered active. The per-thread activation context stack is managed both explicitly, via the *ActivateActCtx* and *DeactivateActCtx* APIs, and implicitly by the system at certain points, such as when the DLL main routine of a binary with embedded dependency information is called. When a Fusion DLL name redirection lookup occurs, the system searches for redirection information in the activation context at the head of the thread's activation context stack, followed by the process and system activation contexts; if redirection information is present, the file identity specified by the activation context is used for the load operation.

- **Known DLL Redirection**   Known DLLs is a mechanism that maps specific DLL base names to files in the system directory, preventing the DLL from being replaced with an alternate version in a different location.

  One edge case in the DLL path search algorithm is the DLL versioning check performed on 64-bit and WOW64 applications. If a DLL with a matching base name is located but is subsequently determined to have been compiled for the wrong machine architecture—for example, a 64-bit image in a 32-bit application—the loader ignores the error and resumes the path search operation, starting with the path element after the one used to locate the incorrect file. This behavior is designed to allow applications to specify both 64-bit and 32-bit entries in the global %PATH% environment variable.

EXPERIMENT: Observing DLL Load Search Order

You can use Sysinternals Process Monitor to watch how the loader searches for DLLs. When the loader attempts to resolve a DLL dependency, you will see it perform CreateFile calls to probe each location in the search sequence until either it finds the specified DLL or the load fails.

Here's the capture of the loader's search when an executable named Myapp.exe has a static dependency on a library named Mylibrary.dll. The executable is stored in C:\Myapp, but the current working directory was C:\ when the executable was launched. For the sake of demonstration, the executable does not include a manifest (by default, Visual Studio has one) so that the loader will check inside the C:\Myapp\Myapp.exe.local subdirectory that was created for the experiment. To reduce noise, the Process Monitor filter includes the myapp.exe process and any paths that contain the string "mylibrary.dll".

Process Name	Operation	Path	Result
myapp.exe	CreateFile	C:\myapp\myapp.exe.local\mylibrary.dll	NAME NOT FOUND
myapp.exe	CreateFile	C:\myapp\mylibrary.dll	NAME NOT FOUND
myapp.exe	CreateFile	C:\myapp\mylibrary.dll	NAME NOT FOUND
myapp.exe	CreateFile	C:\Windows\SysWOW64\mylibrary.dll	NAME NOT FOUND
myapp.exe	CreateFile	C:\Windows\system\mylibrary.dll	NAME NOT FOUND
myapp.exe	CreateFile	C:\Windows\mylibrary.dll	NAME NOT FOUND
myapp.exe	CreateFile	C:\mylibrary.dll	SUCCESS
myapp.exe	QueryBasicInf...	C:\mylibrary.dll	SUCCESS
myapp.exe	CloseFile	C:\mylibrary.dll	SUCCESS
myapp.exe	CreateFile	C:\mylibrary.dll	SUCCESS
myapp.exe	CreateFileMa...	C:\mylibrary.dll	FILE LOCKED WITH ONL...
myapp.exe	QueryStandar...	C:\mylibrary.dll	SUCCESS
myapp.exe	CreateFileMa...	C:\mylibrary.dll	SUCCESS
myapp.exe	Load Image	C:\mylibrary.dll	SUCCESS
myapp.exe	CloseFile	C:\mylibrary.dll	SUCCESS

Note how the search order matches that described. First, the loader checks the .LOCAL subdirectory, then the directory where the executable resides, then C:\Windows\System32 directory (because this is a 32-bit executable, that redirects to C:\Windows\SysWOW64), then the 16-bit Windows directory, then C:\Windows, and finally, the current directory at the time the executable was launched. The Load Image event confirms that the loader successfully resolved the import.

Loaded Module Database

The loader maintains a list of all modules (DLLs as well as the primary executable) that have been loaded by a process. This information is stored in a per-process structure called the process environment block, or PEB (see Chapter 5 for a full description of the PEB)—namely, in a substructure identified by *Ldr* and called PEB_LDR_DATA. In the structure, the loader maintains three doubly-linked lists, all containing the same information but ordered differently (either by load order, memory location, or initialization order). These lists contain structures called *loader data table entries* (LDR_DATA_TABLE_ENTRY) that store information about each module. Table 3-24 lists the various pieces of information the loader maintains in an entry.

TABLE 3-24 Fields in a Loader Data Table Entry

Field	Meaning
BaseDllName	Name of the module itself, without the full path
ContextInformation	Used by *SwitchBranch* (described later) to store the current Windows context GUID associated with this module
DllBase	Holds the base address at which the module was loaded
EntryPoint	Contains the initial routine of the module (such as *DllMain*)
EntryPointActivationContext	Contains the SxS/Fusion activation context when calling initializers
Flags	Loader state flags for this module (See Table 3-25 for a description of the flags.)

Field	Meaning
ForwarderLinks	Linked list of modules that were loaded as a result of export table forwarders from the module
FullDllName	Fully qualified path name of the module
HashLinks	Linked list used during process startup and shutdown for quicker lookups
List Entry Links	Links this entry into each of the three ordered lists part of the loader database
LoadCount	Reference count for the module (that is, how many times it has been loaded)
LoadTime	Stores the system time value when this module was being loaded
OriginalBase	Stores the original base address (set by the linker) of this module, enabling faster processing of relocated import entries
PatchInformation	Information that's relevant during a hotpatch operation on this module
ServiceTagLinks	Linked list of services (see Chapter 4 for more information) referencing this module
SizeOfImage	Size of the module in memory
StaticLinks	Linked list of modules loaded as a result of static references from this one
TimeDateStamp	Time stamp written by the linker when the module was linked, which the loader obtains from the module's image PE header
TlsIndex	Thread local storage slot associated with this module

One way to look at a process' loader database is to use WinDbg and its formatted output of the PEB. The next experiment shows you how to do this and how to look at the LDR_DATA_TABLE_ENTRY structures on your own.

EXPERIMENT: Dumping the Loaded Modules Database

Before starting the experiment, perform the same steps as in the previous two experiments to launch Notepad.exe with WinDbg as the debugger. When you get to the first prompt (where you've been instructed to type **g** until now), follow these instructions:

1. You can look at the PEB of the current process with the *!peb* command. For now, you're interested only in the *Ldr* data that will be displayed. (See Chapter 5 for details about other information stored in the PEB.)

```
0: kd> !peb
PEB at 000007fffffda000
    InheritedAddressSpace:     No
    ReadImageFileExecOptions:  No
    BeingDebugged:             No
    ImageBaseAddress:          00000000ff590000
    Ldr                        0000000076e72640
    Ldr.Initialized:           Yes
    Ldr.InInitializationOrderModuleList: 0000000000212880 . 0000000004731c20
    Ldr.InLoadOrderModuleList:           0000000000212770 . 0000000004731c00
```

```
        Ldr.InMemoryOrderModuleList:        0000000000212780 . 0000000004731c10
              Base TimeStamp                         Module
           ff590000 4ce7a144 Nov 20 11:21:56 2010 C:\Windows\Explorer.EXE
           76d40000 4ce7c8f9 Nov 20 14:11:21 2010 C:\Windows\SYSTEM32\ntdll.dll
           76870000 4ce7c78b Nov 20 14:05:15 2010 C:\Windows\system32\kernel32.dll
         7fefd2d0000 4ce7c78c Nov 20 14:05:16 2010 C:\Windows\system32\KERNELBASE.dll
         7fefee20000 4a5bde6b Jul 14 02:24:59 2009 C:\Windows\system32\ADVAPI32.dll
```

2. The address shown on the Ldr line is a pointer to the PEB_LDR_DATA structure described earlier. Notice that WinDbg shows you the address of the three lists and dumps the initialization order list for you, displaying the full path, time stamp, and base address of each module.

3. You can also analyze each module entry on its own by going through the module list and then dumping the data at each address, formatted as a LDR_DATA_TABLE_ENTRY structure. Instead of doing this for each entry, however, WinDbg can do most of the work by using the *!list* extension and the following syntax:

```
!list -t ntdll!_LIST_ENTRY.Flink -x "dt ntdll!_LDR_DATA_TABLE_ENTRY @$extret\"
0000000076e72640
```

Note that the last number is variable: it depends on whatever is shown on your machine under *Ldr.InLoadOrderModuleList*.

4. You should then see the entries for each module:

```
0:001> !list -t ntdll!_LIST_ENTRY.Flink -x "dt ntdll!_LDR_DATA_TABLE_ENTRY
@$extret\" 001c1cf8
   +0x000 InLoadOrderLinks : _LIST_ENTRY [ 0x1c1d68 - 0x76fd4ccc ]
   +0x008 InMemoryOrderLinks : _LIST_ENTRY [ 0x1c1d70 - 0x76fd4cd4 ]
   +0x010 InInitializationOrderLinks : _LIST_ENTRY [ 0x0 - 0x0 ]
   +0x018 DllBase          : 0x00d80000
   +0x01c EntryPoint       : 0x00d831ed
   +0x020 SizeOfImage      : 0x28000
   +0x024 FullDllName      : _UNICODE_STRING "C:\Windows\notepad.exe"
   +0x02c BaseDllName      : _UNICODE_STRING "notepad.exe"
   +0x034 Flags            : 0x4010
```

Although this section covers the user-mode loader in Ntdll.dll, note that the kernel also employs its own loader for drivers and dependent DLLs, with a similar loader entry structure. Likewise, the kernel-mode loader has its own database of such entries, which is directly accessible through the *PsActiveModuleList* global data variable. To dump the kernel's loaded module database, you can use a similar *!list* command as shown in the preceding experiment by replacing the pointer at the end of the command with "nt!PsActiveModuleList".

Looking at the list in this raw format gives you some extra insight into the loader's *internals*, such as the *flags* field, which contains state information that *!peb* on its own would not show you. See Table 3-25 for their meaning. Because both the kernel and user-mode loaders use this structure, some flags apply only to kernel-mode drivers, while others apply only to user-mode applications (such as .NET state).

TABLE 3-25 Loader Data Table Entry Flags

Flag	Meaning
LDRP_STATIC_LINK (0x2)	This module is referenced by an import table and is required.
LDRP_IMAGE_DLL (0x4)	The module is an image DLL (and not a data DLL or executable).
LDRP_IMAGE_INTEGRITY_FORCED (0x20)	The module was linked with /FORCEINTEGRITY (contains IMAGE_DLLCHARACTERISTICS_FORCE_ INTEGRITY_in its PE header).
LDRP_LOAD_IN_PROGRESS (0x1000)	This module is currently being loaded.
LDRP_UNLOAD_IN_PROGRESS (0x2000)	This module is currently being unloaded.
LDRP_ENTRY_PROCESSED (0x4000)	The loader has finished processing this module.
LDRP_ENTRY_INSERTED (0x8000)	The loader has finished inserting this entry into the loaded module database.
LDRP_FAILED_BUILTIN_LOAD (0x20000)	Indicates this boot driver failed to load.
LDRP_DONT_CALL_FOR_THREADS (0x40000)	Do not send DLL_THREAD_ATTACH/DETACH notifications to this DLL.
LDRP_PROCESS_ATTACH_CALLED (0x80000)	This DLL has been sent the DLL_PROCESS_ATTACH notification.
LDRP_DEBUG_SYMBOLS_LOADED (0x100000)	The debug symbols for this module have been loaded by the kernel or user debugger.
LDRP_IMAGE_NOT_AT_BASE (0x200000)	This image was relocated from its original base address.
LDRP_COR_IMAGE (0x400000)	This module is a .NET application.
LDRP_COR_OWNS_UNMAP (0x800000)	This module should be unmapped by the .NET runtime.
LDRP_SYSTEM_MAPPED (0x1000000)	This module is mapped into kernel address space with System PTEs (versus being in the initial boot loader's memory).
LDRP_IMAGE_VERIFYING (0x2000000)	This module is currently being verified by Driver Verifier.
LDRP_DRIVER_DEPENDENT_DLL (0x4000000)	This module is a DLL that is in a driver's import table.
LDRP_ENTRY_NATIVE (0x8000000)	This module was compiled for Windows 2000 or later. It's used by Driver Verifier as an indication that a driver might be suspect.
LDRP_REDIRECTED (0x10000000)	The manifest file specified a redirected file for this DLL.
LDRP_NON_PAGED_DEBUG_INFO (0x20000000)	The debug information for this module is in non-paged memory.
LDRP_MM_LOADED (0x40000000)	This module was loaded by the kernel loader through *MmLoadSystemImage.*
LDRP_COMPAT_DATABASE_PROCESSED (0x80000000)	The shim engine has processed this DLL.

Import Parsing

Now that we've explained the way the loader keeps track of all the modules loaded for a process, you can continue analyzing the startup initialization tasks performed by the loader. During this step, the loader will do the following:

1. Load each DLL referenced in the import table of the process' executable image.

2. Check whether the DLL has already been loaded by checking the module database. If it doesn't find it in the list, the loader opens the DLL and maps it into memory.

3. During the mapping operation, the loader first looks at the various paths where it should attempt to find this DLL, as well as whether this DLL is a "known DLL," meaning that the system has already loaded it at startup and provided a global memory mapped file for accessing it. Certain deviations from the standard lookup algorithm can also occur, either through the use of a .local file (which forces the loader to use DLLs in the local path) or through a manifest file, which can specify a redirected DLL to use to guarantee a specific version.

4. After the DLL has been found on disk and mapped, the loader checks whether the kernel has loaded it somewhere else—this is called relocation. If the loader detects relocation, it parses the relocation information in the DLL and performs the operations required. If no relocation information is present, DLL loading fails.

5. The loader then creates a loader data table entry for this DLL and inserts it into the database.

6. After a DLL has been mapped, the process is repeated for this DLL to parse its import table and all its dependencies.

7. After each DLL is loaded, the loader parses the IAT to look for specific functions that are being imported. Usually this is done by name, but it can also be done by ordinal (an index number). For each name, the loader parses the export table of the imported DLL and tries to locate a match. If no match is found, the operation is aborted.

8. The import table of an image can also be bound. This means that at link time, the developers already assigned static addresses pointing to imported functions in external DLLs. This removes the need to do the lookup for each name, but it assumes that the DLLs the application will use will always be located at the same address. Because Windows uses address space randomization (see Chapter 10 in Part 2 for more information on Address Space Load Randomization, or ASLR), this is usually not the case for system applications and libraries.

9. The export table of an imported DLL can use a forwarder entry, meaning that the actual function is implemented in another DLL. This must essentially be treated like an import or dependency, so after parsing the export table, each DLL referenced by a forwarder is also loaded and the loader goes back to step 1.

After all imported DLLs (and their own dependencies, or imports) have been loaded, all the required imported functions have been looked up and found, and all forwarders also have been loaded and processed, the step is complete: all dependencies that were defined at compile time by the application and its various DLLs have now been fulfilled. During execution, delayed dependencies (called *delay load*), as well as run-time operations (such as calling *LoadLibrary*) can call into the loader and essentially repeat the same tasks. Note, however, that a failure in these steps will result in an error launching the application if they are done during process startup. For example, attempting to run an application that requires a function that isn't present in the current version of the operating system can result in a message similar to the one in Figure 3-32.

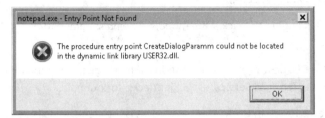

FIGURE 3-32 Dialog box shown when a required (imported) function is not present in a DLL

Post-Import Process Initialization

After the required dependencies have been loaded, several initialization tasks must be performed to fully finalize launching the application. In this phase, the loader will do the following:

1. Check if the application is a .NET application, and redirect execution to the .NET runtime entry point instead, assuming the image has been validated by the framework.

2. Check if the application itself requires relocation, and process the relocation entries for the application. If the application cannot be relocated, or does not have relocation information, the loading will fail.

3. Check if the application makes use of TLS, and look in the application executable for the TLS entries it needs to allocate and configure.

4. If this is a Windows application, the Windows subsystem thread-initialization thunk code is located after loading kernel32.dll, and the Authz/AppLocker enforcement is enabled. (See Chapter 6 for more information on Software Restriction Policies.) If Kernel32.dll is not found, the system is presumably assumed to be running in MinWin and only Kernelbase.dll is loaded.

5. Any static imports are now loaded.

6. At this point, the initial debugger breakpoint will be hit when using a debugger such as WinDbg. This is where you had to type **g** to continue execution in the earlier experiments.

7. Make sure that the application will be able to run properly if the system is a multiprocessor system.

8. Set up the default data execution prevention (DEP) options, including for exception-chain validation, also called "software" DEP. (See Chapter 10 in Part 2 for more information on DEP.)

9. Check whether this application requires any application compatibility work, and load the shim engine if required.

10. Detect if this application is protected by SecuROM, SafeDisc, and other kinds of wrapper or protection utilities that could have issues with DEP (and reconfigure DEP settings in those cases).

11. Run the initializers for all the loaded modules.

12. Run the post-initialization Shim Engine callback if the module is being shimmed for application compatibility.

13. Run the associated subsystem DLL post-process initialization routine registered in the PEB. For Windows applications, this does Terminal Services–specific checks, for example.

Running the initializers is the last main step in the loader's work. This is the step that calls the *DllMain* routine for each DLL (allowing each DLL to perform its own initialization work, which might even include loading new DLLs at run time) as well as processes the TLS initializers of each DLL. This is one of the last steps in which loading an application can fail. If all the loaded DLLs do not return a successful return code after finishing their *DllMain* routines, the loader aborts starting the application. As a very last step, the loader calls the TLS initializer of the actual application.

SwitchBack

As each new version of Windows fixes bugs such as race conditions and incorrect parameter validation checks in existing API functions, an application-compatibility risk is created for each change, no matter how minor. Windows makes use of a technology called SwitchBack, implemented in the loader, which enables software developers to embed a GUID specific to the Windows version they are targeting in their executable's associated manifest. For example, if a developer wants to take advantage of improvements added in Windows 7 to a given API, she would include the Windows 7 GUID in her manifest, while if a developer has a legacy application that depends on Windows Vista–specific behavior, she would put the Windows Vista GUID in the manifest instead. SwitchBack parses this information and correlates it with embedded information in SwitchBack-compatible DLLs (in the .sb_data image section) to decide which version of an affected API should be called by the module. Because SwitchBack works at the loaded-module level, it enables a process to have both legacy and current DLLs concurrently calling the same API, yet observing different results.

Windows currently defines two GUIDs that represent either Windows Vista or Windows 7 compatibility settings:

- {e2011457-1546-43c5-a5fe-008deee3d3f0} for Windows Vista

- {35138b9a-5d96-4fbd-8e2d-a2440225f93a} for Windows 7

These GUIDs must be present in the application's manifest file under the SupportedOS ID present in a compatibility attribute entry. (If the application manifest does not contain a GUID, Windows

Vista is chosen as the default compatibility mode.) Running under the Windows 7 context affects the following components:

- RPC components use the Windows thread pool instead of a private implementation.

- DirectDraw Lock cannot be acquired on the primary buffer.

- Blitting on the desktop is not allowed without a clipping window.

- A race condition in *GetOverlappedResult* is fixed.

Whenever a Windows API is affected by changes that might break compatibility, the function's entry code calls the *SbSwitchProcedure* to invoke the SwitchBack logic. It passes along a pointer to the SwitchBack Module Table, which contains information about the SwitchBack mechanisms employed in the module. The table also contains a pointer to an array of entries for each SwitchBack point. This table contains a description of each branch-point that identifies it with a symbolic name and a comprehensive description, along with an associated mitigation tag. Typically, there will be two branch-points in a module, one for Windows Vista behavior, and one for Windows 7 behavior. For each branch-point, the required SwitchBack context is given—it is this context that determines which of the two (or more) branches is taken at runtime. Finally, each of these descriptors contains a function pointer to the actual code that each branch should execute. If the application is running with the Windows 7 GUID, this will be part of its SwitchBack context, and the *SbSelectProcedure* API, upon parsing the module table, will perform a match operation. It finds the module entry descriptor for the context and proceeds to call the function pointer included in the descriptor.

SwitchBack uses ETW to trace the selection of given SwitchBack contexts and branch-points and feeds the data into the Windows AIT (Application Impact Telemetry) logger. This data can be periodically collected by Microsoft to determine the extent to which each compatibility entry is being used, identify the applications using it (a full stack trace is provided in the log), and notify third-party vendors.

As mentioned, the compatibility level of the application is stored in its manifest. At load time, the loader parses the manifest file, creates a context data structure, and caches it in the *pContextData* member of the process environment block. (For more information on the PEB, see Chapter 5.) This context data contains the associated compatibility GUIDs that this process is executing under and determines which version of the branch-points in the called APIs that employ SwitchBack will be executed.

API Sets

While SwitchBack uses API redirection for specific application-compatibility scenarios, there is a much more pervasive redirection mechanism used in Windows for all applications, called *API Sets*. Its purpose is to enable fine-grained categorization of Windows APIs into sub-DLLs instead of having large multipurpose DLLs that span nearly thousands of APIs that might not be needed on all types of Windows systems today and in the future. This technology, developed mainly to support the refactoring of the bottom-most layers of the Windows architecture to separate it from higher layers, goes hand in hand with the breakdown of Kernel32.dll and Advapi32.dll (among others) into multiple, virtual DLL files.

For example, the following graphic shows that Kernel32.dll, which is a core Windows library, imports from many other DLLs, beginning with API-MS-WIN. Each of these DLLs contain a small subset of the APIs that Kernel32 normally provides, but together they make up the entire API surface exposed by Kernel32.dll. The CORE-STRING library, for instance, provides only the Windows base string functions.

In splitting functions across discrete files, two objectives are achieved: first, doing this allows future applications to link only with the API libraries that provide the functionality that they need, and second, if Microsoft were to create a version of Windows that did not support, for example, Localization (say a non-user-facing, English-only embedded system), it would be possible to simply remove the sub-DLL and modify the API Set schema. This would result in a smaller Kernel32 binary, and any applications that ran without requiring localization would still run.

With this technology, a "base" Windows system called "MinWin" is defined (and, at the source level, built), with a minimum set of services that includes the kernel, core drivers (including file systems, basic system processes such as CSRSS and the Service Control Manager, and a handful of Windows services). Windows Embedded, with its Platform Builder, provides what might seem to be a similar technology, as system builders are able to remove select "Windows components," such as the shell, or the network stack. However, removing components from Windows leaves *dangling dependencies*— code paths that, if exercised, would fail because they depend on the removed components. MinWin's dependencies, on the other hand, are entirely self-contained.

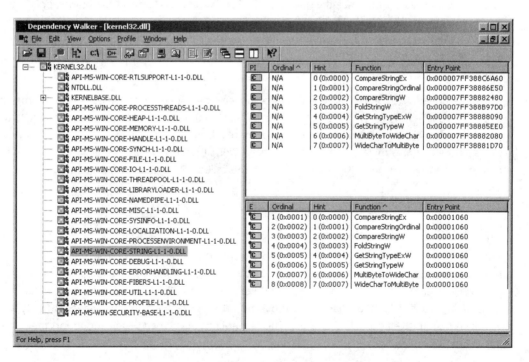

When the process manager initializes, it calls the *PspInitializeApiSetMap* function, which is responsible for creating a section object (using a standard section object) of the API Set redirection table, which is stored in %SystemRoot%\System32\ApiSetSchema.dll. The DLL contains no executable code, but it has a section called *.apiset* that contains API Set mapping data that maps virtual API Set DLLs to logical DLLs that implement the APIs. Whenever a new process starts, the process manager maps the section object into the process' address space and sets the *ApiSetMap* field in the process' PEB to point to the base address where the section object was mapped.

In turn, the loader's *LdrpApplyFileNameRedirection* function, which is normally responsible for the .local and SxS/Fusion manifest redirection that was mentioned earlier, also checks for API Set redirection data whenever a new import library that has a name starting with "API-" loads (either dynamically or statically). The API Set table is organized by library with each entry describing in which logical DLL the function can be found, and that DLL is what gets loaded. Although the schema data is a binary format, you can dump its strings with the Sysinternals Strings tool to see which DLLs are currently defined:

```
C:\Windows\System32>strings apisetschema.dll
...
MS-Win-Core-Console-L1-1-0
kernel32.dllMS-Win-Core-DateTime-L1-1-0
MS-Win-Core-Debug-L1-1-0
kernelbase.dllMS-Win-Core-DelayLoad-L1-1-0
MS-Win-Core-ErrorHandling-L1-1-0
MS-Win-Core-Fibers-L1-1-0
MS-Win-Core-File-L1-1-0
MS-Win-Core-Handle-L1-1-0
MS-Win-Core-Heap-L1-1-0
MS-Win-Core-Interlocked-L1-1-0
MS-Win-Core-IO-L1-1-0
MS-Win-Core-LibraryLoader-L1-1-0
MS-Win-Core-Localization-L1-1-0
MS-Win-Core-LocalRegistry-L1-1-0
MS-Win-Core-Memory-L1-1-0
MS-Win-Core-Misc-L1-1-0
MS-Win-Core-NamedPipe-L1-1-0
MS-Win-Core-ProcessEnvironment-L1-1-0
MS-Win-Core-ProcessThreads-L1-1-0
MS-Win-Core-Profile-L1-1-0
MS-Win-Core-RtlSupport-L1-1-0
ntdll.dll
MS-Win-Core-String-L1-1-0
```

Hypervisor (Hyper-V)

One of the key technologies in the software industry—used by system administrators, developers, and testers alike—is called *virtualization*, and it refers to the ability to run multiple operating systems simultaneously on the same physical machine. One operating system, in which the virtualization software is executing, is called the *host*, while the other operating systems are running as *guests* inside the virtualization software. The usage scenarios for this model cover everything from being able to test an application on different platforms to having fully virtual servers all actually running as part of the same machine and managed through one central point.

Until recently, all the virtualization was done by the software itself, sometimes assisted by hardware-level virtualization technology (called *host-based virtualization)*. Thanks to hardware virtualization, the CPU can do most of the notifications required for trapping instructions and virtualizing access to memory. These notifications, as well as the various configuration steps required for allowing guest operating systems to run concurrently, must be handled by a piece of infrastructure compatible with the CPU's virtualization support. Instead of relying on a piece of separate software running inside a host operating system to perform these tasks, a thin piece of low-level system software, which uses strictly hardware-assisted virtualization support, can be used—a *hypervisor*. Figure 3-33 shows a simple architectural overview of these two kinds of systems.

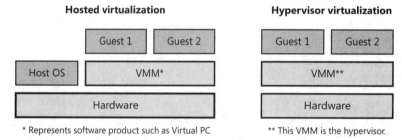

FIGURE 3-33 Two architectures for virtualization

With Hyper-V, Windows server computers can install support for hypervisor-based virtualization as a server role (as long as an edition with Hyper-V support is licensed). Because the hypervisor is part of the operating system, managing the guests inside it, as well as interacting with them, is fully integrated in the operating system through standard management mechanisms such as WMI and services. (See Chapter 4 for more information on these topics.)

Finally, apart from having a hypervisor that allows running other guests managed by a Windows Server host, both client and server editions of Windows also ship with *enlightenments*, which are special optimizations in the kernel and possibly device drivers that detect that the code is being run as a guest under a hypervisor and perform certain tasks differently, or more efficiently, considering this environment. We will look at some of these improvements later; for now, we'll take a look at the basic architecture of the Windows virtualization stack, shown in Figure 3-34.

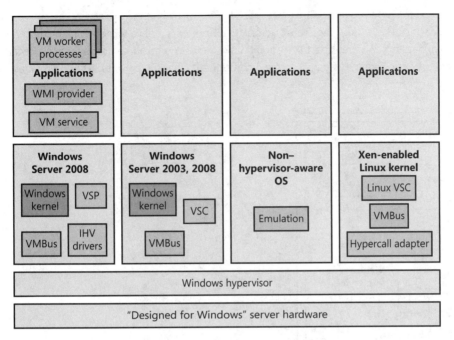

FIGURE 3-34 Windows Hyper-V architectural stack

Partitions

One of the key architectural components behind the Windows hypervisor is the concept of a *partition*. A partition essentially references an instance of an operating system installation, which can refer either to what's traditionally called the host or to the guest. Under the Windows hypervisor model, these two terms are not used; instead, we talk of either a *parent partition* or a *child partition*, respectively. Consequently, at a minimum, a Hyper-V system will have a parent partition, which is recommended to contain a Windows Server Core installation, as well as the virtualization stack and its associated components. Although this installation type is recommended because it allows minimizing patches and reducing the security surface area, resulting in increased availability of the server, a full installation is also supported. Each operating system running within the virtualized environment represents a child partition, which might contain certain additional tools that optimize access to the hardware or allow management of the operating system.

Parent Partition

One of the main goals behind the design of the Windows hypervisor was to have it as small and modular as possible, much like a microkernel, instead of providing a full, monolithic module. This means that most of the virtualization work is actually done by a separate virtualization stack and that there are also no *hypervisor drivers*. In lieu of these, the hypervisor uses the existing Windows driver architecture and talks to actual Windows device drivers. This architecture results in several components that provide and manage this behavior, which are collectively called the *hypervisor stack*.

Logically, it is the parent partition that is responsible for providing the hypervisor, as well as the entire hypervisor stack. Because these are Microsoft components, only a Windows machine can be a root partition, naturally. A parent partition should have almost no resource usage for itself because its role is to run other operating systems. The main components that the parent partition provides are shown in Figure 3-35.

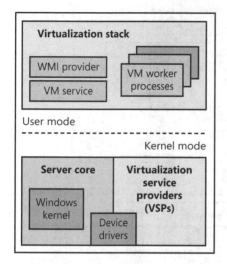

FIGURE 3-35 Components of a parent partition

Parent Partition Operating System

The Windows installation (typically the minimal footprint server installation, called Windows Server Core, to minimize resource usage) is responsible for providing the hypervisor and the device drivers for the hardware on the system (which the hypervisor will need to access), as well as for running the hypervisor stack. It is also the management point for all the child partitions.

Virtual Machine Manager Service and Worker Processes

The virtual machine management service (%SystemRoot%\System32\Vmms.exe) is responsible for providing the Windows Management Instrumentation (WMI) interface to the hypervisor, which allows managing the child partitions through a Microsoft Management Console (MMC) plug-in. It is also responsible for communicating requests to applications that need to communicate to the hypervisor or to child partitions. It controls settings such as which devices are visible to child partitions, how the memory and processor allocation for each partition is defined, and more.

The virtual machine worker processes (VMWPs), on the other hand, perform various virtualization work that a typical monolithic hypervisor would perform (similar to the work of a software-based virtualization solution). This means managing the state machine for a given child partition (to allow support for features such as snapshots and state transitions), responding to various notifications coming in from the hypervisor, performing the emulation of certain devices exposed to child partitions, and collaborating with the VM service and configuration component.

On a system with child partitions performing lots of I/O or privileged operations, you would expect most of the CPU usage to be visible in the parent partition: you can identify them by the name Vmwp.exe (one for each child partition). The worker process also includes components responsible for remote management of the virtualization stack, as well as an RDP component that allows using the remote desktop client to connect to any child partition and remotely view its user interface and interact with it.

Virtualization Service Providers

Virtualization service providers (VSPs) are responsible for the high-speed emulation of certain devices visible to child partitions (the exact difference between VSP-emulated devices and user-mode–process-emulated devices will be explained later), and unlike the VM service and processes, VSPs can also run in kernel mode as drivers. More detail on VSPs will follow in the section that describes device architecture in the virtualization stack.

VM Infrastructure Driver and Hypervisor API Library

Because the hypervisor cannot be directly accessed by user-mode applications, such as the VM service that is responsible for management, the virtualization stack must actually talk to a driver in kernel mode that is responsible for relaying the requests to the hypervisor. This is the job of the VM infrastructure driver (VID). The VID also provides support for certain low-memory memory devices, such as MMIO and ROM emulation.

A library located in kernel mode provides the actual interface to the hypervisor (called *hypercalls).* Messages can also come from child partitions (which will perform their own hypercalls), because there is only one hypervisor for the whole system and it can listen to messages coming from any partition. You can find this functionality in the Winhv.sys device driver.

Hypervisor

At the bottom of the architecture is the hypervisor itself, which registers itself with the processor at system boot-up time and provides its services for the stack to use (through the use of the hypercall interface). This early initialization is performed by the hvboot.sys driver, which is configured to start early on during a system boot. Because Intel and AMD processors have slightly differing implementations of hardware-assisted virtualization, there are actually two different hypervisors—the correct one is selected at boot-up time by querying the processor through CPUID instructions. On Intel systems, the Hvix64.exe binary is loaded, while on AMD systems, the Hvax64.exe image is used.

Child Partitions

The child partition, as discussed earlier, is an instance of any operating system running parallel to the parent partition. (Because you can save or pause the state of any child, it might not necessarily be running, but there will be a worker process for it.) Unlike the parent partition, which has full access to the APIC, I/O ports, and physical memory, child partitions are limited for security and management reasons to their own view of address space (the Guest Virtual Address Space, or GVA, which is managed by the hypervisor) and have no direct access to hardware. In terms of hypervisor access, it is also limited mainly to notifications and state changes. For example, a child partition doesn't have control over other partitions (and can't create new ones).

Child partitions have many fewer virtualization components than a parent partition because they are not responsible for running the virtualization stack—only for communicating with it. Also, these components can also be considered optional because they enhance performance of the environment but are not critical to its use. Figure 3-36 shows the components present in a typical Windows child partition.

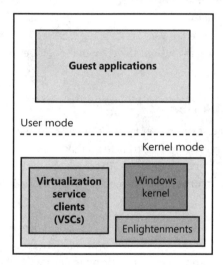

FIGURE 3-36 Components in a child partition

EXPERIMENT: Examining Child Partitions from the Parent with LiveKd

With Sysinternals LiveKd, you can examine a Windows XP or higher virtual machine from the parent partition without having to boot the child operating system in debugging mode. First, specify the *–hvl* option to LiveKd, which has it list the IDs and names of active child partitions:

```
C:\>livekd -hvl

LiveKd v5.0 - Execute kd/windbg on a live system
Sysinternals - www.sysinternals.com
Copyright (C) 2000-2010 Mark Russinovich and Ken Johnson

Partition GUID                           Name
C8FA520B-CBBC-48CE-84EC-14BC2B2C3A74     Win7x64

C:\>
```

Then run LiveKd with the *–hv* switch and specify the ID or name of the child partition that you want to examine. Just as for debugging the local system with Livekd, the contents of the virtual machine's memory can change as you execute LiveKd commands, resulting in LiveKd seeing inconsistencies caused by data reflecting different points in time. If you want LiveKd to see a consistent view, you can specify the –p option to have the child partition paused while LiveKd is running. All commands that work on a local system also work when you use LiveKd to explore a virtual machine. Here's the partial output of the !vm kernel debugger command, which lists various memory-related statistics, when executed on a Hyper-V child partition:

```
C:\>livekd -hv win7x64

LiveKd v5.0 - Execute kd/windbg on a live system
Sysinternals - www.sysinternals.com
Copyright (C) 2000-2010 Mark Russinovich and Ken Johnson

Launching C:\program files\Debugging Tools for Windows (x64)\kd.exe:

Microsoft (R) Windows Debugger Version 6.13.0002.895 AMD64
Copyright (c) Microsoft Corporation. All rights reserved.


Loading Dump File [C:\Windows\livekd.dmp]
Kernel Complete Dump File: Full address space is available

Comment: 'LiveKD live system view (hypervisor partition)'
Symbol search path is: srv*c:\Symbols*http://msdl.microsoft.com/download/symbols
Executable search path is:
Windows 7 Kernel Version 7600 MP (2 procs) Free x64
Product: WinNt, suite: TerminalServer SingleUserTS
Built by: 7600.16617.amd64fre.win7_gdr.100618-1621
Machine Name:
Kernel base = 0xfffff800`02a06000 PsLoadedModuleList = 0xfffff800`02c43e50
Debug session time: Sat Feb 12 19:34:57.897 17420 (UTC - 7:00)
System Uptime: 3 days 7:14:55.312
Loading Kernel Symbols
...............................................................
...............................................................
.........
Loading User Symbols

Loading unloaded module list
......
0: kd> !vm

*** Virtual Memory Usage ***
        Physical Memory:       513422 (    2053688 Kb)
        Page File: \??\C:\pagefile.sys
          Current:   1048576 Kb  Free Space:       792480 Kb
          Minimum:   1048576 Kb  Maximum:         4194304 Kb
        Available Pages:       101260 (    405040 Kb)
        ResAvail Pages:        167196 (    668784 Kb)
        Locked IO Pages:            0 (         0 Kb)
        Free System PTEs:    33533587 ( 134134348 Kb)
        Modified Pages:           898 (      3592 Kb)
```

Virtualization Service Clients

Virtualization service clients (VSCs) are the child partition analogues of VSPs. Like VSPs, VSCs are used for device emulation, which is a topic of later discussion.

Enlightenments

Enlightenments are one of the key performance optimizations that Windows virtualization takes advantage of. They are direct modifications to the standard Windows kernel code that can detect that this operating system is running in a child partition and perform work differently. Usually, these optimizations are highly hardware-specific and result in a hypercall to notify the hypervisor. An example is notifying the hypervisor of a long busy-wait spin loop. The hypervisor can keep some state stale in this scenario instead of keeping track of the state at every single loop instruction. Entering and exiting an interrupt state can also be coordinated with the hypervisor, as well as access to the APIC, which can be enlightened to avoid trapping the real access and then virtualizing it.

Another example has to do with memory management, specifically TLB flushing and changing address space. (See Chapter 9 for more information on these concepts.) Usually, the operating system executes a CPU instruction to flush this information, which affects the entire processor. However, because a child partition could be sharing a CPU with many other child partitions, such an operation would also flush this information for those operating systems, resulting in noticeable performance degradation. If Windows is running under a hypervisor, it instead issues a hypercall to have the hypervisor flush only the specific information belonging to the child partition.

Hardware Emulation and Support

A virtualization solution must also provide optimized access to devices. Unfortunately, most devices aren't made to accept multiple requests coming in from different operating systems. The hypervisor steps in by providing the same level of synchronization where possible and by emulating certain devices when real access to hardware cannot be permitted. In addition to devices, memory and processors must also be virtualized. Table 3-26 describes the three types of hardware that the hypervisor must manage.

TABLE 3-26 Virtualized Hardware

Component	Managed By	Usage
Processor	Hypervisor built-in scheduler and related microkernel components	Manage usage of hardware's processing power, share multiple processors across multiple child partitions, manage and switch processor states (such as registers).
Memory	Hypervisor built-in memory manager and related microkernel components	Manage hardware's RAM usage and availability. Protect memory from child partitions and parent partition. Provide a contiguous view of physical memory starting at address 0.
Devices	VM worker processes—hypervisor responsible only for interception and notification	Provide hardware multiplexing so that multiple child partitions can access the same device on the physical machine. Optimize access to physical devices to be as fast as possible.

Instead of exposing actual hardware to child partitions, the hypervisor exposes virtual devices (called *VDevs*). VDevs are packaged as COM components that run inside a VM worker process, and they are the central manageable object behind the device. (Usually, VDevs expose a WMI interface.) The Windows virtualization stack provides support for two kinds of virtual devices: *emulated devices* and *synthetic devices* (also called *enlightened I/O*). The former provide support for various devices that the operating systems on the child partition would expect to find, while the latter requires specific support from the guest operating system. On the other hand, synthetic devices provide a significant performance benefit by reducing CPU overhead.

Emulated Devices

Emulated devices work by presenting the child partition with a set of I/O ports, memory ranges, and interrupts that are being controlled and monitored by the hypervisor. When access to these resources is detected, the VM worker process eventually gets notified through the virtualization stack (shown earlier in Figure 3-34). The process then emulates whatever action is expected from the device and completes the request, going back through the hypervisor and then to the child partition. From this topological view alone, one can see that there is a definite loss in performance, without even considering that the software emulation of a hardware device is usually slow.

The need for emulated devices comes from the fact that the hypervisor needs to support nonhypervisor-aware operating systems, as well as the early installation steps of even Windows itself. During the boot process, the installer can't simply load all the child partition's required components (such as VSCs) to use synthetic devices, so a Windows installation will always use emulated devices (which is why installation will seem very slow, but once installed the operating system will run quite close to native speed). Emulated devices are also used for hardware that doesn't require high-speed emulation and for which software emulation might even be faster. This includes items such as COM (serial) ports, parallel ports, or the motherboard itself.

> **Note** Hyper-V emulates an Intel i440BX motherboard, an S3 Trio video card, and an Intel 21140 NIC.

Synthetic Devices

Although emulated devices work adequately for 10-Mbit network connections, low-resolution VGA displays, and 16-bit sound cards, the operating systems and hardware that child partitions usually require in today's usage scenarios require a lot more processing power, such as support for 1000-Mbit GbE connections; full-color, high-resolution 3D support; and high-speed access to storage devices. To support this kind of virtualized hardware access at an acceptable CPU usage level and virtualized throughput, the virtualization stack uses a variety of components to optimize device I/Os to their fullest (similar to kernel enlightenments). Three components are part of this support, and they all belong to what's presented to the user as *integration components* or ICs:

- Virtualization service providers (VSPs)

- Virtualization service clients/consumers (VSCs)

- VMBus

Figure 3-37 shows a diagram of how an enlightened, or synthetic storage I/O, is handled by the virtualization stack.

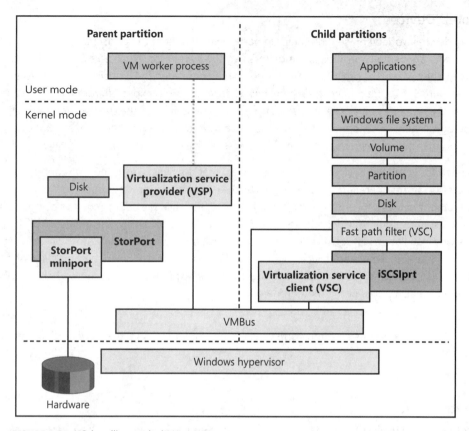

FIGURE 3-37 I/O handling paths in Hyper-V

As shown in Figure 3-37, VSPs run in the parent partition, where they are associated with a specific device that they are responsible for *enlightening*. (We'll use that as a term instead of *emulating* when referring to synthetic devices.) VSCs reside in the child partition and are also associated with a specific device. Note, however, that the term *provider* can refer to multiple components spread across the device stack. For example, a VSP can be any of the following:

- A user-mode service

- A user-mode COM component

- A kernel-mode driver

In all three cases, the VSP will be associated with the actual virtual device inside the VM worker process. VSCs, on the other hand, are almost always designed to be drivers sitting at the lowest level of the device stack (see Chapter 8 in Part 2 for more information on device stacks) and intercept I/Os to a device and redirect them through a more optimized path. The main optimization that is performed by this model is to avoid actual hardware access and use VMBus instead. Under this model, the hypervisor is unaware of the I/O, and the VSP redirects it directly to the parent partition's kernel storage stack, avoiding a trip to user mode as well. Other VSPs can perform work directly on the device, by talking to the actual hardware and bypassing any driver that might have been loaded on the parent partition. Another option is to have a user-mode VSP, which can make sense when dealing with lower-bandwidth devices.

As described earlier, VMBus is the name of the bus transport used to optimize device access by implementing a communications protocol using hypervisor services. VMBus is a bus driver present on both the parent partition and the child partitions responsible for the Plug and Play enumeration of synthetic devices in a child. It also contains the optimized cross-partition messaging protocol that uses a transport method that is appropriate for the data size. One of these methods is to provide a shared ring buffer between each partition—essentially an area of memory on which a certain amount of data is loaded on one side and unloaded on the other side. No memory needs to be allocated or freed because the buffer is continuously reused and simply rotated. Eventually, it might become full with requests, which would mean that newer I/Os would overwrite older I/Os. In this uncommon scenario, VMBus simply delays newer requests until older ones complete. The other messaging transport is direct child memory mapping to the parent address space for large enough transfers.

Virtual Processors

Just as the hypervisor doesn't allow direct access to hardware (or to memory, as you'll see later), child partitions don't really see the actual processors on the machine but have a virtualized view of CPUs as well. On the root machine, the administrator and the operating system deal with *logical processors*, which are the actual processors on which threads can run (for example, a dual quad-core machine has eight logical processors), and assign these processors to various child partitions. For example, one child partition could be scheduled on logical processors 1, 2, 3, and 4, while the second child partition is scheduled on processors 5, 6, 7, and 8. These operations are all made possible through the use of *virtual processors*, or VPs.

Because processors can be shared across multiple child partitions, the hypervisor includes its own scheduler that distributes the workload of the various partitions across each processor. Additionally, the hypervisor maintains the register state for each virtual processor and to an appropriate "processor switch" when the same logical processor is being used by another child partition. The parent partition has the ability to access all these contexts and modify them as required, an essential part of the virtualization stack that must respond to certain instructions and perform actions.

The hypervisor is also directly responsible for virtualizing processor APICs and providing a simpler, less-featured virtual APIC, including support for the timer that's found on most APICs (however, at a slower rate). Because not all operating systems support APICs, the hypervisor also allows for the injection of interrupts through a hypercall, which permits the virtualization stack to emulate a standard i8059 PIC.

Finally, because Windows supports dynamic processor addition, an administrator can add new processors to a child partition at run time to increase the responsiveness of the guest operating systems if it's under heavy load.

Memory Virtualization

The final piece of hardware that must be abstracted away from child partitions is memory, not only for the normal behavior of the guest operating systems, but also for security and stability. Improperly managing the child partitions' access to memory could result in privacy disclosures and data corruption, as well as possible malicious attacks by "escaping" the child partition and attacking the parent (which would then allow attacks on the other child partitions). Apart from this aspect, there is also the matter of the guest operating system's view of physical address space. Almost all operating systems expect memory to begin at address 0 and be somewhat contiguous, so simply assigning chunks of physical memory to each child partition wouldn't work even if enough memory was available on the system.

To solve this problem, the hypervisor implements an address space called the *guest physical address space* (GPA space). The GPA starts at address 0, which satisfies the needs of operating systems inside child partitions. However, the GPA is not a simple mapping to a chunk of physical memory because of the second problem (the lack of contiguous memory). As such, GPAs can point to any location in the machine's physical memory (which is called the *system physical address space*, or SPA space), and there must be a translation system to go from one address type to another. This translation system is maintained by the hypervisor and is nearly identical to the way virtual memory is mapped to physical memory on x86 and x64 processors. (See Chapter 10 in Part 2 for more information on the memory manager and address translation.)

As for actual virtual addresses in the child partition (which are called *guest virtual address space—* GVA space), these continue to be managed by the operating system without any change in behavior. What the operating system believes are real physical addresses in its own page tables are actually SPAs. Figure 3-38 shows an overview of the mapping between each level.

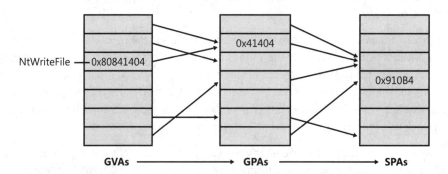

FIGURE 3-38 Guest virtual and physical address translation

This means that when a guest operating system boots up and creates the page tables to map virtual to physical memory, the hypervisor intercepts SPAs and keeps its own copy of the page tables. Conceptually, whenever a piece of code accesses a virtual address inside a guest operating system, the hypervisor does the initial page table translation to go from the guest virtual address to the GPA and then maps that GPA to the respective SPA. In reality, this operation is optimized through the use of *shadow page tables* (SPTs), which the hypervisor maintains to have direct GVA-to-SPA translations and simply loads when appropriate so that the guest accesses the SPA directly.

Second-Level Address Translation and Tagged TLB

Because the translation from GVA to GPA to SPA is expensive (because it must be done in software), CPU manufacturers have worked to curtail this inefficiency by making the processor natively aware of the address translation requirements of a virtual machine—in other words, an advanced processor could understand that the memory access is occurring from a hosted virtual machine and perform the GVA-to-SPA lookup on its own, without requiring assistance from the hypervisor. This lookup technology is called Second-Level Address Translation (SLAT) because it covers both the target-to-host translation (second level) and the host VA–to–host PA translation (first level). For marketing purposes, however, Intel has called this support VT Extended/Nested Page Table (NPT) technology, while AMD calls it AMD-V Rapid Virtualization Indexing (RVI).

The latest version of the Hyper-V stack takes full advantage of this processor support, reducing the complexity of its code and minimizing the number of context switches required to handle page faults in hosted partitions. Additionally, SLAT enables Hyper-V to throw out its shadow page tables and relevant mappings, which allows an additional reduction of memory overhead as well. These changes increase the scalability of Hyper-V on such systems, notably leading to an increase in the maximum number of virtual machines that a single host (Hyper-V server) can serve, or run concurrently. According to tests performed by Microsoft, support for SLAT increases the maximum number of supported sessions between 1.6 and 2.5 times. Furthermore, the processor overhead drops from about 10 percent to 2 percent, and each virtual machine consumes one less megabyte of physical RAM on the host.

In addition, both Intel and AMD introduced a functionality that was typically found only on RISC processors such as ARM, MIPS, or PPC, which is the ability of the processor to differentiate between the processes associated with each cached virtual-to-physical translation entry in the translation look-aside buffer (TLB). On CISC processors such as the x86 and x64, the TLB was built as a systemwide resource—each time the operating system switched the currently executing process, the TLB had to be flushed to invalidate any cached entries that might've belonged to the previous executing process. If the processor, instead, could be told that the process has changed, the TLB would avoid a flush and the processor would simply not use the cached entries that did not correspond to this process. New entries would be created, eventually overriding other processes' older entries. This type of smarter TLB is called a *tagged TLB*, because each cache entry is *tagged* with a per-process identifier.

Flushing the TLB is even worse when dealing with Hyper-V systems because a different process can actually correspond to a completely different VM. In other words, each time the hypervisor and operating system scheduled another VM for execution, the host's TLB had to be flushed, flushing away all the cached translations the previous VM had performed, slowing down memory access, and causing significant latency. When running on a processor that implements a tagged TLB, the Hyper-V can simply notify the processor that a new process/VM is running and that the entries of other VM should not be used. AMD processors with RVI support tagged TLBs through an Address Space Identifier, or ASID, while recent Intel Nehalem-EX processors implement a tagged TLB by using a Virtual Processor Identifier (VPID).

Dynamic Memory

A feature called Dynamic Memory enables systems administrators to make a virtual machine's physical memory allocation variable based on the memory demands of the active virtual machines, in much the same way that the Windows memory manager adjusts the physical memory assigned to each process based on their memory demands. The capability means that administrators do not have to precisely gauge the size of a virtual machine required for optimal performance and that the system's physical memory is more effectively used by the virtual machines that need it.

Dynamic Memory's architecture consists of several components, shown in Figure 3-39.

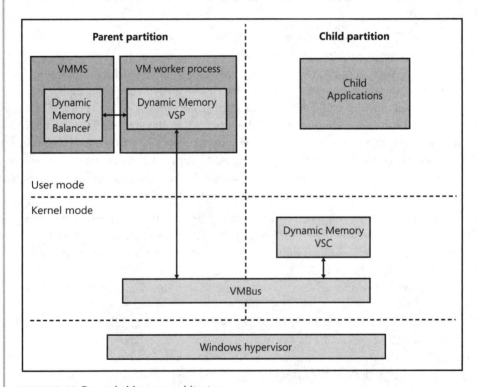

FIGURE 3-39 Dynamic Memory architecture

The principle components of the architecture are as follows:

- The Dynamic Memory balancer, which is implemented in the virtual machine management service. The balancer is responsible for assigning physical memory to child partitions.

- The Dynamic Memory VSP (DM VSP), which runs in the VMWPs of child partitions that have dynamic memory enabled.

- The Dynamic Memory VSC (DM VSC, %SystemRoot%\System32\Drivers\Dmvsc.sys), installed as an enlightenment driver running in the child partitions.

To configure a VM for dynamic memory, an administrator chooses Dynamic in the VM's memory settings as shown in Figure 3-40.

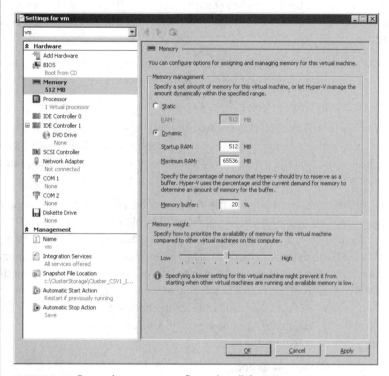

FIGURE 3-40 Dynamic memory configuration dialog

The associated settings include the amount of memory that will be assigned to the VM when it starts (Startup RAM), the maximum amount that it can be assigned (Maximum RAM), the percentage of the VM's memory that should be available for immediate use by the operating system if its memory demand increases, and finally, the weight of the VM with respect to other VMs. In addition to serving as weighting for the distribution of physical memory among virtual machines that have dynamic memory enabled, the hypervisor also uses it as a guide for the startup order of virtual machines configured to start when the system boots. Finally, the available memory percentage is a reference to memory within the VM that the VM's operating system has not assigned to a process, device drivers, or itself, and that can be assigned without incurring a page fault. Chapter 10 in Part 2 describes available memory in more detail.

When the DM VSC starts in a child partition that has dynamic memory enabled in its memory configuration, it first checks to see if the operating system supports dynamic memory capabilities. It performs this check by simply calling the memory manager's hot-add memory function, specifying a block of child physical memory already assigned to the virtual machine. If the memory manager supports hot add, it returns an error indicating that the address range is already in use, and if it doesn't, it reports that the function is not supported. If dynamic memory is supported, the DM VSC establishes a connection to the DM VSP via VMBus. Because the system's memory usage fluctuates during the boot process, after all autostart Windows services have finished initializing, the VSC begins reporting memory statistics once per second that indicate the current system commit level in the virtual machine. (See Chapter 10 in Part 2 for more information on system commit.)

The DM VSP in the parent partition calculates a memory pressure value for its corresponding VM using the following calculation based on the VM's memory report:

Memory Pressure = Committed Memory / Physical Memory

Physical Memory refers to the amount of memory currently assigned to the VM's partition. It also keeps a running exponential average pressure that represents the previous 20 seconds of pressure reports, adjusting the average pressure only when the current pressure deviates from the average by at least a standard deviation.

A component called the *balancer* executes in the VMMS service. Once per second, it analyzes the memory pressures reported by the DM VSPs, considers VM policy configuration, and determines if and how much memory should be redistributed. If a global Hyper-V setting called *NUMA spanning* is enabled, the balancer uses two balancing engines: one engine is the global balancer, and it is responsible for assigning new VMs to NUMA nodes. It does so based on the memory usage and VM pressures of the nodes at the time of the assignment. Each NUMA node has its own local balancer that manages the distribution of the node's memory across the VMs assigned to the node. If the NUMA spanning option is off, the global balancer has no role other than to invoke the only local balancer for the system.

The benefit of assigning VMs to NUMA nodes is that VMs will be guaranteed the fastest memory accesses possible. The tradeoff, however, is that it might not be possible to start or add memory to a VM in the case where the sum of unassigned memory is sufficient but no one node has enough available memory to accommodate the amount of memory requested.

A local balancer increases or decreases a global target memory pressure to use all available memory under its management or to use it until a minimum pressure level is reached that indicates all VMs have ample memory. The balancer then loops over the VMs, determining how much memory to add or remove from each VM to reach the target pressure. During the calculations, the balancer reserves a minimum amount of memory for the host. The host's reservation is a base amount of approximately 400 MB plus 30 MB for each 1 GB of RAM on the system. Factors that can affect the amount of memory reserved include whether or not the system is using SLAT or software paging, and whether multimedia redirection is enabled. Every five minutes, the balancer also removes memory from VMs that have so much memory that their pressure is essentially zero.

Note that if the child partition's operating system is running a 32-bit version of Windows, the dynamic memory engine will not assign the partition more than 4 GB of memory.

Once it has calculated the amounts of memory to add and remove from VMs, it asks each WP to perform the desired operation. If the operation is to remove memory, the WP signals the child DM VSC over VMBUS of the amount to remove and the DM VSC balloons its memory usage by allocating physical memory from the system using the *MmAllocatePagesForMdlEx* function. It retrieves the allocated GPAs and sends that back to the WP, which passes them to the Hyper-V memory manager. The Hyper-V memory manager then converts the GPAs to SPAs and adds the memory to its free memory pool.

If it's a memory add operation, the WP asks the Hyper-V memory manager first if the VM has any physical memory assigned to it but currently allocated by the VSC's balloon. If it does, the WP retrieves the GPAs for an amount that should be *unballooned* and asks the VSC to free those pages, making them available again for use by the VM's operating system. If the amount that can be released by unballooning falls short of the amount of physical memory the balancer wants to give the VM, it asks the Hyper-V memory manager to give the remaining amount from its free memory pool to the child partition via Windows support for hot-add memory and reports the GPAs it added to the WP, which in turn relays them to the child's DM VSC.

EXPERIMENT: Watching Dynamic Memory

You can watch the behavior of Dynamic Memory by configuring Dynamic Memory for a VM running a 64-bit Dynamic Memory-compatible operating system, such as Windows 7 or Windows Server 2008 R2. Hyper-V exposes several Dynamic Memory–related performance counters under Hyper-V Dynamic Memory Balancer and Dynamic Memory VM. Counters include the amount of memory assigned to a guest, the guest operating system–visible memory (the amount of memory it thinks it has), its current and average memory pressure, and the amount of memory added and removed over time:

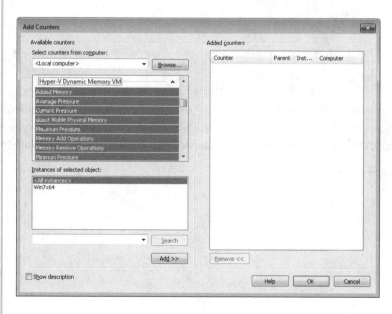

After freshly booting the virtual machine, add the Guest Visible Physical Memory and Physical Memory counters. Set the scale to three times the current Guest Visible Physical Memory value, which will be at least as large as the Physical Memory value. Then run the Sysinternals Testlimit tool in the virtual machine with the following commandline:
testlimit -m 1000 -c 1

Assuming you have enough available physical memory on the system, this causes Testlimit to allocate about 1 GB of virtual memory, raising the memory pressure in the virtual machine. After a few seconds, you will see the guest visible and actual physical memory assigned to the virtual machine jump to the same value. Roughly 30 seconds later, you'll see another jump when the balancer decides that the additional memory is not enough to completely relieve the memory pressure in the virtual machine and, because there's more memory available on the host, gives the virtual machine some more.

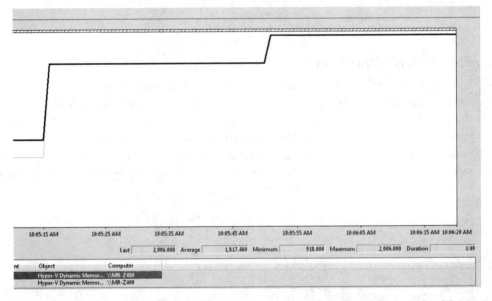

If you terminate Testlimit, the memory levels remain constant for several minutes if there's no memory demands from the host or other virtual machines, but eventually the balancer will respond to the lack of memory pressure in the virtual machine by trimming memory. Note that the Guest Visible Physical Memory counter remains unchanged, but the Physical Memory counter drops back to a level near what it was before Testlimit executed:

Intercepts

We've talked about the various ways in which access to hardware, processors, and memory is virtualized by the hypervisor and sometimes handed off to a VM worker process, but we haven't yet talked about the mechanism that allows this to happen—*intercepts*. Intercepts are configurable *hooks* that a parent partition can install and configure in order to respond to. These can include the following items:

- I/O intercepts, useful for device emulation

- MSR intercepts, useful for APIC emulation and profiling

- Access to GPAs, useful for device emulation, monitoring, and profiling (Additionally, the intercept can be fine-tuned to a specific access, such as read, write, or execute.)

- Exception intercepts such as page faults, useful for maintaining machine state and memory emulation (for example, maintaining copy-on-write)

Once the hypervisor detects an event for which an intercept has been registered, it sends an intercept message through the virtualization stack and puts the VP in a suspended state. The virtualization stack (usually the worker process) must then handle the event and resume the VP (typically with a modified register state that reflects the work performed to handle the intercept).

Live Migration

To support scenarios such as planned hardware upgrades and resource load balancing across servers, Hyper-V includes support for migrating virtual machines between nodes of a Windows Failover Cluster with minimal downtime. The key to Live Migration's efficiency is that the bulk of the transfer of the virtual machine's memory from the source to the target occurs while the virtual machine continues to run on the source node; only when the memory transfer is complete does the virtual machine suspend and resume operating on the target node. This small window when final virtual machine state migrates is typically less than the default TCP timeout value, preserving open connections from clients using services of the virtual machine and making the migration transparent from their perspective. Figure 3-41 shows the Live Migration process.

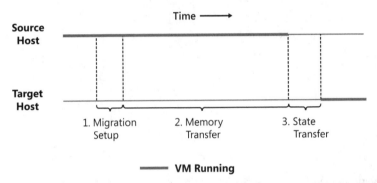

FIGURE 3-41 Live migration transfer steps

The Live Migration process proceeds in a number of steps, shown in Figure 3-41:

1. **Migration Setup**   The VMMS of the hosting (source) node of the virtual machine opens a TCP connection with the destination host. It transfers the virtual machine's configuration information, which includes virtual hardware specifications such as the number of processors and amount of RAM, to the destination. VMMS on the destination (target) node instantiates a paused virtual machine matching the configuration. The VMMS on the source notifies the virtual machine's worker process that the live migration is ready to proceed and hands it the TCP connection. Likewise, the target VMMS hands its end of the connection to the target worker process.

2. **Memory Transfer**   The memory transfer phase consists of several subphases:

    a. The source VMWP creates a bitmap with one bit representing each page of the virtual machine's guest physical memory. It sets every bit to indicate that the page is *dirty*, which means that the page's current contents have not yet been sent to the target.

b. The source VMWP registers a memory-change notification callback with the hypervisor that sets the corresponding bit in the bitmap for each page of the virtual machine that changes.

c. The source VMWP proceeds to walk through the dirty-page bitmap in 16-KB blocks, clearing the dirty bits in the dirty-page bitmap for the pages in the block, reading each dirty page's contents via a hypervisor call, and sending the contents to the target. The target VMWP invokes the hypervisor to inject the memory contents into the target virtual machine's guest physical memory.

d. When it's finished iterating over the dirty-page bitmap, the source VMWP checks to see if any pages have been dirtied during the iteration. If not, it moves to the next phase of the migration, but if any pages have been dirtied, it repeats the iteration. If it's iterated five times, the virtual machine is dirtying memory faster than the worker process can send modifications, so it proceeds to the next phase of the migration.

5. **State Transfer** The source VMWP suspends the virtual machine and makes a final iteration through the dirty-page bitmap to send over any pages that were dirtied since the last pass. Because the virtual machine is suspended during the transfer, no more pages will be dirtied. Then the source worker process sends the virtual machine's state, including the contents of the virtual processor registers. Finally, it notifies VMMS that the migration is complete, waits for acknowledgement, and then sends a message to the target transferring ownership of the virtual machine. As the last migration step, the target worker process moves the virtual machine to the running state.

6. Another aspect of Live Migration is the transfer of ownership of the virtual machine's files, including its VHDs. Traditional Windows Clustering is a shared-nothing model, where each LUN of the cluster's storage system is owned by one node at a time. The LUN's owning node has sole access to the LUN and any files stored on it. This model can lead to management complexity because each virtual machine must be stored on a separate LUN and therefore a separate volume, causing an explosion of volumes in a cluster hosting many virtual machines. It poses an even more significant challenge for Live Migration because LUN ownership transfer is an expensive operation, consisting of the source node flushing any modified file data to the LUN, the source node unmounting the volumes formatted on the LUN, ownership transfer from the source node to target node, and the target node mounting the volumes. Depending on the number of volumes on the LUN and the amount of dirty data that needs to be written back, the entire sequence can take tens of seconds, which would prevent Live Migration from meeting its goal of perceived nearly-instantaneous migrations.

7. To address the limitations of the traditional clustering model and make Live Migration possible, Live Migration leverages a storage feature called Clustered Shared Volumes (CSV). With CSV, one node owns the namespace of the volumes on a LUN while others can have exclusive ownership of individual files. Exclusive ownership permits the node hosting the virtual machine to directly access the on-disk storage of the VHD file, bypassing the network file system accesses normally required to interact with a LUN owned by another node. Only when a node wants to create or delete files, change the size of files (for example, to extend the size of a

dynamic or differencing VHD), or change other file metadata such as timestamps does it need to send a request via the SMB2 protocol to the owning node if it's not the owner.

8. The hybrid sharing model of CSV enables LUN ownership to remain unchanged during Live Migration and enables only ownership of individual migrating virtual machine's file to change, avoiding the unmounts and mount operations. Also, only dirty data specific to the virtual machine files must be written before the migration, something that can typically happen concurrently with the memory migration. Figure 3-42 depicts the storage ownership changes during a Live Migration. CSV's implementation is described in the "File System Filter Drivers" section of Chapter 12, "File Systems," in Part 2.

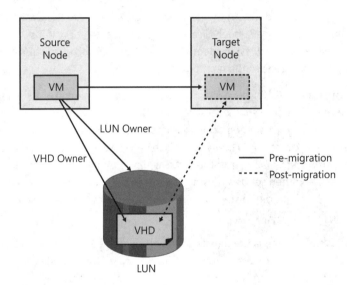

FIGURE 3-42 Clustered Shared Volumes in Live Migration

Kernel Transaction Manager

One of the more tedious aspects of software development is handling error conditions. This is especially true if, in the course of performing a high-level operation, an application has completed one or more subtasks that result in changes to the file system or registry. For example, an application's software updating service might make several registry updates, replace one of the application's executables, and then be denied access when it attempts to update a second executable. If the service doesn't want to leave the application in the resulting inconsistent state, it must track all the changes it makes and be prepared to undo them. Testing the error-recovery code is difficult, and consequently often skipped, so errors in the recovery code can negate the effort.

Applications can, with very little effort, gain automatic error-recovery capabilities by using a kernel mechanism called the *Kernel Transaction Manager* (KTM), which provides the facilities required to perform such transactions and enables services such as the *distributed transaction coordinator* (DTC) in user mode to take advantage of them. Any developer who uses the appropriate APIs can take advantage of these services as well.

KTM does more than solve large-scale issues like the one presented. Even on single-user home computers, installing a service patch or performing a system restore are large operations that involve both files and registry keys. Unplug an older Windows computer during such an operation, and the chances for a successful boot are slim. Even though the NT File System (NTFS) has always had a log file permitting the file system to guarantee atomic operations (see Chapter 12 in Part 2 for more information on NTFS), this only means that whichever file was being written to during the process will get fully written or fully deleted—it does not guarantee the entire update or restore operation. Likewise, the registry has had numerous improvements over the years to deal with corruption (see Chapter 4 for more information on the registry), but the fixes apply only at the key/value level.

As the heart of transaction support, KTM allows transactional resource managers such as NTFS and the registry to coordinate their updates for a specific set of changes made by an application. NTFS uses an extension to support transactions, called TxF. The registry uses a similar extension, called TxR. These kernel-mode resource managers work with KTM to coordinate the transaction state, just as user-mode resource managers use DTC to coordinate transaction state across multiple user-mode resource managers. Third parties can also use KTM to implement their own resource managers.

TxF and TxR both define a new set of file system and registry APIs that are similar to existing ones, except that they include a transaction parameter. If an application wants to create a file within a transaction, it first uses KTM to create the transaction, and then it passes the resulting transaction handle to the new file creation API. Although we'll look at the registry and NTFS implementations of KTM later, these are not its only possible uses. In fact, it provides four system objects that allow a variety of operations to be supported. These are listed in Table 3-27.

TABLE 3-27 KTM Objects

Object	Meaning	Usage
Transaction	Collection of data operations to be performed. Provides *atomic*, *consistent*, *isolated*, and *durable* operations.	Can be associated with the registry and file I/O to make those operations part of the same larger operation.
Enlistment	Association between a resource manager and a transaction.	Register with a transaction to receive notifications on it. The enlistment can specify which notifications should be generated.
Resource Manager (RM)	Container for the transactions and the data on which they operate.	Provides an interface for clients to read and write the data, typically on a database.
Transaction Manager (TM)	Container of all transactions that are part of the associated resource managers. As an instance of a log, it knows about all transaction states but not their data.	Provides an infrastructure through which clients and resource managers can communicate, and provides and coordinates recovery operations after a crash. Clients use the TM for transactions; RMs use the TM for enlistments.

Hotpatch Support

Rebooting a machine to apply the latest patches can mean significant downtime for a server, which is why Windows supports a run-time method of patching, called a *hot patch* (or simply *hotpatch*), in contrast to a *cold patch,* which requires a reboot. Hotpatching doesn't simply allow files to be over-written during execution; instead, it includes a complex series of operations that can be requested (and combined). These operations are listed in Table 3-28.

TABLE 3-28 Hotpatch Operations

Operation	Meaning	Usage
Rename Image	Replacing a DLL that is on the disk and currently used by other applications, or replacing a driver that is on the disk and is currently loaded by the kernel	When an entire library in user mode needs to be replaced, the kernel can detect which processes and services are referencing it, unload them, and then update the DLL and restart the programs and services (which is done through the *restart manager*). When a driver needs to be replaced, the kernel can unload the driver (the driver requires an unload routine), update it, and then reload it.

Operation	Meaning	Usage
Object Swap	Atomically renaming an object in the object directory namespace	When a file (typically a *known DLL*) needs to be renamed atomically but not affect any process that might be using it (so that the process can start using the new file immediately, using the old handle, without requiring an application restart).
Patch Function Code	Replacing the code of one or more functions inside an image file with another version	If a DLL or driver can't be replaced or renamed during run time, functions in the image can be directly patched. A hotpatch DLL that contains the newer code is jumped to whenever an older function is called.
Refresh System DLL	Reload the memory mapped section object for Ntdll.dll	The system native library, Ntdll.dll, is loaded only once during boot-up and then simply duplicated into the address space of every new process. If it has been hotpatched, the system must refresh this section to load the newer version.

Although hotpatches use internal kernel mechanisms, their actual implementation is no different from cold patches. The patch is delivered through Windows Update, typically as an executable file containing a program called Update.exe that performs the extraction of the patch and the update process. For hotpatches, however, an additional hotpatch file, containing the *.hp* extension, will be present. This file contains a special PE header called *.HOT1*. This header contains a data structure describing the various *patch descriptors* present inside the file. Each of these descriptors identifies the offset in the original file that needs to be patched, a validation mechanism (which can include a simple comparison of the old data, a checksum, or a hash), and the new data to be patched. The kernel parses the descriptors and applies the appropriate modifications. In the case of a *protected process* (see Chapter 5 for more information on processes) and other digitally signed images, the hotpatch must also be digitally signed in order to prevent fake patches from being applied to sensitive files or processes.

Note Because the hotpatch file also includes the original data, the hotpatching mechanism can also be used to uninstall a patch at run time.

Compile-time hotpatching support works by adding 7 additional bytes to the beginning of each function—4 are considered part of the end of the previous function, and 2 are part of the *function prolog*—that is, the function's beginning. Here's an example of a function that was built with hotpatching information:

```
lkd> u nt!NtCreateFile - 5
nt!FsRtlTeardownPerFileContexts+0x169:
82227ea5 90              nop
82227ea6 90              nop
82227ea7 90              nop
82227ea8 90              nop
82227ea9 90              nop
nt!NtCreateFile:
82227eaa 8bff            mov     edi,edi
```

Notice that the five *nop* instructions don't actually do anything, while the *mov edi, edi* at the beginning of the *NtCreateFile* function are also essentially meaningless—no actual state-changing operation takes place. Because 7 bytes are available, the *NtCreateFile* prologue can be transformed into a *short jump* to the buffer of five instructions available, which are then converted to a *near jump* instruction to the patched routine. Here's *NtCreateFile* after having been hotpatched:

```
lkd> u nt!NtCreateFile - 5
nt!FsRtlTeardownPerFileContexts+0x169:
82227ea5 e93d020010      jmp     nt_patch!NtCreateFile (922280e7)
nt!NtCreateFile:
82227eaa ebfc            jmp     nt!FsRtlTeardownPerFileContexts+0x169 (82227ea5)
```

This method allows only the addition of 2 bytes to each function by jumping into the previous function's alignment padding that it would most likely have at its end anyway.

There are some limitations to the hotpatching functionality:

- Patches that third-party applications such as security software might block or that might be incompatible with the operation of third-party applications

- Patches that modify a file's export table or import table

- Patches that change data structures, fix infinite loops, or contain inline assembly code

Kernel Patch Protection

Some 32-bit device drivers modify the behavior of Windows in unsupported ways. For example, they patch the system call table to intercept system calls or patch the kernel image in memory to add functionality to specific internal functions. Shortly after the release of 64-bit Windows for x64 and before a rich third-party ecosystem had developed, Microsoft saw an opportunity to preserve the stability of 64-bit Windows. To prevent these kinds of changes, x64 Windows implements Kernel Patch Protection (KPP), also referred to as PatchGuard. KPP's job on the system is similar to what its name implies—it attempts to deter common techniques for patching the system, or hooking it. Table 3-29 lists which components or structures are protected and for what purpose.

TABLE 3-29 Components Protected by KPP

Component	Legitimate Usage	Potential Malicious Usage
Ntoskrnl.exe, Hal.dll, Ci.dll, Kdcom.dll, Pshed.dll, Clfs.sys, Ndis.sys, Tcpip.sys	Kernel, HAL, and their dependencies. Lower layer of network stack.	Patching code in the kernel and/or HAL to subvert normal operation and behavior. Patching Ndis.sys to silently add back doors on open ports.
Global Descriptor Table (GDT)	CPU hardware protection for the implementation of ring privilege levels (Ring 0 vs. Ring 3).	Ability to set up a *callgate*, a CPU mechanism through which user (Ring 3) code could perform operations with kernel privileges (Ring 0).

Component	Legitimate Usage	Potential Malicious Usage
Interrupt Descriptor Table (IDT)	Table read by the CPU to deliver interrupt vectors to the correct handling routine.	Malicious drivers could intercept file I/Os directly at the interrupt level, or hook page faults to hide contents of memory. Rootkits could hook the INT2E handler to hook all system calls from a single point.
System Service Descriptor Table (SSDT)	Table containing the array of pointers for each system call handler.	Rootkits could modify the output or input of calls from user mode and hide processes, files, or registry keys.
Processor Machine State Registers (MSRs)	LSTAR MSR is used to set the handler of the SYSENTER and/ or SYSCALL instructions used for system calls.	LSTAR could be overwritten by a malicious driver to provide a single hook for all system calls performed on the system.
KdpStub, KiDebugRoutine, KdpTrap function pointers	Used for run-time configuration of where exceptions should be delivered, based on whether a kernel debugger is remotely connected to the machine.	Value of the pointers could be overwritten by a malicious rootkit to take control of the system at predetermined times and perform invisible background tasks.
PsInvertedFunctionTable	Cache of exception directories used on x64, allowing quick mapping between code where an exception happened and its handler.	Could be used to take control of the system during the exception handling of unrelated system code, including KPP's own exception code responsible for detecting modifications in the first place.
Kernel stacks	Store function arguments, the call stack (where a function should return), and variables.	A driver could allocate memory on the side, set it as a kernel stack for a thread, and then manipulate its contents to redirect calls and parameters.
Object types	Definitions for the various objects (such as processes and files) that the system supports through the object manager.	Could be used as part of a technique called DKOM (Direct Kernel Object Modification) to modify system behavior—for example, by hooking the object callbacks that each object type has registered.
Other	Code related to bug-checking the system during a KPP violation, executing the DPCs and timers associated with KPP, and more.	By modifying certain parts of the system used by KPP, malicious drivers could attempt to silence, ignore, or otherwise cripple KPP.

Note Because certain 64-bit Intel processors implement a slightly different feature set of the x64 architecture, the kernel needs to perform run-time code patching to work around the lack of a *prefetch* instruction. KPP can deter kernel patching even on these processors, by exempting those specific patches from detection. Additionally, because of hypervisor (Hyper-V) enlightenments (more information on the hypervisor is provided earlier in this chapter), certain functions in the kernel are patched at boot time, such as the *swap context* routine. These patches are also allowed by very explicit checks to make sure they are known patches to the hypervisor-enlightened versions.

When KPP detects a change in any of the structures mentioned (as well as some other internal consistency checks), it crashes the system with code 0x109—CRITICAL_STRUCTURE_CORRUPTION.

For third-party developers who used techniques that KPP deters, the following supported techniques can be used:

- File system minifilters (see Chapter 8 in Part 2 for more information on these) to hook all file operations, including loading image files and DLLs, that can be intercepted to purge malicious code on-the-fly or block reading of known bad executables.

- Registry filter notifications (see Chapter 4 for more information on these notifications) to hook all registry operations. Security software can block modification of critical parts of the registry, as well as heuristically determine malicious software by registry access patterns or known bad registry keys.

- Process notifications (see Chapter 5 for more information on these notifications). Security software can monitor the execution and termination of all processes and threads on the system, as well as DLLs being loaded or unloaded. With the enhanced notifications added for antivirus and other security vendors, they also have the ability to block process launch.

- Object manager filtering (explained in the object manager section earlier). Security software can remove certain access rights being granted to processes and/or threads to defend their own utilities against certain operations.

There is no way to disable KPP once it's enabled. Because device driver developers might need to make changes to a running system as part of debugging, KPP does not enable if the system boots in debugging mode with an active kernel-debugging connection.

Code Integrity

Code integrity is a Windows mechanism that authenticates the integrity and source of executable images (such as applications, DLLs, or drivers) by validating a digital certificate contained within the image's resources. This mechanism works in conjunction with system policies, defining how signing should be enforced. One of these policies is the *Kernel Mode Code Signing* (KMCS) policy, which requires that kernel-mode code be signed with a valid Authenticode certificate rooted by one of several recognized code signing authorities, such as Verisign or Thawte.

To address backward-compatibility concerns, the KMCS policy is only fully enforced on 64-bit machines, because those drivers have to be recompiled recently in order to run on that Windows architecture. This, in turn, implies that a company or individual is still responsible for maintaining the driver and is able to sign it. On 32-bit machines, however, many older devices ship with outdated drivers, possibly from out-of-business companies, so signing those drivers would sometimes be unfeasible. Figure 3-43 shows the warning displayed on 64-bit Windows machines that attempt to load an unsigned driver.

 Note Windows also has a second driver-signing policy, which is part of the Plug and Play manager. This policy is applied solely to Plug and Play drivers, and unlike the kernel-mode code-signing policy, it can be configured to allow unsigned Plug and Play drivers (but not on 64-bit systems, where the KMCS policy takes precedence). See Chapter 8 in Part 2 for more information on the Plug and Play manager.

FIGURE 3-43 Warning when attempting to install an unsigned 64-bit driver

Even on 32-bit Windows, code integrity writes an event to the Code Integrity event log when it loads an unsigned driver.

 Note Protected Media Path applications can also query the kernel for its *integrity state*, which includes information on whether or not unsigned 32-bit drivers are loaded on the system. In such scenarios, they are allowed to disable protected, high-definition media playback as a method to ensure the security and reliability of the encrypted stream.

The code-integrity mechanism doesn't stop at driver load time, however. Stronger measures also exist to authenticate per-page image contents for executable pages. This requires using a special flag while signing the driver binary and will generate a catalog with the cryptographic hash of every executable page on which the driver will reside. (Pages are a unit of protection on the CPU; for more information, see Chapter 10 in Part 2.) This method allows for detection of modification of an existing driver, which might happen either at run time by another driver or through a page file or hibernation file attack (in which the contents of memory are edited on the disk and then reloaded into memory). Generating such per-page hashes is also a requirement for the new filtering model, as well as Protected Media Path components.

Conclusion

In this chapter, we examined the key base system mechanisms on which the Windows executive is built. In the next chapter, we'll look at three important mechanisms involved with the management infrastructure of Windows: the registry, services, and Windows Management Instrumentation (WMI).

CHAPTER 4

Management Mechanisms

This chapter describes four fundamental mechanisms in the Microsoft Windows operating system that are critical to its management and configuration:

- The registry
- Services
- Unified Background Process Manager
- Windows Management Instrumentation
- Windows Diagnostics Infrastructure

The Registry

The registry plays a key role in the configuration and control of Windows systems. It is the repository for both systemwide and per-user settings. Although most people think of the registry as static data stored on the hard disk, as you'll see in this section, the registry is also a window into various in-memory structures maintained by the Windows executive and kernel.

We'll start by providing you with an overview of the registry structure, a discussion of the data types it supports, and a brief tour of the key information Windows maintains in the registry. Then we'll look inside the internals of the configuration manager, the executive component responsible for implementing the registry database. Among the topics we'll cover are the internal on-disk structure of the registry, how Windows retrieves configuration information when an application requests it, and what measures are employed to protect this critical system database.

Viewing and Changing the Registry

In general, you should never have to edit the registry directly: application and system settings stored in the registry that might require manual changes should have a corresponding user interface to control their modification. However, as you've already seen a number of times in this book, some advanced and debug settings have no editing user interface. Therefore, both graphical user interface (GUI) and command-line tools are included with Windows to enable you to view and modify the registry.

Windows comes with one main GUI tool for editing the registry—Regedit.exe—and a number of command-line registry tools. Reg.exe, for instance, has the ability to import, export, back up, and restore keys, as well as to compare, modify, and delete keys and values. It can also set or query flags used in UAC virtualization. Regini.exe, on the other hand, allows you to import registry data based on text files that contain ASCII or Unicode configuration data.

The Windows Driver Kit (WDK) also supplies a redistributable component, Offreg.dll, which hosts the Offline Registry Library. This library allows loading registry hive files in their binary format and applying operations on the files themselves, bypassing the usual logical loading and mapping that Windows requires for registry operations. Its use is primarily to assist in offline registry access, such as for purposes of integrity checking and validation. It can also provide performance benefits if the underlying data is not meant to be visible by the system, because the access is done through local file I/O instead of registry system calls.

Registry Usage

There are four principal times at which configuration data is read:

- During the initial boot process, the boot loader reads configuration data and the list of boot device drivers to load into memory before initializing the kernel. Because the Boot Configuration Database (BCD) is really stored in a registry hive, one could argue that registry access happens even earlier, when the Boot Manager displays the list of operating systems.

- During the kernel boot process, the kernel reads settings that specify which device drivers to load and how various system elements—such as the memory manager and process manager—configure themselves and tune system behavior.

- During logon, Explorer and other Windows components read per-user preferences from the registry, including network drive-letter mappings, desktop wallpaper, screen saver, menu behavior, icon placement, and perhaps most importantly, which startup programs to launch and which files were most recently accessed.

- During their startup, applications read systemwide settings, such as a list of optionally installed components and licensing data, as well as per-user settings that might include menu and toolbar placement and a list of most-recently accessed documents.

However, the registry can be read at other times as well, such as in response to a modification of a registry value or key. Although the registry provides asynchronous callbacks that are the preferred way to receive change notifications, some applications constantly monitor their configuration settings in the registry through polling and automatically take updated settings into account. In general, however, on an idle system there should be no registry activity and such applications violate best practices. (Process Monitor, from Sysinternals, is a great tool for tracking down such activity and the application or applications at fault.)

The registry is commonly modified in the following cases:

- Although not a modification, the registry's initial structure and many default settings are defined by a prototype version of the registry that ships on the Windows setup media that is copied onto a new installation.

- Application setup utilities create default application settings and settings that reflect installation configuration choices.

- During the installation of a device driver, the Plug and Play system creates settings in the registry that tell the I/O manager how to start the driver and creates other settings that configure the driver's operation. (See Chapter 8, "I/O System," in Part 2 for more information on how device drivers are installed.)

- When you change application or system settings through user interfaces, the changes are often stored in the registry.

Registry Data Types

The registry is a database whose structure is similar to that of a disk volume. The registry contains keys, which are similar to a disk's directories, and values, which are comparable to files on a disk. A key is a container that can consist of other keys (subkeys) or values. Values, on the other hand, store data. Top-level keys are root keys. Throughout this section, we'll use the words subkey and key interchangeably.

Both keys and values borrow their naming convention from the file system. Thus, you can uniquely identify a value with the name mark, which is stored in a key called trade, with the name trade\mark. One exception to this naming scheme is each key's unnamed value. Regedit displays the unnamed value as (Default).

Values store different kinds of data and can be one of the 12 types listed in Table 4-1. The majority of registry values are REG_DWORD, REG_BINARY, or REG_SZ. Values of type REG_DWORD can store numbers or Booleans (on/off values); REG_BINARY values can store numbers larger than 32 bits or raw data such as encrypted passwords; REG_SZ values store strings (Unicode, of course) that can represent elements such as names, file names, paths, and types.

TABLE 4-1 Registry Value Types

Value Type	Description
REG_NONE	No value type
REG_SZ	Fixed-length Unicode string
REG_EXPAND_SZ	Variable-length Unicode string that can have embedded environment variables
REG_BINARY	Arbitrary-length binary data

Value Type	Description
REG_DWORD	32-bit number
REG_DWORD_BIG_ENDIAN	32-bit number, with high byte first
REG_LINK	Unicode symbolic link
REG_MULTI_SZ	Array of Unicode NULL-terminated strings
REG_RESOURCE_LIST	Hardware resource description
REG_FULL_RESOURCE_DESCRIPTOR	Hardware resource description
REG_RESOURCE_REQUIREMENTS_LIST	Resource requirements
REG_QWORD	64-bit number

The REG_LINK type is particularly interesting because it lets a key transparently point to another key. When you traverse the registry through a link, the path searching continues at the target of the link. For example, if \Root1\Link has a REG_LINK value of \Root2\RegKey and RegKey contains the value RegValue, two paths identify RegValue: \Root1\Link\RegValue and \Root2\RegKey\RegValue. As explained in the next section, Windows prominently uses registry links: three of the six registry root keys are links to subkeys within the three nonlink root keys.

Registry Logical Structure

You can chart the organization of the registry via the data stored within it. There are six root keys (and you can't add new root keys or delete existing ones) that store information, as shown in Table 4-2.

TABLE 4-2 The Six Root Keys

Root Key	Description
HKEY_CURRENT_USER	Stores data associated with the currently logged-on user
HKEY_USERS	Stores information about all the accounts on the machine
HKEY_CLASSES_ROOT	Stores file association and Component Object Model (COM) object registration information
HKEY_LOCAL_MACHINE	Stores system-related information
HKEY_PERFORMANCE_DATA	Stores performance information
HKEY_CURRENT_CONFIG	Stores some information about the current hardware profile

Why do root-key names begin with an H? Because the root-key names represent Windows handles (H) to keys (KEY). As mentioned in Chapter 1, "Concepts and Tools," HKLM is an abbreviation used for HKEY_LOCAL_MACHINE. Table 4-3 lists all the root keys and their abbreviations. The following sections explain in detail the contents and purpose of each of these six root keys.

TABLE 4-3 Registry Root Keys

Root Key	Abbreviation	Description	Link
HKEY_CURRENT_USER	HKCU	Points to the user profile of the currently logged-on user	Subkey under HKEY_USERS corresponding to currently logged-on user
HKEY_USERS	HKU	Contains subkeys for all loaded user profiles	Not a link
HKEY_CLASSES_ROOT	HKCR	Contains file association and COM registration information	Not a direct link; rather, a merged view of HKLM\SOFTWARE\Classes and HKEY_USERS\<SID>\SOFTWARE\Classes
HKEY_LOCAL_MACHINE	HKLM	Global settings for the machine.	Not a link
HKEY_CURRENT_CONFIG	HKCC	Current hardware profile	HKLM\SYSTEM\CurrentControlSet\Hardware Profiles\Current
HKEY_PERFORMANCE_DATA	HKPD	Performance counters	Not a link

HKEY_CURRENT_USER

The HKCU root key contains data regarding the preferences and software configuration of the locally logged-on user. It points to the currently logged-on user's user profile, located on the hard disk at \Users\<username>\Ntuser.dat. (See the section "Registry Internals" later in this chapter to find out how root keys are mapped to files on the hard disk.) Whenever a user profile is loaded (such as at logon time or when a service process runs under the context of a specific user name), HKCU is created to map to the user's key under HKEY_USERS. Table 4-4 lists some of the subkeys under HKCU.

TABLE 4-4 HKEY_CURRENT_USER Subkeys

Subkey	Description
AppEvents	Sound/event associations
Console	Command window settings (for example, width, height, and colors)
Control Panel	Screen saver, desktop scheme, keyboard, and mouse settings, as well as accessibility and regional settings
Environment	Environment variable definitions
EUDC	Information on end-user defined characters
Identities	Windows Mail account information
Keyboard Layout	Keyboard layout setting (for example, U.S. or U.K.)
Network	Network drive mappings and settings
Printers	Printer connection settings
Software	User-specific software preferences
Volatile Environment	Volatile environment variable definitions

HKEY_USERS

HKU contains a subkey for each loaded user profile and user class registration database on the system. It also contains a subkey named HKU\.DEFAULT that is linked to the profile for the system (which is used by processes running under the local system account and is described in more detail in the section "Services" later in this chapter). This is the profile used by Winlogon, for example, so that changes to the desktop background settings in that profile will be implemented on the logon screen. When a user logs on to a system for the first time and her account does not depend on a roaming domain profile (that is, the user's profile is obtained from a central network location at the direction of a domain controller), the system creates a profile for her account that's based on the profile stored in %SystemDrive%\Users\Default.

The location under which the system stores profiles is defined by the registry value HKLM\Software\Microsoft\Windows NT\CurrentVersion\ProfileList\ProfilesDirectory, which is by default set to %SystemDrive%\Users. The ProfileList key also stores the list of profiles present on a system. Information for each profile resides under a subkey that has a name reflecting the security identifier (SID) of the account to which the profile corresponds. (See Chapter 6, "Security," for more information on SIDs.) Windows shows the list of profiles stored on a system in the User Profiles management dialog box, shown in Figure 4-1, which you access by clicking Settings in the User Profiles section of the Advanced tab in the Advanced System Settings of the System Control Panel applet.

FIGURE 4-1 The User Profiles management dialog box

EXPERIMENT: Watching Profile Loading and Unloading

You can see a profile load into the registry and then unload by using the Runas command to launch a process in an account that's not currently logged on to the machine. While the new process is running, run Regedit and note the loaded profile key under HKEY_USERS. After terminating the process, perform a refresh in Regedit by pressing the F5 key and the profile should no longer be present.

HKEY_CLASSES_ROOT

HKCR consists of three types of information: file extension associations, COM class registrations, and the virtualized registry root for User Account Control (UAC). (See Chapter 6 for more information on UAC.) A key exists for every registered file name extension. Most keys contain a REG_SZ value that points to another key in HKCR containing the association information for the class of files that extension represents.

For example, HKCR\.xls would point to information on Microsoft Office Excel files in a key such as HKCU\.xls\Excel.Sheet.8. Other keys contain configuration details for COM objects registered on the system. The UAC virtualized registry is located in the VirtualStore key, which is not related to the other kinds of data stored in HKCR.

The data under HKEY_CLASSES_ROOT comes from two sources:

- The per-user class registration data in HKCU\SOFTWARE\Classes (mapped to the file on hard disk \Users\<username>\AppData\Local\Microsoft\Windows\Usrclass.dat)

- Systemwide class registration data in HKLM\SOFTWARE\Classes

The reason that there is a separation of per-user registration data from systemwide registration data is so that roaming profiles can contain these customizations. It also closes a security hole: a non-privileged user cannot change or delete keys in the systemwide version HKEY_CLASSES_ROOT, and thus cannot affect the operation of applications on the system. Nonprivileged users and applications can read systemwide data and can add new keys and values to systemwide data (which are mirrored in their per-user data), but they can modify existing keys and values in their private data only.

HKEY_LOCAL_MACHINE

HKLM is the root key that contains all the systemwide configuration subkeys: BCD00000000, COMPONENTS (loaded dynamically as needed), HARDWARE, SAM, SECURITY, SOFTWARE, and SYSTEM.

The HKLM\BCD00000000 subkey contains the Boot Configuration Database (BCD) information loaded as a registry hive. This database replaces the Boot.ini file that was used before Windows Vista and adds greater flexibility and isolation of per-installation boot configuration data. (For more information on the BCD, see Chapter 13, "Startup and Shutdown," in Part 2.)

Each entry in the BCD, such as a Windows installation or the command-line settings for the installation, is stored in the Objects subkey, either as an object referenced by a GUID (in the case of a boot entry) or as a numeric subkey called an element. Most of these raw elements are documented in the BCD reference in the MSDN Library and define various command-line settings or boot parameters. The value associated with each element subkey corresponds to the value for its respective command-line flag or boot parameter.

The BCDEdit command-line utility allows you to modify the BCD using symbolic names for the elements and objects. It also provides extensive help for all the boot options available; unfortunately, it works only locally. Because the registry can be opened remotely as well as imported from a hive file, you can modify or read the BCD of a remote computer by using the Registry Editor. The following experiment shows you how to enable kernel debugging by using the Registry Editor.

EXPERIMENT: Offline or Remote BCD Editing

In this experiment, you enable debugging through editing the BCD inside the registry. For the purposes of this example, you edit the local copy of the BCD, but the point of this technique is that it can be used on any machine's BCD hive. Follow these steps to add the /DEBUG command-line flag:

1. Open the Registry Editor, and then navigate to the HKLM\BCD00000000 key. Expand every subkey so that the numerical identifiers of each Elements key are fully visible.

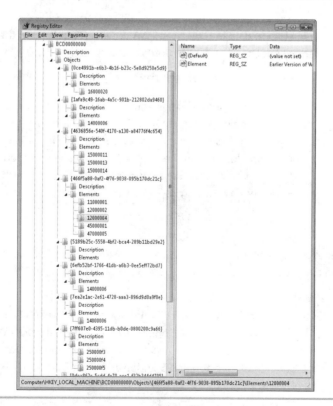

2. Identify the boot entry for your Windows installation by locating the Description with a Type value of 0x10200003, and then check ID 0x12000004 in the Elements tree. In the Element value of that subkey, you should find the name of your version of Windows, such as Windows 7. If you have more than one Windows installation on your machine, you may need to check the 0x22000002 Element, which contains the path, such as \Windows.

3. Now that you've found the correct GUID for your Windows installation, create a new subkey under the Elements subkey for that GUID and name it 0x260000a0. If this subkey already exists, simply navigate to it.

4. If you had to create the subkey, now create a binary value called Element inside it.

5. Edit the value and set it to 01. This will enable kernel-mode debugging. Here's what these changes should look like:

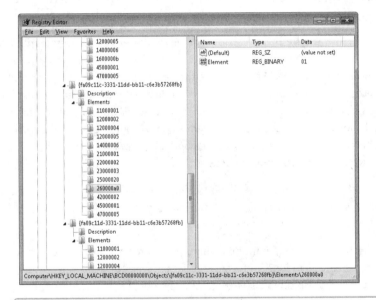

 Note The 0x12000004 ID corresponds to BcdLibraryString_ApplicationPath, while the 0x22000002 ID corresponds to BcdOSLoaderString_SystemRoot. Finally, the ID you added, 0x260000a0, corresponds to BcdOSLoaderBoolean_KernelDebuggerEnabled. These values are documented in the BCD reference in the MSDN Library.

The HKLM\COMPONENTS subkey contains information pertinent to the Component Based Servicing (CBS) stack. This stack contains various files and resources that are part of a Windows installation image (used by the Automated Installation Kit or the OEM Preinstallation Kit) or an active installation. The CBS APIs that exist for servicing purposes use the information located in this key to identify installed components and their configuration information. This information is used whenever components are installed, updated, or removed either individually (called units) or in groups (called packages). To optimize system resources, because this key can get quite large, it is only dynamically loaded and unloaded as needed if the CBS stack is servicing a request.

The HKLM\HARDWARE subkey maintains descriptions of the system's legacy hardware and some hardware device-to-driver mappings. On a modern system, only a few peripherals—such as keyboard, mouse, and ACPI BIOS data—are likely to be found here. The Device Manager tool (which is available by running System from Control Panel and then clicking Device Manager) lets you view registry hardware information that it obtains by simply reading values out of the HARDWARE key (although it primarily uses the HKLM\SYSTEM\CurrentControlSet\Enum tree).

HKLM\SAM holds local account and group information, such as user passwords, group definitions, and domain associations. Windows Server systems that are operating as domain controllers store domain accounts and groups in Active Directory, a database that stores domainwide settings and information. (Active Directory isn't described in this book.) By default, the security descriptor on the SAM key is configured so that even the administrator account doesn't have access.

HKLM\SECURITY stores systemwide security policies and user-rights assignments. HKLM\SAM is linked into the SECURITY subkey under HKLM\SECURITY\SAM. By default, you can't view the contents of HKLM\SECURITY or HKLM\SAM\SAM because the security settings of those keys allow access only by the System account. (System accounts are discussed in greater detail later in this chapter.) You can change the security descriptor to allow read access to administrators, or you can use PsExec to run Regedit in the local system account if you want to peer inside. However, that glimpse won't be very revealing because the data is undocumented and the passwords are encrypted with one-way mapping—that is, you can't determine a password from its encrypted form.

HKLM\SOFTWARE is where Windows stores systemwide configuration information not needed to boot the system. Also, third-party applications store their systemwide settings here, such as paths to application files and directories and licensing and expiration date information.

HKLM\SYSTEM contains the systemwide configuration information needed to boot the system, such as which device drivers to load and which services to start. Because this information is critical to starting the system, Windows also maintains a copy of part of this information, called the last known good control set, under this key. The maintenance of a copy allows an administrator to select a previously working control set in the case that configuration changes made to the current control set prevent the system from booting. For details on when Windows declares the current control set "good," see the section "Accepting the Boot and Last Known Good" later in this chapter.

HKEY_CURRENT_CONFIG

HKEY_CURRENT_CONFIG is just a link to the current hardware profile, stored under HKLM\SYSTEM \CurrentControlSet\Hardware Profiles\Current. Hardware profiles are no longer supported in Windows, but the key still exists to support legacy applications that might be depending on its presence.

HKEY_PERFORMANCE_DATA

The registry is the mechanism used to access performance counter values on Windows, whether those are from operating system components or server applications. One of the side benefits of providing access to the performance counters via the registry is that remote performance monitoring works "for free" because the registry is easily accessible remotely through the normal registry APIs.

You can access the registry performance counter information directly by opening a special key named HKEY_PERFORMANCE_DATA and querying values beneath it. You won't find this key by looking in the Registry Editor; this key is available only programmatically through the Windows registry functions, such as *RegQueryValueEx*. Performance information isn't actually stored in the registry; the registry functions use this key to locate the information from performance data providers.

You can also access performance counter information by using the Performance Data Helper (PDH) functions available through the Performance Data Helper API (Pdh.dll). Figure 4-2 shows the components involved in accessing performance counter information.

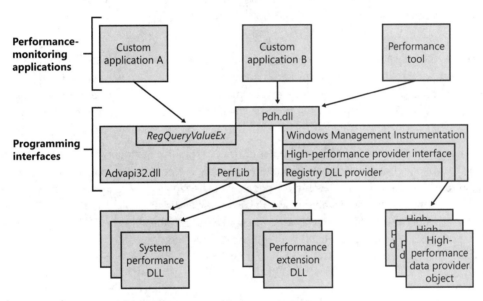

FIGURE 4-2 Registry performance counter architecture

Transactional Registry (TxR)

Thanks to the Kernel Transaction Manager (KTM; for more information see the section about the KTM in Chapter 3, "System Mechanisms"), developers have access to a straightforward API that allows them to implement robust error-recovery capabilities when performing registry operations, which can be linked with nonregistry operations, such as file or database operations.

Three APIs support transactional modification of the registry: *RegCreateKeyTransacted*, *RegOpenKeyTransacted*, and *RegDeleteKeyTransacted*. These new routines take the same parameters as their nontransacted analogs, except that a new transaction handle parameter is added. A developer supplies this handle after calling the KTM function *CreateTransaction*.

After a transacted create or open operation, all subsequent registry operations—such as creating, deleting, or modifying values inside the key—will also be transacted. However, operations on the subkeys of a transacted key will not be automatically transacted, which is why the third API, *RegDeleteKeyTransacted* exists. It allows the transacted deletion of subkeys, which *RegDeleteKeyEx* would not normally do.

Data for these transacted operations is written to log files using the common logging file system (CLFS) services, similar to other KTM operations. Until the transaction itself is committed or rolled back (both of which might happen programmatically or as a result of a power failure or system crash, depending on the state of the transaction), the keys, values, and other registry modifications performed with the transaction handle will not be visible to external applications through the nontransacted APIs. Also, transactions are isolated from each other; modifications made inside one transaction will not be visible from inside other transactions or outside the transaction until the transaction is committed.

> **Note** A nontransactional writer will abort a transaction in case of conflict—for example, if a value was created inside a transaction and later, while the transaction is still active, a nontransactional writer tries to create a value under the same key. The nontransactional operation will succeed, and all operations in the conflicting transaction will be aborted.

The isolation level (the "I" in ACID) implemented by TxR resource managers is read-commit, which means that changes become available to other readers (transacted or not) immediately after being committed. This mechanism is important for people who are familiar with transactions in databases, where the isolation level is predictable-reads (or cursor-stability, as it is called in database literature). With a predictable-reads isolation level, after you read a value inside a transaction, subsequent reads will give you back the same data. Read-commit does not make this guarantee. One of the consequences is that registry transactions can't be used for "atomic" increment/decrement operations on a registry value.

To make permanent changes to the registry, the application that has been using the transaction handle must call the KTM function *CommitTransaction*. (If the application decides to undo the changes, such as during a failure path, it can call the *RollbackTransaction* API.) The changes will then be visible through the regular registry APIs as well.

> **Note** If a transaction handle created with *CreateTransaction* is closed before the transaction is committed (and there are no other handles open to that transaction), the system will roll back that transaction.

Apart from using the CLFS support provided by the KTM, TxR also stores its own internal log files in the %SystemRoot%\System32\Config\Txr folder on the system volume; these files have a .regtrans-ms extension and are hidden by default. Even if there are no third-party applications installed, your system likely will contain files in this directory because Windows Update and Component Based Servicing make use of TxR to atomically write data to the registry to avoid system failure or inconsistent component data in the case of an incomplete update. In fact, if you take a look at some of the transaction files, you should be able to see the key names on which the transaction was being performed.

There is a global registry resource manager (RM) that services all the hives that are mounted at boot time. For every hive that is mounted explicitly, an RM is created. For applications that use registry transactions, the creation of an RM is transparent because KTM ensures that all RMs taking part in the same transaction are coordinated in the two-phase commit/abort protocol. For the global registry RM, the CLFS log files are stored, as mentioned earlier, inside System32\Config\Txr. For other hives, they are stored alongside the hive (in the same directory). They are hidden and follow the same naming convention, ending in .regtrans-ms. The log file names are prefixed with the name of the hive to which they correspond.

Monitoring Registry Activity

Because the system and applications depend so heavily on configuration settings to guide their behavior, system and application failures can result from changing registry data or security. When the system or an application fails to read settings that it assumes it will always be able to access, it might not function properly, display error messages that hide the root cause, or even crash. It's virtually impossible to know what registry keys or values are misconfigured without understanding how the system or the application that's failing is accessing the registry. In such situations, the Process Monitor utility from Windows Sysinternals (*http://technet.microsoft.com/sysinternals*) might provide the answer.

Process Monitor lets you monitor registry activity as it occurs. For each registry access, Process Monitor shows you the process that performed the access; the time, type, and result of the access; and the stack of the thread at the moment of the access. This information is useful for seeing how applications and the system rely on the registry, discovering where applications and the system store configuration settings, and troubleshooting problems related to applications having missing registry keys or values. Process Monitor includes advanced filtering and highlighting so that you can zoom in on activity related to specific keys or values or to the activity of particular processes.

Process Monitor Internals

Process Monitor relies on a device driver that it extracts from its executable image at run time and then starts. Its first execution requires that the account running it have the Load Driver privilege as well as the Debug privilege; subsequent executions in the same boot session require only the Debug privilege because, once loaded, the driver remains resident.

EXPERIMENT: Viewing Registry Activity on an Idle System

Because the registry implements the *RegNotifyChangeKey* function that applications can use to request notification of registry changes without polling for them, when you launch Process Monitor on a system that's idle you should not see repetitive accesses to the same registry keys or values. Any such activity identifies a poorly written application that unnecessarily negatively affects a system's overall performance.

Run Process Monitor, and after several seconds examine the output log to see whether you can spot polling behavior. Right-click on an output line associated with polling, and then choose Process Properties from the context menu to view details about the process performing the activity.

EXPERIMENT: Using Process Monitor to Locate Application Registry Settings

In some troubleshooting scenarios, you might need to determine where in the registry the system or an application stores particular settings. This experiment has you use Process Monitor to discover the location of Notepad's settings. Notepad, like most Windows applications, saves user preferences—such as word-wrap mode, font and font size, and window position—across executions. By having Process Monitor watching when Notepad reads or writes its settings, you can identify the registry key in which the settings are stored. Here are the steps for doing this:

1. Have Notepad save a setting you can easily search for in a Process Monitor trace. You can do this by running Notepad, setting the font to Times New Roman, and then exiting Notepad.

2. Run Process Monitor. Open the filter dialog box and the Process Name filter, and type notepad.exe as the string to match. This step specifies that Process Monitor will log only activity by the notepad.exe process.

3. Run Notepad again, and after it has launched stop Process Monitor's event capture by toggling Capture Events on the Process Monitor File menu.

4. Scroll to the top line of the resultant log and select it.

5. Press Ctrl+F to open a Find dialog box, and search for times new. Process Monitor should highlight a line like the one shown in the following screen that represents Notepad reading the font value from the registry. Other operations in the immediate vicinity should relate to other Notepad settings.

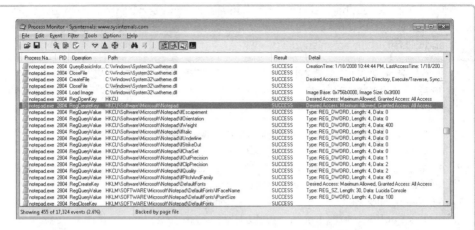

6. Finally, right-click the highlighted line and click Jump To. Process Monitor will execute Regedit (if it's not already running) and cause it to navigate to and select the Notepad-referenced registry value.

Process Monitor Troubleshooting Techniques

Two basic Process Monitor troubleshooting techniques are effective for discovering the cause of registry-related application or system problems:

- Look at the last thing in the Process Monitor trace that the application did before it failed. This action might point to the problem.

- Compare a Process Monitor trace of the failing application with a trace from a working system.

To follow the first approach, run Process Monitor and then run the application. At the point the failure occurs, go back to Process Monitor and stop the logging (by pressing Ctrl+E). Then go to the end of the log and find the last operations performed by the application before it failed (or crashed, hung, or whatever). Starting with the last line, work your way backward, examining the files, registry keys, or both that were referenced—often this will help pinpoint the problem.

Use the second approach when the application fails on one system but works on another. Capture a Process Monitor trace of the application on the working and failing systems, and save the output to a log file. Then open the good and bad log files with Microsoft Excel (accepting the defaults in the Import wizard), and delete the first three columns. (If you don't delete the first three columns, the comparison will show every line as different because the first three columns contain information that is different from run to run, such as the time and the process ID.) Finally, compare the resulting log files. (You can do this by using WinDiff, which is included in the Windows SDK).

Entries in a Process Monitor trace that have values of NAME NOT FOUND or ACCESS DENIED in the Result column are ones you should investigate. NAME NOT FOUND is reported when an application attempts to read from a registry key or value that doesn't exist. In many cases, a missing key or value is innocuous because a process that fails to read a setting from the registry simply falls back on default values. In some cases, however, applications expect to find values for which there is no default and will fail if they are missing.

Access-denied errors are a common source of registry-related application failures and occur when an application doesn't have permission to access a key the way that it wants. Applications that do not validate registry operation results or perform proper error recovery will fail.

A common result string that might appear suspicious is BUFFER OVERFLOW. It does not indicate a buffer-overflow exploit in the application that receives it. Instead, it's used by the configuration manager to inform an application that the buffer it specified to store a registry value is too small to hold the value. Application developers often take advantage of this behavior to determine how large a buffer to allocate to store a value. They first perform a registry query with a zero-length buffer that returns a buffer-overflow error and the length of the data it attempted to read. The application then allocates a buffer of the indicated size and rereads the value. You should therefore see operations that return BUFFER OVERFLOW repeat with a successful result.

In one example of Process Monitor being used to troubleshoot a real problem, it saved a user from doing a complete reinstall of his Windows system. The symptom was that Internet Explorer would hang on startup if the user did not first manually dial the Internet connection. This Internet connection was set as the default connection for the system, so starting Internet Explorer should have caused an automatic dial-up to the Internet (because Internet Explorer was set to display a default home page upon startup).

An examination of a Process Monitor log of Internet Explorer startup activity, going backward from the point in the log where Internet Explorer hung, showed a query to a key under HKCU\Software\Microsoft\RAS Phonebook. The user reported that he had previously uninstalled the dialer program associated with the key and manually created the dial-up connection. Because the dial-up connection name did not match that of the uninstalled dialer program, it appeared that the key had not been deleted by the dialer's uninstall program and that it was causing Internet Explorer to hang. After the key was deleted, Internet Explorer functioned as expected.

Logging Activity in Unprivileged Accounts or During Logon/Logoff

A common application-failure scenario is that an application works when run in an account that has Administrative group membership but not when run in the account of an unprivileged user. As described earlier, executing Process Monitor requires security privileges that are not normally assigned to standard user accounts, but you can capture a trace of applications executing in the logon session of an unprivileged user by using the Runas command to execute Process Monitor in an administrative account.

If a registry problem relates to account logon or logoff, you'll also have to take special steps to be able to use Process Monitor to capture a trace of those phases of a logon session. Applications that are run in the local system account are not terminated when a user logs off, and you can take advantage of that fact to have Process Monitor run through a logoff and subsequent logon. You can launch Process Monitor in the local system account either by using the At command that's built into Windows and specifying the /interactive flag, or by using the Sysinternals PsExec utility, like this:

psexec –i 0 –s –d c:\procmon.exe

The *–i 0* switch directs PsExec to have Process Monitor's window appear on the session 0 interactive window station's default desktop, the *–s* switch has PsExec run Process Monitor in the local system account, and the *–d* switch has PsExec launch Process Monitor and exit without waiting for Process Monitor to terminate. When you execute this command, the instance of Process Monitor that executes will survive logoff and reappear on the desktop when you log back on, having captured the registry activity of both actions.

Another way to monitor registry activity during the logon, logoff, boot, or shutdown process is to use the Process Monitor log boot feature, which you can enable by selecting Log Boot on the Options menu. The next time you boot the system, the Process Monitor device driver logs registry activity from early in the boot to %SystemRoot%\Procmon.pml. It will continue logging to that file until disk space runs out, the system shuts down, or you run Process Monitor. A log file storing a registry trace of startup, logon, logoff, and shutdown on a Windows system will typically be between 50 and 150 MB in size.

Registry Internals

In this section, you'll find out how the configuration manager—the executive subsystem that implements the registry—organizes the registry's on-disk files. We'll examine how the configuration manager manages the registry as applications and other operating system components read and change registry keys and values. We'll also discuss the mechanisms by which the configuration manager tries to ensure that the registry is always in a recoverable state, even if the system crashes while the registry is being modified.

Hives

On disk, the registry isn't simply one large file but rather a set of discrete files called hives. Each hive contains a registry tree, which has a key that serves as the root or starting point of the tree. Subkeys and their values reside beneath the root. You might think that the root keys displayed by the Registry Editor correlate to the root keys in the hives, but such is not the case. Table 4-5 lists registry hives and their on-disk file names. The path names of all hives except for user profiles are coded into the configuration manager. As the configuration manager loads hives, including system profiles, it notes each hive's path in the values under the HKLM\SYSTEM\CurrentControlSet\Control\Hivelist subkey, removing the path if the hive is unloaded. It creates the root keys, linking these hives together to build the registry structure you're familiar with and that the Registry Editor displays.

You'll notice that some of the hives listed in Table 4-5 are volatile and don't have associated files. The system creates and manages these hives entirely in memory; the hives are therefore temporary. The system creates volatile hives every time it boots. An example of a volatile hive is the HKLM\HARDWARE hive, which stores information about physical devices and the devices' assigned resources. Resource assignment and hardware detection occur every time the system boots, so not storing this data on disk is logical.

TABLE 4-5 On-Disk Files Corresponding to Paths in the Registry

Hive Registry Path	Hive File Path
HKEY_LOCAL_MACHINE\BCD00000000	\Boot\BCD
HKEY_LOCAL_MACHINE\COMPONENTS	%SystemRoot%\System32\Config\Components
HKEY_LOCAL_MACHINE\SYSTEM	%SystemRoot%\System32\Config\System
HKEY_LOCAL_MACHINE\SAM	%SystemRoot%\System32\Config\Sam
HKEY_LOCAL_MACHINE\SECURITY	%SystemRoot%\System32\Config\Security
HKEY_LOCAL_MACHINE\SOFTWARE	%SystemRoot%\System32\Config\Software
HKEY_LOCAL_MACHINE\HARDWARE	Volatile hive
HKEY_USERS\<SID of local service account>	%SystemRoot%\ServiceProfiles\LocalService\Ntuser.dat
HKEY_USERS\<SID of network service account>	%SystemRoot%\ServiceProfiles\NetworkService\NtUser.dat
HKEY_USERS\<SID of username>	\Users\<username>\Ntuser.dat
HKEY_USERS\<SID of username>_Classes	\Users\<username>\AppData\Local\Microsoft\Windows\Usrclass.dat
HKEY_USERS\.DEFAULT	%SystemRoot%\System32\Config\Default

EXPERIMENT: Manually Loading and Unloading Hives

Regedit has the ability to load hives that you can access through its File menu. This capability can be useful in troubleshooting scenarios where you want to view or edit a hive from an unbootable system or a backup medium. In this experiment, you'll use Regedit to load a version of the HKLM\SYSTEM hive that Windows Setup creates during the install process.

1. Hives can be loaded only underneath HKLM or HKU, so open Regedit, select HKLM, and choose Load Hive from the Regedit File menu.

2. Navigate to the %SystemRoot%\System32\Config\RegBack directory in the Load Hive dialog box, select System and open it. When prompted, type Test as the name of the key under which it will load.

3. Open the newly created HKLM\Test key, and explore the contents of the hive.

4. Open HKLM\SYSTEM\CurrentControlSet\Control\Hivelist, and locate the entry \Registry\Machine\Test, which demonstrates how the configuration manager lists loaded hives in the Hivelist key.

5. Select HKLM\Test, and then choose Unload Hive from the Regedit File menu to unload the hive.

Hive Size Limits

In some cases, hive sizes are limited. For example, Windows places a limit on the size of the HKLM\SYSTEM hive. It does so because Winload reads the entire HKLM\SYSTEM hive into physical memory near the start of the boot process when virtual memory paging is not enabled. Winload also loads Ntoskrnl and boot device drivers into physical memory, so it must constrain the amount of physical memory assigned to HKLM\SYSTEM. (See Chapter 13 in Part 2 for more information on the role Winload plays during the startup process.) On 32-bit systems, Winload allows the hive to be as large as 400 MB or one-half the amount of physical memory on the system, whichever is lower. On x64 systems, the lower bound is 1.5 GB. On Itanium systems, it is 32 MB.

Registry Symbolic Links

A special type of key known as a registry symbolic link makes it possible for the configuration manager to link keys to organize the registry. A symbolic link is a key that redirects the configuration manager to another key. Thus, the key HKLM\SAM is a symbolic link to the key at the root of the SAM hive. Symbolic links are created by specifying the REG_CREATE_LINK parameter to RegCreateKey or *RegCreateKeyEx*. Internally, the configuration manager will create a REG_LINK value called SymbolicLinkValue, which will contain the path to the target key. Because this value is a REG_LINK instead of a REG_SZ, it will not be visible with Regedit—it is, however, part of the on-disk registry hive.

EXPERIMENT: Looking at Hive Handles

The configuration manager opens hives by using the kernel handle table (described in Chapter 3) so that it can access hives from any process context. Using the kernel handle table is an efficient alternative to approaches that involve using drivers or executive components to access from the System process only handles that must be protected from user processes. You can use Process Explorer to see the hive handles, which will be displayed as being opened in the System process. Select the System process, and then select Handles from the Lower Pane View menu entry on the View menu. Sort by handle type, and scroll until you see the hive files, as shown in the following screen.

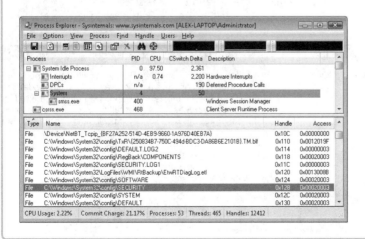

Hive Structure

The configuration manager logically divides a hive into allocation units called blocks in much the same way that a file system divides a disk into clusters. By definition, the registry block size is 4096 bytes (4 KB). When new data expands a hive, the hive always expands in block-granular increments. The first block of a hive is the base block.

The base block includes global information about the hive, including a signature—regf—that identifies the file as a hive, updated sequence numbers, a time stamp that shows the last time a write operation was initiated on the hive, information on registry repair or recovery performed by Winload, the hive format version number, a checksum, and the hive file's internal file name (for example, \Device\HarddiskVolume1\WINDOWS\SYSTEM32\CONFIG\SAM). We'll clarify the significance of the updated sequence numbers and time stamp when we describe how data is written to a hive file.

The hive format version number specifies the data format within the hive. The configuration manager uses hive format version 1.3 (which improved searching by caching the first four characters of the name inside the cell index structure for quick lookups) for all hives except for System and Software for roaming profile compatibility with Windows 2000. For System and Software hives, it uses version 1.5 because of the later format's optimizations for large values (values larger than 1 MB are supported) and searching (instead of caching the first four characters of a name, a hash of the entire name is used to reduce collisions).

Windows organizes the registry data that a hive stores in containers called cells. A cell can hold a key, a value, a security descriptor, a list of subkeys, or a list of key values. A 4-byte character tag at the beginning of a cell's data describes the data's type as a signature. Table 4-6 describes each cell data type in detail. A cell's header is a field that specifies the cell's size as the 1's complement (not present in the CM_ structures). When a cell joins a hive and the hive must expand to contain the cell, the system creates an allocation unit called a bin.

A bin is the size of the new cell rounded up to the next block or page boundary, whichever is higher. The system considers any space between the end of the cell and the end of the bin to be free space that it can allocate to other cells. Bins also have headers that contain a signature, hbin, and a field that records the offset into the hive file of the bin and the bin's size.

TABLE 4-6 Cell Data Types

Data Type	Structure Type	Description
Key cell	CM_KEY_NODE	A cell that contains a registry key, also called a key node. A key cell contains a signature (kn for a key, kl for a link node), the time stamp of the most recent update to the key, the cell index of the key's parent key cell, the cell index of the subkey-list cell that identifies the key's subkeys, a cell index for the key's security descriptor cell, a cell index for a string key that specifies the class name of the key, and the name of the key (for example, CurrentControlSet). It also saves cached information such as the number of subkeys under the key, as well as the size of the largest key, value name, value data, and class name of the subkeys under this key.

Data Type	Structure Type	Description
Value cell	CM_KEY_VALUE	A cell that contains information about a key's value. This cell includes a signature (kv), the value's type (for example, REG_ DWORD or REG_BINARY), and the value's name (for example, Boot-Execute). A value cell also contains the cell index of the cell that contains the value's data.
Subkey-list cell	CM_KEY_INDEX	A cell composed of a list of cell indexes for key cells that are all subkeys of a common parent key.
Value-list cell	CM_KEY_INDEX	A cell composed of a list of cell indexes for value cells that are all values of a common parent key.
Security-descriptor cell	CM_KEY_SECURITY	A cell that contains a security descriptor. Security-descriptor cells include a signature (ks) at the head of the cell and a reference count that records the number of key nodes that share the security descriptor. Multiple key cells can share security-descriptor cells.

By using bins, instead of cells, to track active parts of the registry, Windows minimizes some management chores. For example, the system usually allocates and deallocates bins less frequently than it does cells, which lets the configuration manager manage memory more efficiently. When the configuration manager reads a registry hive into memory, it reads the whole hive, including empty bins, but it can choose to discard them later. When the system adds and deletes cells in a hive, the hive can contain empty bins interspersed with active bins. This situation is similar to disk fragmentation, which occurs when the system creates and deletes files on the disk. When a bin becomes empty, the configuration manager joins to the empty bin any adjacent empty bins to form as large a contiguous empty bin as possible. The configuration manager also joins adjacent deleted cells to form larger free cells. (The configuration manager shrinks a hive only when bins at the end of the hive become free. You can compact the registry by backing it up and restoring it using the Windows *RegSaveKey* and *RegReplaceKey* functions, which are used by the Windows Backup utility.)

The links that create the structure of a hive are called cell indexes. A cell index is the offset of a cell into the hive file minus the size of the base block. Thus, a cell index is like a pointer from one cell to another cell that the configuration manager interprets relative to the start of a hive. For example, as you saw in Table 4-6, a cell that describes a key contains a field specifying the cell index of its parent key; a cell index for a subkey specifies the cell that describes the subkeys that are subordinate to the specified subkey. A subkey-list cell contains a list of cell indexes that refer to the subkey's key cells. Therefore, if you want to locate, for example, the key cell of subkey A, whose parent is key B, you must first locate the cell containing key B's subkey list using the subkey-list cell index in key B's cell. Then you locate each of key B's subkey cells by using the list of cell indexes in the subkey-list cell. For each subkey cell, you check to see whether the subkey's name, which a key cell stores, matches the one you want to locate, in this case, subkey A.

The distinction between cells, bins, and blocks can be confusing, so let's look at an example of a simple registry hive layout to help clarify the differences. The sample registry hive file in Figure 4-3 contains a base block and two bins. The first bin is empty, and the second bin contains several cells. Logically, the hive has only two keys: the root key Root, and a subkey of Root, Sub Key. Root has two values, Val 1 and Val 2. A subkey-list cell locates the root key's subkey, and a value-list cell locates the root key's values. The free spaces in the second bin are empty cells. Figure 4-3 doesn't show the security cells for the two keys, which would be present in a hive.

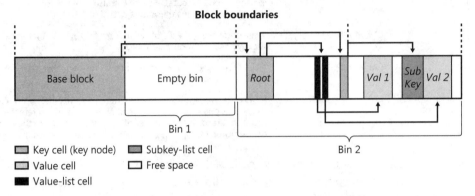

FIGURE 4-3 Internal structure of a registry hive

To optimize searches for both values and subkeys, the configuration manager sorts subkey-list cells alphabetically. The configuration manager can then perform a binary search when it looks for a subkey within a list of subkeys. The configuration manager examines the subkey in the middle of the list, and if the name of the subkey the configuration manager is looking for is alphabetically before the name of the middle subkey, the configuration manager knows that the subkey is in the first half of the subkey list; otherwise, the subkey is in the second half of the subkey list. This splitting process continues until configuration manager locates the subkey or finds no match. Value-list cells aren't sorted, however, so new values are always added to the end of the list.

Cell Maps

If hives never grew, the configuration manager could perform all its registry management on the in-memory version of a hive as if the hive were a file. Given a cell index, the configuration manager could calculate the location in memory of a cell simply by adding the cell index, which is a hive file offset, to the base of the in-memory hive image. Early in the system boot, this process is exactly what Winload does with the SYSTEM hive: Winload reads the entire SYSTEM hive into memory as a read-only hive and adds the cell indexes to the base of the in-memory hive image to locate cells. Unfortunately, hives grow as they take on new keys and values, which means the system must allocate paged pool memory to store the new bins that contain added keys and values. Thus, the paged pool that keeps the registry data in memory isn't necessarily contiguous.

EXPERIMENT: Viewing Hive Paged Pool Usage

There are no administrative-level tools that show you the amount of paged pool that registry hives, including user profiles, are consuming on Windows. However, the !reg dumppool kernel debugger command shows you not only how many pages of the paged pool each loaded hive consumes but also how many of the pages store volatile and nonvolatile data. The command prints the total hive memory usage at the end of the output. (The command shows only the last 32 characters of a hive's name.)

```
kd> !reg dumppool

dumping hive at e20d66a8 (a\Microsoft\Windows\UsrClass.dat)
  Stable Length = 1000
  1/1 pages present
  Volatile Length = 0

dumping hive at e215ee88 (ettings\Administrator\ntuser.dat)
  Stable Length = f2000
  242/242 pages present
  Volatile Length = 2000
  2/2 pages present

dumping hive at e13fa188 (\SystemRoot\System32\Config\SAM)
  Stable Length = 5000
  5/5 pages present
  Volatile Length = 0

...
```

To deal with noncontiguous memory addresses referencing hive data in memory, the configuration manager adopts a strategy similar to what the Windows memory manager uses to map virtual memory addresses to physical memory addresses. The configuration manager employs a two-level scheme, which Figure 4-4 illustrates, that takes as input a cell index (that is, a hive file offset) and returns as output both the address in memory of the block the cell index resides in and the address in memory of the block the cell resides in. Remember that a bin can contain one or more blocks and that hives grow in bins, so Windows always represents a bin with a contiguous region of memory. Therefore, all blocks within a bin occur within the same cache manager view.

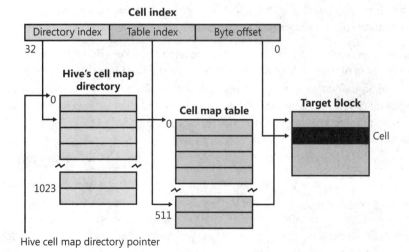

FIGURE 4-4 Structure of a cell index

To implement the mapping, the configuration manager divides a cell index logically into fields, in the same way that the memory manager divides a virtual address into fields. Windows interprets a cell index's first field as an index into a hive's cell map directory. The cell map directory contains 1024 entries, each of which refers to a cell map table that contains 512 map entries. An entry in this cell map table is specified by the second field in the cell index. That entry locates the bin and block memory addresses of the cell. Not all bins are necessarily mapped into memory, and if a cell lookup yields an address of 0, the configuration manager maps the bin into memory, unmapping another on the mapping LRU list it maintains, if necessary.

In the final step of the translation process, the configuration manager interprets the last field of the cell index as an offset into the identified block to precisely locate a cell in memory. When a hive initializes, the configuration manager dynamically creates the mapping tables, designating a map entry for each block in the hive, and it adds and deletes tables from the cell directory as the changing size of the hive requires.

The Registry Namespace and Operation

The configuration manager defines a key object type to integrate the registry's namespace with the kernel's general namespace. The configuration manager inserts a key object named Registry into the root of the Windows namespace, which serves as the entry point to the registry. Regedit shows key names in the form HKEY_LOCAL_MACHINE\SYSTEM\CurrentControlSet, but the Windows subsystem translates such names into their object namespace form (for example, \Registry\Machine\System \CurrentControlSet). When the Windows object manager parses this name, it encounters the key object by the name of Registry first and hands the rest of the name to the configuration manager. The configuration manager takes over the name parsing, looking through its internal hive tree to find the desired key or value. Before we describe the flow of control for a typical registry operation, we need to discuss key objects and key control blocks. Whenever an application opens or creates a registry key, the object manager gives a handle with which to reference the key to the application. The handle corresponds to a key object that the configuration manager allocates with the help of the object manager. By using the object manager's object support, the configuration manager takes advantage of the security and reference-counting functionality that the object manager provides.

For each open registry key, the configuration manager also allocates a key control block. A key control block stores the name of the key, includes the cell index of the key node that the control block refers to, and contains a flag that notes whether the configuration manager needs to delete the key cell that the key control block refers to when the last handle for the key closes. Windows places all key control blocks into a hash table to enable quick searches for existing key control blocks by name. A key object points to its corresponding key control block, so if two applications open the same registry key, each will receive a key object, and both key objects will point to a common key control block.

When an application opens an existing registry key, the flow of control starts with the application specifying the name of the key in a registry API that invokes the object manager's name-parsing routine. The object manager, upon encountering the configuration manager's registry key object in the namespace, hands the path name to the configuration manager. The configuration manager performs a lookup on the key control block hash table. If the related key control block is found there, there's no need for any further work; otherwise, the lookup provides the configuration manager with the closest key control block to the searched key, and the lookup continues by using the in-memory hive data structures to search through keys and subkeys to find the specified key. If the configuration manager finds the key cell, the configuration manager searches the key control block tree to determine whether the key is open (by the same application or another one). The search routine is optimized to always start from the closest ancestor with a key control block already opened. For example, if an application opens \Registry\Machine\Key1\Subkey2, and \Registry\Machine is already opened, the parse routine uses the key control block of \Registry\Machine as a starting point. If the key is open, the configuration manager increments the existing key control block's reference count. If the key isn't open, the configuration manager allocates a new key control block and inserts it into the tree. Then the configuration manager allocates a key object, points the key object at the key control block, and returns control to the object manager, which returns a handle to the application.

When an application creates a new registry key, the configuration manager first finds the key cell for the new key's parent. The configuration manager then searches the list of free cells for the hive in which the new key will reside to determine whether cells exist that are large enough to hold the new key cell. If there aren't any free cells large enough, the configuration manager allocates a new bin and uses it for the cell, placing any space at the end of the bin on the free cell list. The new key cell fills with pertinent information—including the key's name—and the configuration manager adds the key cell to the subkey list of the parent key's subkey-list cell. Finally, the system stores the cell index of the parent cell in the new subkey's key cell.

The configuration manager uses a key control block's reference count to determine when to delete the key control block. When all the handles that refer to a key in a key control block close, the reference count becomes 0, which denotes that the key control block is no longer necessary. If an application that calls an API to delete the key sets the delete flag, the configuration manager can delete the associated key from the key's hive because it knows that no application is keeping the key open.

EXPERIMENT: Viewing Key Control Blocks

You can use the kernel debugger to list all the key control blocks allocated on a system with the command !reg openkeys command. Alternatively, if you want to view the key control block for a particular open key, use !reg findkcb:

```
kd> !reg findkcb \registry\machine\software\microsoft

Found KCB = e1034d40 :: \REGISTRY\MACHINE\SOFTWARE\MICROSOFT
```

You can then examine a reported key control block with the !reg kcb command:

```
kd> !reg kcb e1034d40

Key             : \REGISTRY\MACHINE\SOFTWARE\MICROSOFT
RefCount        : 1f
Flags           : CompressedName, Stable
ExtFlags        :
Parent          : 0xe1997368
KeyHive         : 0xe1c8a768
```

```
KeyCell            : 0x64e598 [cell index]
TotalLevels        : 4
DelayedCloseIndex: 2048
MaxNameLen         : 0x3c
MaxValueNameLen    : 0x0
MaxValueDataLen    : 0x0
LastWriteTime      : 0x 1c42501:0x7eb6d470
KeyBodyListHead    : 0xe1034d70 0xe1034d70
SubKeyCount        : 137
ValueCache.Count   : 0
KCBLock            : 0xe1034d40
KeyLock            : 0xe1034d40
```

The *Flags* field indicates that the name is stored in compressed form, and the *SubKeyCount* field shows that the key has 137 subkeys.

Stable Storage

To make sure that a nonvolatile registry hive (one with an on-disk file) is always in a recoverable state, the configuration manager uses log hives. Each nonvolatile hive has an associated log hive, which is a hidden file with the same base name as the hive and a logN extension. To ensure forward progress, the configuration manger uses a dual-logging scheme. There are potentially two log files: .log1 and .log2. If, for any reason, .log1 was written but a failure occurred while writing dirty data to the primary log file, the next time a flush happens, a switch to .log2 will occur with the cumulative dirty data. If that fails as well, the cumulative dirty data (the data in .log1 and the data that was dirtied in between) is saved in .log2. As a consequence, .log1 will be used again next time around, until a successful write operation is done to the primary log file. If no failure occurs, only .log1 is used.

For example, if you look in your %SystemRoot%\System32\Config directory (and you have the Show Hidden Files And Folders folder option selected), you'll see System.log1, Sam.log1, and other .log1 and .log2 files. When a hive initializes, the configuration manager allocates a bit array in which each bit represents a 512-byte portion, or sector, of the hive. This array is called the dirty sector array because an on bit in the array means that the system has modified the corresponding sector in the hive in memory and must write the sector back to the hive file. (An off bit means that the corresponding sector is up to date with the in-memory hive's contents.)

When the creation of a new key or value or the modification of an existing key or value takes place, the configuration manager notes the sectors of the hive that change in the hive's dirty sector array. Then the configuration manager schedules a lazy write operation, or a hive sync. The hive lazy writer system thread wakes up five seconds after the request to synchronize the hive and writes dirty hive sectors for all hives from memory to the hive files on disk. Thus, the system flushes, at the same time, all the registry modifications that take place between the time a hive sync is requested and the time the hive sync occurs. When a hive sync takes place, the next hive sync will occur no sooner than five seconds later.

Note The *RegFlushKey* API's name implies that the function flushes only modified data for a specified key to disk, but it actually triggers a full registry flush, which has a major performance impact on the system. For that reason and the fact that the registry automatically makes sure that modified data is in stable storage within seconds, application programmers should avoid using it.

If the lazy writer simply wrote all a hive's dirty sectors to the hive file and the system crashed in mid-operation, the hive file would be in an inconsistent (corrupted) and unrecoverable state. To prevent such an occurrence, the lazy writer first dumps the hive's dirty sector array and all the dirty sectors to the hive's log file, increasing the log file's size if necessary. The lazy writer then updates a sequence number in the hive's base block and writes the dirty sectors to the hive. When the lazy writer is finished, it updates a second sequence number in the base block. Thus, if the system crashes during the write operations to the hive, at the next reboot the configuration manager will notice that the two sequence numbers in the hive's base block don't match. The configuration manager can update the hive with the dirty sectors in the hive's log file to roll the hive forward. The hive is then up to date and consistent.

The Windows Boot Loader also contains some code related to registry reliability. For example, it can parse the System.log file before the kernel is loaded and do repairs to fix consistency. Additionally, in certain cases of hive corruption (such as if a base block, bin, or cell contains data that fails consistency checks), the configuration manager can reinitialize corrupted data structures, possibly deleting subkeys in the process, and continue normal operation. If it has to resort to a self-healing operation, it pops up a system error dialog box notifying the user.

Registry Filtering

The configuration manager in the Windows kernel implements a powerful model of registry filtering, which allows for monitoring of registry activity by tools such as Process Monitor. When a driver uses the callback mechanism, it registers a callback function with the configuration manager. The configuration manager executes the driver's callback function before and after the execution of registry system services so that the driver has full visibility and control over registry accesses. Antivirus products that scan registry data for viruses or prevent unauthorized processes from modifying the registry are other users of the callback mechanism.

Registry callbacks are also associated with the concept of altitudes. Altitudes are a way for different vendors to register a "height" on the registry filtering stack so that the order in which the system calls each callback routine can be deterministic and correct. This avoids a scenario in which an antivirus product would be scanning encrypted keys before an encryption product would run its own callback to decrypt them. With the Windows registry callback model, both types of tools are assigned a base altitude corresponding to the type of filtering they are doing—in this case, encryption versus scanning. Secondly, companies that create these types of tools must register with Microsoft so that within their own group, they will not collide with similar or competing products.

The filtering model also includes the ability to either completely take over the processing of the registry operation (bypassing the configuration manager and preventing it from handling the request) or redirect the operation to a different operation (such as Wow64's registry redirection). Additionally, it is also possible to modify the output parameters as well as the return value of a registry operation.

Finally, drivers can assign and tag per-key or per-operation driver-defined information for their own purposes. A driver can create and assign this context data during a create or open operation, which the configuration manager will remember and return during each subsequent operation on the key.

Registry Optimizations

The configuration manager makes a few noteworthy performance optimizations. First, virtually every registry key has a security descriptor that protects access to the key. Storing a unique security-descriptor copy for every key in a hive would be highly inefficient, however, because the same security settings often apply to entire subtrees of the registry. When the system applies security to a key, the configuration manager checks a pool of the unique security descriptors used within the same hive as the key to which new security is being applied, and it shares any existing descriptor for the key, ensuring that there is at most one copy of every unique security descriptor in a hive.

The configuration manager also optimizes the way it stores key and value names in a hive. Although the registry is fully Unicode-capable and specifies all names using the Unicode convention, if a name contains only ASCII characters, the configuration manager stores the name in ASCII form in the hive. When the configuration manager reads the name (such as when performing name lookups), it converts the name into Unicode form in memory. Storing the name in ASCII form can significantly reduce the size of a hive.

To minimize memory usage, key control blocks don't store full key registry path names. Instead, they reference only a key's name. For example, a key control block that refers to \Registry\System\Control would refer to the name Control rather than to the full path. A further memory optimization is that the configuration manager uses key name control blocks to store key names, and all key control blocks for keys with the same name share the same key name control block. To optimize performance, the configuration manager stores the key control block names in a hash table for quick lookups.

To provide fast access to key control blocks, the configuration manager stores frequently accessed key control blocks in the cache table, which is configured as a hash table. When the configuration manager needs to look up a key control block, it first checks the cache table. Finally, the configuration manager has another cache, the delayed close table, that stores key control blocks that applications close so that an application can quickly reopen a key it has recently closed. To optimize lookups, these cache tables are stored for each hive. The configuration manager removes the oldest key control blocks from the delayed close table as it adds the most recently closed blocks to the table.

Services

Almost every operating system has a mechanism to start processes at system startup time that provide services not tied to an interactive user. In Windows, such processes are called services or Windows services, because they rely on the Windows API to interact with the system. Services are similar to UNIX daemon processes and often implement the server side of client/server applications. An example of a Windows service might be a web server, because it must be running regardless of whether anyone is logged on to the computer and it must start running when the system starts so that an administrator doesn't have to remember, or even be present, to start it.

Windows services consist of three components: a service application, a service control program (SCP), and the service control manager (SCM). First, we'll describe service applications, service accounts, and the operations of the SCM. Then we'll explain how auto-start services are started during the system boot. We'll also cover the steps the SCM takes when a service fails during its startup and the way the SCM shuts down services.

Service Applications

Service applications, such as web servers, consist of at least one executable that runs as a Windows service. A user wanting to start, stop, or configure a service uses an SCP. Although Windows supplies built-in SCPs that provide general start, stop, pause, and continue functionality, some service applications include their own SCP that allows administrators to specify configuration settings particular to the service they manage.

Service applications are simply Windows executables (GUI or console) with additional code to receive commands from the SCM as well as to communicate the application's status back to the SCM. Because most services don't have a user interface, they are built as console programs.

When you install an application that includes a service, the application's setup program must register the service with the system. To register the service, the setup program calls the Windows *CreateService* function, a services-related function implemented in Advapi32.dll (%SystemRoot%\System32\Advapi32.dll). Advapi32, the "Advanced API" DLL, implements all the client-side SCM APIs.

When a setup program registers a service by calling *CreateService*, a message is sent to the SCM on the machine where the service will reside. The SCM then creates a registry key for the service under HKLM\SYSTEM\CurrentControlSet\Services. The Services key is the nonvolatile representation of the SCM's database. The individual keys for each service define the path of the executable image that contains the service as well as parameters and configuration options.

After creating a service, an installation or management application can start the service via the *StartService* function. Because some service-based applications also must initialize during the boot process to function, it's not unusual for a setup program to register a service as an auto-start service, ask the user to reboot the system to complete an installation, and let the SCM start the service as the system boots.

When a program calls *CreateService*, it must specify a number of parameters describing the service's characteristics. The characteristics include the service's type (whether it's a service that runs in its own process rather than a service that shares a process with other services), the location of the service's executable image file, an optional display name, an optional account name and password used to start the service in a particular account's security context, a start type that indicates whether the service starts automatically when the system boots or manually under the direction of an SCP, an error code that indicates how the system should react if the service detects an error when starting, and, if the service starts automatically, optional information that specifies when the service starts relative to other services.

The SCM stores each characteristic as a value in the service's registry key. Figure 4-5 shows an example of a service registry key.

FIGURE 4-5 Example of a service registry key

Table 4-7 lists all the service characteristics, many of which also apply to device drivers. (Not every characteristic applies to every type of service or device driver.) If a service needs to store configuration information that is private to the service, the convention is to create a subkey named Parameters under its service key and then store the configuration information in values under that subkey. The service then can retrieve the values by using standard registry functions.

 Note The SCM does not access a service's Parameters subkey until the service is deleted, at which time the SCM deletes the service's entire key, including subkeys like Parameters.

TABLE 4-7 Service and Driver Registry Parameters

Value Setting	Value Name	Value Setting Description
Start	SERVICE_BOOT_START (0)	Winload preloads the driver so that it is in memory during the boot. These drivers are initialized just prior to SERVICE_ SYSTEM_ START drivers.
	SERVICE_SYSTEM_START (1)	The driver loads and initializes during kernel initialization after SERVICE_ BOOT_START drivers have initialized.
	SERVICE_AUTO_START (2)	The SCM starts the driver or service after the SCM process, Services.exe, starts.
	SERVICE_DEMAND_START (3)	The SCM starts the driver or service on demand.
	SERVICE_DISABLED (4)	The driver or service doesn't load or initialize.
ErrorControl	SERVICE_ERROR_IGNORE (0)	Any error the driver or service returns is ignored, and no warning is logged or displayed.
	SERVICE_ERROR_NORMAL (1)	If the driver or service reports an error, an event log message is written.
	SERVICE_ERROR_SEVERE (2)	If the driver or service returns an error and last known good isn't being used, reboot into last known good; otherwise, continue the boot.
	SERVICE_ERROR_CRITICAL (3)	If the driver or service returns an error and last known good isn't being used, reboot into last known good; otherwise, stop the boot with a blue screen crash.
Type	SERVICE_KERNEL_DRIVER (1)	Device driver.
	SERVICE_FILE_SYSTEM_DRIVER (2)	Kernel-mode file system driver.
	SERVICE_ADAPTER (4)	Obsolete.
	SERVICE_RECOGNIZER_DRIVER (8)	File system recognizer driver.
	SERVICE_WIN32_OWN_PROCESS (16)	The service runs in a process that hosts only one service.
	SERVICE_WIN32_SHARE_PROCESS (32)	The service runs in a process that hosts multiple services.
	SERVICE_INTERACTIVE_PROCESS (256)	The service is allowed to display windows on the console and receive user input, but only on the console session (0) to prevent interacting with user/console applications on other sessions.
Group	Group name	The driver or service initializes when its group is initialized.
Tag	Tag number	The specified location in a group initialization order. This parameter doesn't apply to services.
ImagePath	Path to the service or driver executable file	If ImagePath isn't specified, the I/O manager looks for drivers in %SystemRoot%\System32\Drivers. Required for Windows services.

Value Setting	Value Name	Value Setting Description
DependOnGroup	Group name	The driver or service won't load unless a driver or service from the specified group loads.
DependOnService	Service name	The service won't load until after the specified service loads. This parameter doesn't apply to device drivers other than those with a start type of SERVICE_AUTO_START or SERVICE_DEMAND_START.
ObjectName	Usually LocalSystem, but it can be an account name, such as .\Administrator	Specifies the account in which the service will run. If ObjectName isn't specified, LocalSystem is the account used. This parameter doesn't apply to device drivers.
DisplayName	Name of the service	The service application shows services by this name. If no name is specified, the name of the service's registry key becomes its name.
Description	Description of service	Up to 32767-byte description of the service.
FailureActions	Description of actions the SCM should take when the service process exits unexpectedly	Failure actions include restarting the service process, rebooting the system, and running a specified program. This value doesn't apply to drivers.
FailureCommand	Program command line	The SCM reads this value only if FailureActions specifies that a program should execute upon service failure. This value doesn't apply to drivers.
DelayedAutoStart	0 or 1 (TRUE or FALSE)	Tells the SCM to start this service after a certain delay has passed since the SCM was started. This reduces the number of services starting simultaneously during startup.
PreshutdownTimeout	Timeout in milliseconds	This value allows services to override the default preshutdown notification timeout of 180 seconds. After this timeout, the SCM will perform shutdown actions on the service if it has not yet responded.
ServiceSidType	SERVICE_SID_TYPE_NONE (0)	Backward-compatibility setting.
	SERVICE_SID_TYPE_UNRESTRICTED (1)	The SCM will add the service SID as a group owner to the service process' token when it is created.
	SERVICE_SID_TYPE_RESTRICTED (3)	Same as above, but the SCM will also add the service SID to the restricted SID list of the service process, along with the world, logon, and write-restricted SIDs.
RequiredPrivileges	List of privileges	This value contains the list of privileges that the service requires to function. The SCM will compute their union when creating the token for the shared process related to this service, if any.
Security	Security descriptor	This value contains the optional security descriptor that defines who has what access to the service object created internally by the SCM. If this value is omitted, the SCM applies a default security descriptor.

Notice that Type values include three that apply to device drivers: device driver, file system driver, and file system recognizer. These are used by Windows device drivers, which also store their parameters as registry data in the Services registry key. The SCM is responsible for starting drivers with a Start value of SERVICE_AUTO_START or SERVICE_DEMAND_START, so it's natural for the SCM database to include drivers. Services use the other types, SERVICE_WIN32_OWN_PROCESS and SERVICE_WIN32_SHARE_PROCESS, which are mutually exclusive. An executable that hosts more than one service specifies the SERVICE_WIN32_SHARE_PROCESS type.

An advantage to having a process run more than one service is that the system resources that would otherwise be required to run them in distinct processes are saved. A potential disadvantage is that if one of the services of a collection running in the same process causes an error that terminates the process, all the services of that process terminate. Also, another limitation is that all the services must run under the same account (however, if a service takes advantage of service security hardening mechanisms, it can limit some of its exposure to malicious attacks).

When the SCM starts a service process, the process must immediately invoke the *StartServiceCtrlDispatcher* function. *StartServiceCtrlDispatcher* accepts a list of entry points into services, one entry point for each service in the process. Each entry point is identified by the name of the service the entry point corresponds to. After making a named-pipe communications connection to the SCM, *StartServiceCtrlDispatcher* waits for commands to come through the pipe from the SCM. The SCM sends a service-start command each time it starts a service the process owns. For each start command it receives, the *StartServiceCtrlDispatcher* function creates a thread, called a service thread, to invoke the starting service's entry point and implement the command loop for the service. *StartServiceCtrlDispatcher* waits indefinitely for commands from the SCM and returns control to the process' main function only when all the process' services have stopped, allowing the service process to clean up resources before exiting.

A service entry point's first action is to call the *RegisterServiceCtrlHandler* function. This function receives and stores a pointer to a function, called the control handler, which the service implements to handle various commands it receives from the SCM. *RegisterServiceCtrlHandler* doesn't communicate with the SCM, but it stores the function in local process memory for the *StartServiceCtrlDispatcher* function. The service entry point continues initializing the service, which can include allocating memory, creating communications end points, and reading private configuration data from the registry. As explained earlier, a convention most services follow is to store their parameters under a subkey of their service registry key, named Parameters.

While the entry point is initializing the service, it must periodically send status messages, using the *SetServiceStatus* function, to the SCM indicating how the service's startup is progressing. After the entry point finishes initialization, a service thread usually sits in a loop waiting for requests from client applications. For example, a Web server would initialize a TCP listen socket and wait for inbound HTTP connection requests.

A service process' main thread, which executes in the *StartServiceCtrlDispatcher* function, receives SCM commands directed at services in the process and invokes the target service's control handler function (stored by *RegisterServiceCtrlHandler*). SCM commands include stop, pause, resume, interrogate, and shutdown or application-defined commands. Figure 4-6 shows the internal organization of a service process. Pictured are the two threads that make up a process hosting one service: the main thread and the service thread.

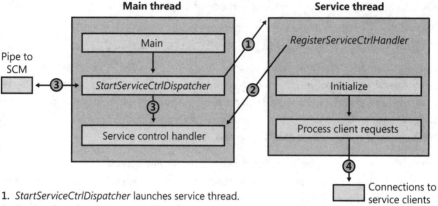

1. *StartServiceCtrlDispatcher* launches service thread.
2. Service thread registers control handler.
3. *StartServiceCtrlDispatcher* calls handlers in response to SCM commands.
4. Service thread processes client requests.

FIGURE 4-6 Inside a service process

Service Accounts

The security context of a service is an important consideration for service developers as well as for system administrators because it dictates what resources the process can access. Unless a service installation program or administrator specifies otherwise, most services run in the security context of the local system account (displayed sometimes as SYSTEM and other times as LocalSystem). Two other built-in accounts are the network service and local service accounts. These accounts have fewer capabilities than the local system account from a security standpoint, and any built-in Windows service that does not require the power of the local system account runs in the appropriate alternate service account. The following subsections describe the special characteristics of these accounts.

The Local System Account

The local system account is the same account in which core Windows user-mode operating system components run, including the Session Manager (%SystemRoot%\System32\Smss.exe), the Windows subsystem process (Csrss.exe), the Local Security Authority process (%SystemRoot%\System32 \Lsass.exe), and the Logon process (%SystemRoot%\System32\Winlogon.exe). For more information on these latter two processes, see Chapter 6.

From a security perspective, the local system account is extremely powerful—more powerful than any local or domain account when it comes to security ability on a local system. This account has the following characteristics:

- It is a member of the local administrators group. Table 4-8 shows the groups to which the local system account belongs. (See Chapter 6 for information on how group membership is used in object access checks.)

- It has the right to enable virtually every privilege (even privileges not normally granted to the local administrator account, such as creating security tokens). See Table 4-9 for the list of privileges assigned to the local system account. (Chapter 6 describes the use of each privilege.)

- Most files and registry keys grant full access to the local system account. (Even if they don't grant full access, a process running under the local system account can exercise the take-ownership privilege to gain access.)

- Processes running under the local system account run with the default user profile (HKU\.DEFAULT). Therefore, they can't access configuration information stored in the user profiles of other accounts.

- When a system is a member of a Windows domain, the local system account includes the machine security identifier (SID) for the computer on which a service process is running. Therefore, a service running in the local system account will be automatically authenticated on other machines in the same forest by using its computer account. (A forest is a grouping of domains.)

- Unless the machine account is specifically granted access to resources (such as network shares, named pipes, and so on), a process can access network resources that allow null sessions—that is, connections that require no credentials. You can specify the shares and pipes on a particular computer that permit null sessions in the NullSessionPipes and NullSessionShares registry values under HKLM\SYSTEM\CurrentControlSet\Services\lanmanserver\parameters.

TABLE 4-8 Service Account Group Membership

Local System	Network Service	Local Service
Everyone	Everyone	Everyone
Authenticated Users	Authenticated Users	Authenticated Users
Administrators	Users	Users
	Local	Local
	Network Service	Local Service
	Service	Service

TABLE 4-9 Service Account Privileges

Local System	Network Service	Local Service
SeAssignPrimaryTokenPrivilege SeAuditPrivilege SeBackupPrivilege SeChangeNotifyPrivilege SeCreateGlobalPrivilege SeCreatePagefilePrivilege SeCreatePermanentPrivilege SeCreateTokenPrivilege SeDebugPrivilege SeImpersonatePrivilege SeIncreaseBasePriorityPrivilege SeIncreaseQuotaPrivilege SeLoadDriverPrivilege SeLockMemoryPrivilege SeManageVolumePrivilege SeProfileSingleProcessPrivilege SeRestorePrivilege SeSecurityPrivilege SeShutdownPrivilege SeSystemEnvironmentPrivilege SeSystemTimePrivilege SeTakeOwnershipPrivilege SeTcbPrivilege SeUndockPrivilege (client only)	SeAssignPrimaryTokenPrivilege SeAuditPrivilege SeChangeNotifyPrivilege SeCreateGlobalPrivilege SeImpersonatePrivilege SeIncreaseQuotaPrivilege SeShutdownPrivilege SeUndockPrivilege (client only) Privileges assigned to the Everyone, Authenticated Users, and Users groups	SeAssignPrimaryTokenPrivilege SeAuditPrivilege SeChangeNotifyPrivilege SeCreateGlobalPrivilege SeImpersonatePrivilege SeIncreaseQuotaPrivilege SeShutdownPrivilege SeUndockPrivilege (client only) Privileges assigned to the Everyone, Authenticated Users, and Users groups

The Network Service Account

The network service account is intended for use by services that want to authenticate to other machines on the network using the computer account, as does the local system account, but do not have the need for membership in the Administrators group or the use of many of the privileges assigned to the local system account. Because the network service account does not belong to the Administrators group, services running in the network service account by default have access to far fewer registry keys and file system folders and files than the services running in the local system account. Further, the assignment of few privileges limits the scope of a compromised network service process. For example, a process running in the network service account cannot load a device driver or open arbitrary processes.

Another difference between the network service and local system accounts is that processes running in the network service account use the network service account's profile. The registry component of the network service profile loads under HKU\S-1-5-20, and the files and directories that make up the component reside in %SystemRoot%\ServiceProfiles\NetworkService.

A service that runs in the network service account is the DNS client, which is responsible for resolving DNS names and for locating domain controllers.

The Local Service Account

The local service account is virtually identical to the network service account with the important difference that it can access only network resources that allow anonymous access. Table 4-9 shows that the network service account has the same privileges as the local service account, and Table 4-8 shows that it belongs to the same groups with the exception that it belongs to the Network Service group instead of the Local Service group. The profile used by processes running in the local service loads into HKU\S-1-5-19 and is stored in %SystemRoot%\ServiceProfiles\LocalService.

Examples of services that run in the local service account include the Remote Registry Service, which allows remote access to the local system's registry, and the LmHosts service, which performs NetBIOS name resolution.

Running Services in Alternate Accounts

Because of the restrictions just outlined, some services need to run with the security credentials of a user account. You can configure a service to run in an alternate account when the service is created or by specifying an account and password that the service should run under with the Windows Services MMC snap-in. In the Services snap-in, right-click on a service and select Properties, click on the Log On tab, and select the This Account option, as shown in Figure 4-7.

Running with Least Privilege

Services typically are subject to an all-or-nothing model, meaning that all privileges available to the account the service process is running under are available to a service running in the process that might require only a subset of those privileges. To better conform to the principle of least privilege, in which Windows assigns services only the privileges they require, developers can specify the privileges their service requires, and the SCM creates a security token that contains only those privileges.

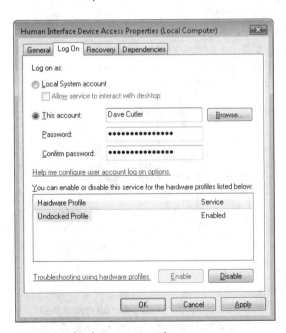

FIGURE 4-7 Service account settings

Note The privileges a service specifies must be a subset of those that are available to the service account in which it runs.

Service developers use the *ChangeServiceConfig2* API to indicate the list of privileges they desire. The API saves that information in the registry under the Parameters key for the service. When the service starts, the SCM reads the key and adds those privileges to the token of the process in which the service is running.

If there is a RequiredPrivileges value and the service is a stand-alone service (running as a dedicated process), the SCM creates a token containing only the privileges that the service needs. For services running as part of a multiservice service process (as are most services that are part of Windows) and specifying required privileges, the SCM computes the union of those privileges and combines them for the service-hosting process' token. In other words, only the privileges not specified by any of the services that are part of that service group will be removed. In the case in which the registry value does not exist, the SCM has no choice but to assume that the service is either incompatible with least privileges or requires all privileges in order to function. In this case, the full token is created, containing all privileges, and no additional security is offered by this model. To strip almost all privileges, services can specify only the Change Notify privilege.

 EXPERIMENT: Viewing Privileges Required by Services

You can look at the privileges a service requires with the Service Control utility, Sc.exe, and the qprivs option. Additionally, Process Explorer can show you information about the security token of any service process on the system, so you can compare the information returned by Sc.exe with the privileges part of the token. The following steps show you how to do this for some of the best locked-down services on the system.

1. Use Sc.exe to take a look at the required privileges specified by Dhcp by typing the following into a command prompt:

   sc qprivs dhcp

   You should see two privileges being requested: the SeCreateGlobalPrivilege and the SeChangeNotifyPrivilege.

2. Run Process Explorer, and take a look at the process list.

   You should see a couple of Svchost.exe processes that are hosting the services on your machine. Process Explorer highlights these in pink.

3. Now locate the service hosting process in which the Dhcp service is running. It should be running alongside other services that are part of the LocalServiceNetworkRestricted service group, such as the Audiosrv service and Eventlog service. You can do this by hovering the mouse over each Svchost process and reading the tooltip, which contains the names of the services running inside the service host.

4. Once you've found the process, double-click to open the Properties dialog box and select the Security tab.

Note that although the service is running as part of the local service account, the list of privileges Windows assigned to it is much shorter than the list available to the local service account shown in Table 4-9.

Because for a service-hosting process the privileges part of the token is the union of the privileges requested by all the services running inside it, this must mean that services such as Audiosrv and Eventlog have not requested privileges other than the ones shown by Process Explorer. You can verify this by running the Sc.exe tool on those other services as well.

Service Isolation

Although restricting the privileges that a service has access to helps lessen the ability of a compromised service process to compromise other processes, it does nothing to isolate the service from resources that the account in which it is running has access to under normal conditions. As mentioned earlier, the local system account has complete access to critical system files, registry keys, and other securable objects on the system because the access control lists (ACLs) grant permissions to that account.

At times, access to some of these resources is indeed critical to a service's operation, while other objects should be secured from the service. Previously, to avoid running in the local system account to obtain access to required resources, a service would be run under a standard user account and ACLs would be added on the system objects, which greatly increased the risk of malicious code attacking the system. Another solution was to create dedicated service accounts and set specific ACLs for each account (associated to a service), but this approach easily became an administrative hassle.

Windows now combines these two approaches into a much more manageable solution: it allows services to run in a nonprivileged account but still have access to specific privileged resources without lowering the security of those objects. In a manner similar to the second pre–Windows Vista solution, the ACLs on an object can now set permissions directly for a service, but not by requiring a dedicated account. Instead, the SCM generates a service SID to represent a service, and this SID can be used to set permissions on resources such as registry keys and files. Service SIDs are implemented in the group SIDs part of the token for any process hosting a service. They are generated by the SCM during system startup for each service that has requested one via the *ChangeServiceConfig2* API. In the case of service-hosting processes (a process that contains more than one service), the process' token will contain the service SIDs of all services that are part of the service group associated with the process, including services that are not started because there is no way to add new SIDs after a token has been created.

The usefulness of having a SID for each service extends beyond the mere ability to add ACL entries and permissions for various objects on the system as a way to have fine-grained control over their access. Our discussion initially covered the case in which certain objects on the system, accessible by a given account, must be protected from a service running within that same account. As we've described to this point, service SIDs prevent that problem only by requiring that Deny entries associated with the service SID be placed on every object that needs to be secured, a clearly unmanageable approach.

To avoid requiring Deny access control entries (ACEs) as a way to prevent services from having access to resources that the user account in which they run does have access, there are two types of service SIDs: the restricted service SID (SERVICE_SID_TYPE_RESTRICTED) and the unrestricted service SID (SERVICE_SID_TYPE_UNRESTRICTED), the latter being the default and the case we've looked at until now.

Unrestricted service SIDs are created as enabled-by-default, group owner SIDs, and the process token is also given a new ACE providing full permission to the service logon SID, which allows the service to continue communicating with the SCM. (A primary use of this would be to enable or disable service SIDs inside the process during service startup or shutdown.)

A restricted service SID, on the other hand, turns the service-hosting process' token into a write-restricted token (see Chapter 6 for more information on tokens), which means that only objects granting explicit write access to the service SID will be writable by the service, regardless of the account it's running as. Because of this, all services running inside that process (part of the same service group) must have the restricted SID type; otherwise, services with the restricted SID type will fail to start. Once the token becomes write-restricted, three more SIDs are added for compatibility reasons:

- The world SID is added to allow write access to objects that are normally accessible by anyone anyway, most importantly certain DLLs in the load path.

- The service logon SID is added to allow the service to communicate with the SCM.

- The write-restricted SID is added to allow objects to explicitly allow any write-restricted service write access to them. For example, Event Tracing for Windows (ETW) uses this SID on its objects to allow any write-restricted service to generate events.

Figure 4-8 shows an example of a service-hosting process containing services that have been marked as having restricted service SIDs. For example, the Base Filtering Engine (BFE), which is responsible for applying Windows Firewall filtering rules, is part of this service because these rules are stored in registry keys that must be protected from malicious write access should a service be compromised. (This could allow a service exploit to disable the outgoing traffic firewall rules, enabling bidirectional communication with an attacker, for example.)

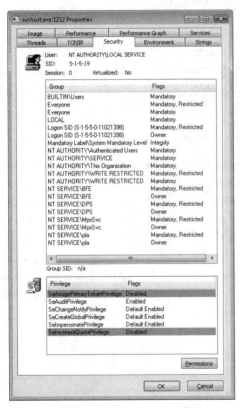

FIGURE 4-8 Service with restricted service SIDs

By blocking write access to objects that would otherwise be writable by the service (through inheriting the permissions of the account it is running as), restricted service SIDs solve the other side of the problem we initially presented because users do not need to do anything to prevent a service running in a privileged account from having write access to critical system files, registry keys, or other objects, limiting the attack exposure of any such service that might have been compromised.

Windows also allows for firewall rules that reference service SIDs linked to one of the three behaviors described in Table 4-10.

TABLE 4-10 Network Restriction Rules

Scenario	Example	Restrictions
Network access blocked	The shell hardware detection service (ShellHWDetection).	All network communications are blocked (both incoming and outgoing).
Network access statically port-restricted	The RPC service (Rpcss) operates on port 135 (TCP and UDP).	Network communications are restricted to specific TCP or UDP ports.
Network access dynamically port-restricted	The DNS service (Dns) listens on variable ports (UDP).	Network communications are restricted to configurable TCP or UDP ports.

Interactive Services and Session 0 Isolation

One restriction for services running under the local system, local service, and network service accounts that has always been present in Windows is that these services could not display (without using a special flag on the *MessageBox* function, discussed in a moment) dialog boxes or windows on the interactive user's desktop. This limitation wasn't the direct result of running under these accounts but rather a consequence of the way the Windows subsystem assigns service processes to window stations. This restriction is further enhanced by the use of sessions, in a model called Session Zero Isolation, a result of which is that services cannot directly interact with a user's desktop.

The Windows subsystem associates every Windows process with a window station. A window station contains desktops, and desktops contain windows. Only one window station can be visible on a console and receive user mouse and keyboard input. In a Terminal Services environment, one window station per session is visible, but services all run as part of the console session. Windows names the visible window station WinSta0, and all interactive processes access WinSta0.

Unless otherwise directed, the Windows subsystem associates services running in the local system account with a nonvisible window station named Service-0x0-3e7$ that all noninteractive services share. The number in the name, 3e7, represents the logon session identifier that the Local Security Authority process (LSASS) assigns to the logon session the SCM uses for noninteractive services running in the local system account.

Services configured to run under a user account (that is, not the local system account) are run in a different nonvisible window station named with the LSASS logon identifier assigned for the service's logon session. Figure 4-9 shows a sample display from the Sysinternals WinObj tool, viewing the object manager directory in which Windows places window station objects. Visible are the interactive window station (WinSta0) and the noninteractive system service window station (Service-0x0-3e7$).

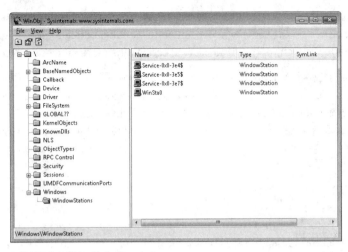

FIGURE 4-9 List of window stations

Regardless of whether services are running in a user account, the local system account, or the local or network service accounts, services that aren't running on the visible window station can't receive input from a user or display windows on the console. In fact, if a service were to pop up a normal dialog box on the window station, the service would appear hung because no user would be able to see the dialog box, which of course would prevent the user from providing keyboard or mouse input to dismiss it and allow the service to continue executing.

> **Note** In the past, it was possible to use the special MB_SERVICE_NOTIFICATION or MB_DEFAULT_DESKTOP_ONLY flags with the *MessageBox* API to display messages on the interactive window station even if the service was marked as noninteractive. Because of session isolation, any service using this flag will receive an immediate IDOK return value, and the message box will never be displayed.

In rare cases, a service can have a valid reason to interact with the user via dialog boxes or windows. To configure a service with the right to interact with the user, the SERVICE_INTERACTIVE_PROCESS modifier must be present in the service's registry key's Type parameter. (Note that services configured to run under a user account can't be marked as interactive.) When the SCM starts a service marked as interactive, it launches the service's process in the local system account's security context but connects the service with WinSta0 instead of the noninteractive service window station.

Were user processes to run in the same session as services, this connection to WinSta0 would allow the service to display dialog boxes and windows on the console and enable those windows to respond to user input because they would share the window station with the interactive services. However, only processes owned by the system and Windows services run in session 0; all other logon sessions, including those of console users, run in different sessions. Any window displayed by processes in session 0 is therefore not visible to the user.

This additional boundary helps prevent shatter attacks, whereby a less privileged application sends window messages to a window visible on the same window station to exploit a bug in a more privileged process that owns the window, which permits it to execute code in the more privileged process.

To remain compatible with services that depend on user input, Windows includes a service that notifies users when a service has displayed a window. The Interactive Services Detection (UI0Detect) service looks for visible windows on the main desktop of the WinSta0 window station of session 0 and displays a notification dialog box on the console user's desktop, allowing the user to switch to session 0 and view the service's UI. (This is akin to connecting to a local Terminal Services session or switching users.)

> **Note** The Interactive Services Detection mechanism is purely for application compatibility, and developers are strongly recommended to move away from interactive services and use a secondary, nonprivileged helper application to communicate visually with the user. Local RPC or COM can be used between this helper application and the service for configuration purposes after UI input has been received.

The dialog box, an example of which is shown in Figure 4-10, includes the process name, the time when the UI message was displayed, and the title of the window being displayed. Once the user connects to session 0, a similar dialog box provides a portal back to the user's session. In the figure, the service displaying a window is Microsoft Paint, which was explicitly started by the Sysinternals PsExec utility with options that caused PsExec to run Paint in session 0. You can try this yourself with the following command:

> *psexec –s –i 0 –d mspaint.exe*

This tells PsExec to run Microsoft Paint as a system process (–s) running on session 0 (–i 0), and to return immediately instead of waiting for the process to finish (–d).

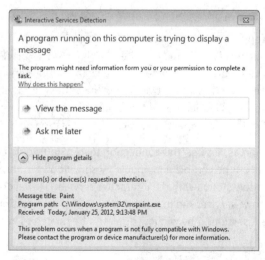

FIGURE 4-10 The Interactive Services Detection service at work

If you click View The Message, you can switch to the console for session 0 (and switch back again with a similar window on the console).

The Service Control Manager

The SCM's executable file is %SystemRoot%\System32\Services.exe, and like most service processes, it runs as a Windows console program. The Wininit process starts the SCM early during the system boot. (Refer to Chapter 13 in Part 2 for details on the boot process.) The SCM's startup function, *SvcCtrlMain*, orchestrates the launching of services that are configured for automatic startup.

SvcCtrlMain first creates a synchronization event named SvcctrlStartEvent_A3752DX that it initializes as nonsignaled. Only after the SCM completes steps necessary to prepare it to receive commands from SCPs does the SCM set the event to a signaled state. The function that an SCP uses to establish a dialog with the SCM is *OpenSCManager*. *OpenSCManager* prevents an SCP from trying to contact the SCM before the SCM has initialized by waiting for SvcctrlStartEvent_A3752DX to become signaled.

Next, *SvcCtrlMain* gets down to business and calls *ScGenerateServiceDB*, the function that builds the SCM's internal service database. *ScGenerateServiceDB* reads and stores the contents of HKLM\SYSTEM\CurrentControlSet\Control\ServiceGroupOrder\List, a REG_MULTI_SZ value that lists the names and order of the defined service groups. A service's registry key contains an optional Group value if that service or device driver needs to control its startup ordering with respect to services from other groups. For example, the Windows networking stack is built from the bottom up, so networking services must specify Group values that place them later in the startup sequence than networking device drivers. The SCM internally creates a group list that preserves the ordering of the groups it reads from the registry. Groups include (but are not limited to) NDIS, TDI, Primary Disk, Keyboard Port, and Keyboard Class. Add-on and third-party applications can even define their own groups and add them to the list. Microsoft Transaction Server, for example, adds a group named MS Transactions.

ScGenerateServiceDB then scans the contents of HKLM\SYSTEM\CurrentControlSet\Services, creating an entry in the service database for each key it encounters. A database entry includes all the service-related parameters defined for a service as well as fields that track the service's status. The SCM adds entries for device drivers as well as for services because the SCM starts services and drivers marked as auto-start and detects startup failures for drivers marked boot-start and system-start. It also provides a means for applications to query the status of drivers. The I/O manager loads drivers marked boot-start and system-start before any user-mode processes execute, and therefore any drivers having these start types load before the SCM starts.

ScGenerateServiceDB reads a service's Group value to determine its membership in a group and associates this value with the group's entry in the group list created earlier. The function also reads and records in the database the service's group and service dependencies by querying its DependOnGroup and DependOnService registry values. Figure 4-11 shows how the SCM organizes the service entry and group order lists. Notice that the service list is alphabetically sorted. The reason this list is sorted alphabetically is that the SCM creates the list from the Services registry key, and Windows stores registry keys alphabetically.

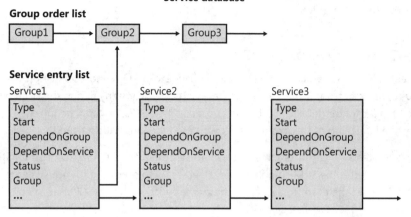

FIGURE 4-11 Organization of a service database

During service startup, the SCM calls on LSASS (for example, to log on a service in a non-local system account), so the SCM waits for LSASS to signal the LSA_RPC_SERVER_ACTIVE synchronization event, which it does when it finishes initializing. Wininit also starts the LSASS process, so the initialization of LSASS is concurrent with that of the SCM, and the order in which LSASS and the SCM complete initialization can vary. Then *SvcCtrlMain* calls *ScGetBootAndSystemDriverState* to scan the service database looking for boot-start and system-start device driver entries.

ScGetBootAndSystemDriverState determines whether or not a driver successfully started by looking up its name in the object manager namespace directory named \Driver. When a device driver successfully loads, the I/O manager inserts the driver's object in the namespace under this directory, so if its name isn't present, it hasn't loaded. Figure 4-12 shows WinObj displaying the contents of the Driver directory. *SvcCtrlMain* notes the names of drivers that haven't started and that are part of the current profile in a list named ScFailedDrivers.

Before starting the auto-start services, the SCM performs a few more steps. It creates its remote procedure call (RPC) named pipe, which is named \Pipe\Ntsvcs, and then RPC launches a thread to listen on the pipe for incoming messages from SCPs. The SCM then signals its initialization-complete event, SvcctrlStartEvent_A3752DX. Registering a console application shutdown event handler and registering with the Windows subsystem process via *RegisterServiceProcess* prepares the SCM for system shutdown.

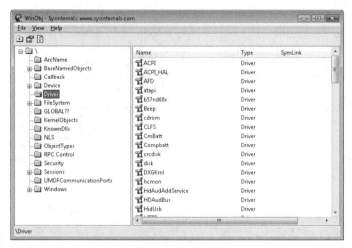

FIGURE 4-12 List of driver objects

> ## Network Drive Letters
>
> In addition to its role as an interface to services, the SCM has another totally unrelated responsibility: it notifies GUI applications in a system whenever the system creates or deletes a network drive-letter connection. The SCM waits for the Multiple Provider Router (MPR) to signal a named event, \BaseNamedObjects\ScNetDrvMsg, which MPR signals whenever an application assigns a drive letter to a remote network share or deletes a remote-share drive-letter assignment. (See Chapter 7, "Networking," for more information on MPR.) When MPR signals the event, the SCM calls the GetDriveType Windows function to query the list of connected network drive letters. If the list changes across the event signal, the SCM sends a Windows broadcast message of type WM_DEVICECHANGE. The SCM uses either DBT_DEVICEREMOVECOMPLETE or DBT_DEVICEARRIVAL as the message's subtype. This message is primarily intended for Windows Explorer so that it can update any open Computer windows to show the presence or absence of a network drive letter.

Service Startup

SvcCtrlMain invokes the SCM function *ScAutoStartServices* to start all services that have a Start value designating auto-start (except delayed auto-start services). *ScAutoStartServices* also starts auto-start device drivers. To avoid confusion, you should assume that the term services means services and drivers unless indicated otherwise. The algorithm in *ScAutoStartServices* for starting services in the correct order proceeds in phases, whereby a phase corresponds to a group and phases proceed in the sequence defined by the group ordering stored in the HKLM\SYSTEM\CurrentControlSet\Control\ServiceGroupOrder\List registry value. The List value, shown in Figure 4-13, includes the names of groups in the order that the SCM should start them. Thus, assigning a service to a group has no effect other than to fine-tune its startup with respect to other services belonging to different groups.

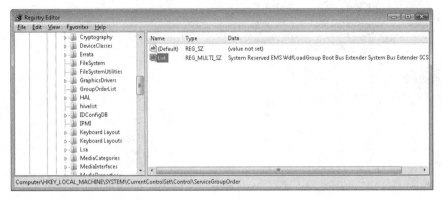

FIGURE 4-13 ServiceGroupOrder registry key

When a phase starts, *ScAutoStartServices* marks all the service entries belonging to the phase's group for startup. Then *ScAutoStartServices* loops through the marked services seeing whether it can start each one. Part of this check includes seeing whether the service is marked as delayed auto-start, which causes the SCM to start it at a later stage. (Delayed auto-start services must also be ungrouped.) Another part of the check it makes consists of determining whether the service has a dependency on another group, as specified by the existence of the DependOnGroup value in the service's registry key. If a dependency exists, the group on which the service is dependent must have already initialized, and at least one service of that group must have successfully started. If the service depends on a group that starts later than the service's group in the group startup sequence, the SCM notes a "circular dependency" error for the service. If *ScAutoStartServices* is considering a Windows service or an auto-start device driver, it next checks to see whether the service depends on one or more other services, and if so, if those services have already started. Service dependencies are indicated with the DependOnService registry value in a service's registry key. If a service depends on other services that belong to groups that come later in the ServiceGroupOrder\List, the SCM also generates a "circular dependency" error and doesn't start the service. If the service depends on any services from the same group that haven't yet started, the service is skipped.

When the dependencies of a service have been satisfied, *ScAutoStartServices* makes a final check to see whether the service is part of the current boot configuration before starting the service. When the system is booted in safe mode, the SCM ensures that the service is either identified by name or by group in the appropriate safe boot registry key. There are two safe boot keys, Minimal and Network, under HKLM\SYSTEM\CurrentControlSet\Control\SafeBoot, and the one that the SCM checks depends on what safe mode the user booted. If the user chose Safe Mode or Safe Mode With Command Prompt at the special boot menu (which you can access by pressing F8 early in the boot process), the SCM references the Minimal key; if the user chose Safe Mode With Networking, the SCM refers to Network. The existence of a string value named Option under the SafeBoot key indicates not only that the system booted in safe mode but also the type of safe mode the user selected. For more information about safe boots, see the section "Safe Mode" in Chapter 13 in Part 2.

Once the SCM decides to start a service, it calls *ScStartService*, which takes different steps for services than for device drivers. When *ScStartService* starts a Windows service, it first determines the name of the file that runs the service's process by reading the ImagePath value from the service's registry key. It then examines the service's Type value, and if that value is SERVICE_WINDOWS_SHARE_PROCESS (0x20), the SCM ensures that the process the service runs in, if already started, is logged on using the same account as specified for the service being started. (This is to ensure that the service is not configured with the wrong account, such as a LocalService account, but with an image path pointing to a running Svchost, such as netsvcs, which runs as LocalSystem.) A service's ObjectName registry value stores the user account in which the service should run. A service with no ObjectName or an ObjectName of LocalSystem runs in the local system account.

The SCM verifies that the service's process hasn't already been started in a different account by checking to see whether the service's ImagePath value has an entry in an internal SCM database called the image database. If the image database doesn't have an entry for the ImagePath value, the SCM creates one. When the SCM creates a new entry, it stores the logon account name used for the service and the data from the service's ImagePath value. The SCM requires services to have an ImagePath value. If a service doesn't have an ImagePath value, the SCM reports an error stating that it couldn't find the service's path and isn't able to start the service. If the SCM locates an existing image database entry with matching ImagePath data, the SCM ensures that the user account information for the service it's starting is the same as the information stored in the database entry—a process can be logged on as only one account, so the SCM reports an error when a service specifies a different account name than another service that has already started in the same process.

The SCM calls *ScLogonAndStartImage* to log on a service if the service's configuration specifies and to start the service's process. The SCM logs on services that don't run in the System account by calling the LSASS function *LogonUserEx*. *LogonUserEx* normally requires a password, but the SCM indicates to LSASS that the password is stored as a service's LSASS "secret" under the key HKLM\SECURITY\Policy \Secrets in the registry. (Keep in mind that the contents of SECURITY aren't typically visible because its default security settings permit access only from the System account.) When the SCM calls *LogonUserEx*, it specifies a service logon as the logon type, so LSASS looks up the password in the Secrets subkey that has a name in the form _SC_<service name>.

The SCM directs LSASS to store a logon password as a secret using the *LsaStorePrivateData* function when an SCP configures a service's logon information. When a logon is successful, *LogonUserEx* returns a handle to an access token to the caller. Windows uses access tokens to represent a user's security context, and the SCM later associates the access token with the process that implements the service.

After a successful logon, the SCM loads the account's profile information, if it's not already loaded, by calling the UserEnv DLL's (%SystemRoot%\System32\Userenv.dll) *LoadUserProfile* function. The value HKLM\SOFTWARE\Microsoft\Windows NT\CurrentVersion\ProfileList\<user profile key>\ ProfileImagePath contains the location on disk of a registry hive that *LoadUserProfile* loads into the registry, making the information in the hive the HKEY_CURRENT_USER key for the service.

An interactive service must open the WinSta0 window station, but before *ScLogonAndStartImage* allows an interactive service to access WinSta0 it checks to see whether the value HKLM\SYSTEM \CurrentControlSet\Control\Windows\NoInteractiveServices is set. Administrators set this value to prevent services marked as interactive from displaying windows on the console. This option is desirable in unattended server environments in which no user is present to respond to the Session 0 UI Discovery notification from interactive services.

As its next step, *ScLogonAndStartImage* proceeds to launch the service's process, if the process hasn't already been started (for another service, for example). The SCM starts the process in a suspended state with the *CreateProcessAsUser* Windows function. The SCM next creates a named pipe through which it communicates with the service process, and it assigns the pipe the name \Pipe\Net\NtControlPipeX, where X is a number that increments each time the SCM creates a pipe. The SCM resumes the service process via the ResumeThread function and waits for the service to connect to its SCM pipe. If it exists, the registry value HKLM\SYSTEM\CurrentControlSet\Control \ServicesPipeTimeout determines the length of time that the SCM waits for a service to call *StartServiceCtrlDispatcher* and connect before it gives up, terminates the process, and concludes that the service failed to start. If ServicesPipeTimeout doesn't exist, the SCM uses a default timeout of 30 seconds. The SCM uses the same timeout value for all its service communications.

When a service connects to the SCM through the pipe, the SCM sends the service a start command. If the service fails to respond positively to the start command within the timeout period, the SCM gives up and moves on to start the next service. When a service doesn't respond to a start request, the SCM doesn't terminate the process, as it does when a service doesn't call *StartServiceCtrlDispatcher* within the timeout; instead, it notes an error in the system Event Log that indicates the service failed to start in a timely manner.

If the service the SCM starts with a call to *ScStartService* has a Type registry value of SERVICE_ KERNEL_DRIVER or SERVICE_FILE_SYSTEM_DRIVER, the service is really a device driver, so *ScStartService* calls *ScLoadDeviceDriver* to load the driver. *ScLoadDeviceDriver* enables the load driver security privilege for the SCM process and then invokes the kernel service *NtLoadDriver*, passing in the data in the ImagePath value of the driver's registry key. Unlike services, drivers don't need to specify an ImagePath value, and if the value is absent, the SCM builds an image path by appending the driver's name to the string %SystemRoot%\System32\Drivers\.

ScAutoStartServices continues looping through the services belonging to a group until all the services have either started or generated dependency errors. This looping is the SCM's way of automatically ordering services within a group according to their DependOnService dependencies. The SCM will start the services that other services depend on in earlier loops, skipping the dependent services until subsequent loops. Note that the SCM ignores Tag values for Windows services, which you might come across in subkeys under the HKLM\SYSTEM\CurrentControlSet\Services key; the I/O manager honors Tag values to order device driver startup within a group for boot-start and system-start drivers. Once the SCM completes phases for all the groups listed in the ServiceGroupOrder\List value, it performs a phase for services belonging to groups not listed in the value and then executes a final phase for services without a group.

After handling auto-start services, the SCM calls *ScInitDelayStart*, which queues a delayed work item associated with a worker thread responsible for processing all the services that *ScAutoStartServices* skipped because they were marked delayed auto-start. This worker thread will execute after the delay. The default delay is 120 seconds, but it can be overridden by the creating an AutoStartDelay value in HKLM\SYSTEM\CurrentControlSet\Control. The SCM performs the same actions as those used during startup of nondelayed auto-start services.

Delayed Auto-Start Services

Delayed auto-start services enable Windows to cope with the growing number of services that are being started when a user logs on, bogging down the boot-up process and increasing the time before a user is able to get responsiveness from the desktop. The design of auto-start services was primarily intended for services required early in the boot process because other services depend on them, a good example being the RPC service, on which all other services depend. The other use was to allow unattended startup of a service, such as the Windows Update service. Because many auto-start services fall in this second category, marking them as delayed auto-start allows critical services to start faster and for the user's desktop to be ready sooner when a user logs on immediately after booting. Additionally, these services run in background mode, which lowers their thread, I/O, and memory priority. Configuring a service for delayed auto-start requires calling the ChangeServiceConfig2 API. You can check the state of the flag for a service by using the qc bits option of sc.exe instead.

Note If a nondelayed auto-start service has a delayed auto-start service as one of its dependencies, the delayed auto-start flag will be ignored and the service will be started immediately in order to satisfy the dependency.

When it's finished starting all auto-start services and drivers, as well as setting up the delayed auto-start work item, the SCM signals the event \BaseNamedObjects\SC_AutoStartComplete. This event is used by the Windows Setup program to gauge startup progress during installation.

Startup Errors

If a driver or a service reports an error in response to the SCM's startup command, the ErrorControl value of the service's registry key determines how the SCM reacts. If the ErrorControl value is SERVICE_ERROR_IGNORE (0) or the ErrorControl value isn't specified, the SCM simply ignores the error and continues processing service startups. If the ErrorControl value is SERVICE_ERROR_NORMAL (1), the SCM writes an event to the system Event Log that says, "The <service name> service failed to start due to the following error:". The SCM includes the textual representation of the Windows error code that the service returned to the SCM as the reason for the startup failure in the Event Log record. Figure 4-14 shows the Event Log entry that reports a service startup error.

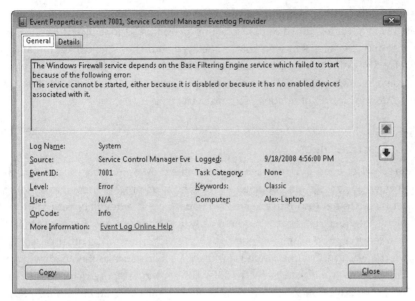

FIGURE 4-14 Service startup failure Event Log entry

If a service with an ErrorControl value of SERVICE_ERROR_SEVERE (2) or SERVICE_ERROR_CRITICAL (3) reports a startup error, the SCM logs a record to the Event Log and then calls the internal function ScRevertToLastKnownGood. This function switches the system's registry configuration to a version, named last known good, with which the system last booted successfully. Then it restarts the system using the NtShutdownSystem system service, which is implemented in the executive. If the system is already booting with the last known good configuration, the system just reboots.

Accepting the Boot and Last Known Good

Besides starting services, the system charges the SCM with determining when the system's registry configuration, HKLM\SYSTEM\CurrentControlSet, should be saved as the last known good control set. The CurrentControlSet key contains the Services key as a subkey, so CurrentControlSet includes the registry representation of the SCM database. It also contains the Control key, which stores many kernel-mode and user-mode subsystem configuration settings. By default, a successful boot consists of a successful startup of auto-start services and a successful user logon. A boot fails if the system halts because a device driver crashes the system during the boot or if an auto-start service with an ErrorControl value of SERVICE_ERROR_SEVERE or SERVICE_ERROR_CRITICAL reports a startup error.

The SCM obviously knows when it has completed a successful startup of the auto-start services, but Winlogon (%SystemRoot%\System32\Winlogon.exe) must notify it when there is a successful logon. Winlogon invokes the NotifyBootConfigStatus function when a user logs on, and

NotifyBootConfigStatus sends a message to the SCM. Following the successful start of the auto-start services or the receipt of the message from *NotifyBootConfigStatus* (whichever comes last), the SCM calls the system function *NtInitializeRegistry* to save the current registry startup configuration.

Third-party software developers can supersede Winlogon's definition of a successful logon with their own definition. For example, a system running Microsoft SQL Server might not consider a boot successful until after SQL Server is able to accept and process transactions. Developers impose their definition of a successful boot by writing a boot-verification program and installing the program by pointing to its location on disk with the value stored in the registry key HKLM\SYSTEM \CurrentControlSet\Control\BootVerificationProgram. In addition, a boot-verification program's installation must disable Winlogon's call to *NotifyBootConfigStatus* by setting HKLM\SOFTWARE \Microsoft\Windows NT\CurrentVersion\Winlogon\ReportBootOk to 0. When a boot-verification program is installed, the SCM launches it after finishing auto-start services and waits for the program's call to *NotifyBootConfigStatus* before saving the last known good control set.

Windows maintains several copies of CurrentControlSet, and CurrentControlSet is really a symbolic registry link that points to one of the copies. The control sets have names in the form HKLM\SYSTEM \ControlSetnnn, where nnn is a number such as 001 or 002. The HKLM\SYSTEM\Select key contains values that identify the role of each control set. For example, if CurrentControlSet points to ControlSet001, the Current value under Select has a value of 1. The LastKnownGood value under Select contains the number of the last known good control set, which is the control set last used to boot successfully. Another value that might be on your system under the Select key is Failed, which points to the last control set for which the boot was deemed unsuccessful and aborted in favor of an attempt at booting with the last known good control set. Figure 4-15 displays a system's control sets and Select values.

NtInitializeRegistry takes the contents of the last known good control set and synchronizes it with that of the CurrentControlSet key's tree. If this was the system's first successful boot, the last known good won't exist and the system will create a new control set for it. If the last known good tree exists, the system simply updates it with differences between it and CurrentControlSet.

Last known good is helpful in situations in which a change to CurrentControlSet, such as the modification of a system performance-tuning value under HKLM\SYSTEM\Control or the addition of a service or device driver, causes the subsequent boot to fail. Users can press F8 early in the boot process to bring up a menu that lets them direct the boot to use the last known good control set, rolling the system's registry configuration back to the way it was the last time the system booted successfully. Chapter 13 in Part 2 describes in more detail the use of last known good and other recovery mechanisms for troubleshooting system startup problems.

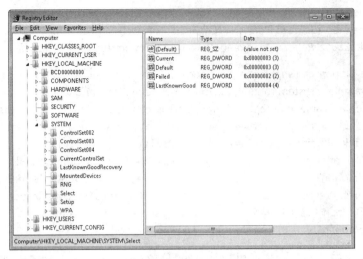

FIGURE 4-15 Control set selection key

Service Failures

A service can have optional *FailureActions* and *FailureCommand* values in its registry key that the SCM records during the service's startup. The SCM registers with the system so that the system signals the SCM when a service process exits. When a service process terminates unexpectedly, the SCM determines which services ran in the process and takes the recovery steps specified by their failure-related registry values. Additionally, services are not only limited to requesting failure actions during crashes or unexpected service termination, since other problems, such as a memory leak, could also result in service failure.

If a service enters the SERVICE_STOPPED state and the error code returned to the SCM is not ERROR_SUCCESS, the SCM will check whether the service has the *FailureActionsOnNonCrashFailures* flag set and perform the same recovery as if the service had crashed. To use this functionality, the service must be configured via the *ChangeServiceConfig2* API or the system administrator can use the Sc.exe utility with the *Failureflag* parameter to set *FailureActionsOnNonCrashFailures* to *1*. The default value being *0*, the SCM will continue to honor the same behavior as on earlier versions of Windows for all other services.

Actions that a service can configure for the SCM include restarting the service, running a program, and rebooting the computer. Furthermore, a service can specify the failure actions that take place the first time the service process fails, the second time, and subsequent times, and it can indicate a delay period that the SCM waits before restarting the service if the service asks to be restarted. The service failure action of the IIS Admin Service results in the SCM running the IISReset application, which performs cleanup work and then restarts the service. You can easily manage the recovery actions for a service using the Recovery tab of the service's Properties dialog box in the Services MMC snap-in, as shown in Figure 4-16.

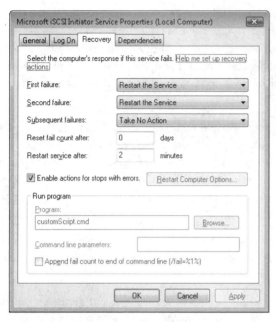

FIGURE 4-16 Service recovery options

Service Shutdown

When Winlogon calls the Windows *ExitWindowsEx* function, *ExitWindowsEx* sends a message to Csrss, the Windows subsystem process, to invoke Csrss's shutdown routine. Csrss loops through the active processes and notifies them that the system is shutting down. For every system process except the SCM, Csrss waits up to the number of seconds specified by HKU\.DEFAULT\Control Panel\Desktop \WaitToKillAppTimeout (which defaults to 20 seconds) for the process to exit before moving on to the next process. When Csrss encounters the SCM process, it also notifies it that the system is shutting down but employs a timeout specific to the SCM. Csrss recognizes the SCM using the process ID Csrss saved when the SCM registered with Csrss using the *RegisterServicesProcess* function during system initialization. The SCM's timeout differs from that of other processes because Csrss knows that the SCM communicates with services that need to perform cleanup when they shut down, so an administrator might need to tune only the SCM's timeout. The SCM's timeout value resides in the HKLM\SYSTEM\CurrentControlSet\Control\WaitToKillServiceTimeout registry value, and it defaults to 12 seconds.

The SCM's shutdown handler is responsible for sending shutdown notifications to all the services that requested shutdown notification when they initialized with the SCM. The SCM function *ScShutdownAllServices* loops through the SCM services database searching for services desiring shutdown notification and sends each one a shutdown command. For each service to which it sends a shutdown command, the SCM records the value of the service's wait hint, a value that a service also specifies when it registers with the SCM. The SCM keeps track of the largest wait hint it receives. After sending the shutdown messages, the SCM waits either until one of the services it notified of shutdown exits or until the time specified by the largest wait hint passes.

If the wait hint expires without a service exiting, the SCM determines whether one or more of the services it was waiting on to exit have sent a message to the SCM telling the SCM that the service is progressing in its shutdown process. If at least one service made progress, the SCM waits again for the duration of the wait hint. The SCM continues executing this wait loop until either all the services have exited or none of the services upon which it's waiting has notified it of progress within the wait hint timeout period.

While the SCM is busy telling services to shut down and waiting for them to exit, Csrss waits for the SCM to exit. If Csrss's wait ends without the SCM having exited (the WaitToKillServiceTimeout time expired), Csrss kills the SCM and continues the shutdown process. Thus, services that fail to shut down in a timely manner are killed. This logic lets the system shut down in the face of services that never complete a shutdown as a result of flawed design, but it also means that services that require more than 20 seconds will not complete their shutdown operations.

Additionally, because the shutdown order is not deterministic, services that might depend on other services to shut down first (called shutdown dependencies) have no way to report this to the SCM and might never have the chance to clean up either.

To address these needs, Windows implements preshutdown notifications and shutdown ordering to combat the problems caused by these two scenarios. Preshutdown notifications are sent, using the same mechanism as shutdown notifications, to services that have requested preshutdown notification via the *SetServiceStatus* API, and the SCM will wait for them to be acknowledged.

The idea behind these notifications is to flag services that might take a long time to clean up (such as database server services) and give them more time to complete their work. The SCM will send a progress query request and wait three minutes for a service to respond to this notification. If the service does not respond within this time, it will be killed during the shutdown procedure; otherwise, it can keep running as long as it needs, as long as it continues to respond to the SCM.

Services that participate in the preshutdown can also specify a shutdown order with respect to other preshutdown services. Services that depend on other services to shut down first (for example, the Group Policy service needs to wait for Windows Update to finish) can specify their shutdown dependencies in the HKLM\SYSTEM\CurrentControlSet\Control\PreshutdownOrder registry value.

Shared Service Processes

Running every service in its own process instead of having services share a process whenever possible wastes system resources. However, sharing processes means that if any of the services in the process has a bug that causes the process to exit, all the services in that process terminate.

Of the Windows built-in services, some run in their own process and some share a process with other services. For example, the LSASS process contains security-related services—such as the Security Accounts Manager (SamSs) service, the Net Logon (Netlogon) service, and the Crypto Next Generation (CNG) Key Isolation (KeyIso) service.

There is also a generic process named Service Host (SvcHost–%SystemRoot%\System32\Svchost.exe) to contain multiple services. Multiple instances of SvcHost can be running in different processes.

Services that run in SvcHost processes include Telephony (TapiSrv), Remote Procedure Call (RpcSs), and Remote Access Connection Manager (RasMan). Windows implements services that run in SvcHost as DLLs and includes an ImagePath definition of the form "%SystemRoot%\System32\svchost.exe –k netsvcs" in the service's registry key. The service's registry key must also have a registry value named ServiceDll under a Parameters subkey that points to the service's DLL file.

All services that share a common SvcHost process specify the same parameter ("–k netsvcs" in the example in the preceding paragraph) so that they have a single entry in the SCM's image database. When the SCM encounters the first service that has a SvcHost ImagePath with a particular parameter during service startup, it creates a new image database entry and launches a SvcHost process with the parameter. The new SvcHost process takes the parameter and looks for a value having the same name as the parameter under HKLM\SOFTWARE\Microsoft\Windows NT\CurrentVersion\Svchost. SvcHost reads the contents of the value, interpreting it as a list of service names, and notifies the SCM that it's hosting those services when SvcHost registers with the SCM.

When the SCM encounters a SvcHost service (by checking the service type value) during service startup with an ImagePath matching an entry it already has in the image database, it doesn't launch a second process but instead just sends a start command for the service to the SvcHost it already started for that ImagePath value. The existing SvcHost process reads the ServiceDll parameter in the service's registry key and loads the DLL into its process to start the service.

Table 4-11 lists all the default service groupings on Windows and some of the services that are registered for each of them.

TABLE 4-11 Major Service Groupings

Service Group	Services	Notes
LocalService	Network Store Interface, Windows Diagnostic Host, Windows Time, COM+ Event System, HTTP Auto-Proxy Service, Software Protection Platform UI Notification, Thread Order Service, LLDT Discovery, SSL, FDP Host, WebClient	Services that run in the local service account and make use of the network on various ports or have no network usage at all (and hence no restrictions).
LocalServiceAndNoImpersonation	UPnP and SSDP, Smart Card, TPM, Font Cache, Function Discovery, AppID, qWAVE, Windows Connect Now, Media Center Extender, Adaptive Brightness	Services that run in the local service account and make use of the network on a fixed set of ports. Services run with a write-restricted token.
LocalServiceNetworkRestricted	DHCP, Event Logger, Windows Audio, NetBIOS, Security Center, Parental Controls, HomeGroup Provider	Services that run in the local service account and make use of the network on a fixed set of ports.
LocalServiceNoNetwork	Diagnostic Policy Engine, Base Filtering Engine, Performance Logging and Alerts, Windows Firewall, WWAN AutoConfig	Services that run in the local service account but make no use of the network at all. Services run with a write-restricted token.

Service Group	Services	Notes
LocalSystemNetworkRestricted	DWM, WDI System Host, Network Connections, Distributed Link Tracking, Windows Audio Endpoint, Wired/WLAN AutoConfig, Pnp-X, HID Access, User-Mode Driver Framework Service, Superfetch, Portable Device Enumerator, HomeGroup Listener, Tablet Input, Program Compatibility, Offline Files	Services that run in the local system account and make use of the network on a fixed set of ports.
NetworkService	Cryptographic Services, DHCP Client, Terminal Services, WorkStation, Network Access Protection, NLA, DNS Client, Telephony, Windows Event Collector, WinRM	Services that run in the network service account and make use of the network on various ports (or have no enforced network restrictions).
NetworkServiceAndNoImpersonation	KTM for DTC	Services that run in the network service account and make use of the network on a fixed set of ports. Services run with a write-restricted token.
NetworkServiceNetworkRestricted	IPSec Policy Agent	Services that run in the network service account and make use of the network on a fixed set of ports.

EXPERIMENT: Viewing Services Running Inside Processes

The Process Explorer utility shows detailed information about the services running within processes. Run Process Explorer, and view the Services tab in the Process Properties dialog box for the following processes: Services.exe, Lsass.exe, and Svchost.exe. Several instances of SvcHost will be running on your system, and you can see the account in which each is running by adding the Username column to the Process Explorer display or by looking at the Username field on the Image tab of a process' Process Properties dialog box. The following screen shows the list of services running within a SvcHost executing in the local service account:

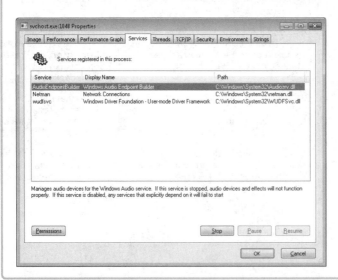

The information displayed includes the service's name, display name, and description, if it has one, which Process Explorer shows beneath the service list when you select a service. Additionally, the path of the DLL containing the service is shown. This information is useful for mapping thread start addresses (shown on the Threads tab) to their respective services, which can help in cases of service-related problems such as troubleshooting high CPU usage.

You can also use the tlist.exe tool from the Debugging Tools for Windows or Tasklist, which ships with Windows, to view the list of services running within processes from a command prompt. The syntax to see services with Tlist is:

```
tlist /s
```

The syntax for tasklist is:

```
tasklist /svc
```

Note that these utilities do not show service display names or descriptions, only service names.

Service Tags

One of the disadvantages of using service-hosting processes is that accounting for CPU time and usage, as well as for the usage of resources, by a specific service is much harder because each service is sharing the memory address space, handle table, and per-process CPU accounting numbers with the other services that are part of the same service group. Although there is always a thread inside the service-hosting process that belongs to a certain service, this association might not always be easy to make. For example, the service might be using worker threads to perform its operation, or perhaps the start address and stack of the thread do not reveal the service's DLL name, making it hard to figure out what kind of work a thread might exactly be doing and to which service it might belong.

Windows implements a service attribute called the service tag, which the SCM generates by calling *ScGenerateServiceTag* when a service is created or when the service database is generated during system boot. The attribute is simply an index identifying the service. The service tag is stored in the SubProcessTag field of the thread environment block (TEB) of each thread (see Chapter 5, "Processes and Threads," for more information on the TEB) and is propagated across all threads that a main service thread creates (except threads created indirectly by thread-pool APIs).

Although the service tag is kept internal to the SCM, several Windows utilities, like Netstat.exe (a utility you can use for displaying which programs have opened which ports on the network), use undocumented APIs to query service tags and map them to service names. Because the TCP/IP stack saves the service tag of the threads that create TCP/IP end points, when you run Netstat with the –b parameter, Netstat can report the service name for end points created by services. Another tool you can use to look at service tags is ScTagQuery from Winsider Seminars & Solutions Inc. (*www.winsiderss.com/tools/sctagquery/sctagquery.htm*). It can query the SCM for the mappings of every service tag and display them either systemwide or per-process. It can also show you to which services all the threads inside a service-hosting process belong. (This is conditional on those threads having a proper service tag associated with them.) This way, if you have a runaway service consuming lots of CPU time, you can identify the culprit service in case the thread start address or stack does not have an obvious service DLL associated with it.

Unified Background Process Manager

Various Windows components have traditionally been in charge of managing hosted or background tasks as the operating system has increased in complexity in features, from the Service Control Manager described earlier to the Task Scheduler, the DCOM Server Launcher, and the WMI Provider—all of which are also responsible for the execution of out-of-process, hosted code. Today, Windows implements a Unified Background Process Manager (UBPM), which handles (at least, for now) two of these mechanisms—the SCM and Task Scheduler—providing the ability for these components to access UBPM functionality.

UBPM is implemented in Services.exe, in the same location as the SCM, but as a separate library providing its own interface over RPC (similarly to how the Plug and Play Manager also runs in Services.exe but is a separate component). It provides access to that interface through a public export DLL, Ubpm.dll, which is exposed to third-party service developers through new Trigger APIs that have been added to the SCM. The SCM then loads a custom SCM Extension DLL (Scext.dll), which calls into Ubpm.dll. This layer of indirection is needed for MinWin support, where Scext.dll is not loaded and the SCM provides only minimal functionality. Figure 4-17 describes this architecture.

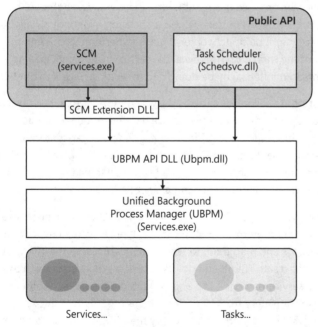

FIGURE 4-17 Overall UBPM architecture

Initialization

UBPM is initialized by the SCM when its UbpmInitialize export is called by *ScExtInitializeTerminateUbpm* in the SCM Extension DLL. As such, it is implemented as a DLL running within the context of the SCM, not as its own separate process.

UBPM first begins initialization by setting up its internal utility library. By leveraging many of the improvements in newer versions of Windows, UBPM uses a thread pool to process the many incoming events we will later see, which allows it to scale from having a single worker thread to having up to 1000 (based on a maximum processing of 10,000 consumers).

Next, UBPM initializes its internal tracing support, which can be configured in the HKLM\Software \Microsoft\Windows NT\CurrentVersion\Tracing\UBPM\Regular key using the Flags value. This is useful for debugging and monitoring the behavior of the UBPM using the WPP tracing mechanism described in the Windows Driver Kit.

Following that, the event manager is set up, which will be used by later components of UBPM to report internal event states. The event manager registers a TASKSCHED GUID on which ETW events can be consumed, and it logs its state to a TaskScheduler.log file.

The next step, critical to UBPM, is to initialize its own real-time ETW consumer, which is the central mechanism used by UBPM to perform its job, as almost all the data it receives comes over as ETW events. UBPM starts an ETW real-time session in secure mode, meaning that it will be the only process capable of receiving its events, and it names its session UBPM. It also enables the first built-in provider (owned by the kernel) in order to receive notifications related to time changes.

It then associates an event callback—UbpmpEventCallback—with incoming events and creates a consumer thread, UbpmpConsumeEvents, that waits for the SCM's event used to signify that auto-start events have completed (which was named previously). Once this happens, the consumer thread calls ProcessTrace, which calls into ETW and blocks the thread until the ETW trace is completed (normally, only once UBPM exists). The event callback, on the other hand, consumes each ETW event as it arrives and processes it according to the algorithm we'll see in the next section.

ETW automatically replays any events that were missed before ProcessTrace was called, which means that kernel events during the boot will all be incoming at once and processed appropriately. UBPM also waits on the SCM's auto-start event, which makes sure that when these events do come in, there will at least have been a couple of services that registered for them; otherwise, starting the trace too early will result in events with no registered consumers, which will cause them to be lost.

Finally, UBPM sets up a local RPC interface to TaskHost—the second component of UBPM, which we'll describe later—and it also sets up its own local RPC interface, which exposes the APIs that allows services to use UBPM functionality (such as registering trigger providers, generating triggers and notifications, and so forth). These APIs are implemented in the Ubpm.dll library and use RPC to communicate to the RPC interface in the UBPM code of Services.exe.

When UBPM exits, the opposite actions in the reverse order are performed to reset the system to its previous state.

UBPM API

UBPM enables the following mechanisms to be used by having services use the UBPM API:

- Registering and unregistering a trigger provider, as well as opening and closing a handle to one

- Generating a notification or a trigger

- Setting and querying the configuration of a trigger provider

- Sending a control command to a trigger provider

Provider Registration

Providers are registered through the SCM Extension DLL, which uses the *ScExtpRegisterProvider* function that is used by *ScExtGenerateNotification*. This opens a handle to UBPM and calls the *UbpmRegisterTriggerProvider* API. When a service registers a provider, it must define a unique name and GUID for the provider, as well as the necessary flags to define the provider (for example, by using the ETW provider flag). Additionally, providers can also have a friendly name as well as a description. Once registration is completed, the provider is inserted into UBPM's provider list, the total count of providers is incremented, and, if this is an ETW provider that's not being started with the disabled flag, the provider's GUID is enabled in the real-time ETW trace that UBPM activated upon initialization. A provider block is created containing all the provider's information that was captured from the registration.

Now that a provider is registered, the open and close API can be used to increment the reference count to the provider and return its provider block. Furthermore, if the provider was not registered in a disabled state, and this is the first reference to it, its GUID is enabled in the real-time ETW trace.

Similarly, unregistering a provider will disable its GUID and unlink it from the provider list, and as soon as all references are closed, the provider block will be deleted.

EXPERIMENT: Viewing UBPM Trigger Providers

You can use the Performance Monitor to see UBPM actively monitoring all the ETW providers that have registered with it. Follow these instructions to do so:

1. Open the Performance Monitor by clicking on the Start button, and then choosing Run.

2. Type perfmon, and click OK.

3. When Performance Monitor launches, expand Data Collector Sets on the left sidebar by clicking the arrow.

4. Choose Event Trace Sessions from the list, and then double click on the UBPM entry.

The following screen shot displays the UBPM trigger providers on the author's machine. You should see a similar display.

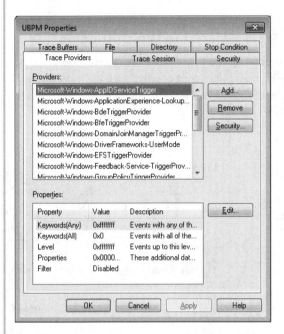

As you can see from the large list, dozens of providers are registered, each of them capable of generating individual events. For example, the BfeTriggerProvider handles Firewall events. In a later experiment, you will see a consumer of such an event.

Consumer Registration

Service consumer registration is initially exposed by the *ScExtRegisterTriggerConsumer* callback that the SCM Extension DLL provides. Its job is to receive all the SCM-formatted trigger information (which service developers provide according to the MSDN API documentation, "Service Trigger Events" available on MSDN) and convert that information into the raw data structures that UBPM internally uses. Once all the processing is finished, the SCM Extension DLL packages the trigger and associates it with two actions: UBPM Start Service and UBPM Stop Service.

The Scheduled Tasks service, which also leverages UBPM, provides similar functionality through an internal UBPM Singleton Class, which calls into Ubpm.dll. It allows its internal RegisterTask API to also register for trigger consumption, and it does similar processing of its input data, with the difference being that it uses the UBPM Start EXE action. Next, to actually perform the registration, both open a handle to UBPM, check if the consumer is already registered (changes to existing consumers are not allowed), and finally register the provider through the *UbpmRegisterTriggerConsumer* API.

Trigger consumer registration is done by *UbpmTriggerProviderRegister*, which validates the request, adds the provider's GUID into the list of providers, and toggles it to enable the ETW trace to now receive events about this provider as well.

EXPERIMENT: Viewing Which Services React to Which Triggers

Certain Windows services are already preconfigured to consume the appropriate triggers to prevent them from staying resident even when they're not needed, such as the Windows Time Service, the Tablet Input Service, and the Computer Browser service. The sc command lets you query information about a service's triggers with the qtriggerinfo option.

1. Open a command prompt.

2. Type the following to see the triggers for the Windows Time Service:

```
sc qtriggerinfo w32time

[SC] QueryServiceConfig2 SUCCESS
SERVICE_NAME: w32time

        START SERVICE
           DOMAIN JOINED STATUS          : 1ce20aba-9851-4421-9430-1ddeb766e809
[DOMAIN JOINED]
        STOP SERVICE
           DOMAIN JOINED STATUS          : ddaf516e-58c2-4866-9574-c3b615d42ea1
[NOT DOMAIN JOINED]
```

3. Now look at the Tablet Input Service:

```
sc qtriggerinfo tabletinputservice
[SC] QueryServiceConfig2 SUCCESS
SERVICE_NAME: tabletinputservice

        START SERVICE
           DEVICE INTERFACE ARRIVAL       : 4d1e55b2-f16f-11cf-88cb-001111000030
[INTERFACE CLASS GUID]
              DATA                        : HID_DEVICE_UP:000D_U:0001
              DATA                        : HID_DEVICE_UP:000D_U:0002
              DATA                        : HID_DEVICE_UP:000D_U:0003
              DATA                        : HID_DEVICE_UP:000D_U:0004
```

4. Finally, here is the Computer Browser Service:

```
sc qtriggerinfo browser
[SC] QueryServiceConfig2 SUCCESS

SERVICE_NAME: browser

        START SERVICE
           FIREWALL PORT EVENT           : b7569e07-8421-4ee0-ad10-86915afdad09
```

```
        [PORT OPEN]
                DATA                            : 139;TCP;System;
                DATA                            : 137;UDP;System;
                DATA                            : 138;UDP;System;
            STOP SERVICE
              FIREWALL PORT EVENT               : a144ed38-8e12-4de4-9d96-e64740b1a524
        [PORT CLOSE]
                DATA                            : 139;TCP;System;
                DATA                            : 137;UDP;System;
                DATA                            : 138;UDP;System;
```

In these three cases, note how the Windows Time Service is waiting for domain join/exit
in order to decide whether or not it should run, while the Tablet Input Service is waiting for a
device with the HID Class ID matching Tablet Device. Finally, the Computer Browser Service will
run only if the firewall policy allows access on ports 137, 138, and 139, which are SMB network
ports that the browser needs.

Task Host

TaskHost receives commands from UBPM living in the SCM. At initialization time, it opens the local
RPC interface that was created by UBPM during its initialization and loops forever, waiting for commands to come through the channel. Four commands are currently supported, which are sent over
the *TaskHostSendResponseReceiveCommand* RPC API:

- Stopping the host

- Starting a task

- Stopping a task

- Terminating a task

Additionally, hosted tasks are supplied with a *TaskHostReportTaskStatus* RPC API, which enables
them to notify UBPM of their current execution state whenever they call *UbpmReportTaskStatus*.

All task-based commands are actually internally implemented by a generic COM Task library, and
they essentially result in the creation and destruction of COM components.

Service Control Programs

Service control programs are standard Windows applications that use SCM service management
functions, including *CreateService*, *OpenService*, *StartService*, *ControlService*, *QueryServiceStatus*,
and *DeleteService*. To use the SCM functions, an SCP must first open a communications channel to
the SCM by calling the *OpenSCManager* function. At the time of the open call, the SCP must specify
what types of actions it wants to perform. For example, if an SCP simply wants to enumerate and
display the services present in the SCM's database, it requests enumerate-service access in its call to
OpenSCManager. During its initialization, the SCM creates an internal object that represents the SCM

database and uses the Windows security functions to protect the object with a security descriptor that specifies what accounts can open the object with what access permissions. For example, the security descriptor indicates that the Authenticated Users group can open the SCM object with enumerate-service access. However, only administrators can open the object with the access required to create or delete a service.

As it does for the SCM database, the SCM implements security for services themselves. When an SCP creates a service by using the *CreateService* function, it specifies a security descriptor that the SCM associates internally with the service's entry in the service database. The SCM stores the security descriptor in the service's registry key as the Security value, and it reads that value when it scans the registry's Services key during initialization so that the security settings persist across reboots. In the same way that an SCP must specify what types of access it wants to the SCM database in its call to *OpenSCManager*, an SCP must tell the SCM what access it wants to a service in a call to *OpenService*. Accesses that an SCP can request include the ability to query a service's status and to configure, stop, and start a service.

The SCP you're probably most familiar with is the Services MMC snap-in that's included in Windows, which resides in %SystemRoot%\System32\Filemgmt.dll. Windows also includes Sc.exe (Service Controller tool), a command-line service control program that we've mentioned multiple times.

SCPs sometimes layer service policy on top of what the SCM implements. A good example is the timeout that the Services MMC snap-in implements when a service is started manually. The snap-in presents a progress bar that represents the progress of a service's startup. Services indirectly interact with SCPs by setting their configuration status to reflect their progress as they respond to SCM commands such as the start command. SCPs query the status with the *QueryServiceStatus* function. They can tell when a service actively updates the status versus when a service appears to be hung, and the SCM can take appropriate actions in notifying a user about what the service is doing.

Windows Management Instrumentation

Windows Management Instrumentation (WMI) is an implementation of Web-Based Enterprise Management (WBEM), a standard that the Distributed Management Task Force (DMTF—an industry consortium) defines. The WBEM standard encompasses the design of an extensible enterprise data-collection and data-management facility that has the flexibility and extensibility required to manage local and remote systems that comprise arbitrary components.

WMI Architecture

WMI consists of four main components, as shown in Figure 4-18: management applications, WMI infrastructure, providers, and managed objects. Management applications are Windows applications that access and display or process data about managed objects. A simple example of a management application is a performance tool replacement that relies on WMI rather than the Performance API to obtain performance information. A more complex example is an enterprise-management tool that lets administrators perform automated inventories of the software and hardware configuration of every computer in their enterprise.

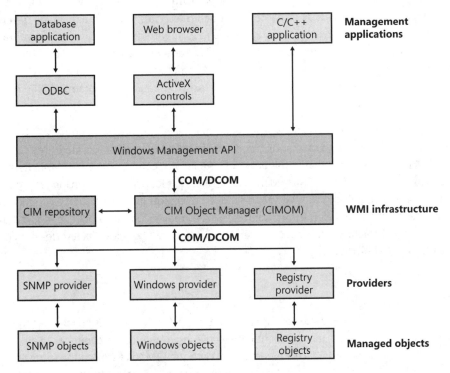

FIGURE 4-18 WMI architecture

Developers typically must target management applications to collect data from and manage specific objects. An object might represent one component, such as a network adapter device, or a collection of components, such as a computer. (The computer object might contain the network adapter object.) Providers need to define and export the representation of the objects that management applications are interested in. For example, the vendor of a network adapter might want to add adapter-specific properties to the network adapter WMI support that Windows includes, querying and setting the adapter's state and behavior as the management applications direct. In some cases (for example, for device drivers), Microsoft supplies a provider that has its own API to help developers leverage the provider's implementation for their own managed objects with minimal coding effort.

The WMI infrastructure, the heart of which is the Common Information Model (CIM) Object Manager (CIMOM), is the glue that binds management applications and providers. (CIM is described later in this chapter.) The infrastructure also serves as the object-class store and, in many cases, as the storage manager for persistent object properties. WMI implements the store, or repository, as an on-disk database named the CIMOM Object Repository. As part of its infrastructure, WMI supports several APIs through which management applications access object data and providers supply data and class definitions.

Windows programs and scripts (such as Windows PowerShell) use the WMI COM API, the primary management API, to directly interact with WMI. Other APIs layer on top of the COM API and include an Open Database Connectivity (ODBC) adapter for the Microsoft Access database application. A database developer uses the WMI ODBC adapter to embed references to object data in the developer's database. Then the developer can easily generate reports with database queries that contain WMI-based data. WMI ActiveX controls support another layered API. Web developers use the ActiveX controls to construct web-based interfaces to WMI data. Another management API is the WMI scripting API, for use in script-based applications and Microsoft Visual Basic programs. WMI scripting support exists for all Microsoft programming language technologies.

As they are for management applications, WMI COM interfaces constitute the primary API for providers. However, unlike management applications, which are COM clients, providers are COM or Distributed COM (DCOM) servers (that is, the providers implement COM objects that WMI interacts with). Possible embodiments of a WMI provider include DLLs that load into WMI's manager process or stand-alone Windows applications or Windows services. Microsoft includes a number of built-in providers that present data from well-known sources, such as the Performance API, the registry, the Event Manager, Active Directory, SNMP, and modern device drivers. The WMI SDK lets developers develop third-party WMI providers.

Providers

At the core of WBEM is the DMTF-designed CIM specification. The CIM specifies how management systems represent, from a systems management perspective, anything from a computer to an application or device on a computer. Provider developers use the CIM to represent the components that make up the parts of an application for which the developers want to enable management. Developers use the Managed Object Format (MOF) language to implement a CIM representation.

In addition to defining classes that represent objects, a provider must interface WMI to the objects. WMI classifies providers according to the interface features the providers supply. Table 4-12 lists WMI provider classifications. Note that a provider can implement one or more features; therefore, a provider can be, for example, both a class and an event provider. To clarify the feature definitions in Table 4-12, let's look at a provider that implements several of those features. The Event Log provider supports several objects, including an Event Log Computer, an Event Log Record, and an Event Log File. The Event Log is an Instance provider because it can define multiple instances for several of its classes. One class for which the Event Log provider defines multiple instances is the Event Log File class (Win32_NTEventlogFile); the Event Log provider defines an instance of this class for each of the system's event logs (that is, System Event Log, Application Event Log, and Security Event Log).

TABLE 4-12 Provider Classifications

Classification	Description
Class	Can supply, modify, delete, and enumerate a provider-specific class. It can also support query processing. Active Directory is a rare example of a service that is a class provider.
Instance	Can supply, modify, delete, and enumerate instances of system and provider-specific classes. An instance represents a managed object. It can also support query processing.

Classification	Description
Property	Can supply and modify individual object property values.
Method	Supplies methods for a provider-specific class.
Event	Generates event notifications.
Event consumer	Maps a physical consumer to a logical consumer to support event notification.

The Event Log provider defines the instance data and lets management applications enumerate the records. To let management applications use WMI to back up and restore the Event Log files, the Event Log provider implements backup and restore methods for Event Log File objects. Doing so makes the Event Log provider a Method provider. Finally, a management application can register to receive notification whenever a new record writes to one of the Event Logs. Thus, the Event Log provider serves as an Event provider when it uses WMI event notification to tell WMI that Event Log records have arrived.

The Common Information Model and the Managed Object Format Language

The CIM follows in the steps of object-oriented languages such as C++ and C#, in which a modeler designs representations as classes. Working with classes lets developers use the powerful modeling techniques of inheritance and composition. Subclasses can inherit the attributes of a parent class, and they can add their own characteristics and override the characteristics they inherit from the parent class. A class that inherits properties from another class derives from that class. Classes also compose: a developer can build a class that includes other classes.

The DMTF provides multiple classes as part of the WBEM standard. These classes are CIM's basic language and represent objects that apply to all areas of management. The classes are part of the CIM core model. An example of a core class is CIM_ManagedSystemElement. This class contains a few basic properties that identify physical components such as hardware devices and logical components such as processes and files. The properties include a caption, description, installation date, and status. Thus, the CIM_LogicalElement and CIM_PhysicalElement classes inherit the attributes of the CIM_ManagedSystemElement class. These two classes are also part of the CIM core model. The WBEM standard calls these classes abstract classes because they exist solely as classes that other classes inherit (that is, no object instances of an abstract class exist). You can therefore think of abstract classes as templates that define properties for use in other classes.

A second category of classes represents objects that are specific to management areas but independent of a particular implementation. These classes constitute the common model and are considered an extension of the core model. An example of a common-model class is the CIM_FileSystem class, which inherits the attributes of CIM_LogicalElement. Because virtually every operating system—including Windows, Linux, and other varieties of UNIX—rely on file-system-based structured storage, the CIM_FileSystem class is an appropriate constituent of the common model.

The final class category, the extended model, comprises technology-specific additions to the common model. Windows defines a large set of these classes to represent objects specific to the

Windows environment. Because all operating systems store data in files, the CIM common model includes the CIM_LogicalFile class. The CIM_DataFile class inherits the CIM_LogicalFile class, and Windows adds the Win32_PageFile and Win32_ShortcutFile file classes for those Windows file types.

The Event Log provider makes extensive use of inheritance. Figure 4-19 shows a view of the WMI CIM Studio, a class browser that ships with the WMI Administrative Tools that you can obtain from the Microsoft download center at the Microsoft website. You can see where the Event Log provider relies on inheritance in the provider's Win32_NTEventlogFile class, which derives from CIM_DataFile. Event Log files are data files that have additional Event Log–specific attributes such as a log file name (LogfileName) and a count of the number of records that the file contains (NumberOfRecords). The tree that the class browser shows reveals that Win32_NTEventlogFile is based on several levels of inheritance, in which CIM_DataFile derives from CIM_LogicalFile, which derives from CIM_LogicalElement, and CIM_LogicalElement derives from CIM_ManagedSystemElement.

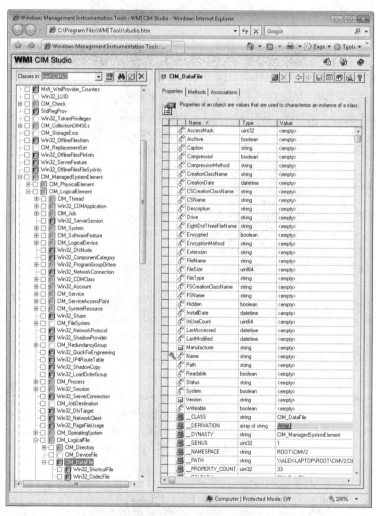

FIGURE 4-19 WMI CIM Studio

As stated earlier, WMI provider developers write their classes in the MOF language. The following output shows the definition of the Event Log provider's Win32_NTEventlogFile, which is selected in Figure 4-19. Notice the correlation between the properties that the right panel in Figure 4-19 lists and those properties' definitions in the MOF file that follows. CIM Studio uses yellow arrows to tag the properties that a class inherits. Thus, you don't see those properties specified in Win32_NTEventlogFile's definition.

```
dynamic: ToInstance, provider("MS_NT_EVENTLOG_PROVIDER"), Locale(1033), UUID("{8502C57B-5FBB-
11D2-AAC1-006008C78BC7}")]
class Win32_NTEventlogFile : CIM_DataFile
{
[read] string LogfileName;
[read, write] uint32 MaxFileSize;
[read] uint32 NumberOfRecords;
[read, volatile, ValueMap{"0", "1..365", "4294967295"}] string OverWritePolicy;
[read, write, Units("Days"), Range("0-365 | 4294967295")] uint32 OverwriteOutDated;
[read] string Sources[];
[implemented, Privileges{"SeSecurityPrivilege", "SeBackupPrivilege"}] uint32 ClearEventlog([in]
string ArchiveFileName);
[implemented, Privileges{"SeSecurityPrivilege", "SeBackupPrivilege"}] uint32 BackupEventlog([in]
string ArchiveFileName);
};
```

One term worth reviewing is dynamic, which is a descriptive designator for the Win32_NTEventlogFile class that the MOF file in the preceding output shows. "Dynamic" means that the WMI infrastructure asks the WMI provider for the values of properties associated with an object of that class whenever a management application queries the object's properties. A static class is one in the WMI repository; the WMI infrastructure refers to the repository to obtain the values instead of asking a provider for the values. Because updating the repository is a relatively expensive operation, dynamic providers are more efficient for objects that have properties that change frequently.

EXPERIMENT: Viewing the MOF Definitions of WMI Classes

You can view the MOF definition for any WMI class by using the WbemTest tool that comes with Windows. In this experiment, we'll look at the MOF definition for the Win32_NTEventLogFile class:

1. Run Wbemtest from the Start menu's Run dialog box.

2. Click the Connect button, change the Namespace to root\cimv2, and connect.

3. Click the Enum Classes button, select the Recursive option button, and then click OK.

4. Find Win32_NTEventLogFile in the list of classes, and then double-click it to see its class properties.

5. Click the Show MOF button to open a window that displays the MOF text.

After constructing classes in MOF, WMI developers can supply the class definitions to WMI in several ways. WDM driver developers compile a MOF file into a binary MOF (BMF) file—a more compact binary representation than a MOF file—and can choose to dynamically give the BMF files to the WDM infrastructure or to statically include it in their binary. Another way is for the provider to compile the MOF and use WMI COM APIs to give the definitions to the WMI infrastructure. Finally, a provider can use the MOF Compiler (Mofcomp.exe) tool to give the WMI infrastructure a classes-compiled representation directly.

The WMI Namespace

Classes define the properties of objects, and objects are class instances on a system. WMI uses a namespace that contains several subnamespaces that WMI arranges hierarchically to organize objects. A management application must connect to a namespace before the application can access objects within the namespace.

WMI names the namespace root directory root. All WMI installations have four predefined namespaces that reside beneath root: CIMV2, Default, Security, and WMI. Some of these namespaces have other namespaces within them. For example, CIMV2 includes the Applications and ms_409 namespaces as subnamespaces. Providers sometimes define their own namespaces; you can see the WMI namespace (which the Windows device driver WMI provider defines) beneath root in Windows.

EXPERIMENT: Viewing WMI Namespaces

You can see what namespaces are defined on a system with WMI CIM Studio. WMI CIM Studio presents a connection dialog box when you run it that includes a namespace browsing button to the right of the namespace edit box. Opening the browser and selecting a namespace has WMI CIM Studio connect to that namespace. Windows defines over a dozen namespaces beneath root, some of which are visible here:

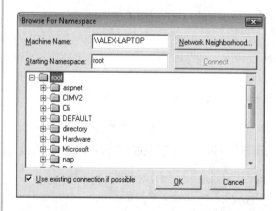

Unlike a file system namespace, which comprises a hierarchy of directories and files, a WMI namespace is only one level deep. Instead of using names as a file system does, WMI uses object properties that it defines as keys to identify the objects. Management applications specify class names with key names to locate specific objects within a namespace. Thus, each instance of a class must be uniquely identifiable by its key values. For example, the Event Log provider uses the Win32_NTLogEvent class to represent records in an Event Log. This class has two keys: Logfile, a string; and RecordNumber, an unsigned integer. A management application that queries WMI for instances of Event Log records obtains them from the provider key pairs that identify records. The application refers to a record using the syntax that you see in this sample object path name:

```
\\DARYL\root\CIMV2:Win32_NTLogEvent.Logfile="Application",
                                    RecordNumber="1"
```

The first component in the name (\\DARYL) identifies the computer on which the object is located, and the second component (\root\CIMV2) is the namespace in which the object resides. The class name follows the colon, and key names and their associated values follow the period. A comma separates the key values.

WMI provides interfaces that let applications enumerate all the objects in a particular class or to make queries that return instances of a class that match a query criterion.

Class Association

Many object types are related to one another in some way. For example, a computer object has a processor, software, an operating system, active processes, and so on. WMI lets providers construct an association class to represent a logical connection between two different classes. Association classes associate one class with another, so the classes have only two properties: a class name and the Ref modifier. The following output shows an association in which the Event Log provider's MOF file associates the Win32_NTLogEvent class with the Win32_ComputerSystem class. Given an object, a management application can query associated objects. In this way, a provider defines a hierarchy of objects.

```
[dynamic: ToInstance, provider("MS_NT_EVENTLOG_PROVIDER"): ToInstance, EnumPrivileges{"Se
SecurityPrivilege"}:
ToSubClass, Locale(1033): ToInstance, UUID("{8502C57F-5FBB-11D2-AAC1-006008C78BC7}"):
ToInstance, Association: DisableOverride ToInstance ToSubClass]
class Win32_NTLogEventComputer
{
    [key, read: ToSubClass] Win32_ComputerSystem ref Computer;
    [key, read: ToSubClass] Win32_NTLogEvent ref Record;
};
```

Figure 4-20 shows the WMI Object Browser (another tool that the WMI Administrative Tools includes) displaying the contents of the CIMV2 namespace. Windows system components typically place their objects within the CIMV2 namespace. The Object Browser first locates the Win32_ComputerSystem object instance ALEX-LAPTOP, which is the object that represents the computer. Then the Object Browser obtains the objects associated with Win32_ComputerSystem and displays them beneath ALEX-LAPTOP. The Object Browser user interface displays association objects with a double-arrow folder icon. The associated class type's objects display beneath the folder.

You can see in the Object Browser that the Event Log provider's association class Win32_NTLogEventComputer is beneath ALEX-LAPTOP and that numerous instances of the Win32_NTLogEvent class exist. Refer to the preceding output to verify that the MOF file defines the Win32_NTLogEventComputer class to associate the Win32_ComputerSystem class with the Win32_NTLogEvent class. Selecting an instance of Win32_NTLogEvent in the Object Browser reveals that class' properties under the Properties tab in the right pane. Microsoft intended the Object Browser to help WMI developers examine their objects, but a management application would perform the same operations and display properties or collected information more intelligibly.

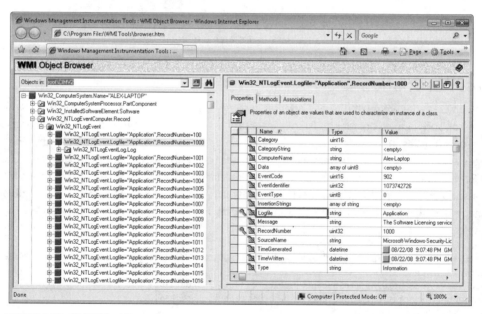

FIGURE 4-20 WMI Object Browser

EXPERIMENT: Using WMI Scripts to Manage Systems

A powerful aspect of WMI is its support for scripting languages. Microsoft has generated hundreds of scripts that perform common administrative tasks for managing user accounts, files, the registry, processes, and hardware devices. The Microsoft TechNet Scripting Center website serves as the central location for Microsoft scripts. Using a script from the scripting center is as easy as copying its text from your Internet browser, storing it in a file with a .vbs extension, and running it with the command cscript script.vbs, where script is the name you gave the script. Cscript is the command-line interface to Windows Script Host (WSH).

Here's a sample TechNet script that registers to receive events when Win32_Process object instances are created, which occurs whenever a process starts, and prints a line with the name of the process that the object represents:

```
strComputer = "."
Set objWMIService = GetObject("winmgmts:" _
    & "{impersonationLevel=impersonate}!\\" & strComputer & "\root\cimv2")
Set colMonitoredProcesses = objWMIService. _
    ExecNotificationQuery("select * from __instancecreationevent " _
        & " within 1 where TargetInstance isa 'Win32_Process'")
i = 0
Do While i = 0
    Set objLatestProcess = colMonitoredProcesses.NextEvent
    Wscript.Echo objLatestProcess.TargetInstance.Name
Loop
```

The line that invokes *ExecNotificationQuery* does so with a parameter that includes a "select" statement, which highlights WMI's support for a read-only subset of the ANSI standard Structured Query Language (SQL), known as WQL, to provide a flexible way for WMI consumers to specify the information they want to extract from WMI providers. Running the sample script with Cscript and then starting Notepad results in the following output:

```
C:\>cscript monproc.vbs
Microsoft (R) Windows Script Host Version 5.7
Copyright (C) Microsoft Corporation. All rights reserved.

NOTEPAD.EXE
```

WMI Implementation

The WMI service runs in a shared Svchost process that executes in the local system account. It loads providers into the Wmiprvse.exe provider-hosting process, which launches as a child of the RPC service process. WMI executes Wmiprvse in the local system, local service, or network service account, depending on the value of the HostingModel property of the WMI Win32Provider object instance that represents the provider implementation. A Wmiprvse process exits after the provider is removed from the cache, one minute following the last provider request it receives.

EXPERIMENT: Viewing Wmiprvse Creation

You can see Wmiprvse being created by running Process Explorer and executing Wmic. A Wmiprvse process will appear beneath the Svchost process that hosts the RPC service. If Process Explorer job highlighting is enabled, it will appear with the job highlight color because, to prevent a runaway provider from consuming all virtual memory resources on a system, Wmiprvse executes in a job object that limits the number of child processes it can create and the amount of virtual memory each process and all the processes of the job can allocate. (See Chapter 5 for more information on job objects.)

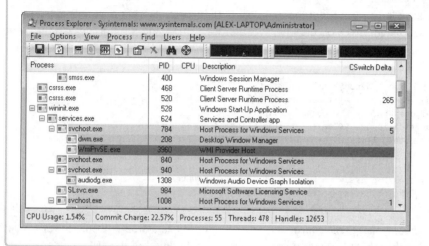

Most WMI components reside by default in %SystemRoot%\System32 and %SystemRoot%\System32\Wbem, including Windows MOF files, built-in provider DLLs, and management application WMI DLLs. Look in the %SystemRoot%\System32\Wbem directory, and you'll find Ntevt.mof, the Event Log provider MOF file. You'll also find Ntevt.dll, the Event Log provider's DLL, which the WMI service uses.

Directories beneath %SystemRoot%\System32\Wbem store the repository, log files, and third-party MOF files. WMI implements the repository—named the CIMOM object repository—using a proprietary version of the Microsoft JET database engine. The database file, by default, resides in %SystemRoot%\System32\Wbem\Repository\.

WMI honors numerous registry settings that the service's HKLM\SOFTWARE\Microsoft\WBEM \CIMOM registry key stores, such as thresholds and maximum values for certain parameters.

Device drivers use special interfaces to provide data to and accept commands—called the WMI System Control commands—from WMI. These interfaces are part of the WDM, which is explained in Chapter 8, "I/O System," in Part 2. Because the interfaces are cross-platform, they fall under the \root \WMI namespace.

WMI Security

WMI implements security at the namespace level. If a management application successfully connects to a namespace, the application can view and access the properties of all the objects in that namespace. An administrator can use the WMI Control application to control which users can access a namespace. Internally, this security model is implemented by using ACLs and Security Descriptors, part of the standard Windows security model that implements Access Checks. (See Chapter 6 for more information on access checks.)

To start the WMI Control application, from the Start menu, select Control Panel. From there, select System And Maintenance, Administrative Tools, Computer Management. Next, open the Services And Applications branch. Right-click WMI Control, and select Properties to launch the WMI Control Properties dialog box, which Figure 4-21 shows. To configure security for namespaces, click on the Security tab, select the namespace, and click Security. The other tabs in the WMI Control Properties dialog box let you modify the performance and backup settings that the registry stores.

FIGURE 4-21 WMI security properties

Windows Diagnostic Infrastructure

The Windows Diagnostic Infrastructure (WDI) helps to detect, diagnose, and resolve common problem scenarios with minimal user intervention. Windows components implement triggers that cause WDI to launch scenario-specific troubleshooting modules to detect the occurrence of a problem scenario. A trigger can indicate that the system is approaching or has reached a problematic state. Once a troubleshooting module has identified a root cause, it can invoke a problem resolver to address it. A resolution might be as simple as changing a registry setting or interacting with the user to perform recovery steps or configuration changes. Ultimately, WDI's main role is to provide a unified framework for Windows components to perform the tasks involved in automated problem detection, diagnosis, and resolution.

WDI Instrumentation

Windows or application components must add instrumentation to notify WDI when a problem scenario is occurring. Components can wait for the results of diagnosis synchronously or can continue operating and let diagnosis proceed asynchronously. WDI implements two different types of instrumentation APIs to support these models:

- Event-based diagnosis, which can be used for minimally invasive diagnostics instrumentation, can be added to a component without requiring any changes to its implementation. WDI supports two kinds of event-based diagnosis: simple scenarios and start-stop scenarios. In a simple scenario, a single point in code is responsible for the failure and an event is raised to trigger diagnostics. In a start-stop scenario, an entire code path is deemed risky and is instrumented for diagnosis. One event is raised at the beginning of the scenario to a real-time Event Tracing for Windows (ETW) session named the DiagLog. At the same time, a kernel facility called the Scenario Event Mapper (SEM) enables a collection of additional ETW traces to the WDI context loggers. A second event is raised to signal the end of the diagnostic scenario, at which time the SEM disables the verbose tracing. This "just-in-time tracing" mechanism keeps the performance overhead of detailed tracing low while maintaining enough contextual information for WDI to find the root cause without a reproduction of the problem, if a failure should occur.

- On-demand diagnosis, which allows applications to request diagnoses on their own, interact with the diagnostic, receive notifications when the diagnostic has completed, and modify its behavior based on the results of the diagnosis. On-demand instrumentation is particularly useful when diagnosis needs to be performed in a privileged security context. WDI facilitates the transfer of context across trust and process boundaries and also supports impersonation of the caller when necessary.

Diagnostic Policy Service

The Diagnostic Policy Service (DPS, %SystemRoot%\System32\Dps.dll) implements most of the WDI scenario back end. DPS is a multithreaded service (running in a Svchost) that accepts on-demand scenario requests and also monitors and watches for diagnostic events delivered via DiagLog.

(See Figure 4-22, which shows the relationship of DPS to the other key WDI components.) In response to these requests, DPS launches the appropriate troubleshooting module, which encodes domain-specific knowledge, such as how to find the root cause of a network problem. In addition, DPS makes all the contextual information related to the scenario available to the modules in the form of captured traces. Troubleshooting modules perform an automated analysis of the data and can request DPS to launch a secondary module called a resolver, which is responsible for fixing the problem, silently if possible.

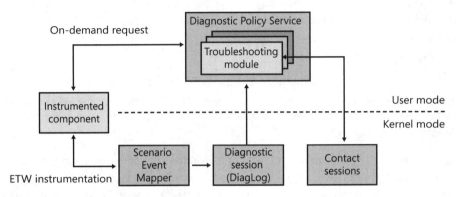

FIGURE 4-22 Windows Diagnostic Infrastructure architecture

DPS controls and enforces Group Policy settings for diagnostic scenarios. You can use the Group Policy Editor (%SystemRoot%\System32\Gpedit.msc) to configure the settings for the diagnostics and automatic recovery options. You can access these settings from Computer Configuration, Administrative Templates, System, Troubleshooting And Diagnostics, shown in Figure 4-23.

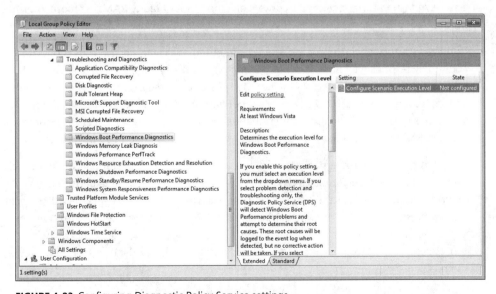

FIGURE 4-23 Configuring Diagnostic Policy Service settings

Diagnostic Functionality

Windows implements several built-in diagnostic scenarios and utilities. Some examples include:

- Disk diagnostics, which include the presence of Self-Monitoring Analysis and Reporting Technology (SMART) code inside the storage class driver (%SystemRoot%\System32\Driver \Classspnp.sys) to monitor disk health. WDI notifies and guides the user through data back-up after an impending disk failure is detected. In addition, Windows monitors application crashes caused by disk corruptions in critical system files. The diagnostic uses the Windows File Protection mechanism to automatically restore such damaged system files from a backup cache when possible. For more information on Windows storage management, see Chapter 9, "Storage Management," in Part 2.

- Network diagnostics and troubleshooting extends WDI to handle different classes of networking-related problems, such as file sharing, Internet access, wireless networks, third-party firewalls, and general network connectivity. For more information on networking, see Chapter 7, "Networking."

- Resource exhaustion prevention, which includes Windows memory leak diagnosis and Windows resource exhaustion detection and resolution. These diagnostics can detect when the commit limit is approaching its maximum and alert the user of the situation, including the top memory and resource consumers. The user can then choose to terminate these applications to attempt to free some resources. For more information on the commit limit and virtual memory, see Chapter 10, "Memory Management," in Part 2.

- Windows memory diagnostic tool, which can be manually executed by the user from the Boot Manager on startup or automatically recommended by Windows Error Reporting (WER) after a system crash that was analyzed as potentially the result of faulty RAM. For more information on the boot process, see Chapter 13 in Part 2.

- Windows startup repair tool, which attempts to automatically fix certain classes of errors commonly responsible for users being unable to boot the system, such as incorrect BCD settings, damaged disk structures such as the MBR or boot sector, and faulty drivers. When system boot is unsuccessful, the Boot Manager automatically launches the startup repair tool, if it is installed, which also includes manual recovery options and access to a command prompt. For more information on the startup repair tool, see Chapter 13 in Part 2.

- Windows performance diagnostics, which include Windows boot performance diagnostics, Windows shutdown performance diagnostics, Windows standby/resume performance diagnostics, and Windows system responsiveness performance diagnostics. Based on certain timing thresholds and the internal behavioral expectations of these mechanisms, Windows can detect problems caused by slow performance and log them to the Event Log, which in turn is used by WDI to provide resolutions and walkthroughs for the user to attempt to fix the problem.

- Program Compatibility Assistant (PCA), which enables legacy applications to execute on newer Windows versions despite compatibility problems. PCA detects application installation failures caused by a mismatch during version checks and run-time failures caused by deprecated binaries and User Account Control (UAC) settings. PCA attempts to recover from these failures by applying the appropriate compatibility setting for the application, which takes effect during the next run. In addition, PCA maintains a database of programs with known compatibility issues and informs the users about potential problems at program startup.

Conclusion

So far, we've examined the overall structure of Windows, the core system mechanisms on which the structure is built, and core management mechanisms. With this foundation laid, we're ready to explore the individual executive components in more detail, starting with processes and threads.

CHAPTER 5

Processes, Threads, and Jobs

In this chapter, we'll explain the data structures and algorithms that deal with processes, threads, and jobs in the Microsoft Windows operating system. The first section focuses on the internal structures that make up a process. The second section outlines the steps involved in creating a process (and its initial thread). The internals of threads and thread scheduling are then described. The chapter concludes with a description of jobs.

Because processes and threads touch so many components in Windows, a number of terms and data structures (such as working sets, objects and handles, system memory heaps, and so on) are referred to in this chapter but are explained in detail elsewhere in the book. To fully understand this chapter, you need to be familiar with the terms and concepts explained in Chapter 1, "Concepts and Tools," and Chapter 2, "System Architecture," such as the difference between a process and a thread, the Windows virtual address space layout, and the difference between user mode and kernel mode.

Process Internals

This section describes the key Windows process data structures maintained by various parts of the system and describes different ways and tools to examine this data.

Data Structures

Each Windows process is represented by an executive process (EPROCESS) structure. Besides containing many attributes relating to a process, an EPROCESS contains and points to a number of other related data structures. For example, each process has one or more threads, each represented by an executive thread (ETHREAD) structure. (Thread data structures are explained in the section "Thread Internals" later in this chapter.)

The EPROCESS and most of its related data structures exist in system address space. One exception is the process environment block (PEB), which exists in the process address space (because it contains information accessed by user-mode code). Additionally, some of the process data structures used in memory management, such as the working set list, are valid only within the context of the current process, because they are stored in process-specific system space. (See Chapter 10, "Memory Management," in Part 2 for more information on process address space.)

For each process that is executing a Win32 program, the Win32 subsystem process (*Csrss*) maintains a parallel structure called the CSR_PROCESS. Finally, the kernel-mode part of the Win32 subsystem (Win32k.sys) maintains a per-process data structure, W32PROCESS. The W32PROCESS structure is created the first time a thread calls a Windows USER or GDI function that is implemented in kernel mode.

With the exception of the idle process, every EPROCESS structure is encapsulated as a process object by the executive object manager (described in Chapter 3, "System Mechanisms"). Because processes are not named objects, they are not visible in the WinObj tool. You can, however, see the Type object called "Process" in the \ObjectTypes directory. A handle to a process provides, through use of the process-related APIs, access to some of the data in the EPROCESS structure and also in some of its associated structures.

Figure 5-1 is a simplified diagram of the process and thread data structures. Each data structure shown in the figure is described in detail in this chapter.

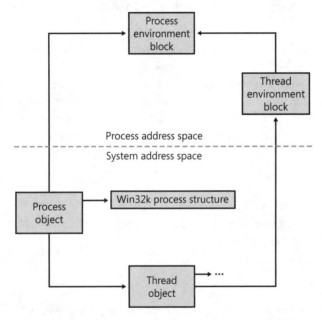

FIGURE 5-1 Data structures associated with processes and threads

Many other drivers and system components, by registering process creation notifications, can choose to create their own data structures to track information they store on a per-process basis. When one discusses the overhead of a process, the size of such data structures must often be taken into consideration, although it is nearly impossible to obtain an accurate number.

First let's focus on the process object. (The thread object is covered in the section "Thread Internals" later in the chapter.) Figure 5-2 shows the key fields in an EPROCESS structure.

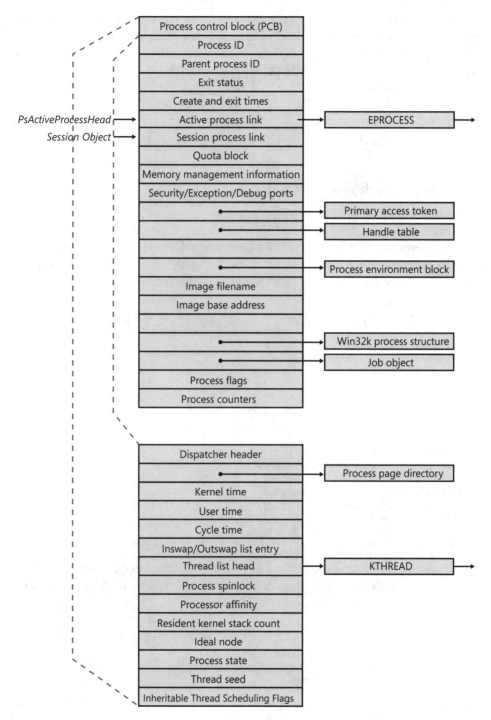

FIGURE 5-2 Important fields of the executive process structure and its embedded kernel process structure

Similar to the way that the kernel's APIs and components are divided into isolated and layered modules with their own naming conventions, the data structures for a process follow a similar design. As shown in Figure 5-2, the first member of the executive process structure is called *Pcb*, for *process control block*. It is a structure of type KPROCESS, for *kernel process*. Although routines in the executive store information in the EPROCESS, the dispatcher, scheduler, and interrupt/time accounting code—being part of the operating system kernel—use the KPROCESS instead. This allows a layer of abstraction to exist between the executive's high-level functionality and its underlying low-level implementation of certain functions, and it helps prevent unwanted dependencies between the layers.

EXPERIMENT: Displaying the Format of an EPROCESS Structure and Its Fields

For a list of the fields that make up an EPROCESS structure and their offsets in hexadecimal, type **dt nt!_eprocess** in the kernel debugger. (See Chapter 1 for more information on the kernel debugger and how to perform kernel debugging on the local system.) The output (truncated for the sake of space) on a 32-bit system looks like this:

```
lkd> dt nt!_eprocess
   +0x000 Pcb              : _KPROCESS
   +0x080 ProcessLock      : _EX_PUSH_LOCK
   +0x088 CreateTime       : _LARGE_INTEGER
   +0x090 ExitTime         : _LARGE_INTEGER
   +0x098 RundownProtect   : _EX_RUNDOWN_REF
   +0x09c UniqueProcessId  : Ptr32 Void
...
   +0x0dc ObjectTable      : Ptr32 _HANDLE_TABLE
   +0x0e0 Token            : _EX_FAST_REF
...
   +0x108 Win32Process     : Ptr32 Void
   +0x10c Job              : Ptr32 _EJOB
...
   +0x2a8 TimerResolutionLink : _LIST_ENTRY
   +0x2b0 RequestedTimerResolution : Uint4B
   +0x2b4 ActiveThreadsHighWatermark : Uint4B
   +0x2b8 SmallestTimerResolution : Uint4B
   +0x2bc TimerResolutionStackRecord : Ptr32 _PO_DIAG_STACK_RECORD
```

The first member of this structure (*Pcb*) is an imbedded structure of type KPROCESS. This is where scheduling and time-accounting data is stored. You can display the format of the kernel process structure in the same way as the EPROCESS:

```
lkd> dt _kprocess
nt!_KPROCESS
   +0x000 Header           : _DISPATCHER_HEADER
   +0x010 ProfileListHead  : _LIST_ENTRY
   +0x018 DirectoryTableBase : Uint4B
   ...
   +0x074 StackCount       : _KSTACK_COUNT
   +0x078 ProcessListEntry : _LIST_ENTRY
   +0x080 CycleTime        : Uint8B
```

```
+0x088 KernelTime       : Uint4B
+0x08c UserTime         : Uint4B
+0x090 VdmTrapcHandler  : Ptr32 Void
```

The *dt* command also enables you to view the specific contents of one field or multiple fields by typing their names following the structure name—such as **dt nt!_eprocess UniqueProcessId**, which displays the process ID field. In the case of a field that represents a structure—such as the *Pcb* field of EPROCESS, which contains the KPROCESS substructure—adding a period after the field name will cause the debugger to display the substructure.

For example, an alternative way to see the KPROCESS is to type **dt nt!_eprocess Pcb**. You can continue to recurse this way by adding more field names (within KPROCESS) and so on. Finally, to recurse through all the substructures, the *−r* switch of the *dt* command allows you to do just that. Adding a number after the switch controls the depth of recursion the command will follow.

The *dt* command used as shown earlier shows the format of the selected structure, not the contents of any particular instance of that structure type. To show an instance of an actual process, you can specify the address of an EPROCESS structure as an argument to the *dt* command. You can get the addresses of almost all of the EPROCESS structures in the system by using the *!process 0 0* command (the exception being the system idle process). Because the KPROCESS is the first thing in the EPROCESS, the address of an EPROCESS will also work as the address of a KPROCESS with *dt _kprocess*.

Processes and threads are such integral parts of Windows that it's impossible to talk about them without referring to many other parts of the system. To keep the length of this chapter manageable, however, those related subjects (such as memory management, security, objects, and handles) are covered elsewhere.

EXPERIMENT: Using the Kernel Debugger *!process* Command

The kernel debugger *!process* command displays a subset of the information in a process object and its associated structures. This output is arranged in two parts for each process. First you see the information about the process, as shown here. (When you don't specify a process address or ID, *!process* lists information for the process owning the thread currently running on CPU 0, which will be WinDbg itself on a single-processor system.)

```
1kd> !process
PROCESS 85857160  SessionId: 1  Cid: 0bcc    Peb: 7ffd9000  ParentCid: 090c
    DirBase: b45b0820  ObjectTable: b94ffda0  HandleCount:  99.
    Image: windbg.exe
    VadRoot 85a1c8e8 Vads 97 Clone 0 Private 5919. Modified 153. Locked 1.
    DeviceMap 9d32ee50
    Token                        ebaa1938
    ...
```

```
'    PageFaultCount              37066
     MemoryPriority              BACKGROUND
     BasePriority                8
     CommitCharge                6242
```

After the basic process output comes a list of the threads in the process. That output is explained in the "Experiment: Using the Kernel Debugger *!thread* Command" section later in the chapter.

Other commands that display process information include *!handle*, which dumps the process handle table (which is described in more detail in the section "Object Handles and the Process Handle Table" in Chapter 3). Process and thread security structures are described in Chapter 6, "Security."

Note that the output gives you the address of the PEB, which you can use with the *!peb* command shown in the next experiment to see the PEB of an arbitrary process. However, because the PEB is in the user-mode address space, it is valid only within the context of its own process. To look at the PEB of another process, you must first switch WinDbg to that process. You can do this with the .process command, followed by the EPROCESS pointer.

The PEB lives in the user-mode address space of the process it describes. It contains information needed by the image loader, the heap manager, and other Windows components that need to access it from user mode. The EPROCESS and KPROCESS structures are accessible only from kernel mode. The important fields of the PEB are illustrated in Figure 5-3 and are explained in more detail later in this chapter.

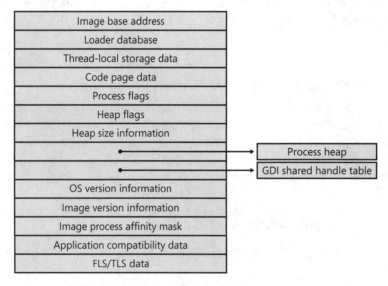

FIGURE 5-3 Fields of the process environment block

EXPERIMENT: Examining the PEB

You can dump the PEB structure with the *!peb* command in the kernel debugger, which displays the PEB of the process that owns the currently running thread on CPU 0. By using the information in the previous experiment, you can also use the PEB pointer as an argument to the command.

```
1kd> !peb 7ffd9000
PEB at 7ffd9000
    InheritedAddressSpace:    No
    ReadImageFileExecOptions: No
    BeingDebugged:            No
    ImageBaseAddress:         002a0000
    Ldr                       77895d00
...
    WindowTitle:  'C:\Users\Alex Ionescu\Desktop\WinDbg.lnk'
    ImageFile:    'C:\Program Files\Debugging Tools for Windows\windbg.exe'
    CommandLine:  '"C:\Program Files\Debugging Tools for Windows\windbg.exe" '
    DllPath:      'C:\Program Files\Debugging Tools for Windows;C:\Windows\
        system32;C:\Windows\system;C:\Windows
    Environment:  001850a8
        ALLUSERSPROFILE=C:\ProgramData
        APPDATA=C:\Users\Alex Ionescu\AppData\Roaming
    ...
```

The CSR_PROCESS structure contains information about processes that is specific to the Windows subsystem (*Csrss*). As such, only Windows applications have a CSR_PROCESS structure associated with them (for example, *Smss* does not). Additionally, because each session has its own instance of the Windows subsystem, the CSR_PROCESS structures are maintained by the *Csrss* process within each individual session. The basic structure of the CSR_PROCESS is illustrated in Figure 5-4 and is explained in more detail later in this chapter.

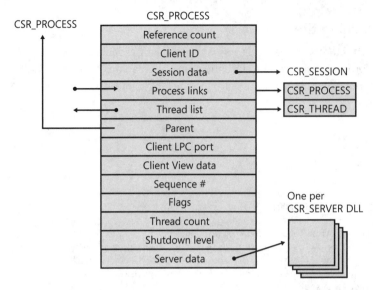

FIGURE 5-4 Fields of the CSR process structure

EXPERIMENT: Examining the CSR_PROCESS

You can dump the CSR_PROCESS structure with the *!dp* command in the user-mode debugger while attached to the *Csrss* process of the session you want to inspect. Use the File, Attach To A Process option to get a list of processes, and select the *Csrss* process for the correct session. (You can see the session of the process by expanding the tree item for it.) Make sure to select the Noninvasive check box to avoid freezing your system.

The *!dp* command takes as input the PID of the process whose CSR_PROCESS structure should be dumped. Alternatively, the structure pointer can be given directly as an argument. Because *!dp* already performs a *dt* command internally, there is no need to use *dt* on your own.

```
0:000> !dp v 0x1c0aa8-8
PCSR_PROCESS @ 001c0aa0:
    +0x000 ClientId          : _CLIENT_ID
    +0x008 ListLink          : _LIST_ENTRY [ 0x1d8618 - 0x1b1b10 ]
    +0x010 ThreadList        : _LIST_ENTRY [ 0x1c0b80 - 0x1c7638 ]
    +0x018 NtSession         : 0x001c0bb8 _CSR_NT_SESSION
...
    +0x054 Luid              : _LUID
    +0x05c ServerDllPerProcessData : [1] (null)
Threads:
Thread 001c0b78, Process 001c0aa0, ClientId 198.19c, Flags 0, Ref Count 1
Thread 001c0e78, Process 001c0aa0, ClientId 198.1cc, Flags 0, Ref Count 1
...
```

The W32PROCESS structure is the final system data structure associated with processes that we'll look at. It contains all the information that the Windows graphics and window management code in the kernel (Win32k) needs to maintain state information about GUI processes (which were defined earlier as processes that have done at least one USER/GDI system call). The basic structure of the W32PROCESS is illustrated in Figure 5-5 and is explained in more detail later in this chapter.

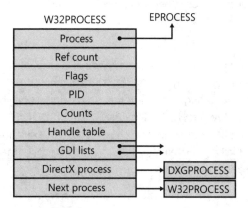

FIGURE 5-5 Fields of the Win32k Process structure

EXPERIMENT: Examining the W32PROCESS

There is no command provided by the debugger extensions to dump the W32PROCESS structure, but it is present in the symbols of the Win32k driver. As such, by using the *dt* command with the appropriate symbol name *win32k!_W32PROCESS*, it is possible to dump the fields as long as the pointer is known. Because the *!process* command does not actually output this pointer (even though it is stored in the EPROCESS object), the field must be inspected manually with *dt nt!_EPROCESS* Win32Process followed by an EPROCESS pointer.

In the following example, the W32PROCESS structure for the shell, Explorer.exe, is shown:

```
lkd> dt win32k!_W32PROCESS 0xff991490
   +0x000 Process            : 0x84a2b030 _EPROCESS
   +0x004 RefCount           : 1
...
   +0x020 W32Pid             : 0x590
   +0x024 GDIHandleCount     : 383
   +0x028 GDIHandleCountPeak : 0x239
   +0x02c UserHandleCount    : 228
   +0x030 UserHandleCountPeak : 0x16c
...
   +0x088 hSecureGdiSharedHandleTable : 0x84a24159
   +0x08c DxProcess          : 0xa2c93980
```

The *DxProcess* field is a pointer to yet another per-process data structure—in this case, maintained by the DirectX Video Card Port Driver—but its description is beyond the scope of this book.

Protected Processes

In the Windows security model, any process running with a token containing the debug privilege (such as an administrator's account) can request any access right that it desires to any other process running on the machine—for example, it can read and write arbitrary process memory, inject code, suspend and resume threads, and query information on other processes. Tools such as Process Explorer and Task Manager need and request these access rights to provide their functionality to users.

This logical behavior (which helps ensure that administrators will always have full control of the running code on the system) clashes with the system behavior for digital rights management requirements imposed by the media industry on computer operating systems that need to support playback of advanced, high-quality digital content such as Blu-ray and HD-DVD media. To support reliable and protected playback of such content, Windows uses protected processes. These processes exist alongside normal Windows processes, but they add significant constraints to the access rights that other processes on the system (even when running with administrative privileges) can request.

Protected processes can be created by any application; however, the operating system will allow a process to be protected only if the image file has been digitally signed with a special Windows Media Certificate. The Protected Media Path (PMP) in Windows makes use of protected processes to provide protection for high-value media, and developers of applications such as DVD players can make use of protected processes by using the Media Foundation API.

The Audio Device Graph process (Audiodg.exe) is a protected process because protected music content can be decoded through it. Similarly, the Windows Error Reporting (or WER, discussed in Chapter 3) client process (Werfault.exe) can also run protected because it needs to have access to protected processes in case one of them crashes. Finally, the System process itself is protected because some of the decryption information is generated by the Ksecdd.sys driver and stored in its user-mode memory. The System process is also protected to protect the integrity of all kernel handles (because the System process' handle table contains all the kernel handles on the system).

At the kernel level, support for protected processes is twofold: first, the bulk of process creation occurs in kernel mode to avoid injection attacks. (The flow for both protected and standard process creation is described in detail in the next section.) Second, protected processes have a special bit set in their EPROCESS structure that modifies the behavior of security-related routines in the process manager to deny certain access rights that would normally be granted to administrators. In fact, the only access rights that are granted for protected processes are PROCESS_QUERY/SET_LIMITED_INFORMATION, PROCESS_TERMINATE, and PROCESS_SUSPEND_RESUME. Certain access rights are also disabled for threads running inside protected processes; we will look at those access rights later in this chapter in the section "Thread Internals."

Because Process Explorer uses standard user-mode Windows APIs to query information on process internals, it is unable to perform certain operations on such processes. On the other hand, a tool like WinDbg in kernel-debugging mode, which uses kernel-mode infrastructure to obtain this information, will be able to display complete information. See the experiment in the "Thread Internals" section on how Process Explorer behaves when confronted with a protected process such as Audiodg.exe.

Note As mentioned in Chapter 1, to perform local kernel debugging, you must boot in debugging mode (enabled by using *bcdedit /debug on* or by using the Msconfig advanced boot options). This protects against debugger-based attacks on protected processes and the Protected Media Path (PMP). When booted in debugging mode, high-definition content playback will not work.

Limiting these access rights reliably allows the kernel to sandbox a protected process from user-mode access. On the other hand, because a protected process is indicated by a flag in the EPROCESS structure, an administrator can still load a kernel-mode driver that disables this bit. However, this would be a violation of the PMP model and considered malicious, and such a driver would likely eventually be blocked from loading on a 64-bit system because the kernel-mode, code-signing policy prohibits the digital signing of malicious code. Even on 32-bit systems, the driver has to be recognized by PMP policy or else the playback will be halted. This policy is implemented by Microsoft and not by any kernel detection. This block would require manual action from Microsoft to identify the signature as malicious and update the kernel.

Flow of *CreateProcess*

So far, this chapter has shown the various data structures involved in process state manipulation and management, and how various tools and debugger commands can inspect this information. In this section, we'll see how and when those data structures are created and filled out, as well as the overall creation and termination behaviors behind processes.

A Windows subsystem process is created when an application calls (or eventually ends up in) one of the process-creation functions, such as *CreateProcess*, *CreateProcessAsUser*, *CreateProcessWithTokenW*, or *CreateProcessWithLogonW*. Creating a Windows process consists of several stages carried out in three parts of the operating system: the Windows client-side library Kernel32.dll (in the case of the *CreateProcessAsUser*, *CreateProcessWithTokenW*, and *CreateProcessWithLogonW* routines, part of the work is first done in Advapi32.dll), the Windows executive, and the Windows subsystem process (*Csrss*).

Because of the multiple-environment subsystem architecture of Windows, creating an executive process object (which other subsystems can use) is separated from the work involved in creating a Windows subsystem process. So, although the following description of the flow of the Windows *CreateProcess* function is complicated, keep in mind that part of the work is specific to the semantics added by the Windows subsystem as opposed to the core work needed to create an executive process object.

The following list summarizes the main stages of creating a process with the Windows *CreateProcess* function. The operations performed in each stage are described in detail in the subsequent sections. Some of these operations might be performed by *CreateProcess* itself (or other helper routines in user mode), while others will be performed by *NtCreateUserProcess* or one of its helper routines in kernel mode. In our detailed analysis to follow, we will differentiate between the two at each step required.

> **Note** Many steps of *CreateProcess* are related to the setup of the process virtual address space and therefore refer to many memory management terms and structures that are defined in Chapter 10 in Part 2.

1. Validate parameters; convert Windows subsystem flags and options to their native counterparts; parse, validate, and convert the attribute list to its native counterpart.

2. Open the image file (.exe) to be executed inside the process.

3. Create the Windows executive process object.

4. Create the initial thread (stack, context, and Windows executive thread object).

5. Perform post-creation, Windows-subsystem-specific process initialization.

6. Start execution of the initial thread (unless the CREATE_ SUSPENDED flag was specified).

7. In the context of the new process and thread, complete the initialization of the address space (such as load required DLLs) and begin execution of the program.

Figure 5-6 shows an overview of the stages Windows follows to create a process.

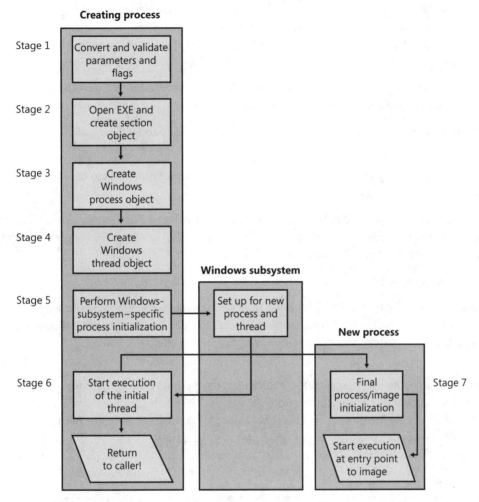

Creating process

Stage 1 — Convert and validate parameters and flags

Stage 2 — Open EXE and create section object

Stage 3 — Create Windows process object

Stage 4 — Create Windows thread object

Windows subsystem

Stage 5 — Perform Windows-subsystem–specific process initialization → Set up for new process and thread

New process

Stage 6 — Start execution of the initial thread

Return to caller!

Final process/image initialization — Stage 7

Start execution at entry point to image

FIGURE 5-6 The main stages of process creation

Stage 1: Converting and Validating Parameters and Flags

Before opening the executable image to run, *CreateProcess* performs the following steps.

In *CreateProcess*, the priority class for the new process is specified as independent bits in the *CreationFlags* parameter. Thus, you can specify more than one priority class for a single *CreateProcess* call. Windows resolves the question of which priority class to assign to the process by choosing the lowest-priority class set.

If no priority class is specified for the new process, the priority class defaults to Normal unless the priority class of the process that created it is Idle or Below Normal, in which case the priority class of the new process will have the same priority as the creating class.

If a Real-time priority class is specified for the new process and the process' caller doesn't have the Increase Scheduling Priority privilege, the High priority class is used instead. In other words, *CreateProcess* doesn't fail just because the caller has insufficient privileges to create the process in the Real-time priority class; the new process just won't have as high a priority as Real-time.

All windows are associated with desktops, the graphical representation of a workspace. If no desktop is specified in *CreateProcess*, the process is associated with the caller's current desktop.

If the process is part of a job object, but the creation flags requested a separate virtual DOS machine (VDM), the flag is ignored.

If the caller is sending a handle to a monitor as an output handle instead of a console handle, standard handle flags are ignored.

If the creation flags specify that the process will be debugged, Kernel32 initiates a connection to the native debugging code in Ntdll.dll by calling *DbgUiConnectToDbg* and gets a handle to the debug object from the current thread's environment block (TEB).

Kernel32.dll sets the default hard error mode if the creation flags specified one.

The user-specified attribute list is converted from Windows subsystem format to native format and internal attributes are added to it. The possible attributes that can be added to the attribute list are listed in Table 5-1, including their documented Windows API counterparts, if any.

 Note The attribute list passed on a *CreateProcess* call permits passing back to the caller information beyond a simple status code, such as the TEB address of the initial thread or information on the image section. This is necessary for protected processes because the parent cannot query this information after the child is created.

TABLE 5-1 Process Attributes

Native Attribute	Equivalent Windows Attribute	Type	Description
PS_CP_PARENT_PROCESS	PROC_THREAD_ATTRIBUTE_ PARENT_PROCESS. Also used when elevating	Input	Handle to the parent process.
PS_CP_DEBUG_OBJECT	N/A – used when using DEBUG_PROCESS as a flag	Input	Debug object if process is being started debugged.
PS_CP_PRIMARY_TOKEN	N/A – used when using *CreateProcessAsUser/ WithToken*	Input	Process token if *CreateProcessAsUser* was used.
PS_CP_CLIENT_ID	N/A – returned by Win32 API as a parameter	Output	Returns the TID and PID of the initial thread and the process.
PS_CP_TEB_ADDRESS	N/A – internally used and not exposed	Output	Returns the address of the TEB for the initial thread.
PS_CP_FILENAME	N/A – used as a parameter in *CreateProcess* API.	Input	Name of the process that should be created.

Native Attribute	Equivalent Windows Attribute	Type	Description
PS_CP_IMAGE_INFO	N/A – internally used and not exposed	Output	Returns SECTION_IMAGE_INFORMATION, which contains information on the version, flags, and subsystem of the executable, as well as the stack size and entry point.
PS_CP_MEM_RESERVE	N/A – internally used by SMSS and CSRSS.	Input	Array of virtual memory reservations that should be made during initial process address space creation, allowing guaranteed availability because no other allocations have taken place yet.
PS_CP_PRIORITY_CLASS	N/A – passed in as a parameter to the *CreateProcess* API.	Input	Priority class that the process should be given.
PS_CP_ERROR_MODE	N/A – passed in through CREATE_DEFAULT_ERROR_MODE flag	Input	Hard error-processing mode for the process.
PS_CP_STD_HANDLE_INFO		Input	Specifies if standard handles should be duplicated, or if new handles should be created.
PS_CP_HANDLE_LIST	PROC_THREAD_ATTRIBUTE_HANDLE_LIST	Input	List of handles belonging to the parent process that should be inherited by the new process.
PS_CP_GROUP_AFFINITY	PROC_THREAD_ATTRIBUTE_GROUP_AFFINITY	Input	Processor group(s) the thread should be allowed to run on.
PS_CP_PREFERRED_NODE	PROC_THREAD_ATTRIBUTES_PRFERRED_NODE	Input	Preferred (ideal) node that should be associated with the process. It affects the node on which the initial process heap and thread stack will be created.
PS_CP_IDEAL_PROCESSOR	PROC_THREAD_ATTTRIBUTE_IDEAL_PROCESSOR	Input	Preferred (ideal) processor that the thread should be scheduled on.
PS_CP_UMS_THREAD	PROC_THREAD_ATTRIBUTE_UMS_THREAD	Input	Contains the UMS attributes, completion list, and context.
PS_CP_EXECUTE_OPTIONS	PROC_THREAD_MITIGATION_POLICY	Input	Contains information on which mitigations (SEHOP, ATL Emulation, NX) should be enabled/disabled for the process.

Once these steps are completed, *CreateProcess* performs the initial call to *NtCreateUserProcess* to attempt creation of the process. Because Kernel32.dll has no idea at this point whether the application image name is a real Windows application or a POSIX, 16-bit, or DOS application, the call might fail—at which point, *CreateProcess* looks at the error reason and attempts to correct the situation.

Stage 2: Opening the Image to Be Executed

As illustrated in Figure 5-7, the first stage in *NtCreateUserProcess* is to find the appropriate Windows image that will run the executable file specified by the caller and to create a section object to later map it into the address space of the new process. If the call failed for any reason, it returns to *CreateProcess* with a failure state (see Table 5-2) that causes *CreateProcess* to attempt execution again.

If the executable file specified is a Windows .exe, *NtCreateUserProcess* tries to open the file and create a section object for it. The object isn't mapped into memory yet, but it is opened. Just because a section object has been successfully created doesn't mean that the file is a valid Windows image, however; it could be a DLL or a POSIX executable. If the file is a POSIX executable, the image to be run changes to Posix.exe, and *CreateProcess* restarts from the beginning of Stage 1. If the file is a DLL, *CreateProcess* fails.

Now that *NtCreateUserProcess* has found a valid Windows executable image, as part of the process creation code described in Stage 3 it looks in the registry under HKLM\SOFTWARE\Microsoft \Windows NT\CurrentVersion\Image File Execution Options to see whether a subkey with the file name and extension of the executable image (but without the directory and path information—for example, Image.exe) exists there. If it does, *PspAllocateProcess* looks for a value named Debugger for that key. If this value is present, the image to be run becomes the string in that value and *CreateProcess* restarts at Stage 1.

> **Tip** You can take advantage of this process creation behavior and debug the startup code of Windows services processes before they start rather than attach the debugger after starting a service, which doesn't allow you to debug the startup code.

On the other hand, if the image is not a Windows .exe (for example, if it's an MS-DOS, a Win16, or a POSIX application), *CreateProcess* goes through a series of steps to find a Windows support image to run it. This process is necessary because non-Windows applications aren't run directly—Windows instead uses one of a few special support images that, in turn, are responsible for actually running the non-Windows program. For example, if you attempt to run a POSIX application, *CreateProcess* identifies it as such and changes the image to be run to the Windows executable file Posix.exe. If you attempt to run an MS-DOS or a Win16 executable, the image to be run becomes the Windows executable Ntvdm.exe. In short, you can't directly create a process that is not a Windows process. If Windows can't find a way to resolve the activated image as a Windows process (as shown in Table 5-2), *CreateProcess* fails.

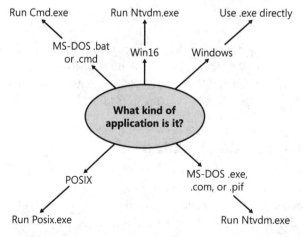

FIGURE 5-7 Choosing a Windows image to activate

TABLE 5-2 Decision Tree for Stage 1 of *CreateProcess*

If the Image . . .	Create State Code	This Image Will Run . . .	. . . and This Will Happen
Is a POSIX executable file	*PsCreateSuccess*	Posix.exe	*CreateProcess* restarts Stage 1.
Is an MS-DOS application with an .exe, .com, or .pif extension	*PsCreateFailOnSectionCreate*	Ntvdm.exe	*CreateProcess* restarts Stage 1.
Is a Win16 application	*PsCreateFailOnSectionCreate*	Ntvdm.exe	*CreateProcess* restarts Stage 1.
Is a Win64 application on a 32-bit system (or a PPC, MIPS, or Alpha Binary)	*PsCreateFailMachineMismatch*	N/A	*CreateProcess* will fail.
Has a Debugger key with another image name	*PsCreateFailExeName*	Name specified in the Debugger key	*CreateProcess* restarts Stage 1.
Is an invalid or damaged Windows EXE	*PsCreateFailExeFormat*	N/A	*CreateProcess* will fail.
Cannot be opened	*PsCreateFailOnFileOpen*	N/A	*CreateProcess* will fail.
Is a command procedure (application with a .bat or .cmd extension)	*PsCreateFailOnSectionCreate*	Cmd.exe	*CreateProcess* restarts Stage 1.

Specifically, the decision tree that *CreateProcess* goes through to run an image is as follows:

- If the image is an MS-DOS application with an .exe, .com, or .pif extension, a message is sent to the Windows subsystem to check whether an MS-DOS support process (Ntvdm.exe, specified in the registry value HKLM\SYSTEM\CurrentControlSet\Control\WOW\cmdline) has already been created for this session. If a support process has been created, it is used to run the MS-DOS application. (The Windows subsystem sends the message to the VDM [Virtual DOS Machine] process to run the new image.) Then *CreateProcess* returns. If a support process hasn't been created, the image to be run changes to Ntvdm.exe and *CreateProcess* restarts at Stage 1.

- If the file to run has a .bat or .cmd extension, the image to be run becomes Cmd.exe, the Windows command prompt, and *CreateProcess* restarts at Stage 1. (The name of the batch file is passed as the first parameter to Cmd.exe.)

- If the image is a Win16 (Windows 3.1) executable, *CreateProcess* must decide whether a new VDM process must be created to run it or whether it should use the default session-wide shared VDM process (which might not yet have been created). The *CreateProcess* flags CREATE_SEPARATE_WOW_VDM and CREATE_SHARED_WOW_VDM control this decision. If these flags aren't specified, the registry value HKLM\SYSTEM\CurrentControlSet\Control \WOW\DefaultSeparateVDM dictates the default behavior. If the application is to be run in a separate VDM, the image to be run changes to ntvdm.exe followed by some configuration parameters and the 16-bit process' name and *CreateProcess* restarts at Stage 1. Otherwise, the Windows subsystem sends a message to see whether the shared VDM process exists and can be used. (If the VDM process is running on a different desktop or isn't running under the same security as the caller, it can't be used and a new VDM process must be created.) If a shared VDM process can be used, the Windows subsystem sends a message to it to run the new image and *CreateProcess* returns. If the VDM process hasn't yet been created (or if it exists but can't be used), the image to be run changes to the VDM support image and *CreateProcess* restarts at Stage 1.

Stage 3: Creating the Windows Executive Process Object (*PspAllocateProcess*)

At this point, *NtCreateUserProcess* has opened a valid Windows executable file and created a section object to map it into the new process address space. Next it creates a Windows executive process object to run the image by calling the internal system function *PspAllocateProcess*. Creating the executive process object (which is done by the creating thread) involves the following substages:

- Setting up the EPROCESS object

- Creating the initial process address space

- Initializing the kernel process structure(KPROCESS)

- Setting up the PEB

- Concluding the setup of the process address space (which includes initializing the working set list and virtual address space descriptors and mapping the image into address space)

> **Note** The only time there won't be a parent process is during system initialization. After that point, a parent process is always required to provide a security context for the new process.

Stage 3A: Setting Up the EPROCESS Object

This substage involves the following steps:

1. Inherit the affinity of the parent process, unless it was explicitly set during process creation (through the attribute list).

2. Choose the ideal node that was specified in the attribute list, if any.

3. Inherit the I/O and page priority from the parent process. If there is no parent process, the default page priority (5) and I/O priority (Normal) are used.

4. Set the new process' exit status to STATUS_PENDING.

5. Choose the hard error processing mode selected by the attribute list; otherwise, inherit the parent's processing mode if none was given. If no parent exists, use the default processing mode which is to display all errors.

6. Store the parent process' process ID in the *InheritedFromUniqueProcessId* field in the new process object.

7. Query the Image File Execution Options key to check if the process should be mapped with large pages. Also, query the key to check if NTDLL has been listed as a DLL that should be mapped with large pages within this process.

8. Query the Image File Execution Options key for a specific NUMA node assignment associated with the process. The assignment can be either based on inheritance (in which the NUMA node will be propagated from the parent) or an explicit NUMA assignment, as long as this assignment does not override the initial NUMA node specified in the attribute list.

9. Disable stack randomization if ASLR was disabled on the executable containing the process.

10. Attempt to acquire all the privileges required for creating the process. Choosing the Real-time process priority class, assigning a token to the new process, mapping the process with large pages, and creating the process within a new session are all operations that require the appropriate privilege.

11. Create the process' primary access token (a duplicate of its parent's primary token). New processes inherit the security profile of their parents. If the *CreateProcessAsUser* function is being used to specify a different access token for the new process, the token is then changed appropriately. This change might happen only if the parent token's integrity level dominates the integrity level of the access token, and if the access token is a true child or sibling of the parent token. Note that if the parent has the *SeAssignPrimaryToken* privilege, this will bypass these checks.

12. The session ID of the new process token is now checked to determine if this is a cross-session create—in which case, the parent process temporarily attaches to the target session to correctly process quotas and address space creation.

13. Set the new process' quota block to the address of its parent process' quota block, and increment the reference count for the parent's quota block. If the process was created through *CreateProcessAsUser*, this step won't occur. Instead, the default quota is created, or a quota matching the user's profile is selected.

14. The process minimum and maximum working set sizes are set to the values of *PspMinimumWorkingSet* and *PspMaximumWorkingSet*, respectively. These values can be overridden if performance options were specified in the *PerfOptions* key part of Image File Execution Options—in which case, the maximum working set is taken from there. Note that the default working set limits are soft limits and are essentially hints, while the *PerfOptions* working set maximum is a hard limit (that is, the working set will not be allowed to grow past that number).

15. Initialize the address space of the process. (See Stage 3B.) Then detach from the target session if it was different.

16. The group affinity for the process is now chosen if group-affinity inheritance was not used. The default group affinity either will inherit from the parent, if NUMA node propagation was set earlier (the group owning the NUMA node will be used) or be assigned round-robin based on the *PspProcessGroupAssignment* seed. If the system is in forced group-awareness mode and group 0 was chosen by the selection algorithm, group 1 is chosen instead, as long as it exists.

17. Initialize the KPROCESS part of the process object. (See Stage 3C.)

18. The token for the process is now set.

19. The process' priority class is set to normal, unless the parent was using idle or the Below Normal process priority class—in which case, the parent's priority is inherited. If a process priority class was set manually through the attribute lists, it is now set.

20. The process handle table is initialized. If the inherit handles flag is set for the parent process, any inheritable handles are copied from the parent's object handle table into the new process. (For more information about object handle tables, see Chapter 3.) A process attribute can also be used to specify only a subset of handles, which is useful when you are using *CreateProcessAsUser* to restrict which objects should be inherited by the child process.

21. If performance options were specified through the *PerfOptions* key, these are now applied. The *PerfOptions* key includes overrides for the working set limit, I/O priority, page priority, and CPU priority class of the process.

22. The final process priority class and the default quantum for its threads are computed and set.

23. The second stage of address space setup is completed, including the initialization of the PEB (Stage 3D/3E).

24. Mitigation options for No-Execute support are now set.

25. The process PID and creation time is set, although the PID is not yet inserted in the PID handle table, nor is the process inserted in the process lists (that is the job of the insertion stage).

Stage 3B: Creating the Initial Process Address Space

The initial process address space consists of the following pages:

- Page directory (and it's possible there'll be more than one for systems with page tables more than two levels, such as x86 systems in PAE mode or 64-bit systems)

- Hyperspace page

- VAD bitmap page

- Working set list

To create these three pages, the following steps are taken:

1. Page table entries are created in the appropriate page tables to map the initial pages.

2. The number of pages is deducted from the kernel variable *MmTotalCommittedPages* and added to *MmProcessCommit*.

3. The systemwide default process minimum working set size (*PsMinimumWorkingSet*) is deducted from *MmResidentAvailablePages*.

4. The page table pages for the global system space (that is, other than the process-specific pages we just described, and except session-specific memory).

Stage 3C: Creating the Kernel Process Structure

The next stage of *PspAllocateProcess* is the initialization of the KPROCESS structure (the *Pcb* member of the EPROCESS). This work is performed by *KeInitializeProcess*, which initializes the following:

- The doubly-linked list which connects all threads part of the process (initially empty).

- The initial value (or reset value) of the process default quantum (which is described in more detail in the "Thread Scheduling" section later in the chapter), which is hard-coded to 6 until it is initialized later (by *PspComputeQuantumAndPriority*).

 Note The default initial quantum differs between Windows client and server systems. For more information on thread quantums, turn to their discussion in the section "Thread Scheduling."

- The process' base priority is set based on what was computed in Stage 3A.

- The default processor affinity for the threads in the process is set, as is the group affinity. The group affinity was calculated earlier in Stage 3A or inherited from the parent.

- The process swapping state is set to resident.

- The thread seed is based on the ideal processor that the kernel has chosen for this process (which is based on the previously created process' ideal processor, effectively randomizing this in a round-robin manner). Creating a new process will update the seed in *KeNodeBlock* (the initial NUMA node block) so that the next new process will get a different ideal processor seed.

Stage 3D: Concluding the Setup of the Process Address Space

Setting up the address space for a new process is somewhat complicated, so let's look at what's involved one step at a time. To get the most out of this section, you should have some familiarity with the internals of the Windows memory manager, which are described in Chapter 10 in Part 2.

1. The virtual memory manager sets the value of the process' last trim time to the current time. The working set manager (which runs in the context of the balance set manager system thread) uses this value to determine when to initiate working set trimming.

2. The memory manager initializes the process' working set list—page faults can now be taken.

3. The section (created when the image file was opened) is now mapped into the new process' address space, and the process section base address is set to the base address of the image.

4. Ntdll.dll is mapped into the process; if this is a Wow64 process, the 32-bit Ntdll.dll is also mapped.

5. A new session, if requested, is now created for the process. This special step is mostly implemented for the benefit of the Session Manager (SMSS) when initializing a new session.

6. The standard handles are duplicated, and the new values are written in the process parameters structure.

7. Any memory reservations listed in the attribute list are now processed. Additionally, two flags allow the bulk reservation of the first 1 or 16 MB of the address space. These flags are used internally for mapping real-mode vectors and ROM code, for example (which must be in the low ranges of virtual address space, where normally the heap or other process structures could be located).

8. The user process parameters are written into the process, copied, and fixed up (meaning converted from absolute form to a relative form so that a single memory block is needed).

9. The affinity information is written into the PEB.

10. The *MinWin* API redirection set is mapped into the process.

> **Note** POSIX processes clone the address space of their parents, so they don't have to go through these steps to create a new address space. In the case of POSIX applications, the new process' section base address is set to that of its parent process and the parent's PEB is cloned for the new process.

Stage 3E: Setting Up the PEB

NtCreateUserProcess calls *MmCreatePeb*, which first maps the systemwide national language support (NLS) tables into the process' address space. It next calls *MiCreatePebOrTeb* to allocate a page for the PEB and then initializes a number of fields, most of them based on internal variables that were configured through the registry, such as *MmHeap** values, *MmCriticalSectionTimeout*, and *MmMinimumStackCommitInBytes*. Some of these fields can be overridden by settings in the linked executable image, such as the Windows version in the PE header or the affinity mask in the load configuration directory of the PE header.

If the image header characteristics IMAGE_FILE_UP_SYSTEM_ONLY flag is set (indicating that the image can run only on a uniprocessor system), a single CPU (*MmRotatingUniprocessorNumber*) is chosen for all the threads in this new process to run on. The selection process is performed by simply cycling through the available processors—each time this type of image is run, the next processor is used. In this way, these types of images are spread evenly across the processors.

Stage 3F: Completing the Setup of the Executive Process Object (*PspInsertProcess*)

Before the handle to the new process can be returned, a few final setup steps must be completed, which are performed by *PspInsertProcess* and its helper functions:

1. If systemwide auditing of processes is enabled (either as a result of local policy settings or group policy settings from a domain controller), the process' creation is written to the Security event log.

2. If the parent process was contained in a job, the job is recovered from the job level set of the parent and then bound to the session of the newly created process. Finally, the new process is added to the job.

3. *PspInsertProcess* inserts the new process object at the end of the Windows list of active processes (*PsActiveProcessHead*).

4. The process debug port of the parent process is copied to the new child process, unless the *NoDebugInherit* flag is set (which can be requested when creating the process). If a debug port was specified, it is attached to the new process at this time.

5. Because job objects can now specify restrictions on which group or groups the threads within the processes part of a job can run on, *PspInsertProcess* must make sure that the group affinity associated with the process would not violate the group affinity associated with the job. An interesting secondary issue to consider is if the job's permissions grant access to modify the process' affinity permissions, because a lesser-privileged job object might interfere with the affinity requirements of a more privileged process.

6. Finally, *PspInsertProcess* creates a handle for the new process by calling *ObOpenObjectByPointer*, and then returns this handle to the caller. Note that no process creation callback is sent until the first thread within the process is created, and the code always sends process callbacks before sending object-managed based callbacks.

Stage 4: Creating the Initial Thread and Its Stack and Context

At this point, the Windows executive process object is completely set up. It still has no thread, however, so it can't do anything yet. It's now time to start that work. Normally, the *PspCreateThread* routine is responsible for all aspects of thread creation and is called by *NtCreateThread* when a new thread is being created. However, because the initial thread is created internally by the kernel without user-mode input, the two helper routines that *PspCreateThread* relies on are used instead: *PspAllocateThread* and *PspInsertThread*.

PspAllocateThread handles the actual creation and initialization of the executive thread object itself, while *PspInsertThread* handles the creation of the thread handle and security attributes and the call to *KeStartThread* to turn the executive object into a schedulable thread on the system. However, the thread won't do anything yet—it is created in a suspended state and isn't resumed until the process is completely initialized (as described in Stage 5).

> **Note** The thread parameter (which can't be specified in *CreateProcess* but can be specified in *CreateThread*) is the address of the PEB. This parameter will be used by the initialization code that runs in the context of this new thread (as described in Stage 6).

PspAllocateThread performs the following steps:

1. It prevents user-mode scheduling (UMS) threads from being created in Wow64 processes, as well as preventing user-mode callers from creating threads in the system process.

2. An executive thread object is created and initialized.

3. If CPU rate limiting is enabled, the CPU quota block is initialized.

4. The various lists used by LPC, I/O Management, and the Executive are initialized.

5. The thread's create time is set, and its thread ID (TID) is created.

6. Before the thread can execute, it needs a stack and a context in which to run, so these are set up. The stack size for the initial thread is taken from the image—there's no way to specify another size. If this is a Wow64 process, the Wow64 thread context will also be initialized.

7. The thread environment block (TEB) is allocated for the new thread.

8. The user-mode thread start address is stored in the ETHREAD. This is the system-supplied thread startup function in Ntdll.dll (*RtlUserThreadStart*). The user's specified Windows start address is stored in the ETHREAD in a different location so that debugging tools such as Process Explorer can query the information.

9. *KeInitThread* is called to set up the KTHREAD structure. The thread's initial and current base priorities are set to the process' base priority, and its affinity and quantum are set to that of the process. This function also sets the initial thread ideal processor. (See the section "Ideal and Last Processor" for a description of how this is chosen.) *KeInitThread* next allocates a kernel stack for the thread and initializes the machine-dependent hardware context for the thread, including the context, trap, and exception frames. The thread's context is set up so that the thread will start in kernel mode in *KiThreadStartup*. Finally, *KeInitThread* sets the thread's state to Initialized and returns to *PspAllocateThread*.

10. If this is a UMS thread, *PspUmsInitThread* is called to initialize the UMS state.

Once that work is finished, *NtCreateUserProcess* calls *PspInsertThread* to perform the following steps:

1. A check is made to ensure that the thread's group affinity does not violate job limitations (which we already described earlier). In the process create path, this check is skipped because it was already done at the earlier stage.

2. Checks are made to ensure that the process hasn't already been terminated, that the thread hasn't already been terminated, or that the thread hasn't even been able to start running. If any of these cases are true, thread creation will fail.

3. The KTHREAD part of the thread object is initialized by calling *KeStartThread*. This involves inheriting scheduler settings from the owner process, setting the ideal node and processor, updating the group affinity, and inserting the thread in the process list maintained by KPROCESS (a separate list from the one in EPROCESS). Additionally, on x64 systems, another systemwide list of processes, *KiProcessListHead*, is used by PatchGuard to maintain the integrity of the executive's *PsActiveProcessHead*. Finally, the stack count of the process is incremented.

4. The thread count in the process object is incremented, and the owner process' I/O priority and page priority are inherited. If this is the highest number of threads the process has ever had, the thread count high watermark is updated as well. If this was the second thread in the process, the primary token is frozen (that is, it can no longer be changed, unless the process is a POSIX subsystem process).

5. If the thread is a UMS thread, the count of UMS threads is incremented.

6. The thread is inserted in the process' thread list, and the thread is suspended if the creating process requested it.

7. If CPU rate limiting is enabled, the rate control APC is initialized and the *CpuThrottled* bit is set in the KTHREAD.

8. The object is inserted, and any registered thread callbacks are called. If this was the first thread in the process (and therefore, the operation happened as part of the *CreateProcess* path), the registered kernel process callbacks are also called.

9. The handle is created with *ObOpenObjectByPointer*.

10. The thread is readied for execution by calling *KeReadyThread*. It enters the deferred ready queue, the process is paged out, and a page in is requested.

Stage 5: Performing Windows Subsystem–Specific Post-Initialization

Once *NtCreateUserProcess* returns with a success code, all the necessary executive process and thread objects have been created. Kernel32.dll then performs various operations related to Windows subsystem–specific operations to finish initializing the process.

First of all, various checks are made for whether Windows should allow the executable to run. These checks include validating the image version in the header and checking whether Windows application certification has blocked the process (through a group policy). On specialized editions of Windows Server 2008 R2, such as Windows Web Server 2008 R2 and Windows HPC Server 2008 R2, additional checks are made to see whether the application imports any disallowed APIs.

If software restriction policies dictate, a restricted token is created for the new process. Afterward, the application-compatibility database is queried to see whether an entry exists in either the registry or system application database for the process. Compatibility shims will not be applied at this point—the information will be stored in the PEB once the initial thread starts executing (Stage 6).

At this point, Kernel32.dll sends a message to the Windows subsystem so that it can set up SxS information (see the end of this section for more information on side-by-side assemblies) such as manifest files, DLL redirection paths, and out-of-process execution for the new process. It also initializes the Windows subsystem structures for the process and initial thread. The message includes the following information:

- Process and thread handles

- Entries in the creation flags

- ID of the process' creator

- Flag indicating whether the process belongs to a Windows application (so that Csrss can determine whether or not to show the startup cursor)

- UI language information

- DLL redirection and .local flags

- Manifest file information

The Windows subsystem performs the following steps when it receives this message:

1. CsrCreateProcess duplicates a handle for the process and thread. In this step, the usage count of the process and the thread is incremented from 1 (which was set at creation time) to 2.

2. If a process priority class isn't specified, CsrCreateProcess sets it according to the algorithm described earlier in this section.

3. The Csrss process structure (CSR_PROCESS) is allocated.

4. The new process' exception port is set to be the general function port for the Windows subsystem so that the Windows subsystem will receive a message when a second-chance exception occurs in the process. (For further information on exception handling, see Chapter 3.)

5. The Csrss thread structure (CSR_THREAD) is allocated and initialized.

6. CsrCreateThread inserts the thread in the list of threads for the process.

7. The count of processes in this session is incremented.

8. The process shutdown level is set to 0x280 (the default process shutdown level—see *SetProcessShutdownParameters* in the MSDN Library documentation for more information).

9. The new *Csrss* process structure is inserted into the list of Windows subsystem-wide processes.

10. The per-process data structure used by the kernel-mode part of the Windows subsystem (W32PROCESS) is allocated and initialized.

11. The application start cursor is displayed. This cursor is the familiar rolling doughnut shape— the way that Windows says to the user, "I'm starting something, but you can use the cursor in the meantime." If the process doesn't make a GUI call after two seconds, the cursor reverts to the standard pointer. If the process does make a GUI call in the allotted time, *CsrCreateProcess* waits five seconds for the application to show a window. After that time, *CsrCreateProcess* resets the cursor again.

After *Csrss* has performed these steps, *CreateProcess* checks whether the process was run elevated (which means it was executed through *ShellExecute* and elevated by the AppInfo service after the consent dialog box was shown to the user). This includes checking whether the process was a setup program. If it was, the process' token is opened, and the virtualization flag is turned on so that the application is virtualized. (See the information on UAC and virtualization in Chapter 6.) If the application contained elevation shims or had a requested elevation level in its manifest, the process is destroyed and an elevation request is sent to the AppInfo service. (See Chapter 6 for more information on elevation.)

Note that most of these checks are not performed for protected processes; because these processes must have been designed for Windows Vista or later, there's no reason why they should require elevation, virtualization, or application-compatibility checks and processing. Additionally, allowing mechanisms such as the shim engine to use its usual hooking and memory-patching techniques on a protected process would result in a security hole if someone could figure how to insert arbitrary shims that modify the behavior of the protected process. Additionally, because the Shim Engine is installed by the parent process, which might not have access to its child protected process, even legitimate shimming cannot work.

Stage 6: Starting Execution of the Initial Thread

At this point, the process environment has been determined, resources for its threads to use have been allocated, the process has a thread, and the Windows subsystem knows about the new process. Unless the caller specified the CREATE_ SUSPENDED flag, the initial thread is now resumed so that it can start running and perform the remainder of the process initialization work that occurs in the context of the new process (Stage 7).

Stage 7: Performing Process Initialization in the Context of the New Process

The new thread begins life running the kernel-mode thread startup routine *KiThreadStartup*. *KiThreadStartup* lowers the thread's IRQL level from deferred procedure call (DPC)/dispatch level to APC level and then calls the system initial thread routine, *PspUserThreadStartup*. The user-specified thread start address is passed as a parameter to this routine.

First, this function disables the ability to swap the primary process token at runtime, which is reserved for POSIX support only (to emulate *setuid* behavior). It then sets the Locale ID and the ideal processor in the TEB, based on the information present in kernel-mode data structures, and then it checks whether thread creation actually failed. Next it calls *DbgkCreateThread*, which checks whether image notifications were sent for the new process. If they weren't, and notifications are enabled, an image notification is sent first for the process and then for the image load of Ntdll.dll. Note that this is done in this stage rather than when the images were first mapped because the process ID (which is required for the kernel callouts) is not yet allocated at that time.

Once those checks are completed, another check is performed to see whether the process is a debuggee. If it is, *PspUserThreadStartup* checks whether the debugger notifications have already been sent for this process. If not, a create process message is sent through the debug object (if one is present) so that the process startup debug event (CREATE_PROCESS_DEBUG_INFO) can be sent to the appropriate debugger process. This is followed by a similar thread startup debug event and by another debug event for the image load of Ntdll.dll. *DbgkCreateThread* then waits for a reply from the debugger (via the *ContinueDebugEvent* function).

Now that the debugger has been notified, *PspUserThreadStartup* looks at the result of the initial check on the thread's life. If it was killed on startup, the thread is terminated. This check is done after the debugger and image notifications to be sure that the kernel-mode and user-mode debuggers don't miss information on the thread, even if the thread never got a chance to run.

Otherwise, the routine checks whether application prefetching is enabled on the system and, if so, calls the prefetcher (and Superfetch) to process the prefetch instruction file (if it exists) and prefetch pages referenced during the first 10 seconds the last time the process ran. (For details on the prefetcher and Superfetch, see Chapter 10 in Part 2.)

PspUserThreadStartup then checks whether the systemwide cookie in the *SharedUserData* structure has been set up yet. If it hasn't, it generates it based on a hash of system information such as the number of interrupts processed, DPC deliveries, and page faults. This systemwide cookie is used in the internal decoding and encoding of pointers, such as in the heap manager to protect against certain classes of exploitation. (For more information on heap manager security, see Chapter 10 in Part 2.)

Finally, *PspUserThreadStartup* sets up the initial thunk context to run the image-loader initialization routine (*LdrInitializeThunk* in Ntdll.dll), as well as the systemwide thread startup stub

(*RtlUserThreadStart* in Ntdll.dll). These steps are done by editing the context of the thread in place and then issuing an exit from system service operation, which loads the specially crafted user context. The *LdrInitializeThunk* routine initializes the loader, the heap manager, NLS tables, thread-local storage (TLS) and fiber-local storage (FLS) arrays, and critical section structures. It then loads any required DLLs and calls the DLL entry points with the DLL_PROCESS_ ATTACH function code.

Once the function returns, *NtContinue* restores the new user context and returns to user mode—thread execution now truly starts.

RtlUserThreadStart uses the address of the actual image entry point and the start parameter and calls the application's entrypoint. These two parameters have also already been pushed onto the stack by the kernel. This complicated series of events has two purposes. First, it allows the image loader inside Ntdll.dll to set up the process internally and behind the scenes so that other user-mode code can run properly. (Otherwise, it would have no heap, no thread-local storage, and so on.)

Second, having all threads begin in a common routine allows them to be wrapped in exception handling so that when they crash, Ntdll.dll is aware of that and can call the unhandled exception filter inside Kernel32.dll. It is also able to coordinate thread exit on return from the thread's start routine and to perform various cleanup work. Application developers can also call *SetUnhandledExceptionFilter* to add their own unhandled exception-handling code.

EXPERIMENT: Tracing Process Startup

Now that we've looked in detail at how a process starts up and the different operations required to begin executing an application, we're going to use Process Monitor to look at some of the file I/O and registry keys that are accessed during this process.

Although this experiment will not provide a complete picture of all the internal steps we've described, you'll be able to see several parts of the system in action, notably prefetch and Superfetch, image-file execution options and other compatibility checks, and the image loader's DLL mapping.

We'll look at a very simple executable—Notepad.exe—and launch it from a Command Prompt window (Cmd.exe). It's important that we look both at the operations inside Cmd. exe and those inside Notepad.exe. Recall that a lot of the user-mode work is performed by *CreateProcess*, which is called by the parent process before the kernel has created a new process object.

To set things up correctly, add two filters to Process Monitor: one for Cmd.exe, and one for Notepad.exe—these are the only two processes you should include. Be sure that you don't have any currently running instances of these two processes so that you know you're looking at the right events. The filter window should look like this:

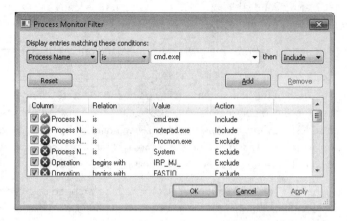

Next, make sure that event logging is currently disabled (clear File, Capture Events), and then start up the command prompt. Enable event logging (using the File menu again, or simply press CTRL+E or click the magnifying glass icon on the toolbar), and then type **Notepad.exe** and press Enter. On a typical Windows system, you should see anywhere between 500 and 1500 events appear. Hide the Sequence and Time Of Day columns so that you can focus your attention on the columns of interest. Your window should look similar to the one shown next.

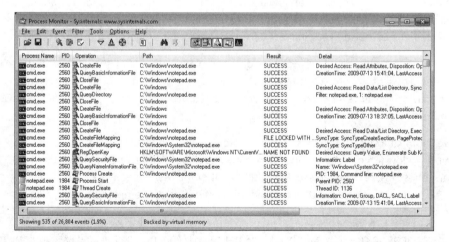

Just as described in Stage 1 of the *CreateProcess* flow, one of the first things to notice is that just before the process is started and the first thread is created, Cmd.exe does a registry read at HKLM\SOFTWARE\Microsoft\Windows NT\CurrentVersion\Image File Execution Options. Because there were no image-execution options associated with Notepad.exe, the process was created as is.

As with this and any other event in Process Monitor's log, you have the ability to see whether each part of the process creation flow was performed in user mode or kernel mode, and by which routines, by looking at the stack of the event. To do this, double-click on the *RegOpenKey* event and switch to the Stack tab. The following screen shows the standard stack on a 32-bit Windows machine.

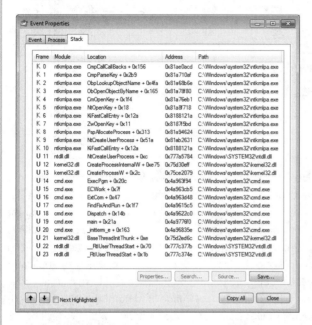

This stack shows that you already reached the part of process creation performed in kernel mode (through *NtCreateUserProcess*) and that the helper routine *PspAllocateProcess* is responsible for this check.

Going down the list of events after the thread and process have been created, you will notice three groups of events. The first is a simple check for application-compatibility flags, which will let the user-mode process creation code know if checks inside the application-compatibility database are required through the shim engine.

This check is followed by multiple reads to Side-By-Side, Manifest, and MUI/Language keys, which are part of the assembly framework mentioned earlier. Finally, you might see file I/O to one or more .sdb files, which are the application-compatibility databases on the system. This I/O is where additional checks are done to see if the shim engine needs to be invoked for this application. Because Notepad is a well-behaved Microsoft program, it doesn't require any shims.

The following screen shows the next series of events, which happen inside the Notepad process itself. These are actions initiated by the user-mode thread startup wrapper in kernel mode, which performs the actions described earlier. The first two are the Notepad.exe and Ntdll.dll image load debug notification messages, which can be generated only now that code is running inside Notepad's process context and not the context for the command prompt.

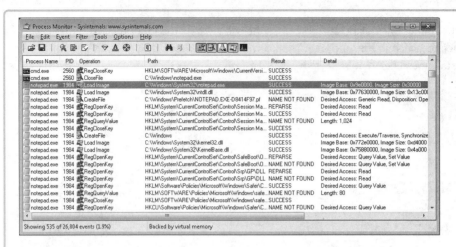

Next, the prefetcher kicks in, looking for a prefetch database file that has already been generated for Notepad. (For more information on the prefetcher, see Chapter 10 in Part 2.) On a system where Notepad has already been run at least once, this database will exist, and the prefetcher will begin executing the commands specified inside it. If this is the case, scrolling down you will see multiple DLLs being read and queried. Unlike typical DLL loading, which is done by the user-mode image loader by looking at the import tables or when an application manually loads a DLL, these events are being generated by the prefetcher, which is already aware of the libraries that Notepad will require. Typical image loading of the DLLs required happens next, and you will see events similar to the ones shown here:

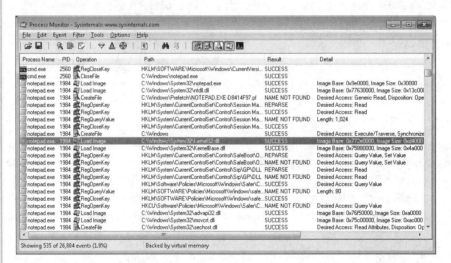

These events are now being generated from code running inside user mode, which was called once the kernel-mode wrapper function finished its work. Therefore, these are the first events coming from *LdrpInitializeProcess*, which we mentioned is the internal system wrapper function for any new process, before the start address wrapper is called. You can confirm this on your own by looking at the stack of these events—for example, the kernel32.dll image load event, which is shown in the next screen:

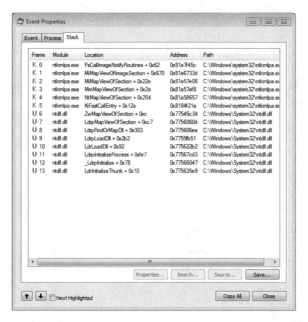

Further events are generated by this routine and its associated helper functions until you finally reach events generated by the *WinMain* function inside Notepad, which is where code under the developer's control is now being executed. Describing in detail all the events and user-mode components that come into play during process execution would fill up this entire chapter, so exploration of any further events is left as an exercise for the reader.

Thread Internals

Now that we've dissected processes, let's turn our attention to the structure of a thread. Unless explicitly stated otherwise, you can assume that anything in this section applies to both user-mode threads and kernel-mode system threads (which are described in Chapter 2).

Data Structures

At the operating-system level, a Windows thread is represented by an executive thread object. The executive thread object encapsulates an ETHREAD structure, which in turn contains a KTHREAD structure as its first member. These are illustrated in Figure 5-8. The ETHREAD structure and the other structures it points to exist in the system address space, with the exception of the thread environment block (TEB), which exists in the process address space (again, because user-mode components need to access it).

The Windows subsystem process (*Csrss*) maintains a parallel structure for each thread created in a Windows subsystem application, called the CSR_THREAD. For threads that have called a Windows subsystem USER or GDI function, the kernel-mode portion of the Windows subsystem (Win32k.sys) maintains a per-thread data structure (called the W32THREAD) that the KTHREAD structure points to.

Note The fact that the executive, high-level, graphics-related, Win32k thread structure is pointed to by the KTHREAD, instead of the ETHREAD, appears to be a layer violation or oversight in the standard kernel's abstraction architecture—the scheduler and other low-level components do not use this field.

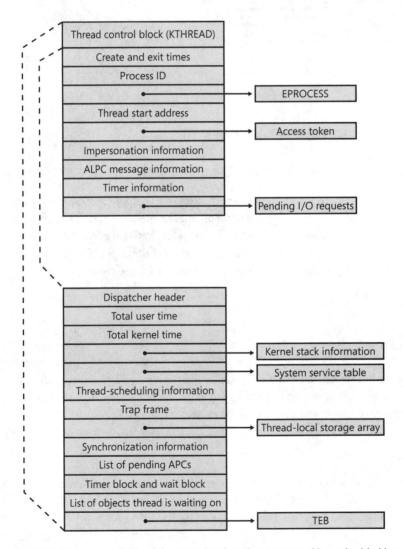

FIGURE 5-8 Important fields of the executive thread structure and its embedded kernel thread structure

Most of the fields illustrated in Figure 5-8 are self-explanatory. The first member of the ETHREAD is called the Tcb, for "Thread control block"; this is a structure of type KTHREAD. Following that are the thread identification information, the process identification information (including a pointer to the owning process so that its environment information can be accessed), security information in the form of a pointer to the access token and impersonation information, and finally, fields relating to Asynchronous Local Procedure Call (ALPC) messages and pending I/O requests. Some of these key fields are covered in more detail elsewhere in this book. For more details on the internal structure of an ETHREAD structure, you can use the kernel debugger *dt* command to display its format.

Let's take a closer look at two of the key thread data structures referred to in the preceding text: the KTHREAD and the TEB. The KTHREAD structure (which is the *Tcb* member of the ETHREAD) contains information that the Windows kernel needs to perform thread scheduling, synchronization, and timekeeping functions.

EXPERIMENT: Displaying ETHREAD and KTHREAD Structures

The ETHREAD and KTHREAD structures can be displayed with the *dt* command in the kernel debugger. The following output shows the format of an ETHREAD on a 32-bit system:

```
lkd> dt nt!_ethread
nt!_ETHREAD
    +0x000 Tcb                  : _KTHREAD
    +0x1e0 CreateTime           : _LARGE_INTEGER
    +0x1e8 ExitTime             : _LARGE_INTEGER
    +0x1e8 KeyedWaitChain       : _LIST_ENTRY
    +0x1f0 ExitStatus           : Int4B
...
    +0x270 AlpcMessageId        : Uint4B
    +0x274 AlpcMessage          : Ptr32 Void
    +0x274 AlpcReceiveAttributeSet : Uint4B
    +0x278 AlpcWaitListEntry : _LIST_ENTRY
    +0x280 CacheManagerCount : Uint4B
```

The KTHREAD can be displayed with a similar command or by typing **dt nt!_ETHREAD Tcb**, as was shown in the EPROCESS/KPROCESS experiment earlier:

```
lkd> dt nt!_kthread
nt!_KTHREAD
    +0x000 Header               : _DISPATCHER_HEADER
    +0x010 CycleTime            : Uint8B
    +0x018 HighCycleTime        : Uint4B
    +0x020 QuantumTarget        : Uint8B
...
    +0x05e WaitIrql             : UChar
    +0x05f WaitMode             : Char
    +0x060 WaitStatus           : Int4B
```

EXPERIMENT: Using the Kernel Debugger *!thread* Command

The kernel debugger *!thread* command dumps a subset of the information in the thread data structures. Some key elements of the information the kernel debugger displays can't be displayed by any utility, including the following information: internal structure addresses; priority details; stack information; the pending I/O request list; and, for threads in a wait state, the list of objects the thread is waiting for.

To display thread information, use either the *!process* command (which displays all the threads of a process after displaying the process information) or the *!thread* command with the address of a thread object to display a specific thread.

EXPERIMENT: Viewing Thread Information

The following output is the detailed display of a process produced by using the Tlist utility in the Debugging Tools for Windows. Notice that the thread list shows Win32StartAddr. This is the address passed to the *CreateThread* function by the application. All the other utilities, except Process Explorer, that show the thread start address show the actual start address (a function in Ntdll.dll), not the application-specified start address.

```
C:\Program Files\Windows Kits\8.0\Debuggers\x86>tlist winword
3232 WINWORD.EXE        648739_Chap05.docx - Microsoft Word
   CWD:     C:\Users\Alex Ionescu\Documents\
   CmdLine: "C:\Program Files\Microsoft Office\Office14\WINWORD.EXE" /n "C:\Users\Alex
Ionescu\Documents\Chapter5.docx
   VirtualSize:    531024 KB   PeakVirtualSize:    585248 KB
   WorkingSetSize:122484 KB   PeakWorkingSetSize:181532 KB
   NumberOfThreads: 12
   2104 Win32StartAddr:0x2fde10ec LastErr:0x00000000 State:Waiting
   2992 Win32StartAddr:0x7778fd0d LastErr:0x00000000 State:Waiting
   3556 Win32StartAddr:0x3877e970 LastErr:0x00000000 State:Waiting
   2436 Win32StartAddr:0x3877e875 LastErr:0x00000000 State:Waiting
   3136 Win32StartAddr:0x3877e875 LastErr:0x00000000 State:Waiting
   3412 Win32StartAddr:0x3877e875 LastErr:0x00000000 State:Waiting
   1096 Win32StartAddr:0x3877e875 LastErr:0x00000000 State:Waiting
    912 Win32StartAddr:0x74497832 LastErr:0x00000000 State:Waiting
   1044 Win32StartAddr:0x389b0926 LastErr:0x00000583 State:Waiting
   1972 Win32StartAddr:0x694532fb LastErr:0x00000000 State:Waiting
   4056 Win32StartAddr:0x75f9c83e LastErr:0x00000000 State:Waiting
   1124 Win32StartAddr:0x777903e9 LastErr:0x00000000 State:Waiting
  14.0.5123.5000 shp  0x2FDE0000  C:\Program Files\Microsoft Office\Office14\WINWORD.EXE
  6.1.7601.17725 shp  0x77760000  C:\Windows\SYSTEM32\ntdll.dll
  6.1.7601.17651 shp  0x75CE0000  C:\Windows\system32\kernel32.dll
```

The TEB, illustrated in Figure 5-9, is one of the data structures explained in this section that exists in the process address space (as opposed to the system space). Internally, it is made up of a header called the *TIB* (Thread Information Block), which mainly existed for compatibility with OS/2 and Win9x applications. It also allows exception and stack information to be kept into a smaller structure when creating new threads by using an *Initial TIB*.

The TEB stores context information for the image loader and various Windows DLLs. Because these components run in user mode, they need a data structure writable from user mode. That's why this structure exists in the process address space instead of in the system space, where it would be writable only from kernel mode. You can find the address of the TEB with the kernel debugger *!thread* command.

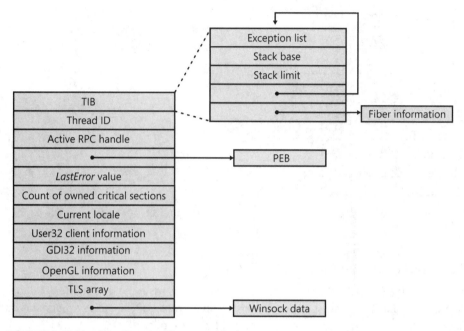

FIGURE 5-9 Fields of the thread environment block

EXPERIMENT: Examining the TEB

You can dump the TEB structure with the *!teb* command in the kernel debugger. The output looks like this:

```
kd> !teb
TEB at 7ffde000
    ExceptionList:          019e8e44
    StackBase:              019f0000
    StackLimit:             019db000
    SubSystemTib:           00000000
    FiberData:              00001e00
...
    PEB Address:            7ffd9000
    LastErrorValue:         0
    LastStatusValue:        c0000139
    Count Owned Locks:      0
    HardErrorMode:          0
```

The CSR_THREAD, illustrated in Figure 5-10 is analogous to the data structure of CSR_PROCESS, but it's applied to threads. As you might recall, this is maintained by each *Csrss* process within a session and identifies the Windows subsystem threads running within it. The CSR_THREAD stores a handle that *Csrss* keeps for the thread, various flags, and a pointer to the CSR_PROCESS for the thread. It also stores another copy of the thread's creation time.

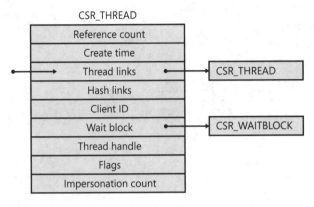

FIGURE 5-10 Fields of the CSR thread

EXPERIMENT: Examining the CSR_THREAD

You can dump the CSR_THREAD structure with the *!dt* command in the user-mode debugger while attached to a *Csrss* process. Follow the instructions in the CSR_PROCESS experiment from earlier to safely perform this operation. The output looks like this:

```
0:000> !dt v 001c7630
PCSR_THREAD @ 001c7630:
   +0x000 CreateTime       : _LARGE_INTEGER 0x1cb9fb6'00f90498
   +0x008 Link             : _LIST_ENTRY [ 0x1c0ab0 - 0x1c0f00 ]
   +0x010 HashLinks        : _LIST_ENTRY [ 0x75f19b38 - 0x75f19b38 ]
   +0x018 ClientId         : _CLIENT_ID
   +0x020 Process          : 0x001c0aa0 _CSR_PROCESS
   +0x024 ThreadHandle     : 0x000005c4
   +0x028 Flags            : 0
   +0x02c ReferenceCount   : 1
   +0x030 ImpersonateCount : 0
```

Finally, the W32THREAD structure, illustrated in Figure 5-11, is analogous to the data structure of WIN32PROCESS, but it's applied to threads This structure mainly contains information useful for the GDI subsystem (brushes and DC attributes) as well as for the User Mode Print Driver framework (UMPD) that vendors use to write user-mode printer drivers. Finally, it contains a rendering state useful for desktop compositing and anti-aliasing.

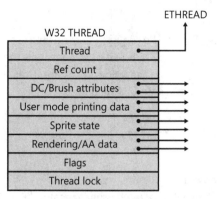

FIGURE 5-11 Fields of the Win32k thread

EXPERIMENT: Examining the W32THREAD

You can dump the W32THREAD structure by looking at the output of the *!thread* command, which gives a pointer to it in the Win32Thread output field. Alternatively, if you use the *dt* command, the KTHREAD block has a field called Win32Thread that contains the pointer to this structure. Recall that only a GUI thread will have a W32THREAD structure, so it's possible that certain threads, such as background or worker threads, will not have an associated W32THREAD. Because there is no extension to view a W32THREAD, you need to use the *dt* command, as shown here:

```
dt win32k!_w32thread ffb79dd8
   +0x000 pEThread          : 0x83ad4b60 _ETHREAD
   +0x004 RefCount          : 1
   +0x008 ptlW32            : (null)
   +0x00c pgdiDcattr        : 0x00130740
   +0x010 pgdiBrushAttr     : (null)
   +0x014 pUMPDObjs         : (null)
   +0x018 pUMPDHeap         : (null)
   +0x01c pUMPDObj          : (null)
...
   +0x0a8 bEnableEngUpdateDeviceSurface : 0 ''
   +0x0a9 bIncludeSprites   : 0 ''
   +0x0ac ulWindowSystemRendering : 0
```

Birth of a Thread

A thread's life cycle starts when a program creates a new thread. The request filters down to the Windows executive, where the process manager allocates space for a thread object and calls the kernel to initialize the thread control block (KTHREAD). The steps in the following list are taken inside the Windows *CreateThread* function in Kernel32.dll to create a Windows thread:

1. *CreateThread* converts the Windows API parameters to native flags and builds a native structure describing object parameters (OBJECT_ATTRIBUTES). See Chapter 3 for more information.

2. *CreateThread* builds an attribute list with two entries: client ID and TEB address. This allows *CreateThread* to receive those values once the thread has been created. (For more information on attribute lists, see the section "Flow of *CreateProcess*" earlier in this chapter.)

3. *NtCreateThreadEx* is called to create the user-mode context and probe and capture the attribute list. It then calls *PspCreateThread* to create a suspended executive thread object. For a description of the steps performed by this function, see the descriptions of Stage 3 and Stage 5 in the section "Flow of *CreateProcess*."

4. *CreateThread* allocates an activation context for the thread used by side-by-side assembly support. It then queries the activation stack to see if it requires activation, and it does so if needed. The activation stack pointer is saved in the new thread's TEB.

5. *CreateThread* notifies the Windows subsystem about the new thread, and the subsystem does some setup work for the new thread.

6. The thread handle and the thread ID (generated during step 3) are returned to the caller.

7. Unless the caller created the thread with the CREATE_SUSPENDED flag set, the thread is now resumed so that it can be scheduled for execution. When the thread starts running, it executes the steps described in the earlier section "Stage 7: Performing Process Initialization in the Context of the New Process" before calling the actual user's specified start address.

Examining Thread Activity

Examining thread activity is especially important if you are trying to determine why a process that is hosting multiple services is running (such as Svchost.exe, Dllhost.exe, or Lsass.exe) or why a process is hung.

There are several tools that expose various elements of the state of Windows threads: WinDbg (in user-process attach and kernel-debugging mode), Performance Monitor, and Process Explorer. (The tools that show thread-scheduling information are listed in the section "Thread Scheduling.")

To view the threads in a process with Process Explorer, select a process and open the process properties (by double-clicking on the process or clicking on the Process, Properties menu item). Then click on the Threads tab. This tab shows a list of the threads in the process and four columns of information. For each thread, it shows its ID, the percentage of CPU consumed (based on the refresh interval configured), the number of cycles charged to the thread, and the thread start address. You can sort by any of these four columns.

New threads that are created are highlighted in green, and threads that exit are highlighted in red. (The highlight duration can be configured with the Options, Difference Highlight Duration menu item.) This might be helpful to discover unnecessary thread creation occurring in a process. (In general, threads should be created at process startup, not every time a request is processed inside a process.)

As you select each thread in the list, Process Explorer displays the thread ID, start time, state, CPU time counters, number of cycles charged, number of context switches, the ideal processor and its group, and the base and current priority. There is a Kill button, which will terminate an individual thread, but this should be used with extreme care. Another option is the Suspend button, which will prevent the thread from forward execution and thus prevent a runaway thread from consuming CPU time. However, this can also lead to deadlocks and should be used with the same care as the Kill button. Finally, the Permissions button allows you to view the security descriptor. (See Chapter 6, "Security," for more information on security descriptors) of the thread.

Unlike Task Manager and all other process/processor monitoring tools, Process Explorer uses the clock cycle counter designed for thread run-time accounting (as described later in this chapter), instead of the clock interval timer, so you will see a significantly different view of CPU consumption using Process Explorer. This is because many threads run for such a short amount of time that they are seldom (if ever) the currently running thread when the clock interval timer interrupt occurs, so they are not charged for much of their CPU time, leading clock-based tools to perceive a CPU usage of 0%. On the other hand, the total number of clock cycles represents the actual number of processor cycles that each thread in the process accrued. It is independent of the clock interval timer's resolution because the count is maintained internally by the processor at each cycle and updated by Windows at each interrupt entry. (A final accumulation is done before a context switch.)

The thread start address is displayed in the form "module!function", where module is the name of the .exe or .dll. The function name relies on access to symbol files for the module. (See "Experiment: Viewing Process Details with Process Explorer" in Chapter 1.) If you are unsure what the module is, click the Module button. This opens an Explorer file properties window for the module containing the thread's start address (for example, the .exe or .dll).

Note For threads created by the Windows *CreateThread* function, Process Explorer displays the function passed to *CreateThread*, not the actual thread start function. That is because all Windows threads start at a common thread startup wrapper function (*RtlUserThreadStart* in Ntdll.dll). If Process Explorer showed the actual start address, most threads in processes would appear to have started at the same address, which would not be helpful in trying to understand what code the thread was executing. However, if Process Explorer can't query the user-defined startup address (such as in the case of a protected process), it will show the wrapper function, so you will see all threads starting at *RtlUserThreadStart*.

However, the thread start address displayed might not be enough information to pinpoint what the thread is doing and which component within the process is responsible for the CPU consumed by the thread. This is especially true if the thread start address is a generic startup function (for example, if the function name does not indicate what the thread is actually doing). In this case, examining the thread stack might answer the question. To view the stack for a thread, double-click on the thread of interest (or select it and click the Stack button). Process Explorer displays the thread's stack (both user and kernel, if the thread was in kernel mode).

 Note While the user mode debuggers (WinDbg, Ntsd, and Cdb) permit you to attach to a process and display the user stack for a thread, Process Explorer shows both the user and kernel stack in one easy click of a button. You can also examine user and kernel thread stacks using WinDbg in local kernel debugging mode.

Viewing the thread stack can also help you determine why a process is hung. As an example, on one system, Microsoft Office PowerPoint was hanging for one minute on startup. To determine why it was hung, after PowerPoint was started, Process Explorer was used to examine the thread stack of the one thread in the process. The result is shown in Figure 5-12.

FIGURE 5-12 Hung thread stack in PowerPoint

This thread stack shows that PowerPoint (line 10) called a function in Mso.dll (the central Microsoft Office DLL), which called the *OpenPrinterW* function in Winspool.drv (a DLL used to connect to printers). Winspool.drv then dispatched to a function *OpenPrinterRPC*, which then called a function in the RPC runtime DLL, indicating it was sending the request to a remote printer. So, without having to understand the internals of PowerPoint, the module and function names displayed on the thread stack indicate that the thread was waiting to connect to a network printer. On this particular system, there was a network printer that was not responding, which explained the delay starting PowerPoint. (Microsoft Office applications connect to all configured printers at process startup.) The connection to that printer was deleted from the user's system, and the problem went away.

Finally, when looking at 32-bit applications running on 64-bit systems as a Wow64 process (see Chapter 3 for more information on Wow64), Process Explorer shows both the 32-bit and 64-bit stack for threads. Because at the time of the system call proper, the thread has been switched to a 64-bit stack and context, simply looking at the thread's 64-bit stack would reveal only half the story—the 64-bit part of the thread, with Wow64's thunking code. So, when examining Wow64 processes, be sure to take into account both the 32-bit and 64-bit stacks. An example of a Wow64 thread inside Microsoft Office Word 2007 is shown in Figure 5-13. The highlighted stack frame and all stack frames below it are the 32-bit stack frames from the 32-bit stack. The stack frames above the highlighted frame are on the 64-bit stack.

FIGURE 5-13 Example Wow64 stack

Limitations on Protected Process Threads

As we discussed in the process internals section, protected processes have several limitations in terms of which access rights will be granted, even to the users with the highest privileges on the system. These limitations also apply to threads inside such a process. This ensures that the actual code running inside the protected process cannot be hijacked or otherwise affected through standard Windows functions, which require access rights that are not granted for protected process threads. In fact, the only permissions granted are THREAD_SUSPEND_RESUME and THREAD_SET/QUERY_LIMITED_INFORMATION.

EXPERIMENT: Viewing Protected Process Thread Information

In the previous section, we took a look at how Process Explorer can be helpful in examining thread activity to determine the cause of potential system or application issues. This time, we'll use Process Explorer to look at a protected process and see how the different access rights being denied affect its ability and usefulness on such a process.

Find the Audiodg.exe service inside the process list. This is a process responsible for much of the core work behind the user-mode audio stack in Windows, and it requires protection to ensure that high-definition decrypted audio content does not leak out to untrusted sources. Bring up the process properties view, and take a look at the Performance tab. Notice how the numbers for WS Private, WS Shareable, and WS Shared are 0, although the total Working Set is still displayed. This is an example of the THREAD_QUERY_INFORMATION versus THREAD_QUERY_LIMITED_INFORMATION rights.

More importantly, take a look at the Threads tab. As you can see here, Process Explorer is unable to show the Win32 thread start address and instead displays the standard thread start wrapper inside Ntdll.dll. If you try clicking the Stack button, you'll get an error, because Process Explorer needs to read the virtual memory inside the protected process, which it can't do.

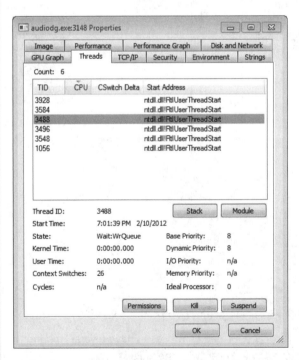

Finally, note that although the Base and Dynamic priorities are shown, the I/O and Memory priorities are not, which is another example of the limited versus full query information access right. As you try to kill a thread inside Audiodg.exe, notice yet another access denied error: recall the lack of THREAD_TERMINATE access.

Worker Factories (Thread Pools)

Worker factories refer to the internal mechanism used to implement user-mode thread pools. The legacy thread pool routines were completely implemented in user mode inside the Ntdll.dll library, and the Windows API provided various routines to call into the relevant routines, which provided waitable timers, wait callbacks, and automatic thread creation and deletion, depending on the amount of work being done.

Because the kernel can have direct control over thread scheduling, creation, and termination without the typical costs associated with doing these operations from user mode, most of the functionality required to support the user-mode thread pool implementation in Windows is now located in the kernel instead, which also simplifies the code that developers need to write. For example, creating a worker pool in a remote process can be done with a single API call, instead of the complex series of virtual memory calls this normally requires. Under this model, Ntdll.dll merely provides the interfaces and high-level APIs required for interfacing with the worker factory code.

This kernel-managed thread pool functionality in Windows is managed by an object manager type called *TpWorkerFactory*, as well as four native system calls for managing the factory and its workers (*NtCreateWorkerFactory*, *NtWorkerFactoryWorkerReady*, *NtReleaseWorkerFactoryWorker*, *NtShutdownWorkerFactory*), two query/set native calls (*NtQueryInformationWorkerFactory* and *NtSetInformationWorkerFactory*), and a wait call (*NtWaitForWorkViaWorkerFactory*).

Just like other native system calls, these calls provide user mode with a handle to the *TpWorkerFactory* object, which contains information such as the name and object attributes, the desired access mask, and a security descriptor. Unlike other system calls wrapped by the Windows API, however, thread-pool management is handled by Ntdll.dll's native code, which means that developers work with an opaque descriptor (a TP_WORK pointer) owned by Ntdll.dll, in which the actual handle is stored.

As its name suggests, the worker factory implementation is responsible for allocating worker threads (and calling the given user-mode worker thread entry point), maintaining a minimum and maximum thread count (allowing for either permanent worker pools or totally dynamic pools), as well as other accounting information. This enables operations such as shutting down the thread pool to be performed with a single call to the kernel, because the kernel has been the only component responsible for thread creation and termination.

Because the kernel dynamically creates new threads as needed, based on minimum and maximum numbers provided, this also increases the scalability of applications using the new thread-pool implementation. A worker factory will create a new thread whenever all of the following conditions are met:

- The number of available workers is lower than the maximum number of workers configured for the factory (default of 500).

- The worker factory has bound objects (a bound object can be, for example, an ALPC port that this worker thread is waiting on) or a thread has been activated into the pool.

- There are pending I/O request packets (IRPs; see Chapter 8, "I/O System," in Part 2, for more information) associated with a worker thread.

- Dynamic thread creation is enabled.

And it will terminate threads whenever they've become idle for more than 10 seconds (by default).

Furthermore, while developers have always been able to take advantage of as many threads as possible (based on the number of processors on the system) through the old implementation, but through support for dynamic processors in Windows Server (see the section on this topic later in this chapter), it's now possible for applications using thread pools to automatically take advantage of new processors added at run time.

Note that the worker factory support is merely a wrapper to manage mundane tasks that would otherwise have to be performed in user mode (at a loss of performance), and much of the logic of the new thread-pool code remains in the Ntdll.dll side of this architecture. (Theoretically, by using undocumented functions, a different thread-pool implementation can be built around worker factories.) Also, it is not the worker factory code that provides the scalability, wait internals, and efficiency of work processing. Instead, it is a much older component of Windows that we already discussed— I/O completion ports, or more correctly, kernel queues (KQUEUE; see Chapter 8 in Part 2 for more information).

In fact, when creating a worker factory, an I/O completion port must have already been created by user mode, and the handle needs to be passed on. It is through this I/O completion port that the user-mode implementation will queue work and also wait for work—but by calling the worker factory system calls instead of the I/O completion port APIs. Internally, however, the "release" worker factory call (which queues work) is a wrapper around *IoSetIoCompletionEx*, which increases pending work, while the "wait" call is a wrapper around *IoRemoveIoCompletion*. Both these routines call into the kernel queue implementation.

Therefore, the job of the worker factory code is to manage either a persistent, static, or dynamic thread pool; wrap the I/O completion port model into interfaces that try to prevent stalled worker queues by automatically creating dynamic threads; and to simplify global cleanup and termination operations during a factory shutdown request (as well as to easily block new requests against the factory in such a scenario).

Unfortunately, the data structures used by the worker factory implementation are not in the public symbols, but it is still possible to look at some worker pools, as we'll show in the next experiment. Additionally, the *NtQueryInformationWorkerFactory* API dumps almost every field in the worker factory structure.

EXPERIMENT: Looking at Thread Pools

Because of the advantages of using the thread-pool mechanism, many core system components and applications make use of it, especially when dealing with resources such as ALPC ports (to dynamically process incoming requests at an appropriate and scalable level). One of the ways to identify which processes are using a worker factory is to look at the handle list in Process Explorer. Follow these steps to look at some details behind them:

1. Run Process Explorer, and select Show Unnamed Handles And Mappings from the View menu. Unfortunately, worker factories aren't named by Ntdll.dll, so you need to take this step in order to see the handles.

2. Select Lsm.exe from the list of processes, and look at the handle table. Make sure that the lower pane is shown (View, Show Lower Pane) and is displaying handle table mode (View, Lower Pane View, Handles).

3. Right-click on the lower pane columns, and then click on Select Columns. Make sure that the Type column is selected to be shown, and click it to sort by type.

4. Now scroll down the handles, looking at the Type column, until you find a handle of type *TpWorkerFactory*. You should see something like this:

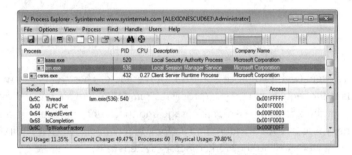

Notice how the *TpWorkerFactory* handle is immediately preceded by an *IoCompletion* handle (numerically; sort by "Handle" to see this). As was described previously, this occurs because before creating a worker factory, a handle to an I/O completion port on which work will be sent must be created.

5. Now double-click Lsm.exe in the list of processes, and click on the Threads tab. You should see something similar to the image here:

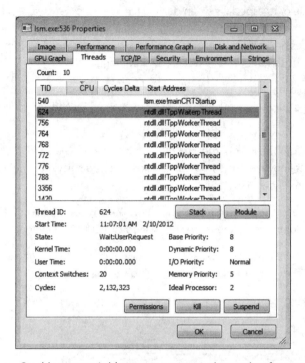

On this system (with two processors), the worker factory has created six worker threads at the request of Lsm.exe (processes can define a minimum and maximum number of threads) and based on its usage and the count of processors on the machine. These threads are identified as *TppWorkerThread*, which is Ntdll.dll's worker entry point when calling the worker factory system calls.

6. Ntdll.dll is responsible for its own internal accounting inside the worker thread wrapper (*TppWorkerThread*) before calling the worker callback that the application has registered. By looking at the Wait reason in the State information for each thread, you

can get a rough idea of what each worker thread might be doing. Double-click on one of the threads inside an LPC wait to look at its stack. Here's an example:

This specific worker thread is being used by Lsm.exe for LPC communication. Because the local session manager needs to communicate with other components such as *Smss* and *Csrss* through LPC, it makes sense that it would want a number of its threads to be busy replying and waiting for LPC messages. (The more threads doing this, the less stalling there is on the LPC pipeline.)

If you look at other worker threads, you'll see some are waiting for objects such as events. A process can have multiple thread pools, and each thread pool can have a variety of threads doing completely unrelated tasks. It's up to the developer to assign work and to call the thread pool APIs to register this work through Ntdll.dll.

Thread Scheduling

This section describes the Windows scheduling policies and algorithms. The first subsection provides a condensed description of how scheduling works on Windows and a definition of key terms. Then Windows priority levels are described from both the Windows API and the Windows kernel points of view. After a review of the relevant Windows utilities and tools that relate to scheduling, the detailed data structures and algorithms that make up the Windows scheduling system are presented, including a description of common scheduling scenarios and how thread selection, as well as processor selection, occurs.

Overview of Windows Scheduling

Windows implements a priority-driven, preemptive scheduling system—at least one of the highest-priority runnable (ready) threads always runs, with the caveat that certain high-priority threads ready to run might be limited by the processors on which they might be allowed or preferred to run on, a phenomenon called *processor affinity*. Processor affinity is defined based on a given processor group, which collects up to 64 processors. By default, threads can run only on any available processors within the processor group associated with the process (to maintain compatibility with older versions of Windows which supported only 64 processors), but developers can alter processor affinity by using the appropriate APIs or by setting an affinity mask in the image header, while users can use tools to change affinity at runtime or at process creation. However, although multiple threads in a process can be associated with different groups, a thread on its own can run only on the processors available within its assigned group. Additionally, developers can choose to create group-aware applications, which use extended scheduling APIs to associate logical processors on different groups with the affinity of their threads. Doing so converts the process into a multigroup process that can theoretically run its threads on any available processor within the machine.

EXPERIMENT: Viewing Ready Threads

You can view the list of ready threads with the kernel debugger *!ready* command. This command displays the thread or list of threads that are ready to run at each priority level. In the following example, generated on a 32-bit machine with a dual-core processor, two threads are ready to run at priority 8 on the first logical processor, and one thread at priority 10, two threads at priority 9, and three threads at priority 8 are ready to run on the second logical processor. Determining which of these threads get to run on their respective processor is a simple matter of picking the first thread on top of the highest priority queue (thread 857d9030 for logical processor 0, and thread 857c0030 for logical processor 1), but why the queues contain the threads they do is a complex result at the end of several algorithms that the scheduler uses. We will cover this topic later in this section.

```
kd> !ready
Processor 0: Ready Threads at priority 8
    THREAD 857d9030  Cid 0ec8.0e30  Teb: 7ffdd000 Win32Thread: 00000000 READY
    THREAD 855c8300  Cid 0ec8.0eb0  Teb: 7ff9c000 Win32Thread: 00000000 READY
Processor 1: Ready Threads at priority 10
    THREAD 857c0030  Cid 04c8.0378  Teb: 7ffdf000 Win32Thread: fef7f8c0 READY
Processor 1: Ready Threads at priority 9
    THREAD 87fc86f0  Cid 0ec8.04c0  Teb: 7ffd3000 Win32Thread: 00000000 READY
    THREAD 88696700  Cid 0ec8.0ce8  Teb: 7ffa0000 Win32Thread: 00000000 READY
Processor 1: Ready Threads at priority 8
    THREAD 856e5520  Cid 0ec8.0228  Teb: 7ff98000 Win32Thread: 00000000 READY
    THREAD 85609d78  Cid 0ec8.09b0  Teb: 7ffd9000 Win32Thread: 00000000 READY
    THREAD 85fdeb78  Cid 0ec8.0218  Teb: 7ff72000 Win32Thread: 00000000 READY
```

After a thread is selected to run, it runs for an amount of time called a quantum. A quantum is the length of time a thread is allowed to run before another thread at the same priority level is given a turn to run. Quantum values can vary from system to system and process to process for any of three reasons:

- System configuration settings (long or short quantums, variable or fixed quantums, and priority separation)

- Foreground or background status of the process

- Use of the job object to alter the quantum

These details are explained in more details in the "Quantum" section later in the chapter, as well as in the "Job Objects" section).

A thread might not get to complete its quantum, however, because Windows implements a preemptive scheduler: if another thread with a higher priority becomes ready to run, the currently running thread might be preempted before finishing its time slice. In fact, a thread can be selected to run next and be preempted before even beginning its quantum!

The Windows scheduling code is implemented in the kernel. There's no single "scheduler" module or routine, however—the code is spread throughout the kernel in which scheduling-related events occur. The routines that perform these duties are collectively called the kernel's dispatcher. The following events might require thread dispatching:

- A thread becomes ready to execute—for example, a thread has been newly created or has just been released from the wait state.

- A thread leaves the running state because its time quantum ends, it terminates, it yields execution, or it enters a wait state.

- A thread's priority changes, either because of a system service call or because Windows itself changes the priority value.

- A thread's processor affinity changes so that it will no longer run on the processor on which it was running.

At each of these junctions, Windows must determine which thread should run next on the logical processor that was running the thread, if applicable, or on which logical processor the thread should now run on. After a logical processor has selected a new thread to run, it eventually performs a context switch to it. A context switch is the procedure of saving the volatile processor state associated with a running thread, loading another thread's volatile state, and starting the new thread's execution.

As already noted, Windows schedules at the thread granularity. This approach makes sense when you consider that processes don't run but only provide resources and a context in which their threads run. Because scheduling decisions are made strictly on a thread basis, no consideration is given to what process the thread belongs to. For example, if process A has 10 runnable threads, process B has 2 runnable threads, and all 12 threads are at the same priority, each thread would theoretically receive one-twelfth of the CPU time—Windows wouldn't give 50 percent of the CPU to process A and 50 percent to process B.

Priority Levels

To understand the thread-scheduling algorithms, one must first understand the priority levels that Windows uses. As illustrated in Figure 5-14, internally Windows uses 32 priority levels, ranging from 0 through 31. These values divide up as follows:

- Sixteen real-time levels (16 through 31)

- Sixteen variable levels (0 through 15), out of which level 0 is reserved for the zero page thread

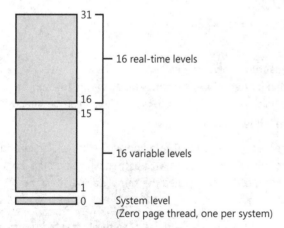

FIGURE 5-14 Thread priority levels

Thread priority levels are assigned from two different perspectives: those of the Windows API and those of the Windows kernel. The Windows API first organizes processes by the priority class to which they are assigned at creation (the numbers represent the internal PROCESS_PRIORITY_CLASS_ index recognized by the kernel): Real-time (4), High (3), Above Normal (7), Normal (2), Below Normal (5), and Idle (1).

It then assigns a relative priority of the individual threads within those processes. Here, the numbers represent a priority delta that is applied to the process base priority: Time-critical (15), Highest (2), Above-normal (1), Normal (0), Below-normal (–1), Lowest (–2), and Idle (–15).

Therefore, in the Windows API, each thread has a base priority that is a function of its process priority class and its relative thread priority. In the kernel, the process priority class is converted to a base priority by using the *PspPriorityTable* and the PROCESS_PRIORITY_CLASS indices shown earlier, which sets priorities of 4, 8, 13, 24, 6, and 10, respectively. (This is a fixed mapping that cannot be changed.) The relative thread priority is then applied as a differential to this base priority. For example, a "Highest" thread will receive a thread base priority of two levels higher than the base priority of its process.

This mapping from Windows priority to internal Windows numeric priority is shown in Table 5-3.

TABLE 5-3 Mapping of Windows Kernel Priorities to the Windows API

Priority Class Relative Priority	Realtime	High	Above Normal	Normal	Below Normal	Idle
Time Critical (+ SATURATION)	31	15	15	15	15	15
Highest (+2)	26	15	12	10	8	6
Above Normal (+1)	25	14	11	9	7	5
Normal (0)	24	13	10	8	6	4
Below Normal (-1)	23	12	9	7	5	3
Lowest (-2)	22	11	8	6	4	2
Idle (- SATURATION)	16	1	1	1	1	1

You'll note that the Time-Critical and Idle relative thread priorities maintain their respective values regardless of the process priority class (unless it is Realtime). This is because the Windows API requests saturation of the priority from the kernel, by actually passing in 16 or -16 as the requested relative priority (instead of 15 or -15). This is then recognized by the kernel as a request for saturation, and the Saturation field in KTHREAD is set. This causes, for positive saturation, the thread to receive the highest possible priority within its priority class (dynamic or real-time), or for negative saturation, the lowest possible one. Additionally, future requests to change the base priority of the process will no longer affect the base priority of these threads, because saturated threads are skipped in the processing code.

Whereas a process has only a single base priority value, each thread has two priority values: current and base. Scheduling decisions are made based on the current priority. As explained in the following section on priority boosting, the system under certain circumstances increases the priority of threads in the dynamic range (0 through 15) for brief periods. Windows never adjusts the priority of threads in the real-time range (16 through 31), so they always have the same base and current priority.

A thread's initial base priority is inherited from the process base priority. A process, by default, inherits its base priority from the process that created it. This behavior can be overridden on the *CreateProcess* function or by using the command-line start command. A process priority can also be changed after being created by using the *SetPriorityClass* function or various tools that expose that function, such as Task Manager and Process Explorer (by right-clicking on the process and choosing a new priority class). For example, you can lower the priority of a CPU-intensive process so that it does not interfere with normal system activities. Changing the priority of a process changes the thread priorities up or down, but their relative settings remain the same.

Normally, user applications and services start with a normal base priority, so their initial thread typically executes at priority level 8. However, some Windows system processes (such as the session manager, service control manager, and local security authentication process) have a base process priority slightly higher than the default for the Normal class (8). This higher default value ensures that the threads in these processes will all start at a higher priority than the default value of 8.

Real-Time Priorities

You can raise or lower thread priorities within the dynamic range in any application; however, you must have the increase scheduling priority privilege to enter the real-time range. Be aware that many important Windows kernel-mode system threads run in the real-time priority range, so if threads spend excessive time running in this range, they might block critical system functions (such as in the memory manager, cache manager, or other device drivers).

Using the standard Windows APIs, once a process has entered the real-time range, all of its threads (even Idle ones) must run at one of the real-time priority levels. It is thus impossible to mix real-time and dynamic threads within the same process through standard interfaces. This is because the *SetThreadPriority* API calls the native *NtSetInformationThread* API with the *ThreadBasePriority* information class, which allows priorities to remain only in the same range. Furthermore, this information class allows priority changes only in the recognized Windows API deltas of –2 to 2 (or real-time/idle), unless the request comes from CSRSS or a real-time process. In other words, this means that a real-time process does have the ability to pick thread priorities anywhere between 16 and 31, even though the standard Windows API relative thread priorities would seem to limit its choices based on the table that was shown earlier.

However, by calling this API with the *ThreadActualBasePriority* information class, the kernel base priority for the thread can be directly set, including in the dynamic range for a real-time process.

 Note As illustrated in Figure 5-15, which shows the interrupt request levels (IRQLs), although Windows has a set of priorities called real-time, they are not real-time in the common definition of the term. This is because Windows doesn't provide true, real-time operating system facilities, such as guaranteed interrupt latency or a way for threads to obtain a guaranteed execution time.

Interrupt Levels vs. Priority Levels

As illustrated in Figure 5-15 of the interrupt request levels (IRQLs) for a 32-bit system, threads normally run at IRQL 0 (called *passive level*, because no interrupts are in process and none are blocked) or IRQL 1 (APC level). (For a description of how Windows uses interrupt levels, see Chapter 3.) User-mode code always runs at passive level. Because of this, no user-mode thread, regardless of its priority, can ever block hardware interrupts (although high-priority, real-time threads can block the execution of important system threads).

Threads running in kernel mode, although initially scheduled at passive level or APC level, can raise IRQL to higher levels—for example, while executing a system call that involves thread dispatching, memory management, or input/output. If a thread does raise IRQL to dispatch level or above, no further thread-scheduling behavior will occur on its processor until it lowers IRQL below dispatch level. A thread executing at dispatch level or above blocks the activity of the thread scheduler and prevents thread context switches on its processor.

A thread running in kernel mode can be running at APC level if it is running a special kernel APC; or it can temporarily raise IRQL to APC level to block the delivery of special kernel APCs. (For more information on APCs, see Chapter 3.) However, executing at APC level does not alter the scheduling behavior of the thread vs. other threads; it affects only the delivery of kernel APCs to that thread. In fact, a thread executing in kernel mode at APC level can be preempted in favor of a higher priority thread running in user mode at passive level.

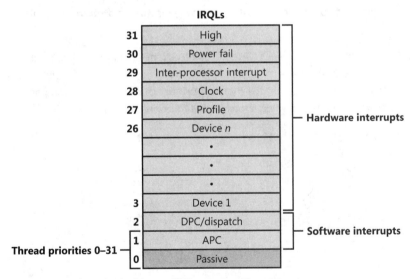

FIGURE 5-15 Thread priorities vs. IRQLs on an x86 system

Using Tools to Interact with Priority

You can change (and view) the base-process priority with Task Manager and Process Explorer. You can kill individual threads in a process with Process Explorer (which should be done, of course, with extreme care).

You can view individual thread priorities with the Performance Monitor, Process Explorer, or WinDbg. Although it might be useful to increase or lower the priority of a process, it typically does not make sense to adjust individual thread priorities within a process, because only a person who thoroughly understands the program (in other words, typically only the developer himself) would understand the relative importance of the threads within the process.

The only way to specify a starting priority class for a process is with the start command in the Windows command prompt. If you want to have a program start every time with a specific priority, you can define a shortcut to use the start command by beginning the command with **cmd /c**. This runs the command prompt, executes the command on the command line, and terminates the command prompt. For example, to run Notepad in the low-process priority, the shortcut is **cmd /c start /low Notepad.exe**.

EXPERIMENT: Examining and Specifying Process and Thread Priorities

Try the following experiment:

1. From an elevated command prompt, type **start /realtime notepad**. Notepad should open.

2. Run Process Explorer, and select Notepad.exe from the list of processes. Double-click on Notepad.exe to show the process properties window, and then click on the Threads tab, as shown here. Notice that the dynamic priority of the thread in Notepad is *24*. This matches the real-time value shown in the following image.

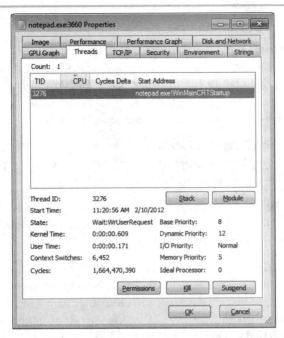

3. Task Manager can show you similar information. Press Ctrl+Shift+Esc to start Task Manager, and click on the Processes tab. Right-click on the Notepad.exe process, and select the Set Priority option. You can see that Notepad's process priority class is Realtime, as shown in the following dialog box:

Windows System Resource Manager

Windows Server 2008 R2 Standard Edition and higher SKUs include an optionally installable component called Windows System Resource Manager (WSRM). It permits the administrator to configure policies that specify CPU utilization, affinity settings, and memory limits (both physical and virtual) for processes. In addition, WSRM can generate resource utilization reports that can be used for accounting and verification of service-level agreements with users.

Policies can be applied for specific applications (by matching the name of the image with or without specific command-line arguments), users, or groups. The policies can be scheduled to take effect at certain periods or can be enabled all the time.

After you set a resource-allocation policy to manage specific processes, the WSRM service monitors CPU consumption of managed processes and adjusts process base priorities when those processes do not meet their target CPU allocations.

The physical memory limitation uses the function *SetProcessWorkingSetSizeEx* to set a hard-working set maximum. The virtual memory limit is implemented by the service checking the private virtual memory consumed by the processes. (See Chapter 10 in Part 2 for an explanation of these memory limits.) If this limit is exceeded, WSRM can be configured to either kill the processes or write an entry to the Event Log. This behavior can be used to detect a process with a memory leak before it consumes all the available committed memory on the system. Note that WSRM memory limits do not apply to Address Windowing Extensions (AWE) memory, large page memory, or kernel memory (nonpaged or paged pool).

Thread States

Before you can comprehend the thread-scheduling algorithms, you need to understand the various execution states that a thread can be in. The thread states are as follows:

- **Ready** A thread in the ready state is waiting to execute (or ready to be in-swapped after completing a wait). When looking for a thread to execute, the dispatcher considers only the pool of threads in the ready state.

- **Deferred ready** This state is used for threads that have been selected to run on a specific processor but have not actually started running there. This state exists so that the kernel can minimize the amount of time the per-processor lock on the scheduling database is held.

- **Standby** A thread in the standby state has been selected to run next on a particular processor. When the correct conditions exist, the dispatcher performs a context switch to this thread. Only one thread can be in the standby state for each processor on the system. Note that a thread can be preempted out of the standby state before it ever executes (if, for example, a higher priority thread becomes runnable before the standby thread begins execution).

- **Running** Once the dispatcher performs a context switch to a thread, the thread enters the running state and executes. The thread's execution continues until its quantum ends (and another thread at the same priority is ready to run), it is preempted by a higher priority thread, it terminates, it yields execution, or it voluntarily enters the waiting state.

- **Waiting** A thread can enter the waiting state in several ways: a thread can voluntarily wait for an object to synchronize its execution, the operating system can wait on the thread's behalf (such as to resolve a paging I/O), or an environment subsystem can direct the thread to suspend itself. When the thread's wait ends, depending on the priority, the thread either begins running immediately or is moved back to the ready state.

- **Transition** A thread enters the transition state if it is ready for execution but its kernel stack is paged out of memory. Once its kernel stack is brought back into memory, the thread enters the ready state.

- **Terminated** When a thread finishes executing, it enters the terminated state. Once the thread is terminated, the executive thread object (the data structure in a nonpaged pool that describes the thread) might or might not be deallocated. (The object manager sets the policy regarding when to delete the object.)

- **Initialized** This state is used internally while a thread is being created.

Table 5-4 describes the state transitions for threads, and Figure 5-16 illustrates a simplified version. (The numeric values shown represent the value of the thread-state performance counter.) In the simplified version, the Ready, Standby, and Deferred Ready states are represented as one. This reflects the fact that the Standby and Deferred Ready states act as temporary placeholders for the scheduling routines. These states are almost always very short-lived; threads in these states always transition quickly to Ready, Running, or Waiting. More details on what happens at each transition are included later in this section.

TABLE 5-4 Thread States and Transitions

	Init	Ready	Running	Standby	Terminated	Waiting	Transition	Deferred Ready	
Init									A thread becomes Initialized during the first few moments of its creation (*KeStartThread*).
Ready								A thread is added in the dispatcher-ready database of its ideal processor.	
Running		Selected by *KiSearch-ForNew-Thread*		Picked up for execution by local CPU		Preemption after wait satisfaction			

	Init	Ready	Running	Standby	Terminated	Waiting	Transition	Deferred Ready	
Standby		Selected by *KiSelect-NextThread*						Selected *by KiDeferred-ReadyThread* for remote CPU	
Terminated	Killed before *PspInsert-Thread* finished		Killed						A thread can kill only itself. It must be in the Running state before entering KeTerminateThread.
Waiting			Thread enters a wait						Only running threads can wait.
Transition						Kernel stack no longer resident			Only waiting threads can transition.
Deferred Ready	Last step in *PspInsert-Thread*	Affinity change	Thread becomes preempted (if old processor is no longer available)	Affinity change		Wait satisfaction (but no preemption)	Kernel stack swap-in completed		

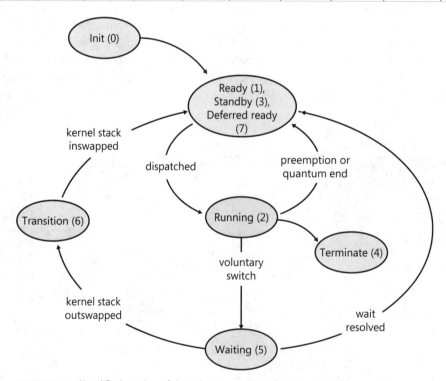

FIGURE 5-16 Simplified version of thread states and transitions

EXPERIMENT: Thread-Scheduling State Changes

You can watch thread-scheduling state changes with the Performance tool in Windows. This utility can be useful when you're debugging a multithreaded application and you're unsure about the state of the threads running in the process. To watch thread-scheduling state changes by using the Performance tool, follow these steps:

1. Run Notepad (Notepad.exe).

2. Start the Performance tool by selecting All Programs from the Start menu and then selecting Performance Monitor from the Administrative Tools menu. Click on the Performance Monitor entry under Monitoring Tools.

3. Select the chart view if you're in some other view.

4. Right-click on the graph, and choose Properties.

5. Click on the Graph tab, and change the chart vertical scale maximum to 7. (As you'll see from the explanation text for the performance counter, thread states are numbered from 0 through 7.) Click OK.

6. Click the Add button on the toolbar to bring up the Add Counters dialog box.

7. Select the Thread performance object, and then select the Thread State counter. Select the Show Description check box to see the definition of the values:

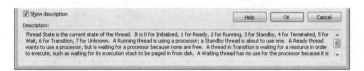

8. In the Instances box, select <All instances> and type Notepad before clicking Search. Scroll down until you see the Notepad process (*notepad/0*); select it, and click the Add button.

9. Scroll back up in the Instances box to the *Mmc* process (the Microsoft Management Console process running the System Monitor), select all the threads (*mmc/0*, *mmc/1*, and so on), and add them to the chart by clicking the Add button. Before you click Add, you should see something like the dialog box that follows.

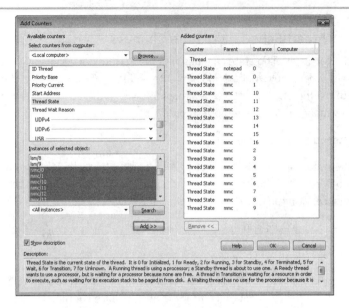

10. Now close the Add Counters dialog box by clicking OK.

11. You should see the state of the Notepad thread (the very top line in the following figure) as a 5. As shown in the explanation text you saw under step 7, this number represents the waiting state (because the thread is waiting for GUI input):

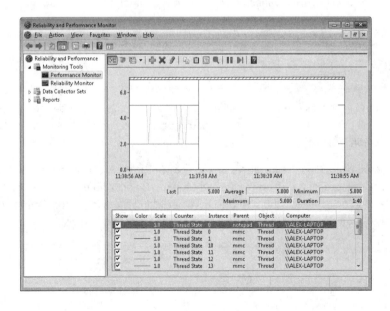

12. Notice that one thread in the *Mmc* process (running the Performance tool snap-in) is in the running state (number 2). This is the thread that's querying the thread states, so it's always displayed in the running state.

13. You'll never see Notepad in the running state (unless you're on a multiprocessor system) because *Mmc* is always in the running state when it gathers the state of the threads you're monitoring.

Dispatcher Database

To make thread-scheduling decisions, the kernel maintains a set of data structures known collectively as the dispatcher database, illustrated in Figure 5-17. The dispatcher database keeps track of which threads are waiting to execute and which processors are executing which threads.

To improve scalability, including thread-dispatching concurrency, Windows multiprocessor systems have per-processor dispatcher ready queues, as illustrated in Figure 5-17. In this way, each CPU can check its own ready queues for the next thread to run without having to lock the systemwide ready queues.

The per-processor ready queues, as well as the per-processor ready summary, are part of the processor control block (PRCB) structure. (To see the fields in the PRCB, type **dt nt!_kprcb** in the kernel debugger.) The names of each component that we will talk about (in italics) are field members of the PRCB structure.

The dispatcher ready queues (*DispatcherReadyListHead*) contain the threads that are in the ready state, waiting to be scheduled for execution. There is one queue for each of the 32 priority levels. To speed up the selection of which thread to run or preempt, Windows maintains a 32-bit bit mask called the ready summary (*ReadySummary*). Each bit set indicates one or more threads in the ready queue for that priority level. (Bit 0 represents priority 0, and so on.)

Instead of scanning each ready list to see whether it is empty or not (which would make scheduling decisions dependent on the number of different priority threads), a single bit scan is performed as a native processor command to find the highest bit set. Regardless of the number of threads in the ready queue, this operation takes a constant amount of time, which is why you might sometimes see the Windows scheduling algorithm referred to as an O(1), or constant time, algorithm.

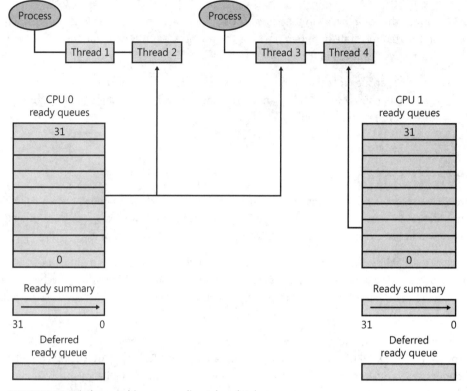

FIGURE 5-17 Windows multiprocessor dispatcher database

The dispatcher database is synchronized by raising IRQL to DISPATCH_LEVEL. (For an explanation of interrupt priority levels, see the "Trap Dispatching" section in Chapter 3.) Raising IRQL in this way prevents other threads from interrupting thread dispatching on the processor because threads normally run at IRQL 0 or 1. However, more is required than just raising IRQL, because other processors can simultaneously raise to the same IRQL and attempt to operate on their dispatcher database. How Windows synchronizes access to the dispatcher database is explained in the "Multiprocessor Systems" section later in the chapter.

Quantum

As mentioned earlier in the chapter, a quantum is the amount of time a thread gets to run before Windows checks to see whether another thread at the same priority is waiting to run. If a thread completes its quantum and there are no other threads at its priority, Windows permits the thread to run for another quantum.

On client versions of Windows, threads run by default for 2 clock intervals; on server systems, by default, a thread runs for 12 clock intervals. (We'll explain how you can change these values later.) The rationale for the longer default value on server systems is to minimize context switching. By having a longer quantum, server applications that wake up as the result of a client request have a better chance of completing the request and going back into a wait state before their quantum ends.

The length of the clock interval varies according to the hardware platform. The frequency of the clock interrupts is up to the HAL, not the kernel. For example, the clock interval for most x86 uniprocessors is about 10 milliseconds (note that these machines are no longer supported by Windows and are only used here for example purposes), and for most x86 and x64 multiprocessors it is about 15 milliseconds. This clock interval is stored in the kernel variable *KeMaximumIncrement* as hundreds of nanoseconds.

Because thread run-time accounting is based on processor cycles, although threads still run in units of clock intervals, the system does not use the count of clock ticks as the deciding factor for how long a thread has run and whether its quantum has expired. Instead, when the system starts up, a calculation is made whose result is the number of clock cycles that each quantum is equivalent to. (This value is stored in the kernel variable *KiCyclesPerClockQuantum*.) This calculation is made by multiplying the processor speed in Hz (CPU clock cycles per second) with the number of seconds it takes for one clock tick to fire (based on the *KeMaximumIncrement* value described earlier).

The result of this accounting method is that threads do not actually run for a quantum number based on clock ticks; they instead run for a quantum target, which represents an estimate of what the number of CPU clock cycles the thread has consumed should be when its turn would be given up. This target should be equal to an equivalent number of clock interval timer ticks because, as you just saw, the calculation of clock cycles per quantum is based on the clock interval timer frequency, which you can check using the following experiment. On the other hand, because interrupt cycles are not charged to the thread, the actual clock time might be longer.

EXPERIMENT: Determining the Clock Interval Frequency

The Windows *GetSystemTimeAdjustment* function returns the clock interval. To determine the clock interval, download and run the Clockres program from Windows Sysinternals (www.microsoft.com/technet/sysinternals). Here's the output from a dual-core 64-bit Windows 7 system:

```
C:\>clockres

ClockRes v2.0 - View the system clock resolution
Copyright (C) 2009 Mark Russinovich
SysInternals - www.sysinternals.com

Maximum timer interval: 15.600 ms
Minimum timer interval: 0.500 ms
Current timer interval: 15.600 ms
```

Quantum Accounting

Each process has a quantum reset value in the process control block (KPROCESS). This value is used when creating new threads inside the process and is duplicated in the thread control block (KTHREAD), which is then used when giving a thread a new quantum target. The quantum reset value is stored in terms of actual quantum units (we'll discuss what these mean soon), which are then multiplied by the number of clock cycles per quantum, resulting in the quantum target.

As a thread runs, CPU clock cycles are charged at different events (context switches, interrupts, and certain scheduling decisions). If at a clock interval timer interrupt, the number of CPU clock cycles charged has reached (or passed) the quantum target, quantum end processing is triggered. If there is another thread at the same priority waiting to run, a context switch occurs to the next thread in the ready queue.

Internally, a quantum unit is represented as one third of a clock tick. (So one clock tick equals three quantums.) This means that on client Windows systems, threads, by default, have a quantum reset value of *6 (2 * 3)*, and that server systems have a quantum reset value of 36 (12 * 3). For this reason, the *KiCyclesPerClockQuantum* value is divided by three at the end of the calculation previously described, because the original value describes only CPU clock cycles per clock interval timer tick.

The reason a quantum was stored internally as a fraction of a clock tick rather than as an entire tick was to allow for partial quantum decay-on-wait completion on versions of Windows prior to Windows Vista. Prior versions used the clock interval timer for quantum expiration. If this adjustment were not made, it would have been possible for threads never to have their quantums reduced. For example, if a thread ran, entered a wait state, ran again, and entered another wait state but was never the currently running thread when the clock interval timer fired, it would never have its quantum charged for the time it was running. Because threads now have CPU clock cycles charged instead of quantums, and because this no longer depends on the clock interval timer, these adjustments are not required.

EXPERIMENT: Determining the Clock Cycles per Quantum

Windows doesn't expose the number of clock cycles per quantum through any function, but with the calculation and description we've given, you should be able to determine this on your own using the following steps and a kernel debugger such as WinDbg in local debugging mode:

1. Obtain your processor frequency as Windows has detected it. You can use the value stored in the PRCB's MHz field, which can be displayed with the *!cpuinfo* command. Here is a sample output of a dual-core Intel system running at 2829 MHz:

```
lkd> !cpuinfo
CP  F/M/S Manufacturer  MHz PRCB Signature     MSR 8B Signature Features
 0  6,15,6 GenuineIntel 2829 000000c700000000 >000000c700000000<a00f3fff
 1  6,15,6 GenuineIntel 2829 000000c700000000                    a00f3fff
                        Cached Update Signature 000000c700000000
                        Initial Update Signature 000000c700000000
```

2. Convert the number to Hertz (Hz). This is the number of CPU clock cycles that occur each second on your system. In this case, 2,829,000,000 cycles per second.

3. Obtain the clock interval on your system by using *clockres*. This measures how long it takes before the clock fires. On the sample system used here, this interval was 15.600100 ms.

4. Convert this number to the number of times the clock interval timer fires each second. One second is 1000 ms, so divide the number derived in step 3 by 1000. In this case, the timer fires every 0.0156001 seconds.

5. Multiply this count by the number of cycles each second that you obtained in step 2. In our case, 44,132,682.9 cycles have elapsed after each clock interval.

6. Remember that each quantum unit is one-third of a clock interval, so divide the number of cycles by three. In our example, this gives us 14,710,894, or 0xE0786E in hexadecimal. This is the number of clock cycles each quantum unit should take on a system running at 2829 MHz with a clock interval of around 15 ms.

7. To verify your calculation, dump the value of *KiCyclesPerClockQuantum* on your system—it should match.

```
1kd> dd nt!KiCyclesPerClockQuantum L1
81d31ae8  00e0786e
```

Controlling the Quantum

You can change the thread quantum for all processes, but you can choose only one of two settings: short (2 clock ticks, which is the default for client machines) or long (12 clock ticks, which is the default for server systems).

Note By using the job object on a system running with long quantums, you can select other quantum values for the processes in the job. For more information on the job object, see the "Job Objects" section later in the chapter.

To change this setting, right-click on your Computer icon on the desktop, or in Windows Explorer, choose Properties, click the Advanced System Settings label, click on the Advanced tab, click the Settings button in the Performance section, and finally click on the Advanced tab. The dialog box displayed is shown in Figure 5-18.

FIGURE 5-18 Quantum configuration in the Performance Options dialog box

The Programs setting designates the use of short, variable quantums—the default for client versions of Windows. If you install Terminal Services on a server system and configure the server as an application server, this setting is selected so that the users on the terminal server have the same quantum settings that would normally be set on a desktop or client system. You might also select this manually if you were running Windows Server as your desktop operating system.

The Background Services option designates the use of long, fixed quantums—the default for server systems. The only reason you might select this option on a workstation system is if you were using the workstation as a server system. However, because changes in this option take effect immediately, it might make sense to use it if the machine is about to run a background/server-style workload. For example, if a long-running computation, encoding or modeling simulation needs to run overnight, Background Services mode could be selected at night, and the system put back in Programs mode in the morning.

Finally, because Programs mode enables variable quantums, let us now explain what controls their variability.

Variable Quantums

When variable quantums are enabled, the variable quantum table (*PspVariableQuantums*) is loaded into the *PspForegroundQuantum* table that is used by the *PspComputeQuantum* function. Its algorithm will pick the appropriate quantum index based on whether or not the process is a foreground process (that is, whether it contains the thread that owns the foreground window on the desktop). If this is not the case, an index of zero is chosen, which corresponds to the default thread quantum described earlier. If it is a foreground process, the quantum index corresponds to the priority separation.

This priority separation value determines the priority boost (described in a later section of this chapter) that the scheduler will apply to foreground threads, and it is thus paired with an appropriate extension of the quantum: for each extra priority level (up to 2), another quantum is given to the thread. For example, if the thread receives a boost of one priority level, it receives an extra quantum as well. By default, Windows sets the maximum possible priority boost to foreground threads, meaning that the priority separation will be 2, therefore selecting quantum index 2 in the variable quantum table, leading to the thread receiving two extra quantums, for a total of 3 quantums.

Table 5-5 describes the exact quantum value (recall that this is stored in a unit representing 1/3rd of a clock tick) that will be selected based on the quantum index and which quantum configuration is in use.

TABLE 5-5 Quantum Values

	Short Quantum Index			Long Quantum Index		
Variable	6	12	18	12	24	36
Fixed	18	18	18	36	36	36

Thus, when a window is brought into the foreground on a client system, all the threads in the process containing the thread that owns the foreground window have their quantums tripled: threads in the foreground process run with a quantum of 6 clock ticks, whereas threads in other processes have the default client quantum of 2 clock ticks. In this way, when you switch away from a CPU-intensive process, the new foreground process will get proportionally more of the CPU, because when its threads run they will have a longer turn than background threads (again, assuming the thread priorities are the same in both the foreground and background processes).

Quantum Settings Registry Value

The user interface to control quantum settings described earlier modifies the registry value HKLM\SYSTEM\CurrentControlSet\Control\PriorityControl\Win32PrioritySeparation. In addition to specifying the relative length of thread quantums (short or long), this registry value also defines whether or not variable quantums should be used, as well as the priority separation (which, as you've seen, will determine the quantum index used when variable quantums are enabled). This value consists of 6 bits divided into the three 2-bit fields shown in Figure 5-19.

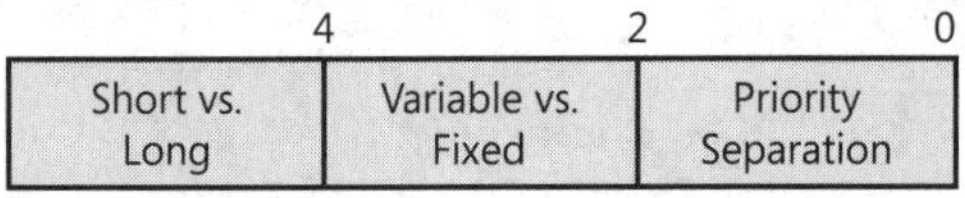

FIGURE 5-19 Fields of the Win32PrioritySeparation registry value

The fields shown in Figure 5-19 can be defined as follows:

- **Short vs. Long** A value of 1 specifies long quantums, and 2 specifies short ones. A setting of 0 or 3 indicates that the default appropriate for the system will be used (short for client systems, long for server systems).

- **Variable vs. Fixed** A setting of 1 means to enable the variable quantum table based on the algorithm shown in the "Variable Quantums" section. A setting of *0* or *3* means that the default appropriate for the system will be used (variable for client systems, fixed for server systems).

- **Priority Separation** This field (stored in the kernel variable *PsPrioritySeparation*) defines the priority separation (up to 2) as explained in the "Variable Quantums" section.

Note that when you're using the Performance Options dialog box (which was shown in Figure 5-18), you can choose from only two combinations: short quantums with foreground quantums tripled, or long quantums with no quantum changes for foreground threads. However, you can select other combinations by modifying the *Win32PrioritySeparation* registry value directly.

Note that the threads part of a process running in the idle process priority class always receive a single thread quantum (2 clock ticks), ignoring any sort of quantum configuration settings, whether set by default or set through the registry.

On Windows Server systems configured as applications servers, the initial value of the *Win32PrioritySeparation* registry value will be hex 26, which is identical to the value set by the Optimize Performance For Programs option in the Performance Options dialog box. This selects quantum and priority boost behavior like that on Windows client systems, which is appropriate for a server primarily used to host users' applications.

On Windows client systems and on servers not configured as application servers, the initial value of the *Win32PrioritySeparation* registry value will be 2. This provides values of 0 for the Short vs. Long and Variable vs. Fixed bit fields, relying on the default behavior of the system (depending on whether it is a client system or a server system) for these options, but it provides a value of 2 for the Priority Separation field. Once the registry value has been changed by use of the Performance Options dialog box, it cannot be restored to this original value other than by modifying the registry directly.

EXPERIMENT: Effects of Changing the Quantum Configuration

Using a local debugger (Kd or WinDbg), you can see how the two quantum configuration settings, Programs and Background Services, affect the *PsPrioritySeparation* and *PspForegroundQuantum* tables, as well as modify the *QuantumReset* value of threads on the system. Take the following steps:

1. Open the System utility in Control Panel (or right-click on your computer name's icon on the desktop, and choose Properties). Click the Advanced System Settings label, click on the Advanced tab, click the Settings button in the Performance section, and finally click on the Advanced tab. Select the Programs option, and click Apply. Keep this window open for the duration of the experiment.

2. Dump the values of *PsPrioritySeparation* and *PspForegroundQuantum*, as shown here. The values shown are what you should see on a Windows system after making the change in step 1. Notice how the variable, short quantum table is being used, and that a priority boost of 2 will apply to foreground applications:

```
lkd> dd PsPrioritySeparation L1
81d3101c  00000002
lkd> db PspForegroundQuantum L3
81d0946c  06 0c 12
...
```

3. Now take a look at the *QuantumReset* value of any process on the system. As described earlier, this is the default, full quantum of each thread on the system when it is replenished. This value is cached into each thread of the process, but the KPROCESS structure is easier to look at. Notice in this case it is 6, because WinDbg, like most other applications, gets the quantum set in the first entry of the *PspForegroundQuantum* table:

```
lkd> .process
Implicit process is now 85b32d90
lkd> dt nt!_KPROCESS 85b32d90 QuantumReset
nt!_KPROCESS
   +0x061 QuantumReset    : 6 ''
```

4. Now change the Performance option to Background Services in the dialog box you opened in step 1.

5. Repeat the commands shown in steps 2 and 3. You should see the values change in a manner consistent with our discussion in this section:

```
lkd> dd nt!PsPrioritySeparation L1
81d3101c  00000000
lkd> db nt!PspForegroundQuantum L3
81d0946c  24 24 24                              $$$
lkd> dt nt!_KPROCESS 85b32d90 QuantumReset
nt!_KPROCESS
   +0x061 QuantumReset    : 36 '$'
```

Priority Boosts

The Windows scheduler periodically adjusts the current priority of threads through an internal priority-boosting mechanism. In many cases, it does so for decreasing various latencies (that is, to make threads respond faster to the events they are waiting on) and increasing responsiveness. In others, it applies these boosts to prevent inversion and starvation scenarios. Here are some of the boost scenarios that will be described in this section (and their purpose):

- Boosts due to scheduler/dispatcher events (latency reduction)

- Boosts due to I/O completion (latency reduction)

- Boosts due to UI input (latency reduction/responsiveness)

- Boosts due to a thread waiting on an executive resource for too long (starvation avoidance)

- Boosts when a thread that's ready to run hasn't been running for some time (starvation and priority-inversion avoidance)

Like any scheduling algorithms, however, these adjustments aren't perfect, and they might not benefit all applications.

> **Note** Windows never boosts the priority of threads in the real-time range (16 through 31). Therefore, scheduling is always predictable with respect to other threads in the real-time range. Windows assumes that if you're using the real-time thread priorities, you know what you're doing.

Client versions of Windows also include another pseudo-boosting mechanism that occurs during multimedia playback. Unlike the other priority boosts, which are applied directly by kernel code, multimedia playback boosts are actually managed by a user-mode service called the MultiMedia Class Scheduler Service (MMCSS), but they are not really boosts—the service merely sets new base priorities for the threads as needed (by calling the user-mode native API to change thread priorities). Therefore, none of the rules regarding boosts apply. We'll first cover the typical kernel-managed priority boosts and then talk about MMCSS and the kind of "boosting" it performs.

Boosts Due to Scheduler/Dispatcher Events

Whenever a dispatch event occurs, the *KiExitDispatcher* routine is called, whose job it is to process the deferred ready list by calling *KiProcessThreadWaitList* and then call *KiCheckForThreadDispatch* to check whether any threads on the local processor should not be scheduled. Whenever such an event occurs, the caller can also specify which type of boost should be applied to the thread, as well as what priority increment the boost should be associated with. The following scenarios are considered as *AdjustUnwait* dispatch events because they deal with a dispatcher object entering a signaled state, which might cause one or more threads to wake up:

- An APC is queued to a thread.

- An event is set or pulsed.

- A timer was set, or the system time was changed, and timers had to be reset.

- A mutex was released or abandoned.

- A process exited.

- An entry was inserted in a queue, or the queue was flushed.

- A semaphore was released.

- A thread was alerted, suspended, resumed, frozen, or thawed.

- A primary UMS thread is waiting to switch to a scheduled UMS thread.

For scheduling events associated with a public API (such as *SetEvent*), the boost increment applied is specified by the caller. Windows recommends certain values to be used by developers, which will be described later. For alerts, a boost of 2 is applied, because the alert API does not have a parameter allowing a caller to set a custom increment.

The scheduler also has two special *AdjustBoost* dispatch events, which are part of the lock ownership priority mechanism. These boosts attempt to fix situations in which a caller that owns the lock at priority X ends up releasing the lock to a waiting thread at priority <= X. In this situation, the new owner thread must wait for its turn (if running at priority X), or worse, it might not even get to run at all if its priority is lower than X. This entails the releasing thread continuing its execution, even though it should have caused the new owner thread to wake up and take control of the processor. The following two dispatcher events cause an *AdjustBoost* dispatcher exit:

- An event is set through the *KeSetEventBoostPriority* interface, which is used by the ERESOURCE reader-writer kernel lock

- A gate is set through the *KeSignalGateBoostPriority* interface, which is used by various internal mechanisms when releasing a gate lock.

Unwait Boosts

Unwait boosts attempt to decrease the latency between a thread waking up due to an object being signaled (thus entering the Ready state) and the thread actually beginning its execution to process the unwait (thus entering the Running state). Because the event that the thread is waiting on could give some sort of information about, say, the state of available memory at the moment, it is important for this state not to change behind the scenes while the thread is still stuck in the Ready state— otherwise, it might become irrelevant or incorrect once the thread does start running.

The various Windows header files specify recommended values that kernel-mode callers of APIs such as *KeSetEvent* and *KeReleaseSemaphore* should use, which correspond to definitions such as MUTANT_INCREMENT and EVENT_INCREMENT. These definitions have always been set to 1 in the headers, so it is safe to assume that most unwaits on these objects result in a boost of 1. In the user-mode API, an increment cannot be specified, nor do the native system calls such as *NtSetEvent* have parameters to specify such a boost. Instead, when these APIs call the underlying *Ke* interface, they use the default _INCREMENT definition automatically. This is also the case when mutexes are abandoned or timers are reset due to a system time change: the system uses the default boost that normally would've been applied when the mutex would have been released. Finally, the APC boost is completely up to the caller. Soon, you'll see a specific usage of the APC boost related to I/O completion.

> **Note** Some dispatcher objects don't have boosts associated with them. For example, when a timer is set or expires, or when a process is signaled, no boost is applied.

All these boosts of +1 attempt to solve the initial problem by making the assumption that both the releasing and waiting threads are running at the same priority. By boosting the waiting thread by one priority level, the waiting thread should preempt the releasing thread as soon as the operation completes. Unfortunately on uniprocessor systems, if this assumption does not hold, the boost might not do much: if the waiting thread is waiting at priority 4 vs. the releasing thread at priority 8, waiting at priority 5 won't do much to reduce latency and force preemption. On multiprocessor systems, however, due to the stealing and balancing algorithms, this higher priority thread may have a higher chance to get picked up by another logical processor. This reality is due to a design choice made in the initial NT architecture, which is not to track lock ownership (except a few locks). That means the scheduler can't be sure who really owns an event, and if it's really being used as a lock. Even with lock ownership tracking, ownership is not usually passed in order to avoid convoy issues, other than in the ERESOURCE case which we'll explain below.

However, for certain kinds of lock objects using events or gates as their underlying synchronization object, the lock ownership boost resolves the dilemma. Also, due to the processor-distribution and load-balancing schemes you'll see later, on a multiprocessor machine, the ready thread might get picked up on another processor, and its high priority might increase the chances of it running on that secondary processor instead.

Lock Ownership Boosts

Because the executive-resource (ERESOURCE) and critical-section locks use underlying dispatcher objects, releasing these locks results in an unwait boost as described earlier. On the other hand, because the high-level implementation of these objects does track the owner of the lock, the kernel can make a more informed decision as to what kind of boost should be applied, by using the *AdjustBoost* reason. In these kinds of boosts, *AdjustIncrement* is set to the current priority of the releasing (or setting) thread, minus any GUI foreground separation boost, and before the *KiExitDispatcher* function is called, *KiRemoveBoostThread* is called by the event and gate code to return the releasing thread back to its regular priority (through the *KiComputeNewPriority* function). This step is needed to avoid a lock convoy situation, in which two threads repeatedly passing the lock between one another get ever-increasing boosts.

Note that pushlocks, which are unfair locks because ownership of the lock in a contended acquisition path is not predictable (rather, it's random, just like a spinlock), do not apply priority boosts due to lock ownership. This is because doing so only contributes to preemption and priority proliferation, which isn't required because the lock becomes immediately free as soon as it is released (bypassing the normal wait/unwait path).

Other differences between the lock ownership boost and the unwait boost will be exposed in the way that the scheduler actually applies boosting, which is the upcoming topic after this section.

Priority Boosting After I/O Completion

Windows gives temporary priority boosts upon completion of certain I/O operations so that threads that were waiting for an I/O have more of a chance to run right away and process whatever was being waited for. Although you'll find recommended boost values in the Windows Driver Kit (WDK) header files (by searching for "#define IO" in Wdm.h or Ntddk.h), the actual value for the boost is up to the device driver. (These values are listed in Table 5-6.) It is the device driver that specifies the boost when it completes an I/O request on its call to the kernel function, *IoCompleteRequest*. In Table 5-6, notice that I/O requests to devices that warrant better responsiveness have higher boost values.

TABLE 5-6 Recommended Boost Values

Device	Boost
Disk, CD-ROM, parallel, video	1
Network, mailslot, named pipe, serial	2
Keyboard, mouse	6
Sound	8

Note You might intuitively expect "better responsiveness" from your video card or disk than a boost of 1, but in fact, the kernel is trying to optimize for *latency*, which some devices (as well as human sensory inputs) are more sensitive to than others. To give you an idea, a sound card expects data around every 1 ms to play back music without perceptible glitches, while a video card needs to output at only 24 frames per second, or once every 40 ms, before the human eye can notice glitches.

As hinted earlier, these I/O completion boosts rely on the unwait boosts seen in the previous section. In Chapter 8 of Part 2, the mechanism of I/O completion will be shown in depth. For now, the important detail is that the kernel implements the signaling code in the *IoCompleteRequest* API through the use of either an APC (for asynchronous I/O) or through an event (for synchronous I/O). When a driver passes in, for example, IO_DISK_INCREMENT to *IoCompleteRequest* for an asynchronous disk read, the kernel calls *KeInsertQueueApc* with the boost parameter set to IO_DISK_INCREMENT. In turn, when the thread's wait is broken due to the APC, it receives a boost of *1*.

Be aware that the boost values given in the previous table are merely recommendations by Microsoft—driver developers are free to ignore them if they choose to do so, and certain specialized drivers can use their own values. For example, a driver handling ultrasound data from a medical device, which must notify a user-mode visualization application of new data, would probably use a boost value of *8* as well, to satisfy the same latency as a sound card.

In most cases, however, due to the way Windows driver stacks are built (again, see Chapter 8, "I/O System," in Part 2 for more information), driver developers often write *minidrivers*, which call into a Microsoft-owned driver that supplies its own boost to *IoCompleteRequest*. For example, RAID or SATA controller card developers would typically call *StorPortCompleteRequest* to complete processing their requests. This call does not have any parameter for a boost value, because the Storport.sys driver fills in the right value when calling the kernel.

Additionally, in newer versions of Windows, whenever any file system driver (identified by setting its device type to FILE_DEVICE_DISK_FILE_SYSTEM or FILE_DEVICE_NETWORK_FILE_SYSTEM) completes its request, a boost of IO_DISK_INCREMENT is always applied if the driver passed in IO_NO_INCREMENT instead. So this boost value has become less of a recommendation and more of a requirement enforced by the kernel.

Boosts During Waiting on Executive Resources

When a thread attempts to acquire an executive resource (ERESOURCE; see Chapter 3 for more information on kernel-synchronization objects) that is already owned exclusively by another thread, it must enter a wait state until the other thread has released the resource. To limit the risk of deadlocks, the executive performs this wait in intervals of five seconds instead of doing an infinite wait on the resource.

At the end of these five seconds, if the resource is still owned, the executive attempts to prevent CPU starvation by acquiring the dispatcher lock, boosting the owning thread or threads to 14 (only if the original owner priority is less than the waiter's and not already 14), resetting their quantums, and performing another wait.

Because executive resources can be either shared or exclusive, the kernel first boosts the exclusive owner and then checks for shared owners and boosts all of them. When the waiting thread enters the wait state again, the hope is that the scheduler will schedule one of the owner threads, which will have enough time to complete its work and release the resource. Note that this boosting mechanism is used only if the resource doesn't have the Disable Boost flag set, which developers can choose to set if the priority-inversion mechanism described here works well with their usage of the resource.

Additionally, this mechanism isn't perfect. For example, if the resource has multiple shared owners, the executive boosts all those threads to priority 14, resulting in a sudden surge of high-priority threads on the system, all with full quantums. Although the initial owner thread will run first (because it was the first to be boosted and therefore is first on the ready list), the other shared owners will run next, because the waiting thread's priority was not boosted. Only after all the shared owners have had a chance to run and their priority has been decreased below the waiting thread will the waiting thread finally get its chance to acquire the resource. Because shared owners can promote or convert their ownership from shared to exclusive as soon as the exclusive owner releases the resource, it's possible for this mechanism not to work as intended.

Priority Boosts for Foreground Threads After Waits

As will be shortly described, whenever a thread in the foreground process completes a wait operation on a kernel object, the kernel boosts its current (not base) priority by the current value of *PsPrioritySeparation*. (The windowing system is responsible for determining which process is considered to be in the foreground.) As described in the section on quantum controls, *PsPrioritySeparation* reflects the quantum-table index used to select quantums for the threads of foreground applications. However, in this case, it is being used as a priority boost value.

The reason for this boost is to improve the responsiveness of interactive applications—by giving the foreground application a small boost when it completes a wait, it has a better chance of running right away, especially when other processes at the same base priority might be running in the background.

EXPERIMENT: Watching Foreground Priority Boosts and Decays

Using the CPU Stress tool (downloadable from *http://live.sysinternals.com/WindowsInternals*), you can watch priority boosts in action. Take the following steps:

1. Open the System utility in Control Panel (or right-click on your computer name's icon on the desktop, and choose Properties). Click the Advanced System Settings label, click on the Advanced tab, click the Settings button in the Performance section, and finally click on the Advanced tab. Select the Programs option. This causes *PsPrioritySeparation* to get a value of *2*.

2. Run Cpustres.exe, and change the activity of thread 1 from Low to Busy.

3. Start the Performance tool by selecting Programs from the Start menu and then selecting Performance Monitor from the Administrative Tools menu. Click on the Performance Monitor entry under Monitoring Tools.

4. Click the Add Counter toolbar button (or press Ctrl+I) to bring up the Add Counters dialog box.

5. Select the Thread object, and then select the % Processor Time counter.

6. In the Instances box, select <All Instances> and click Search. Scroll down until you see the CPUSTRES process. Select the second thread (thread 1). (The first thread is the GUI thread.) You should see something like this:

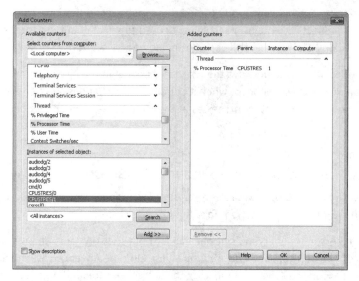

7. Click the Add button, and then click OK.

8. Select Properties from the Action menu. Change the Vertical Scale Maximum to *16* on the Graph tab, and set the interval to *1* in Sample Every box of the Graph Elements area on the General tab.

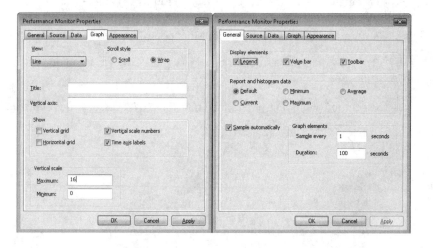

9. Now bring the CPUSTRES process to the foreground. You should see the priority of the CPUSTRES thread being boosted by 2 and then decaying back to the base priority as follows:

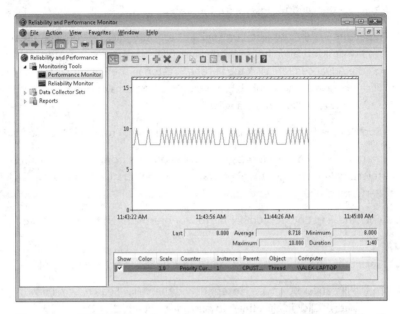

10. The reason CPUSTRES receives a boost of 2 periodically is because the thread you're monitoring is sleeping about 25 percent of the time and then waking up. (This is the Busy Activity level). The boost is applied when the thread wakes up. If you set the Activity level to Maximum, you won't see any boosts because Maximum in CPUSTRES puts the thread into an infinite loop. Therefore, the thread doesn't invoke any wait functions and, as a result, doesn't receive any boosts.

11. When you've finished, exit Performance Monitor and CPU Stress.

Priority Boosts After GUI Threads Wake Up

Threads that own windows receive an additional boost of 2 when they wake up because of windowing activity such as the arrival of window messages. The windowing system (Win32k.sys) applies this boost when it calls *KeSetEvent* to set an event used to wake up a GUI thread. The reason for this boost is similar to the previous one—to favor interactive applications.

EXPERIMENT: Watching Priority Boosts on GUI Threads

You can also see the windowing system apply its boost of 2 for GUI threads that wake up to process window messages by monitoring the current priority of a GUI application and moving the mouse across the window. Just follow these steps:

1. Open the System utility in Control Panel (or right-click on your computer name's icon on the desktop, and choose Properties). Click the Advanced System Settings label, click on the Advanced tab, click the Settings button in the Performance section, and finally click on the Advanced tab. Be sure that the Programs option is selected. This causes *PsPrioritySeparation* to get a value of *2*.

2. Run Notepad from the Start menu by selecting All Programs/Accessories/Notepad.

3. Start the Performance tool by selecting Programs from the Start menu and then selecting Performance Monitor from the Administrative Tools menu. Click on the Performance Monitor entry under Monitoring Tools.

4. Click the Add Counter toolbar button (or press Ctrl+N) to bring up the Add Counters dialog box.

5. Select the Thread object, and then select the Priority Current counter.

6. In the Instances box, type **Notepad**, and then click Search. Scroll down until you see Notepad/0. Click it, click the Add button, and then click OK.

7. As in the previous experiment, select Properties from the Action menu. Change the Vertical Scale Maximum to *16* on the Graph tab, set the interval to *1* in Sample Every box of the Graph Elements area of the General tab, and click OK.

8. You should see the priority of thread 0 in Notepad at 8 or 10. Because Notepad entered a wait state shortly after it received the boost of 2 that threads in the foreground process receive, it might not yet have decayed from 10 to 8.

9. With Performance Monitor in the foreground, move the mouse across the Notepad window. (Make both windows visible on the desktop.) You'll see that the priority sometimes remains at 10 and sometimes at 9, for the reasons just explained. (The reason you won't likely catch Notepad at 8 is that it runs so little after receiving the GUI thread boost of 2 that it never experiences more than one priority level of decay before waking up again because of additional windowing activity and receiving the boost of 2 again.)

10. Now bring Notepad to the foreground. You should see the priority rise to 12 and remain there (or drop to 11, because it might experience the normal priority decay that occurs for boosted threads on the quantum end) because the thread is receiving

two boosts: the boost of 2 applied to GUI threads when they wake up to process windowing input, and an additional boost of 2 because Notepad is in the foreground.

11. If you then move the mouse over Notepad (while it's still in the foreground), you might see the priority drop to 11 (or maybe even 10) as it experiences the priority decay that normally occurs on boosted threads as they complete their turn. However, the boost of 2 that is applied because it's the foreground process remains as long as Notepad remains in the foreground.

12. When you've finished, exit Performance Monitor and Notepad.

Priority Boosts for CPU Starvation

Imagine the following situation: you have a priority 7 thread that's running, preventing a priority 4 thread from ever receiving CPU time; however, a priority 11 thread is waiting for some resource that the priority 4 thread has locked. But because the priority 7 thread in the middle is eating up all the CPU time, the priority 4 thread will never run long enough to finish whatever it's doing and release the resource blocking the priority 11 thread. What does Windows do to address this situation?

You previously saw how the executive code responsible for executive resources manages this scenario by boosting the owner threads so that they can have a chance to run and release the resource. However, executive resources are only one of the many synchronization constructs available to developers, and the boosting technique will not apply to any other primitive. Therefore, Windows also includes a generic CPU starvation-relief mechanism as part of a thread called the balance set manager (a system thread that exists primarily to perform memory-management functions and is described in more detail in Chapter 10 of Part 2).

Once per second, this thread scans the ready queues for any threads that have been in the ready state (that is, haven't run) for approximately 4 seconds. If it finds such a thread, the balance-set manager boosts the thread's priority to 15 and sets the quantum target to an equivalent CPU clock cycle count of 3 quantum units. Once the quantum expires, the thread's priority decays immediately to its original base priority. If the thread wasn't finished and a higher priority thread is ready to run, the decayed thread returns to the ready queue, where it again becomes eligible for another boost if it remains there for another 4 seconds.

The balance-set manager doesn't actually scan all of the ready threads every time it runs. To minimize the CPU time it uses, it scans only 16 ready threads; if there are more threads at that priority level, it remembers where it left off and picks up again on the next pass. Also, it will boost only 10 threads per pass—if it finds 10 threads meriting this particular boost (which indicates an unusually busy system), it stops the scan at that point and picks up again on the next pass.

Note We mentioned earlier that scheduling decisions in Windows are not affected by the number of threads and that they are made in constant time, or O(1). Because the balance-set manager needs to scan ready queues manually, this operation depends on the number of threads on the system, and more threads will require more scanning time. However, the balance-set manager is not considered part of the scheduler or its algorithms and is simply an extended mechanism to increase reliability. Additionally, because of the cap on threads and queues to scan, the performance impact is minimized and predictable in a worst-case scenario.

Will this algorithm always solve the priority-inversion issue? No—it's not perfect by any means. But over time, CPU-starved threads should get enough CPU time to finish whatever processing they were doing and re-enter a wait state.

EXPERIMENT: Watching Priority Boosts for CPU Starvation

Using the CPU Stress tool, you can watch priority boosts in action. In this experiment, you'll see CPU usage change when a thread's priority is boosted. Take the following steps:

1. Run Cpustres.exe. Change the activity level of the active thread (by default, Thread 1) from Low to Maximum. Change the thread priority from Normal to Below Normal. The screen should look like this:

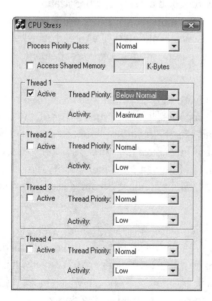

2. Start the Performance tool by selecting Programs from the Start menu and then selecting Performance Monitor from the Administrative Tools menu. Click on the Performance Monitor entry under Monitoring Tools.

3. Click the Add Counter toolbar button (or press Ctrl+N) to bring up the Add Counters dialog box.

4. Select the Thread object, and then select the Priority Current counter.

5. In the Instances box, type CPUSTRES, and then click Search. Scroll down until you see the second thread (thread 1). (The first thread is the GUI thread.) You should see something like this:

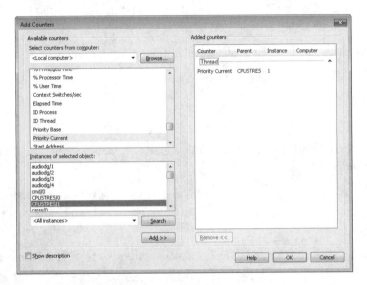

6. Click the Add button, and then click OK.

7. Raise the priority of Performance Monitor to real time by running Task Manager, clicking on the Processes tab, and selecting the Mmc.exe process. Right-click the process, select Set Priority, and then select Realtime. (If you receive a Task Manager Warning message box warning you of system instability, click the Yes button.) If you have a multiprocessor system, you also need to change the affinity of the process: right-click and select Set Affinity. Then clear all other CPUs except for CPU 0.

8. Run another copy of CPU Stress. In this copy, change the activity level of Thread 1 from Low to Maximum.

9. Now switch back to Performance Monitor. You should see CPU activity every six or so seconds because the thread is boosted to priority 15. You can force updates to occur more frequently than every second by pausing the display with Ctrl+F, and then pressing Ctrl+U, which forces a manual update of the counters. Keep Ctrl+U pressed for continual refreshes.

When you've finished, exit Performance Monitor and the two copies of CPU Stress.

EXPERIMENT: "Listening" to Priority Boosting

To "hear" the effect of priority boosting for CPU starvation, perform the following steps on a system with a sound card:

1. Because of MMCSS' priority boosts (which we will describe in the next subsection), you need to stop the MultiMedia Class Scheduler Service by opening the Services management interface (Start, Programs, Administrative Tools, Services).

2. Run Windows Media Player (or some other audio-playback program), and begin playing some audio content.

3. Run Cpustres, and set the activity level of Thread 1 to Maximum.

4. Use Task Manager to set the affinities of both Windows Media Player and Cpustres to a single CPU.

5. Raise the priority of Thread 1 of Cpustres from Normal to Time Critical.

6. You should hear the music playback stop as the computer-bound thread begins consuming all available CPU time.

7. Every so often, you should hear bits of sound as the starved thread in the audio playback process gets boosted to 15 and runs enough to send more data to the sound card.

8. Stop Cpustres and Windows Media Player, and start the MMCSS service again.

Applying Boosts

Back in *KiExitDispatcher*, you saw that *KiProcessThreadWaitList* is called to process any threads in the deferred ready list. It is here that the boost information passed by the caller is processed. This is done by looping through each *DeferredReady* thread, unlinking its wait blocks (only Active and Bypassed blocks are unlinked), and then setting two key values in the kernel's thread control block: *AdjustReason* and *AdjustIncrement*. The reason is one of the two Adjust possibilities seen earlier, and the increment corresponds to the boost value. *KiDeferredReadyThread* is then called, which makes the thread ready for execution, by running two algorithms: the quantum and priority selection algorithm, which you are about to see in two parts, and the processor selection algorithm, which is shown in its respective section later in this topic.

Let's first look at when the algorithm applies boosts, which happens only in the cases where a thread is not in the real-time priority range.

For an *AdjustUnwait* boost, it will be applied only if the thread is not already experiencing an unusual boost and only if the thread has not disabled boosting by calling *SetThreadPriorityBoost*, which sets the *DisableBoost* flag in the KTHREAD. Another situation that can disable boosting in this case is if the kernel has realized that the thread actually exhausted its quantum (but the clock interrupt did not fire to consume it) and the thread came out of a wait that lasted less than two clock ticks.

If these situations are not currently true, the new priority of the thread will be computed by adding the *AdjustIncrement* to the thread's current base priority. Additionally, if the thread is known to be part of a foreground process (meaning that the memory priority is set to MEMORY_PRIORITY_FOREGROUND, which is configured by Win32k.sys when focus changes), this is where the priority-separation boost (*PsPrioritySeparation*) is applied by adding its value on top of the new priority. This is also known as the Foreground Priority boost, which was explained earlier.

Finally, the kernel checks whether this newly computed priority is higher than the current priority of the thread, and it limits this value to an upper bound of 15 to avoid crossing into the real-time range. It then sets this value as the thread's new current priority. If any foreground separation boost was applied, it sets this value in the *ForegroundBoost* field of the KTHREAD, which results in a *PriorityDecrement* equal to the separation boost.

For *AdjustBoost* boosts, the kernel checks whether the thread's current priority is lower than the *AdjustIncrement* (recall this is the priority of the setting thread) and whether the thread's current priority is below *13*. If so, and priority boosts have not been disabled for the thread, the *AdjustIncrement* priority is used as the new current priority, limited to a maximum of *13*. Meanwhile, the *UnusualBoost* field of the KTHREAD contains the boost value, which results in a *PriorityDecrement* equal to the lock ownership boost.

In all cases where a *PriorityDecrement* is present, the quantum of the thread is also recomputed to be the equivalent of only one clock tick, based on the value of *KiLockQuantumTarget*. This ensures that foreground and unusual boosts will be lost after one clock tick instead of the usual two (or other configured value), as will be shown in the next section. This also happens when an *AdjustBoost* is requested but the thread is running at priority 13 or 14 or with boosts disabled.

After this work is complete, *AdjustReason* is now set to *AdjustNone*.

Removing Boosts

Removing boosts is done in *KiDeferredReadyThread* just as boosts and quantum recomputations are being applied (as shown in the previous section). The algorithm first begins by checking the type of adjustment being done.

For an *AdjustNone* scenario, which means the thread became ready due to perhaps a preemption, the thread's quantum will be recomputed if it already hit its target but the clock interrupt has not yet noticed, as long as the thread was running at a dynamic priority level. Additionally, the thread's priority will be recomputed. For an *AdjustUnwait* or *AdjustBoost* scenario on a non-real-time thread, the kernel checks whether the thread silently exhausted its quantum (just as in the prior section). If it did, or if the thread was running with a base priority of 14 or higher, or if no *PriorityDecrement* is present and the thread has completed a wait that lasted longer than two clock ticks, the quantum of the thread is recomputed, as is its priority.

Priority recomputation happens on non-real-time threads, and it's done by taking the thread's current priority, subtracting its foreground boost, subtracting is unusual boost (the combination of these last two items is the *PriorityDecrement*), and finally subtracting one. Finally, this new priority is bounded with the base priority as the lowest bound, and any existing priority decrement is zeroed out (clearing unusual and foreground boosts). This means that in the case of a lock ownership boost, or any of the unusual boosts explained, the entire boost value is now lost. On the other hand, for a regular *AdjustUnwait* boost, the priority naturally trickles down by one due to the subtraction by one. This lowering eventually stops when the base priority is hit due to the lower bound check.

There is another instance where boosts must be removed, which goes through the *KiRemoveBoostThread* function. This is a special-case boost removal, which occurs due to the lock-ownership boost rule, which specifies that the setting thread must lose its boost when donating its current priority to the waking thread (to avoid a lock convoy). It is also used to undo the boost due to targeted DPC-calls as well as the boost against ERESOURCE lock-starvation boost. The only special detail about this routine is that when computing the new priority, it takes special care to separate the *ForegroundBoost* vs. *UnusualBoost* components of the *PriorityDecrement* in order to maintain any GUI foreground-separation boost that the thread accumulated. This behavior, new to Windows 7, ensures that threads relying on the lock-ownership boost do not behave erratically when running in the foreground, or vice-versa.

Figure 5-20 displays an example of how normal boosts are removed from a thread as it experiences quantum end.

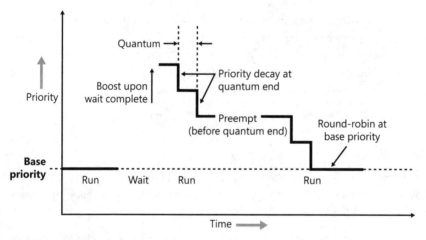

FIGURE 5-20 Priority boosting and decay

Priority Boosts for Multimedia Applications and Games

As you just saw in the last experiment, although Windows' CPU-starvation priority boosts might be enough to get a thread out of an abnormally long wait state or potential deadlock, they simply cannot deal with the resource requirements imposed by a CPU-intensive application such as Windows Media Player or a 3D computer game.

Skipping and other audio glitches have been a common source of irritation among Windows users in the past, and the user-mode audio stack in Windows makes the situation worse because it offers even more chances for preemption. To address this, client versions of Windows incorporate a service (called MMCSS, described earlier in this chapter) whose purpose is to ensure glitch-free multimedia playback for applications that register with it.

MMCSS works by defining several tasks, including the following:

- Audio

- Capture

- Distribution

- Games

- Playback

- Pro Audio

- Window Manager

Note You can find the settings for MMCSS, including a lists of tasks (which can be modified by OEMs to include other specific tasks as appropriate) in the registry keys under HKLM\SOFTWARE\Microsoft\Windows NT\CurrentVersion\Multimedia\SystemProfile. Additionally, the *SystemResponsiveness* value allows you to fine-tune how much CPU usage MMCSS guarantees to low-priority threads.

In turn, each of these tasks includes information about the various properties that differentiate them. The most important one for scheduling is called the Scheduling Category, which is the primary factor determining the priority of threads registered with MMCSS. Table 5-7 shows the various scheduling categories.

TABLE 5-7 Scheduling Categories

Category	Priority	Description
High	23-26	Pro Audio threads running at a higher priority than any other thread on the system except for critical system threads
Medium	16-22	The threads part of a foreground application such as Windows Media Player
Low	8-15	All other threads that are not part of the previous categories
Exhausted	1-7	Threads that have exhausted their share of the CPU and will continue running only if no other higher priority threads are ready to run

The main mechanism behind MMCSS boosts the priority of threads inside a registered process to the priority level matching their scheduling category and relative priority within this category for a guaranteed period of time. It then lowers those threads to the Exhausted category so that other, nonmultimedia threads on the system can also get a chance to execute.

By default, multimedia threads get 80 percent of the CPU time available, while other threads receive 20 percent (based on a sample of 10 ms; in other words, 8 ms and 2 ms, respectively). MMCSS itself runs at priority 27 because it needs to preempt any Pro Audio threads in order to lower their priority to the Exhausted category.

Keep in mind that the kernel still does the actual boosting of the values inside the KTHREAD (MMCSS simply makes the same kind of system call any other application would), and the scheduler is still in control of these threads. It is simply their high priority that makes them run almost uninterrupted on a machine, because they are in the real-time range and well above threads that most user applications run in.

As was discussed earlier, changing the relative thread priorities within a process does not usually make sense, and no tool allows this because only developers understand the importance of the various threads in their programs. On the other hand, because applications must manually register with MMCSS and provide it with information about what kind of thread this is, MMCSS does have the necessary data to change these relative thread priorities (and developers are well aware that this will be happening).

EXPERIMENT: "Listening" to MMCSS Priority Boosting

You'll now perform the same experiment as the prior one but without disabling the MMCSS service. In addition, you'll look at the Performance tool to check the priority of the Windows Media Player threads.

1. Run Windows Media Player (because other playback programs might not yet take advantage of the API calls required to register with MMCSS), and begin playing some audio content.

2. If you have a multiprocessor machine, be sure to set the affinity of the Wmplayer.exe process so that it runs on only one CPU (because you'll use only one CPUSTRES worker thread).

3. Start the Performance tool by selecting Programs from the Start menu and then selecting Performance Monitor from the Administrative Tools menu. Click on the Performance Monitor entry under Monitoring Tools.

4. Click the Add Counter toolbar button (or press Ctrl+N) to bring up the Add Counters dialog box.

5. Select the Thread object, and then select the Priority Current.

6. In the Instances box, type **Wmplayer**, click Search, and then select all its threads. Click the Add button, and then click OK.

7. As in the previous experiment, select Properties from the Action menu. Change the Vertical Scale Maximum to 31 on the Graph tab, set the interval to 1 in Sample Every Seconds of the Graph Elements area on the General tab, and click OK.

   You should see one or more priority 21 threads inside Wmplayer, which will be constantly running unless there is a higher-priority thread requiring the CPU after they are dropped to the Exhausted category.

8. Run Cpustres, and set the activity level of Thread 1 to Maximum.

9. Raise the priority of Thread 1 from Normal to Time Critical.

10. You should notice the system slowing down considerably, but the music playback will continue. Every so often, you'll be able to get back some responsiveness from the rest of the system. Use this time to stop Cpustres.

11. If the Performance tool was unable to capture data during the time Cpustres ran, run it again, but use Highest instead of Time Critical. This change will slow down the system less, but it still requires boosting from MMCSS. Because once the multimedia thread is put in the Exhausted category there will always be a higher priority thread requesting the CPU (CPUSTRES), you should notice Wmplayer's priority 21 thread drop every so often, as shown here:

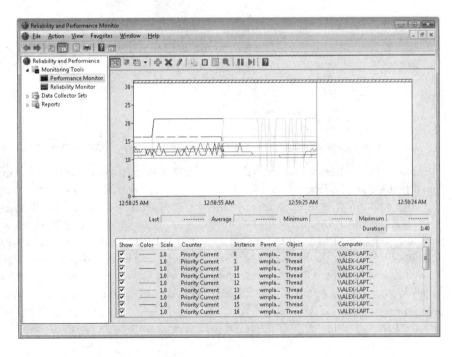

MMCSS' functionality does not stop at simple priority boosting, however. Because of the nature of network drivers on Windows and the NDIS stack, deferred procedure calls (DPCs) are quite common mechanisms for delaying work after an interrupt has been received from the network card. Because DPCs run at an IRQL level higher than user-mode code (see Chapter 3 for more information on DPCs and IRQLs), long-running network card driver code can still interrupt media playback during network transfers or when playing a game, for example.

Therefore, MMCSS also sends a special command to the network stack, telling it to throttle network packets during the duration of the media playback. This throttling is designed to maximize playback performance, at the cost of some small loss in network throughput (which would not be noticeable for network operations usually performed during playback, such as playing an online game). The exact mechanisms behind it do not belong to any area of the scheduler, so we'll leave them out of this description.

> **Note** The original implementation of the network throttling code had some design issues that caused significant network throughput loss on machines with 1000 Mbit network adapters, especially if multiple adapters were present on the system (a common feature of midrange motherboards). This issue was analyzed by the MMCSS and networking teams at Microsoft and later fixed.

Context Switching

A thread's context and the procedure for context switching vary depending on the processor's architecture. A typical context switch requires saving and reloading the following data:

- Instruction pointer

- Kernel stack pointer

- A pointer to the address space in which the thread runs (the process' page table directory)

The kernel saves this information from the old thread by pushing it onto the current (old thread's) kernel-mode stack, updating the stack pointer, and saving the stack pointer in the old thread's KTHREAD structure. The kernel stack pointer is then set to the new thread's kernel stack, and the new thread's context is loaded. If the new thread is in a different process, it loads the address of its page table directory into a special processor register so that its address space is available. (See the description of address translation in Chapter 10 in Part 2.) If a kernel APC that needs to be delivered is pending, an interrupt at IRQL 1 is requested. (For more information on APCs, see Chapter 3.) Otherwise, control passes to the new thread's restored instruction pointer and the new thread resumes execution.

Scheduling Scenarios

Windows bases the question of "Who gets the CPU?" on thread priority, but how does this approach work in practice? The following sections illustrate just how priority-driven preemptive multitasking works on the thread level.

Voluntary Switch

First a thread might voluntarily relinquish use of the processor by entering a wait state on some object (such as an event, a mutex, a semaphore, an I/O completion port, a process, a thread, a window message, and so on) by calling one of the Windows wait functions (such as *WaitForSingleObject* or *WaitForMultipleObjects*). Waiting for objects is described in more detail in Chapter 3.

Figure 5-21 illustrates a thread entering a wait state and Windows selecting a new thread to run. In Figure 5-21, the top block (thread) is voluntarily relinquishing the processor so that the next thread in the ready queue can run (as represented by the halo it has when in the Running column). Although it might appear from this figure that the relinquishing thread's priority is being reduced, it's not—it's just being moved to the wait queue of the objects the thread is waiting for.

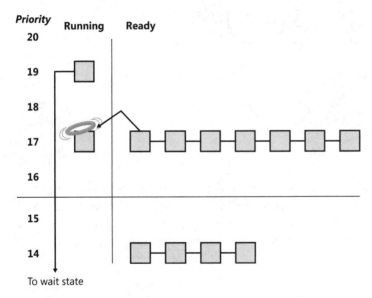

FIGURE 5-21 Voluntary switching

Preemption

In this scheduling scenario, a lower-priority thread is preempted when a higher-priority thread becomes ready to run. This situation might occur for a couple of reasons:

- A higher-priority thread's wait completes. (The event that the other thread was waiting for has occurred.)

- A thread priority is increased or decreased.

In either of these cases, Windows must determine whether the currently running thread should still continue to run or whether it should be preempted to allow a higher-priority thread to run.

> **Note** Threads running in user mode can preempt threads running in kernel mode—the mode in which the thread is running doesn't matter. The thread priority is the determining factor.

When a thread is preempted, it is put at the head of the ready queue for the priority it was running at. Figure 5-22 illustrates this situation.

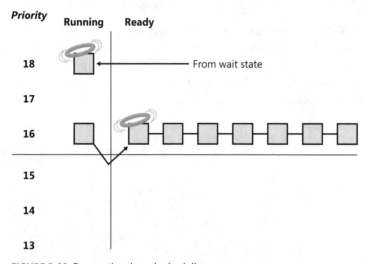

FIGURE 5-22 Preemptive thread scheduling

In Figure 5-22, a thread with priority 18 emerges from a wait state and repossesses the CPU, causing the thread that had been running (at priority 16) to be bumped to the head of the ready queue. Notice that the bumped thread isn't going to the end of the queue but to the beginning; when the preempting thread has finished running, the bumped thread can complete its quantum.

Quantum End

When the running thread exhausts its CPU quantum, Windows must determine whether the thread's priority should be decremented and then whether another thread should be scheduled on the processor.

If the thread priority is reduced, Windows looks for a more appropriate thread to schedule. (For example, a more appropriate thread would be a thread in a ready queue with a higher priority than the new priority for the currently running thread.) If the thread priority isn't reduced and there are other threads in the ready queue at the same priority level, Windows selects the next thread in the ready queue at that same priority level and moves the previously running thread to the tail of that queue (giving it a new quantum value and changing its state from running to ready). This case is illustrated in Figure 5-23. If no other thread of the same priority is ready to run, the thread gets to run for another quantum.

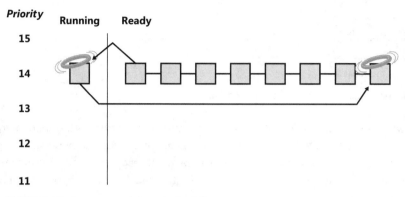

FIGURE 5-23 Quantum end thread scheduling

As you saw, instead of simply relying on a clock interval timer–based quantum to schedule threads, Windows uses an accurate CPU clock cycle count to maintain quantum targets. One factor we haven't yet mentioned is that Windows also uses this count to determine whether quantum end is currently appropriate for the thread—something that might have happened previously and is important to discuss.

Using a scheduling model that relies only on the clock interval timer, the following situation can occur:

■ Threads A and B become ready to run during the middle of an interval. (Scheduling code runs not just at each clock interval, so this is often the case.)

■ Thread A starts running but is interrupted for a while. The time spent handling the interrupt is charged to the thread.

■ Interrupt processing finishes and thread A starts running again, but it quickly hits the next clock interval. The scheduler can assume only that thread A had been running all this time and now switches to thread B.

■ Thread B starts running and has a chance to run for a full clock interval (barring pre-emption or interrupt handling).

In this scenario, thread A was unfairly penalized in two different ways. First, the time it spent handling a device interrupt was accounted to its own CPU time, even though the thread probably had nothing to do with the interrupt. (Recall that interrupts are handled in the context of whichever thread was running at the time.) It was also unfairly penalized for the time the system was idling inside that clock interval before it was scheduled.

Figure 5-24 represents this scenario.

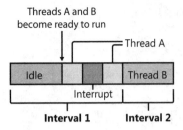

FIGURE 5-24 Unfair time slicing in previous versions of Windows

Because Windows keeps an accurate count of the exact number of CPU clock cycles spent doing work that the thread was scheduled to do (which means excluding interrupts), and because it keeps a quantum target of clock cycles that should have been spent by the thread at the end of its quantum, both of the unfair decisions that would have been made against thread A will not happen in Windows.

Instead, the following situation occurs:

- Threads A and B become ready to run during the middle of an interval.

- Thread A starts running but is interrupted for a while. The CPU clock cycles spent handling the interrupt are not charged to the thread.

- Interrupt processing finishes and thread A starts running again, but it quickly hits the next clock interval. The scheduler looks at the number of CPU clock cycles charged to the thread and compares them to the expected CPU clock cycles that should have been charged at quantum end.

- Because the former number is much smaller than it should be, the scheduler assumes that thread A started running in the middle of a clock interval and might have been additionally interrupted.

- Thread A gets its quantum increased by another clock interval, and the quantum target is recalculated. Thread A now has its chance to run for a full clock interval.

- At the next clock interval, thread A has finished its quantum, and thread B now gets a chance to run.

Figure 5-25 represents this scenario.

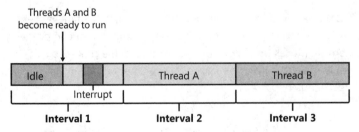

FIGURE 5-25 Fair time slicing in current versions of Windows

Termination

When a thread finishes running (either because it returned from its main routine, called *ExitThread*, or was killed with *TerminateThread*), it moves from the running state to the terminated state. If there are no handles open on the thread object, the thread is removed from the process thread list and the associated data structures are deallocated and released.

Idle Threads

When no runnable thread exists on a CPU, Windows dispatches that CPU's idle thread. Each CPU has its own dedicated idle thread, because on a multiprocessor system one CPU can be executing a thread while other CPUs might have no threads to execute. Each CPU's idle thread is found via a pointer in that CPU's PRCB.

All of the idle threads belong to the idle process. The idle process and idle threads are special cases in many ways. They are, of course, represented by EPROCESS/KPROCESS and ETHREAD/KTHREAD structures, but they are not executive manager processes and thread objects. Nor is the idle process on the system process list. (This is why it does not appear in the output of the kernel debugger's *!process 0 0* command.) However, the idle thread or threads and their process can be found in other ways.

EXPERIMENT: Displaying the Structures of the Idle Threads and Idle Process

The idle thread and process structures can be found in the kernel debugger via the *!pcr* command. "PCR" is short for "processor control region." This command displays a subset of information from the PCR and also from the associated PRCB (processor control block). *!pcr* takes a single numeric argument, which is the number of the CPU whose PCR is to be displayed. The boot processor is processor number 0, and it is always present, so *!pcr 0* should always work. The following output shows the results of this command from a memory dump taken from a 64-bit, four-processor system:

```
3: kd> !pcr 0
KPCR for Processor 0 at fffff800039fdd00:
    Major 1 Minor 1
        NtTib.ExceptionList: fffff80000b95000
         NtTib.StackBase: fffff80000b96080
        NtTib.StackLimit: 000000000008e2d8
      NtTib.SubSystemTib: fffff800039fdd00
           NtTib.Version: 00000000039fde80
       NtTib.UserPointer: fffff800039fe4f0
         NtTib.SelfTib: 000000007efdb000

               SelfPcr: 0000000000000000
                  Prcb: fffff800039fde80
                  Irql: 0000000000000000
                   IRR: 0000000000000000
```

```
                IDR: 0000000000000000
      InterruptMode: 0000000000000000
                IDT: 0000000000000000
                GDT: 0000000000000000
                TSS: 0000000000000000

      CurrentThread: fffffa8007aa8060
         NextThread: 0000000000000000
         IdleThread: fffff80003a0bcc0

          DpcQueue:
```

This output shows that CPU 0 was executing a thread other than its idle thread at the time the memory dump was obtained, because the *CurrentThread* and *IdleThread* pointers are different. (If you have a multi-CPU system you can try *!pcr 1*, *!pcr 2*, and so on, until you run out; observe that each *IdleThread* pointer is different.)

Now use the *!thread* command on the indicated idle thread address:

```
3: kd> !thread fffff80003a0bcc0
THREAD fffff80003a0bcc0  Cid 0000.0000  Teb: 0000000000000000 Win32Thread:
0000000000000000
   RUNNING on processor 0
Not impersonating
DeviceMap               fffff8a000008aa0
Owning Process          fffff80003a0c1c0      Image:         Idle
Attached Process        fffffa800792a040      Image:         System
Wait Start TickCount    50774016      Ticks: 12213 (0:00:03:10.828)
Context Switch Count    1147613282
UserTime                00:00:00.000
KernelTime              8 Days 07:21:56.656
Win32 Start Address nt!KiIdleLoop (0xfffff8000387f910)
Stack Init fffff80000b9cdb0 Current fffff80000b9cd40
Base fffff80000b9d000 Limit fffff80000b97000 Call 0
Priority 16 BasePriority 0 UnusualBoost 0 ForegroundBoost 0 IoPriority 0 PagePriority 0
Child-SP          RetAddr          : Args to Child       [...]: Call Site
fffff800`00b9cd80 00000000`00000000 : fffff800`00b9d000 [...]: nt!KiIdleLoop+0x10d
```

Finally, use the *!process* command on the "Owning Process" shown in the preceding output. For brevity, we'll add a second parameter value of *3*, which causes *!process* to emit only minimal information for each thread:

```
3: kd> !process fffff80003a0c1c0 3
PROCESS fffff80003a0c1c0
    SessionId: none  Cid: 0000    Peb: 00000000  ParentCid: 0000
    DirBase: 00187000  ObjectTable: fffff8a000001630  HandleCount: 1338.
    Image: Idle
    VadRoot fffffa8007846c00 Vads 1 Clone 0 Private 1. Modified 0. Locked 0.
    DeviceMap 0000000000000000
    Token                         fffff8a000004a40
    ElapsedTime                   00:00:00.000
    UserTime                      00:00:00.000
    KernelTime                    00:00:00.000
```

```
    QuotaPoolUsage[PagedPool]          0
    QuotaPoolUsage[NonPagedPool]       0
    Working Set Sizes (now,min,max)   (6, 50, 450) (24KB, 200KB, 1800KB)
    PeakWorkingSetSize                 6
    VirtualSize                        0 Mb
    PeakVirtualSize                    0 Mb
    PageFaultCount                     1
    MemoryPriority                     BACKGROUND
    BasePriority                       0
    CommitCharge                       0

THREAD fffff80003a0bcc0  Cid 0000.0000  Teb: 0000000000000000 Win32Thread:
0000000000000000
  RUNNING on processor 0
THREAD fffff8800310afc0  Cid 0000.0000  Teb: 0000000000000000 Win32Thread:
0000000000000000
  RUNNING on processor 1
THREAD fffff8800317bfc0  Cid 0000.0000  Teb: 0000000000000000 Win32Thread:
0000000000000000
  RUNNING on processor 2
THREAD fffff880031ecfc0  Cid 0000.0000  Teb: 0000000000000000 Win32Thread:
0000000000000000
  RUNNING on processor 3
```

These process and thread addresses can be used with *dt nt!_EPROCESS*, *dt nt!_KTHREAD*, and other such commands as well.

The preceding experiment shows some of the anomalies associated with the idle process and its threads. The debugger indicates an "Image" name of "Idle" (which comes from the EPROCESS structure's *ImageFileName* member), but various Windows utilities report the idle process using different names. Task Manager and Process Explorer call it "System Idle Process," while Tlist calls it "System Process." The process ID and thread IDs (the "client IDs", or "Cid" in the debugger's output) are zero, as are the PEB and TEB pointers, and there are many other fields in the idle process or its threads that might be reported as 0. This occurs because the idle process has no user-mode address space and its threads execute no user-mode code, so they have no need of the various data needed to manage a user-mode environment. Also, the idle process is not an object-manager process object, and its idle threads are not object-manager thread objects. Instead, the initial idle thread and idle process structures are statically allocated and used to bootstrap the system before the process manager and the object manager are initialized. Subsequent idle thread structures are allocated dynamically (as simple allocations from nonpaged pool, bypassing the object manager) as additional processors are brought online. Once process management initializes, it uses the special variable *PsIdleProcess* to refer to the idle process.

Perhaps the most interesting anomaly regarding the idle process is that Windows reports the priority of the idle threads as 0 (16 on x64 systems, as shown earlier). In reality, however, the values of the idle threads' priority members are irrelevant, because these threads are selected for dispatching only when there are no other threads to run. Their priority is never compared with that of any other thread, nor are they used to put an idle thread on a ready queue; idle threads are never part of any ready queues. (Remember, only one thread per Windows system is actually running at priority 0—the zero page thread, explained in Chapter 10 in Part 2.)

Just as the idle threads are special cases in terms of selection for execution, they are also special cases for preemption. The idle thread's routine, *KiIdleLoop*, performs a number of operations that preclude its being preempted by another thread in the usual fashion. When no non-idle threads are available to run on a processor, that processor is marked as idle in its PRCB. After that, if a thread is selected for execution on the idle processor, the thread's address is stored in the *NextThread* pointer of the idle processor's PRCB. The idle thread checks this pointer on each pass through its loop.

Although some details of the flow vary between architectures, the basic sequence of operations of the idle thread is as follows:

1. Enables interrupts briefly, allowing any pending interrupts to be delivered, and then disables them again (using the STI and CLI instructions on x86 and x64 processors). This is desirable because significant parts of the idle thread execute with interrupts disabled.

2. On the debug build on some architectures, checks whether there is a kernel debugger trying to break into the system and, if so, gives it access.

3. Checks whether any DPCs (described in Chapter 3) are pending on the processor. DPCs could be pending if a DPC interrupt was not generated when they were queued. If DPCs are pending, the idle loop calls *KiRetireDpcList* to deliver them. This will also perform timer expiration, as well as deferred ready processing; the latter is explained in the upcoming multiprocessor scheduling section. *KiRetireDpcList* must be entered with interrupts disabled, which is why interrupts are left disabled at the end of step 1. *KiRetireDpcList* exits with interrupts disabled as well.

4. Checks whether a thread has been selected to run next on the processor and, if so, dispatches that thread. This could be the case if, for example, a DPC or timer expiration processed in step 3 resolved the wait of a waiting thread, or if another processor selected a thread for this processor to run while it was already in the idle loop.

5. If requested, checks for threads ready to run on other processors and, if possible, schedules one of them locally. (This operation is explained in the upcoming "Idle Scheduler" section.)

6. Calls the registered power management processor idle routine (in case any power management functions need to be performed), which is either in the processor power driver (such as intelppm.sys) or in the HAL if such a driver is unavailable.

Thread Selection

Whenever a logical processor needs to pick the next thread to run, it calls the *KiSelectNextThread* scheduler function. This can happen in a variety of scenarios:

- A hard affinity change has occurred, making the currently running or standby thread ineligible for execution on its selected logical processor, so another must be chosen.

- The currently running thread reached its quantum end, and the SMT set it was currently running on has now become busy, while other SMT sets within the ideal node are fully idle. (SMT is the abbreviation for Symmetric Multi-Threading, the technical name for the Hyperthreading technology described in Chapter 2.) The scheduler performs a quantum end migration of the current thread, so another must be chosen.

- A wait operation has completed, and there were pending scheduling operations in the wait status register (in other words, the Priority and/or Affinity bits were set).

In these scenarios, the behavior of the scheduler is as follows:

- Call *KiSelectReadyThread* to find the next ready thread that the processor should run, and check whether one was found.

- If a ready thread was not found, the idle scheduler is enabled, and the idle thread is selected for execution.

- Or, if a ready thread was found, it is put in the Standby state and set as the *NextThread* in the KPRCB of the logical processor.

The *KiSelectNextThread* operation is performed only when the logical processor needs to pick, but not yet run, the next schedulable thread (which is why the thread will enter Standby). Other times, however, the logical processor is interested in immediately running the next ready thread or performing another action if one is not available (instead of going idle), such as when the following occurs:

- A priority change has occurred, making the current standby or running thread no longer the highest priority ready thread on its selected logical processor, so a higher priority ready thread must now run.

- The thread has explicitly yielded with *YieldProcessor* or *NtYieldExecution*, and another thread might be ready for execution.

- The quantum of the current thread has expired, and other threads at the same priority level need their chance to run as well

- A thread has lost its priority boost, causing a similar priority change to the scenario just described.

- The idle scheduler is running and needs to check whether a ready thread has not appeared in the interval between which idle scheduling was requested and the idle scheduler ran.

A simple way to remember the difference between which routine runs is to check whether or not the logical processor *must* run a different thread (in which case *KiSelectNextThread* is called) or if it *should, if possible*, run a different thread (in which case *KiSelectReadyThread* is called).

In either case, because each processor has its own database of threads that are ready to run (the dispatcher database's ready queues in the KPRCB), *KiSelectReadyThread* can simply check the current LP's queues, removing the first highest priority thread that it finds, unless this priority is lower than the one of the currently running thread (depending on whether the current thread is still allowed to run, which would not be the case in the *KiSelectNextThread* scenario). If there is no higher priority thread (or no threads are ready at all), no thread is returned.

Idle Scheduler

Whenever the idle thread runs, it checks whether idle scheduling has been enabled, such as in one of the scenarios described in the previous section. If so, the idle thread then begins scanning other processor's ready queues for threads it can run by calling *KiSearchForNewThread*. Note that the runtime costs associated with this operation are not charged as idle thread time, but are instead charged as interrupt and DPC time (charged to the processor), so idle scheduling time is considered system time. The *KiSearchForNewThread* algorithm, which is based on the functions seen in the "Thread Selection" section earlier, will be explained in the upcoming section.

Multiprocessor Systems

On a uniprocessor system, scheduling is relatively simple: the highest-priority thread that wants to run is always running. On a multiprocessor system, it is more complex, because Windows attempts to schedule threads on the most optimal processor for the thread, taking into account the thread's preferred and previous processors, as well as the configuration of the multiprocessor system. Therefore, although Windows attempts to schedule the highest-priority runnable threads on all available CPUs, it guarantees only to be running one of the highest-priority threads somewhere.

Before we describe the specific algorithms used to choose which threads run where and when, let's examine the additional information Windows maintains to track thread and processor state on multiprocessor systems and the three different types of multiprocessor systems supported by Windows (SMT, multicore, and NUMA).

Package Sets and SMT Sets

Windows uses five fields in the KPRCB to determine correct scheduling decisions when dealing with logical processor topologies. The first field, *CoresPerPhysicalProcessor*, determines whether this logical processor is part of a multicore package, and it's computed from the CPUID returned by the processor and rounded to a power of two. The second field, *LogicalProcessorsPerCore* determines whether the logical processor is part of an SMT set, such as on an Intel processor with *HyperThreading* enabled, and is also queried through CPUID and rounded. Multiplying these two numbers yields the number of logical processors per package, or an actual physical processor that fits into a socket. With these numbers, each PRCB can then populate its *PackageProcessorSet* value, which is the affinity mask describing which other logical processors within this group (because packages are constrained to a group) belong to the same physical processor. Similarly, the *CoreProcessorSet* value connects other logical processors to the same core, also called an SMT set. Finally, the *GroupSetMember* value defines which bit mask, within the current processor group, identifies this very logical processor. For example, the logical processor 3 normally has a *GroupSetMember* of 8 (2^3).

NUMA Systems

Another type of multiprocessor system supported by Windows is one with a nonuniform memory access (NUMA) architecture. In a NUMA system, processors are grouped together in smaller units called nodes. Each node has its own processors and memory and is connected to the larger system through a cache-coherent interconnect bus. These systems are called "nonuniform" because each node has its own local high-speed memory. Although any processor in any node can access all of memory, node-local memory is much faster to access.

The kernel maintains information about each node in a NUMA system in a data structure called KNODE. The kernel variable *KeNodeBlock* is an array of pointers to the KNODE structures for each node. The format of the KNODE structure can be shown using the *dt* command in the kernel debugger, as shown here:

```
lkd> dt nt!_KNODE
   +0x000 PagedPoolSListHead : _SLIST_HEADER
   +0x008 NonPagedPoolSListHead : [3] _SLIST_HEADER
   +0x020 Affinity          : _GROUP_AFFINITY
   +0x02c ProximityId       : Uint4B
   +0x030 NodeNumber        : Uint2B
...
   +0x060 ParkLock          : Int4B
   +0x064 NodePad1          : Uint4B
```

EXPERIMENT: Viewing NUMA Information

You can examine the information Windows maintains for each node in a NUMA system using the *!numa* command in the kernel debugger. The following partial output is from a 64-processor NUMA system from Hewlett-Packard with four processors per node:

```
26: kd> !numa
NUMA Summary:
------------
Number of NUMA nodes : 16
Number of Processors : 64
MmAvailablePages      : 0x03F55E67

KeActiveProcessors    : ***********************************************************************
                        (ffffffffffffffff)

NODE 0 (E000000084261900):
    ProcessorMask     : ****------------------------------------------------------------
...
NODE 1 (E0000145FF992200):
    ProcessorMask     : ----****--------------------------------------------------------
...
```

Applications that want to gain the most performance out of NUMA systems can set the affinity mask to restrict a process to the processors in a specific node, although Windows already restricts nearly all threads to a single NUMA node due to its NUMA-aware scheduling algorithms.

How the scheduling algorithms take into account NUMA systems will be covered in the upcoming section "Processor Selection" (and the optimizations in the memory manager to take advantage of node-local memory are covered in Chapter 10 in Part 2).

Processor Group Assignment

While querying the topology of the system to build the various relationships between logical processors, SMT sets, multicore packages and physical sockets, Windows assigns processors to an appropriate group that will describe their affinity (through the extended affinity mask seen earlier). This work is done by the *KePerformGroupConfiguration* routine, which is called during initialization before any other Phase 1 work is done. Note that regardless of the group assignment steps below, NUMA node 0 is always assigned to group 0, no matter what.

First, the function queries all detected nodes (*KeNumberNodes*) and computes the capacity of each node (that is, how many logical processors can be part of the node). This value is stored as the *MaximumProcessors* in the *KeNodeBlock*, which identifies all NUMA nodes on the system. If the system supports NUMA Proximity IDs, the proximity ID is queried for each node as well and saved in the node block. Second, the NUMA distance array is allocated (*KeNodeDistance*), and the distance between each NUMA node is computed as was described in Chapter 3.

The next series of steps deal with specific user-configuration options that override default NUMA assignments. For example, on a system with Hyper-V installed (and the hypervisor configured to auto-start), only one processor group will be enabled, and all NUMA nodes (that can fit) will be associated with group 0. This means that Hyper-V scenarios cannot take advantage of machines with over 64 processors at the moment.

Next, the function checks whether any static group assignment data was passed by the loader (and thus configured by the user). This data specifies the proximity information and group assignment for each NUMA node.

> **Note** Users dealing with large NUMA servers that might need custom control of proximity information and group assignments for testing or validation purposes can input this data through the Group Assignment and Node Distance registry values in the HKLM\SYSTEM \CurrentControlSet\Control\NUMA registry key. The exact format of this data includes a count, followed by an array of proximity IDs and group assignments, which are all 32-bit values.

Before treating this data as valid, the kernel queries the proximity ID to match the node number and then associates group numbers as requested. It then makes sure that NUMA node 0 is associated with group 0, and that the capacity for all NUMA nodes is consistent with the group size. Finally, the function checks how many groups still have remaining capacity.

Next, the kernel dynamically attempts to assign NUMA nodes to groups, while respecting any statically configured nodes if passed-in as we just described. Normally, the kernel tries to minimize the number of groups created, combining as many NUMA nodes as possible per group. However, if this behavior is not desired, it can be configured differently with the /MAXGROUP loader parameter, which is configured through the *maxgroup* BCD option. Turning this value on overrides the default behavior and causes the algorithm to spread as many NUMA nodes as possible into as many groups as possible (while respecting that the currently implemented group limit is 4). If there is only one node, or if all nodes can fit into a single group (and *maxgroup* is off), the system performs the default setting of assigning all nodes to group 0.

If there is more than one node, Windows checks the static NUMA node distances (if any), and then sorts all the nodes by their capacity so that the largest nodes come first. In the group-minimization mode, by adding up all the capacities, the kernel figures out how many maximum processors there can be. By dividing that by the number of processors per group, the kernel assumes there will be this many total groups on the machine (limited to a maximum of 4). In the group-maximization mode, the initial estimate is that there will be as many groups as nodes (limited again to 4).

Now the kernel begins the final assignment process. All fixed assignments from earlier are now committed, and groups are created for those assignments. Next, all the NUMA nodes are reshuffled to minimize the distance between the different nodes within a group. In other words, closer nodes are put in the same group and sorted by distance. Next, the same process is performed for any dynamically configured node to group assignments. Finally, any remaining empty nodes are assigned to group 0.

Logical Processors per Group

Generally, Windows assigns 64 processors per group as explained earlier, but this configuration can also be customized by using different load options, such as the /GROUPSIZE option, which is configured through the *groupsize* BCD element. By specifying a number that is a power of two, groups can be forced to contain fewer processors than normal, for purposes such as testing group awareness in the system (for example, a system with 8 logical processors can be made to appear to have 1, 2, or 4 groups). To force the issue, the /FORCEGROUPAWARE option (BCD element *groupaware*) furthermore makes the kernel avoid group 0 whenever possible, assigning the highest group number available in actions such as thread and DPC affinity selection and process group assignment. Avoid setting a group size of 1, because this will force almost all applications on the system to behave as if they're running on a uniprocessor machine, because the kernel sets the affinity mask of a given process to span only one group until the application requests otherwise (which most applications today will not do).

Note that in the edge case where the number of logical processors in a package cannot fit into a single group, Windows adjusts these numbers so that a package can fit into a single group, shrinking the *CoresPerPhysicalProcessor* number, and if the SMT cannot fit either, doing this as well for *LogicalProcessorsPerCore*. The exception to this rule is if the system actually contains multiple NUMA nodes within a single package. Although this is not a possibility as of this writing, future Multiple-Chip Modules (MCMs, an extension of multicore packages) are due to ship from processor manufacturers in the future. In these modules, two sets of cores as well as two memory controllers are on the same die/package. If the ACPI SRAT table defines the MCM as having two NUMA nodes, depending on group configuration algorithms, Windows might associate the two nodes with two different groups. In this scenario, the MCM package would span more than one group.

Other than causing significant driver and application compatibility problems (which they are designed to identify and root out, when used by developers), these options have an even greater impact on the machine: they will force NUMA behaviors even on a non-NUMA machine. This is because Windows will never allow a NUMA node to span multiple groups, as was shown in the assignment algorithms. So, if the kernel is creating artificially small groups, those two groups must each have their own NUMA node. For example, on a quad-core processor with a group size of two, this will create two groups, and thus two NUMA nodes, which will be subnodes of the main node. This will affect scheduling and memory-management policies in the same way a true NUMA system would, which can be useful for testing.

Logical Processor State

In addition to the ready queues and the ready summary, Windows maintains two bitmasks that track the state of the processors on the system. (How these bitmasks are used is explained in the upcoming section "Processor Selection.") Following are the bitmasks that Windows maintains.

The first one is the active processor mask (*KeActiveProcessors*), which has a bit set for each usable processor on the system. This might be fewer than the number of actual processors if the licensing limits of the version of Windows running supports fewer than the number of available physical processors. To check this, use the variable *KeRegisteredProcessors* to see how many processors are actually licensed on the machine. In this instance, "processors" refers to physical packages. The *KeMaximumProcessors* variable, on the other hand, is the maximum number of logical processors, including all future possible dynamic processor additions, bounded within the licensing limit, and any platform limitations that are queried by calling the HAL and checking with the ACPI SRAT table, if any.

The idle summary (*KiIdleSummary*) is actually an array of two extended bitmasks. In the first entry, called *CpuSet*, each set bit represents an idle processor, while in the second entry, *SMTSet*, each bit describes an idle SMT set.

The nonparked summary (*KiNonParkedSummary*) defines each nonparked logical processor through a bit.

Scheduler Scalability

Because on a multiprocessor system one processor might need to modify another processor's per-CPU scheduling data structures (such as inserting a thread that would like to run on a certain processor), these structures are synchronized by using a per-PRCB queued spinlock, which is held at DISPATCH_LEVEL. Thus, thread selection can occur while locking only an individual processor's PRCB. If needed, up to one more processor's PRCB can also be locked, such as in scenarios of thread stealing, which will be described later. Thread context switching is also synchronized by using a finer-grained per-thread spinlock.

There is also a per-CPU list of threads in the deferred ready state. These represent threads that are ready to run but have not yet been readied for execution; the actual ready operation has been deferred to a more appropriate time. Because each processor manipulates only its own per-processor deferred ready list, this list is not synchronized by the PRCB spinlock. The deferred ready thread list is processed by *KiProcessDeferredReadyList* after a function has already done modifications to process or thread affinity, priority (including due to priority boosting), or quantum values.

This function calls *KiDeferredReadyThread* for each thread on the list, which performs the algorithm shown later in the "Processor Selection" section, which could either cause the thread to run immediately; to be put on the ready list of the processor; or if the processor is unavailable, to be potentially put on a different processor's deferred ready list, in a standby state, or immediately executed. This property is used by the Core Parking engine when parking a core: all threads are put into the deferred ready list, and it is then processed. Because *KiDeferredReadyThread* skips parked cores (as will be shown), it causes all of this processor's threads to wind up on other processors.

Affinity

Each thread has an affinity mask that specifies the processors on which the thread is allowed to run. The thread affinity mask is inherited from the process affinity mask. By default, all processes (and therefore all threads) begin with an affinity mask that is equal to the set of all active processors on their assigned group—in other words, the system is free to schedule all threads on any available processor within the group associated with the process.

However, to optimize throughput, partition workloads to a specific set of processors, or both, applications can choose to change the affinity mask for a thread. This can be done at several levels:

- Calling the *SetThreadAffinityMask* function to set the affinity for an individual thread.

- Calling the *SetProcessAffinityMask* function to set the affinity for all the threads in a process. Task Manager and Process Explorer provide a GUI to this function if you right-click a process and choose Set Affinity. The Psexec tool (from Sysinternals) provides a command-line interface to this function. (See the –a switch in its help output.)

- By making a process a member of a job that has a jobwide affinity mask set using the *SetInformationJobObject* function. (Jobs are described in the upcoming "Job Objects" section.)

- By specifying an affinity mask in the image header when compiling the application. (For more information on the detailed format of Windows images, search for "Portable Executable and Common Object File Format Specification" on *www.microsoft.com*.)

An image can also have the "uniprocessor" flag set at link time. If this flag is set, the system chooses a single processor at process creation time (*MmRotatingProcessorNumber*) and assigns that as the process affinity mask, starting with the first processor and then going round-robin across all the processors within the group. For example, on a dual-processor system, the first time an image marked as uniprocessor is launched, it is assigned to CPU 0; the second time, CPU 1; the third time, CPU 0; the fourth time, CPU 1; and so on. This flag can be useful as a temporary workaround for programs that have multithreaded synchronization bugs that, as a result of race conditions, surface on multiprocessor systems but that don't occur on uniprocessor systems. If an image exhibits such symptoms and is unsigned, the flag can be manually added by editing the image header with a tool such as Imagecfg.exe. A better solution, also compatible with signed executables, is to use the Microsoft Application Compatibility Toolkit and add a shim to force the compatibility database to mark the image as uniprocessor-only at launch time.

EXPERIMENT: Viewing and Changing Process Affinity

In this experiment, you will modify the affinity settings for a process and see that process affinity is inherited by new processes:

1. Run the command prompt (Cmd.exe).

2. Run Task Manager or Process Explorer, and find the Cmd.exe process in the process list.

3. Right-click the process, and select Set Affinity. A list of processors should be displayed. For example, on a dual-processor system you will see this:

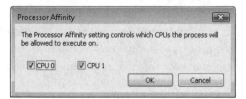

4. Select a subset of the available processors on the system, and click OK. The process' threads are now restricted to run on the processors you just selected.

5. Now run Notepad.exe from the command prompt (by typing **Notepad.exe**).

6. Go back to Task Manager or Process Explorer and find the new Notepad process. Right-click it, and choose Affinity. You should see the same list of processors you chose for the command-prompt process. This is because processes inherit their affinity settings from their parent.

Windows won't move a running thread that could run on a different processor from one CPU to a second processor to permit a thread with an affinity for the first processor to run on the first processor. For example, consider this scenario: CPU 0 is running a priority 8 thread that can run on any processor, and CPU 1 is running a priority 4 thread that can run on any processor. A priority 6 thread that can run on only CPU 0 becomes ready. What happens? Windows won't move the priority 8 thread from CPU 0 to CPU 1 (preempting the priority 4 thread) so that the priority 6 thread can run; the priority 6 thread has to stay in the ready state.

Therefore, changing the affinity mask for a process or a thread can result in threads getting less CPU time than they normally would, because Windows is restricted from running the thread on certain processors. Therefore, setting affinity should be done with extreme care—in most cases, it is optimal to let Windows decide which threads run where.

Extended Affinity Mask

To support more than 64 processors, which is the limit enforced by the affinity mask structure (composed of 64 bits on a 64-bit system), Windows uses an extended affinity mask (KAFFINITY_EX) that is an array of affinity masks, one for each supported processor group (currently defined to 4). When the scheduler needs to refer to a processor in the extended affinity masks, it first de-references the correct bitmask by using its group number and then accesses the resulting affinity directly. In the kernel API, extended affinity masks are not exposed; instead, the caller of the API inputs the group number as a parameter, and receives the legacy affinity mask for that group. In the Windows API, on the other hand, only information about a single group can usually be queried, which is the group of the currently running thread (which is fixed).

The extended affinity mask and its underlying functionality are also how a process can escape the boundaries of its original assigned processor group. By using the extended affinity APIs, threads in a process can choose affinity masks on other processor groups. For example, if a process has 4 threads and the machine has 256 processors, thread 1 can run on processor 4, thread 2 can run on processor 68, thread 3 on processor 132, and thread 4 on processor 196, if each thread set an affinity mask of 0x10 (0b10000 in binary) on groups 0, 1, 2, and 3. Alternatively, the threads can each set an affinity of 0xFFFFFFFF for their given group, and the process then can execute its threads on any available processor on the system (with the limitation, that each thread is restricted to running within its own group only).

Taking advantage of extended affinity must be done at creation time, by specifying a group number in the thread attribute list when creating a new thread. (See the previous topic on thread creation for more information on attribute lists.)

System Affinity Mask

Because Windows drivers usually execute in the context of the calling thread or in the context of an arbitrary thread (that is, not in the safe confines of the System process), currently running driver code might be subject to affinity rules set by the application developer, which are not currently relevant to the driver code and might even prevent correct processing of interrupts and other queued work. Driver developers therefore have a mechanism to temporarily bypass user thread affinity settings, by using the APIs *KeSetSystemAffinityThread(Ex)/KeSetSystemGroupAffinityThread* and *KeRevertToUserAffinityThread(Ex)/KeRevertToUserGroupAffinityThread*.

Ideal and Last Processor

Each thread has three CPU numbers stored in the kernel thread control block:

- Ideal processor, or the preferred processor that this thread should run on

- Last processor, or the processor on which the thread last ran

- Next processor, or the processor that the thread will be, or is already, running on

The ideal processor for a thread is chosen when a thread is created using a seed in the process control block. The seed is incremented each time a thread is created so that the ideal processor for each new thread in the process rotates through the available processors on the system. For example, the first thread in the first process on the system is assigned an ideal processor of 0. The second thread in that process is assigned an ideal processor of 1. However, the next process in the system has its first thread's ideal processor set to 1, the second to 2, and so on. In that way, the threads within each process are spread across the processors.

Note that this assumes the threads within a process are doing an equal amount of work. This is typically not the case in a multithreaded process, which normally has one or more housekeeping threads and then a number of worker threads. Therefore, a multithreaded application that wants to take full advantage of the platform might find it advantageous to specify the ideal processor numbers for its threads by using the *SetThreadIdealProcessor* function. To take advantage of processor groups, developers should call *SetThreadIdealProcessorEx* instead, which allows selection of a group number for the affinity.

64-bit Windows uses the Stride field in the KPRCB to balance the assignment of newly created threads within a process. The stride is a scalar number that represents the number of affinity bits within a given NUMA node that must be skipped to attain a new independent logical processor slice, where "independent" means on another core (if dealing with an SMT system) or another package (if dealing with a non-SMT but multicore system). Because 32-bit Windows doesn't support large processor configuration systems, it doesn't use a stride, and it simply selects the next processor number, trying to avoid sharing the same SMT set if possible. For example, on a dual-processor SMT system with four logical processors, if the ideal processor for the first thread is assigned to logical processor 0, the second thread would be assigned to logical processor 2, the third thread to logical processor 1, the fourth thread to logical process 3, and so forth. In this way, the threads are spread evenly across the physical processors.

Ideal Node

On NUMA systems, when a process is created, an ideal node for the process is selected. The first process is assigned to node 0, the second process to node 1, and so on. Then the ideal processors for the threads in the process are chosen from the process' ideal node. The ideal processor for the first thread in a process is assigned to the first processor in the node. As additional threads are created in processes with the same ideal node, the next processor is used for the next thread's ideal processor, and so on.

Thread Selection on Multiprocessor Systems

Before covering multiprocessor systems in more detail, I should summarize the algorithms discussed in the "Thread Selection" section. They either continued executing the current thread (if no new candidate was found) or started running the idle thread (if the current thread had to block). However, there is a third algorithm for thread selection, which was hinted at in the "Idle Scheduler" section earlier, called *KiSearchForNewThread*. This algorithm is called in one specific instance: when the current thread is about to block due to a wait on an object, including when doing an *NtDelayExecutionThread* call, also known as the Sleep API in Windows.

> **Note** This shows a subtle difference between the commonly used Sleep(1) call, which makes the current thread block until the next timer tick, and the *SwitchToThread()* call, which was shown earlier. The "sleep" will use the algorithm about to be described, while the "yield" uses the previously shown logic.

KiSearchForNewThread initially checks whether there is already a thread that was selected for this processor (by reading the *NextThread* field); if so, it dispatches this thread immediately in the Running state. Otherwise, it calls the *KiSelectReadyThread* routine and, if a thread was found, performs the same steps.

If a thread was not found, however, the processor is marked as idle (even though the idle thread is not yet executing) and a scan of other logical processors queues is initiated (unlike the other standard algorithms, which would now give up). Also, because the processor is now considered idle, if the Dynamic Fair Share Scheduling mode (described in the next topic) is enabled, a thread will be released from the idle-only queue if possible and scheduled instead. On the other hand, if the processor core is now parked, the algorithm will not attempt to check other logical processors, as it is preferable to allow the core to enter the parking state instead keeping it busy with new work.

Barring these two scenarios, the work-stealing loop now runs. This code looks at the current NUMA node and removes any idle processors (because they shouldn't have threads that need stealing). Then, starting from the highest numbered processor, the loop calls *KiFindReadyThread* but points it to the remote KPRCB instead of the current one, causing this processor to find the best ready thread from the other processor's queue. If this is unsuccessful and Dynamic Fair Share Scheduler is enabled, a thread from the idle-only queue of the remote logical processor is released on the current processor instead, if possible.

If no candidate ready thread is found, the next lower numbered logical processor is attempted, and so on, until all logical processors have been exhausted on the current NUMA node. In this case, the algorithm keeps searching for the next closest node, and so on, until all nodes in the current group have been exhausted. (Recall that Windows allows a given thread to have affinity only on a single group.) If this process fails to find any candidates, the function returns NULL and the processor enters the idle thread in the case of a wait (which will skip idle scheduling). If this work was already being done from the idle scheduler, the processor enters a sleep state.

Processor Selection

Up until now, we've described how Windows picks a thread when a logical processor needs to make a selection (or when a selection must be made for a given logical processor) and assumed the various scheduling routines have an existing database of ready threads to choose from. Now we'll see how this database gets populated in the first place—in other words, how Windows chooses which LP's ready queues a given ready thread will be associated with. Having described the types of multiprocessor systems supported by Windows as well as the thread affinity and ideal processor settings, we're now ready to examine how this information is used for this purpose.

Choosing a Processor for a Thread When There Are Idle Processors

When a thread becomes ready to run, the *KiDeferredReadyThread* scheduler function is called, causing Windows to perform two tasks: adjust priorities and refresh quantums as needed, as was explained in the "Priority Boosts" section, and then pick the best logical processor for the thread.

Windows first looks up the thread's ideal processor, and then it computes the set of idle processors within the thread's hard affinity mask. This set is then pruned as follows:

- Any idle logical processors that have been parked by the Core Parking mechanism are removed. (See Chapter 9, "Storage Management," in Part 2 for more information on Core Parking.) If this causes no idle processors to remain, idle processor selection is aborted, and the scheduler behaves as if no idle processors were available (which is described in the upcoming section)

- Any idle logical processors that are not on the ideal node (defined as the node containing the ideal processor) are removed, unless this would cause all idle processors to be eliminated.

- On an SMT system, any non-idle SMT sets are removed, even if this might cause the elimination of the ideal processor itself. In other words, Windows prioritizes a non-ideal, idle SMT set over an ideal processor.

- Windows then checks whether the ideal processor is among the remaining set of idle processors. If it isn't, it must then find the most appropriate idle processor. It does so by first checking whether the processor that the thread last ran on is part of the remaining idle set. If so, this processor is considered to be a temporary ideal processor and chosen. (Recall that the ideal processor attempts to maximize processor cache hits, and picking the last processor a thread ran on is a good way of doing so.)

- If the last processor is not part of the remaining idle set, Windows next checks whether the current processor (that is, the processor currently executing this scheduling code) is part of this set; if so, it applies the same logic as in the prior step.

- If neither the last nor the current processor is idle, Windows performs one more pruning operation, by removing any idle logical processors that are not on the same SMT set as the ideal processor. If there are none left, Windows instead removes any processors not on the SMT set of the current processor, unless this, too, eliminates all idle processors. In other words, Windows prefers idle processors that share the same SMT set as the unavailable ideal processor and/or last processor it would've liked to pick in the first place. Because SMT implementations share the cache on the core, this has nearly the same effect as picking the ideal or last processor from the caching perspective.

- Finally, if this last step results in more than one processor remaining in the idle set, Windows picks the lowest numbered processor as the thread's current processor.

Once a processor has been selected for the thread to run on, that thread is put in the standby state and the idle processor's PRCB is updated to point to this thread. If the processor is idle, but not halted, a DPC interrupt is sent so that the processor handles the scheduling operation immediately.

Whenever such a scheduling operation is initiated, *KiCheckForThreadDispatch* is called, which will realize that a new thread has been scheduled on the processor and cause an immediate context switch if possible (as well as pending APC deliveries), or it will cause a DPC interrupt to be sent.

Choosing a Processor for a Thread When There Are No Idle Processors

If there are no idle processors when a thread wants to run, or if the only idle processors were eliminated by the first pruning (which got rid of parked idle processors), Windows first checks whether the latter situation has occurred. In this scenario, the scheduler calls *KiSelectCandidateProcessor* to ask the Core Parking engine for the best candidate processor. The Core Parking engine selects the highest-numbered processor that is unparked within the ideal node. If there are no such processors, the engine forcefully overrides the park state of the ideal processor and causes it to be unparked. Upon returning to the scheduler, it will check whether the candidate it received is idle; if so, it will pick this processor for the thread, following the same last steps as in the previous scenario.

If this fails, Windows compares the priority of the thread running (or the one in the standby state) on the thread's ideal processor to determine whether it should preempt that thread.

If the thread's ideal processor already has a thread selected to run next (waiting in the standby state to be scheduled) and that thread's priority is less than the priority of the thread being readied for execution, the new thread preempts that first thread out of the standby state and becomes the next thread for that CPU. If there is already a thread running on that CPU, Windows checks whether the priority of the currently running thread is less than the thread being readied for execution. If so, the currently running thread is marked to be preempted, and Windows queues a DPC interrupt to the target processor to preempt the currently running thread in favor of this new thread.

If the ready thread cannot be run right away, it is moved into the ready state on the priority queue appropriate to its thread priority, where it will await its turn to run. As seen in the scheduling scenarios earlier, the thread will be inserted either at the head or the tail of the queue, based on whether it entered the ready state due to preemption.

As such, regardless of the underlying scenario and various possibilities, note that threads are always put on their ideal processor's per-processor ready queues, guaranteeing the consistency of the algorithms that determine how a logical processor picks a thread to run.

Processor Share-Based Scheduling

In the previous section, the standard thread-based scheduling implementation of Windows was described, which has served general user and server scenarios reliably since its appearance in the first Windows NT release (with scalability improvements done throughout each release). However, because thread-based scheduling attempts to fairly share the processor or processors only among competing threads of same priority, it does not take into account higher-level requirements such as the distribution of threads to users and the potential for certain users to benefit from more overall CPU time at the expense of other users. This kind of behavior, as it turns out, is highly sought after in terminal-services environments, where dozens of users can be competing for CPU time and a single high-priority thread from a given user has the potential to starve threads from all users on the machine if only thread-based scheduling is used.

Dynamic Fair Share Scheduling

In this section, two alternative scheduling modes implemented by recent versions of Windows will be described: the session-based Dynamic Fair Share Scheduler (DFSS) and an older, legacy SID-based CPU Rate Limit implementation.

DFSS Initialization

During the very last parts of system initialization, as the SOFTWARE hive is initialized by *Smss*, the process manager initiates the final post-boot initialization in *PsBootPhaseComplete*, which calls *PsInitializeCpuQuota*. It is here that the system decides which of the two CPU quota mechanisms (DFSS or legacy) will be employed. For DFSS to be enabled, the *EnableCpuQuota* registry value must be set to 1 in both of the two quota keys: HKLM\SOFTWARE\Policies\Microsoft\Windows\Session Manager\Quota System for the policy-based setting (that can be configured through the Group Policy Editor under Computer Configuration\Administrative Templates\Windows Components \Remote Desktop Services\Remote Desktop Session Host\Connections - Turn off Fair Share CPU Scheduling), as well as under the system key HKLM\SYSTEM\CurrentControlSet\Control\Session Manager\Quota System, which determines if the system supports the functionality (which, by default, is set to TRUE on Windows Server with the Remote Desktop role).

> **Note** Due to a bug (which you can learn more about at *http://technet.microsoft.com /en-us/library/ee808941(WS.10).aspx*), the group policy setting to turn off DFSS is not honored. The system setting must be manually turned off.

If DFSS is enabled, the *PsCpuFairShareEnabled* variable is set to *true*, which will instruct the kernel, through various scheduling code paths, to behave differently and/or to call into the DFSS engine. Additionally, the default quota is set up to 150 milliseconds for each DFSS cycle, a number called credit that will be explained in more detail shortly.

Once DFSS is enabled, the global *PspCpuQuotaControl* data structure is used to maintain DFSS information, such as the list of per-session CPU quota blocks (as well as a spinlock and count) and the total weight of all sessions on the system. It also stores an array of per-processor DFSS data structures, which you'll see next.

Per-Session CPU Quota Blocks

After DFSS is enabled, whenever a new session is created (other than Session 0), *MiSessionCreate* calls *PsAllocateCpuQuotaBlock* to set up the per-session CPU quota block. The first time this happens on the system (for example, for Session 1), this calls *PspLazyInitializeCpuQuota* to finalize the initialization of DFSS.

This results in the allocation of per-CPU DFSS data structures mentioned in the previous sections, which contain the DPC used for managing the quota (*PspCpuQuotaDpcRoutine*, seen later) and the total number of cycles credited as well as accumulated. This structure also keeps the block generation a monotonically increasing sequence to guarantee atomicity, as well as keeping the idle-only queue lock protecting the list of the same name, which is a central element of the DFSS mechanism yet to be described. Each per-CPU DFSS data structure, in turn, is connected through a sorted doubly-linked list to the various per-session CPU quota blocks that were mentioned at the beginning of this discussion.

When the first-time initialization of DFSS is complete, *PsAllocateCpuQuotaBlock* can continue, first by allocating the actual CPU quota block for this session. This structure maintains overall accounting information on the session, as well as per-CPU tracking—including the cycles remaining and initially allocated, as well as the idle-only queue itself, in a per-CPU quota entry structure.

To begin with, the session ID is stored, and the CPU share weight is set to its default of *5*. You'll see shortly what a weight is, how it can be computed, and its effects on the DFSS engine. Because the quota block has just been created, the initial cycle values are all set to their maximum value for now. Next, this new per-session CPU block must be visible to the system. Therefore, the *PspCpuQuotaControl* data structure is updated with the new total weight of all sessions (by adding this weight), and the quota block is inserted into the block list (sorted by session ID). Finally, *PspCalculateCpuQuotaBlockCycleCredits* enumerates every other session's quota block and captures the new total weight of the system.

Once this is done, the per-session CPU quota block is finalized, and the memory manager sets it in the *CpuQuotaBlock* field of the MM_SESSION_SPACE structure for this session. Likewise, the current EPROCESS (part of this new session's *CpuQuotaBlock* field) is also updated to point to this session's CPU quota block. Now that the process has received a CPU quota block as soon as it became part of the session, future threads created by this process (including the first thread itself) will be allocated with an extra structure after their typical ETHREAD—a per-process CPU Quota APC structure. Additionally, the ETHREAD's *RateApcState* field will be set to *PsRateApcContained*, indicating that this is an embedded Quota APC, as used by the DFSS mechanism (rather than the pool-allocated legacy APC). Finally, the *CpuThrottled* bit is set in the KTHREAD's *ThreadControlFlags*.

At this point, the global quota-control structure contains a pointer to the DFSS per-CPU data structure array, which itself is linked to all the per-session CPU blocks that have been created for each session and associated with the EPROCESS structure of the member processes. In turn, each thread part of such a process has CPU throttling turned on. There is a per-CPU DPC ready to execute, as well as per-thread APCs for each throttled thread.

When the last process in the session loses all its references, *PsDeleteCpuQuotaBlock* is called. It removes the block from the list, refreshes the total weights, and calls *PspCalculateCpuQuotaBlockCycleCredits* to update all other per-session CPU quota blocks.

Charging of Cycles to Throttled Threads

After everything is set up, the entire DFSS mechanism is triggered by the consumption of CPU cycles—something that was already explained in the earlier sections. In other words, not only are consumed cycles used for quantum accounting and providing finer-grained information to thread

APIs, but they also can be "charged" against the thread (and thus against its quota). This operation is done by the *PsChargeProcessCpuCycles* function that is called whenever a thread has completed the accumulation of cycles in its current execution timeline.

The first operation involves accumulating the additional cycles to the per-CPU DFSS data structure for this processor, increasing the *TotalCyclesAccumulated* value. If this accumulation has reached the total credit, the quota DPC is immediately queued. Once the DPC ultimately executes, it calls *PspStartNewFairShareInterval*, which updates the generation, resets the cycles accumulated, and resets the credit to 150 ms. Finally, the idle-only queue is flushed on each processor associated with a given session. (You'll see what this queue is and what flushing it entails, later.) This part of the algorithm manages the 150-ms interval that controls DFSS.

A second possibility is that the generation of the per-CPU quota entry contained in the current process' CPU quota block (owned by the session) does not manage the generation of the current per-CPU DFSS data structure. This generation mismatch suggests that a new interval has been reached and no cycle limits have yet been set, so *PspReplenishCycleCredit* is called to do the work. This reads the per-CPU weight and the total weight that were captured earlier in *PspCalculateCpuQuotaBlockCycleCredits*, and it uses them to set the base cycle allowance for the current per-CPU data inside the process' CPU quota block. To do this, it uses a simple formula: the process receives the equivalent of its cycle credit (150 ms) divided by the total weight of all sessions on the system. Then the amount of cycles it will be permitted to run for (*CyclesRemaining*) is set to the base cycle allowance multiplied by the weight of this particular session. In other words, the process runs for a fairly-divided chunk of time based on the number of other sessions on the system, calculated as a percentage based on its relative weight compared to the overall system weight. When the computation is completed, the generation is set to match.

In all other cases, *PsChargeProcessCpuCycles* merely subtracts the amount of cycles from *CyclesRemaining* and then calls *PsCheckThreadCpuQuota* to see whether these cycles have been exhausted (reaching zero). Note that this function can sometimes also be called directly from the context switch code when control is about to pass to a thread that has CPU throttling enabled.

PsCheckThreadCpuQuota recovers the CPU quota block for this process (that is, for the session), and then further extracts the precise per-CPU information out of it. Once again, it checks whether the generation does not match, which would indicate this is the first charge for this 150-ms credit cycle, and then it calls *PspReplenishCycleCredit*. Next, it checks whether the CPU quota block for the process indicates there are no more cycles remaining. If cycles still remain, the function returns; otherwise, it prepares to suspend the thread's execution.

Before stopping execution, the function extracts the per-CPU DPC, making sure that it (or the associated per-thread APC) is not already running. If this operation is happening due to the context-switch scenario brought up earlier, the per-thread APC is queued, which will preempt the thread's execution as soon as the context switch completes. Otherwise, if this is occurring as result of cycle charging (which happens at DISPATCH_LEVEL or higher), the per-CPU DPC is queued instead, which will later queue the per-thread APC. (This forces a near-immediate response to the CPU quota restriction.) In case further cycle accumulation has occurred past the 150-ms cycle credit, the DPC also calls *PspStartNewFairShareInterval*, which was explained earlier.

CPU Throttling and Quota Enforcement

So far, you've seen how DFSS initializes, how CPU quota blocks are created for each session (and then associated with member processes), and how threads running with the CPU throttling bit (implying they are part of processes that are members of a session with DFSS enabled) will consume cycles out of their total weight-relative allowance, resetting every 150 ms. You also saw how, eventually, an APC is queued in all cases where a thread has exhausted its allowed cycles. You'll now see how the APC enforces the CPU quota restriction.

The APC first enters an infinite loop, creating a stack-allocated Quota Wait Block that contains the current thread being restricted, as well as a resume event. It is this event that ultimately allows the thread to continue its execution. Next, the APC gets the per-CPU DFSS data structure pointer and acquires the idle-only queue lock referenced earlier. It then checks whether the idle-only queue on the current processor (which comes from the per-CPU quota entry contained in the process' CPU quota block) is empty. If the list is empty, it implies that this CPU has never been inserted in the sorted block list that is contained in the per-CPU DFSS data structure (part of the *PspCpuQuotaControl* global array). The *PspInsertQuotaBlockCpuEntry* function is thus called to rectify the situation.

Because the DFSS scheduler itself (which has yet to be described) uses this data structure, it must be inserted in the most optimal way—in this case, sorted by the base cycle allowance of each per-CPU data contained within the per-process CPU quota block. Recall that the base cycle allowance is initially the 150-ms credit cycle divided by the total weight of the system (that is, a full allowance), but you'll see how the allowance can be later modified by the DFSS scheduler.

Next, now that the per-CPU Quota Entry is in the sorted block list (or it might already have been if the idle-only queue was not empty), this thread is inserted at the end of the idle-only queue, and it's connected by a linked list entry that's present in the Quota Wait Block. Because this wait block contains the resume event initialized earlier, the DFSS scheduler is able to control the thread when needed.

Finally, the APC enters a wait on this resume event, with the wait reason *WrCpuRateControl*. By using a tool such as Sysinternals PsList, or Process Explorer—all of which display wait reasons (as well as a kernel debugger)—you can see such threads intermittently blocked on a DFSS system.

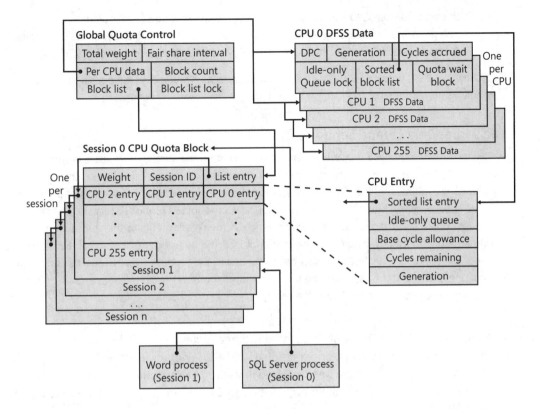

Resuming Execution

With more and more threads possibly hitting their CPU quota restrictions and block on their respective idle-queues, how will they eventually resume execution? One of the possibilities is that a new 150-ms interval has started. Recall from the earlier discussion that *PspStartNewFairShareInterval* was said to "flush the idle-only queue." This operation, performed by *PspFlushProcessorIdleOnlyQueue*, essentially scans every per-CPU quota entry for this processor (which is located in the sorted block list), and then scans the idle-only queue of each such processor. Picking every thread in the list, the function removes the thread and manually sets the resume event. Thus, any blocked thread on the current CPU gets to resume execution after 150 ms.

Obviously, flushing is not the usual mechanism through which the idle-only queue threads are managed. This work typically is done by the DFSS scheduler itself, which provides the *PsReleaseThreadFromIdleOnlyQueue* routine as a callback that the regular thread scheduler, when the system is about to go idle, can use whenever DFSS-related work is required. Specifically, it is the *KiSearchForNewThread* function, thoroughly described earlier, that calls DFSS in the following two scenarios:

- If *KiSelectReadyThread*, which is called initially, has not found a new thread for the current processor, before it checks other processors' dispatcher ready queues, *KiSearchForNewThread* will ask DFSS to release a thread from the idle-only queue.

- Otherwise, as each CPU's dispatcher ready queues are scanned (by looping *KiSelectReadyThread* calls on each PRCB), if once again no thread is found, the DFSS scheduler is called to release a thread from idle-only queue on the target processor as well.

Finally, you'll see what work *PsReleaseThreadFromIdleOnlyQueue* actually does and how the DFSS scheduler is implemented.

DFSS Idle-Only Queue Scheduling

PsReleaseThreadFromIdleOnlyQueue initially checks whether the sorted block list is empty (which would imply there aren't even any valid per-CPU quota entries), and it exits if this is the case. Otherwise, it acquires the idle-only queue spinlock from the per-CPU DFSS data structure and calls *PspFindHighestPriorityThreadToRun*. This function scans the sorted block list, recovering every per-CPU quota entry, and then scans every entry (which, if you recall, points to the Quota Wait Block for the thread). Unfortunately, because threads are not inserted by priority (such as real dispatcher ready queues), the entire idle-only queue must be scanned, and the highest priority found to this point is recorded in each iteration. (Because the lock is acquired, no new per-CPU quota entries or idle-only queue threads can be inserted during the scan.)

> **Note** Because DFSS is not truly integrated with the regular thread scheduler, the reason the threads are not sorted by priority is obvious: DFSS is not aware of priority changes after idle-only queue threads have been inserted in its lists. A user could still modify the priority, and because the thread scheduler does not notify DFSS of this, an incorrect thread would be picked.

Additionally, affinity is carefully checked to ensure only correctly affinitized threads are scanned. Although each idle-only queue contains only threads for the current processor, scenario #2 in the preceding section showed how remote processor idle-only queues can also be scanned. DFSS must ensure that the current CPU will run an appropriate remote-CPU, idle-only thread.

Once the highest priority thread has been found on the current per-CPU quota entry, it is removed from the idle-only queue and returned to the caller. Additionally, if this was the last thread on the idle-only queue, the per-CPU entry is removed from the sorted block list. Therefore, note that the other per-CPU quota entries are not checked unless a runnable highest-priority thread was not found on the first per-CPU quota entry (that is, the one with the highest base cycle allowance).

Once the thread is found, *PsReleaseThreadFromIdleOnlyQueue* resumes its execution and once more queues the DPC responsible for eventually launching the per-thread APC from earlier (after making sure the DPC is not already running). Thus, the APC is never directly queued in this case, because this function runs as part of the thread scheduler, already at DISPATCH_LEVEL. Additionally, it wouldn't make sense to queue another per-thread APC just to notify the original APC; instead, the DPC itself will wake up the thread.

This is done by a special check in the DPC routine that checks whether the *ThreadWaitBlockForRelease* field in the per-CPU DFSS data structure is set. If so, the DPC knows that this is a wake-up, not a stop, request, and it sets the resume event associated with the Quota Wait Block. Additionally, it forces the Idle Scheduler on the current CPU to run, by setting the *IdleSchedule* field in the KPRCB that was brought up in the earlier idle scheduler section.

One detail has been glossed over, however: once the idle-only thread is picked, as soon as a context switch is initiated, the cycle accumulation once again detects that the thread has exhausted its cycles, and it re-inserts the thread in the idle-only queue. Therefore, *PsReleaseThreadFromIdleOnlyQueue* must update the cycles remaining for the current per-CPU quota entry, allowing this CPU to run the thread for a little bit longer. How much longer exactly is determined by the value of *KiCyclesPerClockQuantum*, which was shown in the earlier "Quantum" section. Therefore, this CPU is allowed to run the current thread for an entire quantum, at most.

Additionally, the base cycle allowance for this entry must be updated, because the quota for the CPU is actually exhausted and no longer working on a 150-ms cycle credit. Therefore, the allowance is now updated to include an extra *KiCyclesPerClockQuantum* divided by the weight of the session" cycle. Because the base cycle allowance has changed, the sorted block list is reparsed, and the entries are re-sorted correctly to account for this change. Thus, this block will now migrate to the front of the list and have a higher chance to be picked once a future idle-only thread (within this interval) needs to be picked.

Session Weight Configuration

So far, the weight associated to sessions has been described as its default value of 5. However, this weight can be set to anywhere between 1 and 9, and DFSS provides two internal APIs for managing weight information: *PsQueryCpuInformation* and its *Set* equivalent.

Given an array of session handles (to session objects) and associated weights, the Set API sets the new weight for each session, as well as updating the total weight stored in the *PspCpuQuotaControl* global. By calling *PspCalculateCpuQuotaBlockCycleCredits* again, the new settings will be propagated. Likewise, the Query API returns an array of weights and session IDs. The *SeIncreaseQuotaPrivilege* is required in both cases, as well as SESSION_MODIFY_ACCESS for each session whose weight is being modified. Accessing these APIs is done through the native API function *NtQuerySystemInformation*, with the *SystemCpuQuotaInformation* call.

This API, although not provided by the Windows API directly, is what the Windows System Resource Manager uses when the administrator assigns different priorities to different users when the *Weighted_Remote_Sessions* policy is enabled. The three priorities—Premium, Standard, and Basic—map to the 1, 5, and 9 weights in the internal DFSS scheduler mechanism, respectively.

CPU Rate Limits

As part of the hard quota management system in Windows (based on the original soft-limit quota support present since the first version of Windows NT), support for limiting CPU usage exists in the system in three different ways: per-session, per-user, or per-system. Unfortunately, there is no tool that is part of the operating system that allows you to set these limits—you must modify the registry settings manually. Because all the quotas—save one—are memory quotas, we will cover those in Chapter 10 in Part 2, which deals with the memory manager, and instead focus our attention here on the CPU rate limit.

> **Note** See the topic "CPU rate limits in Windows Server 2008 R2 and Windows 7" in the Microsoft Technet Knowledge Articles at *http://technet.microsoft.com/en-us/library /ff384148(WS.10).aspx* for further documentation and examples on when to use CPU rate limits.

The new quota system can be accessed through the registry key HKLM\SYSTEM \CurrentControlSet\Control\Session Manager\QuotaSystem, as well as through the standard *NtSetInformationProcess* system call. CPU rate limits can therefore be set in one of three ways:

- By creating a new DWORD value called *CpuRateLimit* and entering the rate information.

- By creating a new key with the security ID (SID) of the account you want to limit, and creating a *CpuRateLimit* DWORD value inside that key.

- By calling *NtSetInformationProcess* and giving it the process handle of the process to limit and the CPU rate limiting information, if the process is tied to the system quota block.

In all three cases, the CPU rate limit data is a straightforward value; it is simply a rate limit expressed as a percentage. For example, to limit a user's applications to consume at most 10% of CPU time, you set *CpuRateLimit* to *10*. The process manager, which is responsible for enforcing the CPU rate limit, uses various system mechanisms to do its job. First, rate limiting works reliably because of the CPU cycle count improvements discussed earlier, which allow the process manager to accurately determine how much CPU time a process has taken and know whether the limit should be enforced. It then uses a combination of DPC and APC routines to throttle down DPC and APC CPU usage, which are outside the direct control of user-mode developers but still result in CPU usage in the system (in the case of a systemwide CPU rate limit).

Finally, the main mechanism through which rate limiting works is by creating an artificial wait on an event object (making the thread uniquely bound to this object and putting it in a wait state, which does not consume CPU cycles). Threads that are artificially waiting because of CPU rate limits can be observed because their wait reason code is set to *WrCpuRateControl*. This mechanism operates through the normal routine of an APC object queued to the thread or threads inside the process currently responsible for the work. The event is eventually signaled by the DPC routine associated with a timer (firing every half a second) responsible for replenishing systemwide CPU usage requests.

Dynamic Processor Addition and Replacement

As you've seen, developers can fine-tune which threads are allowed to (and in the case of the ideal processor, should) run on which processor. This works fine on systems that have a constant number of processors during their run time. (For example, desktop machines require shutting down the computer to make any sort of hardware changes to the processor or their count.)

Today's server systems, however, cannot afford the downtime that CPU replacement or addition normally requires. In fact, one example of when adding a CPU is required for a server is at times of high load that is above what the machine can support at its current level of performance. Having to shut down the server during a period of peak usage would defeat the purpose. To meet this requirement, the latest generation of server motherboards and systems support the addition of processors (as well as their replacement) while the machine is still running. The ACPI BIOS and related hardware on the machine have been specifically built to allow and be aware of this need, but operating system participation is required for full support.

Dynamic processor support is provided through the HAL, which notifies the kernel of a new processor on the system through the function *KeStartDynamicProcessor*. This routine does similar work to that performed when the system detects more than one processor at startup and needs to initialize the structures related to them. When a dynamic processor is added, various system components perform some additional work. For example, the memory manager allocates new pages and memory structures optimized for the CPU. It also initializes a new DPC kernel stack while the kernel initializes the global descriptor table (GDT), the interrupt Dispatch table (IDT), the processor control region (PCR), the process control block (PRCB), and other related structures for the processor.

Other executive parts of the kernel are also called, mostly to initialize the per-processor look-aside lists for the processor that was added. For example, the I/O manager, executive look-aside list code, cache manager, and object manager all use per-processor look-aside lists for their frequently allocated structures.

Finally, the kernel initializes threaded DPC support for the processor and adjusts exported kernel variables to report the new processor. Different memory-manager masks and process seeds based on processor counts are also updated, and processor features need to be updated for the new processor to match the rest of the system (for example, enabling virtualization support on the newly added processor). The initialization sequence completes with the notification to the Windows Hardware Error Architecture (WHEA) component that a new processor is online.

The HAL is also involved in this process. It is called once to start the dynamic processor after the kernel is aware of it, and it is called again after the kernel has finished initialization of the processor. However, these notifications and callbacks only make the kernel aware and respond to processor changes. Although an additional processor increases the throughput of the kernel, it does nothing to help drivers.

To handle drivers, the system has a new default executive callback object, the *ProcessorAdd* callback, that drivers can register with for notifications. Similar to the callbacks that notify drivers of power state or system time changes, this callback allows driver code to, for example, create a new worker thread if desirable so that it can handle more work at the same time.

Once drivers are notified, the final kernel component called is the Plug and Play manager, which adds the processor to the system's device node and rebalances interrupts so that the new processor can handle interrupts that were already registered for other processors. CPU-hungry applications are also able to take advantage of newer processors as well.

However, a sudden change of affinity can have potentially breaking changes for a running application (especially when going from a single-processor to a multiprocessor environment) through the appearance of potential race conditions or simply misdistribution of work (because the process might have calculated the perfect ratios at startup, based on the number of CPUs it was aware of). As a result, applications do not take advantage of a dynamically added processor by default—they must request it.

The Windows APIs *SetProcessAffinityUpdateMode* and *QueryProcessAffinityMode* (which use the undocumented *NtSet/QueryInformationProcess* system call) tell the process manager that these applications should have their affinity updated (by setting the *AffinityUpdateEnable* flag in EPROCESS), or that they do not want to deal with affinity updates (by setting the *AffinityPermanent* flag in EPROCESS). Once an application has told the system that its affinity is permanent, it cannot later change its mind and request affinity updates, so this is a one-time change.

As part of *KeStartDynamicProcessor*, a new step has been added after interrupts are rebalanced, which is to call the process manager to perform affinity updates through *PsUpdateActiveProcessAffinity*. Some Windows core processes and services already have affinity updates enabled, while third-party software will need to be recompiled to take advantage of the new API call. The System process, *Svchost* processes, and *Smss* are all compatible with dynamic processor addition.

Job Objects

A job object is a nameable, securable, shareable kernel object that allows control of one or more processes as a group. A job object's basic function is to allow groups of processes to be managed and manipulated as a unit. A process can be a member of only one job object. By default, its association with the job object can't be broken and all processes created by the process and its descendants are associated with the same job object as well. The job object also records basic accounting information for all processes associated with the job and for all processes that were associated with the job but have since terminated.

Jobs can also be associated with an I/O completion port object, which other threads might be waiting for, with the Windows *GetQueuedCompletionStatus* function. This allows interested parties (typically, the job creator) to monitor for limit violation and events that could affect the job's security (such as a new process being created or a process abnormally exiting).

Job Limits

The following are some of the CPU-related and memory-related limits you can specify for a job:

- **Maximum number of active processes**   Limits the number of concurrently existing processes in the job.

- **Jobwide user-mode CPU time limit**   Limits the maximum amount of user-mode CPU time that the processes in the job can consume (including processes that have run and exited). Once this limit is reached, by default all the processes in the job are terminated with an error code and no new processes can be created in the job (unless the limit is reset). The job object is signaled, so any threads waiting for the job will be released. You can change this default behavior with a call to *SetInformationJobObject* to set the *EndOfJobTimeAction* information class and request a notification to be sent through the job's completion port instead.

- **Per-process user-mode CPU time limit**   Allows each process in the job to accumulate only a fixed maximum amount of user-mode CPU time. When the maximum is reached, the process terminates (with no chance to clean up).

- **Job processor affinity**   Sets the processor affinity mask for each process in the job. (Individual threads can alter their affinity to any subset of the job affinity, but processes can't alter their process affinity setting.)

- **Job group affinity**   Sets a list of groups to which the processes in the job can be assigned to. Any affinity changes are then subject to the group selection imposed by the limit. This is treated as a group-aware version of the job processor affinity limit (legacy), and prevents that limit from being used.

- **Job process priority class**   Sets the priority class for each process in the job. Threads can't increase their priority relative to the class (as they normally can). Attempts to increase thread priority are ignored. (No error is returned on calls to *SetThreadPriority*, but the increase doesn't occur.)

- **Default working set minimum and maximum**   Defines the specified working set minimum and maximum for each process in the job. (This setting isn't jobwide—each process has its own working set with the same minimum and maximum values.)

- **Process and job committed virtual memory limit**   Defines the maximum amount of virtual address space that can be committed by either a single process or the entire job.

You can also place security limits on processes in a job. You can set a job so that each process runs under the same jobwide access token. You can then create a job to restrict processes from impersonating or creating processes that have access tokens that contain the local administrator's group. In addition, you can apply security filters so that when threads in processes contained in a job impersonate client threads, certain privileges and security IDs (SIDs) can be eliminated from the impersonation token.

Finally, you can also place user-interface limits on processes in a job. Such limits include being able to restrict processes from opening handles to windows owned by threads outside the job, reading and/or writing to the clipboard, and changing the many user-interface system parameters via the Windows *SystemParametersInfo* function. These user-interface limits are managed by the Windows subsystem GDI/USER driver, Win32k.sys, and are enforced through one of the special callouts that it registers with the process manager, the job callout.

Job Sets

The job implementation also allows for finer grained control of which job object a given process will be associated with by enabling the creation of job sets. A job set is an array that associates a job member level with each job object that was created by the caller. Later, when the process manager attempts to associate a process with a job, it picks the correct job object from the set based on the job member level that was associated with the newly created process (which must be higher than or equal to the parent's job member level. This allows the parent process to have created multiple job objects, and for its children to pick the appropriate one depending on which limits the parent might want to enforce.

EXPERIMENT: Viewing the Job Object

You can view named job objects with the Performance tool. (See the Job Object and Job Object Details performance objects.) You can view unnamed jobs with the kernel debugger *!job* or *dt nt!_ejob* command.

To see whether a process is associated with a job, you can use the kernel debugger *!process* command or Process Explorer. Follow these steps to create and view an unnamed job object:

1. From the command prompt, use the *runas* command to create a process running the command prompt (Cmd.exe). For example, type **runas /user:<domain> \< username> cmd**. You'll be prompted for your password. Enter your password, and a Command Prompt window will appear. The Windows service that executes *runas* commands creates an unnamed job to contain all processes (so that it can terminate these processes at logoff time).

2. From the command prompt, run Notepad.exe.

3. Then run Process Explorer, and notice that the Cmd.exe and Notepad.exe processes are highlighted as part of a job. (You can configure the colors used to highlight

processes that are members of a job by clicking Options, Configure Colors.) Here is a screen shot showing these two processes:

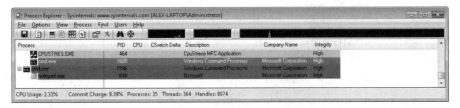

4. Double-click either the Cmd.exe or Notepad.exe process to bring up the process properties. You will see a Job tab in the process properties dialog box.

5. Click the Job tab to view the details about the job. In this case, there are no quotas associated with the job, but there are two member processes:

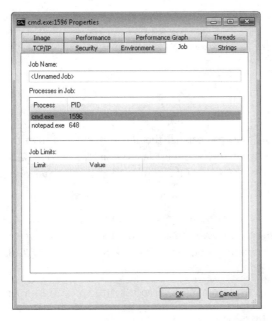

6. Now run the kernel debugger on the live system, display the process list with *!process*, and find the recently created process running Cmd.exe. Then display the process by using *!process <process ID>*, find the address of the job object, and finally display the job object with the *!job* command. Here's some partial debugger output of these commands on a live system:

```
lkd> !process 0 1 cmd.exe
PROCESS 8567b758  SessionId: 1  Cid: 0fc4    Peb: 7ffdf000  ParentCid: 00b0
    DirBase: 1b3fb000  ObjectTable: e18dd7d0  HandleCount:  19.
    Image: Cmd.exe
...
    BasePriority                        8
```

```
        CommitCharge                        636
...     Job                                  85557988

lkd> !job 85557988
Job at 85557988
  TotalPageFaultCount      0
  TotalProcesses           2
  ActiveProcesses          2
  TotalTerminatedProcesses 0
  LimitFlags               0
...
```

7. You can also use the *dt* command to display the job object and see the additional fields shown about the job, such as its member level, if it is part of a job set:

```
lkd> dt nt!_ejob 85557988
nt!_EJOB
   +0x000 Event             : _KEVENT
...
   +0x0b8 EndOfJobTimeAction : 0
   +0x0bc CompletionPort    : 0x87e3d2e8
   +0x0c0 CompletionKey     : 0x07a89508
   +0x0c4 SessionId         : 1
   +0x0c8 SchedulingClass   : 5
...
   +0x120 MemberLevel       : 0
   +0x124 JobFlags          : 0
```

8. Finally, if the job has UI limits, you can use the *dt* command to display the Win32k job structure (*tagW32JOB*). To do this, you must first obtain the W32PROCESS structure pointer as shown in the experiment at the beginning of this chapter, and then display the *pW32Job* field within it.

For example, here is the Win32k job structure for a process using the Block Access To Global Atom Table UI limitation. The structure shows the local atom table this process is using in *pAtomTable*. You can further explore this structure with the *dt nt!_RTL_ATOM_TABLE* command and see which atoms are defined:

```
lkd> ?? ((win32k!tagPROCESSINFO*)(((nt!_EPROCESS*)0x847c4740)->Win32Process))-
>pW32Job
struct tagW32JOB * 0xfd573300
   +0x000 pNext          : 0xff87c5d8 tagW32JOB
   +0x004 Job            : 0x8356ab90 _EJOB
   +0x008 pAtomTable     : 0x8e03eb18
   +0x00c restrictions   : 0xff
   +0x010 uProcessCount  : 1
   +0x014 uMaxProcesses  : 4
   +0x018 ppiTable       : 0xfe5072c0  -> 0xff97db18 tagPROCESSINFO
   +0x01c ughCrt         : 0
   +0x020 ughMax         : 0
   +0x024 pgh            : (null)
```

Conclusion

In this chapter, we examined the structure of processes and threads and jobs, saw how they are created, and looked at how Windows decides which threads should run and for how long, and on which processor or processors.

In the next chapter, we'll look at a part of the system that sometimes receives more attention than anything else: the Windows security reference monitor.

CHAPTER 6

Security

Preventing unauthorized access to sensitive data is essential in any environment in which multiple users have access to the same physical or network resources. An operating system, as well as individual users, must be able to protect files, memory, and configuration settings from unwanted viewing and modification. Operating system security includes obvious mechanisms such as accounts, passwords, and file protection. It also includes less obvious mechanisms, such as protecting the operating system from corruption, preventing less privileged users from performing actions (rebooting the computer, for example), and not allowing user programs to adversely affect the programs of other users or the operating system.

In this chapter, we explain how every aspect of the design and implementation of Microsoft Windows was influenced in some way by the stringent requirements of providing robust security.

Security Ratings

Having software, including operating systems, rated against well-defined standards helps the government, corporations, and home users protect proprietary and personal data stored in computer systems. The current security rating standard used by the United States and many other countries is the Common Criteria (CC). To understand the security capabilities designed into Windows, however, it's useful to know the history of the security ratings system that influenced the design of Windows, the Trusted Computer System Evaluation Criteria (TCSEC).

Trusted Computer System Evaluation Criteria

The National Computer Security Center (NCSC) was established in 1981 as part of the U.S. Department of Defense's (DoD) National Security Agency (NSA). One goal of the NCSC was to create a range of security ratings, listed in Table 6-1, to be used to indicate the degree of protection commercial operating systems, network components, and trusted applications offer. These security ratings, which can be found at *http://csrc.nist.gov/publications/history/dod85.pdf*, were defined in 1983 and are commonly referred to as "the Orange Book."

The TCSEC standard consists of "levels of trust" ratings, where higher levels build on lower levels by adding more rigorous protection and validation requirements. No operating system meets the A1, or "Verified Design," rating. Although a few operating systems have earned one of the B-level ratings, C2 is considered sufficient and the highest rating practical for a general-purpose operating system.

TABLE 6-1 TCSEC Rating Levels

Rating	Description
A1	Verified Design
B3	Security Domains
B2	Structured Protection
B1	Labeled Security Protection
C2	Controlled Access Protection
C1	Discretionary Access Protection (obsolete)
D	Minimal Protection

In July 1995, Windows NT 3.5 (Workstation and Server) with Service Pack 3 was the first version of Windows NT to earn the C2 rating. In March 1999, Windows NT 4 with Service Pack 3 achieved an E3 rating from the U.K. government's Information Technology Security (ITSEC) organization, a rating equivalent to a U.S. C2 rating. In November 1999, Windows NT 4 with Service Pack 6a earned a C2 rating in both stand-alone and networked configurations.

The following were the key requirements for a C2 security rating, and they are still considered the core requirements for any secure operating system:

- A secure logon facility, which requires that users can be uniquely identified and that they must be granted access to the computer only after they have been authenticated in some way.

- Discretionary access control, which allows the owner of a resource (such as a file) to determine who can access the resource and what they can do with it. The owner grants rights that permit various kinds of access to a user or to a group of users.

- Security auditing, which affords the ability to detect and record security-related events or any attempts to create, access, or delete system resources. Logon identifiers record the identities of all users, making it easy to trace anyone who performs an unauthorized action.

- Object reuse protection, which prevents users from seeing data that another user has deleted or from accessing memory that another user previously used and then released. For example, in some operating systems, it's possible to create a new file of a certain length and then examine the contents of the file to see data that happens to have occupied the location on the disk where the file is allocated. This data might be sensitive information that was stored in another user's file but had been deleted. Object reuse protection prevents this potential security hole by initializing all objects, including files and memory, before they are allocated to a user.

Windows also meets two requirements of B-level security:

- Trusted path functionality, which prevents Trojan horse programs from being able to intercept users' names and passwords as they try to log on. The trusted path functionality in Windows comes in the form of its Ctrl+Alt+Delete logon-attention sequence, which cannot be intercepted by nonprivileged applications. This sequence of keystrokes, which is also known as the secure attention sequence (SAS), always displays a system-controlled Windows security screen (if a user is already logged on) or the logon screen so that would-be Trojan horses can easily be recognized. (The secure attention sequence can also be sent programmatically via the *SendSAS* API, if group policy allows it.) A Trojan horse presenting a fake logon dialog box will be bypassed when the SAS is entered.

- Trusted facility management, which requires support for separate account roles for administrative functions. For example, separate accounts are provided for administration (Administrators), user accounts charged with backing up the computer, and standard users.

Windows meets all of these requirements through its security subsystem and related components.

The Common Criteria

In January 1996, the United States, United Kingdom, Germany, France, Canada, and the Netherlands released the jointly developed Common Criteria for Information Technology Security Evaluation (CCITSE) security evaluation specification. CCITSE, which is usually referred to as the Common Criteria (CC), is the recognized multinational standard for product security evaluation. The CC home page is at www.niap-ccevs.org/cc-scheme/.

The CC is more flexible than the TCSEC trust ratings and has a structure closer to the ITSEC standard than to the TCSEC standard. The CC includes the concept of a Protection Profile (PP), used to collect security requirements into easily specified and compared sets, and the concept of a Security Target (ST), which contains a set of security requirements that can be made by reference to a PP. The CC also defines a range of seven Evaluation Assurance Levels (EALs), which indicate a level of confidence in the certification. In this way, the CC (like the ITSEC standard before it) removes the link between functionality and assurance level that was present in TCSEC and earlier certification schemes.

Windows 2000, Windows XP, Windows Server 2003, and Windows Vista Enterprise all achieved Common Criteria certification under the Controlled Access Protection Profile (CAPP). This is roughly equivalent to a TCSEC C2 rating. All received a rating of EAL 4+, the "plus" denoting "flaw remediation." EAL 4 is the highest level recognized across national boundaries.

In March 2011, Windows 7 and Windows Server 2008 R2 were evaluated as meeting the requirements of the US Government Protection Profile for General-Purpose Operating Systems in a Networked Environment, version 1.0, 30 August 2010 (GPOSPP) (*http://www.commoncriteriaportal.org /files/ppfiles/pp_gpospp_v1.0.pdf*). The certification includes the Hyper-V hypervisor, and again Windows achieved Evaluation Assurance Level 4 with flaw remediation (EAL-4+). The validation report can be found at *http://www.commoncriteriaportal.org/files/epfiles/st_vid10390-vr.pdf*, and the description of the security target, giving details of the requirements satisfied, can be found at *http://www.commoncriteriaportal.org/files/epfiles/st_vid10390-st.pdf*.

Security System Components

These are the core components and databases that implement Windows security:

- **Security reference monitor (SRM)** A component in the Windows executive (%SystemRoot%\System32\Ntoskrnl.exe) that is responsible for defining the access token data structure to represent a security context, performing security access checks on objects, manipulating privileges (user rights), and generating any resulting security audit messages.

- **Local Security Authority subsystem (LSASS)** A user-mode process running the image %SystemRoot%\System32\Lsass.exe that is responsible for the local system security policy (such as which users are allowed to log on to the machine, password policies, privileges granted to users and groups, and the system security auditing settings), user authentication, and sending security audit messages to the Event Log. The Local Security Authority service (Lsasrv—%SystemRoot%\System32\Lsasrv.dll), a library that LSASS loads, implements most of this functionality.

- **LSASS policy database** A database that contains the local system security policy settings. This database is stored in the registry in an ACL-protected area under HKLM\SECURITY. It includes such information as what domains are entrusted to authenticate logon attempts, who has permission to access the system and how (interactive, network, and service logons), who is assigned which privileges, and what kind of security auditing is to be performed. The LSASS policy database also stores "secrets" that include logon information used for cached domain logons and Windows service user-account logons. (See Chapter 4, "Management Mechanisms," for more information on Windows services.)

- **Security Accounts Manager (SAM)** A service responsible for managing the database that contains the user names and groups defined on the local machine. The SAM service, which is implemented as %SystemRoot%\System32\Samsrv.dll, is loaded into the LSASS process.

- **SAM database** A database that contains the defined local users and groups, along with their passwords and other attributes. On domain controllers, the SAM does not store the domain-defined users, but stores the system's administrator recovery account definition and password. This database is stored in the registry under HKLM\SAM.

- **Active Directory** A directory service that contains a database that stores information about objects in a domain. A *domain* is a collection of computers and their associated security groups that are managed as a single entity. Active Directory stores information about the objects in the domain, including users, groups, and computers. Password information and privileges for domain users and groups are stored in Active Directory, which is replicated across the computers that are designated as domain controllers of the domain. The Active Directory server, implemented as %SystemRoot%\System32\Ntdsa.dll, runs in the LSASS process. For more information on Active Directory, see Chapter 7, "Networking."

- **Authentication packages**   These include dynamic-link libraries (DLLs) that run both in the context of the LSASS process and client processes, and implement Windows authentication policy. An authentication DLL is responsible for authenticating a user, by checking whether a given user name and password match, and if so, returning to the LSASS information detailing the user's security identity, which LSASS uses to generate a token.

- **Interactive logon manager (Winlogon)**   A user-mode process running %SystemRoot% \System32\Winlogon.exe that is responsible for responding to the SAS and for managing interactive logon sessions. Winlogon creates a user's first process when the user logs on, for example.

- **Logon user interface (LogonUI)**   A user-mode process running %SystemRoot%\System32 \LogonUI.exe that presents users with the user interface they can use to authenticate them-selves on the system. LogonUI uses credential providers to query user credentials through various methods.

- **Credential providers (CPs)**   In-process COM objects that run in the LogonUI process (started on demand by Winlogon when the SAS is performed) and used to obtain a user's name and password, smartcard PIN, or biometric data (such as a fingerprint). The standard CPs are %SystemRoot%\System32\authui.dll and %SystemRoot%\System32 \SmartcardCredentialProvider.dll.

- **Network logon service (Netlogon)**   A Windows service (%SystemRoot%\System32 \Netlogon.dll) that sets up the secure channel to a domain controller, over which security requests—such as an interactive logon (if the domain controller is running Windows NT 4) or LAN Manager and NT LAN Manager (v1 and v2) authentication validation—are sent. Netlogon is also used for Active Directory logons.

- **Kernel Security Device Driver (KSecDD)**   A kernel-mode library of functions that implement the advanced local procedure call (ALPC) interfaces that other kernel mode security components, including the Encrypting File System (EFS), use to communicate with LSASS in user mode. KSecDD is located in %SystemRoot%\System32\Drivers\Ksecdd.sys.

- **AppLocker**   A mechanism that allows administrators to specify which executable files, DLLs, and scripts can be used by specified users and groups. AppLocker consists of a driver (%SystemRoot%\System32\Drivers\Appid.sys) and a service (%SystemRoot%\System32 \AppIdSvc.dll) running in a SvcHost process.

Figure 6-1 shows the relationships among some of these components and the databases they manage.

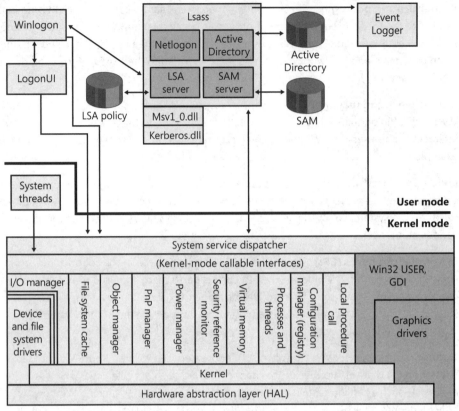

FIGURE 6-1 Windows security components

EXPERIMENT: Looking Inside HKLM\SAM and HKLM\Security

The security descriptors associated with the SAM and Security keys in the registry prevent access by any account other than the local system account. One way to gain access to these keys for exploration is to reset their security, but that can weaken the system's security. Another way is to execute Regedit.exe while running as the local system account. This can be done using the PsExec tool from Windows Sysinternals with the *–s* option, as shown here:

```
C:\>psexec –s –i –d c:\windows\regedit.exe
```

The SRM, which runs in kernel mode, and LSASS, which runs in user mode, communicate using the ALPC facility described in Chapter 3, "System Mechanisms." During system initialization, the SRM creates a port, named SeRmCommandPort, to which LSASS connects. When the LSASS process starts, it creates an ALPC port named SeLsaCommandPort. The SRM connects to this port, resulting in the creation of private communication ports. The SRM creates a shared memory section for messages longer than 256 bytes, passing a handle in the connect call. Once the SRM and LSASS connect to each other during system initialization, they no longer listen on their respective connect ports. Therefore, a later user process has no way to connect successfully to either of these ports for malicious purposes—the connect request will never complete.

Figure 6-2 shows the communication paths as they exist after system initialization.

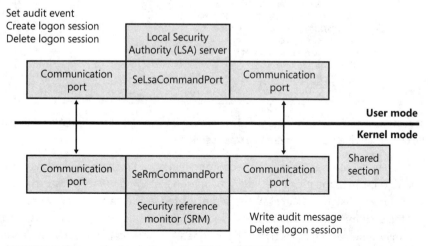

FIGURE 6-2 Communication between the SRM and LSASS

Protecting Objects

Object protection and access logging is the essence of discretionary access control and auditing. The objects that can be protected on Windows include files, devices, mailslots, pipes (named and anonymous), jobs, processes, threads, events, keyed events, event pairs, mutexes, semaphores, shared memory sections, I/O completion ports, LPC ports, waitable timers, access tokens, volumes, window stations, desktops, network shares, services, registry keys, printers, Active Directory objects, and so on—theoretically, anything managed by the executive object manager. In practice, objects that are not exposed to user mode (such as driver objects) are usually not protected. Kernel-mode code is trusted and usually uses interfaces to the object manager that do not perform access checking. Because system resources that are exported to user mode (and hence require security validation) are implemented as objects in kernel mode, the Windows object manager plays a key role in enforcing object security.

We described the object manager in Chapter 3, showing how the object manager maintains the security descriptor for objects. This is illustrated in Figure 6-3 using the Sysinternals Winobj tool, showing the security descriptor for an event object in the user's session. Although files are the resources most commonly associated with object protection, Windows uses the same security model and mechanism for executive objects as it does for files in the file system. As far as access controls are concerned, executive objects differ from files only in the access methods supported by each type of object.

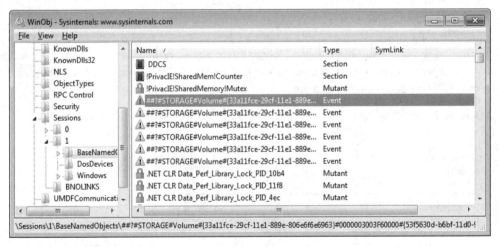

As you will see later, what is shown in Figure 6-3 is actually the object's discretionary access control list, or DACL. We will describe DACLs in detail in a later section.

To control who can manipulate an object, the security system must first be sure of each user's identity. This need to guarantee the user's identity is the reason that Windows requires authenticated logon before accessing any system resources. When a process requests a handle to an object, the object manager and the security system use the caller's security identification and the object's security descriptor to determine whether the caller should be assigned a handle that grants the process access to the object it desires.

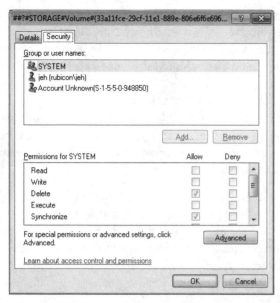

FIGURE 6-3 An executive object and its security descriptor, viewed by Winobj

As discussed later in this chapter, a thread can assume a different security context than that of its process. This mechanism is called impersonation, and when a thread is impersonating, security validation mechanisms use the thread's security context instead of that of the thread's process. When a thread isn't impersonating, security validation falls back on using the security context of the thread's owning process. It's important to keep in mind that all the threads in a process share the same handle table, so when a thread opens an object—even if it's impersonating—all the threads of the process have access to the object.

Sometimes, validating the identity of a user isn't enough for the system to grant access to a resource that should be accessible by the account. Logically, one can think of a clear distinction between a service running under the Alice account and an unknown application that Alice downloaded while browsing the Internet. Windows achieves this kind of intra-user isolation with the Windows integrity mechanism, which implements integrity levels. The Windows integrity mechanism is used by User Account Control (UAC) elevations, Protected Mode Internet Explorer (PMIE), and User Interface Privilege Isolation (UIPI).

Access Checks

The Windows security model requires that a thread specify up front, at the time that it opens an object, what types of actions it wants to perform on the object. The object manager calls the SRM to perform access checks based on a thread's desired access, and if the access is granted, a handle is assigned to the thread's process with which the thread (or other threads in the process) can perform further operations on the object. As explained in Chapter 3, the object manager records the access permissions granted for a handle in the process' handle table.

One event that causes the object manager to perform security access validation is when a process opens an existing object using a name. When an object is opened by name, the object manager performs a lookup of the specified object in the object manager namespace. If the object isn't located in a secondary namespace, such as the configuration manager's registry namespace or a file system driver's file system namespace, the object manager calls the internal function *ObpCreateHandle* once it locates the object. As its name implies, *ObpCreateHandle* creates an entry in the process' handle table that becomes associated with the object. *ObpCreateHandle* first calls *ObpGrantAccess* to see if the thread has permission to access the object; if the thread does, *ObpCreateHandle* calls the executive function *ExCreateHandle* to create the entry in the process handle table. *ObpGrantAccess* calls *ObCheckObjectAccess* to initiate the security access check.

ObpGrantAccess passes to *ObCheckObjectAccess* the security credentials of the thread opening the object, the types of access to the object that the thread is requesting (read, write, delete, and so forth), and a pointer to the object. *ObCheckObjectAccess* first locks the object's security descriptor and the security context of the thread. The object security lock prevents another thread in the system from changing the object's security while the access check is in progress. The lock on the thread's security context prevents another thread (from that process or a different process) from altering the security identity of the thread while security validation is in progress. *ObCheckObjectAccess* then calls the object's security method to obtain the security settings of the object. (See Chapter 3 for a description of object methods.) The call to the security method might invoke a function in a different executive component. However, many executive objects rely on the system's default security management support.

When an executive component defining an object doesn't want to override the SRM's default security policy, it marks the object type as having default security. Whenever the SRM calls an object's security method, it first checks to see whether the object has default security. An object with default security stores its security information in its header, and its security method is *SeDefaultObjectMethod*. An object that doesn't rely on default security must manage its own security information and supply a specific security method. Objects that rely on default security include mutexes, events, and semaphores. A file object is an example of an object that overrides default security. The I/O manager, which defines the file object type, has the file system driver on which a file resides manage (or choose not to implement) the security for its files. Thus, when the system queries the security on a file object that represents a file on an NTFS volume, the I/O manager file object security method retrieves the file's security using the NTFS file system driver. Note, however, that *ObCheckObjectAccess* isn't executed when files are opened, because they reside in secondary namespaces; the system invokes a file object's security method only when a thread explicitly queries or sets the security on a file (with the Windows *SetFileSecurity* or *GetFileSecurity* functions, for example).

After obtaining an object's security information, *ObCheckObjectAccess* invokes the SRM function *SeAccessCheck*. *SeAccessCheck* is one of the functions at the heart of the Windows security model. Among the input parameters *SeAccessCheck* accepts are the object's security information, the security identity of the thread as captured by *ObCheckObjectAccess*, and the access that the thread is requesting. *SeAccessCheck* returns True or False, depending on whether the thread is granted the access it requested to the object.

Another event that causes the object manager to execute access validation is when a process references an object using an existing handle. Such references often occur indirectly, as when a process calls on a Windows API to manipulate an object and passes an object handle. For example, a thread opening a file can request read permission to the file. If the thread has permission to access the object in this way, as dictated by its security context and the security settings of the file, the object manager creates a handle—representing the file—in the handle table of the thread's process. The types of accesses the process is granted through the handle are stored with the handle by the object manager.

Subsequently, the thread could attempt to write to the file using the *WriteFile* Windows function, passing the file's handle as a parameter. The system service *NtWriteFile*, which *WriteFile* calls via Ntdll.dll, uses the object manager function *ObReferenceObjectByHandle* to obtain a pointer to the file object from the handle. *ObReferenceObjectByHandle* accepts the access that the caller wants from the object as a parameter. After finding the handle entry in the process' handle table, *ObReferenceObjectByHandle* compares the access being requested with the access granted at the time the file was opened. In this example, *ObReferenceObjectByHandle* will indicate that the write operation should fail because the caller didn't obtain write access when the file was opened.

The Windows security functions also enable Windows applications to define their own private objects and to call on the services of the SRM (through the AuthZ user-mode APIs, described later) to enforce the Windows security model on those objects. Many kernel-mode functions that the object manager and other executive components use to protect their own objects are exported as Windows user-mode APIs. The user-mode equivalent of *SeAccessCheck* is the AuthZ API *AccessCheck*. Windows applications can therefore leverage the flexibility of the security model and transparently integrate with the authentication and administrative interfaces that are present in Windows.

The essence of the SRM's security model is an equation that takes three inputs: the security identity of a thread, the access that the thread wants to an object, and the security settings of the object. The output is either "yes" or "no" and indicates whether or not the security model grants the thread the access it desires. The following sections describe the inputs in more detail and then document the model's access-validation algorithm.

Security Identifiers

Instead of using names (which might or might not be unique) to identify entities that perform actions in a system, Windows uses security identifiers (SIDs). Users have SIDs, and so do local and domain groups, local computers, domains, domain members, and services. A SID is a variable-length numeric value that consists of a SID structure revision number, a 48-bit identifier authority value, and a variable number of 32-bit subauthority or relative identifier (RID) values. The authority value identifies the agent that issued the SID, and this agent is typically a Windows local system or a domain. Subauthority values identify trustees relative to the issuing authority, and RIDs are simply a way for Windows to create unique SIDs based on a common base SID. Because SIDs are long and Windows takes care to generate truly random values within each SID, it is virtually impossible for Windows to issue the same SID twice on machines or domains anywhere in the world.

When displayed textually, each SID carries an S prefix, and its various components are separated with hyphens:

S-1-5-21-1463437245-1224812800-863842198-1128

In this SID, the revision number is 1, the identifier authority value is 5 (the Windows security authority), and four subauthority values plus one RID (1128) make up the remainder of the SID. This SID is a domain SID, but a local computer on the domain would have a SID with the same revision number, identifier authority value, and number of subauthority values.

When you install Windows, the Windows Setup program issues the computer a machine SID. Windows assigns SIDs to local accounts on the computer. Each local-account SID is based on the source computer's SID and has a RID at the end. RIDs for user accounts and groups start at 1000 and increase in increments of 1 for each new user or group. Similarly, Dcpromo.exe (Domain Controller Promote), the utility used to create a new Windows domain, reuses the computer SID of the computer being promoted to domain controller as the domain SID, and it re-creates a new SID for the computer if it is ever demoted. Windows issues to new domain accounts SIDs that are based on the domain SID and have an appended RID (again starting at 1000 and increasing in increments of 1 for each new user or group). A RID of 1028 indicates that the SID is the twenty-ninth SID the domain issued.

Windows issues SIDs that consist of a computer or domain SID with a predefined RID to many predefined accounts and groups. For example, the RID for the administrator account is 500, and the RID for the guest account is 501. A computer's local administrator account, for example, has the computer SID as its base with the RID of 500 appended to it:

S-1-5-21-13124455-12541255-61235125-500

Windows also defines a number of built-in local and domain SIDs to represent well-known groups. For example, a SID that identifies any and all accounts (except anonymous users) is the Everyone SID: S-1-1-0. Another example of a group that a SID can represent is the network group, which is the group that represents users who have logged on to a machine from the network. The network-group SID is S-1-5-2. Table 6-2, reproduced here from the Windows SDK documentation, shows some basic well-known SIDs, their numeric values, and their use. Unlike users' SIDs, these SIDs are predefined constants, and have the same values on every Windows system and domain in the world. Thus, a file that is accessible by members of the Everyone group on the system where it was created is also accessible to Everyone on any other system or domain to which the hard drive where it resides happens to be moved. Users on those systems must, of course, authenticate to an account on those systems before becoming members of the Everyone group.

 Note See Microsoft Knowledge Base article 243330 for a list of defined SIDs at *http://support.microsoft.com/kb/243330*.

Finally, Winlogon creates a unique logon SID for each interactive logon session. A typical use of a logon SID is in an access control entry (ACE) that allows access for the duration of a client's logon session. For example, a Windows service can use the *LogonUser* function to start a new logon session. The *LogonUser* function returns an access token from which the service can extract the logon SID. The service can then use the SID in an ACE that allows the client's logon session to access the interactive window station and desktop. The SID for a logon session is S-1-5-5-0, and the RID is randomly generated.

TABLE 6-2 A Few Well-Known SIDs

SID	Group	Use
S-1-0-0	Nobody	Used when the SID is unknown.
S-1-1-0	Everyone	A group that includes all users except anonymous users.
S-1-2-0	Local	Users who log on to terminals locally (physically) connected to the system.
S-1-3-0	Creator Owner ID	A security identifier to be replaced by the security identifier of the user who created a new object. This SID is used in inheritable ACEs.
S-1-3-1	Creator Group ID	Identifies a security identifier to be replaced by the primary-group SID of the user who created a new object. Use this SID in inheritable ACEs.
S-1-9-0	Resource Manager	Used by third-party applications performing their own security on internal data (such as Microsoft Exchange).

EXPERIMENT: Using PsGetSid and Process Explorer to View SIDs

You can easily see the SID representation for any account you're using by running the PsGetSid utility from Sysinternals.

PsGetSid's options allow you to translate machine and user account names to their corresponding SIDs and vice versa.

If you run PsGetSid with no options, it prints the SID assigned to the local computer. By using the fact that the Administrator account always has a RID of 500, you can determine the name assigned to the account (in cases where a system administrator has renamed the account for security reasons) simply by passing the machine SID appended with -500 as PsGetSid's command-line argument.

To obtain the SID of a domain account, enter the user name with the domain as a prefix:

```
c:\>psgetsid redmond\daryl
```

You can determine the SID of a domain by specifying the domain's name as the argument to PsGetSid:

```
c:\>psgetsid Redmond
```

Finally, by examining the RID of your own account, you know at least a number of security accounts (equal to the number resulting from subtracting 999 from your RID) have been created in your domain or on your local machine (depending on whether you are using a domain or local machine account). You can determine what accounts have been assigned RIDs by passing a SID with the RID you want to query to PsGetSid. If PsGetSid reports that no mapping between the SID and an account name was possible and the RID is lower than that of your account, you know that the account assigned the RID has been deleted.

For example, to find out the name of the account assigned the twenty-eighth RID, pass the domain SID appended with -1027 to PsGetSid:

```
c:\>psgetsid S-1-5-21-1787744166-3910675280-2727264193-1027
Account for S-1-5-21-1787744166-3910675280-2727264193-1027:
User: redmond\daryl
```

Process Explorer can also show you information on account and group SIDs on your system through its Security tab. This tab shows you information such as who owns this process and which groups the account is a member of. To view this information, simply double-click on any process (for example, Explorer.exe) in the Process list, and then click on the Security tab. You should see something similar to the following:

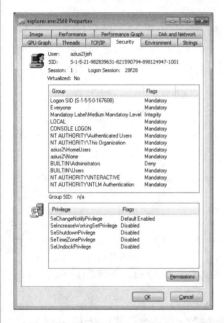

The information displayed in the User field contains the friendly name of the account owning this process, while the SID field contains the actual SID value. The Group list includes information on all the groups that this account is a member of. (Groups are described later in this chapter.)

Integrity Levels

As mentioned earlier, integrity levels can override discretionary access to differentiate a process and objects running as and owned by the same user, offering the ability to isolate code and data within a user account. The mechanism of mandatory integrity control (MIC) allows the SRM to have more detailed information about the nature of the caller by associating it with an integrity level. It also provides information on the trust required to access the object by defining an integrity level for it.

These integrity levels are specified by a SID. Though integrity levels can be arbitrary values, the system uses five primary levels to separate privilege levels, as described in Table 6-3.

TABLE 6-3 Integrity Level SIDs

SID	Name (Level)	Use
S-1-16-0x0	Untrusted (0)	Used by processes started by the Anonymous group. It blocks most write access.
S-1-16-0x1000	Low (1)	Used by Protected Mode Internet Explorer. It blocks write access to most objects (such as files and registry keys) on the system.
S-1-16-0x2000	Medium (2)	Used by normal applications being launched while UAC is enabled.
S-1-16-0x3000	High (3)	Used by administrative applications launched through elevation when UAC is enabled, or normal applications if UAC is disabled and the user is an administrator.
S-1-16-0x4000	System (4)	Used by services and other system-level applications (such as Wininit, Winlogon, Smss, and so forth).

EXPERIMENT: Looking at the Integrity Level of Processes

You can use Process Explorer from Sysinternals to quickly display the integrity level for the processes on your system. The following steps demonstrate this functionality.

1. Launch Internet Explorer in Protected Mode.

2. Open an elevated Command Prompt window.

3. Open Microsoft Paint normally (without elevating it).

4. Now open Process Explorer, right-click on any of the columns in the Process list, and then click Select Columns. You should see a dialog box similar to the one shown here:

5. Select the Integrity Level check box, and click OK to close the dialog box and save the change.

6. Process Explorer will now show you the integrity level of the processes on your system. You should see the Protected Mode Internet Explorer process at Low, Microsoft Paint at Medium, and the elevated command prompt at High. Also note that the services and system processes are running at an even higher integrity level, System.

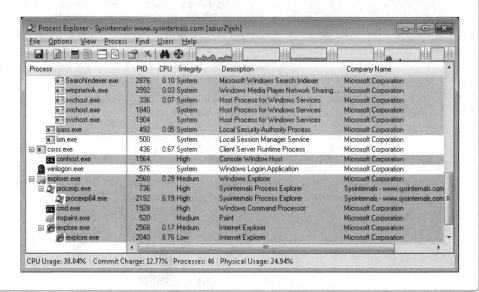

Every process has an integrity level that is represented in the process' token and propagated according to the following rules:

- A process normally inherits the integrity level of its parent (which means an elevated command prompt will spawn other elevated processes).

- If the file object for the executable image to which the child process belongs has an integrity level and the parent process' integrity level is medium or higher, the child process will inherit the lower of the two.

- A parent process can create a child process with an explicit integrity level lower than its own (for example, when launching Protected Mode Internet Explorer from an elevated command prompt). To do this, it uses *DuplicateTokenEx* to duplicate its own access token, it uses *SetTokenInformation* to change the integrity level in the new token to the desired level, and then it calls *CreateProcessAsUser* with that new token.

EXPERIMENT: Understanding Protected Mode Internet Explorer

As mentioned earlier, one of the users of the Windows integrity mechanism is Internet Explorer's Protected Mode, also called Protected Mode Internet Explorer (PMIE). This feature was added in Internet Explorer 7 to take advantage of the Windows integrity levels. This experiment will show you how PMIE utilizes integrity levels to provide a safer Internet experience. To do this, we'll use Process Monitor to trace Internet Explorer's behavior.

1. Make sure that you haven't disabled UAC and PMIE on your systems (they are both on by default), and close any running instances of Internet Explorer.

2. Run Process Monitor, and select Filter, Filter to display the filtering dialog box. Add an include filter for the process name Iexplore.exe, as shown next:

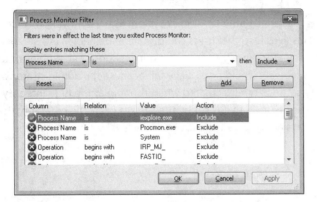

3. Run Process Explorer, and repeat the previous experiment to display the Integrity Level column.

4. Now launch Internet Explorer. You should see a flurry of events appear in the Process Monitor window and a quick succession of events in Process Explorer, showing some processes starting and some exiting.

Once Internet Explorer is running, Process Explorer will show you two new Iexplore.exe processes, the parent Iexplore.exe running at medium integrity level and its child running at low integrity level.

Part of the added protection offered by PMIE is that Iexplore.exe processes that access websites run at low integrity. Because Internet Explorer hosts tabs in multiple processes, if you create additional tabs you might see additional instances of Iexplore.exe. There is one parent Iexplore.exe process that acts as a broker, providing access to parts of the system not accessible by those running at low integrity—for example, to save or open files from other parts of the file system.

Table 6-3 lists the integrity level associated with processes, but what about objects? Objects also have an integrity level stored as part of their security descriptor, in a structure that is called the mandatory label.

To support migrating from previous versions of Windows (whose registry keys and files would not include integrity-level information), as well as to make it simpler for application developers, all objects have an implicit integrity level to avoid having to manually specify one. This implicit integrity level is the medium level, meaning that the mandatory policy (described shortly) on the object will be performed on tokens accessing this object with an integrity level lower than medium.

When a process creates an object without specifying an integrity level, the system checks the integrity level in the token. For tokens with a level of medium or higher, the implicit integrity level of the object remains medium. However, when a token contains an integrity level lower than medium, the object is created with an explicit integrity level that matches the level in the token.

The reason that objects that are created by high or system integrity-level processes have a medium integrity level themselves is so that users can disable and enable UAC: if object integrity levels always inherited their creator's integrity level, the applications of an administrator who disables UAC and subsequently re-enables it would potentially fail because the administrator would not be able to modify any registry settings or files created when running at the high integrity level. Objects can also have an explicit integrity level that is set by the system or by the creator of the object. For example, the following objects are given an explicit integrity level by the kernel when it creates them:

- Processes

- Threads

- Tokens

- Jobs

The reason for assigning an integrity level to these objects is to prevent a process for the same user, but one running at a lower integrity level, from accessing these objects and modifying their content or behavior (for example, DLL injection or code modification).

EXPERIMENT: Looking at the Integrity Level of Objects

You can use the Accesschk tool from Sysinternals to display the integrity level of objects on the system, such as files, processes, and registry keys. Here's an experiment showing the purpose of the LocalLow directory in Windows.

1. Browse to C:\Users\UserName\ in a command prompt.

2. Try running Accesschk on the AppData folder, as follows:

   C:\Users\UserName> accesschk –v appdata

3. Note the differences between Local and LocalLow in your output, similar to the one shown here:

```
C:\Users\UserName\AppData\Local
  Medium Mandatory Level (Default) [No-Write-Up]
  [...]C:\Users\UserName\AppData\LocalLow
  Low Mandatory Level [No-Write-Up]
  [...]
C:\Users\UserName\AppData\Roaming
  Medium Mandatory Level (Default) [No-Write-Up]
  [...]
```

4. Notice that the LocalLow directory has an integrity level that is set to Low, while the Local and Roaming directories have an integrity level of Medium (Default). The default means the system is using an implicit integrity level.

5. You can pass the –e flag to Accesschk so that it displays only explicit integrity levels. If you run the tool on the AppData folder again, you'll notice only the LocalLow information is displayed.

The –o (Object), –k (Registry Key), and –p (Process) flags allow you to specify something other than a file or directory.

Apart from an integrity level, objects also have a mandatory policy, which defines the actual level of protection that's applied based on the integrity-level check. Three types are possible, shown in Table 6-4. The integrity level and the mandatory policy are stored together in the same ACE.

TABLE 6-4 Object Mandatory Policies

Policy	Present on, by Default	Description
No-Write-Up	Implicit on all objects	Used to restrict write access coming from a lower integrity level process to the object.
No-Read-Up	Only on process objects	Used to restrict read access coming from a lower integrity level process to the object. Specific use on process objects protects against information leakage by blocking address space reads from an external process.
No-Execute-Up	Only on binaries implementing COM classes	Used to restrict execute access coming from a lower integrity level process to the object. Specific use on COM classes is to restrict launch-activation permissions on a COM class.

Tokens

The SRM uses an object called a token (or access token) to identify the security context of a process or thread. A security context consists of information that describes the account, groups, and privileges associated with the process or thread. Tokens also include information such as the session ID, the integrity level, and UAC virtualization state. (We'll describe both privileges and UAC's virtualization mechanism later in this chapter.)

During the logon process (described at the end of this chapter), LSASS creates an initial token to represent the user logging on. It then determines whether the user logging on is a member of a powerful group or possesses a powerful privilege. The groups checked for in this step are as follows:

- Built-In Administrators
- Certificate Administrators
- Domain Administrators
- Enterprise Administrators
- Policy Administrators
- Schema Administrators
- Domain Controllers
- Enterprise Read-Only Domain Controllers
- Read-Only Domain Controllers
- Account Operators
- Backup Operators
- Cryptographic Operators
- Network Configuration Operators
- Print Operators
- System Operators
- RAS Servers
- Power Users
- Pre-Windows 2000 Compatible Access

Many of the groups listed are used only on domain-joined systems and don't give users local administrative rights directly. Instead, they allow users to modify domainwide settings.

The privileges checked for are

- SeBackupPrivilege

- SeCreateTokenPrivilege

- SeDebugPrivilege

- SeImpersonatePrivilege

- SeLabelPrivilege

- SeLoadDriverPrivilege

- SeRestorePrivilege

- SeTakeOwnershipPrivilege

- SeTcbPrivilege

These privileges are described in detail in a later section.

If one or more of these groups or privileges are present, LSASS creates a restricted token for the user (also called a filtered admin token), and it creates a logon session for both. The standard user token is attached to the initial process or processes that Winlogon starts (by default, Userinit.exe).

Note If UAC has been disabled, administrators run with a token that includes their administrator group memberships and privileges.

Because child processes by default inherit a copy of the token of their creators, all processes in the user's session run under the same token. You can also generate a token by using the Windows *LogonUser* function. You can then use this token to create a process that runs within the security context of the user logged on through the *LogonUser* function by passing the token to the Windows *CreateProcessAsUser* function. The *CreateProcessWithLogon* function combines these into a single call, which is how the Runas command launches processes under alternative tokens.

Tokens vary in size because different user accounts have different sets of privileges and associated group accounts. However, all tokens contain the same types of information. The most important contents of a token are represented in Figure 6-4.

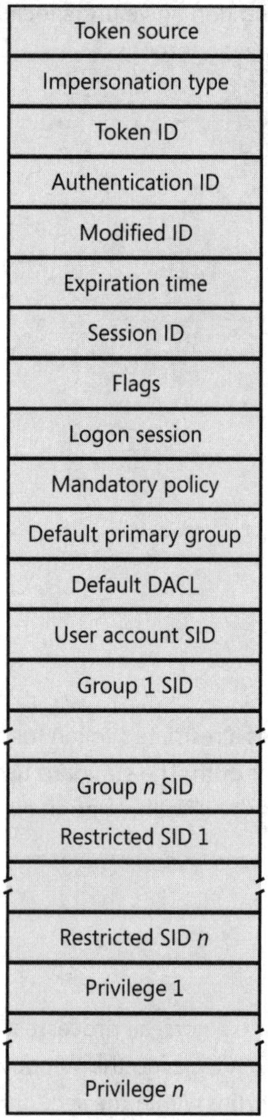

Token source
Impersonation type
Token ID
Authentication ID
Modified ID
Expiration time
Session ID
Flags
Logon session
Mandatory policy
Default primary group
Default DACL
User account SID
Group 1 SID

Group n SID
Restricted SID 1

Restricted SID n
Privilege 1

Privilege n

FIGURE 6-4 Access tokens

The security mechanisms in Windows use two components to determine what objects can be accessed and what secure operations can be performed. One component comprises the token's user account SID and group SID fields. The security reference monitor (SRM) uses SIDs to determine whether a process or thread can obtain requested access to a securable object, such as an NTFS file.

The group SIDs in a token indicate which groups a user's account is a member of. For example, a server application can disable specific groups to restrict a token's credentials when the server application is performing actions requested by a client. Disabling a group produces nearly the same effect as if the group wasn't present in the token. (It results in a deny-only group, described later. Disabled SIDs are used as part of security access checks, described later in the chapter.) Group SIDs can also include a special SID that contains the integrity level of the process or thread. The SRM uses another field in the token, which describes the mandatory integrity policy, to perform the mandatory integrity check described later in the chapter.

The second component in a token that determines what the token's thread or process can do is the privilege array. A token's privilege array is a list of rights associated with the token. An example privilege is the right for the process or thread associated with the token to shut down the computer. Privileges are described in more detail later in this chapter.

A token's default primary group field and default discretionary access control list (DACL) field are security attributes that Windows applies to objects that a process or thread creates when it uses the token. By including security information in tokens, Windows makes it convenient for a process or thread to create objects with standard security attributes, because the process or thread doesn't need to request discrete security information for every object it creates.

Each token's type distinguishes a primary token (a token that identifies the security context of a process) from an impersonation token (a type of token that threads use to temporarily adopt a different security context, usually of another user). Impersonation tokens carry an impersonation level that signifies what type of impersonation is active in the token. (Impersonation is described later in this chapter.)

A token also includes the mandatory policy for the process or thread, which defines how MIC will behave when processing this token. There are two policies:

- TOKEN_MANDATORY_NO_WRITE_UP, which is enabled by default, sets the No-Write-Up policy on this token, specifying that the process or thread will not be able to access objects with a higher integrity level for write access.

- TOKEN_MANDATORY_NEW_PROCESS_MIN, which is also enabled by default, specifies that the SRM should look at the integrity level of the executable image when launching a child process and compute the minimum integrity level of the parent process and the file object's integrity level as the child's integrity level.

Token flags include parameters that determine the behavior of certain UAC and UIPI mechanisms, such as virtualization and user interface access. Those mechanisms will be described later in this chapter.

Each token can also contain attributes that are assigned by the Application Identification service (part of AppLocker) when AppLocker rules have been defined. AppLocker and its use of attributes in the access token are described later in this chapter.

The remaining fields in a token serve informational purposes. The token source field contains a short textual description of the entity that created the token. Programs that want to know where a token originated use the token source to distinguish among sources such as the Windows Session Manager, a network file server, or the remote procedure call (RPC) server. The token identifier is a locally unique identifier (LUID) that the SRM assigns to the token when it creates the token. The Windows executive maintains the executive LUID, a monotonically increasing counter it uses to assign a unique numeric identifier to each token. A LUID is guaranteed to be unique only until the system is shut down.

The token authentication ID is another kind of LUID. A token's creator assigns the token's authentication ID when calling the *LsaLogonUser* function. If the creator doesn't specify a LUID, LSASS obtains the LUID from the executive LUID. LSASS copies the authentication ID for all tokens descended from an initial logon token. A program can obtain a token's authentication ID to see whether the token belongs to the same logon session as other tokens the program has examined.

The executive LUID refreshes the modified ID every time a token's characteristics are modified. An application can test the modified ID to discover changes in a security context since the context's last use.

Tokens contain an expiration time field that can be used by applications performing their own security to reject a token after a specified amount of time. However, Windows itself does not enforce the expiration time of tokens.

Note To guarantee system security, the fields in a token are immutable (because they are located in kernel memory). Except for fields that can be modified through a specific system call designed to modify certain token attributes (assuming the caller has the appropriate access rights to the token object), data such as the privileges and SIDs in a token can never be modified from user mode.

EXPERIMENT: Viewing Access Tokens

The kernel debugger *dt _TOKEN* command displays the format of an internal token object. Although this structure differs from the user-mode token structure returned by Windows API security functions, the fields are similar. For further information on tokens, see the description in the Windows SDK documentation.

The following output is from the kernel debugger's dt nt!_TOKEN command:

```
kd> dt nt!_TOKEN
   +0x000 TokenSource      : _TOKEN_SOURCE
   +0x010 TokenId          : _LUID
   +0x018 AuthenticationId : _LUID
   +0x020 ParentTokenId    : _LUID
   +0x028 ExpirationTime   : _LARGE_INTEGER
   +0x030 TokenLock        : Ptr32 _ERESOURCE
   +0x034 ModifiedId       : _LUID
   +0x040 Privileges       : _SEP_TOKEN_PRIVILEGES
   +0x058 AuditPolicy      : _SEP_AUDIT_POLICY
   +0x074 SessionId        : Uint4B
   +0x078 UserAndGroupCount : Uint4B
   +0x07c RestrictedSidCount : Uint4B
   +0x080 VariableLength   : Uint4B
   +0x084 DynamicCharged   : Uint4B
   +0x088 DynamicAvailable : Uint4B
   +0x08c DefaultOwnerIndex : Uint4B
```

```
+0x090 UserAndGroups      : Ptr32 _SID_AND_ATTRIBUTES
+0x094 RestrictedSids     : Ptr32 _SID_AND_ATTRIBUTES
+0x098 PrimaryGroup       : Ptr32 Void
+0x09c DynamicPart        : Ptr32 Uint4B
+0x0a0 DefaultDacl        : Ptr32 _ACL
+0x0a4 TokenType          : _TOKEN_TYPE
+0x0a8 ImpersonationLevel : _SECURITY_IMPERSONATION_LEVEL
+0x0ac TokenFlags         : Uint4B
+0x0b0 TokenInUse         : UChar
+0x0b4 IntegrityLevelIndex : Uint4B
+0x0b8 MandatoryPolicy    : Uint4B
+0x0bc ProxyData          : Ptr32 _SECURITY_TOKEN_PROXY_DATA
+0x0c0 AuditData          : Ptr32 _SECURITY_TOKEN_AUDIT_DATA
+0x0c4 LogonSession       : Ptr32 _SEP_LOGON_SESSION_REFERENCES
+0x0c8 OriginatingLogonSession : _LUID
+0x0d0 SidHash            : _SID_AND_ATTRIBUTES_HASH
+0x158 RestrictedSidHash  : _SID_AND_ATTRIBUTES_HASH
+0x1e0 VariablePart       : Uint4B
```

You can examine the token for a process with the *!token* command. You'll find the address of the token in the output of the *!process* command, as shown here:

```
lkd> !process d6c 1
Searching for Process with Cid == d6c
PROCESS 85450508  SessionId: 1  Cid: 0d6c    Peb: 7ffda000  ParentCid: 0ecc
    DirBase: cc9525e0  ObjectTable: afd75518  HandleCount:  18.
    Image: cmd.exe
    VadRoot 85328e78 Vads 24 Clone 0 Private 148. Modified 0. Locked 0.
    DeviceMap a0688138
    Token                            afd48470
    ElapsedTime                      01:10:14.379
    UserTime                         00:00:00.000
    KernelTime                       00:00:00.000
    QuotaPoolUsage[PagedPool]        42864
    QuotaPoolUsage[NonPagedPool]     1152
    Working Set Sizes (now,min,max)  (566, 50, 345) (2264KB, 200KB, 1380KB)
    PeakWorkingSetSize               582
    VirtualSize                      22 Mb
    PeakVirtualSize                  25 Mb
    PageFaultCount                   680
    MemoryPriority                   BACKGROUND
    BasePriority                     8
    CommitCharge                     437

lkd> !token afd48470
_TOKEN afd48470
TS Session ID: 0x1
User: S-1-5-21-2778343003-3541292008-524615573-500 (User: ALEX-LAPTOP\Administrator)
Groups:
 00 S-1-5-21-2778343003-3541292008-524615573-513 (Group: ALEX-LAPTOP\None)
    Attributes - Mandatory Default Enabled
 01 S-1-1-0 (Well Known Group: localhost\Everyone)
    Attributes - Mandatory Default Enabled
```

```
02 S-1-5-21-2778343003-3541292008-524615573-1000 (Alias: ALEX-LAPTOP\Debugger Users)
   Attributes - Mandatory Default Enabled
03 S-1-5-32-544 (Alias: BUILTIN\Administrators)
   Attributes - Mandatory Default Enabled Owner
04 S-1-5-32-545 (Alias: BUILTIN\Users)
   Attributes - Mandatory Default Enabled
05 S-1-5-4 (Well Known Group: NT AUTHORITY\INTERACTIVE)
   Attributes - Mandatory Default Enabled
06 S-1-5-11 (Well Known Group: NT AUTHORITY\Authenticated Users)
   Attributes - Mandatory Default Enabled
07 S-1-5-15 (Well Known Group: NT AUTHORITY\This Organization)
   Attributes - Mandatory Default Enabled
08 S-1-5-5-0-89263 (no name mapped)
   Attributes - Mandatory Default Enabled LogonId
09 S-1-2-0 (Well Known Group: localhost\LOCAL)
   Attributes - Mandatory Default Enabled
10 S-1-5-64-10 (Well Known Group: NT AUTHORITY\NTLM Authentication)
   Attributes - Mandatory Default Enabled
11 S-1-16-12288 Unrecognized SID
   Attributes - GroupIntegrity GroupIntegrityEnabled
Primary Group: S-1-5-21-2778343003-3541292008-524615573-513 (Group: ALEX-LAPTOP\None)
Privs:
05 0x000000005 SeIncreaseQuotaPrivilege           Attributes -
08 0x000000008 SeSecurityPrivilege                Attributes -
09 0x000000009 SeTakeOwnershipPrivilege           Attributes -
10 0x00000000a SeLoadDriverPrivilege              Attributes -
11 0x00000000b SeSystemProfilePrivilege           Attributes -
12 0x00000000c SeSystemtimePrivilege              Attributes -
13 0x00000000d SeProfileSingleProcessPrivilege    Attributes -
14 0x00000000e SeIncreaseBasePriorityPrivilege    Attributes -
15 0x00000000f SeCreatePagefilePrivilege          Attributes -
17 0x000000011 SeBackupPrivilege                  Attributes -
18 0x000000012 SeRestorePrivilege                 Attributes -
19 0x000000013 SeShutdownPrivilege                Attributes -
20 0x000000014 SeDebugPrivilege                   Attributes -
22 0x000000016 SeSystemEnvironmentPrivilege       Attributes -
23 0x000000017 SeChangeNotifyPrivilege            Attributes - Enabled Default
24 0x000000018 SeRemoteShutdownPrivilege          Attributes -
25 0x000000019 SeUndockPrivilege                  Attributes -
28 0x00000001c SeManageVolumePrivilege            Attributes -
29 0x00000001d SeImpersonatePrivilege             Attributes - Enabled Default
30 0x00000001e SeCreateGlobalPrivilege            Attributes - Enabled Default
33 0x000000021 SeIncreaseWorkingSetPrivilege      Attributes -
34 0x000000022 SeTimeZonePrivilege                Attributes -
35 0x000000023 SeCreateSymbolicLinkPrivilege      Attributes -
Authentication ID:          (0,be1a2)
Impersonation Level:        Identification
TokenType:                  Primary
Source: User32              TokenFlags: 0x0 ( Token in use )
Token ID: 711076            ParentToken ID: 0
Modified ID:                (0, 711081)
RestrictedSidCount: 0       RestrictedSids: 00000000
OriginatingLogonSession: 3e7
```

You can indirectly view token contents with Process Explorer's Security tab in its process Properties dialog box. The dialog box shows the groups and privileges included in the token of the process you examine.

EXPERIMENT: Launching a Program at Low Integrity Level

When you elevate a program, either by using the Run As Administrator option or because the program is requesting it, the program is explicitly launched at high integrity level; however, it is also possible to launch a program (other than PMIE) at low integrity level by using Psexec from Sysinternals:

1. Launch Notepad at low integrity level by using the following command:

   ```
   c:\psexec –1 notepad.exe
   ```

2. Try opening a file (such as one of the .XML files) in the %SystemRoot%\System32 directory. Notice that you can browse the directory and open any file contained within it.

3. Now use Notepad's File | New command, enter some text in the window, and try saving it in the %SystemRoot%\System32 directory. Notepad should present a message box indicating a lack of permissions and recommend saving the file in the Documents folder.

4. Accept Notepad's suggestion. You will get the same message box again, and repeatedly for each attempt.

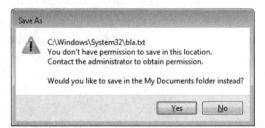

5. Now try saving the file in the LocalLow directory of your user profile, shown in an experiment earlier in the chapter.

In the previous experiment, saving a file in the LocalLow directory worked because Notepad was running with low integrity level, and only the LocalLow directory also had low integrity level. All the other locations where you tried to write the file had an implicit medium integrity level. (You can verify this with Accesschk.) However, reading from the %SystemRoot%\System32 directory, as well as opening files within it, did work, even though the directory and its file also have an implicit medium integrity level.

Impersonation

Impersonation is a powerful feature Windows uses frequently in its security model. Windows also uses impersonation in its client/server programming model. For example, a server application can provide access to resources such as files, printers, or databases. Clients wanting to access a resource send a request to the server. When the server receives the request, it must ensure that the client has permission to perform the desired operations on the resource. For example, if a user on a remote machine tries to delete a file on an NTFS share, the server exporting the share must determine whether the user is allowed to delete the file. The obvious way to determine whether a user has permission is for the server to query the user's account and group SIDs and scan the security attributes on the file. This approach is tedious to program, prone to errors, and wouldn't permit new security features to be supported transparently. Thus, Windows provides impersonation services to simplify the server's job.

Impersonation lets a server notify the SRM that the server is temporarily adopting the security profile of a client making a resource request. The server can then access resources on behalf of the client, and the SRM carries out the access validations, but it does so based on the impersonated client security context. Usually, a server has access to more resources than a client does and loses some of its security credentials during impersonation. However, the reverse can be true: the server can gain security credentials during impersonation.

A server impersonates a client only within the thread that makes the impersonation request. Thread-control data structures contain an optional entry for an impersonation token. However, a thread's primary token, which represents the thread's real security credentials, is always accessible in the process' control structure.

Windows makes impersonation available through several mechanisms. For example, if a server communicates with a client through a named pipe, the server can use the *ImpersonateNamedPipeClient* Windows API function to tell the SRM that it wants to impersonate the user on the other end of the pipe. If the server is communicating with the client through Dynamic Data Exchange (DDE) or RPC, it can make similar impersonation requests using *DdeImpersonateClient* and *RpcImpersonateClient*. A thread can create an impersonation token that's simply a copy of its process token with the *ImpersonateSelf* function. The thread can then alter its impersonation token, perhaps to disable SIDs or privileges. A Security Support Provider Interface (SSPI) package can impersonate its clients with *ImpersonateSecurityContext*. SSPIs implement a network authentication protocol such as LAN Manager version 2 or Kerberos. Other interfaces such as COM expose impersonation through APIs of their own, such as *CoImpersonateClient*.

After the server thread finishes its task, it reverts to its primary security context. These forms of impersonation are convenient for carrying out specific actions at the request of a client and for ensuring that object accesses are audited correctly. (For example, the audit that is generated gives the identity of the impersonated client rather than that of the server process.) The disadvantage to these forms of impersonation is that they can't execute an entire program in the context of a client. In addition, an impersonation token can't access files or printers on network shares unless it is a delegation-level impersonation (described shortly) and has sufficient credentials to authenticate to the remote machine, or the file or printer share supports null sessions. (A null session is one that results from an anonymous logon.)

If an entire application must execute in a client's security context or must access network resources without using impersonation, the client must be logged on to the system. The *LogonUser* Windows API function enables this action. *LogonUser* takes an account name, a password, a domain or computer name, a logon type (such as interactive, batch, or service), and a logon provider as input, and it returns a primary token. A server thread can adopt the token as an impersonation token, or the server can start a program that has the client's credentials as its primary token. From a security standpoint, a process created using the token returned from an interactive logon via *LogonUser*, such as with the *CreateProcessAsUser* API, looks like a program a user starts by logging on to the machine interactively. The disadvantage to this approach is that a server must obtain the user's account name and password. If the server transmits this information across the network, the server must encrypt it securely so that a malicious user snooping network traffic can't capture it.

To prevent the misuse of impersonation, Windows doesn't let servers perform impersonation without a client's consent. A client process can limit the level of impersonation that a server process can perform by specifying a security quality of service (SQOS) when connecting to the server. For instance, when opening a named pipe, a process can specify SECURITY_ANONYMOUS, SECURITY_IDENTIFICATION, SECURITY_IMPERSONATION, or SECURITY_DELEGATION as flags for the Windows *CreateFile* function. Each level lets a server perform different types of operations with respect to the client's security context:

- SecurityAnonymous is the most restrictive level of impersonation—the server can't impersonate or identify the client.

- SecurityIdentification lets the server obtain the identity (the SIDs) of the client and the client's privileges, but the server can't impersonate the client.

- SecurityImpersonation lets the server identify and impersonate the client on the local system.

- SecurityDelegation is the most permissive level of impersonation. It lets the server impersonate the client on local and remote systems.

Other interfaces such as RPC use different constants with similar meanings (for example, RPC_C_IMP_LEVEL_IMPERSONATE).

If the client doesn't set an impersonation level, Windows chooses the SecurityImpersonation level by default. The *CreateFile* function also accepts SECURITY_EFFECTIVE_ONLY and SECURITY_CONTEXT_TRACKING as modifiers for the impersonation setting:

- SECURITY_EFFECTIVE_ONLY prevents a server from enabling or disabling a client's privileges or groups while the server is impersonating.

- SECURITY_CONTEXT_TRACKING specifies that any changes a client makes to its security context are reflected in a server that is impersonating it. If this option isn't specified, the server adopts the context of the client at the time of the impersonation and doesn't receive any changes. This option is honored only when the client and server processes are on the same system.

To prevent spoofing scenarios in which a low integrity process could create a user interface that captured user credentials and then used *LogonUser* to obtain that user's token, a special integrity policy applies to impersonation scenarios: a thread cannot impersonate a token of higher integrity than its own. For example, a low-integrity application cannot spoof a dialog box that queries administrative credentials and then attempt to launch a process at a higher privilege level. The integrity-mechanism policy for impersonation access tokens is that the integrity level of the access token that is returned by *LsaLogonUser* must be no higher than the integrity level of the calling process.

Restricted Tokens

A restricted token is created from a primary or impersonation token using the *CreateRestrictedToken* function. The restricted token is a copy of the token it's derived from, with the following possible modifications:

- Privileges can be removed from the token's privilege array.

- SIDs in the token can be marked as deny-only. These SIDs remove access to any resources for which the SID's access is denied by using a matching access-denied ACE that would otherwise be overridden by an ACE granting access to a group containing the SID earlier in the security descriptor.

- SIDs in the token can be marked as restricted. These SIDs are subject to a second pass of the access-check algorithm, which will parse only the restricted SIDs in the token. The results of both the first pass and the second pass must grant access to the resource or no access is granted to the object.

Restricted tokens are useful when an application wants to impersonate a client at a reduced security level, primarily for safety reasons when running untrusted code. For example, the restricted token can have the shutdown-system privilege removed from it to prevent code executed in the restricted token's security context from rebooting the system.

Filtered Admin Token

As you saw earlier, restricted tokens are also used by UAC to create the filtered admin token that all user applications will inherit. A filtered admin token has the following characteristics:

- The integrity level is set to medium.

- The administrator and administrator-like SIDs mentioned previously are marked as deny-only to prevent a security hole if the group was removed altogether. For example, if a file had an access control list (ACL) that denied the Administrators group all access but granted some access to another group the user belongs to, the user would be granted access if the Administrators group was absent from the token, which would give the standard user version of the user's identity more access than the user's administrator identity.

- All privileges are stripped except Change Notify, Shutdown, Undock, Increase Working Set, and Time Zone.

EXPERIMENT: Looking at Filtered Admin Tokens

You can make Explorer launch a process with either the standard user token or the administrator token by following these steps on a Windows machine with UAC enabled:

1. Log on to an account that's a member of the Administrators group.

2. Click Start, Programs, Accessories, Command Prompt, right-click on the shortcut, and then select Run As Administrator. You will see a command prompt with the word Administrator in the title bar.

3. Now repeat the process, but simply click on the shortcut—this will launch a second command prompt without administrative privileges.

4. Run Process Explorer, and view the Security tab in the Properties dialog boxes for the two command prompt processes you launched. Note that the standard user token contains a deny-only SID and a Medium Mandatory Label, and that it has only a couple of privileges. The properties on the right in the following screen shot are from a command prompt running with an administrator token, and the properties on the left are from one running with the filtered administrative token:

Virtual Service Accounts

Windows provides a specialized type of account known as a virtual service account (or simply virtual account) to improve the security isolation and access control of Windows services with minimal administrative effort. (See Chapter 4 for more information on Windows services.) Without this mechanism, Windows services must run either under one of the accounts defined by Windows for its built-in services (such as Local Service or Network Service) or under a regular domain account. The accounts such as Local Service are shared by many existing services and so offer limited granularity for privilege and access control; furthermore, they cannot be managed across the domain. Domain accounts require periodic password changes for security, and the availability of services during a password change cycle might be affected. Furthermore, for best isolation, each service should run under its own account, but with ordinary accounts this multiplies the management effort.

With virtual service accounts, each service runs under its own account with its own security ID. The name of the account is always "NT SERVICE\" followed by the internal name of the service. Virtual service accounts can appear in access control lists and can be associated with privileges via Group Policy like any other account name. They cannot, however, be created or deleted through the usual account management tools, nor assigned to groups.

Windows automatically sets and periodically changes the password of the virtual service account. Similar to the "Local System and other service accounts" account, there is a password, but the password is unknown to the system administrators

EXPERIMENT: Using Virtual Service Accounts

You can create a service that runs under a virtual service account by using the Sc (service control) tool by following these steps:

1. In an Administrator command prompt, use the create command of the command-line tool Sc (service control) to create a service and a virtual account in which it will run. This example uses the "srvany" service from an earlier Windows Resource Kit:

   ```
   C:\Windows\system32>sc create srvany obj= "NT SERVICE\srvany"  binPath= "d:\a\
   test\srvany.exe"
   [SC] CreateService SUCCESS
   ```

2. The previous command created the service (in the registry and also in the service controller manager's internal list) and also created the virtual service account. Now Run the Services MMC snap-in (services.msc), select the new service, and look at the Log On tab in the Properties dialog.

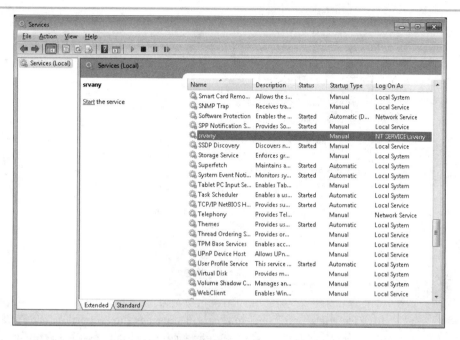

3. You can also use the service properties dialog to create a virtual service account for an existing service. To do so, change the account name to "NT SERVICE\servicename and clear both password fields. Note, however, that existing services might not run correctly under a virtual service account, because that account might not have access to files or other resources needed by the service.

4. If you run Process Explorer and view the Security tab in the Properties dialog boxes for a service that uses a virtual account, you can observe the virtual account name and its security ID (SID).

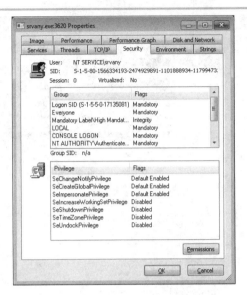

5. The virtual service account can appear in an access control entry for any object (such as a file) the service needs to access. If you open the Properties dialog's Security tab for a file and create an ACL that references the virtual service account, you will find that the account name you typed (for example, NT SERVICE\srvany) is changed to simply the service name (srvany) by the Check Names function, and it appears in the access control list in this shortened form.

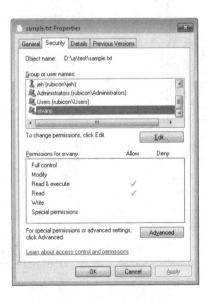

6. The virtual service account can be granted permissions (or user rights) via Group Policy. In this example, the virtual account for the srvany service has been granted the right to create a pagefile.

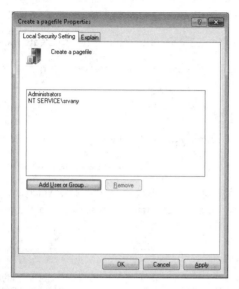

7. You won't see the virtual service account in user administration tools like lusrmgr.msc because it is not stored in the SAM registry hive. However, if you examine the registry within the context of the built-in System account (as described previously), you will see evidence of the account in the HKLM\Security\Policy\Secrets key:

```
C:\>psexec -s -i -d c:\windows\regedit.exe
```

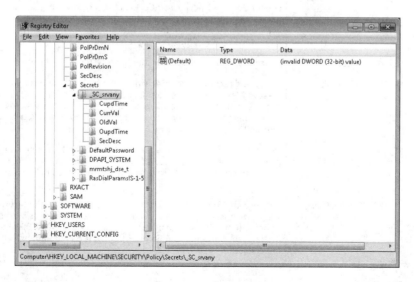

Security Descriptors and Access Control

Tokens, which identify a user's credentials, are only part of the object security equation. Another part of the equation is the security information associated with an object, which specifies who can perform what actions on the object. The data structure for this information is called a security descriptor. A security descriptor consists of the following attributes:

- **Revision number**   The version of the SRM security model used to create the descriptor.

- **Flags**   Optional modifiers that define the behavior or characteristics of the descriptor. These flags are listed in Table 6-5.

- **Owner SID**   The owner's security ID.

- **Group SID**   The security ID of the primary group for the object (used only by POSIX).

- **Discretionary access control list (DACL)**   Specifies who has what access to the object.

- **System access control list (SACL)**   Specifies which operations by which users should be logged in the security audit log and the explicit integrity level of an object.

TABLE 6-5 Security Descriptor Flags

Flag	Meaning
SE_OWNER_DEFAULTED	Indicates a security descriptor with a default owner security identifier (SID). Use this bit to find all the objects that have default owner permissions set.
SE_GROUP_DEFAULTED	Indicates a security descriptor with a default group SID. Use this bit to find all the objects that have default group permissions set.
SE_DACL_PRESENT	Indicates a security descriptor that has a DACL. If this flag is not set, or if this flag is set and the DACL is NULL, the security descriptor allows full access to everyone.
SE_DACL_DEFAULTED	Indicates a security descriptor with a default DACL. For example, if an object creator does not specify a DACL, the object receives the default DACL from the access token of the creator. This flag can affect how the system treats the DACL, with respect to access control entry (ACE) inheritance. The system ignores this flag if the SE_DACL_PRESENT flag is not set.
SE_SACL_PRESENT	Indicates a security descriptor that has a system access control list (SACL).
SE_SACL_DEFAULTED	Indicates a security descriptor with a default SACL. For example, if an object creator does not specify an SACL, the object receives the default SACL from the access token of the creator. This flag can affect how the system treats the SACL with respect to ACE inheritance. The system ignores this flag if the SE_SACL_PRESENT flag is not set.
SE_DACL_UNTRUSTED	Indicates that the ACL pointed to by the DACL of the security descriptor was provided by an untrusted source. If this flag is set and a compound ACE is encountered, the system will substitute known valid SIDs for the server SIDs in the ACEs.
SE_SERVER_SECURITY	Requests that the provider for the object protected by the security descriptor should be a server ACL based on the input ACL, regardless of its source (explicit or defaulting). This is done by replacing all the GRANT ACEs with compound ACEs granting the current server access. This flag is meaningful only if the subject is impersonating.

Flag	Meaning
SE_DACL_AUTO_INHERIT_ REQ	Requests that the provider for the object protected by the security descriptor automatically propagate the DACL to existing child objects. If the provider supports automatic inheritance, the DACL is propagated to any existing child objects, and the SE_DACL_AUTO_INHERITED bit in the security descriptor of the parent and child objects is set.
SE_SACL_AUTO_INHERIT_ REQ	Requests that the provider for the object protected by the security descriptor automatically propagate the SACL to existing child objects. If the provider supports automatic inheritance, the SACL is propagated to any existing child objects, and the SE_SACL_AUTO_INHERITED bit in the security descriptors of the parent object and child objects is set.
SE_DACL_AUTO_ INHERITED	Indicates a security descriptor in which the DACL is set up to support automatic propagation of inheritable ACEs to existing child objects. The system sets this bit when it performs the automatic inheritance algorithm for the object and its existing child objects.
SE_SACL_AUTO_ INHERITED	Indicates a security descriptor in which the SACL is set up to support automatic propagation of inheritable ACEs to existing child objects. The system sets this bit when it performs the automatic inheritance algorithm for the object and its existing child objects.
SE_DACL_PROTECTED	Prevents the DACL of a security descriptor from being modified by inheritable ACEs.
SE_SACL_PROTECTED	Prevents the SACL of a security descriptor from being modified by inheritable ACEs.
SE_RM_CONTROL_VALID	Indicates that the resource control manager bits in the security descriptor are valid. The resource control manager bits are 8 bits in the security descriptor structure that contains information specific to the resource manager accessing the structure.
SE_SELF_RELATIVE	Indicates a security descriptor in self-relative format, with all the security information in a contiguous block of memory. If this flag is not set, the security descriptor is in absolute format.

An access control list (ACL) is made up of a header and zero or more access control entry (ACE) structures. There are two types of ACLs: DACLs and SACLs. In a DACL, each ACE contains a SID and an access mask (and a set of flags, explained shortly), which typically specifies the access rights (Read, Write, Delete, and so forth) that are granted or denied to the holder of the SID. There are nine types of ACEs that can appear in a DACL: access allowed, access denied, allowed object, denied object, allowed callback, denied callback, allowed object callback, denied-object callback, and conditional claims. As you would expect, the access-allowed ACE grants access to a user, and the access-denied ACE denies the access rights specified in the access mask. The callback ACEs are used by applications that make use of the AuthZ API (described later) to register a callback that AuthZ will call when it performs an access check involving this ACE.

The difference between allowed object and access allowed, and between denied object and access denied, is that the object types are used only within Active Directory. ACEs of these types have a GUID (globally unique identifier) field that indicates that the ACE applies only to particular objects or subobjects (those that have GUID identifiers). In addition, another optional GUID indicates what type of child object will inherit the ACE when a child is created within an Active Directory container that has the ACE applied to it. (A GUID is a 128-bit identifier guaranteed to be universally unique.) The conditional claims ACE is stored in a *-callback type ACE structure and is described in the section on the AuthZ APIs.

The accumulation of access rights granted by individual ACEs forms the set of access rights granted by an ACL. If no DACL is present (a null DACL) in a security descriptor, everyone has full access to the object. If the DACL is empty (that is, it has zero ACEs), no user has access to the object.

The ACEs used in DACLs also have a set of flags that control and specify characteristics of the ACE related to inheritance. Some object namespaces have containers and objects. A container can hold other container objects and leaf objects, which are its child objects. Examples of containers are directories in the file system namespace and keys in the registry namespace. Certain flags in an ACE control how the ACE propagates to child objects of the container associated with the ACE. Table 6-6, reproduced in part from the Windows SDK, lists the inheritance rules for ACE flags.

TABLE 6-6 Inheritance Rules for ACE Flags

Flag	Inheritance Rule
CONTAINER_INHERIT_ACE	Child objects that are containers, such as directories, inherit the ACE as an effective ACE. The inherited ACE is inheritable unless the NO_PROPAGATE_INHERIT_ACE bit flag is also set.
INHERIT_ONLY_ACE	This flag indicates an inherit-only ACE that doesn't control access to the object it's attached to. If this flag is not set, the ACE controls access to the object to which it is attached.
INHERITED_ACE	This flag indicates that the ACE was inherited. The system sets this bit when it propagates an inheritable ACE to a child object.
NO_PROPAGATE_INHERIT_ACE	If the ACE is inherited by a child object, the system clears the OBJECT_INHERIT_ACE and CONTAINER_INHERIT_ACE flags in the inherited ACE. This action prevents the ACE from being inherited by subsequent generations of objects.
OBJECT_INHERIT_ACE	Noncontainer child objects inherit the ACE as an effective ACE. For child objects that are containers, the ACE is inherited as an inherit-only ACE unless the NO_PROPAGATE_INHERIT_ACE bit flag is also set.

A SACL contains two types of ACEs, system audit ACEs and system audit-object ACEs. These ACEs specify which operations performed on the object by specific users or groups should be audited. Audit information is stored in the system Audit Log. Both successful and unsuccessful attempts can be audited. Like their DACL object-specific ACE cousins, system audit-object ACEs specify a GUID indicating the types of objects or subobjects that the ACE applies to and an optional GUID that controls propagation of the ACE to particular child object types. If a SACL is null, no auditing takes place on the object. (Security auditing is described later in this chapter.) The inheritance flags that apply to DACL ACEs also apply to system audit and system audit-object ACEs.

Figure 6-5 is a simplified picture of a file object and its DACL.

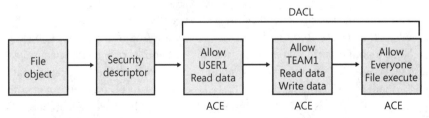

FIGURE 6-5 Discretionary access control list (DACL)

As shown in Figure 6-5, the first ACE allows USER1 to query the file. The second ACE allows members of the group TEAM1 to have read and write access to the file, and the third ACE grants all other users (Everyone) execute access.

EXPERIMENT: Viewing a Security Descriptor

Most executive subsystems rely on the object manager's default security functionality to manage security descriptors for their objects. The object manager's default security functions use the security descriptor pointer to store security descriptors for such objects. For example, the process manager uses default security, so the object manager stores process and thread security descriptors in the object headers of process and thread objects, respectively. The security descriptor pointer of events, mutexes, and semaphores also store their security descriptors. You can use live kernel debugging to view the security descriptors of these objects once you locate their object header, as outlined in the following steps. (Note that both Process Explorer and AccessChk can also show security descriptors for processes.)

1. Start the kernel debugger.

2. Type **!process 0 0 explorer.exe** to obtain process information about Explorer:

```
lkd> !process 0 0 explorer.exe
PROCESS 85a3e030  SessionId: 1  Cid: 0aa4    Peb: 7ffd4000  ParentCid: 0a84
    DirBase: 0f419000  ObjectTable: 952cdd18  HandleCount: 1046.
    Image: explorer.exe
```

3. Type **!object** with the address following the word PROCESS in the output of the previous command as the argument to show the object data structure:

```
lkd> !object 85a3e030
Object: 85a3e030  Type: (842339e0) Process
    ObjectHeader: 85a3e018 (new version)
    HandleCount: 8  PointerCount: 497
```

4. Type **dt _OBJECT_HEADER** and the address of the object header field from the previous command's output to show the object header data structure, including the security descriptor pointer value:

```
lkd> dt _OBJECT_HEADER 85a3e018
nt!_OBJECT_HEADER
    +0x000 PointerCount     : 0n497
    +0x004 HandleCount      : 0n8
    +0x004 NextToFree       : 0x00000008 Void
    +0x008 Lock             : _EX_PUSH_LOCK
    +0x00c TypeIndex        : 0x7 ''
    +0x00d TraceFlags       : 0 ''
    +0x00e InfoMask         : 0x8 ''
    +0x00f Flags            : 0 ''
    +0x010 ObjectCreateInfo : 0x8577e940 _OBJECT_CREATE_INFORMATION
    +0x010 QuotaBlockCharged : 0x8577e940 Void
    +0x014 SecurityDescriptor : 0x97ed0b94 Void
    +0x018 Body             : _QUAD
```

5. Finally, use the debugger's **!sd** command to dump the security descriptor. The security descriptor pointer in the object header uses some of the low-order bits as flags, and these must be zeroed before following the pointer. On 32-bit systems there are three flag bits, so use *& –8* with the security descriptor address displayed in the object header structure, as follows. On 64-bit systems there are four flag bits, so you use *& –10* instead.

```
lkd> !sd 0x97ed0b94 & -8
->Revision: 0x1
->Sbz1    : 0x0
->Control : 0x8814
            SE_DACL_PRESENT
            SE_SACL_PRESENT
            SE_SACL_AUTO_INHERITED
            SE_SELF_RELATIVE
->Owner   : S-1-5-21-1488595123-1430011218-1163345924-1000
->Group   : S-1-5-21-1488595123-1430011218-1163345924-513
->Dacl    :
->Dacl    : ->AclRevision: 0x2
->Dacl    : ->Sbz1       : 0x0
->Dacl    : ->AclSize    : 0x5c
->Dacl    : ->AceCount   : 0x3
->Dacl    : ->Sbz2       : 0x0
->Dacl    : ->Ace[0]: ->AceType: ACCESS_ALLOWED_ACE_TYPE
->Dacl    : ->Ace[0]: ->AceFlags: 0x0
->Dacl    : ->Ace[0]: ->AceSize: 0x24
->Dacl    : ->Ace[0]: ->Mask : 0x001fffff
->Dacl    : ->Ace[0]: ->SID: S-1-5-21-1488595123-1430011218-1163345924-1000

->Dacl    : ->Ace[1]: ->AceType: ACCESS_ALLOWED_ACE_TYPE
->Dacl    : ->Ace[1]: ->AceFlags: 0x0
->Dacl    : ->Ace[1]: ->AceSize: 0x14
->Dacl    : ->Ace[1]: ->Mask : 0x001fffff
->Dacl    : ->Ace[1]: ->SID: S-1-5-18

->Dacl    : ->Ace[2]: ->AceType: ACCESS_ALLOWED_ACE_TYPE
->Dacl    : ->Ace[2]: ->AceFlags: 0x0
->Dacl    : ->Ace[2]: ->AceSize: 0x1c
->Dacl    : ->Ace[2]: ->Mask : 0x00121411
->Dacl    : ->Ace[2]: ->SID: S-1-5-5-0-178173

->Sacl    :
->Sacl    : ->AclRevision: 0x2
->Sacl    : ->Sbz1       : 0x0
->Sacl    : ->AclSize    : 0x1c
->Sacl    : ->AceCount   : 0x1
->Sacl    : ->Sbz2       : 0x0
->Sacl    : ->Ace[0]: ->AceType: SYSTEM_MANDATORY_LABEL_ACE_TYPE
->Sacl    : ->Ace[0]: ->AceFlags: 0x0
->Sacl    : ->Ace[0]: ->AceSize: 0x14
->Sacl    : ->Ace[0]: ->Mask : 0x00000003
->Sacl    : ->Ace[0]: ->SID: S-1-16-8192
```

The security descriptor contains three access-allowed ACEs: one for the current user (S-1-5-21-1488595123-1430011218-1163345924-1000), one for the System account (S-1-5-18), and the last for the Logon SID (S-1-5-5-0-178173). The system access control list has one entry (S-1-16-8192) labeling the process as medium integrity level.

ACL Assignment

To determine which DACL to assign to a new object, the security system uses the first applicable rule of the following four assignment rules:

1. If a caller explicitly provides a security descriptor when creating the object, the security system applies it to the object. If the object has a name and resides in a container object (for example, a named event object in the \BaseNamedObjects object manager namespace directory), the system merges any inheritable ACEs (ACEs that might propagate from the object's container) into the DACL unless the security descriptor has the SE_DACL_PROTECTED flag set, which prevents inheritance.

2. If a caller doesn't supply a security descriptor and the object has a name, the security system looks at the security descriptor in the container in which the new object name is stored. Some of the object directory's ACEs might be marked as inheritable, meaning that they should be applied to new objects created in the object directory. If any of these inheritable ACEs are present, the security system forms them into an ACL, which it attaches to the new object. (Separate flags indicate ACEs that should be inherited only by container objects rather than by objects that aren't containers.)

3. If no security descriptor is specified and the object doesn't inherit any ACEs, the security system retrieves the default DACL from the caller's access token and applies it to the new object. Several subsystems on Windows have hard-coded DACLs that they assign on object creation (for example, services, LSA, and SAM objects).

4. If there is no specified descriptor, no inherited ACEs, and no default DACL, the system creates the object with no DACL, which allows everyone (all users and groups) full access to the object. This rule is the same as the third rule, in which a token contains a null default DACL.

The rules the system uses when assigning a SACL to a new object are similar to those used for DACL assignment, with some exceptions. The first is that inherited system audit ACEs don't propagate to objects with security descriptors marked with the SE_SACL_PROTECTED flag (similar to the SE_DACL_PROTECTED flag, which protects DACLs). Second, if there are no specified security audit ACEs and there is no inherited SACL, no SACL is applied to the object. This behavior is different from that used to apply default DACLs because tokens don't have a default SACL.

When a new security descriptor containing inheritable ACEs is applied to a container, the system automatically propagates the inheritable ACEs to the security descriptors of child objects. (Note that a security descriptor's DACL doesn't accept inherited DACL ACEs if its SE_DACL_PROTECTED flag is enabled, and its SACL doesn't inherit SACL ACEs if the descriptor has the SE_SACL_PROTECTED flag set.) The order in which inheritable ACEs are merged with an existing child object's security descriptor is such that any ACEs that were explicitly applied to the ACL are kept ahead of ACEs that the object inherits. The system uses the following rules for propagating inheritable ACEs:

- If a child object with no DACL inherits an ACE, the result is a child object with a DACL containing only the inherited ACE.

- If a child object with an empty DACL inherits an ACE, the result is a child object with a DACL containing only the inherited ACE.

- For objects in Active Directory only, if an inheritable ACE is removed from a parent object, automatic inheritance removes any copies of the ACE inherited by child objects.

- For objects in Active Directory only, if automatic inheritance results in the removal of all ACEs from a child object's DACL, the child object has an empty DACL rather than no DACL.

As you'll soon discover, the order of ACEs in an ACL is an important aspect of the Windows security model.

Note Inheritance is generally not directly supported by the object stores, such as file systems, the registry, or Active Directory. Windows APIs that support inheritance, including *SetEntriesInAcl*, do so by invoking appropriate functions within the security inheritance support DLL (%SystemRoot%\System32\Ntmarta.dll) that know how to traverse those object stores.

Determining Access

Two methods are used for determining access to an object:

- The mandatory integrity check, which determines whether the integrity level of the caller is high enough to access the resource, based on the resource's own integrity level and its mandatory policy.

- The discretionary access check, which determines the access that a specific user account has to an object.

When a process tries to open an object, the integrity check takes place before the standard Windows DACL check in the kernel's *SeAccessCheck* function because it is faster to execute and can quickly eliminate the need to perform the full discretionary access check. Given the default integrity policies in its access token (TOKEN_MANDATORY_NO_WRITE_UP and TOKEN_MANDATORY_NEW_PROCESS_MIN, described previously), a process can open an object for write access if its integrity level is equal to or higher than the object's integrity level and the DACL also grants the process the accesses it desires. For example, a low-integrity-level process cannot open a medium-integrity-level process for write access, even if the DACL grants the process write access.

With the default integrity policies, processes can open any object—with the exception of process, thread, and token objects—for read access as long as the object's DACL grants them read access. That means a process running at low integrity level can open any files accessible to the user account in which it's running. Protected Mode Internet Explorer uses integrity levels to help prevent malware that infects it from modifying user account settings, but it does not stop malware from reading the user's documents.

Recall that process and thread objects are exceptions because their integrity policy also includes No-Read-Up. That means a process integrity level must be equal to or higher than the integrity level of the process or thread it wants to open, and the DACL must grant it the accesses it wants for an attempt to open it to succeed. Assuming the DACLs allow the desired access, Figure 6-6 shows the types of access that the processes running at medium or low have to other processes and objects.

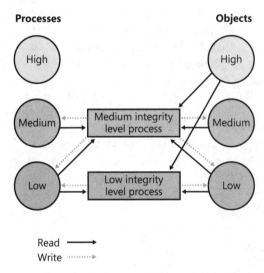

FIGURE 6-6 Access to processes versus objects for medium and low integrity level processes

User Interface Privilege Isolation

The Windows messaging subsystem also honors integrity levels to implement User Interface Privilege Isolation (UIPI). The subsystem does this by preventing a process from sending window messages to the windows owned by a process having a higher integrity level, with the following informational messages being exceptions:

- WM_NULL

- WM_MOVE

- WM_SIZE

- WM_GETTEXT

- WM_GETTEXTLENGTH

- WM_GETHOTKEY

- WM_GETICON

- WM_RENDERFORMAT

- WM_DRAWCLIPBOARD

- WM_CHANGECBCHAIN

- WM_THEMECHANGED

This use of integrity levels prevents standard user processes from driving input into the windows of elevated processes or from performing a *shatter attack* (such as sending the process malformed messages that trigger internal buffer overflows, which can lead to the execution of code at the elevated process' privilege level). UIPI also blocks window hooks from affecting the windows of higher integrity level processes so that a standard user process can't log the keystrokes the user types into an administrative application, for example. Journal hooks are also blocked in the same way to prevent lower integrity level processes from monitoring the behavior of higher integrity level processes.

Processes can choose to allow additional messages to pass the guard by calling the *ChangeWindowMessageEx* API. This function is typically used to add messages required by custom controls to communicate outside native common controls in Windows. An older API, *ChangeWindowMessageFilter* performs a similar function, but it is per-process rather than per-window. With *ChangeWindowMessageFilter* it is possible for two custom controls inside the same process to be using the same internal window messages, which could lead to one control's potentially malicious window message to be allowed through, simply because it happens to be a query-only message for the other custom control.

Because accessibility applications such as the On-Screen Keyboard (Osk.exe) are subject to UIPI's restrictions (which would require the accessibility application to be executed for each kind of visible integrity-level process on the desktop), these processes can enable UI Access. This flag can be present in the manifest file of the image and will run the process at a slightly higher integrity level than medium (between 0x2000 and 0x3000) if launched from a standard user account, or at high integrity level if launched from an administrator account. Note that in the second case, an elevation request won't actually be displayed. For a process to set this flag, its image must also be signed and in one of several secure locations, including %SystemRoot% and %ProgramFiles%.

After the integrity check is complete, and assuming the mandatory policy allows access to the object based on the caller's integrity, one of two algorithms is used for the discretionary check to an object, which will determine the final outcome of the access check:

- Determine the maximum access allowed to the object, a form of which is exported to user mode with the Windows *GetEffectiveRightsFromAcl* function. This is also used when a program specifies a desired access of MAXIMUM_ALLOWED, which is what the legacy APIs that don't have a desired access parameter use.

- Determine whether a specific desired access is allowed, which can be done with the Windows *AccessCheck* function or the *AccessCheckByType* function.

The first algorithm examines the entries in the DACL as follows:

1. If the object has no DACL (a null DACL), the object has no protection and the security system grants all access.

2. If the caller has the take-ownership privilege, the security system grants write-owner access before examining the DACL. (Take-ownership privilege and write-owner access are explained in a moment.)

3. If the caller is the owner of the object, the system looks for an OWNER_RIGHTS SID and uses that SID as the SID for the next steps. Otherwise, read-control and write-DACL access rights are granted.

4. For each access-denied ACE that contains a SID that matches one in the caller's access token, the ACE's access mask is removed from the granted-access mask.

5. For each access-allowed ACE that contains a SID that matches one in the caller's access token, the ACE's access mask is added to the granted-access mask being computed, unless that access has already been denied.

When all the entries in the DACL have been examined, the computed granted-access mask is returned to the caller as the maximum allowed access to the object. This mask represents the total set of access types that the caller will be able to successfully request when opening the object.

The preceding description applies only to the kernel-mode form of the algorithm. The Windows version implemented by *GetEffectiveRightsFromAcl* differs in that it doesn't perform step 2, and it considers a single user or group SID rather than an access token.

Owner Rights

Because owners of an object can normally override the security of an object by always being granted read-control and write-DACL rights, a specialized method of controlling this behavior is exposed by Windows: the Owner Rights SID.

The Owner Rights SID exists for two main reasons: improving service hardening in the operating system, and allowing more flexibility for specific usage scenarios. For example, suppose an administrator wants to allow users to create files and folders but not to modify the ACLs on those objects. (Users could inadvertently or maliciously grant access to those files or folders to unwanted accounts.) By using an inheritable Owner Rights SID, the users can be prevented from editing or even viewing the ACL on the objects they create. A second usage scenario relates to group changes. Suppose an employee has been part of some confidential or sensitive group, has created several files while a member of that group, and has now been removed from the group for business reasons. Because that employee is still a user, he could continue accessing the sensitive files.

As mentioned, Windows also uses the Owner Rights SID to improve service hardening. Whenever a service creates an object at run time, the Owner SID associated with that object is the account the service is running in (such as local system or local service) and not the actual service SID. This means that any other service in the same account would have access to the object by being an owner. The Owner Rights SID prevents that unwanted behavior.

The second algorithm is used to determine whether a specific access request can be granted, based on the caller's access token. Each open function in the Windows API that deals with securable objects has a parameter that specifies the desired access mask, which is the last component of the security equation. To determine whether the caller has access, the following steps are performed:

1. If the object has no DACL (a null DACL), the object has no protection and the security system grants the desired access.

2. If the caller has the take-ownership privilege, the security system grants write-owner access if requested and then examines the DACL. However, if write-owner access was the only access requested by a caller with take-ownership privilege, the security system grants that access and never examines the DACL.

3. If the caller is the owner of the object, the system looks for an OWNER_RIGHTS SID and uses that SID as the SID for the next steps. Otherwise, read-control and write-DACL access rights are granted. If these rights were the only access rights that the caller requested, access is granted without examining the DACL

4. Each ACE in the DACL is examined from first to last. An ACE is processed if one of the following conditions is satisfied:

    a. The ACE is an access-deny ACE, and the SID in the ACE matches an enabled SID (SIDs can be enabled or disabled) or a deny-only SID in the caller's access token.

    b. The ACE is an access-allowed ACE, and the SID in the ACE matches an enabled SID in the caller's token that isn't of type deny-only.

    c. It is the second pass through the descriptor for restricted-SID checks, and the SID in the ACE matches a restricted SID in the caller's access token.

    d. The ACE isn't marked as inherit-only.

5. If it is an access-allowed ACE, the rights in the access mask in the ACE that were requested are granted; if all the requested access rights have been granted, the access check succeeds. If it is an access-denied ACE and any of the requested access rights are in the denied-access rights, access is denied to the object.

6. If the end of the DACL is reached and some of the requested access rights still haven't been granted, access is denied.

7. If all accesses are granted but the caller's access token has at least one restricted SID, the system rescans the DACL's ACEs looking for ACEs with access-mask matches for the accesses the user is requesting and a match of the ACE's SID with any of the caller's restricted SIDs. Only if both scans of the DACL grant the requested access rights is the user granted access to the object.

The behavior of both access-validation algorithms depends on the relative ordering of allow and deny ACEs. Consider an object with only two ACEs, where one ACE specifies that a certain user is allowed full access to an object and the other ACE denies the user access. If the allow ACE precedes the deny ACE, the user can obtain full access to the object, but if the order is reversed, the user cannot gain any access to the object.

Several Windows functions, such as *SetSecurityInfo* and *SetNamedSecurityInfo*, apply ACEs in the preferred order of explicit deny ACEs preceding explicit allow ACEs. Note that the security editor dialog boxes with which you edit permissions on NTFS files and registry keys, for example, use these functions. *SetSecurityInfo* and *SetNamedSecurityInfo* also apply ACE inheritance rules to the security descriptor on which they are applied.

Figure 6-7 shows an example access validation demonstrating the importance of ACE ordering. In the example, access is denied a user wanting to open a file even though an ACE in the object's DACL grants the access because the ACE denying the user access (by virtue of the user's membership in the Writers group) precedes the ACE granting access.

As we stated earlier, because it wouldn't be efficient for the security system to process the DACL every time a process uses a handle, the SRM makes this access check only when a handle is opened, not each time the handle is used. Thus, once a process successfully opens a handle, the security system can't revoke the access rights that have been granted, even if the object's DACL changes. Also keep in mind that because kernel-mode code uses pointers rather than handles to access objects, the access check isn't performed when the operating system uses objects. In other words, the Windows executive trusts itself (and all loaded drivers) in a security sense.

The fact that an object's owner is always granted write-DACL access to an object means that users can never be prevented from accessing the objects they own. If, for some reason, an object had an empty DACL (no access), the owner would still be able to open the object with write-DACL access and then apply a new DACL with the desired access permissions.

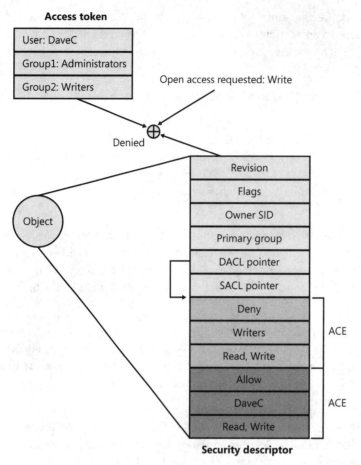

FIGURE 6-7 Access validation example

A Warning Regarding the GUI Security Editors

When you use the GUI permissions editors to modify security settings on a file, a registry, or an Active Directory object, or on another securable object, the main security dialog box shows you a potentially misleading view of the security that's applied to the object. If you allow Full Control to the Everyone group and deny the Administrator group Full Control, the list might lead you to believe that the Everyone group access-allowed ACE precedes the Administrator deny ACE because that's the order in which they appear. However, as we've said, the editors place deny ACEs before allow ACEs when they apply the ACL to the object.

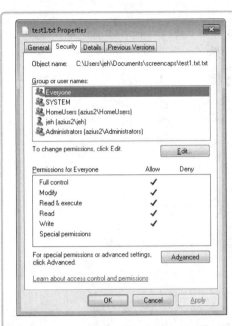

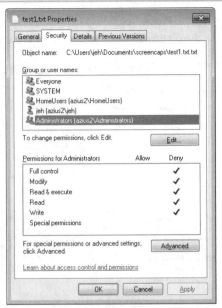

The Permissions tab of the Advanced Security Settings dialog box shows the order of ACEs in the DACL. However, even this dialog box can be confusing because a complex DACL can have deny ACEs for various accesses followed by allow ACEs for other access types.

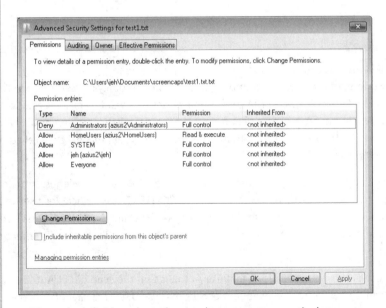

The only definitive way to know what accesses a particular user or group will have to an object (other than having that user or a member of the group try to access the object) is to use the Effective Permissions tab of the dialog box that is displayed when you click the Advanced button in the Properties dialog box. Enter the name of the user or group you want to check, and the dialog box shows you what permissions they are allowed for the object.

The AuthZ API

The AuthZ Windows API provides authorization functions and implement the same security model as the security reference monitor, but it implements the model totally in user mode in the %SystemRoot%\System32\Authz.dll library. This gives applications that want to protect their own private objects, such as database tables, the ability to leverage the Windows security model without incurring the cost of user mode to kernel mode transitions that they would make if they relied on the security reference monitor.

The AuthZ API uses standard security descriptor data structures, SIDs, and privileges. Instead of using tokens to represent clients, AuthZ uses AUTHZ_CLIENT_CONTEXT. AuthZ includes user-mode equivalents of all access-check and Windows security functions—for example, *AuthzAccessCheck* is the AuthZ version of the *AccessCheck* Windows API that uses the *SeAccessCheck* security reference monitor function.

Another advantage available to applications that use AuthZ is that they can direct AuthZ to cache the results of security checks to improve subsequent checks that use the same client context and security descriptor. AuthZ is fully documented in the Windows SDK.

The discretionary access control security mechanisms described previously have been part of the Windows NT family since the beginning, and they work well enough in a static, controlled environment. This type of access checking, using a security ID (SID) and security group membership, is known as *identity-based access control* (IBAC), and it requires that the security system knows the identity of every possible accessor when the DACL is placed in an object's security descriptor.

Windows includes support for Claims Based Access Control (CBAC), where access is granted not based upon the accessor's identity or group membership, but upon arbitrary attributes assigned to the accessor and stored in the accessor's access token. Attributes are supplied by an attribute provider, such as AppLocker. The CBAC mechanism provides many benefits, including the ability to create a DACL for a user whose identity is not yet known or dynamically-calculated user attributes. The CBAC ACE (also known as a conditional ACE) is stored in a *-callback ACE structure, which is essentially private to AuthZ and is ignored by the system *SeAccessCheck* API. The kernel-mode routine *SeSrpAccessCheck* does not understand conditional ACEs, so only applications calling the AuthZ APIs can make use of CBAC. The only system component that makes use of CBAC is AppLocker, for setting attributes such as path, or publisher. Third-party applications can make use of CBAC by taking advantage of the CBAC AuthZ APIs.

Using CBAC security checks allows powerful management policies, such as the following:

- Run only applications approved by the corporate IT department.

- Allow only approved applications to access your Microsoft Outlook contacts or calendar.

- Allow only people on a particular building's floor to access printers on that floor.

- Allow access to an intranet website only to full-time employees (as opposed to contractors).

Attributes can be referenced in what is known as a conditional ACE, where the presence, absence, or value of one or more attributes is checked. An attribute name can contain any alphanumeric Unicode characters, as well as ":/._". The value of an attribute can be one of the following: 64-bit integer, Unicode string, byte string, or array.

Conditional ACEs

The format of SDDL (Security Descriptor Definition Language) strings has been expanded to support ACEs with conditional expressions. The new format of an SDDL string is this: AceType;AceFlags;Rights; ObjectGuid;InheritObjectGuid;AccountSid;(ConditionalExpression).

The AceType for a conditional ACE is either XA (for SDDL_CALLBACK_ACCESS_ALLOWED) or XD (for SDDL_CALLBACK_ACCESS_DENIED). Note that ACEs with conditional expressions are used for claims-type authorization (specifically, the AuthZ APIs and AppLocker) and are not recognized by the object manager or file systems.

A conditional expression can include any of the elements shown in Table 6-7.

TABLE 6-7 Acceptable Elements for a Conditional Expression

Expression Element	Description
AttributeName	Tests whether the specified attribute has a nonzero value.
exists AttributeName	Tests whether the specified attribute exists in the client context.
AttributeName Operator Value	Returns the result of the specified operation. The following operators are defined for use in conditional expressions to test the values of attributes. All of these are binary operators (as opposed to unary) and are used in the form *AttributeName Operator Value*. Operators: Contains any_of , ==, !=, <, <=, >, >=
ConditionalExpression||ConditionalExpression	Tests whether either of the specified conditional expressions is true.
ConditionalExpression && ConditionalExpression	Tests whether both of the specified conditional expressions are true.
!(ConditionalExpression)	The inverse of a conditional expression.
Member_of{SidArray}	Tests whether the SID_AND_ATTRIBUTES array of the client context contains all of the security identifiers (SIDs) in the comma-separated list specified by *SidArray*.

A conditional ACE can contain any number of conditions, and it is either ignored if the resultant evaluation of the condition is false or applied if the result is true. A conditional ACE can be added to an object using the *AddConditionalAce* API and checked using the *AuthzAccessCheck* API.

A conditional ACE could specify that access to certain data records within a program should be granted only to a user who meets the following criteria:

- Holds the *Role* attribute, with a value of Architect, Program Manager, or Development Lead, and the Division attribute with a value of Windows

- Whose *ManagementChain* attribute contains the value John Smith

- Whose *CommissionType* attribute is Officer and whose PayGrade attribute is greater than 6 (that is, the rank of General Officer in the US military)

Windows does not include tools to view or edit conditional ACEs.

Account Rights and Privileges

Many operations performed by processes as they execute cannot be authorized through object access protection because they do not involve interaction with a particular object. For example, the ability to bypass security checks when opening files for backup is an attribute of an account, not of a particular object. Windows uses both privileges and account rights to allow a system administrator to control what accounts can perform security-related operations.

A privilege is the right of an account to perform a particular system-related operation, such as shutting down the computer or changing the system time. An account right grants or denies the account to which it's assigned the ability to perform a particular type of logon, such as a local logon or interactive logon, to a computer.

A system administrator assigns privileges to groups and accounts using tools such as the Active Directory Users and Groups MMC snap-in for domain accounts or the Local Security Policy Editor (%SystemRoot%\System32\secpol.msc). You access the Local Security Policy Editor in the Administrative Tools folder of the Control Panel or the Start menu (if you've configured your Start menu to contain an Administrative Tools link). Figure 6-8 shows the User Rights Assignment configuration in the Local Security Policy Editor, which displays the complete list of privileges and account rights available on Windows. Note that the tool makes no distinction between privileges and account rights. However, you can differentiate between them because any user right that does not contain the words log on is an account privilege.

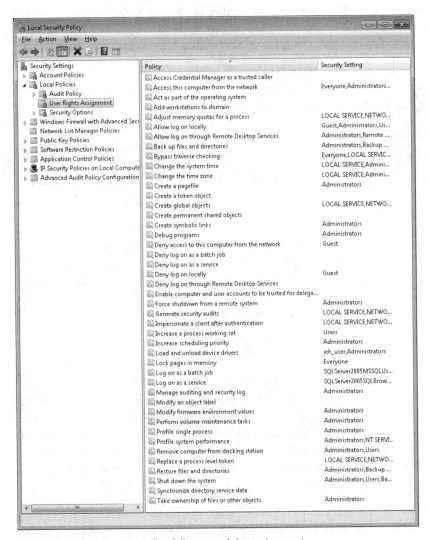

FIGURE 6-8 Local Security Policy Editor user rights assignment

Account Rights

Account rights are not enforced by the security reference monitor, nor are they stored in tokens. The function responsible for logon is *LsaLogonUser*. Winlogon, for example, calls the *LogonUser* API when a user logs on interactively to a computer, and *LogonUser* calls *LsaLogonUser*. *LogonUser* takes a parameter that indicates the type of logon being performed, which includes interactive, network, batch, service, and Terminal Server client.

In response to logon requests, the Local Security Authority (LSA) retrieves account rights assigned to a user from the LSA policy database at the time that a user attempts to log on to the system. LSA checks the logon type against the account rights assigned to the user account logging on and denies the logon if the account does not have the right that permits the logon type or it has the right that denies the logon type. Table 6-8 lists the user rights defined by Windows.

Windows applications can add and remove user rights from an account by using the *LsaAddAccountRights* and *LsaRemoveAccountRights* functions, and they can determine what rights are assigned to an account with *LsaEnumerateAccountRights*.

TABLE 6-8 Account Rights

User Right	Role
Deny logon locally, Allow logon locally	Used for interactive logons that originate on the local machine
Deny logon over the network, Allow logon over the network	Used for logons that originate from a remote machine
Deny logon through Terminal Services, Allow logon through Terminal Services	Used for logons through a Terminal Server client
Deny logon as a service, Allow logon as a service	Used by the service control manager when starting a service in a particular user account
Deny logon as a batch job, Allow logon as a batch job	Used when performing a logon of type batch

Privileges

The number of privileges defined by the operating system has grown over time. Unlike user rights, which are enforced in one place by the LSA, different privileges are defined by different components and enforced by those components. For example, the debug privilege, which allows a process to bypass security checks when opening a handle to another process with the *OpenProcess* Windows API, is checked for by the process manager. Table 6-9 is a full list of privileges, and it describes how and when system components check for them.

When a component wants to check a token to see whether a privilege is present, it uses the *PrivilegeCheck* or *LsaEnumerateAccountRights* APIs if running in user mode and *SeSinglePrivilegeCheck* or *SePrivilegeCheck* if running in kernel mode. The privilege-related APIs are not account-right aware, but the account-right APIs are privilege-aware.

Unlike account rights, privileges can be enabled and disabled. For a privilege check to succeed, the privilege must be in the specified token and it must be enabled. The idea behind this scheme is that privileges should be enabled only when their use is required so that a process cannot inadvertently perform a privileged security operation.

EXPERIMENT: Seeing a Privilege Get Enabled

By following these steps, you can see that the Date and Time Control Panel applet enables the SeTimeZonePrivilege privilege in response to you using its interface to change the time zone of the computer:

1. Run Process Explorer, and set the refresh rate to Paused.

2. Open the Date And Time item by right-clicking on the clock in the system tray region of the taskbar, and then select Adjust Date/Time. A new Rundll32 process will appear with a green highlight when you force a refresh with F5.

3. Hover the mouse over the Rundll32 process, and verify that the target contains the text "Time Date Control Panel Applet" as well as a path to Timedate.cpl. The presence of this argument tells Rundll32, which is a Control Panel DLL hosting process, to load the DLL that implements the user interface that enables you to change the time and date.

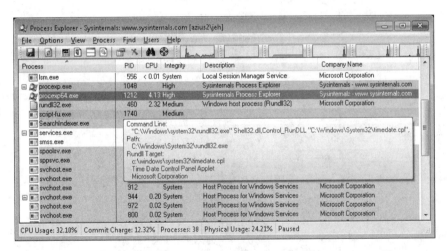

4. View the Security tab of the process Properties dialog box for your Rundll32 process. You should see that the SeTimeZonePrivilege privilege is disabled.

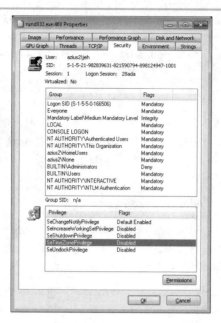

5. Now click the Change Time Zone button in the Control Panel item, close the process Properties dialog box, and then open it again. On the Security tab, you should now see that the SeTimeZonePrivilege privilege is enabled.

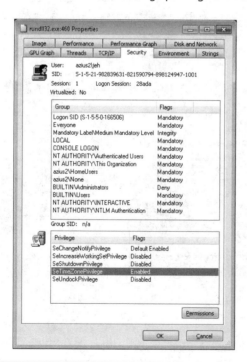

TABLE 6-9 Privileges

Privilege	User Right	Privilege Usage
SeAssignPrimaryTokenPrivilege	Replace a process-level token	Checked for by various components, such as NtSetInformationJob, that set a process' token.
SeAuditPrivilege	Generate security audits	Required to generate events for the Security event log with the ReportEvent API.
SeBackupPrivilege	Back up files and directories	Causes NTFS to grant the following access to any file or directory, regardless of the security descriptor that's present: READ_CONTROL, ACCESS_SYSTEM_SECURITY, FILE_GENERIC_READ, FILE_TRAVERSE Note that when opening a file for backup, the caller must specify the FILE_FLAG_BACKUP_SEMANTICS flag. Also allows corresponding access to registry keys when using RegSaveKey.
SeChangeNotifyPrivilege	Bypass traverse checking	Used by NTFS to avoid checking permissions on intermediate directories of a multilevel directory lookup. Also used by file systems when applications register for notification of changes to the file system structure.
SeCreateGlobalPrivilege	Create global objects	Required for a process to create section and symbolic link objects in the directories of the object manager namespace that are assigned to a different session than the caller.
SeCreatePagefilePrivilege	Create a pagefile	Checked for by NtCreatePagingFile, which is the function used to create a new paging file.
SeCreatePermanentPrivilege	Create permanent shared objects	Checked for by the object manager when creating a permanent object (one that doesn't get deallocated when there are no more references to it).
SeCreateSymbolicLinkPrivilege	Create symbolic links	Checked for by NTFS when creating symbolic links on the file system with the CreateSymbolicLink API.
SeCreateTokenPrivilege	Create a token object	NtCreateToken, the function that creates a token object, checks for this privilege.
SeDebugPrivilege	Debug programs	If the caller has this privilege enabled, the process manager allows access to any process or thread using NtOpenProcess or NtOpenThread, regardless of the process' or thread's security descriptor (except for protected processes).
SeEnableDelegationPrivilege	Enable computer and user accounts to be trusted for delegation	Used by Active Directory services to delegate authenticated credentials.
SeImpersonatePrivilege	Impersonate a client after authentication	The process manager checks for this when a thread wants to use a token for impersonation and the token represents a different user than that of the thread's process token.
SeIncreaseBasePriorityPrivilege	Increase scheduling priority	Checked for by the process manager and is required to raise the priority of a process.
SeIncreaseQuotaPrivilege	Adjust memory quotas for a process	Enforced when changing a process' working set thresholds, a process' paged and nonpaged pool quotas, and a process' CPU rate quota.
SeIncreaseWorkingSetPrivilege	Increase a process working set	Required to call SetProcessWorkingSetSize to increase the minimum working set. This indirectly allows the process to lock up to the minimum working set of memory using VirtualLock.

Privilege	User Right	Privilege Usage
SeLoadDriverPrivilege	Load and unload device drivers	Checked for by the *NtLoadDriver* and *NtUnloadDriver* driver functions.
SeLockMemoryPrivilege	Lock pages in memory	Checked for by *NtLockVirtualMemory*, the kernel implementation of *VirtualLock*.
SeMachineAccountPrivilege	Add workstations to the domain	Checked for by the Security Accounts Manager on a domain controller when creating a machine account in a domain.
SeManageVolumePrivilege	Perform volume maintenance tasks	Enforced by file system drivers during a volume open operation, which is required to perform disk checking and defragmenting activities.
SeProfileSingleProcessPrivilege	Profile single process	Checked by Superfetch and the prefetcher when requesting information for an individual process through the *NtQuerySystemInformation* API.
SeRelabelPrivilege	Modify an object label	Checked for by the SRM when raising the integrity level of an object owned by another user, or when attempting to raise the integrity level of an object higher than that of the caller's token.
SeRemoteShutdownPrivilege	Force shutdown from a remote system	Winlogon checks that remote callers of the *InitiateSystemShutdown* function have this privilege.
SeRestorePrivilege	Restore files and directories	This privilege causes NTFS to grant the following access to any file or directory, regardless of the security descriptor that's present: WRITE_DAC WRITE_OWNER ACCESS_SYSTEM_SECURITY FILE_GENERIC_WRITE FILE_ADD_FILE FILE_ADD_SUBDIRECTORY DELETE Note that when opening a file for restore, the caller must specify the FILE_FLAG_BACKUP_SEMANTICS flag. Allows corresponding access to registry keys when using *RegSaveKey*.
SeSecurityPrivilege	Manage auditing and security log	Required to access the SACL of a security descriptor, and to read and clear the security event log.
SeShutdownPrivilege	Shut down the system	This privilege is checked for by *NtShutdownSystem* and *NtRaiseHardError*, which presents a system error dialog box on the interactive console.
SeSyncAgentPrivilege	Synchronize directory service data	Required to use the LDAP directory synchronization services. It allows the holder to read all objects and properties in the directory, regardless of the protection on the objects and properties.
SeSystemEnvironmentPrivilege	Modify firmware environment variables	Required by *NtSetSystemEnvironmentValue* and *NtQuerySystemEnvironmentValue* to modify and read firmware environment variables using the hardware abstraction layer (HAL).
SeSystemProfilePrivilege	Profile system performance	Checked for by *NtCreateProfile*, the function used to perform profiling of the system. This is used by the Kernprof tool, for example.
SeSystemtimePrivilege	Change the system time	Required to change the time or date.

Privilege	User Right	Privilege Usage
SeTakeOwnershipPrivilege	Take ownership of files and other objects	Required to take ownership of an object without being granted discretionary access.
SeTcbPrivilege	Act as part of the operating system	Checked for by the security reference monitor when the session ID is set in a token, by the Plug and Play manager for Plug and Play event creation and management, by *BroadcastSystemMessageEx* when called with BSM_ALLDESKTOPS, by *LsaRegisterLogonProcess*, and when specifying an application as a VDM with *NtSetInformationProcess*.
SeTimeZonePrivilege	Change the time zone	Required to change the time zone.
SeTrustedCredManAccessPrivilege	Access credential manager as a trusted caller	Checked by the credential manager to verify that it should trust the caller with credential information that can be queried in plain text. It is granted only to Winlogon by default.
SeUndockPrivilege	Remove computer from a docking station	Checked for by the user-mode Plug and Play manager when either a computer undock is initiated or a device eject request is made.
SeUnsolicitedInputPrivilege	Receive unsolicited data from a terminal device	This privilege isn't currently used by Windows.

EXPERIMENT: The Bypass Traverse Checking Privilege

If you are a systems administrator, you must be aware of the Bypass Traverse Checking privilege (internally called *SeNotifyPrivilege*) and its implications. This experiment demonstrates that not understanding its behavior can lead to improperly applied security.

1. Create a folder and, within that folder, a new text file with some sample text.

2. Navigate in Explorer to the new file, and go to the Security tab of its Properties dialog box. Click the Advanced button, and clear the check box that controls inheritance. Select Copy when you are prompted as to whether you want to remove or copy inherited permissions.

3. Next, modify the security of the new folder so that your account does not have any access to the folder. Do this by selecting your account and selecting all the Deny boxes in the permissions list.

4. Run Notepad, and browse using the File, Open dialog box to the new directory. You should be denied access to the directory.

5. In the File Name field of the Open dialog box, type the full path of the new file. The file should open.

If your account does not have the Bypass Traverse Checking privilege, NTFS performs an access check on each directory of the path to a file when you try to open a file, which results in you being denied access to the file in this example.

Super Privileges

Several privileges are so powerful that a user to which they are assigned is effectively a "super user" who has full control over a computer. These privileges can be used in an infinite number of ways to gain unauthorized access to otherwise off-limit resources and to perform unauthorized operations. However, we'll focus on using the privilege to execute code that grants the user privileges not assigned to the user, with the knowledge that this capability can be leveraged to perform any operation on the local machine that the user desires.

This section lists the privileges and discusses the ways that they can be exploited. Other privileges, such as Lock Pages In Physical Memory, can be exploited for denial-of-service attacks on a system, but these are not discussed. Note that on systems with UAC enabled, these privileges will be granted only to applications running at high integrity level or higher, even if the account possesses them:

- **Debug programs**   A user with this privilege can open any process on the system (except for a Protected Process) without regard to the security descriptor present on the process. The user could implement a program that opens the LSASS process, for example, copy executable code into its address space, and then inject a thread with the *CreateRemoteThread* Windows API to execute the injected code in a more-privileged security context. The code could grant the user additional privileges and group memberships.

- **Take ownership**   This privilege allows a holder to take ownership of any securable object (even protected processes and threads) by writing his own SID into the owner field of the object's security descriptor. Recall that an owner is always granted permission to read and modify the DACL of the security descriptor, so a process with this privilege could modify the DACL to grant itself full access to the object and then close and reopen the object with full access. This would allow the owner to see sensitive data and to even replace system files that execute as part of normal system operation, such as LSASS, with his own programs that grant a user elevated privileges.

- **Restore files and directories**   A user assigned this privilege can replace any file on the system with her own. She could exploit this power by replacing system files as described in the preceding paragraph.

- **Load and unload device drivers**   A malicious user could use this privilege to load a device driver into the system. Device drivers are considered trusted parts of the operating system that can execute within it with System account credentials, so a driver could launch privileged programs that assign the user other rights.

- **Create a token object**   This privilege can be used in the obvious way to generate tokens that represent arbitrary user accounts with arbitrary group membership and privilege assignment.

- **Act as part of operating system**   *LsaRegisterLogonProcess*, the function a process calls to establish a trusted connection to LSASS, checks for this privilege. A malicious user with this privilege can establish a trusted-LSASS connection and then execute *LsaLogonUser*, a function used to create new logon sessions. *LsaLogonUser* requires a valid user name and password and accepts an optional list of SIDs that it adds to the initial token created for a new logon session.

The user could therefore use her own user name and password to create a new logon session that includes the SIDs of more privileged groups or users in the resulting token.

Note that the use of an elevated privilege does not extend past the machine boundary to the network, because any interaction with another computer requires authentication with a domain controller and validation of domain passwords. Domain passwords are not stored on a computer either in plain text or encrypted form, so they are not accessible to malicious code.

Access Tokens of Processes and Threads

Figure 6-9 brings together the concepts covered so far in this chapter by illustrating the basic process and thread security structures. In the figure, notice that the process object and the thread objects have ACLs, as do the access token objects themselves. Also in this figure, thread 2 and thread 3 each have an impersonation token, whereas thread 1 uses the default process access token.

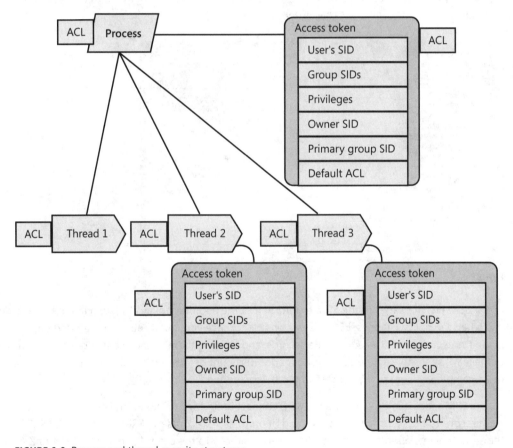

FIGURE 6-9 Process and thread security structures

Security Auditing

The object manager can generate audit events as a result of an access check, and Windows functions available to user applications can generate them directly. Kernel-mode code is always allowed to generate an audit event. Two privileges, SeSecurityPrivilege and SeAuditPrivilege, relate to auditing. A process must have the SeSecurityPrivilege privilege to manage the security Event Log and to view or set an object's SACL. Processes that call audit system services, however, must have the SeAuditPrivilege privilege to successfully generate an audit record.

The audit policy of the local system controls the decision to audit a particular type of security event. The audit policy, also called the local security policy, is one part of the security policy LSASS maintains on the local system, and it is configured with the Local Security Policy Editor as shown in Figure 6-10.

The audit policy configuration (both the basic settings under Local Policies and the Advanced Audit Policy Configuration to be described later) is stored in the registry as a bitmapped value in the key HKEY_LOCAL_MACHINE\SECURITY\Policy\PolAdtEv.

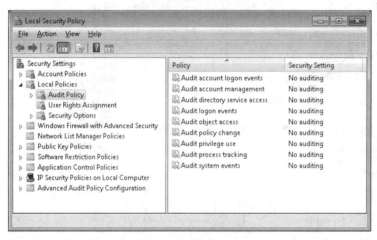

FIGURE 6-10 Local Security Policy Editor audit policy configuration

LSASS sends messages to the SRM to inform it of the auditing policy at system initialization time and when the policy changes. LSASS is responsible for receiving audit records generated based on the audit events from the SRM, editing the records, and sending them to the Event Logger. LSASS (instead of the SRM) sends these records because it adds pertinent details, such as the information needed to more completely identify the process that is being audited.

The SRM sends audit records via its ALPC connection to LSASS. The Event Logger then writes the audit record to the security Event Log. In addition to audit records the SRM passes, both LSASS and the SAM generate audit records that LSASS sends directly to the Event Logger, and the AuthZ APIs allow for applications to generate application-defined audits. Figure 6-11 depicts this overall flow.

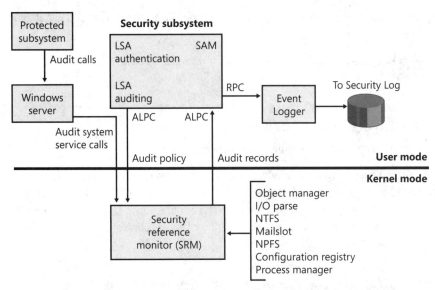

FIGURE 6-11 Flow of security audit records

Audit records are put on a queue to be sent to the LSA as they are received—they are not submitted in batches. The audit records are moved from the SRM to the security subsystem in one of two ways. If the audit record is small (less than the maximum ALPC message size), it is sent as an ALPC message. The audit records are copied from the address space of the SRM to the address space of the LSASS process. If the audit record is large, the SRM uses shared memory to make the message available to LSASS and simply passes a pointer in an ALPC message.

Object Access Auditing

An important use of the auditing mechanism in many environments is to maintain a log of accesses to secured objects, files in particular. To do this, the Audit Object Access policy must be enabled, and there must be audit ACEs in System Access Control Lists that enable auditing for the objects in question.

When an accessor attempts to open a handle to an object, the security reference monitor first determines whether the attempt is allowed or denied. If object access auditing is enabled, the SRM then scans the System ACL of the object. There are two types of audit ACEs, access allowed and access denied. An audit ACE must match any of the security IDs held by the accessor, it must match any of the access methods requested, and its type (access allowed or access denied) must match the result of the access check in order to generate an object access audit record.

Object access audit records include not just the fact of access allowed or denied, but also the reason for the success or failure. This "reason for access" reporting generally takes the form of an access control entry, specified in SDDL (Security Descriptor Definition Language), in the audit record. This allows for a diagnosis of scenarios in which an object to which you believe access should be denied is being permitted, or vice versa, by identifying the specific access control entry that caused the attempted access to succeed or fail.

As can be seen in Figure 6-10, object access auditing is disabled by default (as are all other auditing policies).

EXPERIMENT: Object Access Auditing

You can demonstrate object access auditing by following these steps:

1. In Explorer, navigate to a file to which you would normally have access. In its Properties dialog box, click on the Security tab and then select the Advanced settings. Click on the Auditing tab, and click through the administrative privileges warning. The resulting dialog box allows you to add auditing of access control entries to the file's System Access Control List.

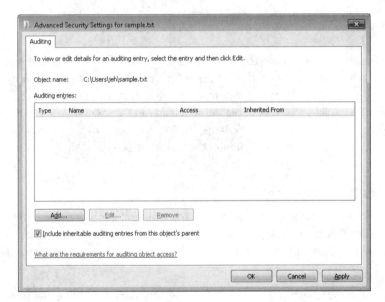

2. Click the Add button. In the resulting Select User Or Group dialog box, enter your own user name or a group to which you belong, such as Everyone, and click Check Names and then OK. This presents a dialog box for creating an Auditing Access Control Entry for this user or group for this file.

3. In the Successful column, select Full control (which will cause all of the other access methods to be selected as well). Click OK four times to close the file Properties dialog box.

4. In Explorer, double-click on the file to open it with its associated program.

5. In Event Viewer, navigate to the Security log. Note that there is no entry for access to the file. This is because the audit policy for object access is not yet configured.

6. In the Local Security Policy Editor, navigate to Local Policies, Audit Policy. Double-click on Audit Object Access, and then click Success to enable auditing of successful access to files.

7. In Event Viewer, click Action, Refresh. Note that the changes to audit policy resulted in audit records.

8. In Explorer, double-click on the file to open it again.

9. In Event Viewer, click Action, Refresh. Note that several file access audit records are now present.

Find one of the file access audit records for Event ID 4656, This shows up as "a handle to an object was requested." Scroll down in the text box to find the Access Reasons section. The following example shows that two access methods, READ_CONTROL and ReadAttributes, were requested. The former was granted because the accessor was the owner of the file, and the latter was granted because of the indicated Access Control Entry. The ACE includes the SID of the user who attempted the access and includes the designation A:FA, indicating that this SID is Allowed (A) all file access methods (FA) to the file.

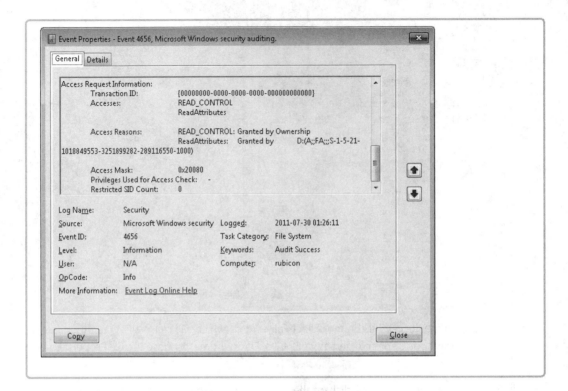

Global Audit Policy

In addition to object-access ACEs on individual objects, a global audit policy can be defined for the system that enables object access auditing for all file system objects, for all registry keys, or for both. A security auditor can therefore be certain that the desired auditing will be performed, without having to set or examine SACLs on all of the individual objects of interest.

An administrator can set or query the global audit policy via the AuditPol command with the /resourceSACL option. This can also be done with a program calling the *AuditSetGlobalSacl* and *AuditQueryGlobalSacl* APIs. As with changes to objects' SACLs, changing these global SACLs requires SeSecurityPrivilege.

EXPERIMENT: Setting Global Audit Policy

You can use the AuditPol command to enable global audit policy.

1. If not already done in the previous experiment, in the Local Security Policy Editor, navigate to the Audit Policy settings (as shown in Figure 6-10), double-click Audit Object Access, and enable auditing for both success and failure. Note that on most systems, SACLs specifying object access auditing are uncommon, so few if any object access audit records will be produced at this point.

2. In an elevated command prompt window, enter the following command:

```
C:\> auditpol /resourceSACL
```

This will produce a summary of the commands for setting and querying global audit policy.

3. In the same elevated command prompt window, enter the following commands:

```
C:\> auditpol /resourceSACL /type:File /view
C:\> auditpol /resourceSACL /type:Key /view
```

On a typical system, each of these commands will report that no Global SACL exists for the respective resource type. (Note that the keywords "File" and "Key" are case-sensitive.)

4. In the same elevated command prompt window, enter the following command:

```
C:\> auditpol /resourceSACL /set /type:File /user:yourusername /success /failure
/access:FW
```

This will set a global audit policy such that all attempts to open files for write access (FW) by the indicated user will result in audit records, whether the open attempts succeed or fail. The user name can be a specific user name on the system, a group such as Everyone, a domain-qualified user name such as domainname\username, or a SID.

5. While running under the user name indicated, use Explorer or other tools to open a file. Then look at the security log in the system Event Log to find the audit records.

6. At the end of the experiment, use the auditpol command to remove the global SACL you created in step 4, as follows:

```
C:\> auditpol /resourceSACL /remove /type:File /user:yourusername
```

The global audit policy is stored in the registry as a pair of system access control lists in HKEY_LOCAL_MACHINE\SECURITY\Policy\GlobalSaclNameFile and HKEY_LOCAL_MACHINE \SECURITY\Policy\GlobalSaclNameKey. These keys can be examined by running Regedit.exe under the System account, as described earlier in the "Security System Components" section. These keys will not exist until the corresponding global SACLs have been set at least once.

The global audit policy cannot be overridden by SACLs on objects, but object-specific SACLs can allow for additional auditing. For example, global audit policy could require auditing of read access by all users to all files, but SACLs on individual files could add auditing of write access to those files by specific users or by more specific user groups.

Global audit policy can also be configured via the Local Security Policy Editor in the Advanced Audit Policy settings, described in the next subsection.

Advanced Audit Policy Settings

In addition to the Audit Policy settings described previously, the Local Security Policy Editor offers a much more fine-grained set of audit controls under the Advanced Audit Policy Configuration heading, as shown in Figure 6-12.

FIGURE 6-12 Local Security Policy Editor Advanced Audit Policy Configuration settings

Each of the nine audit policy settings under Local Policies, as illustrated previously in Figure 6-10, maps to a group of settings here that provide more detailed control. For example, while the Audit Object Access settings under Local Policies allow access to all objects to be audited, the settings here allow auditing of access to various types of objects to be controlled individually. Enabling one of the audit policy settings under Local Policies implicitly enables all of the corresponding advanced audit policy events, but if finer control over the contents of the audit log is desired, the advanced settings can be set individually. The standard settings then become a product of the advanced settings; however, this is not visible in the Local Security Policy Editor. Attempts to specify audit settings by using both the basic and the advanced options can cause unexpected results.

The Global Object Access Auditing option under the Advanced Audit Policy Configuration item can be used to configure the Global SACLs described in the previous section, using a graphical interface identical to that seen in Explorer or the Registry Editor for security descriptors in the file system or the registry.

Logon

Interactive logon (as opposed to network logon) occurs through the interaction of the logon process (Winlogon), the logon user interface process (LogonUI) and its credential providers, LSASS, one or more authentication packages, and the SAM or Active Directory. Authentication packages are DLLs that perform authentication checks. Kerberos is the Windows authentication package for interactive logon to a domain, and MSV1_0 is the Windows authentication package for interactive logon to a local computer, for domain logons to trusted pre–Windows 2000 domains, and for times when no domain controller is accessible.

Winlogon is a trusted process responsible for managing security-related user interactions. It coordinates logon, starts the user's first process at logon, handles logoff, and manages various other operations relevant to security, including launching LogonUI for entering passwords at logon, changing passwords, and locking and unlocking the workstation. The Winlogon process must ensure that operations relevant to security aren't visible to any other active processes. For example, Winlogon guarantees that an untrusted process can't get control of the desktop during one of these operations and thus gain access to the password.

Winlogon relies on the credential providers installed on the system to obtain a user's account name or password. Credential providers are COM objects located inside DLLs. The default providers are %SystemRoot%\System32\authui.dll and %SystemRoot%\System32\SmartcardCredentialProvider.dll, which support both password and smartcard PIN authentication. Allowing other credential providers to be installed allows Windows to use different user-identification mechanisms. For example, a third party might supply a credential provider that uses a thumbprint recognition device to identify users and extract their passwords from an encrypted database.

To protect Winlogon's address space from bugs in credential providers that might cause the Winlogon process to crash (which, in turn, will result in a system crash, because Winlogon is considered a critical system process), a separate process, LogonUI.exe, is used to actually load the credential providers and display the Windows logon interface to users. This process is started on demand whenever Winlogon needs to present a user interface to the user, and it exits after the action has finished. It also allows Winlogon to simply restart a new LogonUI process should it crash for any reason.

Winlogon is the only process that intercepts logon requests from the keyboard, which are sent through an RPC message from Win32k.sys. Winlogon immediately launches the LogonUI application to display the user interface for logon. After obtaining a user name and password from credential providers, Winlogon calls LSASS to authenticate the user attempting to log on. If the user is authenticated, the logon process activates a logon shell on behalf of that user. The interaction between the components involved in logon is illustrated in Figure 6-13.

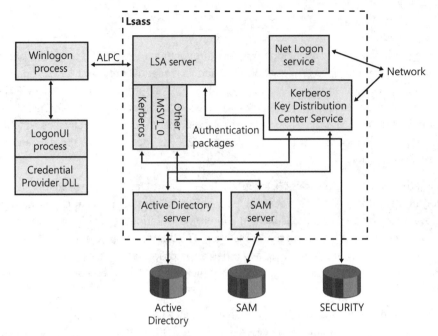

FIGURE 6-13 Components involved in logon

In addition to supporting alternative credential providers, LogonUI can load additional network provider DLLs that need to perform secondary authentication. This capability allows multiple network providers to gather identification and authentication information all at one time during normal logon. A user logging on to a Windows system might simultaneously be authenticated on a UNIX server. That user would then be able to access resources of the UNIX server from the Windows machine without requiring additional authentication. Such a capability is known as one form of single sign-on.

Winlogon Initialization

During system initialization, before any user applications are active, Winlogon performs the following steps to ensure that it controls the workstation once the system is ready for user interaction:

1. Creates and opens an interactive window station (for example, \Sessions\1\Windows \WindowStations\WinSta0 in the object manager namespace) to represent the keyboard, mouse, and monitor. Winlogon creates a security descriptor for the station that has one and only one ACE containing only the System SID. This unique security descriptor ensures that no other process can access the workstation unless explicitly allowed by Winlogon.

2. Creates and opens two desktops: an application desktop (\Sessions\1\Windows\WinSta0 \Default, also known as the interactive desktop) and a Winlogon desktop (\Sessions\1 \Windows\WinSta0\Winlogon, also known as the secure desktop). The security on the Winlogon desktop is created so that only Winlogon can access that desktop. The other desktop allows both Winlogon and users to access it. This arrangement means that any time the Winlogon desktop is active, no other process has access to any active code or data

associated with the desktop. Windows uses this feature to protect the secure operations that involve passwords and locking and unlocking the desktop.

3. Before anyone logs on to a computer, the visible desktop is Winlogon's. After a user logs on, pressing Ctrl+Alt+Delete switches the desktop from Default to Winlogon and launches LogonUI. (This explains why all the windows on your interactive desktop seem to disappear when you press Ctrl+Alt+Delete, and then return when you dismiss the Windows Security dialog box.) Thus, the SAS always brings up a secure desktop controlled by Winlogon.

4. Establishes an ALPC connection with LSASS's LsaAuthenticationPort. This connection will be used for exchanging information during logon, logoff, and password operations and is made by calling *LsaRegisterLogonProcess*.

5. Registers the Winlogon RPC message server, which listens for SAS, logoff, and workstation lock notifications from Win32k. This measure prevents Trojan horse programs from gaining control of the screen when the SAS is entered.

> **Note** The Wininit process performs steps similar to steps 1 and 2 to allow legacy interactive services running on session 0 to display windows, but it does not perform any other steps because session 0 is not available for user logon. (See Chapter 3 for more information on Wininit and session isolation.)

How SAS Is Implemented

The SAS is secure because no application can intercept the Ctrl+Alt+Delete keystroke combination or prevent Winlogon from receiving it. Win32k.sys reserves the Ctrl+Alt+Delete key combination so that whenever the Windows input system (implemented in the raw input thread in Win32k) sees the combination, it sends an RPC message to Winlogon's message server, which listens for such notifications. The keystrokes that map to a registered hot key are otherwise not sent to any process other than the one that registered it, and only the thread that registered a hot key can unregister it, so a Trojan horse application cannot deregister Winlogon's ownership of the SAS.

A Windows function, *SetWindowsHook*, enables an application to install a hook procedure that's invoked every time a keystroke is pressed, even before hot keys are processed, and it allows the hook to squash keystrokes. However, the Windows hot key processing code contains a special case for Ctrl+Alt+Delete that disables hooks so that the keystroke sequence can't be intercepted. In addition, if the interactive desktop is locked, only hot keys owned by Winlogon are processed.

Once the Winlogon desktop is created during initialization, it becomes the active desktop. When the Winlogon desktop is active, it is always locked. Winlogon unlocks its desktop only to switch to the application desktop or the screen-saver desktop. (Only the Winlogon process can lock or unlock a desktop.)

User Logon Steps

Logon begins when a user presses the SAS (Ctrl+Alt+Delete). After the SAS is pressed, Winlogon starts LogonUI, which calls the credential providers to obtain a user name and password. Winlogon also creates a unique local logon SID for this user that it assigns to this instance of the desktop (keyboard, screen, and mouse). Winlogon passes this SID to LSASS as part of the *LsaLogonUser* call. If the user is successfully logged on, this SID will be included in the logon process token—a step that protects access to the desktop. For example, another logon to the same account but on a different system will be unable to write to the first machine's desktop because this second logon won't be in the first logon's desktop token.

When the user name and password have been entered, Winlogon retrieves a handle to a package by calling the LSASS function *LsaLookupAuthenticationPackage*. Authentication packages are listed in the registry under HKLM\SYSTEM\CurrentControlSet\Control\Lsa. Winlogon passes logon information to the authentication package via *LsaLogonUser*. Once a package authenticates a user, Winlogon continues the logon process for that user. If none of the authentication packages indicates a successful logon, the logon process is aborted.

Windows uses two standard authentication packages for interactive logons: Kerberos and MSV1_0. The default authentication package on a stand-alone Windows system is MSV1_0 (%SystemRoot% \System32\Msv1_0.dll), an authentication package that implements LAN Manager 2 protocol. LSASS also uses MSV1_0 on domain-member computers to authenticate to pre–Windows 2000 domains and computers that can't locate a domain controller for authentication. (Computers that are disconnected from the network fall into this latter category.) The Kerberos authentication package, %SystemRoot% \System32\Kerberos.dll, is used on computers that are members of Windows domains. The Windows Kerberos package, with the cooperation of Kerberos services running on a domain controller, supports the Kerberos protocol. This protocol is based on Internet RFC 1510. (Visit the Internet Engineering Task Force [IETF] website, *www.ietf.org*, for detailed information on the Kerberos standard.)

The MSV1_0 authentication package takes the user name and a hashed version of the password and sends a request to the local SAM to retrieve the account information, which includes the hashed password, the groups to which the user belongs, and any account restrictions. MSV1_0 first checks the account restrictions, such as hours or type of accesses allowed. If the user can't log on because of the restrictions in the SAM database, the logon call fails and MSV1_0 returns a failure status to the LSA.

MSV1_0 then compares the hashed password and user name to that obtained from the SAM. In the case of a cached domain logon, MSV1_0 accesses the cached information by using LSASS functions that store and retrieve "secrets" from the LSA database (the SECURITY hive of the registry). If the information matches, MSV1_0 generates a LUID for the logon session and creates the logon session by calling LSASS, associating this unique identifier with the session and passing the information needed to ultimately create an access token for the user. (Recall that an access token includes the user's SID, group SIDs, and assigned privileges.)

Note MSV1_0 does not cache a user's entire password hash in the registry because that would enable someone with physical access to the system to easily compromise a user's domain account and gain access to encrypted files and to network resources the user is authorized to access. Instead, it caches half of the hash. The cached half-hash is sufficient to verify that a user's password is correct, but it isn't sufficient to gain access to EFS keys and to authenticate as the user on a domain because these actions require the full hash.

If MSV1_0 needs to authenticate using a remote system, as when a user logs on to a trusted pre–Windows 2000 domain, MSV1_0 uses the Netlogon service to communicate with an instance of Netlogon on the remote system. Netlogon on the remote system interacts with the MSV1_0 authentication package on that system, passing back authentication results to the system on which the logon is being performed.

The basic control flow for Kerberos authentication is the same as the flow for MSV1_0. However, in most cases, domain logons are performed from member workstations or servers (rather than on a domain controller), so the authentication package must communicate across the network as part of the authentication process. The package does so by communicating via the Kerberos TCP/IP port (port 88) with the Kerberos service on a domain controller. The Kerberos Key Distribution Center service (%SystemRoot%\System32\Kdcsvc.dll), which implements the Kerberos authentication protocol, runs in the LSASS process on domain controllers.

After validating hashed user name and password information with Active Directory's user account objects (using the Active Directory server %SystemRoot%\System32\Ntdsa.dll), Kdcsvc returns domain credentials to LSASS, which returns the result of the authentication and the user's domain logon credentials (if the logon was successful) across the network to the system where the logon is taking place.

Note This description of Kerberos authentication is highly simplified, but it highlights the roles of the various components involved. Although the Kerberos authentication protocol plays a key role in distributed domain security in Windows, its details are outside the scope of this book.

After a logon has been authenticated, LSASS looks in the local policy database for the user's allowed access, including interactive, network, batch, or service process. If the requested logon doesn't match the allowed access, the logon attempt will be terminated. LSASS deletes the newly created logon session by cleaning up any of its data structures and then returns failure to Winlogon, which in turn displays an appropriate message to the user. If the requested access is allowed, LSASS adds the appropriate additional security IDs (such as Everyone, Interactive, and the like). It then checks its policy database for any granted privileges for all the SIDs for this user and adds these privileges to the user's access token.

When LSASS has accumulated all the necessary information, it calls the executive to create the access token. The executive creates a primary access token for an interactive or service logon and an impersonation token for a network logon. After the access token is successfully created, LSASS duplicates the token, creating a handle that can be passed to Winlogon, and closes its own handle. If necessary, the logon operation is audited. At this point, LSASS returns success to Winlogon along with a handle to the access token, the LUID for the logon session, and the profile information, if any, that the authentication package returned.

```
[3] Logon session 00000000:000003e5:
    User name:    NT AUTHORITY\LOCAL SERVICE
    Auth package: Negotiate
    Logon type:   Service
    Session:      0
    Sid:          S-1-5-19
    Logon time:   2012-01-16 22:03:40
    Logon server:
    DNS Domain:
    UPN:

[4] Logon session 00000000:00021ed2:
    User name:    NT AUTHORITY\ANONYMOUS LOGON
    Auth package: NTLM
    Logon type:   Network
    Session:      0
    Sid:          S-1-5-7
    Logon time:   2012-01-16 22:03:46
    Logon server:
    DNS Domain:
    UPN:

[5] Logon session 00000000:000882c2:
    User name:    LAPT8\jeh
    Auth package: NTLM
    Logon type:   Interactive
    Session:      1
    Sid:          S-1-5-21-1488595123-1430011218-1163345924-1000
    Logon time:   2012-01-17 01:34:46
    Logon server: LAPT8
    DNS Domain:
    UPN:

[6] Logon session 00000000:000882e3:
    User name:    LAPT8\jeh
    Auth package: NTLM
    Logon type:   Interactive
    Session:      1
    Sid:          S-1-5-21-1488595123-1430011218-1163345924-1000
    Logon time:   2012-01-17 01:34:46
    Logon server: LAPT8
    DNS Domain:
    UPN:
```

Information reported for a session includes the SID and name of the user associated with the session, as well as the session's authentication package and logon time. Note that the Negotiate authentication package, seen in logon session 2 in the preceding output, will attempt to authenticate via Kerberos or NTLM, depending on which is most appropriate for the authentication request.

The LUID for a session is displayed on the "Logon Session" line of each session block, and using the Handle utility (also from Sysinternals), you can find the tokens that represent a particular logon session. For example, to find the tokens for logon session 5 in the example output just shown, you could enter this command:

```
C:\Windows\system32>handle -a 882c2

Handle v3.46
Copyright (C) 1997-2011 Mark Russinovich
Sysinternals - www.sysinternals.com

System           pid: 4      type: Directory      D60: \Sessions\0\DosDevices\00000000-
000882c2
winlogon.exe     pid: 440    type: Event          DC:
 \BaseNamedObjects\00000000000882c2_WlballoonSmartCardUnlockNotificationEventName
winlogon.exe     pid: 440    type: Event          E4:
 \BaseNamedObjects\00000000000882c2_WlballoonKerberosNotificationEventName
winlogon.exe     pid: 440    type: Event          1D4:
 \BaseNamedObjects\00000000000882c2_WlballoonAlternateCredsNotificationEventName
lsass.exe        pid: 492    type: Token          508: LAPT8\jeh:882c2
lsass.exe        pid: 492    type: Token          634: LAPT8\jeh:882c2
svchost.exe      pid: 892    type: Token          7C4: LAPT8\jeh:882c2
svchost.exe      pid: 960    type: Token          E70: LAPT8\jeh:882c2
svchost.exe      pid: 960    type: Token          1034: LAPT8\jeh:882c2
svchost.exe      pid: 960    type: Token          1194: LAPT8\jeh:882c2
svchost.exe      pid: 960    type: Token          1384: LAPT8\jeh:882c2
```

Winlogon then looks in the registry at the value HKLM\SOFTWARE\Microsoft\Windows NT \Current Version\Winlogon\Userinit and creates a process to run whatever the value of that string is. (This value can be several .EXEs separated by commas.) The default value is Userinit.exe, which loads the user profile settings and then creates a process to run whatever the value of HKCU\SOFTWARE \Microsoft\Windows NT\Current Version\Winlogon\Shell is, if that value exists. That value does not exist by default. If it doesn't exist, Userinit.exe does the same for HKLM\SOFTWARE\Microsoft \Windows NT\Current Version\Winlogon\Shell, which defaults to Explorer.exe. Userinit then exits (which is why Explorer.exe shows up as having no parent when examined in Process Explorer). For more information on the steps followed during the user logon process, see Chapter 13, "Startup and Shutdown," in Part 2.

Assured Authentication

A fundamental problem with password-based authentication is that passwords can be revealed, or stolen, and used by malicious third parties. New in Windows 7 and Windows Server 2008/R2 is a mechanism that tracks the authentication strength of how a user authenticated with the system, which allows objects to be protected from access if a user did not authenticate securely. (Smartcard authentication is considered to be a stronger form of authentication than password authentication.)

On systems that are joined to a domain, the domain administrator can specify a mapping between an Object Identifier (OID), which is a unique numeric string representing a specific object type, on a certificate used for authenticating a user (such as on a smartcard or hardware security token) and a

Security ID (SID) that is placed into the user's access token when the user successfully authenticates with the system. An ACE in a DACL on an object can specify such a SID be part of a user's token in order for the user to gain access to the object. Technically, this is known as a group claim. In other words, the user is claiming membership in a particular group, which is allowed certain access rights on specific objects, with the claim based upon the authentication mechanism. This feature is not enabled by default, and it must be configured by the domain administrator in a domain with certificate-based authentication.

Assured Authentication builds upon existing Windows security features in a way that provides a great deal of flexibility to IT administrators and anyone concerned with enterprise IT security. The enterprise decides which OIDs to embed in the certificates it uses for authenticating users and the mapping of particular OIDs to Active Directory universal groups (SIDs). A user's group membership can be used to identify whether a certificate was used during the logon operation. Different certificates can have different issuance policies and, thus, different levels of security, which can be used to protect highly sensitive objects (such as files or anything else that might have a security descriptor).

Authentication protocols (APs) retrieve OIDs from certificates during certificate-based authentication. These OIDs must be mapped to SIDs, which are in turn processed during group membership expansion, and placed in the access token. The mapping of OID to universal group is specified in Active Directory.

As an example, an organization might have several certificate issuance policies with the names Contractor, Full Time Employee, and Senior Management, which map to the universal groups Contractor-Users, FTE-Users, and SM-Users, respectively. A user named Abby has a smartcard with a certificate issued using the Senior Management issuance policy, and when she logs in using her smartcard, she receives an additional group membership (which is represented by a SID in her access token) indicating that she is a member of the SM-Users group. Permissions can be set on objects (using an ACL) such that only members of the FTE-Users or SM-Users group (identified by their SIDs within an ACE) are granted access. If Abby logs in using her smartcard, she can access those objects, but if she logs in with just her user name and password (without the smartcard), she cannot access those objects because she will not have either the FTE-Users or SM-Users group in her access token. A user named Toby who logs in with a smartcard that has a certificate issued using the Contractor issuance policy would not be able to access an object that has an ACE requiring FTE-Users or SM-Users group membership.

Biometric Framework for User Authentication

Windows provides a standardized mechanism for supporting certain types of biometric devices—specifically, fingerprint scanners—to support user identification via a fingerprint swipe. Like many other such frameworks, the Windows Biometric Framework was developed to isolate the various functions involved in supporting such devices, so as to minimize the code required to implement a new device.

The primary components of the Windows Biometric Framework are shown in Figure 6-14. Except as noted in the following list, all of these components are supplied by Windows:

- **The Windows Biometric Service (%SystemRoot%\System32\Wbiosrvc.dll** This provides the process execution environment in which one or more biometric service providers can execute.

- **The Windows Biometric API** This allows existing Windows components such as WinLogon and LoginUI to access the biometric service. Third-party applications have access to the biometric API and can use the biometric scanner for functions other than logging in to Windows. An example of a function in this API is *WinBioEnumServiceProviders*. The Biometric API is exposed by %SystemRoot%\System32\Winbio.dll.

- **The Fingerprint Biometric Service Provider** This wraps the functions of biometric-type-specific adapters so as to present a common interface, independent of the type of biometric, to the Windows Biometric Service. In the future, additional types of biometrics, such as retinal scans or voiceprint analyzers, might be supported by additional Biometric Service Providers. The Biometric Service Provider in turn uses three adapters, which are user-mode DLLs:

  - The sensor adapter exposes the data-capture functionality of the scanner. The sensor adapter will usually use Windows I/O calls to access the scanner hardware. Windows provides a sensor adapter that can be used with simple sensors, those for which a Windows Biometric Device Interface (WBDI) driver exists. For more complex sensors, the sensor adapter is written by the sensor vendor.

  - The engine adapter exposes processing and comparison functionality specific to the scanner's raw data format and other features. The actual processing and comparison might be performed within the engine adapter DLL, or the DLL might communicate with some other module. The engine adapter is always provided by the sensor vendor.

  - The storage adapter exposes a set of secure storage functions. These are used to store and retrieve templates against which scanned biometric data is matched by the engine adapter. Windows provides a storage adapter using Windows cryptography services and standard disk file storage. A sensor vendor might provide a different storage adapter.

- **The Windows Biometric Driver Interface** This is a set of interface definitions (IRP major function codes, *DeviceIoControl* codes, and so forth) to which any driver for a biometric scanner device must conform if it is to be compatible with the Windows Biometric Service. WBDI is described in the Windows Driver Kit documentation. The Windows Driver Kit includes a sample WBDI driver.

- **The functional device driver for the actual biometric scanner device** This exposes the WBDI at its upper edge, and it usually uses the services of a lower-level bus driver, such as the USB bus driver, to access the scanner device. It can be a User-Mode Driver Framework (UMDF) driver, a Kernel-Mode Driver Framework (KMDF) driver, or a Windows Driver Model (WDM) driver. This driver is always provided by the sensor vendor. Microsoft recommends the use of UMDF and a USB hardware interface for the scanner.

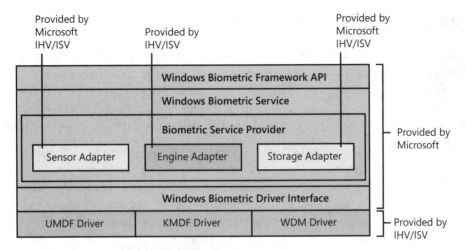

FIGURE 6-14 Windows Biometric Framework components and architecture

A typical sequence of operations to support logging in via a fingerprint scan might be as follows:

1. After initialization, the sensor adapter receives from the service provider a request for capture data. The sensor adapter in turn sends a *DeviceIoControl* request with the IOCTL_BIOMETRIC_ CAPTURE_DATA control code to the WBDI driver for the fingerprint scanner device.

2. The WBDI driver puts the scanner into capture mode and queues the IOCTL_BIOMETRIC_ CAPTURE_DATA request until a fingerprint scan occurs.

3. A prospective user swipes a finger across the scanner. The WBDI driver receives notification of this, obtains the raw scan data from the sensor, and returns this data to the sensor driver in a buffer associated with the IOCTL_BIOMETRIC_CAPTURE_DATA request.

4. The sensor adapter provides the data to the Fingerprint Biometric Service Provider, which in turn passes the data to the engine adapter.

5. The engine adapter processes the raw data into a form compatible with its template storage.

6. The Fingerprint Biometric Service Provider uses the storage adapter to obtain templates and corresponding security IDs from secure storage. It invokes the engine adapter to compare each template to the processed scan data. The engine adapter returns a status indicating whether it's a match or not a match.

7. If a match is found, the Biometric Service notifies WinLogon, via a credential provider DLL, of a successful login and passes it the security ID of the identified user. This notification is sent via an Advanced Local Procedure Call message, providing a path that cannot be spoofed

User Account Control and Virtualization

UAC is meant to enable users to run with standard user rights, as opposed to administrative rights. Without administrative rights, users cannot accidentally (or deliberately) modify system settings, malware can't normally alter system security settings or disable antivirus software, and users can't compromise the sensitive information of other users on shared computers. Running with standard user rights can thus mitigate the impact of malware and protect sensitive data on shared computers.

UAC had to address several problems to make it practical for a user to run with a standard user account. First, because the Windows usage model has been one of assumed administrative rights, software developers assumed their programs would run with those rights and so could access and modify any file, registry key, or operating system setting. The second problem UAC had to address was that users sometimes need administrative rights to perform such operations as installing software, changing the system time, and opening ports in the firewall.

The UAC solution to these problems is to run most applications with standard user rights, even though the user is logged in to an account with administrative rights; but at the same time, UAC makes it possible for standard users to access administrative rights when they need them—whether for legacy applications that require them or for changing certain system settings.

As described previously, UAC accomplishes this by creating a filtered admin token as well as the normal admin token when a user logs in to an administrative account. All processes created under the user's session will normally have the filtered admin token in effect so that applications that can run with standard user rights will do so. However, the administrative user can run a program or perform other functions that require full administrator rights by performing UAC Elevation.

Windows also allows certain tasks that were previously considered reserved for administrators to be performed by standard users, enhancing the usability of the standard user environment. For example, Group Policy settings exist that can enable standard users to install printer and other device drivers approved by IT administrators and to install ActiveX controls from administrator-approved sites.

Finally, when software developers test in the UAC environment, they are encouraged to develop applications that can run without administrative rights. Fundamentally, nonadministrative programs should not need to run with Administrator privileges; programs that often require Administrator privileges are typically legacy programs using old APIs or techniques, and they should be updated.

Together, these changes obviate the need for users to run with administrative rights all the time.

File System and Registry Virtualization

Although some software legitimately requires administrative rights, many programs needlessly store user data in system-global locations. When an application executes, it can be running in different user accounts, and it should therefore store user-specific data in the per-user %AppData% directory and save per-user settings in the user's registry profile under HKEY_CURRENT_USER\Software. Standard user accounts don't have write access to the %ProgramFiles% directory or HKEY_LOCAL_MACHINE \Software, but because most Windows systems are single-user and most users have been administrators until UAC was implemented, applications that incorrectly saved user data and settings to these locations worked anyway.

Windows enables these legacy applications to run in standard user accounts through the help of file system and registry namespace virtualization. When an application modifies a system-global location in the file system or registry and that operation fails because access is denied, Windows redirects the operation to a per-user area. When the application reads from a system-global location, Windows first checks for data in the per-user area and, if none is found, permits the read attempt from the global location.

Windows will always enable this type of virtualization unless

■   The application is 64-bit. Because virtualization is purely an application-compatibility technology meant to help legacy applications, it is enabled only for 32-bit applications. The world of 64-bit applications is relatively new and developers should follow the development guidelines for creating standard user-compatible applications.

■   The application is already running with administrative rights. In this case, there is no need for any virtualization.

■   The operation came from a kernel-mode caller.

■   The operation is being performed while the caller is impersonating. For example, any operations not originating from a process classified as legacy according to this definition, including network file-sharing accesses, are not virtualized.

■   The executable image for the process has a UAC-compatible manifest (specifying a *requestedExecutionLevel* setting, described in the next section).

■   The administrator does not have write access to the file or registry key. This exception exists to enforce backward compatibility, because the legacy application would have failed before UAC was implemented even if the application was run with administrative rights.

■   Services are never virtualized.

You can see the virtualization status (as discussed previously, the process' virtualization status is stored as a flag in its token) of a process by adding the UAC Virtualization column to Task Manager's Processes page, as shown in Figure 6-15. Most Windows components—including the Desktop Window Manager (Dwm.exe), the Client Server Run-Time Subsystem (Csrss.exe), and Explorer—have virtualization disabled because they have a UAC-compatible manifest or are running with administrative rights and so do not allow virtualization. Internet Explorer (Iexplore.exe) has virtualization enabled because it can host multiple ActiveX controls and scripts and must assume that they were not written to operate correctly with standard user rights.

In addition to file system and registry virtualization, some applications require additional help to run correctly with standard user rights. For example, an application that tests the account in which it's running for membership in the Administrators group might otherwise work, but it won't run if it's not in that group. Windows defines a number of application-compatibility shims to enable such applications to work anyway. The shims most commonly applied to legacy applications for operation with standard user rights are shown in Table 6-10. Note that, if required, virtualization can be completely disabled for a system using a local security policy setting.

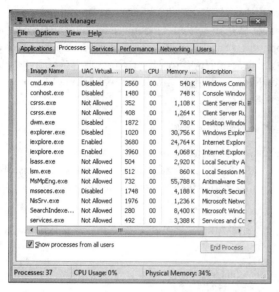

FIGURE 6-15 Using Task Manager to view virtualization status

TABLE 6-10 UAC Virtualization Shims

Flag	Meaning
ElevateCreateProcess	Changes *CreateProcess* to handle ERROR_ELEVATION_REQUIRED errors by calling the application information service to prompt for elevation
ForceAdminAccess	Spoofs queries of Administrator group membership
VirtualizeDeleteFile	Spoofs successful deletion of global files and directories
LocalMappedObject	Forces global section objects into the user's namespace
VirtualizeHKCRLite	Redirects global registration of COM objects to a per-user location
VirtualizeRegisterTypeLib	Converts per-machine *typelib* registrations to per-user registrations

File Virtualization

The file system locations that are virtualized for legacy processes are %ProgramFiles%, %ProgramData%, and %SystemRoot%, excluding some specific subdirectories. However, any file with an executable extension—including .exe, .bat, .scr, .vbs, and others—is excluded from virtualization. This means that programs that update themselves from a standard user account fail instead of creating private versions of their executables that aren't visible to an administrator running a global updater.

Note To add additional extensions to the exception list, enter them in the HKEY_LOCAL_
MACHINE\System\CurrentControlSet\Services\Luafv\Parameters\ExcludedExtensionsAdd
registry key and reboot. Use a multistring type to delimit multiple extensions, and do not
include a leading dot in the extension name.

Modifications to virtualized directories by legacy processes are redirected to the user's virtual
root directory, %LocalAppData%\VirtualStore. The Local component of the path highlights the fact
that virtualized files don't roam with the rest of the profile when the account has a roaming profile. If you navigate in Explorer to a directory containing virtualized files, Explorer displays a button
labeled Compatibility Files in its toolbar, as shown in Figure 6-16. Clicking the button takes you to the
corresponding VirtualStore subdirectory to show you the virtualized files.

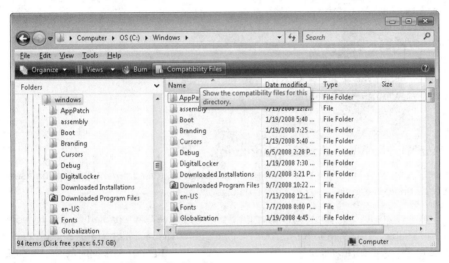

FIGURE 6-16 Virtualized files are displayed here

The UAC File Virtualization Filter Driver (%SystemRoot%\System32\Drivers\Luafv.sys) implements
file system virtualization. Because this is a file system filter driver, it sees all local file system
operations, but it implements functionality only for operations from legacy processes. As shown in
Figure 6-17, the filter driver changes the target file path for a legacy process that creates a file in a
system-global location but does not for a nonvirtualized process with standard user rights. Default
permissions on the \Windows directory deny access to the application written with UAC support, but
the legacy process acts as though the operation succeeds, when it really created the file in a location
fully accessible by the user.

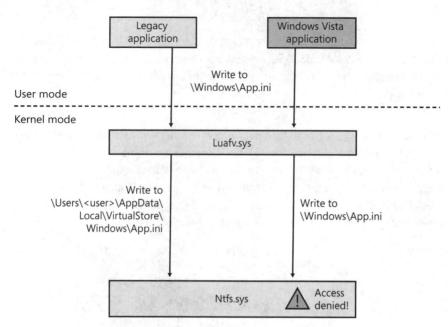

FIGURE 6-17 UAC File Virtualization Filter Driver operation

EXPERIMENT: File Virtualization Behavior

In this experiment, we will enable and disable virtualization on the command prompt and see several behaviors to demonstrate UAC file virtualization:

1. Open a nonelevated command prompt (you must have UAC enabled for this to work), and enable virtualization for it. You can change the virtualization status of a process by selecting UAC Virtualization from the shortcut menu that appears when you right-click the process in Task Manager.

2. Navigate to the C:\Windows directory, and use the following command to write a file:

   ```
   echo hello-1 > test.txt
   ```

3. Now list the contents of the directory:

   ```
   dir test.txt
   ```

   You'll see that the file appears.

4. Now disable virtualization by right-clicking on the process on the Processes page in Task Manager and deselecting UAC Virtualization, and then list the directory as in step 3. Notice that the file is gone. However, a directory listing of the VirtualStore directory will reveal the file:

   ```
   dir %LOCALAPPDATA%\VirtualStore\Windows\test.txt
   ```

5. Enable virtualization again for this process.

6. To take a look at a more complex scenario, create a new command prompt window, but elevate it this time, and then repeat steps 2 and 3 using the string "hello-2".

7. Examine the text inside these files by using the following command in both command prompts:

    ```
    echo test.txt
    ```

    The following two screen shots show the expected output.

8. Finally, from your elevated command prompt, delete the test.txt file:

    ```
    del test.txt
    ```

9. Repeat step 6 of the experiment. Notice that the elevated command prompt cannot find the file anymore, while the standard user command prompt shows the old contents of the file again. This demonstrates the failover mechanism described earlier—read operations will look in the per-user virtual store location first, but if the file doesn't exist, read access to the system location will be granted.

Registry Virtualization

Registry virtualization is implemented slightly differently from file system virtualization. Virtualized registry keys include most of the HKEY_LOCAL_MACHINE\Software branch, but there are numerous exceptions, such as the following:

- HKLM\Software\Microsoft\Windows

- HKLM\Software\Microsoft\Windows NT

- HKLM\Software\Classes

Only keys that are commonly modified by legacy applications, but that don't introduce compatibility or interoperability problems, are virtualized. Windows redirects modifications of virtualized keys by a legacy application to a user's registry virtual root at HKEY_CURRENT_USER \Software\Classes\VirtualStore. The key is located in the user's Classes hive, %LocalAppData% \Microsoft\Windows\UsrClass.dat, which, like any other virtualized file data, does not roam with a roaming user profile. Instead of maintaining a fixed list of virtualized locations as Windows does for the file system, the virtualization status of a key is stored as a combination of flags, shown in Table 6-11.

TABLE 6-11 Registry Virtualization Flags

Flag	Meaning
REG_KEY_DONT_VIRTUALIZE	Specifies whether virtualization is enabled for this key. If the flag is set, virtualization is disabled.
REG_KEY_DONT_SILENT_FAIL	If the REG_KEY_DONT_VIRTUALIZE flag is set (virtualization is disabled), this key specifies that a legacy application that would be denied access performing an operation on the key is instead granted MAXIMUM_ALLOWED rights to the key (any access the account is granted), instead of the rights the application requested. If this flag is set, it implicitly disables virtualization as well.
REG_KEY_RECURSE_FLAG	Determines whether the virtualization flags will propagate to the child keys (subkeys) of this key.

You can use the Reg.exe utility included in Windows, with the flags option, to display the current virtualization state for a key or to set it. In Figure 6-18, note that the HKLM\Software key is fully virtualized, but the Windows subkey (and all its children) have only silent failure enabled.

FIGURE 6-18 UAC registry virtualization flags on the Software and Windows keys

Unlike file virtualization, which uses a filter driver, registry virtualization is implemented in the configuration manager. (See Chapter 4 for more information on the registry and the configuration manager.) As with file system virtualization, a legacy process creating a subkey of a virtualized key is redirected to the user's registry virtual root, but a UAC-compatible process is denied access by default permissions. This is shown in Figure 6-19.

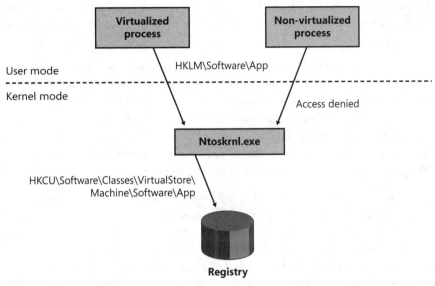

FIGURE 6-19 UAC registry virtualization operation

Elevation

Even if users run only programs that are compatible with standard user rights, some operations still require administrative rights. For example, the vast majority of software installations require administrative rights to create directories and registry keys in system-global locations or to install services or device drivers. Modifying system-global Windows and application settings also requires administrative rights, as does the parental controls feature. It would be possible to perform most of these operations by switching to a dedicated administrator account, but the inconvenience of doing so would likely result in most users remaining in the administrator account to perform their daily tasks, most of which do not require administrative rights.

It's important to be aware that UAC elevations are conveniences and not security boundaries. A security boundary requires that security policy dictate what can pass through the boundary. User accounts are an example of a security boundary in Windows, because one user can't access the data belonging to another user without having that user's permission.

Because elevations aren't security boundaries, there's no guarantee that malware running on a system with standard user rights can't compromise an elevated process to gain administrative rights. For example, elevation dialog boxes only identify the executable that will be elevated; they say nothing about what it will do when it executes.

Running with Administrator Rights

Windows includes enhanced "run as" functionality so that standard users can conveniently launch processes with administrative rights. This functionality requires giving applications a way to identify operations for which the system can obtain administrative rights on behalf of the application, as necessary. (We'll say more on this topic shortly.)

To enable users acting as system administrators to run with standard user rights but not have to enter user names and passwords every time they want to access administrative rights, Windows makes use of a mechanism called Admin Approval Mode (AAM). This feature creates two identities for the user at logon: one with standard user rights and another with administrative rights. Since every user on a Windows system is either a standard user or acting for the most part as a standard user in AAM, developers must assume that all Windows users are standard users, which will result in more programs working with standard user rights without virtualization or shims.

Granting administrative rights to a process is called elevation. When elevation is performed by a standard user account (or by a user who is part of an administrative group but not the actual Administrators group), it's referred to as an over-the-shoulder (OTS) elevation because it requires the entry of credentials for an account that's a member of the Administrators group, something that's usually completed by a user typing over the shoulder of a standard user. An elevation performed by an AAM user is called a consent elevation because the user simply has to approve the assignment of his administrative rights.

Stand-alone systems, which are typically home computers, and domain-joined systems treat AAM access by remote users differently because domain-connected computers can use domain administrative groups in their resource permissions. When a user accesses a stand-alone computer's file share, Windows requests the remote user's standard user identity, but on domain-joined systems, Windows honors all the user's domain group memberships by requesting the user's administrative identity. Executing an image that requests administrative rights causes the application information service (AIS, contained in %SystemRoot%\System32\Appinfo.dll), which runs inside a service host process (%SystemRoot%\System32\Svchost.exe), to launch Consent.exe (%SystemRoot%\System32\Consent.exe). Consent captures a bitmap of the screen, applies a fade effect to it, switches to a desktop that's accessible only to the local system account (the secure desktop), paints the bitmap as the background, and displays an elevation dialog box that contains information about the executable. Displaying this dialog box on a separate desktop prevents any application present in the user's account from modifying the appearance of the dialog box.

If an image is a Windows component digitally signed by Microsoft and the image is in the Windows system directory, the dialog box displays a blue stripe across the top, as shown at the top of Figure 6-20, with a blue and gold shield at the left end of the stripe. If the image is signed by someone other than Microsoft, or if it is signed by Microsoft but resides in a directory tree other than the Windows directory tree, the shield becomes solid blue with a question mark over it. If the image is unsigned, the shield background and the stripe both become orange, the shield has an exclamation point over it, and the prompt stresses the unknown origin of the image. The elevation dialog box shows the image's icon, description, and publisher for digitally signed images, but it shows only the file name and "Unknown publisher" for unsigned images. This difference makes it harder for malware to mimic the appearance of legitimate software. The Details button at the bottom of the dialog box expands it to show the command line that will be passed to the executable if it launches.

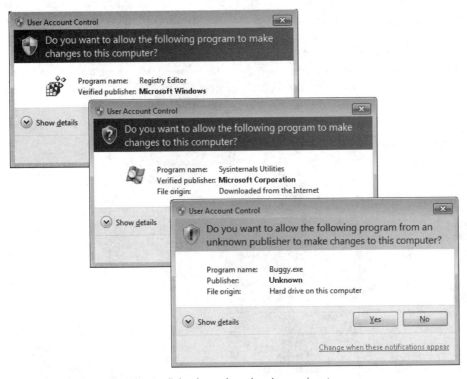

FIGURE 6-20 AAC UAC elevation dialog boxes based on image signature

The OTS consent dialog box, shown in Figure 6-21, is similar, but prompts for administrator credentials. It will list any accounts with administrator rights.

FIGURE 6-21 OTS consent dialog box

If a user declines an elevation, Windows returns an access-denied error to the process that initiated the launch. When a user agrees to an elevation by either entering administrator credentials or clicking Continue, AIS calls *CreateProcessAsUser* to launch the process with the appropriate administrative identity. Although AIS is technically the parent of the elevated process, AIS uses new support in the *CreateProcessAsUser* API that sets the process' parent process ID to that of the process that originally launched it. (See Chapter 5, "Processes and Threads," for more information on processes and this mechanism.) That's why elevated processes don't appear as children of the AIS service-hosting process in tools such as Process Explorer that show process trees. Figure 6-22 shows the operations involved in launching an elevated process from a standard user account.

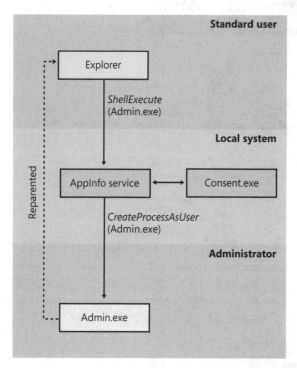

FIGURE 6-22 Launching an administrative application as a standard user

Requesting Administrative Rights

There are a number of ways the system and applications identify a need for administrative rights. One that shows up in the Explorer user interface is the Run As Administrator context menu command and shortcut option. These items also include a blue and gold shield icon that should be placed next to any button or menu item that will result in an elevation of rights when it is selected. Choosing the Run As Administrator command causes Explorer to call the *ShellExecute* API with the "runas" verb.

The vast majority of installation programs require administrative rights, so the image loader, which initiates the launch of an executable, includes installer-detection code to identify likely legacy installers. Some of the heuristics it uses are as simple as detecting internal version information or whether the image has the words setup, install, or update in its file name. More sophisticated means of detection involve scanning for byte sequences in the executable that are common to third-party installation wrapper utilities. The image loader also calls the application compatibility library to see if the target executable requires administrator rights. The library looks in the application compatibility database to see whether the executable has the *RequireAdministrator* or *RunAsInvoker* compatibility flag associated with it.

The most common way for an executable to request administrative rights is for it to include a *requestedExecutionLevel* tag in its application manifest file. The element's level attribute can have one of the three values shown in Table 6-12.

TABLE 6-12 Requested Elevation Levels

Elevation Level	Meaning	Usage
As Invoker	No need for administrative rights; never ask for elevation.	Typical user applications that don't need administrative privileges—for example, Notepad.
Highest Available	Request approval for highest rights available. If the user is logged on as a standard user, the process will be launched as invoker; otherwise, an AAM elevation prompt will appear, and the process will run with full administrative rights.	Applications that can function without full administrative rights but expect users to want full access if it's easily accessible. For example, the Registry Editor, Microsoft Management Console, and the Event Viewer use this level.
Require Administrator	Always request administrative rights—an OTS elevation dialog box prompt will be shown for standard users; otherwise, AAM.	Applications that require administrative rights to work, such as the Firewall Settings editor, which affects systemwide security.

The presence of the *trustInfo* element in a manifest (which you can see in the excerpted string dump of eventvwr.exe discussed next) denotes an executable that was written with support for UAC and the *requestedExecutionLevel* element nests within it. The *uiAccess* attribute is where accessibility applications can use the UIPI bypass functionality mentioned earlier.

```
C:\>strings c:\Windows\System32\eventvwr.exe
...
<trustInfo xmlns="urn:schemas-microsoft-com:asm.v3">
    <security>
        <requestedPrivileges>
            <requestedExecutionLevel
                level="highestAvailable"
                uiAccess="false"
            />
        </requestedPrivileges>
    </security>
</trustInfo>
<asmv3:application>
    <asmv3:windowsSettings xmlns="http://schemas.microsoft.com/SMI/2005/WindowsSettings">
        <autoElevate>true</autoElevate>
    </asmv3:windowsSettings>
</asmv3:application>
...
```

An easier way to determine the values specified by an executable is to view its manifest with the Sysinternals Sigcheck utility, like this:

```
sigcheck -m <executable>
```

EXPERIMENT: Using Application-Compatibility Flags

In this experiment, we will use an application-compatibility flag to run the Registry Editor as a standard user process. This will bypass the *RequireAdministrator* manifest flag and force virtualization on Regedit.exe, allowing you to make changes to the virtualized registry directly.

1. Navigate to your %SystemRoot% directory, and copy the Regedit.exe file to another path on your system (such as C:\ or your Desktop folder).

2. Go to the HKLM\Software\Microsoft\Windows NT\CurrentVersion\AppCompatFlags \Layers registry key, and create a new string value whose name is the path where you copied Regedit.exe, such as c:\regedit.exe

3. Set the value of this key to RUNASINVOKER.

4. Now start Regedit.exe from its location. (Be sure to close any running copies of the Registry Editor first.) You will not see the typical AAM dialog box, and Regedit.exe will now run with standard user rights. You will also be subject to the virtualized view of the registry, meaning you can now see what legacy applications see when accessing the registry.

Auto-Elevation

In the default configuration (see the next section for information on changing this), most Windows executables and control panel applets do not result in elevation prompts for administrative users, even if they need administrative rights to run. This is because of a mechanism called auto-elevation. Auto-elevation is intended to preclude administrative users from seeing elevation prompts for most of their work; the programs will automatically run under the user's full administrative token.

Auto-elevation has several requirements. The executable in question must be considered as a Windows executable. This means it must be signed by the Windows publisher (not just by Microsoft), and it must be in one of several directories considered secure: %SystemRoot%\System32 and most of its subdirectories, %Systemroot%\Ehome, and a small number of directories under %ProgramFiles%—for example, those containing Windows Defender and Windows Journal.

There are additional requirements, depending on the type of executable.

.exe files other than Mmc.exe auto-elevate if they are requested via an *autoElevate* element in their manifest. The string dump of EventVwr.exe in the previous section illustrates this.

Windows also includes a short internal list of executables that are auto-elevated without the autoElevate element. Two examples are Spinstall.exe, the service pack installer, and Pkgmgr. exe, the package manager. They are handled this way because they are also supplied external to Windows 7; they must be able to run on earlier versions of Windows where the autoExecute element in their manifest might cause an error. These executables must still meet the signing and directory requirements for Windows executables as described previously.

Mmc.exe is treated as a special case, because whether it should auto-elevate or not depends on which system management snap-ins it is to load. Mmc.exe is normally invoked with a command line specifying an .msc file, which in turn specifies which snap-ins are to be loaded. When Mmc.exe is run from a protected administrator account (one running with the limited administrator token), it asks Windows for administrative rights. Windows validates that Mmc.exe is a Windows executable and then checks the .msc. The .msc must also pass the tests for a Windows executable, and furthermore must be on an internal list of auto-elevate .msc's. This list includes nearly all .msc files in Windows.

Finally, COM objects can request administrative rights within their registry key. To do so requires a subkey named Elevation with a REG_DWORD value named Enabled, having a value of 1. Both the COM object and its instantiating executable must meet the Windows executable requirements, though the executable need not have requested auto-elevation.

Controlling UAC Behavior

UAC can be modified via the dialog box shown in Figure 6-23. This dialog box is available under Control Panel, Action Center, Change User Account Control Settings. Figure 6-23 shows the control in its default position for Windows 7.

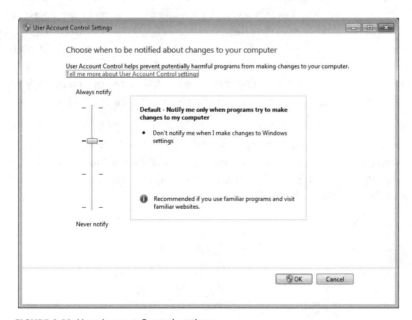

FIGURE 6-23 User Account Control settings

The four possible settings have the effects described in Table 6-13.

TABLE 6-13 User Account Control Options

| Slider Position | When administrative user not running with administrative rights... | | Remarks |
	...attempts to change Windows settings, for example, use certain Control Panel applets	...attempts to install software, or run a program whose manifest calls for elevation, or uses Run As Administrator	
Highest position ("Always notify")	UAC elevation prompt appears on the secure desktop	UAC elevation prompt appears on the secure desktop	This was the Windows Vista behavior
Second position	UAC elevation occurs automatically with no prompt or notification	UAC elevation prompt appears on the secure desktop	Windows 7 default setting
Third position	UAC elevation occurs automatically with no prompt or notification	UAC elevation prompt appears on the user's normal desktop	Not recommended
Lowest position ("Never notify")	UAC is turned off for administrative users	UAC is turned off for administrative users	Not recommended.

The third position is not recommended because the UAC elevation prompt appears not on the secure desktop but on the normal user's desktop. This could allow a malicious program running in the same session to change the appearance of the prompt. It is intended for use only in systems where the video subsystem takes a long time to dim the desktop or is otherwise unsuitable for the usual UAC display.

The lowest position is strongly discouraged because it turns UAC off completely as far as administrative accounts are concerned. All processes run by a user with an administrative account will be run with the user's full administrative rights in effect; there is no filtered admin token. Registry and file system virtualization are disabled as well for these accounts, and the Protected mode of Internet Explorer is disabled. However, virtualization is still in effect for nonadministrative accounts, and nonadministrative accounts will still see an OTS elevation prompt when they attempt to change Windows settings, run a program that requires elevation, or use the Run As Administrator context menu option in Explorer.

The UAC setting is stored in four values in the registry under HKEY_LOCAL_MACHINE \SOFTWARE\Microsoft\Windows\CurrentVersion\Policies\System, as shown in Table 6-14. ConsentPromptBehaviorAdmin controls the UAC elevation prompt for administrators running with a filtered admin token, and ConsentPromptBehaviorUser controls the UAC prompt for users other than administrators.

TABLE 6-14 User Account Control Registry Values

Slider Position	ConsentPrompt BehaviorAdmin	ConsentPrompt BehaviorUser	EnableLUA	PromptOnSecureDesktop
Highest position ("Always notify")	2 (display AAC UAC elevation prompt)	3 (display OTS UAC elevation prompt)	1 (enabled)	1 (enabled)
Second position	5 (display AAC UAC elevation prompt, except for changes to Windows settings)	3	1	1
Third position	5	3	1	0 (disabled; UAC prompt appears on user's normal desktop)
Lowest position ("Never notify")	0	3	0 (disabled. Logins to administrative accounts do not create a restricted admin access token)	0

Application Identification (AppID)

Historically, security decisions in Windows have been based upon a user's identity (in the form of the user's SID and group membership), but a growing number of security components (AppLocker, firewall, antivirus, antimalware, Rights Management Services, and others) need to make security decisions based upon what code is to be run. In the past, each of these security components used their own proprietary method for identifying applications, which led to inconsistent and overly-complicated policy authoring. The purpose of AppID is to bring consistency to how the security components recognize applications by providing a single set of APIs and data structures.

> **Note** This is not the same as the AppID used by DCOM/COM+ applications, where a GUID represents a process that is shared by multiple CLSIDs, nor is it the AppID used by Windows Live applications.

Just as a user is identified when she logs in, an application is identified just before it is started by generating the main program's AppID. An AppID can be generated from any of the following attributes of the application: Fields within a code-signing certificate embedded within the file allow for different combinations of publisher name, product name, file name, and version. APPID://FQBN is a Fully Qualified Binary Name, and it is a string in the following form: {Publisher\Product\Filename,Version}. The Publisher name is the Subject field of the x.509 certificate used to sign the code, using the following fields: O = Organization, L = Locality, S = State or Province, and C = Country.

File hash. There are several methods that can be used for hashing. The default is APPID://SHA256HASH. However, for backward compatibility with SRP and most x.509 certificates, SHA-1 (APPID://SHA1HASH) is still supported. APPID://SHA256HASH specifies the SHA-256 hash of the file.

The partial or complete path to the file. APPID://Path specifies a path with optional wildcard characters ("*").

> **Note** An AppID does not serve as a means for certifying the quality or security of an application. An AppID is simply a way of identifying an application so that administrators can reference the application in security policy decisions.

The AppID is stored in the process's access token, allowing any security component to make authorization decisions based upon a single, consistent identification. AppLocker uses conditional ACEs (described earlier) for specifying whether a particular program is allowed to be run by the user.

When an AppID is created for a signed file, the certificate from the file is cached and verified to a trusted root certificate. The certificate path is re-verified daily to ensure the certificate path remains valid. Certificate caching and verification are recorded in the system event log. See Figure 6-24.

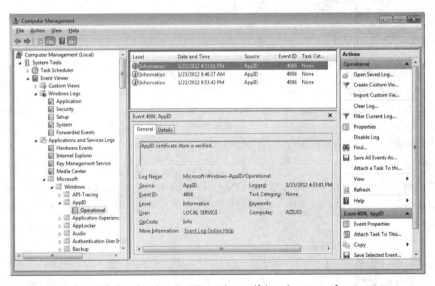

FIGURE 6-24 Event Viewer showing AppID service verifying signature of a program.

AppLocker

New to Windows 7 and Windows Server 2008/R2 (Enterprise and Ultimate editions) is a feature known as AppLocker, which allows an administrator to lockdown a system to prevent unauthorized programs from being run. Windows XP introduced Software Restriction Policies (SRP), which was the first step toward this capability, but SRP suffered from being difficult to manage, and it couldn't be applied to specific users or groups. (All users were affected by SRP rules.) AppLocker is a replacement for SRP, and yet coexists alongside SRP, with AppLocker's rules being stored separately from SRP's rules. If both AppLocker and SRP rules are in the same Group Policy object (GPO), only the AppLocker rules will be applied. Another feature that makes AppLocker superior to SRP is AppLocker's auditing mode, which allows an administrator to create an AppLocker policy and examine the results (stored in the system event log) to determine whether the policy will perform as expected—without actually performing the restrictions. AppLocker auditing mode can be used to monitor which applications are being used by one, or more, users on a system.

AppLocker allows an administrator to restrict the following types of files from being run:

- Executable images (.EXE and .COM)

- Dynamic-Link Libraries (.DLL and .OCX)

- Microsoft Software Installer (.MSI and .MSP) for both install and uninstall

- Scripts

- Windows PowerShell (.PS1)

- Batch (.BAT and .CMD)

- VisualBasic Script (.VBS)

- Java Script (.JS)

AppLocker provides a simple GUI rule-based mechanism, which is very similar to network firewall rules, for determining which applications or scripts are allowed to be run by specific users and groups, using conditional ACEs and AppID attributes. There are two types of rules in AppLocker:

- Allow the specified files to run, denying everything else.

- Deny the specified files from being run, allowing everything else. "Deny" rules take precedence over "allow" rules.

Each rule can also have a list of exceptions to exclude files from the rule. Using an exception, you could create a rule to "Allow everything in the C:\Windows or C:\Program Files directories to be run, except the built-in games."

AppLocker rules can be associated with a specific user or group. This allows an administrator to support compliance requirements by validating and enforcing which users can run specific applications. For example, you can create a rule to "Allow users in the Finance security group to run the finance line-of-business applications." This blocks everyone who is not in the Finance security group from running finance applications (including administrators) but still provides access for those that have a business need to run the applications. Another useful rule would be to prevent users in the Receptionists group from installing or running unapproved software.

AppLocker rules depend upon conditional ACEs and attributes defined by AppID. Rules can be created using the following criteria:

- Fields within a code-signing certificate embedded within the file, allowing for different combinations of publisher name, product name, file name, and version. For example, a rule could be created to "Allow all versions greater than 9.0 of Contoso Reader to run" or "Allow anyone in the graphics group to run the installer or application from Contoso for GraphicsShop as long as the version is 14.*". For example, the following SDDL string denies execute access to any signed programs published by Contoso for the user account RestrictedUser (identified by the user's SID):

```
D:(XD;;FX;;;S-1-5-21-3392373855-1129761602-2459801163-1028;((Exists APPID://FQBN)
&& ((APPID://FQBN) >= ({"O=CONTOSO, INCORPORATED, L=REDMOND,
S=CWASHINGTON, C=US\*\*",0})))))
```

- Directory path, allowing only files within a particular directory tree to run. This can also be used to identify specific files. For example, the following SDDL string denies execute access to the programs in the directory C:\Tools for the user account RestrictedUser (identified by the user's SID):

```
D:(XD;;FX;;;S-1-5-21-3392373855-1129761602-2459801163-1028;(APPID://PATH
Contains "%OSDRIVE%\TOOLS\*"))
```

- File hash. Using a hash will also detect if a file has been modified and prevent it from running, which can also be a weakness if files are changed frequently, because the hash rule will need to be updated frequently. File hashes are often used for scripts because few scripts are signed. For example, this SDDL string denies execute access to programs with the specified hash values for the user account RestrictedUser (identified by the user's SID):

```
D:(XD;;FX;;;S-1-5-21-3392373855-1129761602-2459801163-1028;(APPID://SHA256HASH
Any_of {#7a334d2b99d48448eedd308dfca63b8a3b7b44044496ee2f8e236f5997f1b647,
#2a782f76cb94ece307dc52c338f02edbbfdca83906674e35c682724a8a92a76b}))
```

AppLocker rules can be defined on the local machine using the Security Policy MMC snap-in (%SystemRoot%\System32\secpol.msc) or a Windows PowerShell script, or they can be pushed to machines within a domain using group policy. AppLocker rules are stored in multiple locations within the registry:

- **HKLM\Software\Policies\Microsoft\Windows\SrpV2** This key is also mirrored to HKLM\SOFTWARE\Wow6432Node\Policies\Microsoft\Windows\SrpV2. The rules are stored in XML format.

- **HKLM\SYSTEM\CurrentControlSet\Control\Srp\Gp\Exe** The rules are stored as SDDL and a binary ACE.

- **HKEY_CURRENT_USER\Software\Microsoft\Windows\CurrentVersion\Group Policy Objects\{GUID}Machine\Software\Policies\Microsoft\Windows\SrpV2** AppLocker policy pushed down from a domain as part of a Group Policy Object (GPO) are stored here in XML format.

Certificates for files that have been run are cached in the registry under the key HKLM\SYSTEM\CurrentControlSet\Control\AppID\CertStore. AppLocker also builds a certificate chain (stored in HKLM\SYSTEM\CurrentControlSet\Control\AppID\CertChainStore) from the certificate found in a file back to a trusted root certificate. See Figure 6-25.

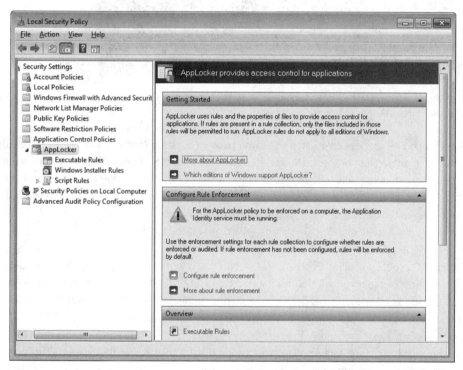

FIGURE 6-25 AppLocker configuration page in Local Security Policy

There are also AppLocker-specific PowerShell commands (also known as cmdlets) to enable deployment and testing via scripting. Figure 6-26 demonstrates using PowerShell commands to determine which files in a directory tree have been signed, saving the current AppLocker policy in an XML file, and displaying which executable files in a directory tree could be run by a user named RestrictedUser.

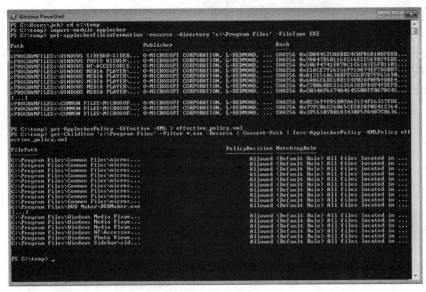

FIGURE 6-26 Powershell cmdlets used to examine executables for signatures, save AppLocker policies in an XML file, and test the ability of a user to run the executables

The AppID and SRP services co-exist in the same binary (%SystemRoot%\System32\AppIdSvc.dll), which runs within an SvcHost process. The service requests a registry change notification to monitor any changes under that key, which is written by either a GPO or the AppLocker UI in the Local Security Policy MMC snap-in. When a change is detected, the AppID service triggers a user-mode task (%SystemRoot%\System32\AppIdPolicyConverter.exe), which reads the new XML rules and translates them into binary format ACEs and SDDL strings, which are understandable by both the user-mode and kernel-mode AppID and AppLocker components. The task stores the translated rules under HKLM\SYSTEM\CurrentControlSet\Control\Srp\Gp. This key is writable only by SYSTEM and Administrators, and it is marked read-only for authenticated users. Both user-mode and kernel-mode AppID components read the translated rules from the registry directly. The service also monitors the local machine trusted root certificate store, and it invokes a user-mode task (%SystemRoot%\System32 \AppIdCertStoreCheck.exe) to reverify the certificates at least once per day and whenever there is a change to the certificate store. The AppID kernel-mode driver (%SystemRoot%\System32\drivers \AppId.sys) is notified about rule changes by the AppID service through an APPID_POLICY_CHANGED DeviceIoControl request. See Figure 6-27.

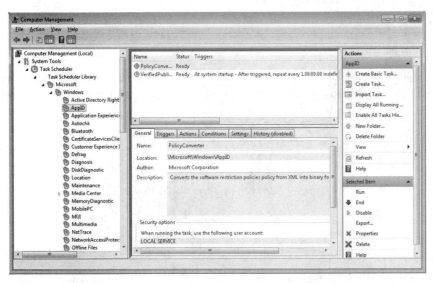

FIGURE 6-27 Scheduled task that runs every day to convert software restriction policies stored in XML to binary format

An administrator can track which applications are being allowed or denied by looking at the system Event Log using the event viewer (once AppLocker has been configured and the service started). See Figure 6-28.

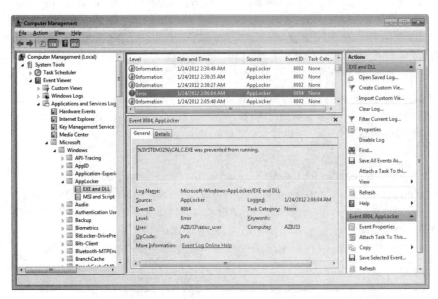

FIGURE 6-28 Event Viewer showing AppLocker allowing and denying access to various applications. Event ID 8004 is "denied"; 8002 is "allowed."

The implementations of AppID, AppLocker, and SRP are somewhat blurred and violate strict layering, with various logical components co-existing within the same executables, and the naming is not as consistent as one would like.

The AppID service runs as LocalService so that it has access to the Trusted Root Certificate Store on the system. This also enables it to perform certificate verification. The AppID service is responsible for the following:

- Verification of publisher certificates

- Adding new certificates to the cache

- Detecting AppLocker rule updates, and notifying the AppID driver

The AppID driver performs the majority of the AppLocker functionality and relies upon communication (via *DeviceIoControl* requests) from the AppID service, so its device object is protected by an ACL, granting access only to the NT SERVICE\AppIDSvc, NT SERVICE\LOCAL SERVICE and BUILTIN\Administrators groups. Thus, the driver cannot be spoofed by malware.

When the AppID driver is first loaded, it requests a process creation callback (*CreateProcessNotifyEx*) by calling *PsSetCreateProcessNotifyRoutineEx*. When the *CreateProcessNotifyEx* routine is called, it is passed a PPS_CREATE_NOTIFY_INFO structure (describing the process being created). It then gathers the AppID attributes that identify the executable image and writes them to the process' access token. Then it calls the undocumented routine *SeSrpAccessCheck*, which examines the process token and the conditional ACE AppLocker rules, and determines whether the process should be allowed to run. If the process should not be allowed to run, the driver writes STATUS_ACCESS_DISABLED_BY_POLICY_OTHER to the Status field of the PPS_CREATE_NOTIFY_INFO structure, which causes the process creation to be canceled (and sets the process' final completion status).

To perform DLL restriction, the image loader will send a *DeviceIoControl* request to the AppID driver whenever it loads a DLL into a process. The driver then checks the DLL's identity against the AppLocker conditional ACEs, just like it would for an executable.

> **Note** Performing these checks for every DLL load is time consuming and might be noticeable to end users. For this reason, DLL rules are normally disabled, and they must be specifically enabled via the Advanced tab in the AppLocker properties page in the Local Security Policy snap-in.

The scripting engines and the MSI installer have been modified to call the user-mode SRP APIs whenever they open a file, to check whether a file is allowed to be opened. The user-mode SRP APIs call the AuthZ APIs to perform the conditional ACE access check.

Software Restriction Policies

Windows also contains a user-mode mechanism called Software Restriction Policies that enables administrators to control what images and scripts execute on their systems. The Software Restriction Policies node of the Local Security Policy Editor, shown in Figure 6-29, serves as the management interface for a machine's code execution policies, although per-user policies are also possible using domain group policies.

Several global policy settings appear beneath the Software Restriction Policies node:

- The Enforcement policy configures whether restriction policies apply to libraries, such as DLLs, and whether policies apply to users only or to administrators as well.

- The Designated File Types policy records the extensions for files that are considered executable code.

- Trusted Publishers control who can select which certificate publishers are trusted.

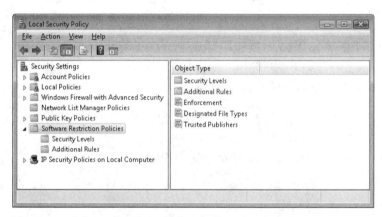

FIGURE 6-29 Software Restriction Policy configuration

When configuring a policy for a particular script or image, an administrator can direct the system to recognize it using its path, its hash, its Internet Zone (as defined by Internet Explorer), or its cryptographic certificate, and she can specify whether it is associated with the Disallowed or Unrestricted security policy.

Enforcement of Software Restriction Policies takes place within various components where files are treated as containing executable code. Some of these components are listed here:

- The user-mode Windows *CreateProcess* function in %SystemRoot%\System32\Kernel32.dll enforces it for executable images.

- The DLL loading code of Ntdll (%SystemRoot%\System32\Ntdll.dll) enforces it for DLLs.

- The Windows command prompt (%SystemRoot%\System32\Cmd.exe) enforces it for batch file execution.

- Windows Scripting Host components that start scripts—%SystemRoot%\System32\Cscript.exe (for command-line scripts), %SystemRoot%\System32\Wscript.exe (for UI scripts), and %SystemRoot%\System32\Scrobj.dll (for script objects)—enforce it for script execution.

Each of these components determines whether the restriction policies are enabled by reading the registry value HKEY_LOCAL_MACHINE\Software\Microsoft\Policies\Windows\Safer\CodeIdentifiers \TransparentEnabled, which if set to 1 indicates that policies are in effect. Then it determines whether the code it's about to execute matches one of the rules specified in a subkey of the CodeIdentifiers key and, if so, whether or not the execution should be allowed. If there is no match, the default policy, as specified in the DefaultLevel value of the CodeIdentifiers key, determines whether the execution is allowed.

Software Restriction Policies are a powerful tool for preventing the unauthorized access of code and scripts, but only if properly applied. Unless the default policy is set to disallow execution, a user can make minor changes to an image that's been marked as disallowed so that he can bypass the rule and execute it. For example, a user can change an innocuous byte of a process image so that a hash rule fails to recognize it, or copy a file to a different location to avoid a path-based rule.

EXPERIMENT: Watching Software Restriction Policy Enforcement

You can indirectly see Software Restriction Policies being enforced by watching accesses to the registry when you attempt to execute an image that you've disallowed.

1. Run secpol.msc to open the Local Security Policy Editor, and navigate to the Software Restriction Policies node.

2. Choose Create New Policies from the context menu if no policies are defined.

3. Create a path-based disallow restriction policy for %SystemRoot%\System32\Notepad.exe.

4. Run Process Monitor, and set an include filter for Safer. (See Chapter 4 for a description of Process Monitor.)

5. Open a command prompt, and run Notepad from the prompt.

Your attempt to run Notepad should result in a message telling you that you cannot execute the specified program, and Process Monitor should show the command prompt (cmd.exe) querying the local machine restriction policies.

Conclusion

Windows provides an extensive array of security functions that meet the key requirements of both government agencies and commercial installations. In this chapter, we've taken a brief tour of the internal components that are the basis of these security features. In the next chapter, we'll look at the I/O system.

CHAPTER 7

Networking

Microsoft Windows was designed with networking in mind, and it includes broad networking support that is integrated with the I/O system and the Windows APIs. The four basic types of network software components are services, APIs, protocols, and drivers for network adapters—with each component layered on top of the next to form a network stack. Windows has well-defined interfaces for each layer, so in addition to using the wide variety of APIs, protocols, and network adapter device drivers that ship with Windows, third parties can extend the operating system's networking capabilities by developing their own components.

In this chapter, we take you from the top of the Windows networking stack to the bottom. First, we present the mapping between the Windows networking software components and the Open Systems Interconnection (OSI) reference model. Then we briefly describe the networking APIs available on Windows and explain how they are implemented. You'll learn how multiple redirector support and name resolution work, see how to access and cache remote files, and learn how a multitude of drivers interact to form a network protocol stack. After looking at the implementation of network adapter device drivers, we examine *binding*, which is the glue that connects services, protocol stacks, and network adapters.

Windows Networking Architecture

The goal of network software is to take a request (in the form of an I/O request) from an application on one machine, pass it to another machine, execute the request on the remote machine, and return the results to the first machine. In the course of this process, the request must be transformed several times. A high-level request, such as "read *x* number of bytes from file *y* on machine *z*," requires software that can determine how to get to machine *z* and what communication software that machine understands. Then the request must be altered for transmission across a network—for example, divided into short packets of information. When the request reaches the other side, it must be checked for completeness, decoded, and sent to the correct operating system component for execution. Finally, the reply must be encoded for sending back across the network.

The OSI Reference Model

To help different computer manufacturers standardize and integrate their networking software, in 1984 the International Organization for Standardization (ISO) defined a software model for sending messages between machines. The result was the *Open Systems Interconnection* (OSI) *reference model*. The model defines six layers of software and one physical layer of hardware, as shown in Figure 7-1.

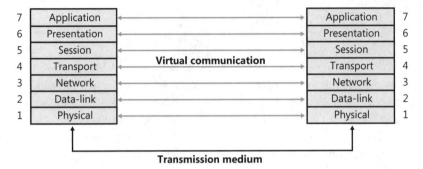

FIGURE 7-1 OSI reference model

The OSI reference model is an idealized scheme that few systems implement precisely, but it's often used to frame discussions of networking principles. Each layer on one machine assumes that it is "talking to" the same layer on the other machine. Both machines "speak" the same language, or protocol, at the same level. In reality, however, a network transmission must pass down each layer on the client machine, be transmitted across the network, and then pass up the layers on the destination machine until it reaches a layer that can understand and implement the request.

The purpose of each layer in the OSI model is to provide services to higher layers and to abstract how the services are implemented at lower layers. Describing the details of each layer is beyond the scope of this book, but following is a brief description of each layer in the OSI model.

Note Most network descriptions start with the top-most layer and work down to the lowest layer; however, here the description of the layers will start at the bottom and work toward the top, to demonstrate how each layer builds upon the services provided by the layer beneath it.

- **Physical** This is the lowest layer in the OSI model, and it exchanges signals between cooperating network entities over some physical medium (wire, radio, fiber, or other type). The physical layer specifies the mechanical, electrical, functional, and procedural standards for accessing the medium, such as connectors, cabling, signaling, and so on. Common examples are Ethernet (IEEE 802.3) and Wi-Fi (IEEE 802.11).

- **Datalink** This layer exchanges data frames (also called *packets*) between *physically adjacent* network entities (known as *stations*) using the services provided by the physical layer. By its nature, the datalink layer is tightly tied to the physical layer and is really more of an architectural abstraction than the other layers within the model. The datalink layer provides each station with its own unique address on the network, and it provides point-to-point communications between stations (such as between two systems connected to the same Ethernet). The capabilities of the datalink layer vary considerably, depending upon the physical layer. Typically, transmit and receive errors are detected by the datalink layer, and in some instances, the error might be corrected. A datalink layer can be connection oriented, which is typically used in wide area networks (WANs), or connectionless, which is typically used in local area networks (LANs). The IEEE (Institute of Electrical and Electronics Engineers) 802 committee is responsible for the majority of the LAN architectures used throughout the world, and they specify the physical and datalink layers of most networking equipment. They divide the datalink layer into two sublayers: the Logical Link Control (LLC) and the Medium Access Control (MAC). The LLC layer provides a single access method for the network layer to communicate with any 802.x MAC, insulating the network layer from the physical LAN type. The MAC layer provides access-control functions to the shared network medium, and it specifies signaling, the sharing protocol, address recognition, frame generation, CRC generation, and so on. The datalink layer does not guarantee that frames will be delivered to their destination.

- **Network** The network layer implements node addresses and routing functions to allow packets to traverse multiple datalinks. This layer understands the network topology (hiding it from the transport layer) and knows how to direct packets to the nearest router. Any network entity containing the network, datalink, and physical layers is considered to be a *node*, and the network layer can transfer data between any two nodes on the network. There are two types of nodes implemented by the network layer: end nodes, which are the source or destination of data, and intermediate nodes (usually referred to as *routers*), which route packets between end nodes. Network-layer service can be either connection oriented, where all packets traveling between the end nodes follow the same path through the network, or connectionless, where each packet is routed independently. The network layer does not guarantee that packets will be delivered to their destination.

- **Transport** The transport layer provides a transparent data-transfer mechanism between end nodes. On the sending side, the transport layer receives an unstructured stream of data from the layer above and segments the data into discrete packets, which can be sent across the network, using the services of the network layer beneath it. On the receiving side, the transport layer reassembles the packets received from the network layer into a stream of data and provides it to the layer above. This layer provides *reliable* data transfer and will re-transmit lost or corrupted packets to ensure that the data stream received is identical to the data stream that was sent.

- **Session** This layer implements a *connection* or *pipe* between cooperating applications. Each connection endpoint has its own address (often called a *port*), which is unique on that system. There are a variety of communications services provided by session layers, such as two-way simultaneous (full-duplex), two-way alternate (single-duplex), or one-way. Once a connection is established, the systems typically send periodic messages to each other to ensure that each end of the connection is functioning. If an uncorrectable transmission error is detected over a connection, the connection is typically terminated and disconnected.

- **Presentation**   The presentation layer is responsible for preserving the information content of data sent over the network. It handles data formatting, including issues such as whether lines end in a carriage return/line feed (CR/LF) or just a carriage return (CR), whether data is to be compressed or encrypted, converting binary data from little-endian to big-endian, and so on. This layer is not present in most network protocol stacks, so its functionality is implemented at the application layer.

- **Application**   This is a layer that handles the information transfer between two network applications, including functions such as security checks, identification of the participating machines, and initiation of the data exchange. This is the protocol that is used by two communicating applications, and is application specific.

The gray lines in Figure 7-1 represent protocols used in transmitting a request to a remote machine. As stated earlier, each layer of the hierarchy assumes that it is speaking to the same layer on another machine and uses a common protocol. The collection of protocols through which a request passes on its way down and back up the layers of the network is called a *protocol stack*.

Not all network protocol suites implement all the layers in the OSI model. (The presentation layer is rarely provided.) In particular, the TCP/IP protocol stack (which predates the OSI model) matches poorly to the abstractions of OSI. As data travels down the network stack, each layer adds a header (and possibly a trailer) to the data payload, building up a structure that is very similar to the layers of an onion. When this structure is received on a remote node, it travels up the network stack, with each layer stripping off its header (and trailer) until the data payload is delivered to the receiving application.

Windows Networking Components

Figure 7-2 provides an overview of the components of Windows networking, showing how each component fits into the OSI reference model and which protocols are used between layers. The mapping between OSI layers and networking components isn't precise, which is the reason that some components cross layers. The various components include the following:

- *Networking APIs* provide a protocol-independent way for applications to communicate across a network. Networking APIs can be implemented in user mode or in both user mode and kernel mode. In some cases, they are wrappers around another networking API that implements a specific programming model or provides additional services. (Note that the term *networking API* also describes any programming interfaces provided by networking-related software.)

- *Transport Driver Interface (TDI) clients* are legacy kernel-mode device drivers that usually implement the kernel-mode portion of a networking API's implementation. TDI clients get their name from the fact that the I/O request packets (IRPs) they send to protocol drivers are formatted according to the Windows Transport Driver Interface standard (documented in the Windows Driver Kit). This standard specifies a common programming interface for kernel-mode device drivers. (See Chapter 8, "I/O System," in Part 2 for more information about IRPs.) The TDI interface is deprecated and will be removed in a future version of Windows. The TDI interface is now being exported by the TDI Extension (TDX) Driver. Kernel-mode network clients should now use the Winsock Kernel (WSK) interface for accessing the network stack.

- *TDI transports* (also known as *transports*) and Network Driver Interface Specification (NDIS) protocol drivers (or protocol drivers) are kernel-mode network protocol drivers. They accept IRPs from TDI clients and process the requests these IRPs represent. This processing might require network communications with a peer, prompting the TDI transport to add protocol-specific headers (for example, TCP, UDP, and/or IP) to data passed in the IRP, and to communicate with adapter drivers using NDIS functions (also documented in the Windows Driver Kit). TDI transports generally facilitate application network communications by transparently performing message operations such as segmentation and reassembly, sequencing, acknowledgment, and retransmission.

- Microsoft has decided that TCP/IP has won the network protocol wars, so it has re-architected the network protocol portion of the network stack from being protocol-neutral to being TCP/IP-centric. The interface between the TCP/IP protocol driver and Winsock is known as the *Transport Layer Network Provider Interface (TLNPI)* and is currently undocumented.

- *Winsock Kernel (WSK)* is a transport-independent, kernel-mode networking API that replaces the legacy TDI. WSK provides network communication by using socket-like programming semantics similar to user-mode Winsock, while also providing unique features such as asynchronous I/O operations built on IRPs and event callbacks. WSK also natively supports IP version 6 (IPv6) functionality in the Next Generation TCP/IP network stack in Windows.

- The *Windows Filtering Platform (WFP)* is a set of APIs and system services that provide the ability to create network filtering applications. The WFP allows applications to interact with packet processing at different levels of the Windows networking stack, much like file system filters. Similarly, network data can be traced, filtered, and also modified before it reaches its destination.

- *WFP callout drivers* are kernel-mode drivers that implement one or more *callouts*, which extend the capabilities of the WFP by processing TCP/IP-based network data in ways that extend the basic functionality provided by the WFP.

- The *NDIS library* (Ndis.sys) provides an abstraction mechanism that encapsulates Network Interface Card (NIC) drivers (also known as *NDIS miniports*), hiding from them the specifics of the Windows kernel-mode environment. The NDIS library exports functions for use by TCP/IP and legacy TDI transports.

- *NDIS miniport drivers* are kernel-mode drivers that are responsible for interfacing the network stack to a particular NIC. NDIS miniport drivers are written so that they are wrapped by the Windows NDIS library. NDIS miniport drivers don't process IRPs; rather, they register a call-table interface to the NDIS library that contains pointers to functions that perform simple operations on the NIC, such as sending a packet or querying properties. NDIS miniport drivers communicate with network adapters by using NDIS library functions that resolve to hardware abstraction layer (HAL) functions.

As Figure 7-2 shows, the OSI layers don't correspond to actual software. WSK transport providers, for example, frequently cross several boundaries. In fact, the bottom three layers of software and the hardware layer are often referred to collectively as *the transport*. Software components residing in the upper three layers are referred to as *users* or *clients* of the transport."

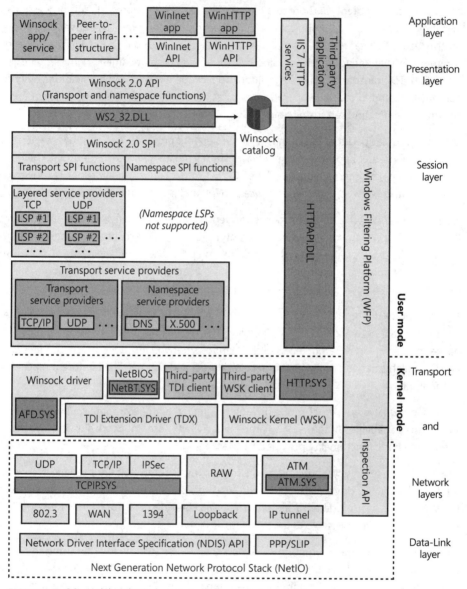

FIGURE 7-2 OSI model and Windows networking components

In the remainder of this chapter, we'll examine the networking components shown in Figure 7-2 (as well as others not shown in the figure), looking at how they fit together and how they relate to Windows as a whole.

Networking APIs

Windows implements multiple networking APIs to provide support for legacy applications and compatibility with industry standards. In this section, we'll briefly look at the networking APIs and describe how applications use them. Keep in mind that the decision about which API an application uses depends on characteristics of the API, such as which protocols the API can layer over, whether the API supports reliable (or bidirectional) communication, and the API's portability to other Windows platforms the application might run on. We'll discuss the following networking APIs:

- Windows Sockets (Winsock)

- Winsock Kernel (WSK)

- Remote procedure call (RPC)

- Web access APIs

- Named pipes and mailslots

- NetBIOS

- Other networking APIs

Windows Sockets

The original Windows Sockets (Winsock) (version 1.0) was Microsoft's implementation of BSD (Berkeley Software Distribution) Sockets, a programming API that became the standard by which UNIX systems have communicated over the Internet since the 1980s. Support for sockets on Windows makes the task of porting UNIX networking applications to Windows relatively straightforward. The modern versions of Winsock include most of the functionality of BSD Sockets but also include Microsoft-specific enhancements, which continue to evolve. Winsock supports reliable, connection-oriented communication as well as unreliable, connectionless communication. ("Reliable," in this sense, indicates whether the sender is notified of any problems in the delivery of data to the receiver.) Windows provides Winsock 2.2, which adds numerous features beyond the BSD Sockets specification, such as functions that take advantage of Windows asynchronous I/O, to offer far better performance and scalability than straight BSD Sockets programming.

Winsock includes the following features:

- Support for scatter-gather and asynchronous application I/O.

- Quality of Service (QoS) conventions so that applications can negotiate latency and bandwidth requirements when the underlying network supports QoS.

- Extensibility so that Winsock can be used with third-party protocols (deprecated).

- Support for integrated namespaces with third-party namespace providers. A server can publish its name in Active Directory, for example, and by using namespace extensions, a client can look up the server's address in Active Directory.

- Support for multicast messages, where messages transmit from a single source to multiple receivers.

We'll examine typical Winsock operation and then describe ways that Winsock can be extended.

Winsock Client Operation

The first step a Winsock application takes is to initialize the Winsock API with a call to an initialization function. A Winsock application's next step is to create a *socket* that will represent a communications endpoint. The application obtains the address of the server to which it wants to connect by calling *getaddrinfo* (and later calling *freeaddrinfo* to release the information). The *getaddrinfo* function returns the list of protocol-specific addresses assigned to the server, and the client attempts to connect to each one in turn until it is able to establish a connection with one of them. This ensures that a client that supports both IP version 4 (IPv4) and IPv6 will connect to the appropriate and/or most efficient address on a server that might have both IPv4 and IPv6 addresses assigned to it. (IPv6 is preferred over IPv4.) Winsock is a protocol-independent API, so an address can be specified for any protocol installed on the system over which Winsock operates. After obtaining the server address, a connection-oriented client attempts to connect to the server by using *connect* and specifying the server address.

When a connection is established, the client can send and receive data over its socket using the *recv* and *send* APIs. A connectionless client specifies the remote address with connectionless APIs, such as the connectionless equivalents of *send* and *recv*, and *sendto* and *recvfrom*. Clients can also use the *select* and *WSAPoll* APIs to wait on or poll multiple sockets for synchronous I/O operations, or to check their state.

Winsock Server Operation

The sequence of steps for a server application differs from that of a client. After initializing the Winsock API, the server creates a socket and then binds it to a local address by using *bind*. Again, the address family specified—whether it's TCP/IPv4, TCP/IPv6, or some other address family—is up to the server application.

If the server is connection oriented, it performs a *listen* operation on the socket, indicating the *backlog*, or the number of connections the server asks Winsock to hold until the server is able to accept them. Then it performs an *accept* operation to allow a client to connect to the socket. If there is a pending connection request, the *accept* call completes immediately; otherwise, it completes when a connection request arrives. When a connection is made, the *accept* function returns a new socket that represents the server's end of the connection. (The original socket used for listening is not used for communications, only for receiving connection requests.) The server can perform receive and send operations by using functions such as *recv* and *send*. Like Winsock clients, servers can use the *select* and *WSAPoll* functions to query the state of one or more sockets; however, the Winsock *WSAEventSelect* function and overlapped (asynchronous) I/O extensions are preferred for better scalability. Figure 7-3 shows connection-oriented communication between a Winsock client and server.

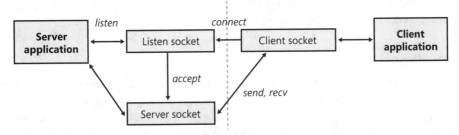

FIGURE 7-3 Connection-oriented Winsock operation

After binding an address, a connectionless server is no different from a connectionless client: it can send and receive data over the socket simply by specifying the remote address with each operation. Most connectionless protocols are unreliable and, in general, will not know whether the destination actually received the sent data packets (which are known as *datagrams*). Datagram protocols are ideal for quick message passing, where the overhead of establishing a connection is too much and reliability is not required (although an application can build reliability on top of the protocol).

Winsock Extensions

In addition to supporting functions that correspond directly to those implemented in BSD Sockets, Microsoft has added a handful of functions that aren't part of the BSD standard. Two of these functions, *AcceptEx* (the *Ex* suffix is short for *Extended*) and *TransmitFile*, are worth describing because many Web servers on Windows use them to achieve high performance. *AcceptEx* is a version of the *accept* function that, in the process of establishing a connection with a client, returns the client's address and the client's first message. *AcceptEx* allows the server application to queue multiple accept operations so that high volumes of incoming connection requests can be handled. With this function, a web server avoids executing multiple Winsock functions that would otherwise be required.

After establishing a connection with a client, a web server frequently sends a file, such as a web page, to the client. The *TransmitFile* function's implementation is integrated with the Windows cache manager so that a file can be sent directly from the file system cache. Sending data in this way is called *zero-copy* because the server doesn't have to read the file data to send it; it simply specifies a handle to a file and the byte range (offset and length) of the file to send. In addition, *TransmitFile* allows a server to add prefix or suffix data to the file's data so that the server can send header information, trailer information, or both, which might include the name of the web server and a field that indicates to the client the size of the message the server is sending. Internet Information Services (IIS), which is included with Windows, uses both *AcceptEx* and *TransmitFile* to achieve better performance.

Windows also supports a handful of other multifunction APIs, including *ConnectEx*, *DisconnectEx*, and *TransmitPackets*. *ConnectEx* establishes a connection and sends the first message on the connection. *DisconnectEx* closes a connection and allows the socket handle representing the connection to be reused in a call to *AcceptEx* or *ConnectEx*. Finally, *TransmitPackets* is similar to *TransmitFile*, except that it allows for the sending of in-memory data in addition to, or in lieu of, file data. Finally, by using the *WSAImpersonateSocketPeer* and *WSARevertImpersonation* functions, Winsock servers can perform impersonation (described in Chapter 6, "Security") to perform authorization or to gain access to resources based on the client's security credentials.

Extending Winsock

Winsock is an extensible API on Windows because third parties can add a *transport service provider* that interfaces Winsock with other protocols, or layers on top of existing protocols, to provide functionality such as proxying. Third parties can also add a *namespace service provider* to augment Winsock's name-resolution facilities. Service providers plug in to Winsock by using the Winsock *service provider interface* (SPI). When a transport service provider is registered with Winsock, Winsock uses the transport service provider to implement socket functions, such as *connect* and *accept*, for the address types that the provider indicates it implements. There are no restrictions on how the transport service provider implements the functions, but the implementation usually involves communicating with a transport driver in kernel mode.

> **Note** Layered service providers are not secure and can be bypassed; secure network protocol layering must be done in kernel mode. Installing itself as a Winsock layered service provider (LSP) is a technique used frequently by malware and spyware.

A requirement of any Winsock client/server application is for the server to make its address available to clients so that the clients can connect to the server. Standard services that execute on the TCP/IP protocol use *well-known addresses* to make their addresses available. As long as a browser knows the name of the computer a Web server is running on, it can connect to the web server by specifying the well-known web server address (the IP address of the server concatenated with :80, the port number used for HTTP). Namespace service providers make it possible for servers to register their presence in other ways. For example, one namespace service provider might on the server side register the server's address in Active Directory and on the client side look up the server's address in Active Directory. Namespace service providers supply this functionality to Winsock by implementing standard Winsock name-resolution functions such as *getaddrinfo* and *getnameinfo*.

EXPERIMENT: Looking at Winsock Service and Namespace Providers

The Network Shell (Netsh.exe) utility included with Windows is able to show the registered Winsock transport and namespace providers by using the *netsh winsock show catalog* command. For example, if there are two TCP/IP transport service providers, the first one listed is the default provider for Winsock applications using the TCP/IP protocol. Here's sample output from Netsh showing the registered transport service providers:

```
C:\Users\Toby>netsh winsock show catalog
```

```
Winsock Catalog Provider Entry
----------------------------------------------------
Entry Type:            Base Service Provider
Description:           MSAFD Tcpip [TCP/IP]
Provider ID:           {E70F1AA0-AB8B-11CF-8CA3-00805F48A192}
Provider Path:         %SystemRoot%\system32\mswsock.dll
Catalog Entry ID:      1001
Version:               2
Address Family:        2
Max Address Length:    16
Min Address Length:    16
Socket Type:           1
Protocol:              6
Service Flags:         0x20066
Protocol Chain Length: 1

Winsock Catalog Provider Entry
----------------------------------------------------
Entry Type:            Base Service Provider
Description:           MSAFD Tcpip [UDP/IP]
Provider ID:           {E70F1AA0-AB8B-11CF-8CA3-00805F48A192}
Provider Path:         %SystemRoot%\system32\mswsock.dll
Catalog Entry ID:      1002
Version:               2
Address Family:        2
Max Address Length:    16
Min Address Length:    16
Socket Type:           2
Protocol:              17
Service Flags:         0x20609
Protocol Chain Length: 1

Winsock Catalog Provider Entry
----------------------------------------------------
Entry Type:            Base Service Provider
Description:           MSAFD Tcpip [RAW/IP]
Provider ID:           {E70F1AA0-AB8B-11CF-8CA3-00805F48A192}
Provider Path:         %SystemRoot%\system32\mswsock.dll
Catalog Entry ID:      1003
Version:               2
Address Family:        2
Max Address Length:    16
Min Address Length:    16
Socket Type:           3
Protocol:              0
Service Flags:         0x20609
Protocol Chain Length: 1
.
.
.
Name Space Provider Entry
----------------------------------------------------
Description:           Network Location Awareness Legacy (NLAv1) Namespace
Provider ID:           {6642243A-3BA8-4AA6-BAA5-2E0BD71FDD83}
Name Space:            15
Active:                1
Version:               0
```

```
Name Space Provider Entry
-----------------------------------------------------
Description:            E-mail Naming Shim Provider
Provider ID:           {964ACBA2-B2BC-40EB-8C6A-A6DB40161CAE}
Name Space:            37
Active:                1
Version:               0


Name Space Provider Entry
-----------------------------------------------------
Description:            PNRP Cloud Namespace Provider
Provider ID:           {03FE89CE-766D-4976-B9C1-BB9BC42C7B4D}
Name Space:            39
Active:                1
Version:               0
     .
     .
     .
```

You can also use the Autoruns utility from Windows Sysinternals (*www.microsoft.com /technet/sysinternals*) to view namespace and transport providers, as well as to disable or delete those that might be causing problems or unwanted behavior on the system.

Winsock Implementation

Winsock's implementation is shown in Figure 7-4. Its application interface consists of an API DLL, Ws2_32.dll (%SystemRoot%\System32\Ws2_32.dll), which provides applications access to Winsock functions. Ws2_32.dll calls on the services of namespace and transport service providers to carry out name and message operations. The Mswsock.dll (%SystemRoot%\System32\mswsock.dll) library acts as a transport service provider for the protocols supported by Microsoft and uses *Winsock Helper* libraries that are protocol specific to communicate with kernel-mode protocol drivers. For example, Wshtcpip.dll (%SystemRoot%\System32\wshtcpip.dll) is the TCP/IP helper. Mswsock.dll implements the Microsoft Winsock extension functions, such as *TransmitFile*, *AcceptEx*, and *WSARecvEx*.

Windows ships with helper DLLs for TCP/IPv4, TCPv6, Bluetooth, NetBIOS, IrDA (Infrared Data Association), and PGM (Pragmatic General Multicast). It also includes namespace service providers for DNS (TCP/IP), Active Directory (NTDS), NLA (Network Location Awareness), PNRP (Peer Name Resolution Protocol), and Bluetooth.

Like the named-pipe and mailslot APIs (described later in this chapter), Winsock integrates with the Windows I/O model and uses file handles to represent sockets. This support requires the aid of a kernel-mode driver, so Msafd.dll (%SystemRoot%\System32\msafd.dll) uses the services of the Ancillary Function Driver (AFD—%SystemRoot%\System32\Drivers\Afd.sys) to implement socket-based functions. AFD is a Transport Layer Network Provider Interface (TLNPI) client and executes network socket operations, such as sending and receiving messages. TLNPI is the undocumented interface between AFD and the TCP/IP protocol stack. If a legacy protocol driver is installed, Windows will use the TDI-TLNPI translation driver TDX (%SystemRoot%\System32\Drivers\tdx.sys) to map TDI IRPs to TLNPI requests.

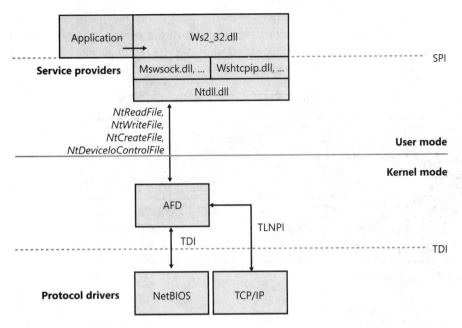

FIGURE 7-4 Winsock implementation

Winsock Kernel

To enable kernel-mode drivers and modules to have access to networking API interfaces similar to those available to user-mode applications, Windows implements a socket-based networking programming interface called Winsock Kernel (WSK). WSK replaces the legacy TDI API interface present on older versions of Windows but maintains the TDI API interface for transport providers. Compared to TDI, WSK provides better performance, better security, better scalability, and a much easier programming paradigm, because it relies less on internal kernel behavior and more on socket-based semantics. Additionally, WSK was written to take full advantage of the latest technologies in the Windows TCP/IP stack, which TDI was not originally anticipated to support. As shown in Figure 7-5, WSK makes use of the Network Module Registrar (NMR) component of Windows (part of %SystemRoot%\System32\drivers\NetIO.sys) to attach and detach from transport protocols, and it can be used, just like Winsock, to support many types of network clients—for example, the Http.sys driver for the HTTP Server API (mentioned later in the chapter) is a WSK client. Using NMR with WSK is rather complicated, so registration-support APIs are provided to register with WSK (*WskRegister, WskDeregister, WskCaptureProviderNPI,* and *WskReleaseProviderNPI*).

> **Note** The Raw transport protocol is not really a protocol and does not perform any encapsulation of the user data. This allows the client to directly control the contents of the frames transmitted and received by the network interface.

WSK enhances security by restricting address sharing—which allows multiple sockets to use the same transport (TCP/IP) address—through the use of nondefault sharing and security descriptors on addresses. WSK uses the security descriptor specified by the first socket for an address, and it checks the owning process and thread for each subsequent attempt to use that address.

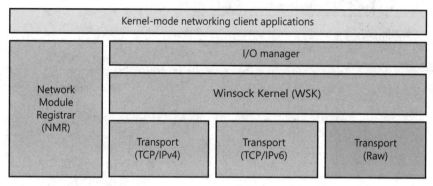

FIGURE 7-5 WSK overview

WSK Implementation

WSK's implementation is shown in Figure 7-6. At its core is the WSK subsystem itself, which uses the Next Generation TCP/IP Stack (%SystemRoot%\System32\Drivers\Tcpip.sys) and the NetIO support library (%SystemRoot%\System32\Drivers\NetIO.sys) but is actually implemented in AFD. The subsystem is responsible for the provider side of the WSK API. The subsystem interfaces with the TCP/IP transport protocols (shown at the bottom of Figure 7-5). Attached to the WSK subsystem are WSK clients, which are kernel-mode drivers that implement the client-side WSK API in order to perform network operations. The WSK subsystem calls WSK clients to notify them of asynchronous events.

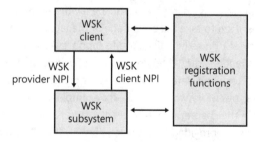

FIGURE 7-6 WSK implementation

WSK clients are bound to the WSK subsystem through the NMR or through the WSK's registration functions, which allow WSK clients to dynamically detect when the WSK subsystem becomes available and then load their own dispatch table to describe the provider and client-side implementations of the WSK API. These implementations provide the standard WSK socket-based functions, such as *WskSocket, WskAccept, WskBind, WskConnect, WskReceive,* and *WskSend,* which have similar semantics (but not necessarily similar parameters) as their user-mode Winsock counterparts. However, unlike user-mode Winsock, the WSK subsystem defines four kinds of *socket categories*, which identify which functions and events are available:

- Basic sockets, which are used only to get and set information on the transport. They cannot be used to send or receive data or be bound to an address.

- Listening sockets, which are used for sockets that accept only incoming connections.

- Datagram sockets, which are used solely for sending and receiving datagrams.

- Connection-oriented sockets, which support all the functionality required to send and receive network traffic over an established connection.

Apart from the socket functions described, WSK also provides events through which clients are notified of network status. Unlike the model for socket functions, in which a client controls the connection, events allow the subsystem to control the connection and merely notify the client. These include the *WskAcceptEvent*, *WskInspectEvent*, *WskAbortEvent*, *WskReceiveFromEvent*, *WskReceiveEvent*, *WskDisconnectEvent*, and *WskSendBacklogEvent* routines.

Finally, like user-mode Winsock, WSK can be extended through *extension interfaces* that clients can associate with sockets. These extensions can enhance the default functionality provided by the WSK subsystem.

Remote Procedure Call

Remote procedure call (RPC) is a network programming standard originally developed in the early 1980s. The Open Software Foundation (now The Open Group) made RPC part of the distributed computing environment (DCE) distributed computing standard. Although there is a second RPC standard, SunRPC, the Microsoft RPC implementation is compatible with the OSF/DCE standard. RPC builds on other networking APIs, such as named pipes or Winsock, to provide an alternate programming model that in some respects hides the details of networking programming from an application developer. Fundamentally, RPC provides a mechanism for creating programs that are distributed across a network, with portions of the application running transparently on one or more systems.

RPC Operation

An RPC facility is one that allows a programmer to create an application consisting of any number of procedures, some that execute locally and others that execute on remote computers via a network. It provides a procedural view of networked operations rather than a transport-centered view, thus simplifying the development of distributed applications.

Networking software is traditionally structured around an I/O model of processing. In Windows, for example, a network operation is initiated when an application issues an I/O request. The operating system processes the request accordingly by forwarding it to a *redirector*, which acts as a remote file system by making the client interaction with the remote file system invisible to the client. The redirector passes the operation to the remote file system, and after the remote system fulfills the request and returns the results, the local network card interrupts. The kernel handles the interrupt, and the original I/O operation completes, returning results to the caller.

RPC takes a different approach altogether. RPC applications are like other structured applications, with a main program that calls procedures or procedure libraries to perform specific tasks. The difference between RPC applications and regular applications is that some of the procedure libraries in an RPC application are stored and execute on remote computers, as shown in Figure 7-7, whereas others execute locally.

To the RPC application, all the procedures appear to execute locally. In other words, instead of making a programmer actively write code to transmit computational or I/O-related requests across a network, handle network protocols, deal with network errors, wait for results, and so forth, RPC software handles these tasks automatically. And the Windows RPC facility can operate over any available transport protocols loaded into the system.

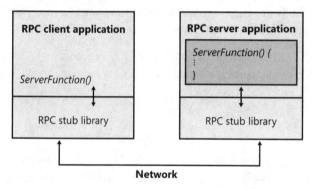

FIGURE 7-7 RPC operation

To write an RPC application, the programmer decides which procedures will execute locally and which will execute remotely. For example, suppose an ordinary workstation has a network connection to a supercomputer (a very fast machine usually designed for high-speed vector operations). If the programmer were writing an application that manipulated large matrices, it would make sense from a performance perspective to offload the mathematical calculations to the supercomputer by writing the program as an RPC application.

RPC applications work like this: As an application runs, it calls local procedures as well as procedures that aren't present on the local machine. To handle the latter case, the application is linked to a local library or DLL that contains *stub procedures*, one for each remote procedure. For simple applications, the stub procedures are statically linked with the application, but for bigger components the stubs are included in separate DLLs. In DCOM, covered later in the chapter, the latter method is typically used. The stub procedures have the same name and use the same interface as the remote procedures, but instead of performing the required operations, the stub takes the parameters passed to it and *marshals* them for transmission across the network. Marshaling parameters means ordering and packaging them in a particular way to suit a network link, such as resolving references and picking up a copy of any data structures that a pointer refers to.

The stub then calls RPC run-time procedures that locate the computer where the remote procedure resides, determines which network transport mechanisms that computer uses, and sends the request to it using local transport software. When the remote server receives the RPC request, it *unmarshals* the parameters (the reverse of marshaling), reconstructs the original procedure call, and calls the procedure with the parameters passed from the calling system. When the server finishes, it performs the reverse sequence to return results to the caller.

In addition to the synchronous function-call-based interface described here, Windows RPC also supports *asynchronous RPC*. Asynchronous RPC lets an RPC application execute a function but not wait until the function completes to continue processing. Instead, the application can execute other code and later, when a response has arrived from the server, the RPC runtime notifies the client that the operation has completed. The RPC runtime uses the notification mechanism requested by the client. If the client uses an event synchronization object for notification, it waits for the signaling of the event object by calling either *WaitForSingleObject* or *WaitForMultipleObjects*. If the client provides an asynchronous procedure call (APC), the runtime queues the execution of the APC to the thread that executed the RPC function. (The APC will not be delivered until the requesting thread enters an *alertable* wait state. See Chapter 3, "System Mechanisms," for more information on APCs.) If the client program uses an I/O completion port as its notification mechanism, it must call *GetQueuedCompletionStatus* to learn of the function's completion. Alternatively, a client can poll for completion by calling *RpcAsyncGetCallStatus*.

In addition to the RPC runtime, Microsoft's RPC facility includes a compiler, called the *Microsoft Interface Definition Language* (MIDL) compiler. The MIDL compiler simplifies the creation of an RPC application by generating the necessary stub routines. The programmer writes a series of ordinary function prototypes (assuming a C or C++ application) that describe the remote routines and then places the routines in a file. The programmer then adds some additional information to these prototypes, such as a network-unique identifier for the package of routines and a version number, plus attributes that specify whether the parameters are input, output, or both. The embellished prototypes form the developer's Interface Definition Language (IDL) file.

Once the IDL file is created, the programmer compiles it with the MIDL compiler, which produces client-side and server-side stub routines (mentioned previously), as well as header files to be included in the application. When the client-side application is linked to the stub routines file, all remote procedure references are resolved. The remote procedures are then installed, using a similar process, on the server machine. A programmer who wants to call an existing RPC application need only write the client side of the software and link the application to the local RPC run-time facility.

The RPC runtime uses a generic RPC *transport provider interface* to talk to a transport protocol. The provider interface acts as a thin layer between the RPC facility and the transport, mapping RPC operations onto the functions provided by the transport. The Windows RPC facility implements transport provider DLLs for named pipes, HTTP, TCP/IP, and UDP. In a similar fashion, the RPC facility is designed to work with different network security facilities.

Most of the Windows networking services are RPC applications, which means that both local applications and applications on remote computers might call them. Thus, a remote client computer might call the server service to list shares, open files, write to print queues, or activate users on your server, all subject to security constraints, of course. The majority of client-management APIs are implemented using RPC.

Server name publishing, which is the ability of a server to register its name in a location accessible for client lookup, is in RPC and is integrated with Active Directory. If Active Directory isn't installed, the RPC name locator services fall back on NetBIOS broadcast. This behavior allows RPC to function on stand-alone servers and workstations.

RPC Security

Windows RPC includes integration with security support providers (SSPs) so that RPC clients and servers can use authenticated or encrypted communications. When an RPC server wants secure communication, it tells the RPC runtime what authentication service to add to the list of available *authentication services*. When a client wants to use secure communication, it binds to the server. At that time, it must tell the RPC runtime the authentication service and *authentication level* it wants. Various authentication levels exist to ensure that only authorized clients connect to a server, verify that each message a server receives originates at an authorized client, check the integrity of RPC messages to detect manipulation, and even encrypt RPC message data. Obviously, higher authentication levels require more processing. The client can also optionally specify the server *principal name*. A principal is an entity that the RPC security system recognizes. The server must register its SSP-specific principal name with an SSP.

An SSP handles the details of performing network communication authentication and encryption, not only for RPC but also for Winsock. Windows includes a number of built-in SSPs, including a Kerberos SSP to implement Kerberos version 5 authentication (including AES support) and Secure Channel (SChannel), which implements Secure Sockets Layer (SSL) and the Transport Layer Security (TLS) protocols. SChannel also supports TLS and SSL extensions, which allow you to use the AES cipher as well as elliptic curve cryptographic (ECC) ciphers on top of the protocols. Also, because it supports an *open cryptographic interface* (OCI) and crypto-agile capabilities, SChannel allows an administrator to replace or add to the existing cryptographic algorithms. In the absence of a specified SSP, RPC software uses the built-in security of the underlying transport. Some transports, such as named pipes or local RPC, have built-in security. Others, like TCP, do not, and in this case RPC makes unsecure calls in the absence of a specified SSP.

> **Note** The use of unencrypted RPC might pose serious security issues for your organization.

Another feature of RPC security is the ability of a server to impersonate the security identity of a client with the *RpcImpersonateClient* function. After a server has finished performing impersonated operations on behalf of a client, it returns to its own security identity by calling *RpcRevertToSelf* or *RpcRevertToSelfEx*. (See Chapter 6 for more information on impersonation.)

RPC Implementation

RPC implementation is depicted in Figure 7-8, which shows that an RPC-based application links with the RPC run-time DLL (%SystemRoot%\System32\Rpcrt4.dll). The RPC run-time DLL provides marshaling and unmarshaling functions for use by an application's RPC function stubs as well as functions for sending and receiving marshaled data. The RPC run-time DLL includes support routines to handle RPC over a network as well as a form of RPC called *local RPC*. Local RPC can be used for communication between two processes located on the same system, and the RPC run-time DLL uses the advanced local procedure call (ALPC) facilities in kernel mode as the local networking API. (See Chapter 3 for more information on ALPCs.) When RPC is based on nonlocal communication mechanisms, the RPC run-time DLL uses the Winsock or named pipe APIs.

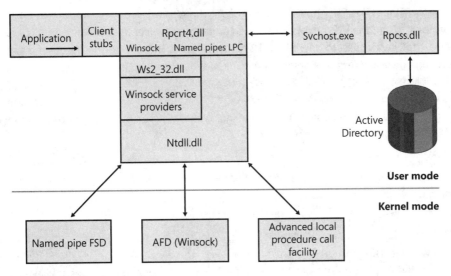

FIGURE 7-8 RPC implementation

The RPC subsystem (RPCSS—%SystemRoot%\System32\Rpcss.dll) is implemented as a Windows service. RPCSS is itself an RPC application that communicates with instances of itself on other systems to perform name lookup, registration, and dynamic endpoint mapping. (For clarity, Figure 7-8 doesn't show RPCSS linked with the RPC run-time DLL.)

Windows also includes support for RPC in kernel mode through the kernel-mode RPC driver (%SystemRoot%\System32\Drivers\Msrpc.sys). Kernel-mode RPC is for internal use by the system and is implemented on top of ALPC. Winlogon includes an RPC server with a documented set of interfaces that user-mode RPC clients might call, while Win32k.sys includes an RPC client that communicates with Winlogon for internal notifications, such as the secure attention sequence (SAS). (See Chapter 6 for more information.) The TCP/IP stack in Windows (as well as the WFP) also uses kernel-mode RPC to communicate with the *Network Storage Interface (NSI)* service, which handles network configuration information.

Web Access APIs

To ease the development of Internet applications, Windows provides both client and server Internet APIs. By using the APIs, applications can provide HTTP services and use FTP and HTTP services without knowledge of the intricacies of the corresponding protocols. The client APIs include *Windows Internet*, also known as *WinInet*, which enables applications to interact with the FTP and HTTP protocols, and WinHTTP, which enables applications to interact with the HTTP protocol and is more suitable than WinInet in certain situations (Windows services and middle-tier applications). HTTP Server is a server-side API that enables the development of web server applications.

WinInet

WinInet supports the HTTP, FTP, and Gopher protocols. The APIs break down into sub-API sets specific to each protocol. Using the FTP-related APIs—such as *InternetConnect* to connect to an HTTP server, followed by *HttpOpenRequest* to open an HTTP request handle, *HttpSendRequestEx* to send a request to the sever and receive a response, *InternetWriteFile* to send a file, and *InternetReadFileEx* to receive a file—an application developer avoids the details of establishing a connection and formatting TCP/IP messages to the various protocols. The HTTP-related APIs also provide cookie persistence, client-side file caching, and automatic credential dialog handling. WinInet is used by core Windows components such as Windows Explorer and Internet Explorer.

> **Note** WinINet does not support server implementations or use by services. For these types of usage, use WinHTTP instead.

WinHTTP provides an abstraction of the HTTP v1.1 protocol for HTTP client applications similar to what the WinInet HTTP-related APIs provide. However, whereas the WinInet HTTP API is intended for user-interactive, client-side applications, the WinHTTP API is designed for server applications that communicate with HTTP servers. Server applications are often implemented as Windows services that do not provide a user interface and so do not desire the dialog boxes that WinInet APIs display. In addition, the WinHTTP APIs are more scalable (such as supporting uploads of greater than 4 GB) and offer security functionality, such as thread impersonation, that is not available from the WinInet APIs.

HTTP

Using the HTTP Server API implemented by Windows, server applications can register to receive HTTP requests for particular URLs, receive HTTP requests, and send HTTP responses. The HTTP Server API includes SSL support so that applications can exchange data over secure HTTP connections. The API includes server-side caching capabilities, synchronous and asynchronous I/O models, and both IPv4 and IPv6 addressing. The HTTP server APIs are used by IIS and other Windows services that rely on HTTP as a transport.

The HTTP Server API, which applications access through %SystemRoot%\System32\Httpapi.dll, relies on the kernel-mode %SystemRoot%\System32\Drivers\Http.sys driver. Http.sys starts on demand the first time any application on the system calls *HttpInitialize*. Applications then call *HttpCreateServerSession* to initialize a server session for the HTTP Server API. Next they use *HttpCreateRequestQueue* to create a private request queue and *HttpCreateUrlGroup* to create a URL group, specifying the URLs that they want to handle requests for with *HttpAddUrlToUrlGroup*. Using the request queues and their registered URLs (which they associate by using *HttpSetUrlGroupProperty*), Http.sys allows more than one application to service HTTP requests on a given port (port 80 for example), with each servicing HTTP requests to different parts of the URL namespace, as shown in Figure 7-9.

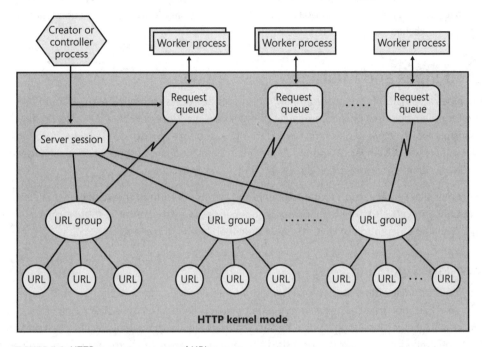

FIGURE 7-9 HTTP request queues and URL groups

HttpReceiveHttpRequest receives incoming requests directed at registered URLs, and *HttpSendHttpResponse* sends HTTP responses. Both functions offer asynchronous operation so that an application can use *GetOverlappedResult* or I/O completion ports to determine when an operation is completed.

Applications can use Http.sys to cache data in nonpaged physical memory by calling *HttpAddFragmentToCache* and associating a *fragment name* (specified as a URL prefix) with the cached data. Http.sys invokes the memory manager function *MmAllocatePagesForMdlEx* to allocate unmapped physical pages. (For large requests, Http.sys also attempts to use large pages to optimize access to the buffered data.) When Http.sys requires a virtual address mapping for the physical memory described by an entry in the cache—for instance, when it copies data to the cache or sends data from the cache—it uses *MmMapLockedPagesSpecifyCache* and then *MmUnmapLockedPages* after it completes its access. Http.sys maintains cached data until an application invalidates it or an optional application-specified timeout associated with the data expires. Http.sys also trims cached data in a worker thread that wakes up when the low-memory notification event is signaled. (See Chapter 10, "Memory Management," in Part 2 for information on the low-memory notification event.) When an application specifies one or more fragment names in a call to *HttpSendHttpResponse*,

Http.sys passes a pointer to the cached data in physical memory to the TCP/IP driver and avoids a copy operation. Http.sys also contains code for performing server-side authentication, including full SSL support, which removes the need to call back to the user-mode API to perform encryption and decryption of traffic.

Finally, the HTTP Server API contains many configuration options that clients can use to set functionality, such as authentication policies, bandwidth throttling, logging, connection limits, server state, response caching, and SSL certificate binding.

Named Pipes and Mailslots

Named pipes and mailslots are programming APIs for interprocess communication. Named pipes provide for reliable bidirectional communications, whereas mailslots provide unreliable, unidirectional data transmission. An advantage of mailslots is that they support broadcast capability. In Windows, both APIs make use of standard Windows security authentication and authorization mechanisms, which allow a server to control precisely which clients can connect to it.

The names that servers assign to named pipes and clients conform to the Windows Universal Naming Convention (UNC), which is a protocol-independent way to identify resources on a Windows network. The implementation of UNC names is described later in the chapter.

Named-Pipe Operation

Named-pipe communication consists of a named-pipe server and a named-pipe client. A named-pipe server is an application that creates a named pipe to which clients can connect. A named pipe's name has the format \\Server\Pipe\PipeName. The *Server* component of the name specifies the computer on which the named-pipe server is executing. (A named-pipe server can't create a named pipe on a remote system.) The name can be a DNS name (for example, *mspress.microsoft.com*), a NetBIOS name (*mspress*), or an IP address (131.107.0.1). The *Pipe* component of the name must be the string "Pipe", and *PipeName* is the unique name assigned to a named pipe. The unique portion of the named pipe's name can include subdirectories; an example of a named-pipe name with a subdirectory is \\MyComputer\Pipe\MyServerApp\ConnectionPipe.

A named-pipe server uses the *CreateNamedPipe* Windows function to create a named pipe. One of the function's input parameters is a pointer to the named-pipe name, in the form \\.\Pipe\PipeName. The "\\.\" is a Windows-defined alias for "this system," because a pipe must be created on the local system (although it can be accessed from a remote system). Other parameters the function accepts include an optional security descriptor that protects access to the named pipe, a flag that specifies whether the pipe should be bidirectional or unidirectional, a value indicating the maximum number of simultaneous connections the pipe supports, and a flag specifying whether the pipe should operate in *byte mode* or *message mode*.

Most networking APIs operate only in byte mode, which means that a message sent with one send function might require the receiver to perform multiple receive operations, building up the complete message from fragments. A named pipe operating in message mode simplifies the implementation of a receiver because there is a one-to-one correspondence between send and receive requests. A receiver therefore obtains an entire message each time it completes a receive operation and doesn't have to concern itself with keeping track of message fragments.

The first call to *CreateNamedPipe* for a particular name creates the first instance of that name and establishes the behavior of all named-pipe instances having that name. A server creates additional instances, up to the maximum specified in the first call, with additional calls to *CreateNamedPipe*. After creating at least one named-pipe instance, a server executes the *ConnectNamedPipe* Windows function, which enables the named pipe the server created to establish connections with clients. *ConnectNamedPipe* can be executed synchronously or asynchronously, and it doesn't complete until a client establishes a connection with the instance (or an error occurs).

A named-pipe client uses the Windows *CreateFile* or *CallNamedPipe* function, specifying the name of the pipe a server has created, to connect to a server. If the server has performed a *ConnectNamedPipe* call, the client's security profile and the access it requests to the pipe (read, write) are validated against the named pipe's security descriptor. (See Chapter 6 for more information on the security-check algorithms Windows uses.) If the client is granted access to a named pipe, it receives a handle representing the client side of a named-pipe connection and the server's call to *ConnectNamedPipe* completes.

After a named-pipe connection is established, the client and server can use the *ReadFile* and *WriteFile* Windows functions to read from and write to the pipe. Named pipes support both synchronous and asynchronous operations for message transmittal, depending upon how the handle to the pipe was opened. Figure 7-10 shows a server and client communicating through a named-pipe instance.

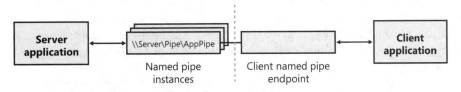

FIGURE 7-10 Named-pipe communications

Another characteristic of the named-pipe networking API is that it allows a server to impersonate a client by using the *ImpersonateNamedPipeClient* function. See the "Impersonation" section in Chapter 6 for a discussion of how impersonation is used in client/server applications. A second advanced area of functionality of the named-pipe API is that it allows for atomic send and receive operations through the *TransactNamedPipe* API, which behaves according to a simple transactional model in which a message is both sent and received in the same operation. In other words, it combines a write operation and a read operation into a single operation by not completing a write request until it has been read by the recipient.

Mailslot Operation

Mailslots provide an unreliable, unidirectional, multicast network transport. *Multicast* is a term used to describe a sender sending a message on the network to one or more specific listeners, which is different from a *broadcast*, which all systems would receive. One example of an application that can use this type of communication is a time-synchronization service, which might send a source time across the domain every few seconds. Such a message would be received by all applications listening on the particular mailslot. Receiving the source-time message isn't crucial for every computer on the network (because time updates are sent relatively frequently); therefore, a source-time message is a good example for the use of mailslots, because the loss of a message will not cause any harm.

Like named pipes, mailslots are integrated with the Windows API. A mailslot server creates a mailslot by using the *CreateMailslot* function. *CreateMailslot* accepts a UNC name of the form "\\.\Mailslot\MailslotName" as an input parameter. Again like named pipes, a mailslot server can create mailslots only on the machine it's executing on, and the name it assigns to a mailslot can include subdirectories. *CreateMailslot* also takes a security descriptor that controls client access to the mailslot. The handles returned by *CreateMailslot* are *overlapped*, which means that operations performed on the handles, such as sending and receiving messages, are asynchronous.

Because mailslots are unidirectional and unreliable, *CreateMailslot* doesn't take many of the parameters that *CreateNamedPipe* does. After it creates a mailslot, a server simply listens for incoming client messages by executing the *ReadFile* function on the handle representing the mailslot.

Mailslot clients use a naming format similar to that used by named-pipe clients but with variations that make it possible to send messages to all the mailslots of a given name within the client's domain or a specified domain. To send a message to a particular instance of a mailslot, the client calls *CreateFile*, specifying the computer-specific name. An example of such a name is "\\Server\Mailslot \MailslotName". (The client can specify "\\.\" to represent the local computer.) If the client wants to obtain a handle representing all the mailslots of a given name on the domain it's a member of, it specifies the name in the format "*\Mailslot\MailslotName", and if the client wants to broadcast to all the mailslots of a given name within a different domain, the format it uses is "\\DomainName \Mailslot\MailslotName".

After obtaining a handle representing the client side of a mailslot, the client sends messages by calling *WriteFile*. Because of the way mailslots are implemented, only messages smaller than 424 bytescan be sent. If a message is larger than 424 bytes, the mailslot implementation uses a reliable communications mechanism that requires a one-to-one client/server connection, which precludes multicast capability. This limitation makes mailslots generally unsuitable for messages larger than 424 bytes. Figure 7-11 shows an example of a client broadcasting to multiple mailslot servers within a domain.

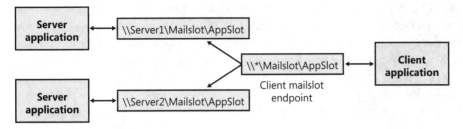

FIGURE 7-11 Mailslot broadcast

Named Pipe and Mailslot Implementation

As evidence of their tight integration with Windows, named-pipe and mailslot functions are all implemented in the Kernel32.dll Windows client-side DLL. *ReadFile* and *WriteFile*, which are the functions applications use to send and receive messages using named pipes or mailslots, are the primary Windows I/O routines. The *CreateFile* function, which a client uses to open either a named pipe or a mailslot, is also a standard Windows I/O routine. However, the names specified by named-pipe and mailslot applications specify file-system namespaces managed by the named-pipe file-system driver (%SystemRoot%\System32\Drivers\Npfs.sys) and the mailslot file-system driver (%SystemRoot% \System32\Drivers\Msfs.sys), as shown in Figure 7-12.

The name- pipe file-system driver creates a device object named \Device\NamedPipe and a symbolic link to that object named \Global??\Pipe. The mailslot file-system driver creates a device object named \Device\Mailslot and a symbolic link named "\Global??\Mailslot", which points to that device object. (See Chapter 3 for an explanation of the \Global?? object manager directory.) Names passed to *CreateFile* of the form "\\.\Pipe\..." and "\\.\Mailslot\..." have their prefix of "\\.\" translated to "\Global??\" so that the names resolve through a symbolic link to a device object. The special functions *CreateNamedPipe* and *CreateMailslot* use the corresponding native functions *NtCreateNamedPipeFile* and *NtCreateMailslotFile*, which ultimately call *IoCreateFile*.

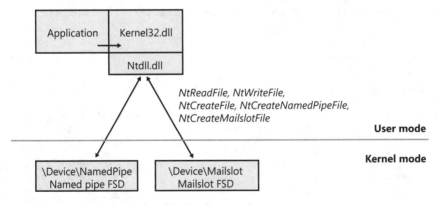

FIGURE 7-12 Named-pipe and mailslot implementation

Later in the chapter, we'll discuss how the redirector file system driver is involved when a name that specifies a remote named pipe or mailslot resolves to a remote system. However, when a named pipe or mailslot is created by a server or opened by a client, the appropriate file-system driver (FSD) on the machine where the named pipe or mailslot is located is eventually invoked. The reason that named pipes and mailslots are implemented as FSDs is that they can take advantage of the existing infrastructure in the object manager, the I/O manager, the redirector (covered later in this chapter), and the Server Message Block (SMB) protocol. (For more information about SMB, see Chapter 12, "File Systems," in Part 2.) This integration results in several benefits:

- The FSDs use kernel-mode security functions to implement standard Windows security for named pipes and mailslots.

- Applications can use *CreateFile* to open a named pipe or mailslot because FSDs integrate with the object manager namespace.

- Applications can use Windows functions such as *ReadFile* and *WriteFile* to interact with named pipes and mailslots.

- The FSDs rely on the object manager to track handle and reference counts for file objects representing named pipes and mailslots.

- The FSDs can implement their own named pipe and mailslot namespaces, complete with subdirectories.

EXPERIMENT: Listing the Named-Pipe Namespace and Watching Named-Pipe Activity

It's not possible to use the Windows API to open the root of the named-pipe FSD and perform a directory listing, but you can do this by using native API services. The PipeList tool from Sysinternals shows you the names of the named pipes defined on a computer as well as the number of instances that have been created for a name and the maximum number of instances as defined by a server's call to *CreateNamedPipe*. Here's an example of PipeList output:

```
C:\>pipelist

PipeList v1.01
by Mark Russinovich
http://www.sysinternals.com

Pipe Name                           Instances     Max Instances
---------                           ---------     -------------
InitShutdown                            3             -1
lsass                                   6             -1
protected_storage                       3             -1
ntsvcs                                  3             -1
scerpc                                  3             -1
```

net\NtControlPipe1	1	1
plugplay	3	-1
net\NtControlPipe2	1	1
Winsock2\CatalogChangeListener-394-0	1	1
epmapper	3	-1
Winsock2\CatalogChangeListener-25c-0	1	1
LSM_API_service	3	-1
net\NtControlPipe3	1	1
eventlog	3	-1
net\NtControlPipe4	1	1
Winsock2\CatalogChangeListener-3f8-0	1	1
net\NtControlPipe5	1	1
net\NtControlPipe6	1	1
net\NtControlPipe0	1	1
atsvc	3	-1
Winsock2\CatalogChangeListener-438-0	1	1
Winsock2\CatalogChangeListener-2c8-0	1	1
net\NtControlPipe7	1	1
net\NtControlPipe8	1	1
net\NtControlPipe9	1	1
net\NtControlPipe10	1	1
net\NtControlPipe11	1	1
net\NtControlPipe12	1	1
142CDF96-10CC-483c-A516-3E9057526912	1	1
net\NtControlPipe13	1	1
net\NtControlPipe14	1	1
TSVNCache-000000000001b017	20	-1
TSVNCacheCommand-000000000001b017	2	-1
Winsock2\CatalogChangeListener-2b0-0	1	1
Winsock2\CatalogChangeListener-468-0	1	1
TermSrv_API_service	3	-1
Ctx_WinStation_API_service	3	-1
PIPE_EVENTROOT\CIMV2SCM EVENT PROVIDER	2	-1
net\NtControlPipe15	1	1
keysvc	3	-1

It's clear from this output that several system components use named pipes as their communications mechanism. For example, the *InitShutdown* pipe is created by WinInit to accept remote shutdown commands, and the *Atsvc* pipe is created by the Task Scheduler service to enable applications to communicate with it to schedule tasks. You can determine what process has each of these pipes open by using the object search facility in Process Explorer.

Note A Max Instances value of –1 means that there is no upper limit on the number of instances.

NetBIOS

Until the 1990s, the Network Basic Input/Output System (NetBIOS) programming API had been the most widely used network programming API on PCs. NetBIOS allows for both reliable connection-oriented and unreliable connectionless communication. Windows supports NetBIOS for its legacy applications. Microsoft discourages application developers from using NetBIOS because other APIs, such as named pipes and Winsock, are much more flexible and portable. NetBIOS is supported by the TCP/IP protocol on Windows.

NetBIOS Names

NetBIOS relies on a naming convention whereby computers and network services are assigned a 16-byte NetBIOS name. The sixteenth byte of a NetBIOS name is treated as a modifier that can specify a name as unique or as part of a group. Only one instance of a unique NetBIOS name can be assigned to a network, but multiple applications can assign the same group name. A client can send multicast messages by sending them to a group name.

To support interoperability with Windows NT 4 systems as well as Windows 9x/Me, Windows automatically defines a NetBIOS name for a domain that includes up to the first 15 bytes of the left-most Domain Name System (DNS) name that an administrator assigns to the domain. For example, if a domain were named *mspress.microsoft.com*, the NetBIOS name of the domain would be *mspress*.

Another concept used by NetBIOS is that of LAN adapter (LANA) numbers. A LANA number is assigned to every NetBIOS-compatible protocol that layers above a network adapter. For example, if a computer has two network adapters and TCP/IP and NWLink can use either adapter, there would be four LANA numbers. LANA numbers are important because a NetBIOS application must explicitly assign its service name to each LANA through which it's willing to accept client connections. If the application listens for client connections on a particular name, clients can access the name only via protocols on the network adapters for which the name is registered.

NetBIOS Operation

A NetBIOS server application uses the NetBIOS API to enumerate the LANAs present on a system and assign a NetBIOS name representing the application's service to each LANA. If the server is connection oriented, it performs a NetBIOS listen command to wait for client connection attempts. After a client is connected, the server executes NetBIOS functions to send and receive data. Connectionless communication is similar, but the server simply reads messages without establishing connections.

A connection-oriented client uses NetBIOS functions to establish a connection with a NetBIOS server and then executes further NetBIOS functions to send and receive data. An established NetBIOS connection is also known as a *session*. If the client wants to send connectionless messages, it simply specifies the NetBIOS name of the server with the send function.

NetBIOS consists of a number of functions, but they all route through the same interface: *Netbios*. This routing scheme is the result of a legacy left over from the time when NetBIOS was implemented on MS-DOS as an MS-DOS interrupt service. A NetBIOS application would execute an MS-DOS interrupt and pass a data structure to the NetBIOS implementation that specified every aspect of the command being executed. As a result, the *Netbios* function in Windows takes a single parameter, which is a data structure that contains the parameters specific to the service the application requests.

EXPERIMENT: Using *Nbtstat* to See NetBIOS Names

You can use the *Nbtstat* command, which is included with Windows, to list the active sessions on a system, the NetBIOS-to-TCP/IP name mappings cached on a computer, and the NetBIOS names defined on a computer. Here's an example of the *Nbtstat* command with the −n option, which lists the NetBIOS names defined on the computer:

```
C:\Users\Toby>nbtstat -n

Local Area Connection:
Node IpAddress: [192.168.0.193] Scope Id: []

            NetBIOS Local Name Table

      Name               Type         Status
   ---------------------------------------------
   WIN-NLRTEOW2ILZ<00>  UNIQUE       Registered
   WORKGROUP     <00>   GROUP        Registered
   WIN-NLRTEOW2ILZ<20>  UNIQUE       Registered
```

NetBIOS API Implementation

The components that implement the NetBIOS API are shown in Figure 7-13. The *Netbios* function is exported to applications by %SystemRoot%\System32\Netbios.dll. Netbios.dll opens a handle to the kernel-mode driver named the *NetBIOS emulator* (%SystemRoot%\System32\Drivers\Netbios. sys) and issues Windows *DeviceIoControl* file commands on behalf of an application. The NetBIOS emulator translates NetBIOS commands issued by an application into TDI commands that it sends to protocol drivers.

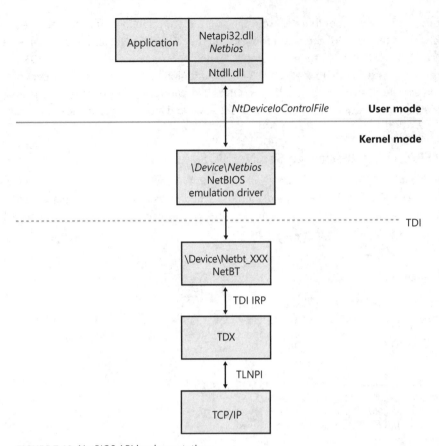

FIGURE 7-13 NetBIOS API implementation

If an application wants to use NetBIOS over the TCP/IP protocol, the NetBIOS emulator requires the presence of the NetBT driver (%SystemRoot%\System32\Drivers\Netbt.sys). NetBT is known as the NetBIOS over TCP/IP driver and is responsible for supporting NetBIOS semantics that are inherent to the NetBIOS Extended User Interface (NetBEUI) protocol (included in previous versions of Windows) but not the TCP/IP protocol. For example, NetBIOS relies on NetBEUI's message-mode transmission and NetBIOS name-resolution facilities, so the NetBT driver implements them on top of the TCP/IP protocol.

Other Networking APIs

Windows includes other networking APIs that are used less frequently or are layered on the APIs already described (and outside the scope of this book). Five of these, however—Background Intelligent Transfer Service (BITS), Distributed Component Object Model (DCOM), Message Queuing (MSMQ), Peer-to-Peer Infrastructure (P2P), and Universal Plug and Play (UPnP) with Plug and Play Extensions (PnP-X)—are important enough to the operation of a Windows system and many applications to merit brief descriptions.

Background Intelligent Transfer Service

BITS is a service and an API that provides reliable asynchronous transfer of files between systems, using either the SMB, HTTP, or HTTPS protocol. BITS normally runs in the background, making use of unutilized network bandwidth by monitoring network utilization and throttling itself so that it consumes only resources that would otherwise be unused; however, BITS transfers might also take place in the foreground and compete for resources with other processes running on the system.

BITS keeps track of ongoing, or scheduled, transfers in what are known as *transfer jobs* (not to be confused with jobs and job objects as described in Chapter 5, "Processes and Threads") for each user. Each job is an entry in a queue and describes the files to transfer, the security context (access tokens) to run under, and the priority of the job. BITS version 4.0 is integrated into BranchCache (described later in this chapter) to further reduce network bandwidth.

BITS is used by many other components in Windows, such as Microsoft Update, Windows Update, Internet Explorer (version 9 and later, for downloading files), Microsoft Outlook (for downloading address books), Microsoft Security Essentials (for downloading daily virus signature updates), and others, making BITS the most widely used network file-transfer system in use today.

BITS provides the following capabilities:

- **Seamless data transfer**   Components create BITS transfer jobs that will then run until the files are transferred. When a user logs out, the system restarts, or the system loses network connectivity, BITS pauses the transfer. The transfer resumes from where it left off once the user logs in again or network connectivity is restored. The application that created a transfer job does not need to remain running, but the user must remain logged in, while the transfer is taking place. Transfer jobs created under service accounts (such as Windows Update) are always considered to be logged on, allowing those jobs to run continuously.

- **Multiple transfer types**   BITS supports three transfer types: download (server to client), upload (client to server), and upload-reply (client to server, with a notification receipt from the server).

- **Prioritization of transfers**   When a transfer job is created, the priority is specified (either Foreground, Background High, Background Normal, or Background Low). All background priority jobs make use only of unutilized network resources, while jobs with foreground priority compete with applications for network resources. If there are multiple jobs, BITS processes them in priority order, using a round-robin scheduling system within a particular priority so that all jobs make progress on their transfers.

- **Secure data transfer**   BITS normally runs the transfer job using the security context of the job's creator, but you can also use the BITS API to specify the credentials to use for impersonating a user. For privacy across the network, you should use the HTTPS protocol.

- **Management**   The BITS API consists of methods for creating, starting, stopping, monitoring, enumerating, modifying, or requesting notification of transfer-job status changes. Tools include BITSAdmin (which is deprecated and will be removed in a future version of Windows), and Windows PowerShell *cmdlets* (the preferred management mechanism).

When downloading files, BITS writes the file to a temporary hidden file in the destination directory. Of course, BITS will impersonate the user to ensure that file-system security and quotas are enforced properly. When the application calls the *IBackgroundCopyJob::Complete* method (or the *Complete-BitsTransfer* cmdlet in PowerShell), BITS renames the temporary files to their destination names, and the files are available to the client. If there is already a file in the destination directory with the same name, BITS overwrites the file.

When uploading files, by default, BITS does not allow overwriting an existing file. When the transfer is finished and BITS would overwrite the file, an error is returned to the client. To allow overwrites, set the *BITSAllowOverwrites* property to *True* in the Internet Information Services (IIS) metabase using PowerShell or Windows Management Instrumentation (WMI) scripting.

The BITS server is a server-side component that lets you configure an IIS server to allow BITS clients to perform file transfers to IIS virtual directories. Upon completion of a file upload, the BITS server can notify a web application of the new file's presence (via an HTTP POST message) so the web application can process the uploaded files.

The BITS server extends IIS to support throttled, restartable uploads of files. To make use of the upload feature, you must create an IIS virtual directory on the server where you want the clients to upload their files. BITS adds properties to the IIS metabase for the virtual directory you create and uses these properties to determine how to upload the files.

For security reasons, BITS will not permit uploading files to a virtual directory that has scripting and execute permissions enabled. If you upload a file to a virtual directory that has these permissions enabled, the job will fail. Also, BITS does not require the virtual directory to be write-enabled, so it is recommended that you turn off write access to the virtual directory; however, the user must have write access to the physical directory.

In some cases, the BITS Compact Server might be used instead of IIS. The Compact Server is intended for use by enterprise and small business customers that meet the following conditions:

- The anticipated usage is a maximum of 25 URL groups, and each URL group supports up to three simultaneous file transfers

- File transfers occur between systems in the same domain or mutually trusted domains

- File transfers are not intended for Internet-facing clients

Figure 7-14 demonstrates how to load the BITS module within PowerShell, and some of the BITS PowerShell cmdlets.

Figure 7-15 demonstrates the use of the BITSAdmin tool, which is now deprecated in favor of PowerShell for managing and using BITS.

FIGURE 7-14 Using BITS from PowerShell

FIGURE 7-15 BitsAdmin tool

Figure 7-16 shows BITS messages written to the event log.

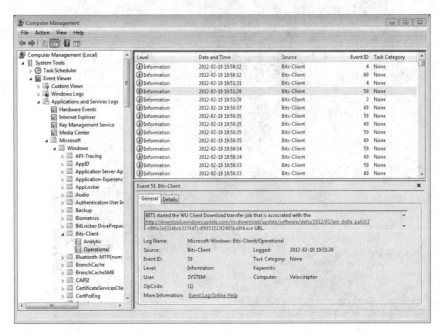

FIGURE 7-16 BITS messages in the event log

Peer-to-Peer Infrastructure

Peer-to-Peer Infrastructure is a set of APIs that cover different technologies to enhance the Windows networking stack by providing flexible peer-to-peer (P2P) support for applications and services. The P2P infrastructure covers four major technologies, shown in Figure 7-17.

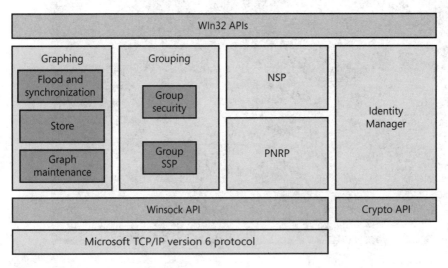

FIGURE 7-17 Peer-to-peer architecture

Here are the major peer-to-peer components:

- **Peer-to-Peer Graphing**   Allows applications to pass data between peers efficiently and reliably by using nodes and events.

- **Peer-to-Peer Namespace Provider**   Enables serverless name resolution of peers and their services (described later in the "Name Resolution" section).

- **Peer-to-Peer Grouping**   Combines graphing and namespace technologies to group and isolate services and/or peers into a defined group and uniquely identify it.

- **Peer-to-Peer Identity Manager**   Enhances the services offered by the namespace provider to securely create, publish, and identify peer names, as well as to identify group members that are part of the grouping API.

The Peer-to-Peer Infrastructure in Windows is also paired with the Peer-to-Peer Collaboration Interface, which adds support for creating collaborative P2P applications (such as online games and group instant messaging) and supersedes the Real-Time Communications (RTC) architecture in earlier versions of Windows. It also provides presence capabilities through the People Near Me (PNM) architecture.

DCOM

Microsoft's COM API lets applications consist of different components, each component being a replaceable, self-contained module. A COM object exports an object-oriented interface to methods for manipulating the data within the object. Because COM objects present well-defined interfaces, developers can implement new objects to extend existing interfaces and dynamically update applications with the new support.

DCOM (Distributed Component Object Model) extends COM by letting an application's components reside on different computers, which means that applications don't need to be concerned that one COM object might be on the local computer and another might be across the network. DCOM thus provides location transparency, which simplifies developing distributed applications. DCOM isn't a self-contained API but relies on RPC to carry out its work.

Message Queuing

Message Queuing is a general-purpose platform for developing distributed applications that take advantage of loosely coupled messaging. Message Queuing is therefore an API and a messaging infrastructure. Its flexibility comes from the fact that its queues serve as message repositories in which senders can queue messages for receivers, and receivers can de-queue the messages at their discretion. Senders and receivers do not need to establish connections to use Message Queuing, nor do they need to be executing at the same time, which allows for disconnected asynchronous message exchange.

A notable feature of Message Queuing is that it is integrated with Microsoft Transaction Server (MTS) and SQL Server, so it can participate in Microsoft Distributed Transaction Coordinator (MS DTC) coordinated transactions. Using MS DTC with Message Queuing allows you to develop reliable transaction functionality for three-tier applications.

UPnP with PnP-X

Universal Plug and Play is an architecture for peer-to-peer network connectivity of intelligent appliances, devices, and *control points*. It is designed to bring easy-to-use, flexible, standards-based connectivity to ad-hoc, managed, or unmanaged networks, whether these networks are in the home, in small businesses, or attached directly to the Internet. Universal Plug and Play is a distributed, open networking architecture that uses existing TCP/IP and Web technologies to enable seamless proximity networking in addition to control and data transfer among networked devices.

Universal Plug and Play supports zero-configuration, invisible networking, and automatic discovery for a range of device categories from a wide range of vendors. This enables a device to dynamically join a network, obtain an IP address, and convey its capabilities upon request. Then other control points can use the Control Point API with UPnP technology to learn about the presence and capabilities of other devices. A device can leave a network smoothly and automatically when it is no longer in use.

Plug and Play Extensions (PnP-X), shown in Figure 7-18, is an additional component of Windows that allows network-attached devices to integrate with the Plug and Play manager in the kernel. With PnP-X, network-connected devices are shown in the Device Manager like locally attached devices and provide the same installation, management, and behavioral experience as a local device. (For example, installation is performed through the standard Add New Hardware Wizard.)

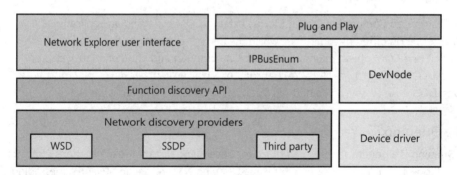

FIGURE 7-18 PnP-X implementation

PnP-X uses a virtual network bus driver that uses an IP bus enumerator service (%SystemRoot% \System32\Ipbusenum.dll) to discover PnP-X compatible devices, which include UPnP devices (through the Simple Service Discovery Protocol) and the newer Device Profile for Web Services (DPWS) devices (using the WS-Discovery protocol). The IP bus enumerator reports devices it discovers to the Plug and Play manager, which uses user-mode Plug and Play manager services if needed (such as for driver installation). It's similar to wireless discovery (like Bluetooth) and unlike wired device discovery (like USB), however, PnP-X enumeration and driver installation must be explicitly requested by a user from the Network Explorer.

 Note DPWS v1.1 became an OASIS standard in June 2009 and has goals similar to those of UPnP, but it is tightly integrated with web services standards and frameworks and allows greater extensibility than UPnP.

Multiple Redirector Support

Applications access file-system resources on remote systems (often called *file shares*) using UNC paths—for example, \\servername\sharename\file. Resources can be accessed directly using the UNC name if it is already known and the logged-on user's credentials are sufficient. Optionally, the Windows Networking (WNet) API can be used to enumerate computers and resources that those computers export for sharing, map drive letters to UNC paths, and explicitly specify credentials. To access SMB servers from a client, Microsoft supplies an SMB client, which has a kernel-mode component called the *mini-redirector* and a user-mode component called the *Workstation service*. (SMB is described in Chapter 12 in Part 2.) Microsoft also makes available redirectors that can access WebDAV resources, NFS v2/v3 resources (Windows Professional and Enterprise editions only), and Terminal Services–shared drives. Third parties can add their own redirectors to Windows. In this section, we'll examine the software that decides which redirector to invoke for file access using UNC paths. Here are the responsible components:

- *Multiple Provider Router* (MPR) is a DLL (%SystemRoot%\System32\Mpr.dll) that determines which network to access when an application uses the Windows WNet API for browsing remote file resources.

- *Multiple UNC Provider* (MUP) is a driver (%SystemRoot%\System32\Drivers\Mup.sys) that determines which network to access when an application uses the Windows I/O APIs to open remote files through UNC paths or drive letters mapped to UNC paths.

Multiple Provider Router

The Windows WNet functions allow applications (including the Network and Sharing Center) to connect to network resources, such as file servers and printers, and to browse the different share points. Because the WNet API can be called to work across different networks using different transport protocols, software must be present to send the request to the correct network and to understand the results that the remote server returns. Figure 7-19 shows the redirector software responsible for these tasks.

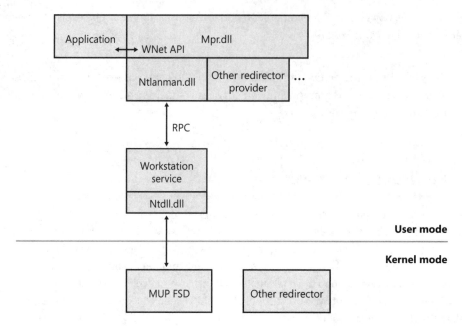

FIGURE 7-19 MPR components

A *provider* is software that establishes Windows as a client of a remote network server. Some of the operations a WNet provider performs include making and breaking network connections, as well as supporting network printing. The built-in SMB WNet provider includes a DLL, the Workstation service, and the redirector. Other network vendors need to supply only a DLL and a redirector.

When an application calls a WNet routine, the call passes directly to the MPR DLL. MPR takes the call and determines which network provider recognizes the resource being accessed. Each provider DLL beneath MPR supplies a set of standard functions collectively called the *network provider interface*. This interface allows MPR to determine which network the application is trying to access and to direct the request to the appropriate WNet provider software. The SMB Workstation service's provider is %SystemRoot%\System32\Ntlanman.dll, as specified by the *ProviderPath* value under the HKLM\SYSTEM\CurrentControlSet\Services\LanmanWorkstation\NetworkProvider registry key.

When called by the *WNetAddConnection2* or *WNetAddConnection3* API function to connect to a remote network resource, MPR checks the HKLM\SYSTEM\CurrentControlSet\Control \NetworkProvider\HwOrder\ProviderOrder registry value to determine which network providers are loaded. It polls them one at a time, in the order in which they're listed in the registry, until a provider recognizes the resource or until all available providers have been polled. You can change the *ProviderOrder* by using the Advanced Settings dialog box shown in Figure 7-20. You can access the dialog box by opening the Start menu, typing **view network connections** in the search box, and pressing Enter. This brings up the Network Connections dialog box. Press the Alt key on the keyboard, which will display the menus in the dialog box. Click on the Advanced drop-down menu, and choose Advanced Settings, and then click on the Provider Order tab.

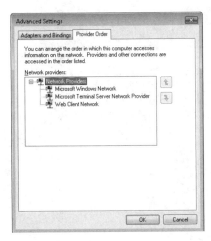

FIGURE 7-20 The provider order editor

The *WNetAddConnection* function can also assign a drive letter or device name to a remote resource. When called to do so, *WNetAddConnection* routes the call to the appropriate network provider. The provider, in turn, creates a symbolic-link object in the object manager's namespace that maps the drive letter being defined to the redirector (that is, the remote FSD) for that network.

Figure 7-21 shows the Session 0 DosDevices directory corresponding to the LUID of the user who performed the drive-letter mapping, which is where connections to remote file shares are stored. The symbolic link created by network providers relies on MUP to serve as the connection between a network path and the corresponding redirector. The figure shows that MUP creates a device object named *Device**LanmanRedirector*, which is itself a symbolic link to \\Device\\MUP (which is not shown in the figure because the symbolic link is in the \\Device directory), with additional text included in the symbolic link's value indicating to the MUP redirector which mini-redirector the drive letter corresponds to. The "\\Global??" directory shows you the drive letters available to the system session—others will be mapped in the session-specific DosDevices directory.

Then, when the WNet or other API calls the object manager to open a resource on a different network, the object manager uses the device object as a jumping-off point into the remote file system. It calls an I/O manager parse method associated with the device object to locate the redirector FSD that can handle the request. (See Chapter 12 in Part 2 for more information on file system drivers.)

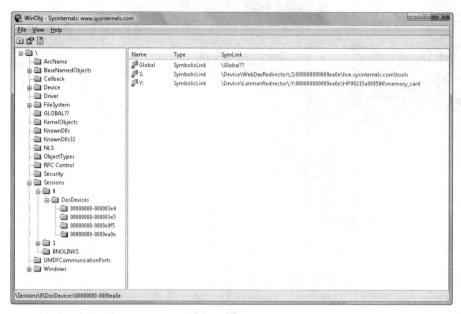

FIGURE 7-21 Resolving a network resource name

Multiple UNC Provider

The Multiple UNC Provider (MUP, %SystemRoot%\System32\Drivers\mup.sys) is a file-system driver that exposes remote file systems to Windows. It is a single point where file system filter drivers can be layered to filter any and all I/O requests made to remote file systems. (Prior to Windows Vista, there were many inconsistencies and difficulties regarding filtering remote file systems.) MUP receives I/O requests for access to remote file systems (via UNC paths or drive letters mapped to them) and determines which redirector will handle the request. The term *redirector* is used because it redirects an I/O request to a remote system. Before, and optionally after, calling the redirector, MUP will call any registered *surrogate providers* that might provide file caching and path rewriting.

MUP implements what is known as a *prefix cache*, which is a list of which remote file system paths (\\<server name>[\<share name>]) that are handled by each redirector. It is possible that multiple redirectors could handle a particular prefix, so there is a list in the registry (HKLM\System \CurrentControlSet\Control\NetworkProvider\Order\ProviderOrder) containing a comma-separated list of the priority order in which MUP forwards requests to the redirectors. This list is also used to load the providers. Under *ProviderOrder*, there are two subkeys (*HwOrder* and *Order*) containing identical information in a value named *ProviderOrder*. A typical value is the following:

```
ProviderOrder    REG_SZ    RDPNP,LanmanWorkstation,webClient
```

Each entry specifies the name of a service in HKLM\System\CurrentControlSet\Services, where another subkey named *NetworkProvider* is found. For example, in the key HKLM\System \CurrentControlSet\Services\RDPNP\NetworkProvider are the following values:

```
DeviceName      REG_SZ           \Device\RdpDr
DisplayName     REG_EXPAND_SZ        @%systemroot%\system32\drprov.dll,-100
Name               REG_SZ           Microsoft Terminal Services
ProviderPath    REG_EXPAND_SZ     %SystemRoot%\System32\drprov.dll
```

The *DeviceName* value is the name assigned to the kernel-mode redirector's device object. *DisplayName* is the formal name of the provider. (This can be either a string or the location of a string in the resource section of a DLL, as seen here.) *Name* is the name that will be displayed by *net use* to identify which redirector owns a particular drive. *ProviderPath* specifies the path where the provider DLL is located.

> **Note** Not all redirectors are, or have to be, listed in provider order. (Typically, you will see only *RDPNP, LanmanWorkstation, webclient* listed.) The priority of the redirectors not listed in the registry follows those that are listed in decreasing order and is then based upon the order in which the mini-redirector registered with MUP via *FsRtlRegisterUncProviderEx* via *RxRegisterMinirdr*.

The components of a prefix (server name and share name) that are claimed by a redirector varies; most redirectors usually claim both the server name and the share name of a UNC path (\\<server name>\<share name>[\<path>]). For example, for the path \\Server\Users\Brian \Documents, a redirector might claim the prefix \\Server\Users, which would cause MUP to route all requests containing that prefix to that particular redirector, such as \\Server\Users\David\Documents \Chapter7.doc; however, a path with the prefix \\Server\Backups will have to be resolved by query-ing the redirectors in priority order. If a redirector claims a prefix consisting of just a server name (for example, \\Server), MUP sends requests for all shares (for example, \\Server\Users, \\Server\WebDAV, and so on) on that server to the redirector.

MUP uses the names found in *ProviderOrder* to look up the name of the device implementing the redirector, by looking in HKLM\System\CurrentControlSet\Services\<redirector name> \NetworkProvider\DeviceName. *DeviceName* is a symbolic link, pointing back to MUP—for example, \Device\MUP\;LanmanRedirector. (The semicolon identifies this as a "targeted open," meaning that MUP will not look in the prefix cache.)

The relationships between MUP and the other components that are part of the remote file system are shown in Figure 7-22.

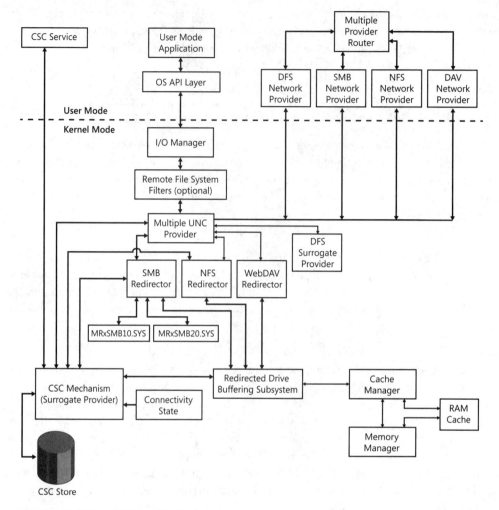

FIGURE 7-22 MPR and UNC architecture

Surrogate Providers

Prior to Windows Vista, the caching of remote file systems (Offline Files) was implemented inside the SMB mini-redirector, and the DFS-N (Distributed File System Namespace) client was implemented inside MUP. A unified cache was needed, so the remote file system architecture was redesigned for Windows Vista. The DFS-N client was moved into a separate driver component known as a *MUP surrogate provider*, and Offline Files became a separate driver acting both as a mini-redirector and a surrogate provider. Currently, there are two surrogate providers:

- Offline Files (%SystemRoot%\System32\Drivers\csc.sys), which determines whether a requested file should be or has been cached locally. Offline Files is hardcoded to be the highest priority surrogate.

- Distributed File System Client (%SystemRoot%\System32\Drivers\dfsc.sys), which determines whether the path to a requested file needs to be changed (rewritten) to point to another server or share. (The essence of DFS-N is that it collects one or more network shares in the same namespace.) DFSCDFS is hardcoded to be the second highest priority surrogate.

It might appear that having surrogates in the path between MUP and the redirectors would cause a performance penalty, but Offline Files does not process paths that are not enabled for offline access, and after rejecting a path, MUP will not forward Offline Files further I/Os directed at the path. Likewise, DFS does not process non-DFS paths.

The list of surrogates is hardcoded, so MUP does not support the addition of additional surrogates.

Redirector

A network redirector consists of software components installed on a system that support access to various types of resources on remote systems, using various network file protocols. The types of resources a redirector supports depends upon the redirector and the capabilities of the protocol system. Virtually all redirectors support UNC names, which allows the remote sharing of resources such as files, printers, named pipes, and mailslots (although a redirector might opt out of supporting pipes and mailslots, while still supporting printers and files). All redirectors shipping as part of Windows include the following components:

- A DLL loaded by MPR in user mode, to perform non-file-related operations such as determining the capabilities of the network provider, enumerating remote network resources, logging on to a remote network, and mounting remote network shares.

- A kernel-mode driver known as a *mini-redirector* that imports the RDBSS (Redirected Drive Buffering SubSystem) export driver (%SystemRoot%\System32\Drivers\rdbss.sys). The mini-redirector services file I/O requests directed at remote systems.

Some redirectors require one or more of the following optional components:

- A service process to assist the DLL and possibly store sensitive information or information that is global across client applications using a particular network or share. For example, the Workstation service (running in an SVCHOST process) keeps track of drive-letter to \\server\share mappings.

- A network protocol driver that implements the legacy Transport Driver Interface (TDI) on its upper edge is required if the redirector uses a network protocol not supplied by Windows. (In essence, this means anything other than TCP/IP.) Such a protocol driver is responsible for implementing communications with the remote system.

- A service process to assist the redirector. For example, the WebDav redirector forwards file-access operations to the WebClient user-mode service, which in turn issues the actual WebDav network protocol requests using HTTP APIs.

A redirector presents resources that are attached to remote systems as if they were attached to the local system. In Windows, there are no special file I/O APIs required to access resources on a remote system. When accessing a resource, an application generally does not know—nor does it care—whether the resource is located on the local system or on a remote system. The name "redirector" is used because it redirects file system operations to the remote system and returns to the application the responses from the remote system.

All redirectors that ship with Windows are implemented using the mini-redirector architecture, where protocol-specific code is implemented in a mini-redirector driver that imports the RDBSS library. RDBSS is implemented like a class driver, and the mini-redirectors are akin to port drivers. RDBSS registers with MUP by calling *FsRtlRegisterUncProviderEx*.

When a mini-redirector registers with RDBSS via *RxRegisterMiniRdr*, RDBSS in turn registers with MUP by calling *FsRtlRegisterUncProviderEx*. MUP routes requests (IRPs) to RDBSS, which performs processing that is common to all remote file systems, and then issues simplified requests via callback routines that mini-redirectors linked against it have registered. RDBSS provides common functionality such as a data structure and locking model, Cache Manager and Memory Manager integration, and handling of IRPs. This simplifies the implementation of the mini-redirectors, and it vastly reduces the amount of code that needs to be written and debugged.

Because RDBSS integrates with Cache Manager, RDBSS mini-redirectors might not directly see read and write requests on buffered handles (handles opened *without* specifying the FILE_FLAG_NO_BUFFERING flag to the *CreateFile* API); changes are cached by the cache manager on the local system until they need to be written back to the remote system. This improves response time, and it saves network bandwidth by aggregating writes and eliminating duplicate reads. RDBSS relies on the mini-redirector to tell it when it is safe to cache data for read and/or write. For example, the SMB mini-redirector uses opportunistic locks (more commonly known as *oplocks*, which are discussed in Chapter 12 in Part 2) to manage caching. An oplock is a cache coherency mechanism that allows file-system consumers to dynamically alter their caching state for a given file or stream (see Chapter 12 in Part 2 for more information about file system streams), while maintaining cache coherency between multiple concurrent users of a file. If the file (or stream) is not currently opened for read or write by another accessor (either locally or remotely), a client can locally cache reads, writes, and byte range locks. If the file is open by others but is not being written, writes and locks will not be locally cached, but reads can still be cached.

Mini-Redirectors

A mini-redirector implements a protocol necessary to contact a remote system and access its shared resources. The mini-redirector tries to make access to remote resources as transparent as possible to the local client application. For example, if there are network problems, a redirector might retry a request multiple times before it returns an error to the client application.

There are several mini-redirectors included with Windows:

- RDPDR (Remote Desktop Protocol Device Redirection), which allows access from a Terminal Server system to the client system's files and printers (%SystemRoot%\System32\Drivers\rdpdr.sys)

- SMB (Server Message Block), which is the standard remote file system used by Windows (also known as CIFS, or Common Internet File System) (%SystemRoot%\System32\Drivers\MRxSMB.SYS). MRxSMB.SYS will load sub-redirectors, which are covered in the next section.

- WebDAV (Web Differencing and Versioning), which enables access to files over the HTTP(S) protocol (%SystemRoot%\System32\Drivers\MRxDAV.SYS).

- MailSlot (part of MRxSMB.SYS). Mailslots are handled very differently from named pipes. The surrogates are not called for I/Os sent to a mailslot, and prefix caching is not used. (All paths having "mailslot" as the share name are targeted directly at the mailslot mini-redirector.) There can be, at most, one mailslot mini-redirector, and it is currently reserved for the SMB redirector.

- Network File System (NFS) is an optional component that was formerly installed with Services For Unix (SFU) and is now an optional Windows component (available on all Server editions, but only Enterprise and Ultimate editions of Windows client) that can be installed using the Programs and Features control panel. (Click Turn Windows Features On Or Off, and then select Services For NFS.) NFS protocol versions 2 and 3 are supported.

Offline Files, covered in a following section, optionally enables disk caching and offline access to files accessed through the SMB protocol. Offline Files also registers as a MUP surrogate provider.

Server Message Block and Sub-Redirectors

The Server Message Block (SMB) protocol is the primary remote file-access protocol used by Windows clients and servers, and dates back to the 1980s. SMB version 1.0 (generally referred to as just *SMB*) was designed to operate in a friendly LAN environment, where speeds were typically 10 Mb/s and no one was trying to steal your data. To accomplish many common tasks required a series of synchronous messages between the client and the server. Little thought was given to WANs, because WANs were scarce at the time. In 1996, SMB was submitted to the IETF as the Common Internet File System (CIFS). Microsoft documents the CIFS/SMB protocol in the MS-CIFS and MS-SMB protocol documents.

The SMB 2.0 protocol was released in Windows Vista and Windows Server 2008, and it was a complete redesign of the main remote file protocol for Windows. SMB 2.0 provides a number of improvements over SMB, such as the following:

- Greatly reduced complexity. The number of opcodes was reduced from over 100 to just 19.

- Reduced the *chattiness* of the protocol to make it more suitable for running across WANs, which generally have much longer latencies and lower bandwidth than LANs.

- *Compound requests* allow multiple requests to be sent in a single network packet.

- *Pipelining requests* allow multiple requests and data to be sent before the answer to a previous request is received (also known as *credit-based flow control*).

- Larger reads and writes.

- Caching of folder and file properties.

- Improved message-signing algorithm (HMAC SHA-256 replaced MD5).

- Improved scalability of file sharing.

- Works well with Network Address Translation (NAT).

- Support for symbolic links.

Version 2.1 of the SMB protocol (released with Windows 7 and Windows Server 2008/R2) is a minor release (documented in the MS-SMB2 protocol specification). It adds the following improvements:

- A new opportunistic lock (oplock) leasing model, which allows greater file and handle caching opportunities—without requiring changes to existing applications

- Support for even larger transmission units (large MTU), from a previous maximum of 64 KB to 1 MB (by default, but configurable up to 8 MB via the registry).

To maintain backward compatibility with SMB servers, an SMB2 client uses the existing SMB connection setup mechanisms, and then advertises that it supports a higher version of the protocol. The SMB mini-redirector contains all the functionality that is common between the different versions of the protocol, with a separate sub-redirector implementing each variant of the SMB protocol. An SMB2 client establishes a connection and sends an SMB negotiate request that contains both the supported SMB and SMB2 dialects. If the server supports SMB2, it responds with an SMB2 negotiate response, and the client hands the connection to the SMB2 sub-redirector. At that point, all messages on the connection are SMB2. If the server does not support SMB2, it responds with an SMB negotiate response, and the client hands the connection to the SMB1 sub-redirector:

- The common portions are implemented by %SystemRoot%\System32\Drivers\MRxSMB.sys.

- The SMB 1 protocol is implemented by %SystemRoot%\System32\Drivers\MRxSMB10.sys.

- The SMB 2 protocol is implemented by %SystemRoot%\System32\Drivers\MRxSMB20.sys.

Distributed File System Namespace

Distributed File System Namespace (DFS-N) is a namespace aggregation and availability feature of Windows. As organizations grow, the number of file servers tends to increase, and users find it increasingly difficult to find the files they need because the files might be spread over a number of different servers with completely unrelated names. DFS-N allows an administrator to create a new file share (also known as a *root* or *namespace*) that aggregates multiple file shares, from the same or different servers, into a single namespace. For example, assume the Aura Corporation had the following shares: \\Development\Projects, \\Accounting\FY2012, and \\Marketing\CoolStuff. These shares could be presented to users through a DFS-N *namespace* \\Aura\Teams containing DFS-N *links* called \\Aura\Teams\\Aura\Development, \\Aura\Teams\Accounting, and \\Aura\Teams \Marketing. The redirection of a client accessing the path \\Aura\Teams\Marketing to the real share path \\Marketing\CoolStuff is invisible to the user. In this example, \\Marketing\CoolStuff is the *link target* of \\Aura\Teams\Marketing. Link targets can, in fact, refer to paths below the root of a share like \\Marketing\CoolStuff\Presentations.

Other benefits that DFS-N provides are redundancy and location-aware redirection. Another major capability of DFS is availability, through a feature known as DFS Replication (DFSR). Replication provides two benefits: high availability in case of a failure, and load balancing. As an organization grows geographically, accessing file servers from remote offices with wide area network (WAN) connections might be slow and inefficient. An administrator could create a replicated version of a file server within the remote office, providing high-speed access to the files from the users within the remote office. A DFS-N link, such as \\Aura\Teams\Accounting in the preceding example, might have multiple *link targets* associated with it—for example, \\AccountingEurope\FY2012 and \\AccountingUS\FY2012. In this case, the DFS-N server returns to the client an ordered list of available target servers and takes into account the location of the client and the target servers (using Active Directory site information) when ordering the list so that the client can access the closest target first. If access to one link target fails, DFS-N tries the next available target, if available. When a DFS-N link has multiple target shares, the targets should normally contain the same data because the client accessing the namespace will access only one of the targets at a time. This can be accomplished using DFS Replication (DFS-R), discussed in the next section. A server-side implementation of DFS-N consists of a Windows service (%SystemRoot%\System32\Dfssvc.exe) and a device driver (%SystemRoot%\System32\Drivers\Dfs.sys). The DFSSVC service is responsible for exporting DFS topology-management interfaces and maintaining the DFS topology in either the registry (on non–Active Directory systems) or Active Directory. The DFS driver performs topology lookups when it receives a client request touching a link so that it can direct the client to the share where the file it is requesting resides.

On the client side, DFS-N support is implemented in a MUP surrogate provider driver (%SystemRoot%\System32\Drivers\Dfsc.sys) and an MPR/WNet provider implemented in %SystemRoot%\System32\Ntlanman.dll. The Distributed File System Client (DFSC) driver is responsible for determining if a UNC path is a DFS namespace, and if so, it translates the specified path into the name of one or more target shares. Communication with DFS-N servers is accomplished using the SMB redirector. The DFS-N client is only part of the I/O path when a file or directory is being created or opened. Once it returns the name of a target share to MUP, DFSC is not involved with subsequent I/O to the file.

The DFS-N protocols are documented in the MS-DFSC and MS-DFSNM protocol documents.

Distributed File System Replication

Distributed File System Replication (DFS-R) provides bandwidth-efficient, asynchronous, multimaster replication of file-system changes between servers. In addition to general-purpose, file-system replication (for example, keeping data on multiple DFS-N link target shares in sync), DFS-R is also used for replicating a domain controller's \SYSVOL directory, which is where Windows domain controllers store logon scripts and Group Policy files. (Group Policy permits administrators to define usage and security policies for the computers that belong to a domain.) Because DFS-R supports multimaster replication, file-system changes can occur on any server, potentially simultaneously, and DFS-R will automatically handle conflicts and maintain synchronization of the file-system contents.

The fundamental unit of DFS replication is a DFS replicated folder, which is a directory tree whose contents will be synchronized across multiple servers according to an administratively defined schedule and replication topology. Replication schedules allow administrators to restrict replication activity to specific windows of time or restrict the amount of bandwidth that DFS-R will use.

Replication topologies allow administrators to define the network connections between a set of servers (called a *replication group*). Arbitrary topologies are supported, including common topologies such as ring, star, or mesh. The replication topology configuration is stored in Active Directory. Only directories on NTFS volumes can be replicated because DFS-R relies on the NTFS USN journal to detect changes to the contents of a replicated folder.

DFS-R uses several technologies to conserve network bandwidth, making it well-suited to replication over WANs that might have high latency and low bandwidth. Remote Differential Compression (RDC) allows DFS-R to identify and replicate only those pieces of a file that have changed, rather than the whole file. DFS-R also compresses content before sending it to a remote partner, providing additional bandwidth savings. On Enterprise or Datacenter SKUs, DFS-R makes use of an extended version of RDC called RDC Similarity to provide further bandwidth savings; if content is modified in a replicated folder on server A, and chunks of the modified content are similar to chunks of any file in partner server B's replicated folder, server B satisfies the similar chunks of the update's content locally from the similar files, rather than downloading all of the modified content from server A.

New capabilities for DFS-R in Windows Server 2008 R2 include support for clustering and true read-only replicas.

DFS-R is implemented as a Windows service (%SystemRoot%\System32\DfsrS.exe) that uses authenticated RPC with encryption to communicate between instances of itself running on different computers. There is also a WMI interface for configuration and management of the service, a file system minifilter used to protect read-only replicas from modification, and a cluster resource DLL for integration with MSCS. The DFS-R protocol is documented in the MS-FRS2 specification.

Offline Files

Offline Files (also known internally as client-side caching, or CSC) transparently caches files from a remote system (a file server) on the local machine to make the files available when the local machine is not connected to the network. Offline Files caches files for remote files accessed over the SMB protocol. Files can be cached by users by simply right-clicking on a remote file, folder, or drive and selecting Always Available Offline, thus *pinning* the selected files to the cache. Cached items can be viewed in the Sync Center control panel. Caching also can be specified administratively using Group Policy.

There is a single Offline Files cache on the system, which is shared by all users of the system. All cached files are stored in an ACL-protected directory, which by default is %SystemRoot%\CSC. If you choose, you can encrypt the files in the Offline Files cache (accessed by going to Control Panel, Sync Center, and then clicking Manage Offline Files, clicking on the Encryption tab, and clicking the Encrypt button). Access to the cache is permitted only by using Offline File tools and the IOfflineFilesXxx COM APIs. The easiest way to examine the contents of the cache is to use the Sync Center control panel interface (click Manage Offline Files, and then click the View Your Offline Files button).

Offline Files understands two types of objects:

- **Files** Includes files, folders, and symbolic links. Caching is not done at the NTFS level, so not all file NTFS attributes are cached or are cacheable. Cacheable attributes include the standard Win32 file attributes (*metadata*), such as the name, ACL, and the contents—only a file's (unnamed) data stream will be cached.

- **Scope** A scope is the portion of a namespace that corresponds to a physical share. In a DFS namespace, the root of a scope is the object that is pointed to by a DFS link, which can contain additional DFS links to other scopes. If DFS is not being used, a scope and a share are the same thing.

Offline Files does not support complete NTFS semantics for cached files and has the following limitations:

- Offline Files does not cache alternate data streams, which are therefore not available offline. When online, access to alternate data streams works because I/O requests for streams go directly to the server.

- Offline Files does not cache Extended Attributes (EAs). An implication of this is that if a file containing EAs is cached and the cached version is modified while the server is offline, any EAs on the server are deleted when changes are written back to the server.

Offline Files consists of the following components, as shown in Figure 7-23:

- A user-mode agent (%SystemRoot%\System32\cscsvc.dll) running as a service in an SVCHOST process. This service is primarily concerned with maintaining synchronization between the cache and remote file systems. It also implements the COM interfaces used to interact with the Offline Files cache.

- A remote file system driver (%SystemRoot%\System32\Drivers\csc.sys) that acts as both a MUP surrogate provider and a mini-redirector. This driver is responsible for controlling when I/O requests are sent to the cache or to the remote file system. The driver also implements the local cache, updating the cached data as appropriate based on the I/O requests seen.

- An Explorer extension DLL (%SystemRoot%\System32\cscui.dll) for selecting which files, folders, or drives to pin in the Offline Files cache, and for displaying icon overlays to identify offline (cached) files. CSCUI links against %SystemRoot%\System32\cscobj.dll, which provides the interface to the Offline Files service.

- A DLL (%SystemRoot%\System32\cscapi.dll) containing publicly available Win32 APIs for interacting with the Offline Files from applications.

- An in-process COM object (%SystemRoot%\System32\cscobj.dll) used by application clients of Offline Files COM APIs.

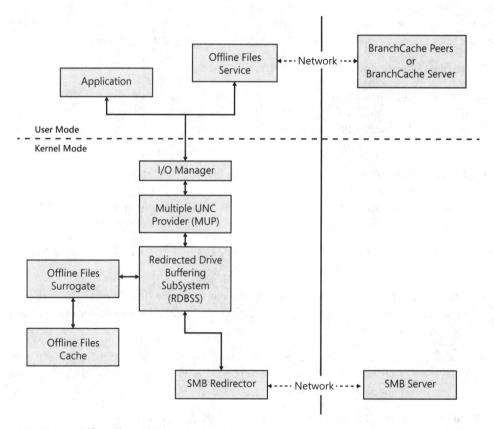

FIGURE 7-23 Offline Files architecture

Caching Modes

Offline Files has five caching modes. The mode for an object is dependent upon the object's connection status, which is determined by whether or not the local system has a network connection to the file server.

Online

This is the default mode for objects cached by Offline Files. In this mode, the server is available. The file system metadata operations and write operations flow to the server, and the cache state is updated as required. Read operations are serviced from the cache. When working online, Offline Files attempt to cache data only if the SMB client has been granted at least read-caching privileges from the file server.

Offline (Slow Connection)

To isolate the user from fluctuations in network performance, Offline Files transition into Offline (Slow Connection) mode when the network performance meets the configured slow-link latency or bandwidth thresholds. In Windows 7, a default slow-link latency threshold is configured at 80 milliseconds (ms). The latency and bandwidth thresholds can be controlled via the Group Policy editor (%SystemRoot%\gpedit.msc) via the Configure Slow-Link Mode policy.

When working in this mode, all file-system operations are serviced by the Offline Files cache. The data is synchronized back to the server every six hours by default, but this synchronization frequency can be controlled through Group Policy via the Configure Background Sync policy.

The Offline Files Service periodically checks the network performance of the shares in the Offline Files cache. If the network latency improves to be less than half the configured slow-link latency threshold, the user will transition back to working online.

The slow-link behavior can be controlled via the Group Policy editor (%SystemRoot%\gpedit.msc) as shown in Figure 7-24.

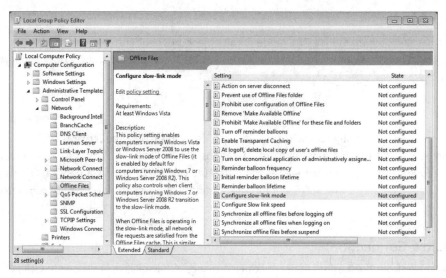

FIGURE 7-24 Offline Files Group Policy settings

Offline (Working Offline)

The user can force the client to work offline by clicking the Work Offline button in Explorer. When running in this mode, all file-system operations are satisfied from the cache. Periodic background synchronization of the data can be enabled in this mode through the Configure Background Sync policy, but by default they are not enabled. If the user wants to work online again, he must click the Work Online button in Explorer.

Offline (Not Connected)

A cached object is in Offline (Not Connected) mode when the server is not accessible. The transition to offline is transparently satisfied through the Offline Files cache, without the application knowing. When the network connection to the server is re-established, any changes written to the file are synchronized back to the server by the Offline Files agent. If a file is modified on both the client and the remote system while the file was offline, the conflict must be resolved by the user through Sync Center.

Offline (Need to Sync)

When a user transitions back online after making changes to the version of the file in the local cache, the status of this file will be Offline (Need to Sync) until the changes are synchronized back to the server. Offline Files keep the user working offline for the affected files until that synchronization is complete to ensure that the user sees a consistent view of the files, include the changes made while working offline.

Ghosts

When files are selected to be available offline, they must be copied from the server to the client. Until the transfer is complete, not all the files will be visible on the client. This can cause confusion for the user if the server drops offline and the user tries to access a file before it is in the cache. To address this case, Offline Files creates *ghosts* of the files and directories on the server within the cache as soon as caching is enabled. The ghosts are markers for files and directories that have not been copied and are unavailable in the cache. Explorer displays ghosted files with an overlay on the file's icon. As the cache is filled, the ghost entries eventually disappear. If the user tries to access a ghosted file and the server is online, the file is copied immediately to the cache and the ghost overlay is removed.

When a subdirectory of a share is pinned into the Offline Files cache, ghosts are also used to provide the user context to the surrounding namespace that is not cached. When offline, the sibling files and directories appear in a ghosted state so that the user does not think that this other content somehow disappeared. When files and directories are ghosted for this purpose, they are neither cached by Offline Files nor are they available while working offline, unless they are explicitly pinned in the Offline Files cache.

Data Security

The goal of Offline Files is to provide the same file-access experience for remote files that the user experience for local files. To achieve that end, Offline Files caches the users and their effective access for each file and directory in the cache. This information is used by the Offline Files driver to enforce the appropriate access on the objects in the cache. Encrypted files using EFS on the server are also encrypted in the cache.

Offline Files caches access for a given user as the data is accessed or synchronized on behalf of that user. For example, if two users, Able and Baker, share a laptop, and user Able marks a file on the server to be available offline, the file is copied to the cache and only Able's access is cached. If the server drops offline, user Baker would not be able to access the file in the cache; however, when the server is online again, and Baker tries to access the file, Offline Files updates the cache to reflect user Baker's access, allowing both users to access the file when working offline.

Files protected with EFS remain protected but are encrypted in the security context of the first user to bring the data into the cache. When working offline, only this user will be able to access the data in the cache.

Cache Structure

By default, the root directory for the Offline Files cache is located in %SystemRoot%\CSC and is protected with a DACL that grants Administrators full control of the directory and everyone else read, Read & Execute, and List Folder Contents access. As shown in Figure 7-25, beneath the root directory is a subdirectory with a name equal to the current version of the database schema (currently, 2.0.6) and a security descriptor specifying an owner SID of S-1-5-12, which is used to indicate it is owned by *restricted code* and cannot be accessed by anyone other than the Offline Files service. This security descriptor is inherited by all files and subdirectories beneath the schema version directory.

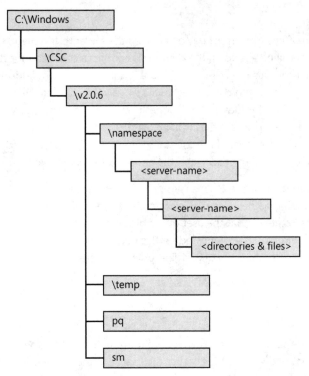

FIGURE 7-25 Default Offline Files directory structure

In the schema version directory are two files and two directories. The files consist of the Priority Queue (pq) and SID Map (sm) databases. The Priority Queue is a database that tracks the usage of the files within the cache and orders them from most recently used to least recently used. The Offline Files agent threads walk the queue tail to head when pushing files out of the cache when the cache's disk quota has been exceeded. Within the Offline Files cache, an internal user ID is used to represent a user when storing that user's access. The SID Map is used to map these internal user IDs to SIDs. This becomes important when the server is offline and Offline Files must validate the user's access itself.

The *namespace* directory is the root of the cache and contains a directory for each server that Offline Files is caching. The *temp* directory is for encryption and is also used as a temporary location for files that are removed from the namespace before they are deleted. The temp directory is used as a scratch area by Offline Files.

For every file in the Offline Files cache, Offline Files adds a sparse NTFS alternate data stream named *CscBitmapStream*, which contains a bitmap indicating which pages of the file have been modified while the file was "offline" (server not reachable). Each bit in the bitmap represents a 4-KB page within the file. This bitmap is not created until the first offline write to a file. Writes that extend the file are not included in the bitmap. If the file is truncated while offline, the bitmap is also truncated to match the new length of the file. When the server is next online, only the changed pages are written to the server.

BranchCache

BranchCache is a generalized content-caching mechanism designed to reduce network bandwidth, especially over WANs. The name *BranchCache* comes from the concept of branch offices within a company connecting to the company's centralized servers via WAN links, which are typically hundreds of times slower than LAN links and caching content used by computers in the branch office within that branch office. Moving the content cache to the branch office drastically reduces the time to access the content because the data does not have to traverse the WAN.

Unlike Offline Files, which caches only files, BranchCache caches *content*, which is anything that can be identified by a URL, such as files, web pages, an HTTP video stream, or even a blob accessed from a database or cloud service.

BranchCache does not access the files in the CSC cache, because CSC is a client of BranchCache. Instead, Offline Files uses BranchCache to populate its own cache.

A variety of protocols make use of BranchCache, including the following ones:

- **Server Message Block (SMB)**   Used to access files on file servers

- **HTTP(S)**   Web pages, video streams, and other content identified by a URL

- **Background Intelligent Transfer Service (BITS)**   Used to transfer files, and runs over HTTP/TLS 1.1

Figure 7-26 depicts the BranchCache architecture.

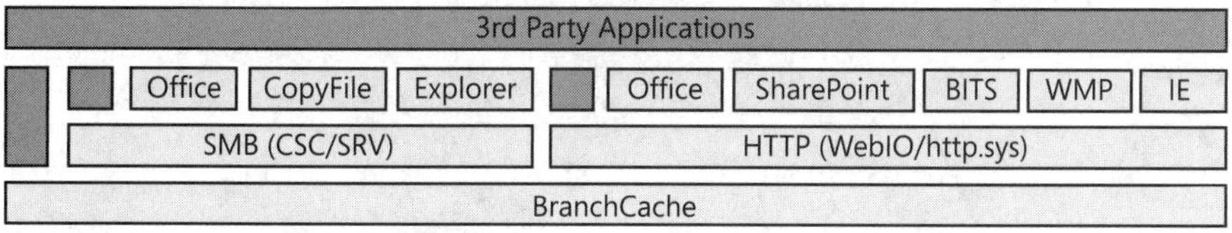

FIGURE 7-26 BranchCache architecture

BranchCache's operation is transparent to the applications accessing the content being cached, as shown in Figure 7-26. When BranchCache is enabled on a client, a request made by that client to a content server carries headers/metadata (the exact mechanism depends upon the protocol used) to let the remote content server know that the client has BranchCache enabled. In this case, the content server returns content information (CI) describing that content, rather than the requested content. The CI contains hashes of all the segments and blocks in which the content is chunked. (This is covered in more detail later.) The client uses the CI for retrieving part, or all, of the content from the local BranchCache. If any part of the content is not available locally, the client goes back to the remote content server to retrieve the data that was not present in the local BranchCache and, once the data is retrieved, offers the missing data to the local BranchCache so that the same data can be served to other clients in the future.

BranchCache operates in two caching modes, as shown in Figure 7-27:

- **Hosted Cache** A single server in a branch office (running Windows Server 2008/R2, or later), with the BranchCache feature enabled, contains the entire content cache for all BranchCache-enabled systems within that branch office.

- **Distributed Cache** Instead of a hosted cache server caching content for the remote office, the clients within the remote office cache the content files themselves. The cache is spread across all the clients on the same subnet. There is no effort to evenly distribute the contents of the cache among peers within a branch office. In general, until the maximum local cache size is reached, each client has a copy of all the content it has accessed (resulting in content being duplicated throughout the distributed cache). This is desirable because it adds redundancy and some resiliency to the cache, especially when clients join and leave the branch office network frequently, as is often the case when the users are working on laptops. The distributed cache is implemented using peer-to-peer networking, using the Web Services Discovery (WS-D) multicast protocol to locate which client has the content in its cache, with a 300-millisecond timeout.

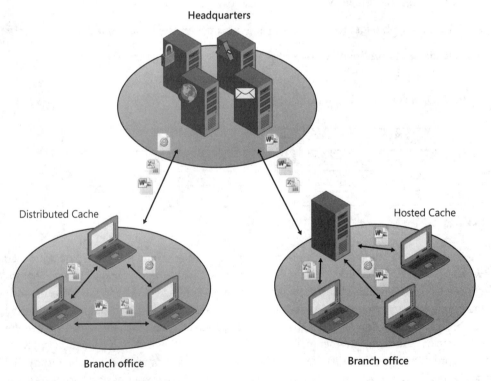

FIGURE 7-27 Types of BranchCache caching

BranchCache is fully compatible with end-to-end encryption, such as IPsec. Just like with CSC, Windows' existing security mechanisms are used to ensure that access to cached content operates the same way that it would if the content were not cached.

BranchCache is similar to Offline Files, but it differs in several important ways. The most important of which is that content in the BranchCache is not available if the WAN is down. This is because the content is identified by a hash list generated and stored on the server, which the client uses to locate the cached content within the BranchCache (distributed or hosted). Some BranchCache features the following behaviors:

- Data transfer uses AES encryption.

- For content that is not file-based, BranchCache caches only content that is larger than 64 KB. (This can be changed by editing the registry value HKLM\System\CurrentControlSet\Services \PeerDistKM\Parameters\MinContentLength on the server.)

Caching Modes

BranchCache maintains two different local caches on each BranchCache-enabled system (which can be BranchCache content servers on one side of the WAN link, and BranchCache clients and BranchCache hosted cache servers on other side):

- The *publication cache* stores content information metadata for content published using the BranchCache Server APIs (*PeerDistServerXxx*). The content information structure contains hashes of the various segments and blocks in which BranchCache breaks up the content into chunks, along with the secret needed to generate public and private content identifiers and the encryption key.

- Publishing is usually thought of as a server-side operation, though any BranchCache client can publish content. With regard to publishing, BranchCache offers two different approaches to its client applications/protocols for generating/managing/storing BranchCache content information metadata:

  - An application and/or protocol that uses BranchCache acceleration can ask BranchCache to store content information metadata on its behalf (in the BranchCache publication cache), allowing BranchCache to manage the lifetime of that metadata according to rules, timelines, and limits shared across multiple applications using BranchCache. This is achieved by publishing via the *PeerDistServerXxx* APIs, and it is what the HTTP-BranchCache and BITS-BranchCache integrations do.

  - Alternatively, an application/protocol that wants to use BranchCache acceleration can ask BranchCache to generate only content information metadata without storing it, and instead simply return the metadata to the application or protocols. In this case, the application or protocol has to implement its own way to store or manage that metadata. This is what the SMB-BranchCache integrations does.

  In both cases, the protocol integrated with BranchCache or the application using BranchCache directly is responsible for transporting that content information metadata through the WAN link from the publishing content server to the clients in the remote branches. BranchCache does not have, or control, a data channel crossing the WAN link. The transport of content information metadata is intentionally left to the protocol or application using BranchCache acceleration, so that the metadata can be transported with the same level of security, authentication, and authorization that would have been used for retrieving the actual content when BranchCache is not used. This is consistent with the fact that, from a security standpoint, owning a copy of the BranchCache content information for a given content is equivalent to owning the entire content and therefore being authorized to retrieve a copy of it from other BranchCache entities (clients, hosted cache servers, or third-party implementations).

The publication cache does not store any actual data of the published content; it stores only content information metadata. Publications tend to last for long periods of time, though the actual length of time is determined by the application that publishes the content. By default, the publication cache is constrained to consume no more than one percent of the volume on which it is located, which is specified by %SystemRoot%\ServiceProfiles\NetworkService \AppData\Local\PeerDistPub. The size and location of the publication cache can be changed using NetSh:

- netsh branchcache set publicationcache directory=C:\PublicationCacheFolder

- netsh branchcache set publicationcachesize size=20 percent=TRUE

■ The *republication cache* contains both metadata (but no secrets) and actual data (chunked in segments and blocks) for the BranchCache content retrieved by the local BranchCache client. It is stored with the purpose of making those chunks of content available to other BranchCache clients. Republished content is stored for up to 28 days, but it can be flushed out earlier if the republication cache has reached its limit and space is needed for newer content to be republished. By default, the republication cache is constrained to consume no more than five percent of the volume on which it is located, which is by specified by %SystemRoot% \ServiceProfiles\NetworkService\AppData\Local\PeerDistRepub. The location and the size of the republication cache can be changed using NetSh:

- netsh branchcache set localcache directory=C:\BranchCache\Localcache

- netsh branchcache set localcache size=20 percent=TRUE

BranchCache attempts to persist the republication cache across system reboots through the use of an index file that contains the database of segment descriptors. When the system reboots, BranchCache validates the general integrity of the republication cache by checking that it was properly closed. If the republication cache fails this consistency check, it is discarded. The publication cache is not persisted across reboots. The private SMB-BranchCache publication cache needs no explicit persistence; persistence comes for free, as a result of the SMB-BranchCache integration (which was covered previously) and the fact that with the SMB all published content is actual files. The hashes are validated before access to the files in the cache is allowed.

Configuration

BranchCache can be configured using the Local Security Group Policy editor as shown in Figure 7-28, using the network shell (NetSh) as shown in Figure 7-29, or as part of Group Policy pushed by an administrator (within a domain).

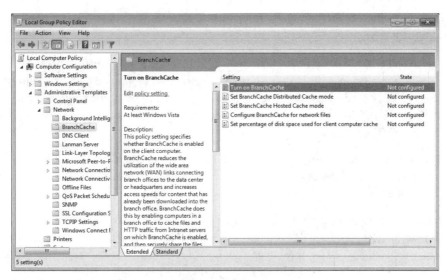

FIGURE 7-28 Configuring BranchCache using the Group Policy editor

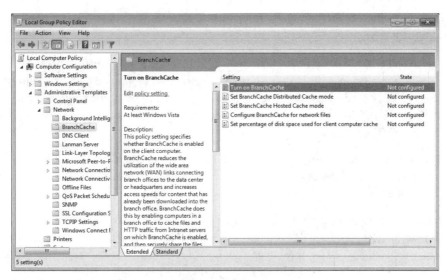

FIGURE 7-29 Configuring BranchCache using the network shell

- BranchCache Implementationservice in %SystemRoot%\PeerDistSvc.dll. This service starts when the BranchCache is enabled on both clients and servers, and it interacts with the kernel-mode components (drivers).

- HTTP extension driver in %SystemRoot%\System32\Drivers\PeerDistKM.sys. This driver registers with the Network Module Registrar (NMR) as a client of the http.sys driver and examines all HTTP packets going into and out of the system. It adds files to the cache and retrieves cached content information for published content from the BranchCache service, rather than sending the request to the web server.

- BranchCache APIs (*PeerDistXxx*) are exported by %SystemRoot%\System32\PeerDist.dll, which uses LRPC/ALPC to communicate with the BranchCache service.

- The BranchCache HTTP transport in %SystemRoot%\System32\PeerDistHttpTrans.dll implements the transport on top of which the Peer Content Caching and Retrieval: Retrieval Protocol [MS-PCCRR] exchanges data between BranchCache clients and/or hosted cache servers. Each MS-PCCRR message is encapsulated in a simple transport message, which in turn, is sent over an HTTP request.

- The Web Services Discovery Provider in %SystemRoot%\System32\PeerDistWSDDiscoProv.dll implements the WS-D protocol to discover which clients on the LAN are caching a particular file (or part of a file).

- The BranchCache Network Shell Helper in %SystemRoot%\System32\PeerDistSh.dll is an extension to the Network Shell (%SystemRoot%\System32\Netsh.exe) application that provides users with a means of monitoring and configuring the BranchCache service. Network Shell helper DLLs are installed by adding a string value to HKEY_LOCAL_MACHINE \SOFTWARE\Microsoft\NetSh, which provides the Network Shell with the path to the helper DLL.

- A standalone variant of all the BranchCache APIs are implemented in %SystemRoot% \System32\PeerDistHashPeerDistHash.dll (only present on Windows Server systems), which contains all of the BranchCache APIs and functionality and does not require the use of the BranchCache service. This component is designed for use by other Windows features that are tightly integrated with BranchCache, such as the SMB Groveler, which generates the hashes on the server.

- Hash groveler service in %SystemRoot%\System32\smbhash.exe (only on Windows Server systems). The groveler runs on the file or web server and generates hashes when clients request a hash list. The groveler monitors a given namespace or share and ensures that the BranchCache hashes are updated for all files within that namespace. All groveler I/O runs at low I/O priority so as not to interfere with the normal operation of the system.

BranchCache uses the following protocols, which are documented at *www.microsoft.com*:

Peer Content Caching and Retrieval: Content Identification, as defined in [MS-PCCRC], defines the content information structures previously described. Peer Content Caching and Retrieval: Discovery Protocol, as defined in [MS-PCCRD], specifies a multicast to discover and locate services based on the Web Services Dynamic Discovery (WS-Discovery) protocol [WS-Discovery]. There are two modes of operations in WS-Discovery: client-initiated probes and service-initiated announcements. Both are sent through IP multicast to a predefined group. The primary role in the Content Caching and Retrieval System is Content Discovery.

- Peer Content Caching and Retrieval: Retrieval Protocol, as defined in [MS-PCCRR], specifies the messages that are necessary for querying peer-role servers or a hosted cache server for the availability of certain content, and for retrieving the content. The primary role in the Content Caching and Retrieval System is Content Retrieval.

- Peer Content Caching and Retrieval: Hosted Cache Protocol, as defined in [MS-PCHC], specifies an HTTPS-based mechanism for clients to notify a hosted cache server regarding the availability of content and for a hosted cache server to indicate interest in the content. The primary role in the Content Caching and Retrieval System is Content Notification.

- Peer Content Caching and Retrieval: Hypertext Transfer Protocol (HTTP) Extensions, as defined in [MS-PCCRTP], specifies a content encoding known as *PeerDist* that is used by an HTTP/1.1 client and an HTTP/1.1 server to communicate content to each other. The primary role in the Content Caching and Retrieval System is Metadata (Hash) Retrieval.

- Server Message Block (SMB) Version 2.1 Protocol, as defined in [MS-SMB2]. Version 2.1 of this protocol has enhancements for the detection of content caching-enabled shares and retrieval of metadata related to content caching. The primary role in the Content Caching and Retrieval System is Metadata (Hash) Retrieval.

Supporting SMB-BranchCache integration requires the following changes on both the clients and servers. On the client, the functionality of the existing client-side caching (CSC) components were extended. On the server, the SMB Server Driver (srv2.sys) was extended to support hash list retrieval from the server, and a new service was added, the SMB Hash Generation Service (also known as the Groveler), to manage the generation, updating, and deletion of hashes for content on an SMB share.

BranchCache Optimized Application Retrieval: SMB Sequence

The following sequence describes how content that is cached by BranchCache is delivered to an application without requiring any changes to the application, as shown in Figure 7-30. This sequence refers to the case when the channel/protocol of choice for that application is SMB—for example, the application opens the file from the remote share with *CreateFile* (or something that calls *CreateFile*, such as *fopen*) and reads from the file. If the application decides to retrieve the data via an HTTP request (backed by either *WinHTTP* or *WinInet*), the sequence is very different, but it is still a sequence completely transparent to the application.

BranchCache and SMB are integrated through the Offline Files component in Windows. The Offline Files service opportunistically tries to prefetch files accessed via SMB to optimize network usage and user experience on the client side. The offline files driver might temporarily delay the application's read to give the prefetch from BranchCache an opportunity to stay ahead of the application's read position. This delay is calculated based on the measured latency to the file server.

Data retrieval begins with an application reading data from a file on a remote SMB share. When Offline Files is enabled on the client and BranchCache is not enabled, the application's read request flow through the offline files driver to the SMB server. When both offline files and BranchCache are enabled on the client, the following steps occur:

1. The offline files driver intercepts the read I/O request and determines whether the following specific conditions have been met to initiate prefetching the file:

   a. The data is not already stored in the offline files cache. If the data is already present, the application's read will be satisfied by this data without making any data requests to the file server.

   b. The latency to the server (as observed by the client so far) is above the configured threshold.

   c. BranchCache hash generation is enabled on the file share.

   d. The target file size is at least 64 KB.

   e. The read is beyond the first 64 KB of the file.

2. If the preceding conditions are met, the offline files driver notifies the offline files service to start prefetching the file.

3. The offline files service then retrieves the content information from the file server. If the server has the up-to-date content information for the specified file, it returns it to the client. If there is no content information for the specified file or if it is out of date, the SMB hash-generation service on the file server will be requested to generate new content information for this file, and no content information is returned to the client, causing offline files to skip BranchCache retrieval for this file.

4. If content information is retrieved from the file server, the offline files service then uses that information to attempt to retrieve data from BranchCache.

5. BranchCache attempts to retrieve the data either from peers or the hosted cache (depending on the configuration). If data is found, it is returned to the offline files service; otherwise, an error is returned.

6. If data is found in BranchCache, the data is written to the offline files cache and the prefetch thread continues to attempt to retrieve data from BranchCache until it has retrieved up to 8 MB of data or it fails to retrieve data.

7. When the application's read operation is allowed to proceed, it attempts to read the data from the offline files cache, which is prepopulated by data from BranchCache if the prefetch thread successfully retrieved data. Otherwise, the application's read is allowed to flow to the server to retrieve data. Data retrieved from the file server is then cached in the offline files cache for later publication to BranchCache.

8. When the Offline Files Service is requested to prefetch data from BranchCache, it also attempts to publish any data to BranchCache for the file from the offline files cache. File data is stored in the offline files cache until the offline files cache needs to reclaim space for newer files. The same data is also stored in BranchCache's republication cache so that it can be shared with other BranchCache clients and across different protocols/applications integrated with BranchCache.

If the client accesses the same content again (after closing the file and opening it again) and the content has not been changed on the server, the application will be able to retrieve the data from the Offline Files cache without doing the BranchCache lookup. This is called *transparent caching*.

If the requested data cannot be found through BranchCache, once it is retrieved from the SMB server it will be republished to the BranchCache for access by other clients. (These steps are not shown in Figure 7-30.)

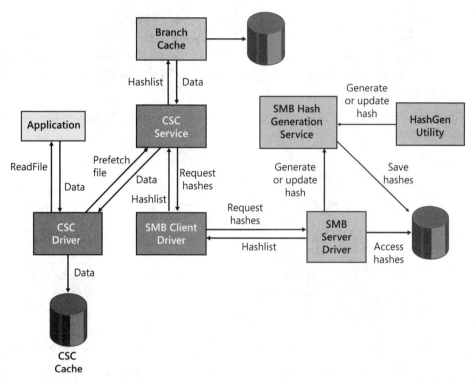

FIGURE 7-30 BranchCache request flows

BranchCache Optimized Application Retrieval: HTTP Sequence

The following sequence describes how content that is cached by BranchCache is delivered to an application without requiring any changes to the application. This sequence covers the case when the channel/protocol of choice for that application is HTTP, for example the application retrieves the content via an HTTP request based on either WinInet or WinHTTP APIs.

BranchCache and HTTP are tightly integrated, both in terms of HTTP.sys on the server side and WinInet and WinHTTP on the client side. In contrast with the SMB-BranchCache integration, when BranchCache is enabled on both client and server, an application's HTTP requests are always stalled, waiting for BranchCache retrievals. The HTTP-BranchCache integration is focuses on minimizing the usage of the WAN's bandwidth (even when the WAN happens to be very fast and has very low latency), and all the data that can be retrieved via BranchCache will be transferred via BranchCache.

1. Data retrieval begins with an application issuing an HTTP Request.

2. When BranchCache is enabled on the client, the HTTP client stack (either WinInet or WinHTTP) adds headers to the request indicating that the client is capable of understanding the PeerDist HTTP encoding (as defined in [MS-PCCRTP]).

3. The HTTP client stack sends the request to the remote content server, typically across the WAN link.

4. The kernel-mode HTTP driver (HTTP.sys) receives the request on the content server. If BranchCache is enabled on that server, HTTP.sys forwards a copy of the request to the BranchCache HTTP extension driver (PeerDistKM.sys), which keeps track of the request and retrieves content information for that content (identified by its URL and content tags) from the BranchCache service.

5. The kernel-mode HTTP driver delivers the HTTP request to the associated web server in user mode (typically, IIS or a web service) and waits for a response.

6. The HTTP server authenticates and authorizes the client, it generates the response accordingly, and it starts streaming the response down to HTTP.sys.

7. Because BranchCache is enabled, HTTP.sys redirects the response through PeerDistKM.sys.

8. If the content information for that HTTP content is not available (or not yet available) or if the content tags do not match, the following steps occur:

    a. PeerDistKM.sys sends a copy of the response stream to the BranchCache service for publication so that the next request for the same URL will find the content information.

    b. It allows the response stream to go back to HTTP.sys unchanged.

    c. HTTP.sys sends out the response with actual data in it and no BranchCache metadata.

9. If, instead, the content information for that HTTP content is available and, based on content tags, it is found to be up to date with the content returned, the following steps occur:

    a. PeerDistKM.sys replaces the body of the response with the content information describing it in BranchCache terms.

    b. It modifies the response headers adding that the response is now PeerDist-encoded.

    c. It returns the modified (and, in general, much shorter) response stream to HTTP.sys.

    d. HTTP.sys sends out the modified response, containing only BranchCache content information metadata, but not any actual content data.

10. The response is received on the client side. If the response contains BranchCache content information, the HTTP client stack passes that metadata to the BranchCache service, and it

starts serving the first application read for the actual contents of that response by asking BranchCache to retrieve the content data associated with the size of that first read.

11. BranchCache retrieves that data from the local republication cache (if available), or it retrieves a superset including the requested data either from other BranchCache clients in the LAN or from the hosted cache server (depending on the configuration).

12. If any of the requested data is missing, BranchCache signals to the HTTP stack the range of missing data, and the HTTP stack issues a range request back to the remote server for the missing data (or a superset including it).

13. Once all the data is reassembled for the specific application read, it is returned to the application in a way completely transparent to the application.

14. The last three steps are repeated until all the application's reads on the HTTP response in question are completed.

Name Resolution

Name resolution is the process by which a character-based name, such as www.microsoft.com or Mycomputer, is translated into a numeric address, such as 192.168.1.1, that the network protocol stack can recognize. This section describes the three TCP/IP-related name resolution protocols provided by Windows: Domain Name System (DNS), Windows Internet Name Service (WINS), and Peer Name Resolution Protocol (PNRP).

Domain Name System

Domain Name System (DNS) is the standard (RFC 1035, et al.) by which Internet names (such as *www.microsoft.com*) are translated to their corresponding IP addresses. A network application that wants to resolve a DNS name to an IP address sends a DNS lookup request using the UDP/IP protocol (TCP/IP is used for requests whose response size exceeds 512 bytes) to a DNS server. DNS servers implement a distributed database of name/IP address pairs that are used to perform translations, and each server maintains the translations for a particular *zone*. Describing the details of DNS is outside the scope of this book, but DNS is the foundation of naming in Windows and so it is the primary Windows name resolution protocol.

The Windows DNS server is implemented as a Windows service (%SystemRoot%\System32 \Dns.exe) that is included in server versions of Windows. Standard DNS server implementation relies on a text file as the translation database, but the Windows DNS server can be configured to store zone information in Active Directory.

Peer Name Resolution Protocol

The *Peer Name Resolution Protocol (PNRP)* is a distributed peer-to-peer protocol that allows for dynamic name resolution and publication exclusively across IPv6 networks. It allows Internet-connected devices to publish *peer names* and their associated IPv6 address, as well as optional information. Other devices will then resolve the peer name, retrieve the IPv6 address, and establish a connection.

PNRP offers significant advantages over DNS, mainly by being distributed, which means that it is essentially serverless (other than for early bootstrapping), can scale to potentially millions of names, and is fault tolerant and bottleneck free. Because it includes secure name publication services, changes to name records can be performed from any system. DNS generally requires contacting a DNS server administrator to perform updates. PNRP name updates also occur in real time, making it appropriate for highly mobile devices, whereas DNS caches results. Finally, PNRP allows for naming more than just computers and services by allowing extended information to be published with name records. The specification for the Peer Name Resolution Protocol [MS-PNRP] can be found at *www.microsoft.com*.

Windows exposes PNRP via a PNRP API for applications and services, as well as by extending the *getaddrinfo* Winsock API described earlier in the chapter to perform resolution of PNRP IDs (described next) when an address includes the reserved *.pnrp.net* domain suffix.

PNRP peer names (also called *P2P IDs*) are made up of two components:

- **Authority**   For *secure clients* (which have their name records signed by a certifying authority), the authority is identified by a SHA-1 hash of an associated public key, and for *unsecured clients*, it is zero. If a client is secure, PNRP validates the name record before publishing it.

- **Classifier**   The classifier uses a simple string to identify a service provided by a peer, which allows multiple services to be provided by the same device.

To create a PNRP ID, PNRP hashes the P2P ID and combines it with a unique 128-bit ID called the *service location*, as shown in Figure 7-31. The service location identifies different instances of the same P2P ID in the same *cloud*. (PNRP uses two clouds: a *global cloud,* which corresponds to all IPv6 addresses on the Internet, and the *link-local cloud,* which corresponds to IPv6 addresses with the *fe80::/10* prefix and is analogous to an IPv4 subnet.)

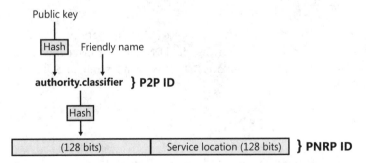

FIGURE 7-31 PNRP ID generation

PNRP Resolution and Publication

PNRP name resolution occurs in two phases:

- **Endpoint determination**   In this phase, the requesting peer determines the IPv6 address associated with the peer responsible for publishing the PNRP ID of the desired service.

- **PNRP ID resolution**   In this phase, once the requesting peer has located and confirmed the availability of the peer associated with the IPv6 address, it sends a PNRP request message for the PNRP ID of the service being requested. The peer providing the service replies to confirm the PNRP ID and can supply a comment and up to 4 KB of additional data, such as context information related to the service.

During the first phase, PNRP iterates over nodes while locating the publishing node, such that the node performing name resolution will be responsible for contacting nodes that are successively closer to the desired PNRP ID. Each iteration works as follows: Once a peer receives a request message, it performs a lookup in its cache for the requested PNRP ID. If a match is found, the request message is sent directly; otherwise, it is sent to the next closest PNRP ID (by seeing how much of the ID matches).

When a node receives a request message for which it cannot find a PNRP ID, it checks the distance of any other IDs in the cache to the target ID. If it finds a node that is closer, the requested node sends a reply to the requesting node, where the reply contains the IPv6 address of the peer that most closely matches the target PNRP ID. The requesting node can then use the IPv6 address to send another query to that address' node. If no node is closer, the requesting node is notified, and that node sends the request to the next closest node. Assuming PNRP IDs of 200, 350, 450, 500, and 800, Figure 7-32 depicts a possible endpoint determination phase for an example in which peer A is trying to find the endpoint for PNRP 800 (peer E).

To publish its PNRP ID(s), a peer first sends PNRP publication messages to its closest neighbors (entries in its cache that have IDs that are in the lowest levels) to seed their caches. It then randomly chooses nodes in the cloud that are not neighbors and sends them PNRP name resolution requests for its own PNRP ID. Through a mechanism described earlier, the endpoint determination phase results in the seeding of the PNRP ID across the caches of the random nodes that were chosen in the cloud.

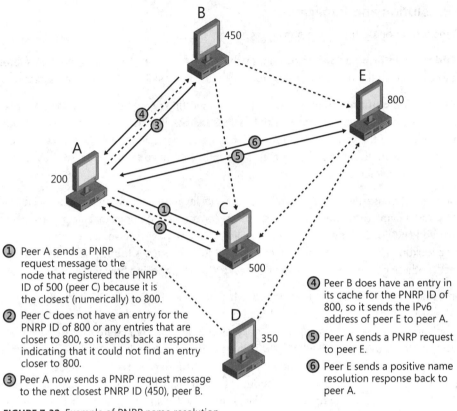

① Peer A sends a PNRP request message to the node that registered the PNRP ID of 500 (peer C) because it is the closest (numerically) to 800.

② Peer C does not have an entry for the PNRP ID of 800 or any entries that are closer to 800, so it sends back a response indicating that it could not find an entry closer to 800.

③ Peer A now sends a PNRP request message to the next closest PNRP ID (450), peer B.

④ Peer B does have an entry in its cache for the PNRP ID of 800, so it sends the IPv6 address of peer E to peer A.

⑤ Peer A sends a PNRP request to peer E.

⑥ Peer E sends a positive name resolution response back to peer A.

FIGURE 7-32 Example of PNRP name resolution

Location and Topology

Today, networked computers often move between networks that require different configuration settings—for example, a corporate LAN and a home-based wireless network. Windows includes the Network Location Awareness (NLA) service to enable the dynamic configuration of network applications and settings based on location, and Link-Layer Topology Discovery (LLTD) to enable the intelligent discovery and mapping of networked devices.

Network Location Awareness

The Network Location Awareness (NLA) service provider is implemented as a Winsock Namespace Provider (NSP) and provides the necessary framework for allowing computers and devices that move across different networks to select the most appropriate configuration settings. For example, an application taking advantage of NLA can detect when the user moves from a high-speed LAN to a high-latency wireless network and fine-tune its bandwidth use appropriately. NLA can also detect when a home computer on a LAN might also have a secondary VPN connection to the office and select the proper configuration options.

Instead of having developers rely on manual network interface information to figure out the type of network, and the IP addresses or DNS names associated with them, NLA provides a standardized query API for enumerating all the local network attachment information and correlating it with network interface information. The NLA API also includes notifications that enable applications to respond to changes when they occur. NLA provides applications two pieces of location information:

- **Logical network identity** This identity is based on the logical network's DNS domain name. If one does not exist, NLA uses custom static information stored in the registry together with the network's subnet address as the identity.

- **Logical network interfaces** For each network that a device is attached to, NLA creates an *adapter name* that identifies interfaces such as NICs or RAS connections in a unique fashion. Applications use adapter names with the IP Helper API (%SystemRoot%\System32\iphlpapi.dll) to query interface information and characteristics.

Each logical network is implemented as a service class with an associated GUID and properties. NLA creates instances of that service class when it returns information about a logical network. Service classes are schemas that describe a namespace; they define the name, identifier, and namespace-specific information that is common to all instances. These classes are then used in combination with the *WSALookupServiceXxx* APIs when performing name resolution.

The best way to get network location information programmatically is to use the Network List Manager (NLM) APIs—for example *INetworkListManager*, *INetwork*, *IEnumNetworks*, *INetworkEvents*, and so on.

Network Connectivity Status Indicator

Network Connectivity Status Indicator (NCSI) determines in real time the connectivity level of network connections on a system. It is loaded by the NLA service and functions solely as an information provider for NLA. NLA enables network-interacting programs to change their behavior based on how the computer is connected to the network. NCSI does not register as a client of NLA, but it does receive certain private notifications directly from it. NCSI detects local vs. Internet connectivity, hotspot networks, and corporate connectivity detection and level.

The connectivity level of a network connection is assessed and is based on whether or not the system has access to the Internet and to network devices such as the default gateway, DNS servers, and web proxy servers. This network connectivity information is used by various applications such as the Networking Tray Icon, Mini Map, Network Connection Wizard, Windows Media Center, DirectAccess, Windows Update, and Outlook. NCSI information is displayed in the tray as an overlay on the network icon. Most of NCSI's activity is disabled if a user is not logged in.

NCSI performs the primary tasks described in the following sections.

Passive Poll

Every five seconds (configurable in the registry), NCSI activates to perform its general processing. The main purpose of this action is to query the network stack using the Network Storage Interface (NSI), and looks for:

1. Evidence that some traffic has been received. NSI returns packet counts for each network interface. If any packets have been received on an interface, that interface will have at least *local* connectivity.

2. Evidence that traffic has been received from either the Internet or corporate network. This is a little more complex and is determined by calculating the average number of hops a packet takes to depart from a system's local ISP network (in a home/nondomain environment) or intranet (in a corporate environment). NSI returns the largest hop count seen since the last time the hop counts were requested. If this value exceeds the average for a given IP family (for example, IPv4 vs. IPv6) on a given interface, that interface has *internet* connectivity.

3. Evidence that the host is communicating with a web proxy. The IP addresses for web proxies will have been identified using Web Proxy AutoDetect (WPAD), or DNS, and proxies configured manually through Internet control panel. NSI returns details of the current TCP paths from the network stack. If this is a new path to a proxy, that interface has *internet* connectivity.

4. Evidence that an IPSEC Security Association (SA) has been established between the system and a host that has an IPv6 address matching the corporate network prefix defined in the registry. (This is passive corporate connectivity detection.)

5. Evidence that there is a reachable path reported by NSI to a host with an IPv6 prefix matching the corporate network prefix in the registry. The interface is marked with *corporate* connectivity.

In addition to handling the NSI queries, the passive poll is also used by NCSI to carry out most time-based processing. If there are no networks connected, NCSI continues to poll, but stops polling three polling periods after the last data is received.

Network Change Monitoring

NCSI has to be aware of changes to the configuration of interfaces on the system. This is handled by two event monitors that watch for NSI interface change notifications and DHCP status change notifications.

When NCSI detects that the network has changed, it records the current time in a data structure associated with each interface. The passive poll task queries this value and, if it is older than 15 seconds, it will perform an active probe. The 15-second delay (for example, three poll periods have elapsed) is used to re-evaluate the Internet connectivity state if it has seen one or more unreachable paths.

NCSI registers for DHCP events and responds to them immediately (that is, there is no dampening that happens). If in that callback, DHCP reports that an interface is stable, an active probe is queued for that interface.

Registry Change Monitoring

NCSI monitors two parent keys in the registry for any changes to themselves or their children using the registry change notification API. Any changes trigger NCSI to reload all values under each key:

- HKLM\System\CurrentControlSet\Services\NlaSvc\Parameters\Internet

- HKLM\SOFTWARE\Policies\Microsoft\Windows\NetworkConnectivityStatusIndicator

Active Probe

NCSI has two mechanisms for actively testing an interface to determine whether it has Internet connectivity, both of which are configurable (and can be disabled) using the registry keys.

The first time an active probe is performed on an interface, it will be a web probe. This consists of an attempt to download the file *http://www.msftncsi.com/ncsi.txt,* and it compares the contents of that file with the expected value of "Microsoft NCSI". If the comparison succeeds, the active probe is considered successful.

If NCSI has detected proxy servers, it checks to see if the interface being probed is the best interface over which to reach the first proxy server. If so, it applies the proxy settings to the HTTP request. Otherwise, it first tries without the proxy settings, only applying them and making a second attempt if the first failed with name resolution failure. This is to support multihomed scenarios, where one interface is connected via proxy and the interface being probed is not.

If an active probe succeeds, either the IPv4 or IPv6 Internet state will be brought to *internet* connectivity. Because NCSI does not know whether the request was satisfied using IPv4 or IPv6 connectivity, it makes a guess based on the existence of default gateways for each address family, with IPv4 being selected if an exact determination cannot be made.

The next time an active probe is to be performed, if the hardware address of the default gateway is already in the list of known proxy-less gateways, a DNS probe is performed instead of a web probe. This is an optimization that produces quicker results. A DNS probe performs a simple DNS lookup for the name listed in the registry, with the default being *dns.msftncsi.com*.

HTTP probe behavior changes in multihomed scenarios when a proxy is detected. When an active probe is executed on an interface, a check is made whether or not that interface is preferred by the network stack to reach the first proxy server address. If so, the web probe is continued as normal. If not, the web probe is first attempted without the use of the proxy. If that fails because the name could not be resolved via DNS, NCSI concludes it must be behind the proxy after all and applies the proxy server settings and retries the probe.

The content retrieved by the HTTP request is compared to known content in the registry. If the content does not match, NCSI assumes that the interface is connected to a hotspot network (which has rerouted the HTTP request to a login page). It then uses the Network List Manager (NLM) APIs to send a message to the PNIDUI (%SystemRoot%\System32\pnidui.dll) Shell Service Object (SSO), which then displays a balloon to indicate to the user that she needs to log in before connecting to the Internet. The gateway MAC address is also recorded in a known hotspot gateway list for proxy detection optimization later.

NSCI can be configured via Group Policy, as shown in Figure 7-33, or via the registry.

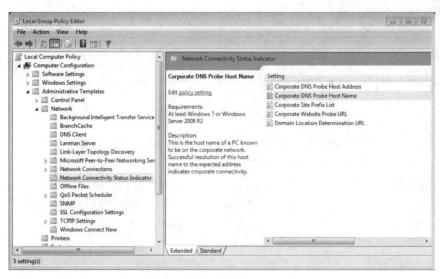

FIGURE 7-33 NCSI parameters in the Group Policy editor

Link-Layer Topology Discovery

The Link-Layer Topology Discovery (LLTD) protocol operates over both wired and wireless networks and enables applications to discover the topology of a network. For example, the *Network Map* functionality in Windows uses LLTD to draw the local network topology for the connected devices that support the LLTD protocol. Additionally, LLTD supports Quality of Service (QoS) extensions, which allow applications to diagnose network problems such as low signal strength on a wireless network and bandwidth constraints on home networks. Because it operates on the OSI data-link layer, LLTD works only on a single LAN or subnet and cannot cross routers, but its capabilities make it suitable for most home and small-office networks. The specification for the Link-Layer Topology Discovery protocol [MS-LLTD] can be found at *www.microsoft.com*.

The *LLTD Mapper I/O* and the *LLTD Responder* components implement LLTD. The former is responsible for the discovery process and for generating network maps. Because it uses a protocol different from IP, the LLTD Mapper uses NDIS APIs to directly send commands to the network via the network adapter. The LLTD Responder listens for and responds to discovery commands with information about the computer. As mentioned earlier, only devices that have a responder are shown in the network map.

Protocol Drivers

Network drivers take high-level I/O requests and translate them into low-level network protocol requests for transmission across the network. The network APIs rely on transport protocol drivers in kernel mode to perform the actual translation. Separating APIs from underlying protocols gives the networking architecture the flexibility of letting each API use a number of different protocols. The Internet's explosive growth and reliance on the TCP/IP protocol has made TCP/IP the preeminent protocol in Windows. The Defense Advanced Research Projects Agency (DARPA) developed TCP/IP in 1969, specifically as the foundation for a large-scale, fault-tolerant network that became the Internet; therefore, TCP/IP has WAN-friendly characteristics such as routability and good WAN performance. TCP/IP is the preferred Windows protocol and is installed by default.

The 4-byte network addresses used by the IPv4 protocol on the legacy TCP/IP stack limits the number of public IP addresses to roughly four billion, which is nearly exhausted as more and more devices, such as cell phones and PDAs, acquire an Internet presence. For this reason, the IPv6 protocol, which has 16-byte addresses, is gaining adoption. Windows includes a combined TCP/IP stack, called the *Next Generation TCP/IP Stack*, which supports both IPv4 and IPv6 simultaneously, with IPv6 being the preferred protocol. When operating on IPv6 networks, the stack also supports coexistence with IPv4 networks through the use of tunneling. The Next Generation TCP/IP Stack offers several advanced features to improve network performance, some of which are outlined in the following list:

- **Receive Window Auto Tuning** The TCP protocol defines a *receive window size*, which determines how much data a receiver can accept before the server requires an acknowledgment. Optimally, the receive window size should be equal to the bandwidth-delay product, which is the network link's capacity multiplied by its end-to-end delay. This calculates the amount of data that can be "in transit" between the sender and receiver at any given time. The Windows TCP/IP stack analyzes the conditions of a network link and chooses the optimal receive window size, adjusting it as needed if the network conditions change.

- **Compound TCP (CTCP)** Network congestion occurs when a node or link reaches its carrying capacity. CTCP implements a congestion-avoidance algorithm that monitors network bandwidth, latency, and packet losses. It aggressively increases the amount of data that can be sent by a machine when the network will support it, and it backs off when the network is congested. Using CTCP on a high-bandwidth, low-latency network can significantly improve transfer speeds

- **Explicit Congestion Notification (ECN)** Whenever a TCP packet is lost (unacknowledged), the TCP protocol assumes that the data was dropped because of router congestion and enforces congestion control, which dramatically lowers the sender's transmission rate. ECN allows routers to explicitly mark packets as being forwarded during congestion, which is read by the Windows TCP/IP stack as a sign that transmission rates should be lowered. Lowering rates in this manner results in better performance than relying on loss-based congestion control. ECN is disabled by default, because many outdated routers might drop packets with the ECN bit set instead of ignoring the bit. To determine whether your network supports ECN, you can use the Microsoft Internet Connectivity Evaluation Tool (*http://www.microsoft.com/windows/using/tools/igd/default.mspx*). You can examine and modify the ECN capability using the network shell (from an Admin command window), as shown in Figure 7-34.

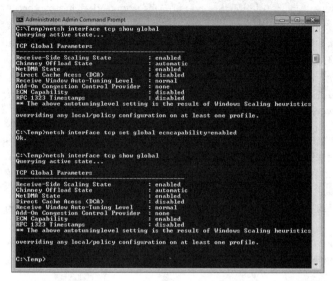

FIGURE 7-34 Using the network shell to examine and configure TCP parameters

- High-loss throughput improvements, including the NewReno Fast Recovery Algorithm, Enhanced Selective Acknowledgment (SACK), Forward RTO-Recovery (F-RTO), and Limited Transit. These algorithms reduce the overall retransmission of acknowledgments or TCP segments during high-loss scenarios while still maintaining the integrity of the TCP stream. This allows for greater bandwidth in these environments and preserves TCP's reliable transport semantics.

The Next Generation TCP/IP Stack (%SystemRoot%\System32\Drivers\Tcpip.sys), shown in Figure 7-35, implements TCP, UDP, IP, ARP, ICMP, and IGMP. To support legacy protocols such as NetBIOS, which make use of the deprecated TDI interface, the network stack also includes a component called TDX (TDI translation), which creates device objects that represent legacy protocols so that clients can obtain a file object representing a protocol and issue network I/O to the protocol using TDI IRPs. The TDX component creates several device objects that represent various TDI client–accessible protocols: \Device\Tcp6, \Device\Tcp, \Device\Udp6, \Device\Udp, \Device\Rawip, and \Device\Tdx.

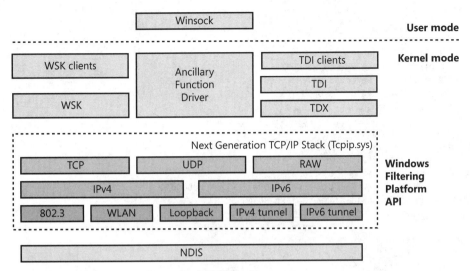

FIGURE 7-35 Windows Next Generation TCP/IP Stack

EXPERIMENT: Looking at TCP/IP's Device Objects

Using the kernel debugger to look at a live system, you can examine TCP/IP's device objects. After performing the *!drvobj* command to see the addresses of each of the driver's device objects, execute *!devobj* to view the name and other details about the device object.

```
kd> !drvobj tdx
Driver object (861d9478) is for:
 \Driver\tdx
Driver Extension List: (id , addr)

Device Object list:
861db310  861db440  861d8440  861d03e8
861cd440  861d2318  861d9350
lkd> !devobj 861cd440
Device object (861cd440) is for:
 Tcp6 \Driver\tdx DriverObject 861d9478
Current Irp 00000000 RefCount 7 Type 00000012 Flags 00000050
Dacl 8b1bc54c DevExt 861cd4f8 DevObjExt 861cd500
ExtensionFlags (0x00000800)
                         Unknown flags 0x00000800
Device queue is not busy.
lkd> !devobj 861db440
Device object (861db440) is for:
 RawIp \Driver\tdx DriverObject 861d9478
Current Irp 00000000 RefCount 0 Type 00000012 Flags 00000050
Dacl 8b1bc54c DevExt 861db4f8 DevObjExt 861db500
ExtensionFlags (0x00000800)
                         Unknown flags 0x00000800
```

```
Device queue is not busy.
lkd> !devobj 861d8440
Device object (861d8440) is for:
 Udp6 \Driver\tdx DriverObject 861d9478
Current Irp 00000000 RefCount 0 Type 00000012 Flags 00000050
Dacl 8b1bc54c DevExt 861d84f8 DevObjExt 861d8500
ExtensionFlags (0x00000800)
                            Unknown flags 0x00000800
Device queue is not busy.
lkd> !devobj 861d03e8
Device object (861d03e8) is for:
 Udp \Driver\tdx DriverObject 861d9478
Current Irp 00000000 RefCount 6 Type 00000012 Flags 00000050
Dacl 8b1bc54c DevExt 861d04a0 DevObjExt 861d04a8
ExtensionFlags (0x00000800)
                            Unknown flags 0x00000800
Device queue is not busy.
lkd> !devobj 861cd440
Device object (861cd440) is for:
 Tcp6 \Driver\tdx DriverObject 861d9478
Current Irp 00000000 RefCount 7 Type 00000012 Flags 00000050
Dacl 8b1bc54c DevExt 861cd4f8 DevObjExt 861cd500
ExtensionFlags (0x00000800)
                            Unknown flags 0x00000800
Device queue is not busy.
lkd> !devobj 861d2318
Device object (861d2318) is for:
 Tcp \Driver\tdx DriverObject 861d9478
Current Irp 00000000 RefCount 167 Type 00000012 Flags 00000050
Dacl 8b1bc54c DevExt 861d23d0 DevObjExt 861d23d8
ExtensionFlags (0x00000800)
                            Unknown flags 0x00000800
Device queue is not busy.
lkd> !devobj 861d9350
Device object (861d9350) is for:
 Tdx \Driver\tdx DriverObject 861d9478
Current Irp 00000000 RefCount 0 Type 00000021 Flags 00000050
Dacl 8b0649a8 DevExt 00000000 DevObjExt 861d9408
ExtensionFlags (0x00000800)
                            Unknown flags 0x00000800
Device queue is not busy.
```

Windows Filtering Platform

Windows includes a rich and extensible platform for monitoring, intercepting, and processing network traffic at all levels in the network stack. Other Windows networking services extend basic networking features of the TCP/IP protocol driver by relying on Windows Filtering Platform (WFP). These include Network Address Translation (NAT), IP filtering, IP inspection, and Internet Protocol Security (IPsec). Figure 7-36 shows how the different components of the WFP are integrated with the TCP/IP stack. These include

- **Filter engine** The filter engine is implemented in both user mode and kernel mode and performs all the filtering operations on the network. Each filter engine component consists of filtering layers, one for each component of the network stack. The user-mode engine, responsible for RPC and IPsec keying policy, among other things, contains approximately 10 filters, while the kernel-mode engine, which performs the network and transport layer filtering of the TCP/IP stack, contains around 50.

- **Shims** Shims are the kernel-mode components that reside between the network stack and the filter engine. They are responsible for making the decision to allow or block network traffic based on their filtering behavior, which is defined by the filter engine. A shim operates in three steps: it parses the incoming data to match incoming values with entries in the filter engine, calls the filter engine to return an action based on the incoming values, and then interprets the action (drop the packet, for example).

- **Base filtering engine (BFE)** The BFE is a user-mode service (%SystemRoot%\System32\Bfe. dll) that manages all WFP operations. It is responsible for adding and removing filters from the WFP stack, managing the filter configuration, and enforcing security on the filter database.

- **Callout drivers** Callout drivers are kernel-mode components that add custom filtering functionality outside the basic support provided by the WFP. Callout drivers associate callout functions with one or more kernel-mode filtering layers, and the WFP enables callout functions to perform deep packet inspection and modification. Network Address Translation (described next) and IPsec are implemented as callout drivers, for example.

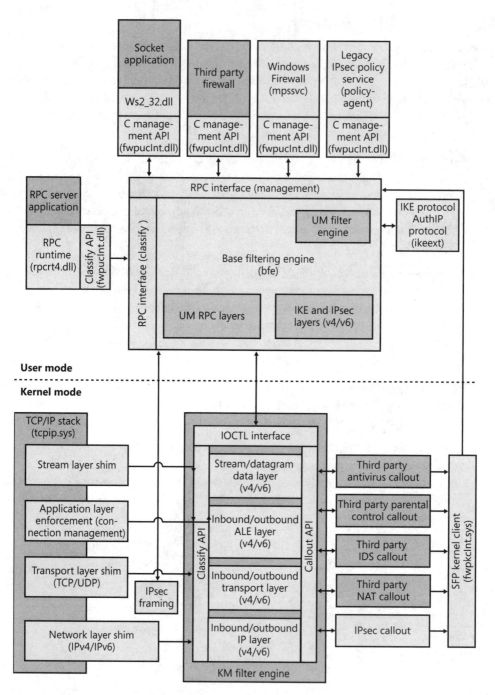

FIGURE 7-36 Windows Filtering Platform architecture

Network Address Translation

Network Address Translation (NAT) is a routing service that allows multiple private IP addresses to map to a single public IP address. Without NAT, each computer of a LAN must be assigned a public IP address to communicate across the Internet. NAT allows one computer of the LAN to be assigned an IP address and the other computers to use private IP addresses and be connected to the Internet through that computer. NAT translates between private IP addresses and the public IP address as necessary, routing packets between LAN computers and the Internet.

NAT components on Windows consist of a NAT device driver, %SystemRoot%\System32\Drivers \ipnat.sys, that interfaces with the WFP stack as a callout driver, as well as packet editors that can perform additional packet processing beyond address and port translation.

IP Filtering

Windows includes a very basic IP filtering capability with which a user can choose to allow only certain ports or IP protocols into or out of the network. Although this capability can serve to protect a computer from unauthorized network accesses, its drawback is that it is static and does not automatically create new filters for traffic initiated by applications running on the computer.

Windows also includes a host firewall capability, called Windows Firewall, that goes beyond the basic filtering just described. Windows Firewall uses WFP to provide a *stateful firewall*, which is one that keeps track of traffic flow so that it distinguishes between TCP/IP traffic that originates on the local LAN and unsolicited traffic that originates on the Internet. When Windows Firewall is enabled on an interface, one of three profiles can be applied—public, private, and domain. By default, when the public profile is chosen (or until a profile is selected), all unsolicited incoming traffic received by the computer is discarded. A user or application can define exceptions so that services running on the computer, such as file and printer sharing or a website, can be accessed from other computers.

The Windows Firewall service, which executes in a Svchost process, uses the BFE to pass exception rules defined in the configuration user interface to the IPNat driver. The WFP filter engine executes the callback functions of each registered callout driver as it processes both inbound and outbound IP packets. A callback function can provide NAT functionality by modifying source and destination addresses in a packet, or as a firewall by returning a status code to TCP/IP that requests that TCP/IP drop the packet and cease processing for it. In kernel mode, Windows Firewall uses the Microsoft Protection Service driver (%SystemRoot%\System32\Drivers\Mpsdrv.sys) that provides support for PPTP and FTP filtering, because those protocols provide their own independent control and data channels. The driver must analyze the control channel to figure out which data channel to manipulate. The driver is also used for displaying notification windows when an application starts listening on a socket.

Internet Protocol Security

Internet Protocol Security (IPsec), which is integrated with the Windows TCP/IP stack, helps protect unicast (IPsec itself supports multicast, but the Windows implementation does not) IP data against attacks such as eavesdropping, sniffer attacks, data modification, IP address spoofing, and man-in-the-middle attacks (as long as the identity of the remote machine can be verified, such as a VPN).

You can use IPsec to provide defense-in-depth against network-based attacks from untrusted computers; certain attacks that can result in the denial-of-service of applications, services, or the network; data corruption, data theft, and user-credential theft; and the administrative control over servers, other computers, and the network. IPsec helps defend against network-based attacks through cryptography-based security services, security protocols, and dynamic key management.

IPsec provides the following properties for unicast IP packets sent between trusted hosts:

- Data origin authentication, which verifies the origin of an IP packet and ensures that unauthenticated parties cannot access data.

- Data integrity, which protects an IP packet from being modified in transit without being detected.

- Data confidentiality, which encrypts the payload of IP packets before transmission. Data confidentiality ensures that only the IPsec peer with which a computer is communicating can read and interpret the contents of the packets. This property is optional.

- Anti-replay (or replay protection), which ensures that each IP packet is unique and can't be reused. This property prevents an attacker from intercepting IP packets and inserting modified packets into a data stream between a source computer and a destination computer. When anti-replay is used, attackers cannot reply to captured messages to establish a session or gain unauthorized access to data.

You can use IPsec to help defend against network-based attacks by configuring host-based IPsec packet filtering and enforcing trusted communications. When you use IPsec for host-based IPsec packet filtering, IPsec can permit or block specific types of unicast IP traffic based on source and destination address combinations and specific protocols and specific ports.

In an Active Directory environment, Group Policy can be used to configure domains, sites, and organizational units (OUs), and IPsec policies (called *connection security rules*) can then be assigned as required to Group Policy objects (GPOs) through Windows Firewall with Advanced Security configuration settings. Alternatively, you can configure and assign local IPsec policies. Active Directory–based connection security rules are stored in Active Directory, and a copy of the current policy is maintained in a cache in the local registry. Local connection security rules are stored in the local system registry.

To establish trusted communications, IPsec uses mutual authentication, and it supports the following authentication methods through AuthIP, Microsoft's extension to Internet Key Exchange (IKE):

- Interactive user Kerberos 5 credentials or interactive user NTLMv2 credentials

- User x.509 certificates

- Computer SSL certificates

- NAP health certificates

- Anonymous authentication (optional authentication)

- Preshared key

If AuthIP is not available, plain IKE is also supported by IPsec. The Windows implementation of IPsec is based on IPsec Requests for Comments (RFCs). The Windows IPsec architecture includes Windows Firewall with Advanced Security, the legacy IPsec Policy Agent, the IKE and Authenticated Internet Protocol (AuthIP) protocols, and an IPsec WFP callout driver, which are described in the following list:

- **Windows Firewall with Advanced Security**   In addition to the filtering functionality described earlier, the Windows Firewall service is also responsible for providing the security and policy configuration settings for IPsec, which can be configured through Group Policy either locally or on an Active Directory domain.

- **Legacy IPsec Policy Agent**   The legacy IPsec Policy Agent runs as a service. In the Services snap-in in the Microsoft Management Console (MMC), the IPsec Policy Agent appears in the list of computer services under the name IPsec Policy Agent. The IPsec Policy Agent obtains the legacy IPsec policy from an Active Directory domain or the local registry and then passes IP address filters to the IPsec driver and authentication and security settings to IKE. These policies are honored to enable compatibility with older versions of Windows, which implement IPsec management through Active Directory.

- **IKE and AuthIP**   IKE is a protocol that supports the authentication and key negotiation services required by IPsec. For outgoing traffic, IKE waits for requests to negotiate security associations (SAs) from the IPsec driver, negotiates the SAs, and then sends the SA settings back to the IPsec driver. For incoming traffic, IKE receives a negotiation request directly from the remote peer, and all other traffic from the peer is dropped until the SAs have been successfully negotiated. SAs are a combination of mutually agreeable IPsec policy settings and keys that defines the security services, mechanisms, and keys that are used to help secure communications between IPsec peers. Each SA is a one-way or simplex connection that secures the traffic it carries. IKE negotiates main mode SAs and quick mode SAs when requested by the IPsec driver. The IKE main mode (or ISAKMP) SA protects the IKE negotiation. The quick mode (or IPsec) SAs protect application traffic. AuthIP is a proprietary extension to IKE supported by Windows Vista and later, while Windows 7 and Windows Server 2008 R2 also add support for IKEv2, an equivalent standardized extension. It adds a secondary authentication mechanism to increase security and simplify maintenance and configuration of IPsec.

- **IPsec WFP callout driver**   The IPsec WFP callout driver is a device driver (%SystemRoot% \System32\Drivers\Fwpkclnt.sys) that is bound to WFP and processes packets that pass through the TCP/IP driver. The IPsec driver monitors and secures outbound unicast IP traffic, and it monitors, decrypts, and validates inbound unicast IP packets. WFP receives filters from the IPsec Policy Agent and invokes the callout, which then permits, blocks, or secures packets as required. To secure traffic, the IPsecl driver uses active SA settings, or it requests that new SAs be created.

You can use the Windows Firewall with Advanced Security (%SystemRoot%\System32\Wf.msc) snap-in that is available in MMC to create and manage connection security rules by using the New Connection Security Rule Wizard, shown in Figure 7-37. This snap-in can be used to create, modify, and store local connection security rules or Active Directory–based connection security rules, and to modify connection security rules on remote computers. Alternatively, you can use the Netsh utility with the *netsh advfirewall consec* command to manage connection security rules. After IPsec-secured communication is established, you can monitor IPsec information for local computers and for remote computers by using the Windows Firewall with Advanced Security snap-in or the Netsh utility with the *netsh advfirewall monitor* command.

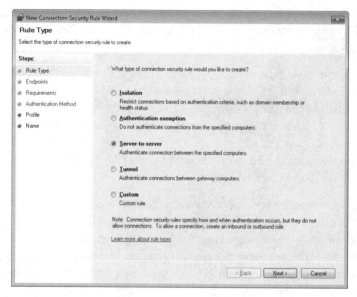

FIGURE 7-37 New Connection Security Rule Wizard

NDIS Drivers

When a protocol driver wants to read or write messages formatted in its protocol's format from or to the network, the driver must do so using a network adapter. Expecting protocol drivers to understand the nuances of every network adapter on the market (proprietary network adapters number in the thousands) is not reasonable, so network adapter vendors provide device drivers that can take network messages and transmit them via the vendors' proprietary hardware. In 1989, Microsoft and 3Com jointly developed the Network Driver Interface Specification (NDIS), which lets protocol drivers communicate with network adapter drivers in a device-independent manner. Network adapter drivers that conform to NDIS are called *NDIS drivers* or *NDIS miniport drivers*. The version of NDIS that ships with Windows 7 and Windows Server 2008 R2 is NDIS 6.20.

The NDIS library (%SystemRoot%\System32\Drivers\Ndis.sys) implements the boundary that exists between network transports, such as the TCP/IP driver, and adapter drivers. The NDIS library is a helper library that NDIS driver clients use to format commands they send to NDIS drivers. NDIS drivers interface with the library to receive requests and send back responses. Figure 7-38 shows the relationship between various NDIS-related components.

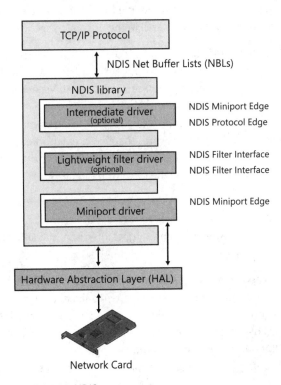

FIGURE 7-38 NDIS components

Instead of merely providing the NDIS boundary helper routines, the NDIS library provides NDIS drivers with an entire execution environment. NDIS drivers do not follow the standard Windows device driver I/O model, and they cannot function without the encapsulation the NDIS library gives them. This insulation layer wraps NDIS drivers so thoroughly that NDIS drivers don't accept and process IRPs. Rather, protocol drivers such as TCP/IP call a function in the NDIS library, *NdisAllocateNetBufferList*, and pass the packets to an NDIS miniport by calling an NDIS library function (*NdisSendNetBufferLists*). Additionally, to make development simpler, all components of the Windows Next Generation TCP/IP stack make use of the NET_BUFFER_LIST structure, including TCP/IP and WSK, which streamlines communications with NDIS.

NDIS includes the following features:

- NDIS drivers can report whether or not their network medium is active, which allows Windows to display a network connected/disconnected icon on the taskbar. This feature also allows protocols and other applications to be aware of this state and react accordingly. The TCP/IP transport, for example, uses this information to determine when it should reevaluate addressing information it receives from DHCP.

- NDIS drivers can be paused and resumed, which enables run-time reconfiguration, such as adding or removing an NDIS Lightweight Filter driver. A lightweight filter replaces most instances of NDIS intermediate drivers used prior to NDIS version 6. (Intermediate drivers are still supported in NDIS 6, but their complexity makes them suitable for only a small class of problems.) Lightweight filter drivers are covered in more detail in the upcoming sections.

- TCP/IP offloading, including task and chimney offloading. Task offloading allows a network interface card to implement some or all of the TCP/IP protocol stack, providing a substantial increase in network performance. NDIS includes support for IPsec Task Offload Version 2, which includes support for additional cryptography suites used in IPsec, such as AES, as well as IPv6 support. Chimney offloading provides a direct connection (the so-called *chimney*) between network applications and the network card hardware, enabling greater offloading and connection state management to be implemented by the network card. These offloading operations can improve system performance by relieving the CPU from the tasks.

- Receive-side scaling enables systems with multiple processors to perform packet receive operations based on the most efficient use of available target processors. NDIS supports the receive-side scaling (RSS) interface at the hardware level and targets interrupts and DPCs to the appropriate processors.

- Wake-on-LAN allows a wake-on-LAN-capable network adapter to bring the system out of a suspended power state. Events that can trigger the network adapter to signal the system include media connections (such as plugging a network cable into the adapter), the receipt of protocol-specific patterns registered by a protocol (the TCP/IP transport asks to be woken for Address Resolution Protocol [ARP] requests), and, for Ethernet adapters, the receipt of a *magic* packet (a network packet that contains 16 contiguous copies of the adapter's Ethernet address).

- Header-data split allows compatible network cards to improve network performance by splitting the data and header part of an Ethernet frame into different buffers and subsequently combining the buffers into smaller regions of memory than if the buffers were combined. This allows more efficient memory usage as well as better caching because multiple headers can fit in a single page.

- Connection-oriented NDIS (CoNDIS) allows NDIS drivers to manage connection-oriented media (typically, a WAN), such as ISDN or PPP devices. (CoNDIS is described in more detail shortly.)

The interfaces that the NDIS library provides for NDIS drivers to interface with network adapter hardware are available via functions that translate directly to corresponding functions in the HAL.

EXPERIMENT: Listing the Loaded NDIS Miniports

The Ndiskd kernel debugger extension library includes the *!miniports* and *!miniport* commands, which let you list the loaded miniports using a kernel debugger and, given the address of a miniport block (a data structure Windows uses to track miniports), see detailed information about the miniport driver. The following example shows the *!miniports* and *!miniport* commands being used to list all the miniports and then specifics about the miniport responsible for interfacing the system to a PCI Ethernet adapter. (Note that WAN miniport drivers work with dial-up connections.)

```
lkd> .load ndiskd
Loaded ndiskd extension DLL


lkd> !miniports
NDIS Driver verifier level: 0
NDIS Failed allocations    : 0
Miniport Driver Block: 86880d78, Version 0.0
  Miniport: 868cf0e8, NetLuidIndex: 1, IfIndex: 9, RAS Async Adapter
Miniport Driver Block: 84c3be60, Version 4.0
  Miniport: 84c3c0e8, NetLuidIndex: 3, IfIndex: 15, VMware Virtual Ethernet Adapter
Miniport Driver Block: 84c29240, Version 0.0
  Miniport: 84c2b438, NetLuidIndex: 0, IfIndex: 2, WAN Miniport (SSTP)
...
lkd> !miniport 84bcc0e8


 Miniport 84bcc0e8 : Broadcom NetXtreme 57xx Gigabit Controller, v6.0


    AdapterContext : 85f6b000
    Flags          : 0c452218
                     BUS_MASTER, 64BIT_DMA, IGNORE_TOKEN_RING_ERRORS
                     DESERIALIZED, RESOURCES_AVAILABLE, SUPPORTS_MEDIA_SENSE
                     DOES_NOT_DO_LOOPBACK, SG_DMA,
                     NOT_MEDIA_CONNECTED,
    PnPFlags       : 00610021
                     PM_SUPPORTED, DEVICE_POWER_ENABLED, RECEIVED_START
                     HARDWARE_DEVICE, NDIS_WDM_DRIVER,
    MiniportState      : STATE_RUNNING
    IfIndex            : 10
    Ndis5MiniportInNdis6Mode : 0
    InternalResetCount   : 0000
    MiniportResetCount   : 0000
    References           : 5
    UserModeOpenReferences: 0
    PnPDeviceState       : PNP_DEVICE_STARTED
    CurrentDevicePowerState : PowerDeviceD0
    Bus PM capabilities
    DeviceD1:        0
    DeviceD2:        0
    WakeFromD0:        0
```

```
WakeFromD1:         0
WakeFromD2:         0
WakeFromD3:         1

SystemState          DeviceState
PowerSystemUnspecified    PowerDeviceUnspecified
S0          D0
S1          PowerDeviceUnspecified
S2          PowerDeviceUnspecified
S3          D3
S4          D3
S5          D3
SystemWake: S5
    DeviceWake: D3

WakeupMethods Enabled 2:
    WAKE_UP_PATTERN_MATCH
WakeUpCapabilities:
MinMagicPacketWakeUp: 4
MinPatternWakeUp: 4
MinLinkChangeWakeUp: 0
Current PnP and PM Settings:          : 00000030
                DISABLE_WAKE_UP, DISABLE_WAKE_ON_RECONNECT,
Translated Allocated Resources:
    Memory: ecef0000, Length: 10000
    Interrupt Level: 9, Vector: a8
MediaType       : 802.3
DeviceObject    : 84bcc030, PhysDO : 848fd6b0   Next DO: 848fc7b0
MapRegisters    : 00000000
FirstPendingPkt: 00000000
DriverVerifyFlags   : 00000000
Miniport Interrupt : 85f72000
Miniport version 6.0
Miniport Filter List:
Miniport Open Block Queue:
   8669bad0: Protocol 86699530 = NDISUIO, ProtocolBindingContext 8669be88, v6.0
   86690008: Protocol 86691008 = VMNETBRIDGE, ProtocolBindingContext 866919b8, v5.0
   84f81c50: Protocol 849fb918 = TCPIP6, ProtocolBindingContext 84f7b930, v6.1
   84f7b230: Protocol 849f43c8 = TCPIP, ProtocolBindingContext 84f7b5e8, v6.1
```

The *Flags* field for the miniport that was examined indicates that the miniport supports 64-bit direct memory access operation (64BIT_DMA), that the media is currently not active (NOT_MEDIA_CONNECTED), and that it can dynamically detect whether the media is connected or disconnected (SUPPORTS_MEDIA_SENSE). Also listed are the adapter's system-to-device power-state mappings and the bus resources that the Plug and Play manager assigned to the adapter. (See the section "The Power Manager" in Chapter 8 in Part 2 for more information on power-state mappings.)

Variations on the NDIS Miniport

The NDIS model also supports hybrid network transport NDIS drivers, called *NDIS intermediate drivers*. These drivers lie between transport drivers and NDIS miniport drivers. To an NDIS miniport driver, an NDIS intermediate driver looks like a transport driver; to a transport driver, an NDIS intermediate driver looks like an NDIS miniport driver. NDIS intermediate drivers can see all network traffic taking place on a system because the drivers lie between protocol drivers and network drivers. Software that provides fault-tolerant and load-balancing options for network adapters, such as Microsoft's Network Load Balancing Provider, are based on NDIS intermediate drivers. Finally, the NDIS model also implements *lightweight filter drivers* (LWF), which are similar to intermediate drivers but specifically designed for filtering network traffic. LWFs support dynamic insertion and removal while the protocol stack is running. Filter drivers have the ability to filter all communications to and from the underlying miniport adapter. They also have the ability to select specify types of filtering (packet data or control messages) and to be bypassed for those that they are not interested in.

Connection-Oriented NDIS

Support for connection-oriented network hardware (for example, PPP) is native in Windows, which makes connection management and establishment standard in the Windows network architecture. Connection-oriented NDIS drivers use many of the same APIs that standard NDIS drivers use; however, connection-oriented NDIS drivers send packets through established network connections rather than placing them on the network medium.

In addition to miniport support for connection-oriented media, NDIS includes definitions for drivers that work to support a connection-oriented miniport driver:

- Call managers are NDIS drivers that provide call setup and teardown services for connection-oriented clients (described shortly). A call manager uses a connection-oriented miniport to exchange signaling messages with network switches or another connection-oriented network medium. A call manager supports one or more signaling protocols. A call manager is implemented as a network protocol driver.

- An integrated miniport call manager (MCM) is a connection-oriented miniport driver that also provides call manager services to connection-oriented clients. An MCM is essentially an NDIS miniport driver with a built-in call manager.

- A connection-oriented client uses the call setup and teardown services of a call manager or MCM and the send and receive services of a connection-oriented NDIS miniport driver. A connection-oriented client can provide its own protocol services to higher levels in the network stack, or it can implement an emulation layer that interfaces connectionless legacy protocols and connection-oriented media.

Figure 7-39 shows the relationships between these components.

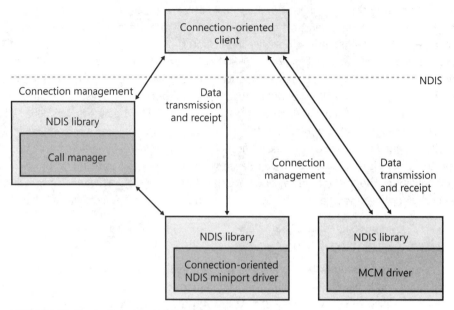

FIGURE 7-39 Connection-oriented NDIS drivers

EXPERIMENT: Using Network Monitor to Capture Network Packets

Microsoft provides a tool named Network Monitor that lets you capture packets that flow through one or more NDIS miniport drivers on your system by installing an NDIS lightweight filter driver (Netmon). You can obtain the latest version of Network Monitor by going to *http://www.microsoft.com/download/en/details.aspx?id=4865*. Don't forget to download the NetMon protocol parsers from *http://nmparsers.codeplex.com/*; otherwise, you won't be able to decode the Microsoft protocols. When you first start Network Monitor, you'll see a window similar to the one shown in Figure 7-40.

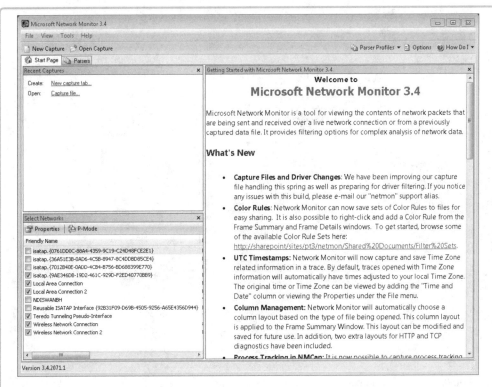

FIGURE 7-40 Network monitor

In the Select Networks pane, Network Monitor lets you select which network connection you want to monitor. After selecting one or more, start the capture environment by clicking the New Capture button on the toolbar. You can now initiate monitoring by clicking the Start button on the toolbar. Perform operations that generate network activity on the connection you're monitoring (such as browsing to a website), and after you see that Network Monitor has captured packets, stop monitoring by clicking the Stop button. In the Frame Summary pane, you will see all the raw network traffic during the capture period. The Network Conversations pane displays network traffic isolated by process, whenever possible. By clicking on the Iexplore.exe process in this example, Network Monitor shows only the relevant frames in the Frame Summary view, as shown in Figure 7-41.

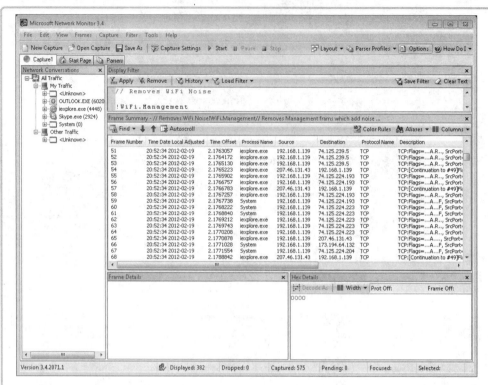

FIGURE 7-41 Capturing packets with Network Monitor

The window shows the HTTP packets that Network Monitor captured as the Microsoft website was accessed through Internet Explorer. If you click on a frame, Network Monitor displays a view of the packet that breaks it apart to show various layered application and protocol headers in the Frame Details pane, as shown in the previous screen shot.

Network Monitor also includes a number of other features, such as capture triggers and filters, that make it a powerful tool for troubleshooting network problems. You can also add parsers for other protocols, as well as view and modify their source code. Network Monitor parsers are hosted on CodePlex (*http://nmparsers.codeplex.com*), the Microsoft open source project site.

Remote NDIS

Prior to the development of Remote NDIS, a vendor that developed a USB network device had to provide a driver that interfaced with NDIS as a miniport driver as well as interfacing with a USB WDM bus driver, as shown in Figure 7-42.

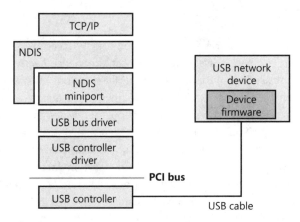

FIGURE 7-42 NDIS miniport driver for a USB network device

Remote NDIS is a specification for network devices on USB. The specification eliminates the need for a hardware vendor to write an NDIS miniport driver by defining messages and the mechanism by which the messages are transmitted over USB. Remote NDIS messages mirror the NDIS interface and include messages for initializing and resetting a device, transmitting and receiving packets, setting and querying device parameters, and indicating media link status.

The Remote NDIS architecture, in Figure 7-43, relies on a Microsoft-supplied NDIS miniport driver, %SystemRoot%\System32\Drivers\Rndismp.sys, that translates NDIS commands and forwards them to a USB device. The architecture allows for a single NDIS miniport driver to be used for all Remote NDIS devices on USB.

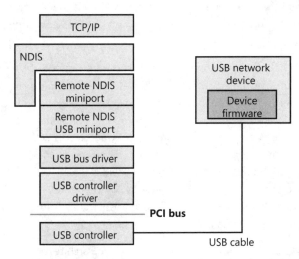

FIGURE 7-43 Remote NDIS architecture for USB network devices

Currently, USB is the only bus supported by RNDIS on Windows.

QoS

If no special measures are taken, IP network traffic is delivered on a first-come, first-served basis. Applications have no control over the priority of their messages, and they can experience *bursty* network behavior, where they occasionally obtain high throughput and low latencies but otherwise receive poor network performance. While this level of service is acceptable in most situations (such as transferring files or browsing the Web), an increasing number of network applications demand more consistent service levels, or *Quality of Service* (QoS) guarantees. Video conferencing, media streaming, and enterprise resource planning (ERP) are examples of applications that require consistent network performance. QoS allows an application to specify minimum bandwidth and maximum latencies, which can be satisfied only if every networking software and hardware component between a sender and a receiver supports QoS standards such as IEEE 802.1P, an industry standard that specifies the format of QoS packets and how OSI layer 2 devices (switches and network adapters) respond to them.

Windows supports QoS through a *policy-based QoS* implementation that takes full advantage of the Next Generation TCP/IP network stack, WFP, and NDIS lightweight filter drivers. The implementation allows for managing or prioritizing bandwidth use based on different conditions, such as the application, the source or destination IP address, the protocol being used, and the source or destination ports. Network administrators typically apply QoS settings to a logon session or a computer with Active Directory–based Group Policy, but they can be applied locally as well.

Policy-based QoS provides two methods through which bandwidth can be managed. The first uses a special field in the IP header called the Differentiated Services Code Point (DSCP). Routers that support DSCP read the value and separate packets into specific priority queues. The QoS architecture in Windows can mark outgoing packets with the appropriate DSCP field so that network devices can provide differentiated levels of service. The other bandwidth management method is the ability to simply throttle outgoing traffic based on the conditions outlined earlier, where the QoS components limit bandwidth to a specified rate.

The Windows QoS implementation consists of several components, as shown in Figure 7-44. First, the QoS Client Side Extension (%SystemRoot%\System32\Gptext.dll) notifies the Group Policy client and the QoS Inspection Module that QoS settings have changed. Next, the QoS Inspection Module (Enterprise Quality of Service, eQoS), which is a WFP packet-inspection component implemented in the TCP/IP driver that reacts to policy changes, retrieves the updated policy and works with the transport layer and QoS Packet Scheduler to mark traffic that matches the policy. Finally, the QoS Packet Scheduler, or Pacer (%SystemRoot%\System32\Drivers\Pacer.sys), provides the NDIS lightweight filter functionality, such as throttling and setting the DSCP value, to control packet scheduling based on the QoS policies. Pacer also provides the GQoS (Generic QoS) and TC (Traffic Control) API support for legacy Windows applications that used these mechanisms.

In addition to the systemwide, policy-based QoS support provided by the QoS architecture, Windows enables specific classes of socket-based applications to have individual and specific control of QoS behavior through an API called the Quality Windows Audio/Video Experience, or qWAVE.

Network-based multimedia applications, such as Voice over IP (VoIP), can use the qWAVE API to query information on real-time network bandwidth and adapt to changing network conditions, as well as to prioritize packets to efficiently use the available bandwidth. qWAVE also takes advantage of the topology protocols described earlier to dynamically determine if the current network devices will support the required bandwidth for a video stream, for example. It can notify applications of diminishing bandwidth, at which point the multimedia application is expected to reduce the stream quality, for example.

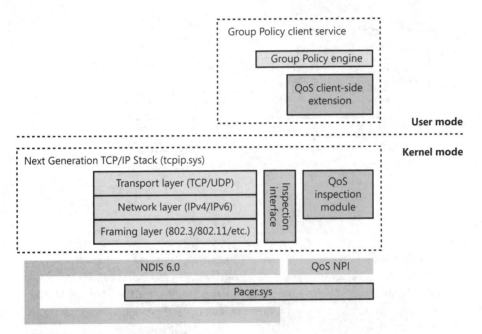

FIGURE 7-44 Policy-based QoS architecture

qWAVE is implemented in the QoS2 (%SystemRoot%\System32\Qwave.dll) API library and provides four main components:

- Admission control, which determines, when a new network multimedia stream is started, if the current network can support the sustained bandwidth requested.

- Caching, which allows the detailed admission control checks to be bypassed if similar usage patterns occurred in the past and the calculation result was already cached.

- Monitoring and probing, which keep track of available bandwidth and notify applications during low-bandwidth or high-latency situations.

- Traffic tagging and shaping, which uses the 802.11p and DSCP technologies mentioned earlier to tag packets with the appropriate priority to ensure timely delivery.

Figure 7-45 shows the general overview of the qWAVE architecture:

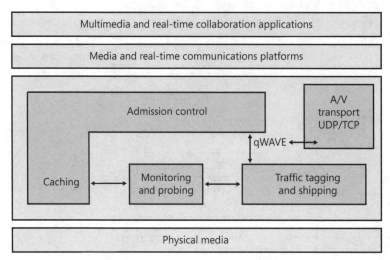

FIGURE 7-45 qWAVE architecture

Binding

The final piece in the Windows networking architecture puzzle is the way in which the components at the various layers—networking API layer, transport driver layer, NDIS driver layer—locate one another. The name of the process that connects the layers is *binding*. You've witnessed binding taking place if you've changed your network configuration by adding or removing a component using the Network Connections folder.

When you install a networking component, you must supply an INF file for the component. (INF files are described in Chapter 8 in Part 2.) This file includes directions that setup API routines must follow to install and configure the component, including binding dependencies or binding relationships. A developer can specify binding dependencies for a proprietary component so that the Service Control Manager (the Service Control Manager is described in Chapter 4, "Management Mechanisms") will not only load the component in the correct order but will load the component only if other dependent components are present on the system. Binding relationships, which the bind engine determines with the aid of additional information in a component's INF file, establish connections between components at the various layers. The connections specify which components a network component on one layer can use on the layer beneath it.

For example, the Workstation service (redirector) automatically binds to the TCP/IP protocol. The order of the binding, which you can examine on the Adapters And Bindings tab in the Advanced Settings dialog box (shown in Figure 7-46), determines the priority of the binding. (See the section "Multiple Redirector Support" earlier in this chapter for instructions on how to launch the Advanced Settings dialog box.) When the redirector receives a request to access a remote file, it submits the request to both protocol drivers simultaneously. When the response comes, the redirector waits until it has also received responses from any higher-priority protocol drivers. Only then will the redirector return the result to the caller. Thus, it can be advantageous to reorder bindings so that bindings of high priority are also the most performance efficient or applicable to most of the computers in your network. You can also manually remove bindings with the Advanced Settings dialog box.

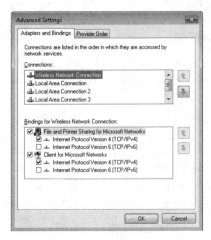

FIGURE 7-46 Editing bindings with the Advanced Settings dialog box

The *Bind* value, in the Linkage subkey of a network component's registry configuration key, stores binding information for that component. For example, if you examine HKLM\SYSTEM \CurrentControlSet\Services\LanmanWorkstation\Linkage\Bind, you'll see the binding information for the Workstation service.

Layered Network Services

Windows includes network services that build on the APIs and components we've presented in this chapter. Describing the capabilities and detailed internal implementation of all these services is outside the scope of this book, but this section provides a brief overview of remote access, Active Directory, Network Load Balancing, and Distributed File System (DFS), including DFS Replication (DFSR).

Remote Access

Remote access, which is available with Windows Server with the Routing and Remote Access service, allows remote access clients to connect to remote access servers and access network resources such as files, printers, and network services as if the client were physically connected to the remote access server's network. Windows provides two types of remote access:

- Dial-up remote access is used by clients that connect to a remote access server via a telephone or other telecommunications infrastructure. The telecommunications medium is used to create a temporary physical or virtual connection between the client and the server.

- Virtual private network (VPN) remote access lets a VPN client establish a virtual point-to-point connection to the server over an IP network such as the Internet. Windows also supports the Secure Socket Transmission Protocol (SSTP), which is a newer tunneling protocol for VPN connections that has the ability to pass through most firewalls and routers that block PPTP or L2TP/IPsec traffic. It does so by packaging PPP data over the SSL channel of the HTTPS protocol. Because the latter operates on port 443 and is usually part of typical Web browsing behavior, it is much more likely to be available than traditional VPN tunneling protocols.

Remote access differs from remote control solutions because remote access acts as a proxy connection to a Windows network, whereas remote control software executes applications on a server, presenting a user interface to the client.

Active Directory

Active Directory is the Windows implementation of Lightweight Directory Access Protocol (LDAP) directory services (RFC 4510). Fundamentally, Active Directory is a database that stores objects representing resources defined by applications in a Windows network. For example, the structure and membership of a Windows domain, including user accounts and password information, are stored in Active Directory.

Object classes and the attributes that define properties of objects are specified by a *schema*. The objects in the Active Directory are hierarchically arranged, much like the registry's logical organization, where container objects can store other objects, including other container objects. (See Chapter 6 for more information on container objects.)

Active Directory supports a number of APIs that clients can use to access objects within an Active Directory database:

- The LDAP C API is a C language API that uses the LDAP networking protocol. Applications written in C or C++ can use this API directly, and applications written in other languages can access the APIs through translation layers.

- Active Directory Service Interfaces (ADSI) is a COM interface to Active Directory implemented on top of LDAP that abstracts the details of LDAP programming. ADSI supports multiple languages, including Microsoft Visual Basic, C, and Microsoft Visual C++. ADSI can also be used by Microsoft Windows Script Host (WSH) applications.

- Messaging API (MAPI) is supported for compatibility with Microsoft Exchange client and Outlook Address Book client applications.

- Security Account Manager (SAM) APIs are built on top of Active Directory to provide an interface to logon authentication packages such as MSV1_0 (%SystemRoot%\System32\Msv1_0.dll, which is used for legacy NT LAN Manager authentication) and Kerberos (%SystemRoot%\System32\Kdcsvc.dll).

- Windows NT 4 networking APIs (Net APIs) are used by Windows NT 4 clients to gain access to Active Directory through SAM.

- NTDS API is used to look up SIDs and GUIDs in an Active Directory implementation (via *DsCrackNames* mostly) as well as for its main purposes, Active Directory management and replication. Several third parties have written applications that monitor Active Directory from these APIs.

Active Directory is implemented as a database file that, by default, is named %SystemRoot%\Ntds \Ntds.dit and replicated across the domain controllers in a domain. The Active Directory directory service, which is a Windows service that executes in the Local Security Authority Subsystem (LSASS) process, manages the database, using DLLs that implement the on-disk structure of the database as well as provide transaction-based updates to protect the integrity of the database. The Active Directory database store is based on a version of the Extensible Storage Engine (ESE), also known as the JET Blue, database used by Microsoft Exchange Server 2007, Desktop Search, and Windows Mail. The ESE library (%SystemRoot%\System32\Esent.dll) provides routines for accessing the database, which are open for other applications to use as well. Figure 7-47 shows the Active Directory architecture.

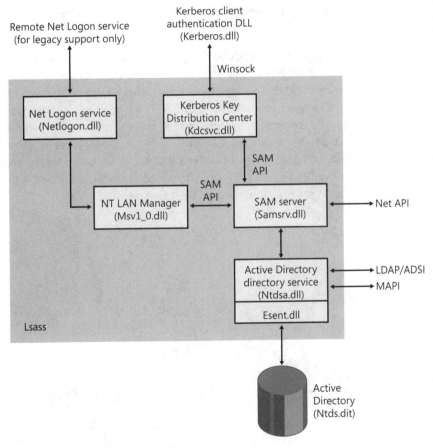

FIGURE 7-47 Active Directory architecture

Network Load Balancing

As stated earlier in the chapter, Network Load Balancing, which is included with server versions of Windows, is based on NDIS lightweight filter technology. Network Load Balancing allows for the creation of a cluster containing up to 32 computers, which are called *cluster hosts* in Network Load Balancing. The cluster can maintain multiple dedicated IP addresses and a single virtual IP address that is published for access by clients. Client requests go to all the computers in the cluster, but only one cluster host responds to the request. The Network Load Balancing NDIS drivers effectively partition the client space among available cluster hosts in a distributed manner. This way, each host handles its portion of incoming client requests, and every client request always gets handled by one and only one host. The cluster host that determines it should handle a client request allows the request to propagate up to the TCP/IP protocol driver and eventually a server application; the other cluster hosts don't. If a cluster host fails, the rest of the cluster realizes that the cluster host is no longer a candidate for processing requests and redistributes the incoming client requests to the remaining cluster hosts. No new client requests are sent to the failed cluster host. Another cluster host can be added to the cluster as a replacement, and it will then seamlessly start handling client requests.

Network Load Balancing isn't a general-purpose clustering solution because the server application that clients communicate with must have certain characteristics: the first is that it must be based on protocols supported by the Windows TCP/IP stack, and the second is that it must be able to handle client requests on any system in a Network Load Balancing cluster. This second requirement typically means that an application that must have access to shared state in order to service client requests must manage the shared state itself—Network Load Balancing doesn't include services for automatically distributing shared state across cluster hosts. Applications that are ideally suited for Network Load Balancing include a web server that serves static content, Windows Media Server, and Terminal Services. Figure 7-48 shows an example of a Network Load Balancing operation.

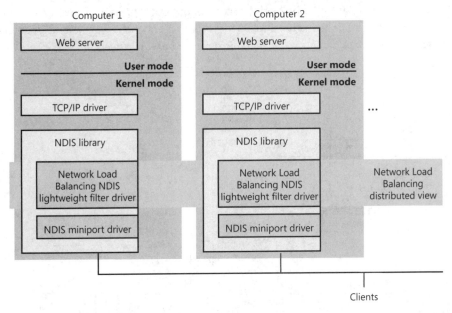

FIGURE 7-48 Network Load Balancing operation

Network Access Protection

One of the most difficult challenges that network administrators face is ensuring that systems
that connect to their private networks are up to date and meet the organization's health policy
requirements. A health policy contains the specific requirements that a system must meet, such as
the minimum required system hotfixes, or a minimum antivirus signature version. Enforcing these
requirements is even more difficult when the systems, such as home computers or laptops, are not
under the network administrator's control. Attackers often create malware that targets out-of-date
software, so users who do not keep their systems up to date with the most recent operating system
updates or antivirus signatures risk exposing the organization's private network assets to attacks and
viruses.

Network Access Protection (NAP) provides a mechanism that helps network administrators enforce
compliance with health requirement policies for all systems that require network access. Systems that
do not meet the required health policies are isolated from the network and are placed in quarantine.
While in quarantine, the noncompliant system's network connectivity is severely limited, and it can
only see the remediation servers from which it can receive the necessary updates to bring it back
into compliance. This ensures that only systems that comply with the health policy requirements are
allowed to access the organization's network. NAP is not designed to protect a network from malicious users; it is designed to help administrators maintain the health of the systems on the network,
which in turn helps maintain the network's overall integrity. NAP is a multivendor system, with clients
running on other operating systems, such as Mac OS X and Linux, and several third-party System
Health Agents, System Health Validators, and Enforcement Clients.

An exhaustive description of NAP is beyond the scope of this book; however, Figures 7-49 and 7-50 illustrate the various components that implement NAP on client and server systems. A detailed description of NAP can be found at *http://technet.microsoft.com/en-us/network/bb545879.aspx*.

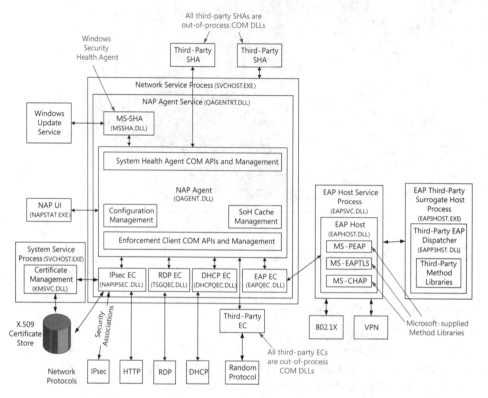

FIGURE 7-49 NAP client-side architecture

In brief, the components of NAP on the client include the following:

- **System Health Agent (SHA)**   Monitors one or more aspects of a client's health, and provides one or more Statements of Health (SoH) to the local system's NAP Agent. For example, an antivirus SHA might examine the version numbers of the antivirus engine and virus signature file, and place that information in its SoH. A SHA can be matched to a remediation server so that a noncompliant system will know how to become compliant. For example, a SHA for checking antivirus signatures could be matched to a server that contains the latest antivirus signature file and the antivirus application package. Some SHAs do not need to be matched with a remediation server. For example, a SHA might just report local system settings that a System Health Validator (SHV) running on the NAP server SHV can use to determine whether the system's firewall is enabled. Windows XP Service Pack 3 and later provide a SHA (%SystemRoot%\System32\Mssha.dll) that monitors the settings of the Windows Action Center (SHA-WAC). This SHA is typically referred to as the Windows SHA, or WSH. To write a SHA, look at the *INapSystemHealthAgentBinding2*, *INapSystemHealthAgentCallback*, and

INapSystemHealthAgentRequest APIs. The SHA is dependent upon the System Health Validator (SHV), and it is expected that the author of a SHA also provide a SHV.

> **Note** SHA vendors should understand that the evaluation process can happen before the system has an IP address (for example, using 802.1x), so the SHA cannot look for data outside the client system. In addition, the IP address can change at any point in time (for example, if NAP causes the client to move to the quarantine VLAN), so the SHA should not cache sockets or make any assumptions about its IP address.

- **NAP Agent**   %SystemRoot%\System32\qagentRT.dll (quarantine agent service runtime). Runs on each client computer, collects the SoH from each SHA, and relays that information to the NAP Server. The NAP Agent communicates with the NAP Server running on the Network Policy Server using the Microsoft Statement of Health protocol [MS-SoH].

- **Enforcement Client (EC)**   Responsible for communicating with an Enforcement Point when trying to connect to a network, and for enforcing machine compliance with NAP policies. An Enforcement Point is a server or network access device that can be used with NAP to require the evaluation of a NAP client's health state and provide restricted network access or communication. If the machine's health is not compliant, the NAP EC indicates the restricted status to the NAP Agent. Windows provides ECs for IPsec (%SystemRoot%\System32\NapIPsec.dll), 802.1X and VPN EAP-authenticated connections (%SystemRoot%\System32\Eapqec.dll), DHCP (%SystemRoot%\System32\Dhcpqec.dll), and a Remote Desktop gateway (%SystemRoot% \System32\Tsgqec.dll). To write an EC, look at the *INapEnforcementClientBinding*, *INapEnforcementClientCallback*, and *INapEnforcementClientConnection2* APIs.

> **Note** The name "enforcement client" can be somewhat confusing. The name refers to its role as a client of a network enforcement point, so it is more about how a client system accesses a network (although access control is generally part of its function).

The following diagram shows the NAP components on a server. On the server side, the entire mechanism is an add-on to the Network Policy Server (NPS) Server (part of the IAS service). In general, the health requests arrive at the NPS as an addition to RADIUS requests sent to the NPS by the enforcement point. The servers, the NPS then passes the Statement of Health (SoH) to the health validation layer, which passes the SoH to the appropriate SHV.

From the NPS perspective, the requests are coming from RADIUS clients (for example, 802.1x network switch, VPN server, DHCP server, and so on) in RADIUS UDP packets. Or it allows private ALPC calls. (Instead of going through UDP, the ALPC is used by the other Windows

Server roles—for example, DHCP server—to simplify the programming model.) The RADIUS specification (RFC 2865) provides for a maximum packet size of 4096, which has a significant impact on the amount of data that a SHA can send.

The client IPsec EC talks to a Health Registration Authority (HRA) server over HTTP. The HRA is an IIS ISAPI filter, which passes the SoH to the NPS (using the ALPC interface) and is responsible for issuing the certificates (when the machine is identified as qualified for a certificate). The HRA server list can be configured using DNS, by adding HRA server records and configuring the client to get the list from DNS. Third parties can implement a RADIUS client to talk to the NPS over UDP.

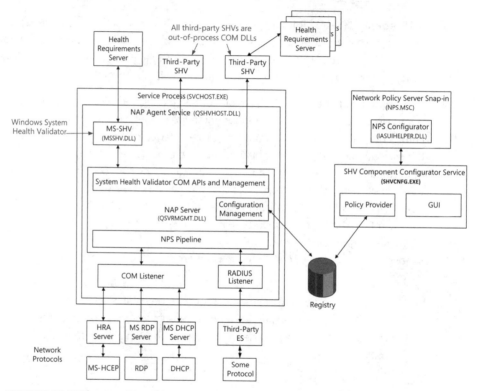

FIGURE 7-50 NAP server-side architecture

- **System Health Validator (SHV)** Evaluates a SoH received from the corresponding SHA on a client and determines whether the client is in compliance with the organization's health policy by checking with a Health Requirements Server (HRS). For example, an antivirus HRS might specify the minimum antivirus engine version and virus signature file version.

Note The presence of a Health Requirements Server is an implementation detail; an SHV can perform all the necessary work on its own.

The SHV uses this information to determine whether the SoH provided by the client SHA is in compliance with the health policy provided by the HRS. To write a SHV, look at the *INapSystemHealthValidator* and *INapSystemHealthValidationRequest2* APIs. The SHV is dependent upon the System Health Agent (SHA), and it is expected that the author of a SHA also provide a SHV.

Not pictured in the diagram are one or more Remediation Servers, which allow a client to be brought into compliance (for example, a Windows Update server). The SHV is not connected to the Remediation Servers, but it is aware of their existence (configured administratively). It passes information about the servers to the client when the SoH indicates that the client is not compliant with the current policy requirements.

NAP client configuration is typically done in the Group Policy editor with the Enforcement Client snap-in, but it can also be performed using the NAP client configuration MMC snap-in (%SystemRoot%\System32\Napclcfg.msc) or the network shell (%SystemRoot%\System32\Netsh.exe), as shown in Figures 7-51, 7-52, and 7-53.

 Note Group Policy always takes precedence over other configurations, followed by the local configuration, and then by DNS auto-discovery.

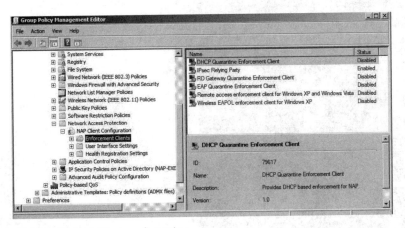

FIGURE 7-51 NAP Client configuration

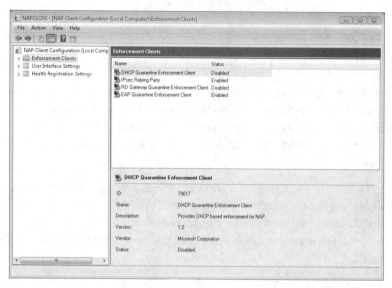

FIGURE 7-52 NAP Client configuration

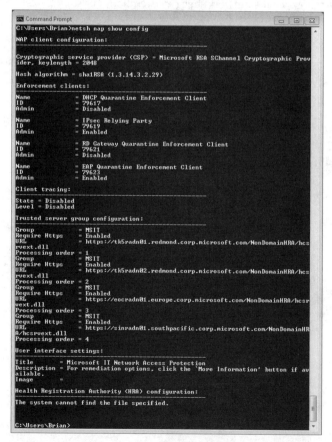

FIGURE 7-53 Configuring NAP using the network shell

Direct Access

In Windows 7 Ultimate and Enterprise editions, Microsoft added an always-on Virtual Private Network (VPN) capability known as DirectAccess (DA), which allows a remote client on the Internet access to a corporate domain-based network. A DA connection to a corporate network is created when the client system boots, and it lasts for as long as the client is running and connected to the Internet. If network problems cause the connection to be dropped, the connection will be automatically re-established when network connections permit. DA uses IPsec running over IPv6, which can be encapsulated in IPv4 using a variety of mechanisms (described later) if the local system does not have end-to-end IPv6 connectivity to the private network. Remote systems can even use DA when they are behind a firewall, because DA can use HTTPS (TCP port 443) as a transport (IP-HTTPS).

Unlike traditional VPN products, remote systems using DA to access a corporate network are always visible and manageable—just as if the machine was directly plugged into the corporate network. The corporate IT department can manage remote systems by updating Group Policy settings or push software updates at any time the remote systems are attached to the Internet. The IT department can also specify which corporate network resources (applications, servers, subnets, and so on) can be accessed by a user or remote system that is connected using DA.

For enhanced security, Authentication Mechanism Assurance (described in Chapter 6) can be required on DA clients. This requires two-factor authentication (for example, a smart card or other hardware token) to log on or unlock a system.

As shown in Figure 7-54, there are many mechanisms available for connecting a DA client to a corporate network: IPv6, Intra-Site Automatic Tunnel Addressing Protocol (ISATAP), IPv4 encrypted with IPsec, 6to4 tunnel, or Teredo. In all cases, a connection is made between the remote client and a DA server. This server provides Denial of Service (DoS) protection by rate-limiting connection negotiation traffic used to connect to it, and it acts as an IPv6 tunnel gateway between the remote client and the corporate network. The DA server also functions as an IPv6-based IPsec security gateway, similar to a VPN server or VPN client access concentrator, to control access to the corporate network

A client typically has two IPv6 tunnels to the DA server: an *infrastructure* tunnel and an *intranet* tunnel. The infrastructure tunnel is for communicating with corporate infrastructure servers, such as a Domain Name System (DNS) server, and domain controllers. The infrastructure tunnel is created automatically when the client boots, and it does not require the user to be logged in. The intranet tunnel is established when a user logs in, and it carries network traffic for the user.

DA also works with NAP. In this case, a Health Registration Authority (HRA) server is placed outside the corporate firewall (often referred to as the DMZ, or DeMilitarized Zone). The client is configured with the name of the HRA (which can be resolved to an IP address using a public DNS server). When the client boots, it contacts the HRA and sends its Statement of Health. If the client is not healthy, it must access remediation servers, which are also in the DMZ. Once the client is healthy, it obtains a health certificate that can then be used with IPsec to connect to the DA server.

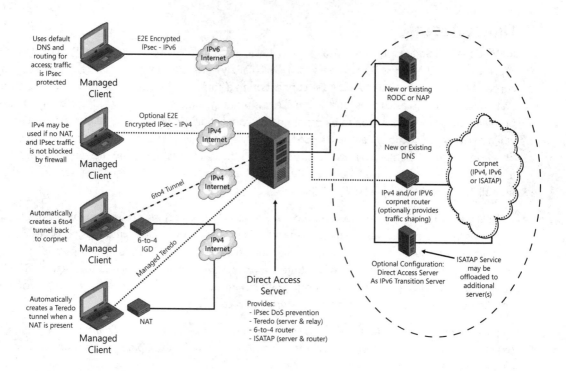

FIGURE 7-54 Connecting a DA client to a corporate network

Conclusion

The Windows network architecture provides a flexible infrastructure for networking APIs, network protocol drivers, and network adapter drivers. The Windows networking architecture takes advantage of I/O layering to give networking support the extensibility to evolve as computer networking evolves. Similarly, new APIs can interface to existing Windows protocol drivers. Finally, the range of networking APIs implemented on Windows affords network application developers a range of possible implementations, each with different programming models and protocol support.

Index

Symbols

About the Authors

Mark Russinovich is a Technical Fellow in Windows Azure at Microsoft, working on Microsoft's cloud operating system. He is the author of the cyberthriller *Zero Day* (Thomas Dunne Books, 2011) and coauthor of *Windows Sysinternals Administrator's Reference* (Microsoft Press, 2011). Mark joined Microsoft in 2006 when Microsoft acquired Winternals Software, the company he cofounded in 1996, as well as Sysinternals, where he still authors and publishes dozens of popular Windows administration and diagnostic utilities. He is a featured speaker at major industry conferences. Follow Mark on Twitter at @markrussinovich and on Facebook at *http://facebook.com/markrussinovich*.

David Solomon, president of David Solomon Expert Seminars (*www.solsem.com*), has focused on explaining the internals of the Microsoft Windows NT operating system line since 1992. He has taught his world-renowned Windows internals classes to thousands of developers and IT professionals worldwide. His clients include all the major software and hardware companies, including Microsoft. He was nominated a Microsoft Most Valuable Professional in 1993 and from 2005 to 2008.

Prior to starting his own company, David worked for nine years as a project leader and developer in the VMS operating system development group at Digital Equipment Corporation. His first book was entitled *Windows NT for Open VMS Professionals* (Digital Press/Butterworth Heinemann, 1996). It explained Windows NT to VMS-knowledgeable programmers and system administrators. His second book, *Inside Windows NT, Second Edition* (Microsoft Press, 1998), covered the internals of Windows NT 4.0. Since the third edition (*Inside Windows 2000*) David has coauthored this book series with Mark Russinovich.

In addition to organizing and teaching seminars, David is a regular speaker at technical conferences such as Microsoft TechEd and Microsoft PDC. He has also served as technical chair for several past Windows NT conferences. When he's not researching Windows, David enjoys sailing, reading, and watching Star Trek.

 **Alex Ionescu** is the founder of Winsider Seminars & Solutions Inc., specializing in low-level system software for administrators and developers as well as reverse engineering and security training for government and infosec clients. He also teaches Windows internals courses for David Solomon Expert Seminars, including at Microsoft. From 2003 to 2007, Alex was the lead kernel developer for ReactOS, an open source clone of Windows XP/Server 2003 written from scratch, for which he wrote most of the Windows NT-based kernel. While in school and part-time in summers, Alex worked as an intern at Apple on the iOS kernel, boot loader, firmware, and drivers on the original core platform team behind the iPhone, iPad, and AppleTV. Returning to his Windows security roots, Alex is now chief architect at CrowdStrike, a startup based in Seattle and San Francisco.

Alex continues to be very active in the security research community, discovering and reporting several vulnerabilities related to the Windows kernel, and presenting talks at conferences such as Blackhat, SyScan, and Recon. His work has led to the fixing of many critical kernel vulnerabilities, as well as to fixing over a few dozen nonsecurity bugs. Previous to his work in the security field, Alex's early efforts led to the publishing of nearly complete NTFS data structure documentation, as well as the Visual Basic metadata and pseudo-code format specifications.

SIT DOWN WITH THE EXPERTS
who literally wrote the book on Windows internals!

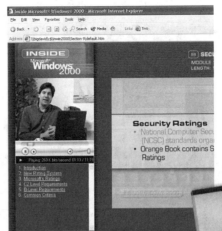

If you liked their book, you'll love hearing them in person. Get one of their video tutorials or come to a live class.

LIVE, INSTRUCTOR LED CLASSES

If you're an IT professional deploying and supporting Windows servers and workstations, you need to be able to dig beneath the surface when things go wrong. In our classes, you'll gain a deep understanding of the internals of the operating system and how to leverage advanced troubleshooting tools to solve system and application problems and understand performance issues more effectively. Attend a public class or schedule a private on site seminar at your location. For dates, course details, pricing, and registration information, see www.solsem.com.

> "The information given in this class should be required for all Windows engineers/administrators."

> "This course holds the key to understanding Windows."

> "Should be required training for anyone responsible for Windows software development, administration, or design."

INTERACTIVE DVD TUTORIAL

Sit down with the experts who literally wrote the book on Windows internals. Windows Internals COMPLETE consists of 12 hours of interactive training taking you under the hood of the operating system to learn how the kernel components work. As the ultimate compliment, Microsoft Corporation licensed these videos for their corporate training worldwide.

The Sysinternals Video Library (also 12 hours) covers essential Windows troubleshooting topics such as crash dump analysis and memory troubleshooting as well as how to leverage key Sysinternals tools.

> "These videos drill into the core of the platform, capture its technical essence and present it in a powerful interactive video format."–Rob Short, Vice President Core Technologies, Microsoft Corporation

To view video samples or for a detailed outline, visit www.solsem.com or email videos@solsem.com

What do you think of this book?

We want to hear from you!
To participate in a brief online survey, please visit:

microsoft.com/learning/booksurvey

Tell us how well this book meets your needs—what works effectively, and what we can do better. Your feedback will help us continually improve our books and learning resources for you.

Thank you in advance for your input!